JOSEF FRANK

JOSEF

FRANK

L I F E   A N D   W O R K

Christopher Long

The University of Chicago Press
Chicago and London

CHRISTOPHER LONG is assistant professor of
architectural history and theory at the University of Texas at
Austin.

The University of Chicago Press, Chicago 60637
The University of Chicago Press, Ltd., London
© 2002 by The University of Chicago
All rights reserved. Published 2002
Printed in Hong Kong
10 09 08 07 06 05 04 03 02   1 2 3 4 5
ISBN: 0-226-49266-4 (cloth)

Publication of this book was supported in part by grants from
the University Cooperative Society Subvention Grant of The
University of Texas at Austin and the Kjell and Märta Beijers
Foundation of Stockholm, Sweden.

Library of Congress Cataloging-in-Publication Data
Long, Christopher.
   Josef Frank : life and work / by Christopher Long.
      p.   cm.
   Includes bibliographical references and index.
   ISBN 0-226-49266-4 (alk. paper)
   1. Frank, Josef, 1885–1967. 2. Architects—Austria—Biography.
3. Modern movement (Architecture) 4. Interior decoration—Swe-
den—History—20th century. I. Frank, Josef, 1885–1967. II. Title.
   NA1011.5.F7 L66 2002
   720'.92—dc21   2001002130

FOR H. L. + H. L.

CONTENTS

ILLUSTRATIONS

PLATES

ACKNOWLEDGMENTS This book has been long in the making, and I would like to extend my gratitude to the many people who have helped me over the years. For assisting me in locating information, photographs, or sharing their memories of Frank with me, I would like to acknowledge the following: Dr. Petra Albrecht (Berlin), Dr. Eva-Maria Amberger (Berlin), Renata Antoniou (Vienna), Mikael Bergquist (Stockholm), Prof. Karl A. Bieber (Graz; d. 1995), Valarie Brocato (Chicago), Dr. Richard Bösel (Vienna), Elisabeth Pelc-Bunzl (Pettswood, Kent), Prof. Martin Bunzl (Princeton), Prof. Robert Cohen (Boston), Kenneth D. Craven (Austin), Hermann Czech (Vienna), Helene Eisenkolb (Vienna; d. 1997); Gabriele Fabiankowitsch (Vienna), Anni Feilendorf (Sydney), Stephanie Feilendorf (New York; d. 1988), Pat Fox (Austin), June Fraydas (New Rochelle, New York), Prof. Peter Galison (Stanford), Angela Giral (New York), Mary M. Goodwin (Atlanta), Prof. Otto Antonia Graf (Vienna), Sabine Hartmann (Berlin), Sylvia Herkt (Vienna), W. Gerald Heverly (Pittsburgh), Anna Holian (Chicago), Prof. Gerald Holton (Cambridge, Mass.), Gun Jacobson (Tyresö, Sweden), Mag. Claus Jesina (Vienna), Dipl.-Ing. Erich Jiresch (Vienna), Jane Kallir (New York), Prof. Martin Kermacy (Austin), Peter Klinger (Vienna), Markus Kristan (Vienna), Dr. Gabrielle Koller (Vienna), Dr. Uta Krammer (Vienna), Prof. Carol Herselle Krinsky (New York),

Paul Lampl (New York), Dr. Alfred Lechner (Vienna), Rebecca Lehrman (New York), Jöran Lindvall (Stockholm), Michael D. Lisser (New York), Dr. Dieter Litschauer (Vienna), Daniel Meyer (Chicago), Olof Michélsen (Stockholm), Dr. Juliane Mikoletzky (Vienna), Prof. Henk Mulder (Amsterdam), Dr. Roswitha Neu-Kock (Cologne), Paul Neurath (New York), Andreas Nutz (Weil am Rhein, Germany), Nicholas Olsberg (Montreal), Dr. Erika Patka (Vienna), Daniel Philipson (Stockholm), Ernst A. Plischke (Vienna; d. 1992), Kathrin Pokorny-Nagel (Vienna), Prof. Marco Pozzetto (Trieste), Dr. Marian Bisanz-Prakken (Vienna), Alice Schreyer (Chicago), Werner J. Schweiger (Vienna), Gustav Szekely (Vienna), Prof. Eduard F. Sekler (Cambridge, Mass.), Helena Smedberg (Stockholm), Prof. Johannes Spalt (Vienna), Therese Schweizer (Zurich), Dr. Christoph Tepperberg (Vienna), Bo Theen (Stockholm), Prof. Peter Vignau-Wilberg (Munich), Cecilia Währner (Stockholm), Tobias Walch (Boulder, Colorado), Ann Wall (Stockholm), Dipl.-Ing. Helmut Weihsmann (Vienna), Ulla Fischer-Westhauser (Vienna), Dr. Ulrich Wiesner (Cologne), Ruth Wilson-Kalmár (Vienna), Sascha Windholz (Vienna), Dr. Wim de Wit (Los Angeles), and Dr. Christian Witt-Dörring (Vienna).

In addition, I would like to extend my thanks to the staffs of the following institutions: Graphische Sammlung Albertina, Vienna; Arkitekturmuseet, Stockholm; Avery Architectural and Fine Arts Library, Columbia University, New York; CIAM-Archiv, ETH, Zurich; Getty Research Institute, Los Angeles; Historisches Museum der Stadt Wien; Sammlung und Bibliothek, Universität für angewandte Kunst, Vienna; Harry Ransom Humanities Research Center, Austin; Museum of Modern Art, New York; Österreichische Nationalbibliothek, Vienna; Rheinisches Bildarchiv, Cologne; Bibliothek und Archiv, Technische Universität, Vienna; and the Wiener Stadt- und Landesbibliothek. I am also deeply indebted to Janine Henri and Daniel Orozco, at the Architecture and Planning Library at the University of Texas at Austin, for their help over many years.

This book began as a doctoral dissertation, and I would like to acknowledge my advisors, Anthony Alofsin and Peter Jelavich, whose wise counsel and advice greatly improved it. Since that time, I have had many discussions with Anthony Alofsin, who shares my interest in the architecture and culture of Central Europe. I have learned an immense amount from our conversations, and they have greatly shaped my views about modernism and the building of the region. I also benefited from the suggestions of my other committee members, David Crew, Bruce Hunt, Eleftherios Ikonomou, and Jeffrey L. Meikle. I am fortunate to have learned a great deal from my colleagues and students at the School of Architecture at the University of Texas, among them Richard Cleary, W. Owen Harrod, Danielle Langston, Timothy Parker, Monica Penick, Dan Roush, and Danilo Udovicki-Selb.

My initial research in Vienna was generously supported by a grant from the Austrian Fulbright Commission; and a grant from the American Alpbach Foundation allowed me to return to Austria in the summer of 1990 to undertake further research. I am also grateful for the financial support I received from the Kjell and Märta Beijers Foundation and Svenskt Tenn, both in Stockholm, which helped to offset the costs of the illustrations. The publication of this book was generously aided by a University Cooperative Society Subvention Grant award by the University of Texas at Austin.

I also want to express my appreciation to those at the University of Chicago Press who, with patience and skill, worked to make this book a reality, in particular, Susan Bielstein, Anthony Burton, Maia Rigas, and Jill Shimabukuro.

I owe a very special debt of gratitude to Dr. Kristina Wängberg-Eriksson and Professor-Dr. Jan Christer Eriksson, who not only helped me to understand Frank's work in Sweden and shared many documents and photographs but who also graciously hosted me during my visits there and who carefully read the entire manuscript. Their comments and suggestions vastly improved the book. I would also like thank Monika Platzer, my frequent host in Vienna, for all of her help over the years.

I cannot end without acknowledging an immense debt of gratitude to Dr. Martin Enge, to whom, more than anyone else, I owe my interest in Austria and its culture. Finally, I would like to thank Gia Marie Houck, whose assistance, encouragement, and remarkable forbearance were crucial to helping me to complete this work.

PROLOGUE

In the summer of 1930, the German Werkbund held its annual conference in Vienna. The honor of presenting the keynote address was accorded to the Viennese architect and designer Josef Frank, who, along with Josef Hoffmann, was the animating force behind the Werkbund's sister organization in Austria. Frank, just a few weeks short of his forty-fifth birthday, was at the time widely looked upon not only as the foremost representative of the younger generation of Austrian modernists but also as one of the leading progressive architects in Europe. Three years before, in 1927, he had been among the select group of architects chosen to build at the Weissenhofsiedlung housing exhibition; the following year he had represented Austria at the inaugural meeting of the Congrés Internationaux d'Architecture Moderne (CIAM).

But instead of delivering the customary speech for such occasions, one filled with light pleasantries and fulsome praise, Frank startled those assembled—including Ludwig Mies van der Rohe and Walter Gropius, who were seated on either side of him on the speaker's rostrum—with a withering attack on many of the modern movement's core convictions. Dismissing the growing chorus of voices calling for a unified modern style, Frank insisted that it was pluralism, not uniformity, that most characterized life in the new machine age. The modern world, he declared, was too multifaceted and modern life too diverse to be encompassed by a single style: "The striving for complete simplicity is pathetic, it is pathetic to want to make everything the same so that variations are no longer possible, to want to organize everything to force all people into a large homogeneous mass."[1] Frank similarly rejected the notion that architects should abandon the past and begin anew. It was senseless for architects and designers to disregard the rich legacy of history; what separated the modern age from earlier times was not its distance from history but an unprecedented knowledge of it.[2] To the idea that the advent of the machine necessitated a new rational approach to life and art, Frank responded that, on the contrary, the increasing emphasis on rationalism meant that freedom and leisure had become all the more important and that, as a result, architects and designers had an even greater responsibility to meet the everyday needs of people.

Although some in the large audience believed that Frank had gone too far, many welcomed his repudiation of the ideas of those he called the "Radikal-Modernen," and over the next several months the talk unleashed a public debate within the Werkbund about the nature and course of modernism. The discussion soon abated, however, a casualty not only to the rise of Fascism in Germany but also to a growing trend, particularly conspicuous in the CIAM meetings of the 1930s, to promote the idea of a single, uniform modern movement and to conceal differences among its members. While Frank continued to advocate greater freedom in architecture and design, he became an increasingly marginal figure after he went into exile in Sweden in 1933 and, despite the seminal role he later played in forging what became known as Swedish, or Scandinavian, Modern design, he was almost wholly excluded from the standard histories of modernism.

This book is a study of Josef Frank's work and ideas; but in the broadest sense it is also about the rise and fall of modern architecture and design. Born in the 1880s, Frank was reared and educated at the turn of the century and began practicing just at the time when the new language of rationalism and purism was beginning to emerge. During the 1920s and early 1930s, he was on the crests of most of the important waves of the development of modernism; and in spite of his mounting criticism of many of the modern movement's basic premises, he remained, until his death in the mid-1960s, committed to the cause of creating a new architecture. In pointing out what he thought were the modern movement's shortcomings, Frank cut himself off from its mainstream; but for this reason he was able to see it with a coruscating clarity. In his works, in his writings, and in his life, Frank summed up the experience of twentieth-century architecture in a singular way, charting not only its visions and successes but also its shortsightedness and failures. His story, his critique, and the evolution of the modern movement form the central themes of this book.

JOSEF FRANK

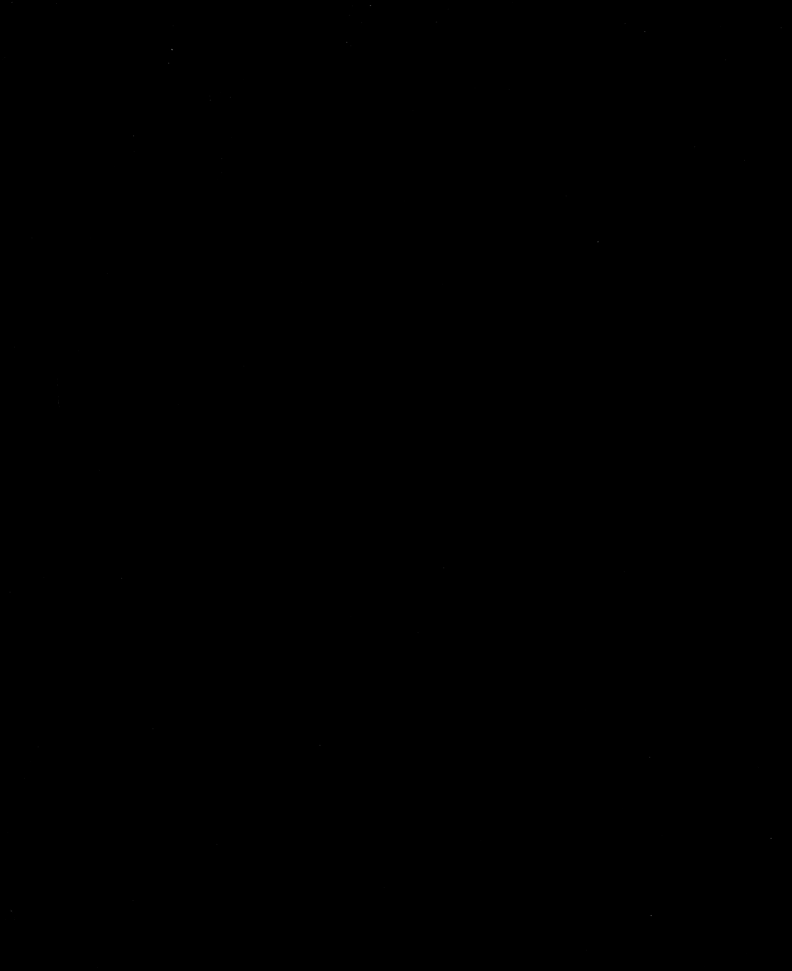

1

GENESIS Although Josef Frank spent nearly half of his adult life in exile, mostly in Sweden, his personality and work were deeply etched by his upbringing during the Viennese fin de siècle. For much of his working life, even after he left Austria in the early 1930s, Frank struggled to come to terms with the legacy left by Otto Wagner, Joseph Maria Olbrich, Josef Hoffmann, Adolf Loos, and the other architects and designers of the early Viennese modern movement. In many respects, Frank carried on and even broadened the revolution they inaugurated in the 1890s. Yet if he continued to bear the torch of Viennese modernism well after most of its original leaders had passed from the scene, Frank also questioned many of its guiding ideas. Indeed, much like Loos, he adopted a course that not only often ran counter to the prevailing currents of Viennese architecture and design but also stood in opposition to the wider modern movement. While he never completely shed the cultural and intellectual assumptions of the Vienna of his youth, in the end he plotted his own direction, one that led to a unique, complex, and personal vision of the modern.

FRANK'S EARLY YEARS Josef Frank (fig. 1) was a product of the assimilated Jewish middle class. His father, Ignaz Frank, was a well-to-do industrialist and textile wholesaler. Born in

1. Josef Frank, 1903.
Universitätsarchiv, Technische
Universität, Vienna.

1851 in Heves, a rural province in northeastern Hungary, he moved to Vienna as a young man and opened a textile shop in the Westbahnstraße. By the mid-1870s, he had become a partner in Freistadl & Company, a cloth manufacturing and wholesale tailor supply firm headquartered in the Zelinkagasse in the city's textile quarter.[1] Frank's mother, Jenny Feilendorf, born in 1861, was the daughter of a prosperous upper middle class Jewish family originally from the nearby town of Preßburg (Bratislava) in Slovakia. A strong-willed, imaginative woman who was superior to her husband in social status and cultural attainments, she studied to be a teacher—an unusual pursuit for a young woman of her class at the time—but married young and never practiced her profession.[2]

Josef was the second of the couple's four children. The eldest, Philipp (1884–1966), born only fifteen months earlier, became a prominent physicist and philosopher of science. Two years after Josef's birth, another child followed, a sister, Hedwig (1887–1966), who would marry into a wealthy industrialist family that would provide Frank with several important commissions. Three years after her birth a younger brother, Rudolf (1890–1942?), arrived.[3]

Josef's birthplace was not Vienna but the small spa town of Baden (fig. 2), where the Franks often spent the summer months. Located some thirty kilometers to the south, the picturesque resort was a favored destination of the Viennese haute bourgeoisie, who flocked there to take the waters and enjoy the fresh air. Over the years many of Vienna's leading artists and musicians—Beethoven, Salieri, Kreutzer, and Schubert—had been frequent guests in the town. Its principal attractions, aside from its thermal baths, were its charming Biedermeier buildings, many of them the work of one of the leading exponents of the style, the Viennese architect Josef Kornhäusel. In the summer of 1885, the Franks rented rooms in a Biedermeier house at Braitnerstrasse 6 near the center of town, and Josef was born there on 15 July with a Viennese doctor in attendance.[4]

The Franks were typical of the ascendant Jewish middle class living in Central Europe on the cusp of the new century—assimilated, worldly, cultured, interested in the newest trends and ideas. As for many affluent families of the "Mosaic persuasion," Judaism for the Franks was little more than a formality.[5] Although the specter of anti-Semitism was never far from the surface, the family's Jewishness, at least during Frank's early years, caused them little inconvenience. While barriers to advancement for Jews remained, especially in the army and civil service, the marginalization and social dislocation that they later experienced were not yet in evidence. Indeed, the years between 1860 and 1890 marked the heyday for assimilated Jews in Austria; the emancipation decree of 1867 and the rise of liberal politics in Austria opened new vistas of opportunity, allowing many to make the extraordinary climb from peddlers and artisans to jurists, professors, businessmen, and politicians. Frank's family exemplified this new social mobility: his father struggled up from modest circumstances to become a man of some means, one of Frank's maternal uncles became a high official with the Austrian State Railways, and an-

2. Baden, Lower Austria, main square, c. 1890. Österreichische Nationalbibliothek, Bildarchiv, Vienna.

other uncle was an engineer who oversaw the construction of the Riesenrad, the city's great Ferris wheel, and who later became a successful manufacturer of car batteries.[6]

Frank attended a public primary school (*Volkschule*), and in 1895, at the age of 10, he entered the *Staatsoberrealschule* (higher secondary school) in the inner city. The school was one of the group of *Realschulen* founded during the period of reform that followed the 1848 revolution to provide a technical education for the sons of the new industrial middle class. In contrast to the humanistic *Gymnasien*, which sought to give students a thorough grounding in the classics, the curriculum of the *Realschulen* stressed mathematics, the natural sciences, and modern languages, all intended to prepare their graduates for careers in the various technical fields or manufacturing.

The reasons Frank's parents' elected to enroll their second son in the *Realschule* remain obscure. His brother Philipp, who early showed signs of the brilliance that would lead to his meteoric rise in the world of mathematical physics, attended the prestigious Wasa Gymnasium. Perhaps the Franks hoped that Josef would follow his father into the family textile business. Among Frank's schoolmates was the future writer Hermann Broch, who from a young age was groomed to take over the running of his family's textile mill.[7]

From the start, however, Frank exhibited little aptitude for business.[8] To judge from his transcripts, he was a rather desultory student. His grades in his first six years were, on the whole, average or just below, and he was forced to repeat the fifth form after failing English and mathematics. In his final two years, however, his grades improved: on his last report he received the mark of "lobenswert" (praiseworthy) in several subjects, including natural science and history, while earning the grade of "superior" (*vorzüglich*) in German.[9]

It was evident, nonetheless, that Frank's talents lay elsewhere. During his final years at the school, he excelled at both freehand drawing and model-making. Indeed, early on, he displayed a talent for drawing. He often sat by himself doodling or sketching, and he even briefly considered studying art.[10] A surviving watercolor from 1900 (plate 1), made when Frank was fifteen, testifies to his developing facility in both drawing and painting. Upon completing his final secondary school examinations, however, Frank opted to study architecture, perhaps in an attempt to please his practical-minded father.

THE KÖNIGSCHULE Frank's years at the *Realschule* coincided with the rapid rise of the Viennese modern movement. In 1896, a year after he entered the school, Otto Wagner published his book *Moderne Architektur* proclaiming a new era in architecture and design. "The basis of today's predominant outlook on architecture must be adjusted," Wagner demanded, "and we must be fully aware that the sole point of departure for our artistic work can only be modern life."[11] This shift was most fully apparent in the series of stations Wagner designed in the later 1890s for the *Stadtbahn*, the city's urban rail network. Lean and spare, incorporating the newest materials and construction methods, they announced, in spite of their vestigial classicism, a clear and abrupt change of direction.

A year after Wagner's summons to action, Gustav Klimt and many of the city's other progressive artists, architects, and designers broke away from the conservative Künstlergenossenschaft (Artist's Association) and founded the Vienna Secession. Their critical attack on historical revivalism, expressed through a new stylistic language, the *Jugendstil*, the German and Austrian equivalent of art nouveau, inaugurated a full-blown search for a contemporary aesthetic. But if young Frank registered the events then transforming the Viennese artistic world, he left no record at the time—either written or drawn—of their impact on him.

In October 1903, Frank enrolled in the architecture faculty at the Vienna Technische Hochschule, or Polytechnic Institute. Founded a century earlier, the institution was among the preeminent polytechnic universities in Central Europe, rivaling those in Munich, Dresden, and Berlin. The architecture faculty included many of Austria's leading practitioners, and its standing as the "first school of the monarchy" attracted students from throughout the Habsburg realm and from Eastern and Southern Europe. A diploma from the school was almost a prerequisite for those intending to enter the state building ministry or to teach at one of the other universities or building trade schools. But compared with the nearby Kunstgewerbeschule (School of Arts and Crafts), whose faculty included many of the leading Secessionists, among them Josef Hoffmann and Koloman Moser, or the Akademie der bildenden Künste (Academy of Fine Arts), where Otto Wagner and Friedrich Ohmann conducted the two architecture classes, the Technische Hochschule remained a conservative bastion. Most of the professors belonged to the late Viennese historicist school—the generation that followed after the great builders of the Ringstrasse—and many were openly hostile to the modernists and their ideas. The curriculum of the school, little changed from the time of the professors' own student years, was still heavily weighted toward the study of history. Students were required to sign up for 420 hours of history courses spread over four of the five years of the program; in addition, as part of the regular requirements, they spent an entire semester building models of classical Greek and Roman temples and other historical structures.[12]

3. Carl König, c. 1910. *Bauten und Entwürfe von Carl König* (Vienna, 1910).

The roster of the young Frank's professors included many of the school's best-known personalities: Max von Ferstel, Karl Mayreder, Alexander Wielemans, and Josef Neuwirth. But it was Carl König (fig. 3), the school's doyen and holder of the chair for classical and Renaissance architecture, who was to have the most lasting influence on him. König belonged to the same generation as Wagner: both were born in the same year, 1841, and until the early 1890s, when Wagner had mounted his first assault on historicism, their careers had followed similar paths.[13] A promising painter as a youth, König studied architecture at the Technische Hochschule and at the Academy of Fine Arts. He soon achieved professional recognition with a series of well-designed works in the neo-Renaissance style, and in 1885 he was appointed as Heinrich von Ferstel's successor at the Technische Hochschule. Unlike Wagner, however, König remained firmly committed to the historical canon. By the turn of the century, his works—among them, the much-praised Philipphof and Agricultural Products Exchange and an addition to the Technische Hochschule (fig. 4)—had earned him a reputation as one of the city's foremost interpreters of the reigning historical *Stilarchitektur*.

The charismatic König exercised a powerful hold over his students. In spite of his introverted manner, he was widely admired both for his encyclopedic knowledge and his wide experience as an architect. One student later remembered that every one of König's lectures or critiques of his students' works "was an event."[14]

As an assimilated Jew who had overcome considerable obstacles to attain a position of prestige and respect, König also held a particularly strong attraction for young Jewish students like Frank, who saw in him a model for the dream of complete emancipation. Indeed, König counted among his students a large percentage of the Jews studying architecture in Vienna in the period after the turn of the century, among them Oskar Strnad, Oskar Wlach, and Walter Sobotka, all of whom would go on to play significant roles

4. Carl König, addition to the Technische Hochschule, Vienna, 1907–10. *Bauten und Entwürfe von Carl König* (Vienna, 1910).

in the architectural scene. König's outstanding ability as a teacher no doubt explained part of the attraction Frank and many others had for him. Perhaps just as important, he offered young Jews opportunities and encouragement that they likely would not have found elsewhere.[15]

In his lectures, König stressed the importance of studying history, above all the architecture and art of classical Greece and Renaissance Italy, which he viewed as the twin pinnacles of the Western tradition. In the spirit of Eugène-Emmanuel Viollet-le-Duc and Gottfried Semper (both of whom König admired), he championed the notion of a thorough, scientific study of the past as the basis for any new architecture. Yet he was also outspokenly critical of those who used history as a model book, charging that they denied the spirit of the old masters. He called instead for an architecture that would reflect the honesty and comprehensibility of past building but, at the same time, conform to the needs of modern life.

Unlike Wagner, however, König rejected the notion that a modern architecture could be forged on the basis of a novel artistic style. He assailed the attempts of the modernists to invent a wholly new architectural language, calling their ideas "repulsive" and "at best, empty whim. . . . The assertion that the forms of architecture are pure products of fantasy," König declared in a speech when he became rector of the university in 1901, "is absurd; it is based on the erroneous notion that they exist apart from [their] empirical content." History alone, he contended, gives architectural forms their meaning: the "arbitrary products of the imagination" are not only incomprehensible, but also "belong to the realm of the grotesque." To abandon the past "means the destruction of architecture."[16]

Not surprisingly, Frank's training under König at the Technische Hochschule stressed the study of architectural history. In addition to regularly offering lectures on Greek and Roman classicism and the Renaissance, König in his studio classes often drew examples from the past, which he sought to apply to contemporary building situations.[17] His pronounced emphasis on classical antiquity and the Renaissance left its mark. As one former student recalled, "[W]e, all of his students, were indoctrinated on the highest level of classical tradition."[18]

If König remained firm in his belief in the importance of history, he underscored not only the necessity of gaining fluency in the visual language of classicism, but also—much like Semper—the importance of understanding the process through which the basic forms of antique building had been derived. The purpose of studying historical motifs, König insisted, was not to learn how to imitate them but to understand how and why they had come about; only when armed with this knowledge could the architect rework these qualities in a new spirit.

König's notion that the forms themselves were only a screen that concealed their inner meaning had a lasting impact on Frank's thinking. The sense that history was not a warehouse of motifs to be "appropriated" but a source for endless dialogue never left him; it lingers behind even the most seemingly original and austere of his works. Although he soon jettisoned the visual language of classicism and any other outward signs of König's teachings, he maintained throughout his life a deep respect for the achievements of the past. It was this commitment to history, to continuity rather than to revolution, that was among the most important lessons Frank took from König.

For all of König's teachings about the uses of the past, his classes proved to be a fertile training ground for future modernists. In his design exercises he stressed—as did the majority of the professors at the Technische Hochschule—the technical aspects of building. This emphasis on building practice rather than on stylistic issues opened the students up to a wide range of influences—including the ideas of the Wagner School (Wagnerschule) at the Academy of Fine Arts—and made it easier for them to find their way to modernism in later years.[19]

König also offered other lessons that proved critical for Frank. Among these was a pronounced emphasis on functionality. As a true son of the nineteenth-century Viennese middle class, König shared a view of architecture that was at its center rational and instrumental. For König, clarity and simplicity defined the best aspects of architecture. Although he believed in the power of architecture as art, he spurned caprice and arbitrariness. His application of the formal inflections of the Baroque notwithstanding, the plans of his buildings were invariably straightforward and remarkably pragmatic; his use of structural and decorative elements, logical and efficient.[20] König pursued these qualities not only in his own designs, but he also underscored them in his teaching; they proved to be potent ideas for many of his followers who worked in the same spirit but to very different ends.

König's most important lesson, however, may have been one that he imparted to his students only implicitly. By demonstrating that style could be applied independently of other architectural qualities, he opened up the possibility that it might be regarded as relative or even extraneous. Frank, like all of König's students, gained fluency in the language of the neo-Baroque and other historical styles, but he also learned that he could manipulate these styles, using the forms and elements freely.

5. Max Fabiani, Portois & Fix Building, Vienna, 1899–1900. *Die Architektur des XX. Jahrhunderts* (Berlin, 1903).

THE INFLUENCE OF MAX FABIANI König's assistant Max Fabiani also left his mark on Frank. During Frank's years at the Technische Hochschule, König served as rector of the university, and he turned over much of the day-to-day teaching of his studio classes to Fabiani.[21] Fabiani also presented his own lectures on a variety of topics, including construction and interior design, and he often accompanied the architecture students on study trips— usually visits to the classical monuments of Italy.

As an architect, Fabiani had followed a very different course than König. After studying at the Technische Hochschule, he had worked in Wagner's atelier during the period from 1894 to 1896 when Wagner was laying the basis for his architectural revolution; he became part of Wagner's inner circle, assisting him in the writing of *Moderne Architektur,* and under Wagner's influence, he produced one of the first examples of the incipient functionalist aesthetic, the radically pared-down Portois & Fix Building (1899–1900) (fig. 5). After the turn of the century, Fabiani abandoned the Wagnerian idiom for a modernized variant of the neo-Baroque. But his commitment to structural integrity and to clearly articulated spatial form remained paramount in his work: even his most "traditional" façades conceal manifestly modern construction techniques and interior spaces.[22]

Like König, Fabiani concentrated on tectonics and practical design issues. He sought to provide his students with a full understanding of the various materials and methods used in modern building, carefully exploring in lectures and in studio exercises their individual qualities and constructive possibilities.

Fabiani also underscored the need for developing, as he put it, "a sense of simplicity and the search for the unified concept."[23] Ornamental detailing and the arrangement of the interior spaces, he taught, should be subordinate to functional considerations and the overall design concept. For Frank, as for many of his fellow students, Fabiani's accent on the technical and programmatic aspects of building was liberating. Many years later he would remember how one of his first forays into a new architectural conception was "the showing of the construction instead of classical symbolizing."[24]

But perhaps even more important for Frank was Fabiani's message about the importance of keeping human needs at the forefront of architecture and design. Fabiani regarded cities and their buildings as living organisms that should grow with their human inhabitants: fixed systems or absolute ideals, he argued, were incapable of responding to the ever-changing demands placed upon them.[25] Fabiani's call for a human-centered design ethos and his skeptical and undogmatic attitude were important lessons for young Frank: not only did these ideas help to free him from the constraints of academicism, but they also provided him with a powerful and readily adaptable approach to the problems of building in the modern age.

ADOLF LOOS However enriching the teachings he encountered at the Technische Hochschule, the young Frank was also attentive to the newest currents in art and culture. In his student years, he was a regular at the Café Museum, a favored gathering place of the city's revolutionary architects, artists, thinkers, and musicians, including Wagner, Hoffmann, Olbrich, Oskar Kokoschka, Klimt, Egon Schiele, Max Oppenheimer, Alfred Adler, and Alban Berg.[26] It was during this time that Frank also came to know Adolf Loos, another of the café's regulars.

Although Loos had built very little, his reputation as a firebrand and his outspoken and irreverent iconoclasm attracted many students from the nearby Hochschule and the Academy of Fine Arts. He would often offer impromptu lectures on building and design, expounding his own ideas and—not infrequently in the process—disparaging the works of both the Secessionists and the historicists. König, in fact, became so concerned about the pernicious influence Loos was having on his students that he once posted a notice forbidding them from attending Loos's private lectures.[27]

Given Frank's training at the Technische Hochschule, Loos's faith in the historical tradition and his belief in the importance of grafting the architecture of the new age onto the past must have had a strong appeal for him. But Frank also shared Loos's pronounced Anglophilia, his admiration for the American way of life, his love of good craftsmanship and sumptuous materials, and his belief that the culture of everyday life and not the machine should be at the center of modern design.

Exactly when Frank first met Loos is not known, but the two were well acquainted by the summer of 1908.[28] In the years prior to the First World War, Frank visited many of

Loos's works, including his Michaelerplatz Building and the Steiner, Horner, and Scheu Houses, and he was familiar with Loos's writings and ideas. Yet Frank never attended Loos's private "Bauschule"; and if some of his later buildings and writings show the unmistakable signs of Loos's influence, Frank carefully preserved his intellectual independence. Though he no doubt learned a great deal from Loos, the older architect's work and ideas were only one of many sources of generative stimulation for Frank.

THE ZEDLITZHALLE PROJECT Frank's early years at the Technische Hochschule coincided with the high period of the Viennese *Jugendstil*. Like many of the students at the school, he was attracted to the densely intertwining vegetal forms popularized by Klimt, Hoffmann, Olbrich, Moser, and the other Secessionists. A drawing of the Stock-im-Eisen monument (fig. 6), which he published in a school almanac in 1904—one of the very few surviving examples of work from Frank's student years—shows the imprint of the new *Secessionsstil*.

Secessionist motifs also appear in the only extant original architectural work from Frank's years at the Technische Hochschule, a project for an art exhibition hall he executed in 1907 (fig. 7). Frank produced the design for a competition to replace the old Zedlitzhalle with an art gallery. Although no prize money was offered, a number of prominent architects took part in the competition, including Wagner, Otto Schönthal, Max Hegele, and Ernst von Gotthilf.[29] Wagner eventually won the competition, but the editors of *Der Architekt* selected Frank's design as one of the best entries, and it was reproduced in the September 1907 issue of the journal.[30]

The site was a narrow parcel of land extending back from the Zedlitzgasse in Vienna's inner city. Frank proposed a long, rectangular structure divided into two functional zones (fig. 8). The three-story front portion was to house offices, a cloakroom, and other service areas; the larger, two-story rear block would contain the actual gallery, storage areas, and sales rooms. What stands out is Frank's simple, rational distribution of the spaces, especially in the rear gallery, which is clearly articulated in the structure.

The most striking aspect of Frank's design, however, is the composite arrangement of its main façade. While Wagner's winning entry was a scrupulously controlled exercise in harmony and equipoise, Frank's project gives the impression of being a mélange of separate, seemingly contrasting elements. Dominating the center is a formal entry with a superimposed entablature supported by caryatids and bearing the inscription "Für Volk und Kunst" (For People and Art). But the areas on either side are much more casually treated: the windows are irregularly arranged and, with their simple unadorned frames, seem better suited to a common house or apartment building than to a monumental structure in the center of the city.

The design also reveals how much Frank still remained under the influence of his conservative education. Despite the applied *Jugendstil*-inspired ornamental flourishes, it

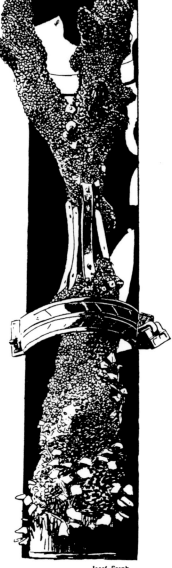

Josef Frank.

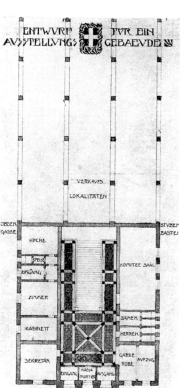

6. (left) Book decoration (Stock-im-Eisen monument) from *Wiener Türmer. Ein Almanach auf das Jahr 1904.* (Vienna, 1904). Collection Dr. Alfred Lechner, Vienna.

7. (top, right) Project for the renovation of the Zedlitzhalle, Vienna, 1907; elevation. *Der Architekt* 13 (1907).

8. (bottom, right) Project for the renovation of the Zedlitzhalle, Vienna, 1907; plan. *Der Architekt* 13 (1907).

belongs much more to the stylistic world of late Viennese historicism than to that of the Wagnerschule: both the overall conception and much of the detailing show the imprint of König and Fabiani's teachings, as well as Frank's own emerging interest in the architecture of the early Renaissance.

Concealed beneath the welter of stylistic and formal ideas are many of the hallmarks of Frank's later work: his interest in the complex and the contradictory; his penchant for asymmetry and disproportion; his readiness to undermine traditional rules of composition. Perhaps most immediately, the design testifies to Frank's strong absorption with history and his ardent desire to find a means to reconcile the building of the past with the needs of the present—concerns that would occupy him for much of the remainder of his life.

APPRENTICESHIP IN BERLIN Frank's abiding interest in history is also reflected in the surviving records from his student years. In a brief curriculum vitae written in 1910, he noted that he had "devoted himself to the study of art and architecture of the Italian Renaissance" and that as part of his studies he had "made a number of short trips to Italy."[31] His attraction to architectural history is also evident in the results of his comprehensive state examinations, which he took in July 1908. He received the highest mark of "very good" in classical and Renaissance architecture, "adequate" in medieval architecture and architectural composition, and a failing grade in building construction.[32]

Frank spent the following year, probably from the late summer or fall of 1908 through the first half of 1909, in Berlin. Of his time in the German capital very little is known; in his vita of 1910, he mentions only that he worked in the office of architect Bruno Möhring.[33]

Möhring was a prominent figure in Berlin architecture circles, well-known as the editor and copublisher of *Berliner Architekturwelt,* which was among the most influential journals in Germany at the time. His reputation as an architect rested above all on a series of innovative industrial buildings, bridges, and transportation projects, including the Rhine Bridge at Bonn and the Berlin city railway (fig. 9), which made use of the latest advances in structural engineering. Like Wagner's designs for the Vienna city railway system, Möhring's works celebrated technology without sacrificing the imperatives of art. Combining *Jugendstil* motifs with a pared-down historical vocabulary, they sought to dignify the new iron and glass constructions while affirming their utilitarian function. In his work as editor, Möhring kept abreast of the latest developments in architecture and design, and he played a key role in disseminating the work of leading modernists, including Frank Lloyd Wright, in Germany.[34] His renown as a progressive drew apprentices from both Germany and abroad, among them, Bruno Taut and the young Swedish architect Sigurd Lewerentz, whose stay in Möhring's office overlapped with Frank's.[35]

9. Bruno Möhring, Bülowstraße
Station, Berlin-Schöneberg, 1900–1.
Berlinische Galerie.

Möhring's practice was a large and active one, and Frank would have had the opportunity to assist on a wide range of projects. Works on the boards at the time included a concert hall in the Berlin Zoologischer Garten and a bank building in Budapest, as well as designs for exhibitions in Berlin and Buenos Aires.[36] Frank left no record of what he did in Möhring's employ, but a perspective view (fig. 10) of a massive hangar for the Zeppelin works in Friedrichshafen published in *Stein und Eisen,* a folio of Möhring's works, is almost certainly the work of Frank.[37] It is also likely that Frank assisted in the preparation of the *Plan for Greater Berlin* that Möhring, along with economist Rudolf Eberstadt and traffic engineer Richard Petersen, submitted in 1910 for a competition to design a regulation scheme for the city.[38]

While in Berlin, Frank saw the works of Peter Behrens, Alfred Messel, and Bruno Paul, as well as those of Karl Friedrich Schinkel. But his time there left little, if any, direct impact on his work. Nonetheless, Frank must have been struck by the very different atmosphere of the city. The air of practicality, sobriety, and utility that was increasingly coming to define the German capital posed a stark contrast to the aestheticism of Vienna. Moreover, the growing influence of mass-production and industrialization on architecture and design in Berlin represented a very different situation than in Vienna, where the majority of manufacturing concerns were small and where the traditional crafts still clung to life. For Frank, the question of how to reconcile these two divergent visions—be-

10. Zeppelin hangar, Zeppelin Werke, Friedrichshafen, 1909; perspective. *Stein und Eisen* (Berlin, 1908). Department of Special Collections, University of Chicago Library.

tween industrial collectivism on the one hand and an enduring faith in art and the individual on the other—would present a problem to which he would return again and again.

DISSERTATION ON ALBERTI After almost a full year in Möhring's office, Frank embarked on an extended trip to Italy, where he conducted research for his dissertation, a study of the churches of the Florentine Renaissance architect Leon Battista Alberti.[39] Frank's interest in Alberti no doubt was fired by König, who was himself deeply enamored of Alberti and the architecture of the quattrocento. But while König stressed Alberti's role in reviving and expanding the classical tradition, Frank seems to have been equally interested in Alberti's sensitivity and almost puritanical restraint. Many years later, Frank would write that the "modern style" had "originated in the year 1420."[40]

Frank remained in Italy for seven months, spending time in Florence, Mantua, and Rimini. Relying on Alberti's writings and other documents as well as on a meticulous examination of the buildings themselves, he sought to piece together clues to their original appearance. He made a careful survey of the churches' façades and interiors, noting alterations that had been made over time. To illustrate the work, he prepared twenty ink and wash renderings of the exteriors and interiors of Alberti's most important churches, including Santa Maria Novella and Santissima Annunziata in Florence, San Sebastiano in Mantua, and San Francesco in Rimini, showing his reconstructions of the building's original states (plate 2, fig. 11). The carefully executed drawings reveal Frank's strong interest in color schemes and primary forms; especially noteworthy is his attention to Alberti's polychromatic decorative patterning, which seems to presage the richly colored ornamental schemes of Frank's mature work.

In late 1909 or early 1910, Frank returned to Vienna, where he put the final touches on his dissertation. In the fall of 1910, König formally accepted the work, and in December, Frank stood for his final examination (*Rigorosum*) before a board consisting of König, Mayreder, Neuwirth, and Emil Artmann. Although Neuwirth and Artmann gave him failing

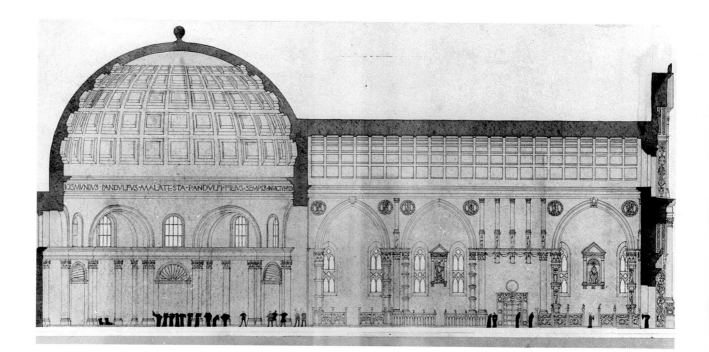

11. Reconstruction of the interior
of San Francesco, Rimini, by Leon
Battista Alberti, c. 1910; longitudinal section. Pencil, pen and ink,
watercolor on paper, 32 × 32 cm.
Universitätsarchiv, Technische
Universität, Vienna.

marks on portions of the exam, Frank passed by a majority of votes and was awarded his doctorate two weeks before Christmas.[41]

In his six years of study at the Technische Hochschule, Frank had acquired a strong technical education that grounded him in the basics of architecture and design practice. The stylistic influences he had encountered during his years there—the neo-Baroque and the *Jugendstil*—he very soon abandoned. Many of the other lessons he learned, however, would remain with him. Echoes of König's and Fabiani's teachings and of the ideas of Wagner, Loos, and their contemporaries often resounded in Frank's later writings, and they account in no small part for the substance of his later thinking. But as both architect and theorist, Frank was to draw very different conclusions from them.

12. Book decoration from *Wiener
Türmer. Ein Almanach auf das Jahr
1904* (Vienna, 1904). Collection Dr.
Alfred Lechner, Vienna.

2

EXPLORATION The period from 1906 to 1910, Frank's last years at the Technische Hochschule, was a time of sharp transition in Viennese architecture and design. After 1904, the abstracted, rectilinear variant of the *Jugendstil* that had come to define the *Wiener Moderne* during the first years of the new century began to give way to a whole array of other stylistic directions. On the one hand, there was a decided movement—particularly evident in the work of Hoffmann and many of Wagner's younger students—toward a new pared-down classicism, one that drew especially on Biedermeier models. But also discernible in the work of a wide range of Viennese architects and designers was a developing interest in other stylistic influences, including historical and vernacular motifs, a new primitivism, and the English "freestyle." The years between 1910 and the outbreak of the First World War was a time of restless experimentation, as progressive architects tried out new forms and ideas. It was also a time of exploration for young Frank as he sought to define his own ideas and attitudes toward architecture and design. Over the course of the next four years, he experimented with a welter of different sources and approaches, gradually developing his own distinctive vision of the modern.

13. Strömberg-Palm Swedish Gymnastics School, Vienna, 1910, gymnasium. *Das Interieur* 13 (1912).

THE SWEDISH TURNSCHULE AND THE TEDESCO APARTMENT By the middle of 1910, even before he stood for his final examinations, Frank was already at work on two commissions. One of the commissions was for the interiors of a private gymnastics school, the Strömberg-Palm Swedish Turnschule. Operated by two Swedes, Esther Strömberg and Harald Palm, the school was housed on the top floor of a newly constructed building (designed, coincidentally, by another former König student, Arthur Baron) in the center of the city.[1] Frank's light and cheery design (fig. 13) took full advantage of the rooms' high ceilings and large windows. In other respects, however, it was a seemingly inauspicious debut for a young modernist in the making. Not only did Frank cover the reinforced concrete ceilings with brightly colored folk motifs, but he also concealed many of the other modern architectonic features with wood paneling, patterned draperies, and inlay work. In keeping with the Swedish theme of the school, the ornamental scheme was based on traditional Swedish folk motifs, probably inspired by the work of the Swedish painter Carl Larsson and an exhibition of Swedish folk arts held at the Österreichisches Museum für Kunst und Industrie (Austrian Museum of Art and Industry) the same year.[2] Frank altered and refined the designs, both simplifying and abstracting them. The overall look was that of an old-fashioned country rusticity; but the serial repetition of the various motifs, despite their still discernible folk origins, evoked the geometric stylizations of the high Viennese *Jugendstil.*

14. Apartment for Karl and Hedwig Tedesco, Vienna, 1910; lady's drawing room. Collection Professor Johannes Spalt, Vienna.

In most other ways, the school's interiors were a departure from the Viennese design of the early years of the century. Frank's blending of disparate forms, colors, and textures and his interest in the vernacular echoed a wider trend away from the purist reductiveness that had dominated the work of Hoffmann, Moser, and others only a few years before. After the short-lived triumph of the *Moderne,* a reaction had begun to set in, and by 1906 even Hoffmann and Olbrich were experimenting with a new historical eclecticism. Like König's other students, Frank had been imbued with a deep faith in the historical tradition as a generator of ideas, and he responded with particular enthusiasm to the shift in sensibility. The interiors of the school evoked this new spirit.

An even more complete demonstration of Frank's emerging design idiom was his other project of the same period, the apartment of his sister Hedwig and her husband, the industrialist Karl Tedesco. The two were married in 1910, and they asked Frank to design their spacious apartment in the Untere Viaduktstraße. Frank responded with an exuberant, and to modern eyes, oddly discordant arrangement. As one of the surviving photographs shows, the rooms (fig. 14) encompassed a hodgepodge of styles, forms, and materials. At first glance, the results seem to be a retreat to the historicism of the 1890s. Although unmistakable vestiges of the *Jugendstil* remain—for example, in the design of the glass vitrine, which borrowed from Hoffmann's purist style—the apartment as a whole represented a decided move away from the earlier works of the Secessionists.[3]

Yet a closer inspection reveals that the rooms were also a break from late historicist design. While a broad array of historical influences is discernible—ranging from the Italian Renaissance to neoclassicism and Biedermeier—Frank blended them together in seemingly indiscriminate fashion; even some of the individual pieces of furniture exhibit the influence of several different styles. Moreover, the furnishings are arranged casually, with little or no reference to the other objects in the room.

This eclectic mélange, as Oskar Wlach, one of Frank's former classmates at the Technische Hochschule, wrote in a review of Frank's early work, was in part an effort to break free of the "tyranny" of "architectonically composed rooms" ruled by the "laws" of "symmetry" and "rhythm."[4] But it was just as manifestly an attempt to undermine the *Gesamtkunstwerk* (total work of art) ideals that Hoffmann and the other Secessionists had championed at the turn of the century. The notion of the interior as a "symphony" of elements sounding together, as the critic Hermann Bahr had expressed it,[5] gave way in Frank's work to a new stylelessness, a look that was unquestionably modern but lacking specific rules. "A room like the salon in the Tedesco apartment," Wlach noted, "in which a Persian carpet, an English table, a Chinese lamp, and Swedish ceiling, etc., form a resonant harmony . . . cannot be damaged, one may add what one will. It remains mutable and lives along with the life of its owners."[6]

Like Loos, who had never embraced the Secessionist style, Frank sanctioned the use not only of elements that were expressly "modern" but also pieces based on historical models. Frank, however, sought in his designs to break down the connection between architecture and interior decoration: whereas Loos conceived of his furnishings in relation to their architectural surroundings, often arranging them formally or symmetrically to frame or accentuate various architectonic details, Frank placed his pieces casually about the rooms. He also dispensed with large built-in furnishings, preferring instead those that were light and freestanding; and he rejected the wainscoting and other formal framing devices that Loos employed, opting instead for minimal wall treatments, which allowed the rooms to serve as more or less neutral containers.

In his review of Frank's early works, Wlach spelled out these ideas: "The only immobile element of the living space is its defining surfaces: ceiling, wall, and floor. All of the objects must appear to be moveable . . . The walls are borders within which all things must be subject to the changing needs and moods of the occupants. The objects in the room must not be arranged according to the fixed principles of some external architectonic composition that deny people's free choices . . . The controlling measure is man."[7]

THE STRNAD CIRCLE Frank was not alone in his call for a new approach to interior design. While still at the Technische Hochschule, he had joined a small circle of like-minded young architects and designers that included Oskar Strnad, Viktor Lurje, Hugo Gorge, and Wlach. All of the members of the group, aside from Gorge, had been students of König's, and, like Frank, all came from middle-class Jewish backgrounds.[8] Strnad, who was the eldest, assumed the leading role. At the age of thirty-one, he had already earned a reputation as one of the rising stars of a new generation of Viennese modernists. After graduating, he had worked for several years for Friedrich Ohmann and for theater architects Ferdinand Fellner and Hermann Helmer, along the way designing several highly praised projects of his own, including a synagogue in Trieste and the Empress Elisabeth Monument in Vienna. In 1909, on Hoffmann's recommendation, he was appointed to a teaching post at the Kunstgewerbeschule, where he took over the school's basic design course.[9] From 1907 on, Strnad also collaborated sporadically with Wlach and Lurje on various competitions and projects.[10]

As the youngest member of the circle, Frank was influenced by the work and ideas of the others: his emerging views on the design of furnishings and spaces seem, in particular, to owe a debt to Strnad. Frank's Tedesco interiors show unmistakable parallels with Strnad's own apartment of the same year (fig. 15), and many of his early writings echo the ideas in Strnad's prewar lectures.[11] What united all of the members of the group was the belief—appropriated from König—that reform in architecture and interior design could only result from coming to terms with historical tradition. In contrast to the Secessionists, they rejected the search for new forms for novelty's sake, preferring instead to develop their work out of a careful consideration of older models. They drew a sharp distinction, however, between "imitating" and "being inspired by" a given source. Although they borrowed more or less directly from the earlier works, what interested them above all was the underlying raison d'être of a form or motif, the cultural and functional considerations that had given rise to it. By gaining insight into the "inner mean-

15. Oskar Strnad, Living room, Strnad apartment, c. 1912. *The Studio Yearbook of Decorative Art* (London, 1913).

ing" of historical artworks, they believed that they could discern certain principles that could then become the basis for new works.

Strnad, Frank, and the other members of the circle took these lessons from a wide variety of sources. They concentrated on the Western classical tradition, but like the Secessionists, they were also interested in cultures more remote in time and place, from ancient Sumer and the Minoan and Mycenaean worlds to European folk traditions and the art of the Far East.

Evidence of this new interior design style was on display in the fall of 1911 in a room Frank, Gorge, Lurje, and Strnad designed for the *Exhibition of Austrian Applied Arts* held at the Österreichisches Museum für Kunst und Industrie. The space (fig. 16), which combined painted and metal-laminated furniture (designed by Frank) with a ceiling and balcony richly decorated with geometric motifs, provided a working demonstration of their effort to recast past sources in an up-to-date fashion. The unambiguous but pared-down historical references of the case pieces and ceiling and the highly restrained handling of the wall surfaces and light fixture contributed to what critic Hartwig Fischel described as a "striving to approach the effects of old art with modern, objectively (*sachlich*) applied design principles."[12] Although Fischel detected a "strong archaistic tendency" in the installation, it was still possible, he observed, to recognize an "overcoming of the old form elements with the requirements of our time."[13]

This new "modernized traditionalism" was also apparent in the room Frank designed for the 1912 *Frühjahrsausstellung* (spring exhibition) at the Österreichisches Museum für Kunst und Industrie. The exhibit, organized by Hoffmann's assistant Karl Witzmann, was an attempt to sum up recent developments in Viennese design.[14] The designs of a number of the participants, including Hoffmann and Strnad, reflected the trend toward a new, denuded classicism that had become increasingly popular in Vienna after 1905. Frank's contribution, a living room (*Wohnhalle*) for a country house (fig. 17), on the other hand, with its quaint simplicity, offered a dramatic contrast with the other exhibits. Not only was he the only exhibitor to place his installation out of the axis of the enfilade of displays, but the room's informality and avoidance of stereometric and decorative details represented an almost total break with earlier Viennese modernism.[15] In place of the geometric purism that had formed the basis for much of Viennese design for the preceding decade, Frank substituted a new vocabulary based on historical and contemporary English design.[16]

Frank was by no means alone in turning to England for models: English design and, more generally, the English way of life were widely admired in Viennese architectural circles in the years prior to the First World War. Both Hoffmann and Loos had been stimulated by English precedents, as had many others.[17] Frank, however, looked not only to Morris and his followers for inspiration, but also back to earlier English vernacular forms. The chairs, table, and settee were based on seventeenth-century English and

American Colonial models; and the design of the sideboard was influenced by the work of Cotswold furniture makers Ernest Gimson and Sidney and Ernest Barnsley, who themselves had been inspired by earlier designs.[18]

  With its ladder-back chairs and English country ambiance, Frank's design struck one reviewer as "touchingly old-fashioned."[19] Yet the sense of refinement and simplicity of the arrangement also gave the room a distinctly modern cast, one that most observers immediately recognized. Another reviewer praised the design, noting that "Dr. Frank knows how to make a room intimate and comfortable with the simplest means . . . His furnishings are distinguished by a particularly strong emphasis on their constructive elements. In these [pieces] the taste, the sense of form, and color of our times are alive, and yet he has not lost sight of the needs of the present."[20]

  This attempt to reconcile past and present is also behind Frank's design for his own apartment the following year (fig. 18). Making use of several pieces from the 1912 exhibition, including the arts and crafts–inspired sideboard, the Carl Larsson watercolors, and the framed view of Florence, the rooms presented an even more refined essay on the possibilities of mixing together different elements, both old and new. Many of the objects,

16. (left) Josef Frank, Hugo Gorge, Viktor Lurje, and Oskar Strnad, Room 2, *Exhibition of Austrian Applied Arts*, Österreichisches Museum für Kunst und Industrie, Vienna, 1911–12. MAK-Österreichisches Museum für angewandte Kunst, Vienna.

17. (right) Living hall of a country house, Room 13, *Spring Exhibition of Austrian Arts and Crafts*, Österreichisches Museum für Kunst und Industrie, 1912. MAK-Österreichisches Museum für angewandte Kunst, Vienna.

18. Living room, Frank apartment, Wiedener Hauptstraße 64, Vienna, 1913. MAK-Österreichisches Museum für angewandte Kunst, Vienna.

such as the Oriental carpets and patterned cretonnes, would become standard features in Frank's later interiors.

The most striking aspect of the apartment is the free placement of the furnishings. "Living spaces," Frank wrote a few years later, "are not artworks, nor are they well-tuned harmonies in color and form, whose individual elements (wallpaper, carpets, furniture, pictures) constitute a completed whole." Rather, they are spaces that must not only serve the immediate needs of their occupants, but also house both handcrafted objects of art and machine-made objects of everyday life. Modern living spaces "require a maximum of movement and brightness, a wealth of colors and forms, objects and materials."[21] Frank insisted that interiors should present the impression of having evolved naturally over time, as a part of the process of living. It was the client, he maintained, not the architect, who should ultimately decide what should be included in the modern home. "The architect," he wrote, "can have no influence on what form these objects take." He can only

offer a framework or setting for a domicile. The home of an insensitive person, in which the architect has placed the most exquisite objects, tastefully and symmetrically ordered, placed, laid, and hung, will forever remain unfeeling and sober. The living space is never unfinished and never finished; it lives with those who live within.[22]

One other feature of the design, which pointed firmly in the direction of Frank's later work, is worth mentioning: the configuration of the spaces. The apartment was on the top floor of a new building in the Wiedener Hauptstraße designed by Arthur Baron. The arrangement of the turret, mansard roof, and gables yielded a complex assembly of spaces; in fact, none of the main rooms was a regular rectangle. Frank, who in later years would repeatedly write of the need to break free of the straightjacket of the regular four-cornered room, chose the apartment precisely for its unusual spaces; and he would use it as a model for his experiments in spatial planning.

THE EAST ASIAN ART MUSEUM   Around the same time as the 1912 spring exhibition, Frank received his first major commission: the interiors for the new Museum of East Asian Art in Cologne. The museum, the first in Germany devoted solely to East Asian art, had been founded in 1909 by Adolf Fischer. The son of a Viennese industrial magnate, Fischer had assembled an impressive collection of Chinese, Japanese, Indian, and other East Asian artworks while serving as scientific attaché at the German Embassy in Beijing at the turn of the century. After returning to Germany, he sought a permanent exhibition space for his works, entering into negotiations with several cities, including Berlin and Kiel, before eventually settling on Cologne.[23]

The museum was housed in a newly constructed four-story wing of the city's Museum of Arts and Crafts designed by German architect Franz Brantzky. Fischer requested, however, that the interiors be left unfinished so that they could be specially adapted for the requirements of his collection. His choice for the job fell on the young Frank, who had been recommended to him by Hoffmann, a close friend of Fischer's.[24]

But when Frank arrived in Cologne, he found that the construction on the annex was well underway and that much of the detailing was already completed.[25] In a letter to Hoffmann, he complained that the meager budget for the job allowed him only to fabricate the vitrines and to make minor changes to the rooms. Frank found himself further restricted by the plan of the rooms (fig. 19), which had already been determined.[26] In the end, the limitations proved to be an advantage. Fischer was particularly concerned that the installations would not in any way detract from the artworks.[27] Accordingly, Frank's treatment of the rooms was highly restrained, even ascetic (figs. 20–22). He had the walls painted white or a neutral gray-ochre; the floors, a natural gray or brown. He outlined several of the rooms with spare black wooden moldings (recalling both Japanese traditional architecture and Hoffmann's contemporary exhibition designs); otherwise, he left them devoid of ornamentation. Frank also installed three complete original rooms that Fischer had crafted in Japan.[28]

Aside from the vaguely Oriental touches that Frank gave the display cases, the rooms constituted a neutral frame for the art. The larger sculptures were mounted on simple stone or wooden bases, most freestanding, and the smaller works were installed in spe-

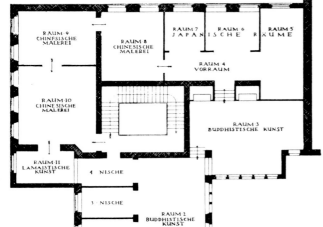

19. Museum für Ostasiatische Kunst, Cologne, 1912–13; plan of the ground floor. Adolf Fischer, *Führer durch das Museum für ostasiatische Kunst der Stadt Cöln* (Cologne, 1913).

20. Museum für Ostasiatische Kunst, Cologne, 1912–13; entrance from the main building looking toward Room 1. Museum der Stadt Köln, Rheinisches Bildarchiv, Cologne.

21. Museum für Ostasiatische Kunst, Cologne, 1912–13; Room 3, Buddhist sculptures. Museum der Stadt Köln, Rheinisches Bildarchiv, Cologne.

22. Museum für Ostasiatische Kunst, Cologne, 1912–13; Room 13, lacquered objects. Museum der Stadt Köln, Rheinisches Bildarchiv, Cologne.

cially made vitrines. The cases, designed by Frank and executed by local cabinetmakers, were arranged to allow the viewer to see the artworks from all sides, in some instances even from below. His painstaking attention to the objects is particularly evident in the textiles room, for which Frank created a special storage system with glass drawers, enabling museumgoers to inspect each piece individually (fig. 23). Although some of the detailing drew from contemporary Viennese and English design, the overall effect was a stunning departure from the fustian museum interiors of the time.

Frank spent ten months in Cologne, from the second half of 1912 through the early fall of 1913, planning and overseeing every aspect of the installations. When the museum finally opened its doors in late October 1913, the response to Frank's design in the press and in scholarly circles was universally positive. One reviewer, Curt Glaser, writing in *Kunst und Künstler*, remarked that "nowhere is there a museum presented in such a comfortable and tasteful fashion as this one."[29] Other critics praised Frank's restrained handling of the interiors and the museum's simplicity and unity of conception, comparing it with the recently opened Museum of Arts and Crafts in Frankfurt, considered a model of museum design at the time.[30]

For the twenty-eight-year-old Frank, the museum project was a triumph, one that brought him newfound status and recognition. The time he spent in Germany also

23. Museum für Ostasiatische Kunst, Cologne, 1912–13; Room 30, fabric display cases. Museum der Stadt Köln, Rheinisches Bildarchiv, Cologne.

brought changes to his personal life. In December 1912, while in Cologne, he married a Swedish woman, Anna Regina Sebenius.

Frank had met Anna in Vienna through his work on the Swedish gymnastics school two years before.[31] Born in 1880 in Dragsfjärd, Finland, she spent her childhood in Stockholm. Later, she trained to become a music teacher.[32] Though five years older than her husband and a Lutheran, Anna shared a background similar to her husband's: she was from a well-to-do, worldly, and cultured middle-class family. At thirty-two years of age, she was already well past the age when most women of her time married. But Anna's independence and her good-natured and sociable manner made her an excellent match for Frank. What she offered, further, was intellectual companionship. Like Frank, Anna was interested in the newest currents and ideas.[33] Perhaps more important, she also played a central role in Frank's developing connections with Scandinavian design. During their numerous trips to Sweden, he was able to observe both historical and contemporary works of the region's designers—sources that would become increasingly influential in his work.

THE PARTNERSHIP OF STRNAD-WLACH-FRANK

After returning from Cologne in the fall of 1913, Frank joined a working partnership with Strnad and Wlach. They set up an office in Strand's studio at the annex of the Kunstgewerbeschule at Fichtegasse 4. Although both Strnad and Wlach had some experience in working on large public buildings, they specialized in private houses and interiors. Their clientele, like that of the earlier Secessionist generation, was drawn almost exclusively from the ranks of the haute bourgeoisie—the industrialists, bankers, bureaucrats, and managers who were coming increasingly to supplant the old aristocracy as patrons of the arts.

The three architects worked together occasionally, but they also pursued their own individual projects. When Frank returned to Vienna, Strnad and Wlach had recently finished an apartment building on the Stuckgasse, and they were in the process of completing a single-family house on the Cobenzlgasse. Strnad, possibly with the assistance of Frank and Wlach, also provided some of the furnishings for Hoffmann's Primavesi Country House (1913–14) in Winkelsdorf (Kouty, Czech Republic).[34]

Most of the three architects' surviving drawings from these years bear the stamp of the partnership, "Strnad-Wlach-Frank." Ordinarily, however, they signed their drawings individually. They were also careful to credit each partner's designs in publications. But the similarities of many of their works of this period suggest that there was a good deal of cross-fertilization in the office. It was not merely that they drew ideas from each other: all three architects borrowed from the same historical sources, and they had developed similar design strategies going back to their time at the Technische Hochschule.

Yet there were evident differences in their works as well. From the start, Frank showed a much stronger tendency toward eclecticism: his interiors were more formally varied, and they were often more radical in their statement of a new modernity. Frank, too, was more strongly drawn to folk design and to exotic models, especially Asian sources—a not surprising development, given his recent work on the East Asian Museum. Strnad's works, by contrast, evinced a greater reliance on classicism, especially the Biedermeier and Baroque. Wlach, for his part, often displayed an allegiance to traditional German forms. Despite these dissimilarities, the three architects offered their own distinctive architectural and design idiom, "differing," as Wlach later described, "from the work of all other Viennese architects, such as Wagner, Hofmann [*sic*], Loos, etc."[35]

THE BUNZL HOUSE By the end of 1913, Frank was at work on several houses. One of these was a country house for industrialist Hugo Bunzl. Bunzl, to whom Frank was related both through his mother and by marriage,[36] was owner and director of a large paper factory near the small Lower Austrian town of Ortmann bei Pernitz in the Piesting Valley some forty kilometers southwest of Vienna. He commissioned Frank to design not only the house, which he intended to use during the summers and while at the factory on business, but also the interiors, including the fixtures, furniture, and fabrics.

Frank responded with what was surely one of the most unusual houses built in Austria on the eve of the war. Situated in a clearing on the crest of a small wooded hill a short distance from the factory complex (fig. 24), the two-story, hipped-roofed structure was

24. Summer house for Hugo Bunzl, Ortmann, Lower Austria, 1913–14. Graphische Sammlung Albertina, Vienna.

built entirely of wood except for the foundation and chimneys. The outer walls were large squared logs thirteen centimeters thick, with dovetail joints at the corners. First seen, the rustic log members, red tile roof, and casual composition suggest a borrowing from local vernacular styles. On closer inspection, another influence also becomes apparent: the house's sloping chimney, asymmetrical arrangement, and hipped roof reveal the impact of the English arts and crafts movement, especially the works of C. F. A. Voysey.

Like many other Austrian and German architects of his generation, Frank shared a strong regard for the rural residences of the contemporary English "freestyle" designers. His interest had been stimulated above all by Hermann Muthesius, whose three-volume work, *Das englische Haus* (1905), documented in exhaustive detail the recent history of English domestic architecture.[37] Muthesius, like many of his contemporaries, was drawn to the informality of English domestic architecture. What attracted Frank, however, was less the picturesque quality of English country houses than their habitability, homeyness, comfort, and ease. The matter-of-factness of English houses, their lack of pretension and, above all, their avoidance of a controlling theory seemed to him to pose an alternative to the rigid formality and ostentatiousness of Central European historicism.

But if Frank sometimes borrowed directly from British models, he was more concerned with learning and applying their underlying principles. He was especially interested in the ideas of M. H. Baillie Scott, and the Bunzl House can be read as an attempt to interpret the precepts spelled out in Scott's 1906 book *Houses and Gardens*.[38] In the work, which appeared in German in 1912,[39] Scott urged that practicality and comfort replace style and representational character as the central issues in residential design. In the 1890s, he had begun to work out the possibilities of a new spaciousness, opening up his interiors to provide an uninterrupted field for daily activities. The modern house, he wrote, is merely a "roomy cottage," which balances the "opposing qualities of privacy and spaciousness."[40]

The average house should not be a place primarily for the reception of visitors, but a dwelling for the family. . . . [It] should then be designed essentially for its occupants and should consist mainly of one good-sized apartment, with plenty of floor space and elbow room, with only such furniture as may be actually required.[41]

Not only should the rooms of the house "be well designed and arranged in due relation to their functions," Scott wrote, but "it is important also that the routes of passage . . . should be carefully studied and arranged without undue waste of space in passages." The house ultimately was not a rational container but "a congeries of conveniences."[42]

With its lack of pretension and emphasis on comfort, the Bunzl House fulfilled Scott's call to meet the "actual requirements" of its occupants.[43] Its furnishings (fig. 25) were simple and straightforward, with the visual stress on creating a pleasant, hospitable atmosphere. Beamed ceilings, Oriental carpets, and upholstered furniture, similar to

those one might have found in any contemporary British middle class country home, created an atmosphere of ease and warmth. As befit a summer house, the rooms were also open and airy. "It was my intention," Frank wrote in a short article in *Innen-Dekoration,* "to join the living rooms of the ground floor with the garden by means of large glass doors, and to open the bedrooms on the upper floor to all sides with added-on balconies." Frank further underscored this feeling of lightness by painting most of the interior walls and ceilings white and using simple unadorned furnishings. "The few furnishings are placed independently of the space," Frank noted.

To avoid any sense of heaviness, they are made of the most diverse materials. But the wood is neither stained nor painted, so that none of the freshness and natural character of the wood is lost. Similarly, the curtains on the windows and the lampshades are white so that the light can fall into the room in its natural color . . . The fabrics and carpets are multicolored, like the gardens outside the windows, but are mostly red and yellow, and thus provide a warm-toned contrast to the broad expanses of sky and forest on all sides of the house.[44]

This same general air of informality and comfort is also evident in the house's plan (fig. 26). The rooms were large, and most were irregularly shaped. Their arrangement, though clearly well thought out, appears casual at first, even a little haphazard. Here again, Frank drew on English and American precedents, specifically the free or irregular

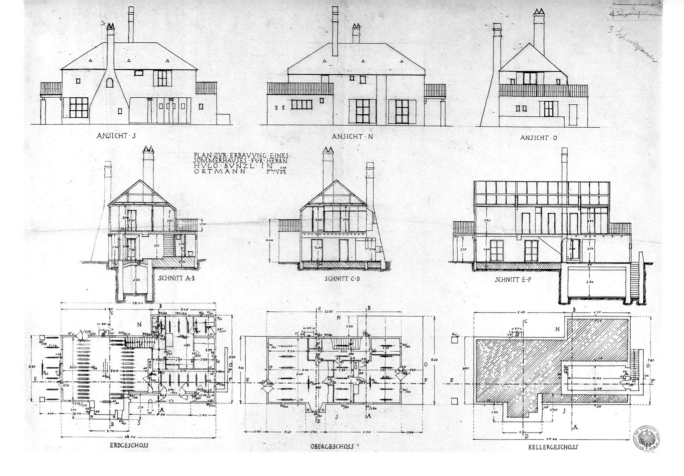

ANSICHT·S · ANSICHT·N · ANSICHT·O

PLAN·ZVR·ERBAVVNG·EINES·
SOMMERHAVSES·FVR·HERRN
HVGO·BVNZL·IN
ORTMANN

SCHNITT A-B · SCHNITT C-D · SCHNITT E-F

ERDGESCHOSS · OBERGESCHOSS · KELLERGESCHOSS

plan with which Philip Webb, Richard Norman Shaw, H. H. Richardson, and others had experimented in their houses of the latter half of the nineteenth century to achieve a rambling effect, with each space freely flowing into the next.[45] Frank reinforced this element of spatial play by linking the rooms to terraces and balconies, fostering a sense of spatial continuity both within the house and between the interior and exterior. It was an idea he would return to again and again, and it became one of the fundamental organizing principles of his later houses.

THE SCHOLL AND STRAUß HOUSES At the same time he was designing the Bunzl House, Frank was also at work on two villas in Vienna. The houses, for two upper-middle-class couples, Emil and Agnes Scholl and Oskar and Hanny Strauß, were situated on a hill facing the Wilbrandtgasse in Vienna's eighteenth district on what was then the western edge of the city.

If the Bunzl House was expressly a "country house," Frank intended the formal language of the Wilbrandtgasse houses (figs. 27–31) to articulate a new urbanism. In an article published after the First World War, Frank explained that he had sought to produce a house type that would readily fit into the city context. "It was my aim," he wrote, "to leave out everything, or at least to simplify to the utmost, anything that in any way could be viewed as incidental . . . The endless fantasies" being constructed in various historical

26. Summer house for Hugo Bunzl, Ortmann, Lower Austria, 1913–14, elevations, plans and sections 1:100. Pencil, pen and ink on tracing paper, 44 × 61 cm. Sammlung, Universität für angewandte Kunst, Vienna.

27. Scholl House, Vienna,
1913–14. Bauhaus-Archiv, Berlin.

28. Scholl House, Vienna,
1913–14; view from the rear garden.
Bauhaus-Archiv, Berlin.

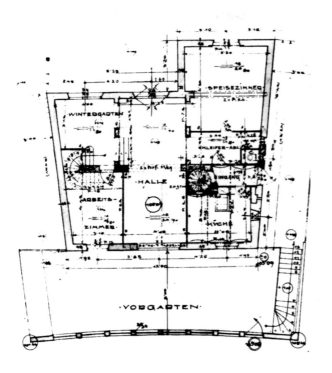

29. Scholl House, Vienna,
1913–14, plan and sections.
Collection Professor Johannes
Spalt, Vienna.

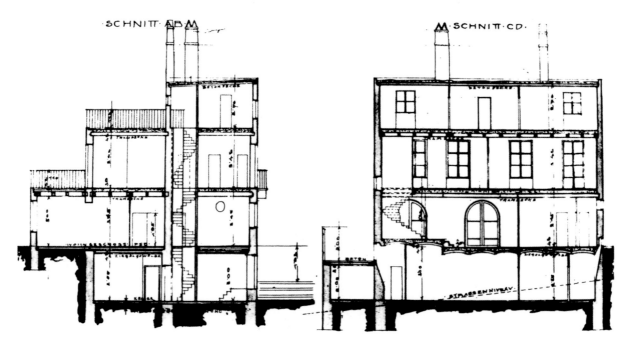

30. Strauß House, Vienna,

1913–14. Bauhaus-Archiv, Berlin.

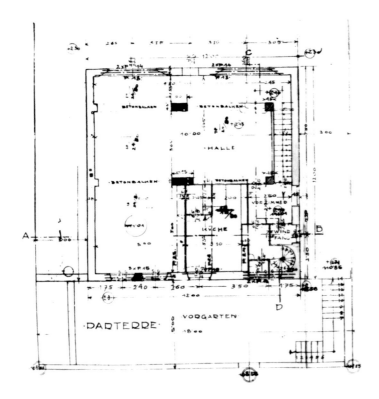

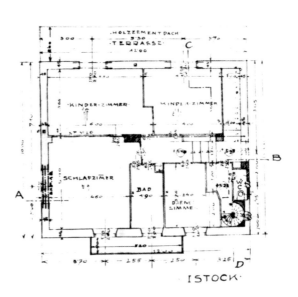

31. Strauß House, Vienna,

1913–14; plans. Collection Professor

Johannes Spalt, Vienna.

styles "destroy that sense of unity that we love so much in old cities."[46] The house's flat roofs and understated façades, Frank explained, were an attempt to foster a coherence lost amid the jumble of different house styles and roof shapes that pervaded such suburban districts.[47] A drawing Frank made in 1914 or early 1915 (fig. 32) showing both the Scholl and Strauß Houses (the first and fourth from the left, respectively) with two projected houses of the same basic type in between, was intended to illustrate this new unity.

The differences between the Bunzl House, with its picturesque massing and pitched roof, and the Scholl and Strauß Houses, with their pared-down lines and flats roofs, resulted from their disparate settings and functions. A summer house in the country and a suburban villa, Frank believed, had discrete formal requirements that demanded differentiated appearances. This fundamental distinction between the needs of town and country can also be found in Loos's work of the same period—demonstrated, for example, by the contrast between his simple, unadorned prewar villas and his project for the supervisor's cabin for the Schwarzwald School on the Semmering from 1913, with its almost literal use of regional dialect.[48] In the Bunzl House, however, Frank showed a much greater willingness than Loos to break free of local vernacular codes and to experiment with what, in some respects, was a novel architectonic language.

While the Bunzl summer house drew on English precedents, Frank's two suburban villas bore quite obvious parallels with Loos's houses of the preceding years, especially his 1910 Horner House and the 1912 Steiner and Scheu Houses. The massing of the Scholl House, with its cascading rear terraces, in particular, is strikingly similar to Loos's Scheu House (fig. 33). (The Scholl House, however, is rotated ninety degrees so that the terraces face the rear [south] garden, rather than the side, an alteration that, in fact, gave the two houses—despite their evident formal kinship—quite different looks.)

Frank, who saw Loos regularly throughout this period, was no doubt aware of Loos's residences and his ideas. The unmistakable similarities in the outward appearances of their houses suggest that Frank, at the very least, was in his own way trying to come to

32. Sketch showing the possible further development of the Wilbrandtgasse, Vienna XVIII, c. 1914; perspective. Author's collection.

33. Adolf Loos, Scheu House,
Vienna, 1912–13, rear façade.
Heinrich Kulka, *Adolf Loos: Das
Werk des Architekten*
(Vienna, 1931).

terms with the precedent Loos had set. Yet it is also possible to understand the work of
both architects as a response to the same underlying issues. The designs of both Loos
and Frank grew out of a critique of the Viennese bourgeois culture and architecture establishment. Both shared a rejection of a domineering, form-giving art, whether *Jugendstil* or a later conception; and both were confronted with the question of how to escape
from the apparent dead end of historicism without merely resorting to a newly invented
architectural vocabulary. Frank and Loos tended, moreover, to draw on the same reper-
tory of historical sources, including classicism and—particularly notable in the case of
their prewar house projects—the Mediterranean vernacular. During his many trips to
Italy, Frank had had the opportunity to observe firsthand the simple and unaffected building forms of the region. Hoffmann, too, had shown a decided interest in the folk architecture of Southern Europe and a number of his early buildings, including the Purkers-
dorf Sanatorium, were an attempt to bring this idiom up-to-date. Indeed, as Eduard
Sekler has written, for many of the Viennese architects of the time this anonymous
Mediterranean architecture "demonstrated a direct relationship between need and design
response which was the very antithesis of the relationship that followed from the formal-
istic design method of historicizing stylistic eclecticism based on imitation." The simple,
honest architectural forms of vernacular building "were believed to owe nothing to the
historic styles of 'high art,'" and thus appeared as "acceptable sources of inspiration."[49]
Frank's Wilbrandtgasse houses, like Loos's prewar villas, grew out of a shared desire to

EXPLORATION

find an idiom that had not been corrupted by decades of stylistic imitation and that could provide the starting point for a new, modern urban architecture.

But if Frank and Loos both began with many of the same assumptions and formal ideas, they proceeded in quite dissimilar ways. In fact, a careful examination of their houses of this period reveals telling differences. Whereas Loos, for example, simply cut the windows into the façade and avoided all further elaboration, Frank framed his windows and door with broad white bands, a tactic that served to soften the appearance of the walls. Loos's villas have smooth plaster surfaces, wholly concealing their underlying block and mortar structure; Frank, on the other hand, chose to employ a thin plaster that reveals the brick courses underneath. As a result, the sense of the tectonic is preserved; it is neither abstracted nor masked. Frank also retained a number of clearly legible historical quotations, including string courses, moldings, and, in the case of the Scholl House, corner pilasters.

The most significant differences, however, involve the composition of the façades. While Loos preferred symmetrical—or at least balanced—arrangements, Frank deliberately sought to undermine any sense of traditional proportion or symmetry. This is especially evident on the front façade of the Scholl House: the windows line up neither vertically nor horizontally; and the door to the second story balcony is set off insistently to one side, a strategy that establishes a dynamic tension absent in Loos's prewar compositions. The façades of the smaller Strauß House also show this same willful warping and displacing of the elements, though in a more subtle fashion. But in either case the effect, which Frank clearly intended as a repudiation of conventional symmetrical ordering, lends the houses a look that was quite unlike anything else being constructed in Vienna at the time.

MOVEMENT AND SPACE It was not only the arrangement of the façades of Frank's Wilbrandtgasse houses that stood out. The interior plans of the two houses were a radical departure from tradition. This was particularly evident on the main level of the Scholl House, which was dominated by a large living area (*Halle*) extending the full width of the house. Adjacent to the *Halle* on either side were a dining room and conservatory, which together formed a continuous volume. The large expanse of open space, afforded by Frank's use of a massive reinforced concrete beam that extended the width of the house and carried much of the weight of the upper floor, allowed a reduction in the number and size of interior load-bearing walls.

This openness and interconnection, however, did not entail the elimination of spatial fragmentation and differentiation, as it would in later "open plan" designs. Instead, as in Wright's houses at the turn of the century, it provided for a series of contiguous spaces or zones, which were linked together in complex patterns. By adopting different vantage points or merely by turning one's head, the occupant would be confronted with a wide variety of views. The unusual, slightly wedge-shaped footprint of the house—evidently a result of Frank's attempt to squeeze the most usable area out of the narrow, trapezoidal lot—also served to underscore the sense of spatial play.

To further increase the amount of "living space," Frank reduced the size of the service areas, and he largely dispensed with hallways. As in the Bunzl House, the organizing principle in the house is an attempt to foster a sense of spatial diversity and flow. Frank achieved this by arranging the rooms along a carefully thought-out route of penetration extending from the entry through the house to the main living areas, and from there upstairs or out into the rear garden. Along this route, the individual rooms flowed into each other, forming an intricate sequence of volumes.

Frank apparently derived this idea of arranging the house along a path of ever-changing spatial effects from Strnad. Strnad had begun to experiment with the notion of a perceptual architectural promenade in his design for the Hock House on the Cobenzl-gasse in Vienna (fig. 34), produced in collaboration with Wlach around 1912–13. Although the house maintained a regular horizontal layering of floors, Strand and Wlach took advantage of the hilly site to create a winding path of entry extending from the street to the upper piano nobile containing the principal public rooms. By controlling the direction of the pathway, the intervals between the stairs and landings, and the amount of light within the passageway, they were able to achieve a rich and highly varied experience.

The route of the stair in the Hock House is confined largely to the exterior, but in other designs for residences in the same period Strnad investigated the possibilities of related interior sequences. In a house he designed for the writer Jakob Wassermann (fig. 35) in 1914, Strnad devised an extended, straight axis leading from the street through a small vestibule and along a series of French doors into a large L-shaped living area. Along this main route, he introduced various pavements and floorings, vistas, and lighting effects; the path also involved a gradual climb upward, with (if one counts the various stair landings) as many as eight different levels from the street to the rear *Halle*.

In a lecture delivered in 1913, Strnad contended that opportunities for movement (*das Sichbewegen*) constituted one of the "essential" ingredients of "comfortable living space."[50] For Strnad, this "shifting movement" (*Verschiebungsbewegung*) resulted in a more profound awareness of space, which in turn served to heighten the observer's architectural experience. "The more possibilities for movement a plan offered," he asserted, "the more discontinuities [*Verschneidungen*] and displacements [*Verschiebungen*] that are evident, the richer the spatial structure" and, by extension, the more interesting and "livable" the resulting spaces.[51] In another lecture of the same year, "Gedanken beim Entwurf eines Grundrisses" (Thoughts on the design of a ground plan), Strnad argued that the effects of such a promenade were not merely visual, but also that they involved the other senses, as well as producing certain psychological impressions:

34. (top) Oskar Strnad and
Oskar Wlach, Hock House, Vienna,
1912–13. Max Eisler, *Oskar Strnad*
(Vienna, 1910).

35. (bottom) Oskar Strnad,
Wassermann House, Vienna, 1914;
stair. Österreichische
Nationalbibliothek, Bildarchiv,
Vienna.

Architecture is by no means a purely visual medium, but is made up of an endless number of imponderables. An architectural conception arises from the combined impact of our impression [of a space] as well as the possibilities for movement (providing a complete feeling of space) as well as the effect of light (the color of the material), of smell, of sound, and of touch (of the material world). . . . The treatment of the surface of the material must proceed not only from aesthetic considerations, but also from a much deeper, inexplicable spirit.[52]

Strnad's notion of the experience of kinetic space almost certainly drew from the new concepts of psychological and physiological perception first developed in the writings of German theorists Adolf Hildebrand, August Schmarsow, and others around the turn of the century.[53] Hildebrand, in his book *Das Problem der Form in der bildenden Künste* (The problem of form in the fine arts; 1893), had proposed that spatial perception through motion of the eye—kinetic perception (*Bewegungsvorstellung*)—was essential to grasping an object's plasticity and thus its three-dimensional reality.[54] In a series of writings published after the turn of the century, Schmarsow extended this notion, insisting that the essence of the human experience of architecture resided in bodily movement through space rather than stationary observation. Our sense of depth—and, thus, our sense of space—emerged through movement within a particular volume. Only by moving from place to place in the third dimension, Schmarsow contended, could one develop full spatial awareness.[55]

Schmarsow, however, was not concerned solely with how we perceive space but also with how our bodily experiences determine the way in which we frame and arrange our spaces. Among the most striking features of Schmarsow's writings is his assertion that architecture could be understood as both an expression and an outcome of our bodily structure, perceptive apparatus, and patterns of movement, as well as of our needs and desires. Because of this, Schmarsow showed a preference in his writings for vital spaces, whose forms were an expression of human activity.[56]

Such assertions, of course, had a powerful appeal for young modernists like Frank, who sought to reshape traditional building plans in accord with contemporary living conditions. Strnad and Frank were no doubt aware of these ideas, which were widely discussed and debated within Viennese art and architectural circles after the turn of the century.[57]

A more immediate source of new ideas of space and form for both was likely Loos himself.[58] By 1909, Frank's last year as a student, Loos was already at work on his Michaelerplatz building. What initially influenced both Strnad and Frank, however, was evidently not Loos's use of differentiated room heights and interlocking volumes, but his conviction that interior spaces should convey sundry mental and emotional states. This concept is spelled out perhaps most clearly in Loos's 1898 essay "Das Prinzip der Bekleidung" (The principle of cladding):

The architect's task is to provide a warm and livable space. . . . But the artist, the architect, first senses the effect he intends to realize and sees the rooms he wants to create in his mind's eye. He senses the effects he wants to exert upon the spectator: fear and horror, if it is a dungeon; reverence, if a church; respect for the power of the state, if a government building; piety, if a tomb; homeyness, if a residence; gaiety, if a tavern. These effects are produced by both the material and the form of the space.[59]

Loos derived this notion of the emotional impact of both wall covering and space from Gottfried Semper. But he was also influenced—at least indirectly—by the contemporary discussions of the role of subjective feelings in conditioning our perceptions of space developed in the writings of Robert Vischer, Theodor Lipps, and others in the 1880s and 1890s.[60] This idea of *Einfühlung,* or empathy, as applied to the observer's impression of space, suggested not only new paths for the interpretation of architectural works but also the possibility of manipulating space to provoke certain impressions or emotions. For Loos, most of whose works were designed for the urban middle class, chief among these impressions was livability—the need to foster the feeling of a warm and comforting environment. Both the arrangement of the spaces themselves and the movement sequence assumed a role in enhancing these feelings in his designs.

Strnad and Frank were also aware of this principle of subjective psychology of architectural space. In Strnad and Wlach's Hock and Wassermann Houses, the feeling of livability is enhanced though the variety and ambience of the extended movement sequence leading into and through the main living spaces. The impressions are not merely visually arresting; they are also designed to provoke different physical and psychological responses. Whether Strnad developed the concept of the "empathic" architectural promenade independently or, which is also possible, in discussions with Frank, the two began to translate these ideas of kinetic vision, spatial perception, and subjective response into a design strategy, putting great stress on circulation and the progression of experiences a person undergoes while moving through built volumes.

In his plan for the Scholl House, Frank only partially exploited the possibilities of this concept: both the route into and through the house and the resulting spaces were still conventional in many respects, in spite of the irregularity and openness of the rooms. The interiors of the smaller Strauß House were arranged in like manner, though the resulting spaces were less complex. The living and dining areas, which opened into each other, formed a simple L-shape. The weight of the upper floor was supported by two reinforced concrete beams, which rested on central piers that served to partially define the transition from the *Halle* to the dining area. As in the Bunzl and Scholl Houses, Frank avoided any sort of regular or axial planning, while at the same time undermining any representational quality for the main living areas—in studied defiance to the standard maxims of contemporary Viennese planning. Instead, much of the focus was on creating connections with the rear garden: all of the rooms either had windows that faced the rear or opened out onto the terrace or balcony.

This emphasis on establishing a direct linkage with the garden—which for Frank constituted an extension of the interior living spaces—is also conveyed on the façades. The street sides of the two Wilbrandtgasse houses were largely closed and uncommunicative; the rear façades, by contrast, were open, inviting, and animated. This opposition arose not only out of the distinction that Frank, like Loos, sought to make between public and private; it was also a byproduct of his attempt to remove any overtly symbolic meaning from the houses. The intentionally "ordinary" appearance of the street façades of the Wilbrandtgasse houses resulted from Frank's desire to foster a new urban uniformity. Concealed behind the outer shell was another world, the private sphere, where inhabitants could live as they wished and where they could indulge their needs for the sentimental and old-fashioned objects.

THE OFFICE BUILDING NEAR THE CHURCH OF MARIA AM GESTADE By the end of 1913, Frank was also collaborating with Strnad and Wlach on another project, an office building in Vienna's inner city (fig. 36). The building was intended to replace an older structure located on a narrow site facing the Tiefer Graben adjacent to the Gothic Church of Maria am Gestade.[61] As in their other works, they largely dispensed with the standard historical vocabulary, paring the structure down to its bare essentials. The simple, planar walls of the eight-story building are interrupted by rows of identical windows, set almost flush with the walls, and by a series of regular string courses that divide the floors. Only the main entry, which occupies a narrow wall where the building juts out into the square, is singled out for special treatment. Though no plan of the project has survived, the configuration of the window walls on the ground floor suggests that the architects intended the building to be supported by a reinforced concrete frame. The lack of any readily observable indication of the interior structure, however, provides a striking atectonic visual effect, not unlike Hoffmann's Palais Stoclet (1905–11).[62]

The building was never realized. The pronounced contrast with the Gothic Maria am Gestade Church provoked storms of protest, and resistance from the authorities and the outbreak of the war doomed the project.[63] The critic Max Eisler (who was a close friend of the three architects), in spite of the outcry, publicly praised the design, noting that its strong horizontal orientation and simple masses actually would have served to accentuate the church's verticality and ornate façade, "demonstrating a new form of respect for the older building."[64]

Though it still has the weightiness of most of the prewar modernist architecture, Strnad, Wlach, and Frank's office building project clearly looked toward the taut plaster and glass-skin constructions of the 1920s. Its impact at the time, however, was barely felt;

36. Oskar Strnad, Oskar Wlach, and Josef Frank (Strnad-Wlach-Frank), Project for an office building near the church of Maria am Gestade, Vienna, photomontage, 1913–14. MAK-Österreichisches Museum für angewandte Kunst, Vienna.

photographs of the project were not published until 1921, and it received scant notice outside Vienna.[65] Frank's prewar houses suffered a similar fate: photographs of the Scholl and Bunzl Houses appeared in *Wasmuths Monatshefte* in 1915 and in *Österreichische Werkkultur,* a commemorative volume published by the Austrian Werkbund the following year.[66] But little was written about the houses elsewhere, and their influence was largely confined to Vienna.[67]

Nonetheless, by the eve of the First World War Frank had already established himself as one of the leaders of a new generation of architects. Indeed, everything seemed to indicate that he could look forward to a promising future: Vienna was in the midst of a prolonged building boom, and the prospect of further commissions seemed bright.

The outbreak of the war in August, however, brought an abrupt end to the opening phase of Frank's life and career. Work on the two Wilbrandtgasse houses stretched into the late summer of 1915. But Frank, who had turned twenty-nine the previous July, was unable to supervise the final stages of construction.[68] At the end of January 1915, he was called up for military service. In view of his technical training, he was assigned to the Imperial army's railroad engineering regiment based in nearby Korneuburg. After a short training period, he was promoted to the rank of reserve lieutenant and assigned to a unit of bridge engineers and railroad builders stationed near the border of Austria-Hungary and Serbia.[69]

Frank saw no combat, and his duties often left him time to work on his own projects.[70] Between 1915 and 1918, he made a number of sketches for furniture designs, most of them intended for friends and acquaintances. From 1916 on, he also produced designs for the Wiener Werkstätte, including several textile patterns.[71] The war put a hold on his development as an architect and designer, however, and his few surviving works from the period—such as his design for "Schöpfung" (Creation; plate 3)—were more in tune with the prewar spirit than a glance into the future.

If the period from 1915 to 1918 was a time of enforced idleness for Frank, it nevertheless marked a decisive break in his life. The war and its aftermath brought to a close the long era of stability and prosperity that he had till then experienced. The visions of a secure and promising future faded, and Frank found himself forced to confront vastly different circumstances in the postwar years.

3

RED VIENNA After the First World War, both the shape and direction of Frank's work changed. For the next six years, until 1925, much of his time and energy were taken up with designing housing projects for the city of Vienna and for various private housing cooperatives. When called up for military service in 1915, Frank had expected that the war would soon end and that he could reestablish his practice designing single-family houses and interiors. But the realities of postwar Austria dashed any such hopes. The war that had engulfed Europe had not only brought an interruption to his private life and career; it had also seriously undermined the social foundation upon which Vienna's prewar culture had rested. The comfortable middle-class existence Frank had known in his early years and the political order that had sustained it crumbled away, leaving only a deep sense of uncertainty for the future.

The collapse of the Habsburg empire and the loss of the non-German provinces left the new Austrian Republic with grave economic problems. The abrupt cessation of trade between Austria and the new successor states of Czechoslovakia, Hungary, Yugoslavia, and Romania spelled disaster for the country's economy, which had traditionally been dependent on its outlying provinces for raw materials and markets. The Allied blockade, which continued until the middle of 1919, prevented the importation of aid from abroad, aggravating the country's already severe food and fuel shortages. There was, as novelist Stefan Zweig later recalled, "no flour, bread, coal, or oil; there appeared to be no solution other than revolution or else some other catastrophe."[1]

For a time it seemed that either revolution or civil war was imminent. The country was rent by deep divisions between "Red Vienna" and the conservative provinces, between the Social Democratic and Christian Social parties. But while Soviet-style workers' republics were established in neighboring Hungary and Bavaria, in Austria the Socialists and Christian Socialists, ignoring for the moment their differences, formed a coalition government in March 1919 and chose Socialist leader Karl Renner as chancellor. Over the course of the next year, the two parties managed to head off challenges from both the far left and the far right. An attempted putsch by the Communists in April 1919 was quickly suppressed, and by the end of the year a measure of political stability had been restored. The economic situation, however, remained bleak. Spiraling inflation, which reached its apex at the end of 1922, wiped out the savings of the middle class, putting a virtual halt to private construction.

37. Josef Frank, c. 1920. Sammlung, Universität für angewandte Kunst, Vienna.

PROFESSOR AT THE KUNSTGEWERBESCHULE In the early postwar years, Frank (fig. 37) managed to secure a few commissions from private clients—most of them friends and relatives—for furnishings and interiors. Until the end of 1919, he also continued to produce designs for the Wiener Werkstätte, including brass bowls, lamps, small boxes, and several textiles.[2] Due to the economic situation, however, there was simply no possibility for him to reestablish his prewar practice designing single-family houses. Strnad, Wlach, and Frank dissolved their partnership, and Frank found himself compelled to turn to other pursuits to make a living. In the fall of 1919, with the support of Hoffmann and Strnad, he was appointed an adjunct professor (Hilfslehrer mit Professorentitel) at the Kunstgewerbeschule. The position provided a modest but steady source of income, and for the next half-dozen years, he taught courses in construction and design.

Frank's tenure coincided with a period of reform at the school. Working together with Strnad, who taught one of the school's two architecture classes, Frank helped to usher in a new and more rigorous intellectual climate. Although it had been an important training ground for up-and-coming young modernists, the institution prior to the war had had the status of a secondary school. Strnad and Frank inaugurated a comprehensive training program aimed to provide students with a knowledge of the fundamentals of architectural practice comparable to that of the graduates of the nearby Technische Hochschule.

Frank proved to be an energetic and effective teacher. Although only of medium height—he was barely five feet seven inches tall—his authoritative presence and intensity made him stand out. He spoke quietly, but deliberately—and with great fluency. Indeed, it was Frank's facile manner of speaking, lightly accented with Viennese dialect, that struck most who encountered him. Incisive and quick-witted, he was usually jovial, but, if annoyed, he could also be derisive.

Karl Augustinus Bieber, who studied at the school in the early 1920s, recalled that Frank's knowledge, lack of "personal whim," and "aversion to formulas" earned him the respect of the students. But many also quickly became aware of Frank's sometimes prickly personality. As Bieber recounted, Frank could be "sarcastic, even sometimes intellectually brutal." Once Bieber recalled that Frank came up to his desk in class and stood looking at a drawing he was making. It was just after the war, and high-quality paper was difficult to obtain. After examining his work for a few moments, he quipped, "Well, at least Bieber always has good supplies."[3] Nonetheless, as Herbert Thurner, another of Frank's students, remembered, he was "instantly recognized" by students at the school as the "most modern of the many important teachers on the faculty," and "we followed him and his ideas blindly."[4]

Although Frank officially taught "building construction" (*Baukonstruktionslehre*), he dealt with a wide array of subjects in his classes, from the history and theory of architecture to furniture and interior design. Rather than lecturing, he preferred to hold discussions with small groups of students or to go from desk to desk, critiquing their work and offering suggestions. Frank taught his students to approach design problems by posing basic questions: How should a door open? What should a window look like? What is the best shape for a living room? He emphasized discipline and responsibility, often repeating his admonition that "the architect is the one who creates order."[5] Frank, however, left his students a considerable degree of freedom, allowing them to develop their own solutions and personal styles.

The six years Frank spent at the Kunstgewerbeschule witnessed the rapid development of the modern movement. He encouraged his students to explore the possibilities of the new architecture but cautioned them repeatedly about what he viewed as its excesses. "He taught us," Thurner recalled, "that a house was not a functioning machine, but a living, constantly changing organism, which was there to serve the well-being of the inhabitants. He taught us that a building that fulfills its purpose must not necessarily be a work of art, but on the other hand—like the product of any other human endeavor—can be a work of art."[6]

Like König, Frank also stressed the importance of learning the lessons of history. At a time when Johannes Itten and others at the fledgling Bauhaus were exhorting their students to liberate themselves from "dead conventions,"[7] Frank would sometimes take his students on walks through Vienna's old city, pointing out various features of the buildings that might be reapplied to new works. Bieber later recounted how Frank had once led students through Vienna's inner city discussing its development. Suddenly, he stopped, pointing out how the windows on the old Baroque buildings, set flush with the façades, reflected the light back into the street, while the later historicist structures, with their windows deeply inset, cast dark looming shadows.[8] Frank also stressed the importance of absorbing the legacy of Wagner, Olbrich, Loos, and the other early Viennese modernists, "whose works," he declared, "lead in a straight line to the architecture of the present."[9]

RESPONSE TO THE HOUSING CRISIS Although Frank cared little for teaching, he applied himself conscientiously to the task, and he often assisted Strnad or sat in for him while the latter was away. After 1919, however, Frank devoted himself more and more to searching for solutions to Vienna's acute housing shortage.

The disastrous economic situation in the country and a huge influx of German-speaking refugees from the outlying provinces during and after the war had combined to exacerbate the city's already severe housing problem. At the end of the war, as many as ten thousand Viennese families were homeless or living in temporary accommodations. While the authorities debated what to do about the ever-worsening situation, the city's legions of homeless took matters into their own hands. Desperate for shelter and food and emboldened by the successful revolution, they occupied fields and woods on the city's periphery, building shacks and planting small vegetable gardens. By the end of 1919, whole makeshift villages had grown up on open land around the capital. The *Siedlerbewegung,* or settlers' movement, as Loos recorded, "fell over all of the city's inhabitants like a fever,"[10] and within a short time it emerged as a potent political force. During the winter of 1918–1919, many of the *Siedler* formed self-governing unions, loosely modeled on the workers' councils of revolutionary Russia and Germany, and in the first months of 1919, they began to appeal to the city authorities for additional land, as well as for building materials and technical support.[11]

From the start, Frank was sympathetic to the plight of the *Siedler.* Both he and his older brother Philipp had joined the Austrian Socialist party when they were still in their teens, and after the war Frank was increasingly identified with the radical wing of the party.[12] Like many of the city's leftist intelligentsia, he was attracted to the *Siedlerbewegung* because he believed that it represented a genuine proletarian movement. But he also saw a very real opportunity to improve living standards in the city—to fashion a new type of working-class dwelling. Frank recognized, however, that the makeshift *Siedlungen,* or settlements, despite their independence from bourgeois codes, had stopped well short of real housing reform. Not only were the "wild" settlements unsightly and unsafe, but they also lacked public amenities, such as streets, squares, and landscaping.

In response to the mounting crisis, Frank published an article in *Der Architekt* in early 1919 calling for the construction of a series of city-financed housing projects. The centerpiece of the proposal, which he coauthored with two architectural engineers, Hugo Fuchs and Franz Zettinig, was to employ poured concrete and standardized elements—

rather than traditional brick and stucco construction—to erect large numbers of housing units rapidly and inexpensively. The idea of using concrete was in part a response to a shortage of bricks resulting from the lack of coal to fire kilns. However, Frank also recognized that concrete construction offered a means to industrialize the building process.[13] Although reinforced concrete was certainly not a new technology, up to that time in Austria it had been almost exclusively confined to commercial and industrial structures. Citing U.S. examples of poured concrete construction for residential use, Frank and his coauthors argued not only that concrete would be less expensive than other building materials, but that construction practices could be rationalized, providing additional savings by reducing the amount of labor required and cutting down on construction time.[14] To further economize, they proposed using cinder-concrete, made from coal ash, which would be less expensive than traditional concrete and provide better insulation. In place of standard wooden forms, they called for the use of a system of special metal forms designed by Fuchs, which could be quickly assembled, removed, and reused. To speed the process and minimize costs, they proposed as well that the windows, doors, stairwells, and other finishing elements be standardized.[15]

Frank drew up plans for a prototypical *Siedlung,* which were published in the article. He divided the site into an irregular grid of streets, leaving a large open square at the center. The identical three-story apartment buildings were arranged in straight rows, set either parallel or perpendicular to each other; at the rear of each building was a space for a garden plot for each family to enable them to grow as much of their own food as possible. The standard apartment unit had a total area of sixty-five square meters and included a tiny vestibule, a combined kitchen and living area, and two bedrooms.

38. Project for a poured concrete housing settlement, 1919; perspective. *Der Architekt* 22 (1919).

The design of the buildings' façades (fig. 38) was guided by what Frank described as the "Niedrig-Praktische" (basely practical): aside from simple frames around the doors and windows, they were devoid of decorative elements or picturesque modulations. Frank, however, stopped short of calling for typification.[16] Although convinced that the changing social and economic order necessitated new architectonic forms, he believed that a truly proletarian architecture would only emerge gradually.

THE ORTMANN SIEDLUNG Nothing came of the proposal, but the same year Frank was asked by his cousin Hugo Bunzl (for whom Frank had designed the summer house in Ortmann before the war) to design a small housing complex for the workers at his nearby paper factory.

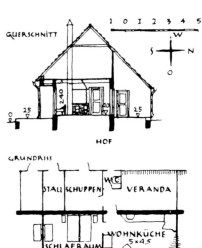

39. Workers' *Siedlung* (Phase 1), Ortmann, Lower Austria, 1919. Arkitekturmuseet, Stockholm.

40. Workers' *Siedlung* (Phase 1), Ortmann, Lower Austria, 1919, plan and section. *Deutsche Kunst und Dekoration* 48 (1921).

Two years older than Frank, Bunzl had studied in Manchester, but he had returned to Austria in 1905 to run the family company. In spite of his wealth and position, Bunzl harbored strong socialist sympathies, and the housing settlement was one of a series of postwar projects he undertook to help improve the lives of his six thousand workers—earning him the unlikely nickname, the "Roter Industrie-Baron" (Red Baron of Industry).[17]

The first phase of the project (fig. 39), completed in 1921, consisted of eight small row houses. The complex was arranged in a U-shape around a small courtyard, with a well at the center. Though more modest in scale than the blocks Frank had proposed in the *Architekt* article, the one-story structures shared numerous similarities, including the same basic, unadorned façades, pitched roofs, and small garden plots. The walls were constructed of poured concrete, twenty-six centimeters thick, with a fourteen-centimeter-wide hollow space at the center for better insulation.[18] The individual dwellings (fig. 40) were minimal, consisting of an open living area and kitchen, a bedroom, a toilet, and a storage space for garden implements; attached to the rear was a stall area to enable the residents to keep pigs, chickens, and other small livestock.

Even before construction on the first phase of the housing for the Ortmann factory was completed, Frank was at work on a second housing complex nearby. The new development, which was considerably larger, comprised a row of six one-story row houses similar to those in the first building phase, and a second, longer row, set perpendicular to it, of two-story row house units of several different types. All of the buildings (fig. 41) featured simple, unadorned façades and conventional pitched roofs; each unit, too, had

41. Workers' *Siedlung* (Phase II),
Ortmann, Lower Austria, 1922.
Moderne Bauformen 26 (1927).

its own garden as well as a tiny shed for small livestock. Frank, however, experimented with several different plans, varying the disposition of the rooms, terraces, and outbuildings.

In stylistic terms, both the 1919 concrete housing project and the Ortmann *Siedlung* were a departure from Frank's prewar Wilbrandtgasse villas. While still retaining the same elemental austerity, they were more closely related to the unornamented vernacular building style that Paul Mebes, Paul Schultze-Naumburg, Heinrich Tessenow, and others had promoted before the war.[19] Frank was particularly drawn to the community planning and design principles of Tessenow, who had taught at the Kunstgewerbeschule from 1913 to 1919.[20] Indeed, the Ortmann estate and several of Frank's subsequent housing projects bore an obvious resemblance to Tessenow's row houses for the prewar garden city at Hellerau (fig. 42). Frank was guided by similar considerations: the simple composition of the houses grew out of the same attempt to find the most fundamental architectonic expression, the *Ur-Ausdruck*.

Aside from their more rudimentary materials and finishes, Frank's Ortmann *Siedlung* houses differed from the prewar garden cities in Germany in at least one vital respect: whereas Tessenow and the others had regarded their houses as expressions of a new *kleinbürgerlich* (petite-bourgeois) culture, Frank saw his efforts merely as a stopgap solution. In an essay written shortly after their completion, he observed that the Ortmann houses represented "the smallest type," reflecting the hard times in which they had arisen; and he added that they were not intended as a model for the "ideal working-class domicile of the future." In subsequent construction at the factory complex, he noted, efforts would be made to increase the size of the houses in order to "raise the overall living standard."[21]

This difference is revealed in the houses' plans. Not only were Tessenow's units larger, but in accord with the standard arrangement in bourgeois homes, they provided separate living and kitchen spaces. Frank, by contrast, opted for a *Wohnküche*, the combined living, dining, and cooking space that was a traditional feature of Austrian vernacular dwellings. The provision of a *Wohnküche* not only afforded a significant saving of space, but it also—which was equally important for Frank—corresponded to the real living patterns of the working-class families who would inhabit the houses.

In his writings of the early 1920s, Frank repeatedly returned to the idea that new working-class domiciles not merely be scaled down versions of middle-class housing. He assailed the previous attempts of Viennese architects and builders to design proletarian housing: "Right up to the present day," he noted, "the *kleinbürgerlich* ideal has remained a flat consisting of a small kitchen and a large room, the kitchen serving as the family room and storage space, and the room, which serves both as a bedroom and formal space for entertaining guests."[22] Such an arrangement was based neither on practicality nor on comfort, but on "the Viennese ardor for courtly splendor, which values representation above all."[23] For Frank, this long-standing practice to replicate the features of the palaces of the nobility was a symptom of the general low standard of domestic design in Vienna. The *Siedlerbewegung* offered an opportunity to rethink the arrangement of the small dwelling, to develop more sensible and livable accommodations.

42. Heinrich Tessenow, Hellerau *Siedlung*, 1910–11. Heinrich Tessenow, *Der Wohnhausbau* (Munich, 1927)

The interiors Frank designed for the Ortmann *Siedlung* demonstrated his concern for practicality and comfort. To make the tiny dwellings less cluttered, he provided built-in cabinets as well as a full range of simple, light furnishings. Many of the pieces, like those in his prewar interiors, were patterned after older models, but they were adapted to bring them up-to-date and to make them inexpensive to produce.

Throughout the early 1920s, Frank continued to refine his ideas about what might constitute the best form for the *Siedlung* house interior. The *Wohnküche* Frank designed for the first phase of the Ortmann *Siedlung* (fig. 43) amounted to a new "proletarian" version of his prewar aesthetic. The same English arts and crafts ambiance is still discernible, but now in a reduced form. Frank recognized, however, that such furnishings were only an interim solution: new forms would eventually come to the fore that better expressed the values and needs of the working class. In the meantime, he asserted, it was preferable to forgo attempts to design something that "would only stand in the way of future advances."[24]

FRANK AND THE SIEDLERVERBAND By the end of 1920, Frank had also begun to work directly with various organizations allied with the *Siedlerbewegung*. Over the next three years, he assisted in the planning and design of a number of housing estates in and around Vienna. Frank carried out most of the projects under the auspices of the Österreichischer Verband für Siedlungs- und Kleingartenwesen (Austrian Union of Settlers and Small Gardeners, or Siedlerverband), which was formed in September 1921 to serve as an umbrella organization for the more than two hundred settlers' cooperatives in the country.

The executive secretary of the Siedlerverband was Frank's close friend, the economist and sociologist Otto Neurath. Frank had met Neurath before the war through his older brother Philipp, who, along with Neurath and the mathematicians Hans Hahn and Richard von Mises, had belonged to an informal philosophical discussion group.[25] Frank would sometimes meet up with them at one of the coffeehouses they frequented, and he and Neurath, who had similar left-wing social and political interests, soon formed a lasting friendship.[26]

A huge, exuberant man with bright red hair—a genuine "Hun," as Margarete Schütte-Lihotzky once affectionately described him—Neurath's extraordinary range of interests and remarkable intellect brought him into contact with many of the city's bright-

43. *Wohnküche*, Workers' *Siedlung*, Ortmann, Lower Austria, 1919. MAK-Österreichisches Museum für angewandte Kunst, Vienna.

est minds.[27] Born in Vienna in 1882, the son of the sociologist and reformer, Wilhelm Neurath, he studied mathematics, natural science, economics, and history at the Universities of Vienna and Berlin. From 1907 to 1914, he taught economics at the Vienna Handelsakademie (School of Business), and during the war he served for a time on the Eastern front. After the war, Neurath became a technical advisor on economic questions for the short-lived revolutionary *Räterepublik* in Munich. Arrested after its overthrow, he was imprisoned for high treason only to be released through the intercession of Max Weber and Austrian Socialist leader Otto Bauer on the proviso that he not return to Germany.[28]

Like Frank, Neurath was a practical reformer with a sincere desire to improve the plight of the masses. But he also shared Frank's basic underlying skepticism and his aversion to sloganeering and easy solutions, a position that sometimes made both men critical of the Socialists and the modernists. Over the next decade, Frank's ideas were more strongly colored by Neurath than by anyone else in his life. Their close relationship brought Frank into immediate contact with the emerging world of scientific philosophy, an encounter that would decisively influence his design views.

Under Neurath's energetic leadership the Siedlerverband quickly developed into a formidable organization, effectively lobbying the municipal and federal governments for land, building supplies, and financial support. In addition to its function as a clearing house for information and funds, the Siedlerverband operated an architectural planning office, headed by Franz Schuster, that was responsible for overseeing the design of the *Siedlungen*. Neurath enlisted the aid of a number of the city's progressive architects, including Frank, Loos, and Margarete Lihotzky, to provide technical assistance and advice to the various housing cooperatives. Frank and several other architects also gave informal courses at a school Neurath launched in the fall of 1921 to instruct the various *Siedler* organizations in the principles of building and design. In all, nineteen courses were offered, taught by the organization's staff and volunteers, including a class on the economic issues of the settlement movement, taught by Neurath, and one on furnishing the *Siedlung* house, taught by Lihotzky. Frank, for his part, provided instruction in "economical building techniques."[29] Beginning in late 1921, he also became a consultant to the architectural planning office (*Baubüro*) of the Siedlerverband on construction questions.[30]

THE HOFFINGERGASSE *SIEDLUNG* Between 1921 and 1923, Frank received more than a half-dozen commissions through the Siedlerverband to design housing estates. When the opportunities presented themselves, he also worked on private commissions. Frank's designs of this period not only record his developing ideas of how to promote a genuine proletarian culture; they also illustrate his growing commitment to modern architecture. In spite of the economic limitations and hardships of the times, Frank continued to explore the possibilities of a new idiom, gradually breaking his way through to modernism.

44. Hoffingergasse *Siedlung*,
Vienna, 1921–24. Collection
Professor Johannes Spalt, Vienna.

45. Hoffingergasse *Siedlung*,
Vienna, 1921–24. *Moderne
Bauformen* 26 (1927).

By the middle of 1921, Frank was already hard at work on his largest work to date, a row house settlement in the working-class district of Meidling on Vienna's southern edge. In the spring of that year, he and Erich Faber, an architect with the municipal building office, were commissioned by the Altmannsdorf and Hetzendorf Housing Association (one of the independent housing collectives that made up the Siedlerverband) to design and oversee the construction of the project. The Hoffingergasse *Siedlung*, as it became known, consisted of 284 row house units and a small community center.

The site, a large open field bounded by existing streets, incorporated a number of pre-existing garden allotments, and Frank was forced to accommodate the layout to preserve as many of the gardens as possible. In its overall planning and design, the Hoffingergasse *Siedlung* resembled the second phase of the Ortmann settlement (figs. 44, 45). Most of the houses were situated on narrow rectangular lots of approximately 465 square meters (the size deemed large enough for the average family to be self-sufficient in food production), with only about one-tenth of the site occupied by the buildings. In accord with the wishes of the cooperative, Frank put special emphasis on the gardens, positioning the houses at the edge of the street so that the entire available land area was at the rear.

Frank's site plan (fig. 46), however, deviated from the standard planning ideas of the time. Rather than arranging the houses in north-south rows, as Loos suggested, or east-west, as was the common practice in Germany, Frank oriented most of the houses at a roughly forty-five degree angle so that the rows ran northeast-southwest. This ensured not only that all of the gardens would receive sufficient light, but also that the façades would not be exposed to the prevailing north wind.[31] In contrast to most of the other *Siedlungen* constructed in Vienna in the early 1920s, Frank's site plan also avoided tradi-

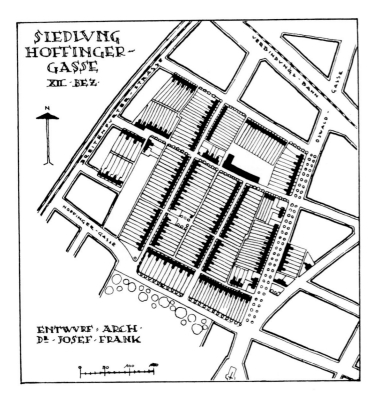

SIEDLVNG
HOFFINGER-
GASSE
XII · BEZ ·

N

HOFFINGER · GASSE

ENTWVRF · ARCH ·
D^r · JOSEF · FRANK

46. Hoffingergasse *Siedlung*,
Vienna, 1921–24; site plan. *Das
neue Wien* (Vienna, 1926).

tional monumental axes or symmetry, producing an antipicturesque and matter-of-fact effect. Although the distribution of the streets corresponded to the existing grid, the lack of framed prospects or enclosed squares gave the *Siedlung* a provisional and unified appearance, one very different from the villagelike designs of most of the other Vienna *Siedlungen*.[32]

The individual houses, as in all of Vienna's early postwar *Siedlungen*, were small. Nevertheless, they represented a considerable improvement over the tenements and shacks most of the occupants had previously inhabited. Occupying the ground floor of the two-story units was an anteroom, a *Wohnküche,* and a toilet; on the second floor were three small bedrooms. Each unit also had a small shed to house livestock and store garden tools. The basic configuration followed the standard *Siedlung* house type in Vienna. However, Frank placed the stairs along the inside wall of the street front, an arrangement that provided for a larger ground-floor living area and allowed the main downstairs rooms and the three upstairs bedrooms to face onto the gardens.

From the outset, Frank intended that the Hoffingergasse *Siedlung* be more than a collection of houses and gardens. His design introduced playgrounds (set within the gardens and reached through narrow pathways), as well as space for a community building, cooperative store, and daycare center. To encourage the development of a genuine Socialist culture, the residents were also encouraged to join one of the many community groups, which included a choral union, gymnastics club, and a freethinkers' association.[33]

Because much of the construction work was undertaken by the settlers themselves (each adult was required to contribute two thousand hours of labor to the project), Frank kept the design as simple as possible, relying on conventional building methods and materials. Except for the units at the ends of the rows, which featured projecting balconies, all of the houses were identical, achieving the homogeneous effect Frank had sought with his prewar villas. The uniformity of the settlement, as Neurath described, was "an expression of frugality, but also an expression of a feeling of equality. . . . Each individual house is not an object of design, but rather the entire collection of houses. The individual house is like a brick in a building."[34] Frank's statement of his belief in democracy and equality met strong resistance from the settlers, however. Dissatisfied with the uniformity and plainness of the houses, they gradually altered them to provide a more "volkstümlich" (folkish, popular) appearance.[35]

THE *KINDERHEIM* IN ORTMANN By 1921, Frank was also at work on several other projects, among them, an unrealized *Siedlung* in the nearby town of Traiskirchen and a nursery school for the Ortmann factory complex. The Traiskirchen *Siedlung* project (fig. 47), which he designed in the spring of that year, introduced several new features: a kindergarten, a swimming pool, and an infirmary. Frank also developed an extensive planting scheme, for the first time considering landscape design beyond merely providing pathways and space for garden allotments. Aside from its more refined site plan, however, the Traiskirchen settlement was virtually identical to the Hoffingergasse *Siedlung*, consisting of a series of simple two-story row houses dominated by high, pitched roofs.

The nursery school (*Kinderheim*; fig. 48) for the Ortmann housing complex, on which Frank started work in the summer or early fall of 1921, marked the beginning of a new phase in his postwar work. He reverted once more to the use of the flat roof, adopting a vocabulary similar to that of his earlier Wilbrandtgasse houses. But though the simple cubic massing and irregular arrangement of the façades looked back to his prewar designs, the school's taut white surfaces (achieved through the use of smooth stucco over masonry walls) produced an impression that was at once more manifestly "modern." Despite the red brick door surround on the main entrance and the irregular arrangement of the entrance (fig. 49), the building displayed the crisp, machined appearance that was already coming to define the modern movement in the early 1920s.

The new look ended at the entry, however. The central hall of the school (plate 4) repeated many of the elements that had characterized Frank's prewar interiors: a brightly painted beamed ceiling, checkerboard motifs, and Windsor-inspired settee. These vivid accents served to subvert the otherwise spare treatment of the room's surfaces, to both enrich and enliven the space. What stands out even more is the unconventional circulation route in the entry hall (fig. 50), which contained both a stairway to the roof terrace and a separate balcony connecting the roof terrace's two halves. It was an awkward solution, but one that yielded both a rich architectural promenade and a visually complex image.

In other, less conspicuous ways, the school's interior also pointed toward the future. The straightforward articulation of the spaces and the simple linear arrangement of the rooms attested to Frank's evolving interest in functionality. The decorative touches in the entry hall notwithstanding, the overall design of the *Kinderheim* was utilitarian, a fact further demonstrated through his use of inexpensive doors, windows, and other details.

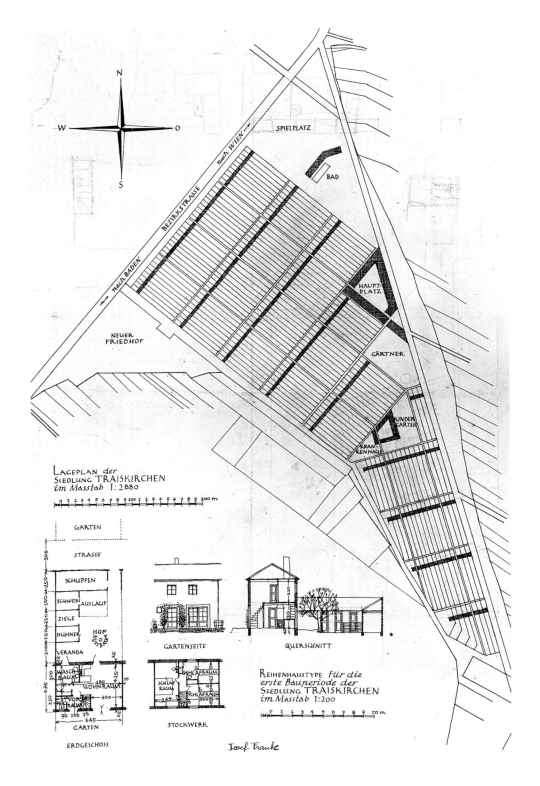

47. Project for a *Siedlung* in
Traiskirchen, Lower Austria, c. 1921;
site plan 1:2880, elevation, plans,
section of a typical house 1:200.
Pencil, pen and ink on tracing
paper, 36 × 25.5 cm. Graphische
Sammlung Albertina, Vienna.

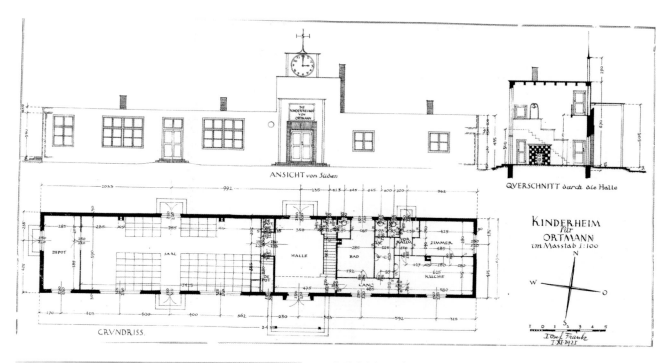

ANSICHT von Süden

QVERSCHNITT durch die Halle

GRVNDRISS.

KINDERHEIM
für
ORTMANN
im Masstab 1:100

DEPOT

SAAL

HALLE

DEPOT

BAD

W.C.

ZIMMER

KUCHE

LANG

48. Kinderheim, Workers' *Siedlung*,
Ortmann, Lower Austria, 1921;
ground plan, elevation, and section
1:100. Collection Professor
Johannes Spalt, Vienna.

49. Kinderheim, Workers' *Siedlung*,
Ortmann, Lower Austria, 1921,
entry. Arkitekturmuseet,
Stockholm.

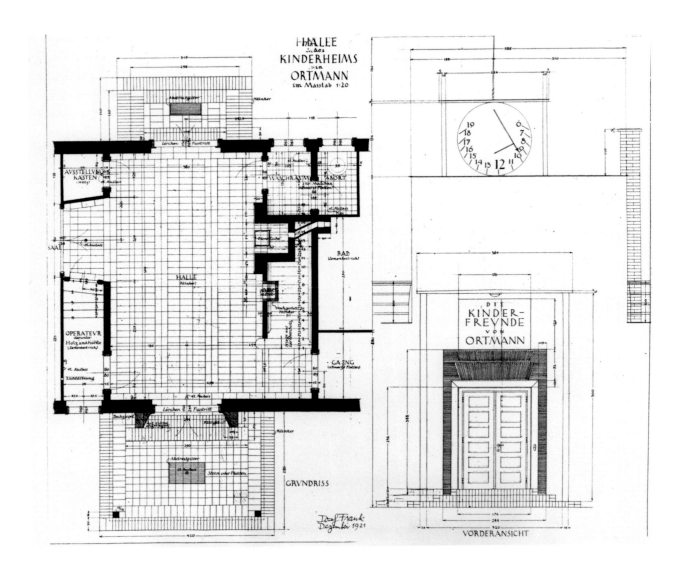

HALLE zu des **KINDERHEIMS** in **ORTMANN** im Maßstab 1:20

GRVNDRISS

VORDERANSICHT

DIE KINDER-FREVNDE VON ORTMANN

50. Kinderheim, Workers' *Siedlung*, Ortmann, Lower Austria, 1921; entry hall, plan, and elevation 1:20. Collection Professor Johannes Spalt, Vienna.

More understated was another work Frank designed for the Ortmann complex in May 1922, an unrealized project for a small apartment building for the factory's clerical staff (fig. 51). Though repeating the blocky format and stair detail from the hall of the *Kinderheim,* it made little attempt to go beyond the "basely practical." With its small rooms and shared toilet and washroom facilities, it could be readily mistaken for a worker's dormitory. Even Frank's use of the small square windows on the north façade was probably intended not as an affectation but an effort to minimize the building's exposure to the winter wind. Indeed, the overtly sober character of the apartment block as

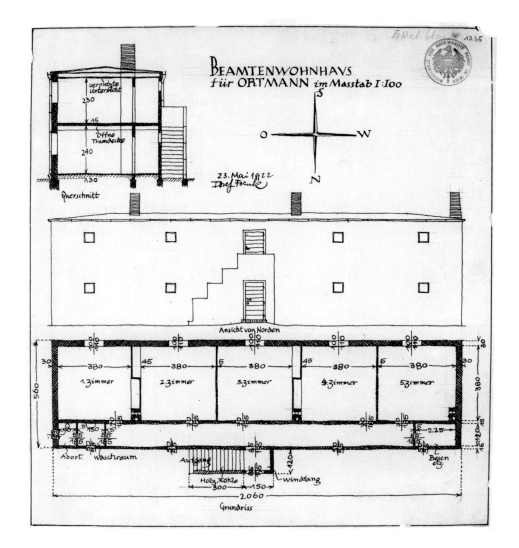

51. Project for a housing block for clerical workers, Ortmann, Lower Austria, 1922; section, elevation, plan 1:100. Pencil, pen and ink on tracing paper, 26 × 23.5 cm. Sammlung, Universität für angewandte Kunst, Vienna.

a whole was perhaps as much a concession to the limited construction funds available in Austria at the time as it was a response to the *neue Sachlichkeit*.

THE SCHOOL IN TIBERIAS AND OTHER PROJECTS

By early 1922, Frank was occupied with several new projects, including various row house models for the Siedlerverband (figs. 52, 53). He also commenced work on an elementary school for the town of Tiberias in Palestine (fig. 54). The exact circumstances of the commission are not known; it likely came from a Viennese acquaintance of Frank's associated

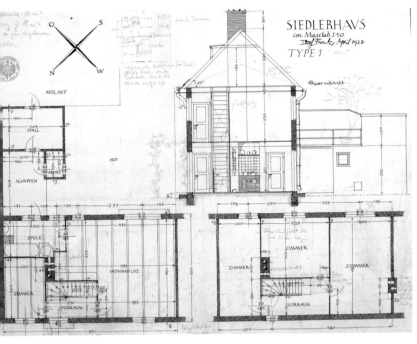

SIEDLERHAVS
im Masstab 1:50
Josef Frank, April 1922
TYPE 1

Querschnitt

AVSLAVF

STALL

SCHVPFEN

HOF

SPVLE

WOHNKVCHE

ZIMMER

ZIMMER

ZIMMER

ZIMMER

VORRAVM

VORRAVM

SPEIS

VOLKSSCHVLE
für TIBERIAS
März 1922
Josef Frank

LAGEPLAN 1:1000

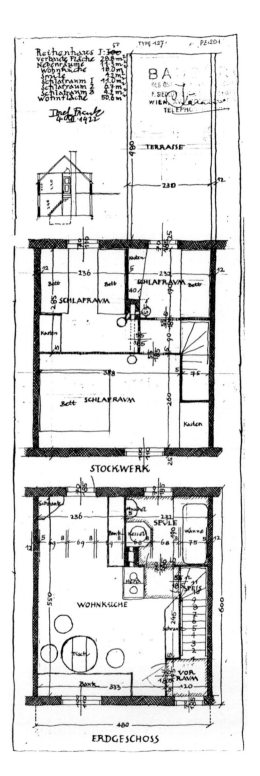

Reihenhaus 1:100   TYPE 127   PZ 1291
verbaute Fläche   20.8 m²
Nebenräume   11.3 m²
Wohnküche   18.0 m²
Spule   1.2 m²
Schlafraum 1   11.0 m²
Schlafraum 2   6.7 m²
Schlafraum 3   4.3 m²
Wohnfläche   50.6 m²

Josef Frank
4. XII. 1922

BA
OES. OST.
F. SIEDL
WIEN
TELEPHO

TERRASSE

SCHLAFRAVM

SCHLAFRAVM

SCHLAFRAVM

Kasten

Kasten

Kasten

Bett

Bett

Bett

Bett

STOCKWERK

SPVLE

WANNE

WOHNKVCHE

VORRAVM

SPEIS

Tisch

Bank

HERD

Schrank

Schrank

ERDGESCHOSS

with the Zionist movement. The only surviving drawing of the school is dated March 1922, indicating that it was on the boards at the same time the Ortmann *Kinderheim* was already entering the construction phase. The two buildings in fact share certain formal parallels, especially their long narrow footprint and the asymmetrical arrangement of their entries.

To these Frank added several new elements, including an open gallery at the street level and an upper-story veranda. He apparently intended the gallery and veranda to produce a Near Eastern affect, but the combination of the jauntily placed roof pavilion—evidently intended to house a water tank—and oversized oculi produced an odd mannerism. The building also departed from the Ortmann *Kinderheim* in terms of its intended constructional system—reinforced concrete—which allowed Frank to attenuate the building's features, giving it a much lighter appearance. It is unclear why the school was never built; the absence of plans or of any other drawings suggests that it never advanced beyond the early stages. However, certain features of the design, most notably the roof terraces, would carry over into Frank's works of the next several years.

Although the unmistakable signature of the *neue Sachlichkeit* was already evident in the Ortmann *Kinderheim* and the Tiberias school project, Frank also continued to employ traditional forms in the early 1920s. A villa he designed in 1923 for Dr. Theo Herzberg-Fränkl (fig. 55), manager of the Bunzl and Biach Paper Factory in Ortmann, provides a case in point. The interior, which featured a large, beamed-ceiling living room and irregular second-floor landing, attested to Frank's continuing interest in the look and form of the English freestyle house. But in most other respects, the rectangular, hipped-roofed

ON FACING PAGE:

52. (top, left) Project for a settlement house, "Type 1," 1922; section, plans 1:50. Pencil, pen and ink on tracing paper, 34.5 × 43 cm. Sammlung, Universität für angewandte Kunst, Vienna.

53. (right) Project for a settlement house, "Type 127," 1922. Collection Professor Johannes Spalt Vienna.

54. (bottom, left) Project for an elementary school in Tiberias, Palestine, 1922; elevation, site plan 1:1000. Pencil, pen and ink on tracing paper, 46.5 × 46 cm. Graphische Sammlung Albertina, Vienna.

55. House for Dr. Theo Herzberg-Fränkel, Ortmann, Lower Austria, 1923. *Moderne Bauformen* 26 (1927).

house was a step backward from his two prewar Wilbrandtgasse villas. The dormers, window and door surrounds, and brick columns all pointed back to the stripped-down neoclassical idiom that had been developed by Hoffmann, Strnad, and others after 1905; and the overall character of the house—despite its asymmetrical façades—was more in keeping with prewar Viennese design than with the emerging modernist style.

More noteworthy was another of Frank's designs from this period, an unrealized synagogue in Antwerp (fig. 56). Frank submitted the design to a competition for Jewish architects held in 1923. The blocky massing and simple fenestration bore visible parallels with his other early postwar works, but many of the design's other features constituted unabashed historical references. Especially conspicuous in this regard were the rounded pylons (evoking the tablets of the law) and the stair-stepped form of the roof, which, as Carol Herselle Krinsky has pointed out, resembles ancient Near Eastern ziggurats.[36] Frank's use of these motifs recalls his early interest in archaic sources, but it also discloses the important distinction that he still drew in his work between monumental and everyday architecture.

During this period, Frank also produced preliminary designs for housing estates in the Viennese suburb of Rodaun and in the nearby towns of Stockerau and St. Veit an der Triesting. In both their overall planning and the design of the individual units, all three projects represented variations of the Hoffingergasse Siedlung. However, in one version of the Rodaun Siedlung (fig. 57), Frank substituted flat roofs for the steeply pitched ones he had been using for his Siedlung units up to that time. Although the change in structural terms was relatively minor, the effect was very different, producing a decidedly more modern look.

Frank returned to the use of the flat roof in his proposal for a main square for the Ortmann Siedlung of the following year. A perspective drawing dated June 1923 (fig. 58) shows the already completed Kinderheim at the rear; arrayed around the large central courtyard are a gymnastics hall, library, tavern, cooperative store, school, kindergarten, and a small hospital. Not only had Frank now completely converted to the Flachdach (flat roof), but a number of other changes in the design of the buildings are discernible: all traces of traditional detailing have been removed, and the windows have been greatly enlarged, so much so that a considerable amount of the wall surface is given over to glazing.

This breakthrough to a more expressly "modern" conception is evident in another of Frank's projects of this period, a Siedlung for the town of Klosterneuburg. He first labored on the project during the winter of 1921–22, and over the course of the next year and a half he produced several related schemes. A perspective view of the Siedlung Frank prepared in June 1923 (fig. 59), the same month as the proposal for the main square of the Ortmann project, replicated many of its principal features. The row houses, which can be seen at the rear, have the identical profile, although their windows are considerably smaller and the gardens are walled off from the street. Apart from the dissimilar layout

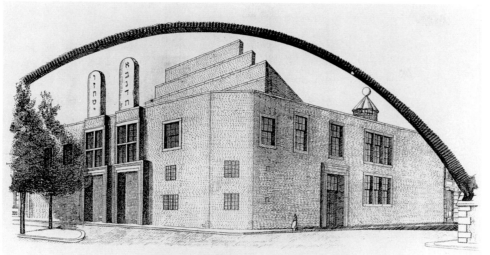

PROJET
pour la construction
de la
NOVVELLE SYNAGOGVE
à
ANVERS

VVE PERSPECTIVE

BOAS

56. Project for a synagogue in Antwerp, Belgium, c. 1922; perspective. Collection Professor Johannes Spalt, Vienna.

57. Project for a *Siedlung* in Rodaun, 1922; section, elevations, plans 1:250. *Der Neubau* 6 (1924).

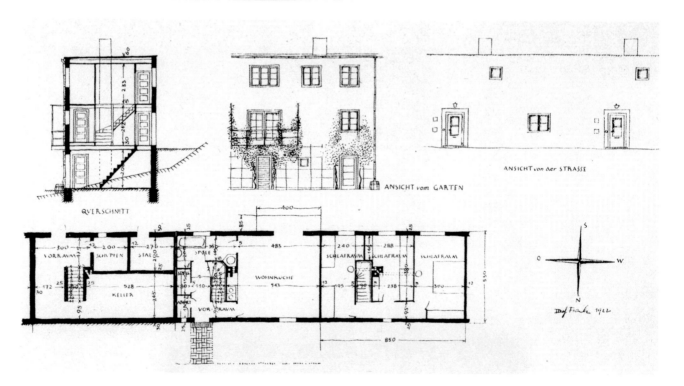

QVERSCHNITT

ANSICHT *vom* GARTEN

ANSICHT *von der* STRASSE

58. Project for the main square, Workers' *Siedlung*, Ortmann, Lower Austria, 1923; aerial perspective. Pencil, pen and ink on tracing paper, 43 × 42.5 cm. Sammlung, Universität für angewandte Kunst, Vienna.

59. Project for a *Siedlung* in Klosterneuburg, Lower Austria, 1922–23; perspective. Pencil, pen and ink on tracing paper, 42.5 × 82.5 cm. Graphische Sammlung Albertina, Vienna.

of the main square, however, the most notable difference can be seen in the two-story community center shown in the right foreground. No plan or other drawings of the building has survived, but it was clearly intended to be a concrete frame structure with a brick veneer, the first time Frank had proposed to use more advanced construction methods for a *Siedlung* project. Another drawing for the Klosterneuburg project (fig. 60), probably dating from the middle of 1923, shows a modified version of the row house prototype, now with much more modern detailing—not unlike the *sachlich* row house developments German architect Ludwig Hilbersheimer published in his book *Groß-stadtarchitektur* around the same time.

PROLETARIAN WOHNKULTUR Frank's published plan of the individual units for the Klosterneuburg *Siedlung* (fig. 61), which appeared in *Innen-Dekoration* in 1923, betray his mounting interest in clarifying and rationalizing the houses' interiors. But unlike Hilbersheimer and other radical modernists in Germany, he continued to reject the notion of incorporating machine-age imagery into the inner domain of his houses.

Frank's alternate vision of a future proletarian *Wohnkultur* (domestic culture) was announced in three drawings of idealized interiors accompanying the plans for the proposed *Siedlung*.[37] One, a design for a *Wohnküche* (fig. 62), reproduced the main outlines of his Ortmann interiors. The other two renderings—both for living rooms (figs. 63, 64)—pointed toward a

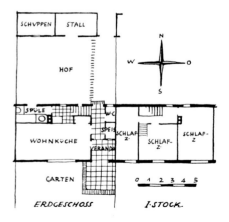

62. (top) Project for a *Wohnküche* for a *Siedlung* house; perspective. *Innen-Dekoration* 34 (1923).

63. (bottom, left) Project for a living room for a *Siedlung* house; perspective. *Innen-Dekoration* 34 (1923).

64. (bottom, right) Project for a living room for a *Siedlung* house; perspective. *Innen-Dekoration* 34 (1923).

new, more elaborate working-class interior. As in his prewar bourgeois dwellings, Frank relied on light "reform furniture," mostly derived from seventeenth- and eighteenth-century English and American Windsor models. But his reductive handling of the room's framing surfaces—walls, ceilings, floors, and windows—and his casual arrangement of the various elements reinforced an appearance of austerity.

The basis of this new proletarian dwelling was once more a modernized traditionalism, this time an attempt to meld older forms with the new language of *Sachlichkeit*. However, Frank continued to maintain that the architect should not prescribe how people should live or arrange their furniture and objects. Frank's model *Siedlung* rooms thus were intended only to offer a framework for dwelling; for that reason they were presented, as he wrote, only "schematically."[38]

Implicit in Frank's designs, however, was not only his belief in diversity and freedom, but also his conviction that the working class was entitled to more than "stereotyped uniformity"—at least in the houses' interiors. The two living rooms retain unmistakable vestiges of Frank's earlier, prewar design aesthetic: airy spaces, genteel settings, and, in one of the rooms, even a grand piano. On the one hand, this specific look grew out of Frank's desire to preserve the nineteenth-century ideal of the home as a place of peaceful affluence—an ideal that would continue to guide his work in the coming decades. But it derived, too, from his fervent belief in the importance of providing for the lower classes the comforts and opportunities for leisure once reserved only for the well-to-do.

Such a position flew in the face of the leftist critique of bourgeois culture in the postwar era. Echoing other contemporary attacks on middle-class dwelling, left radical architects Franz Schuster and Franz Schacherl contended that a genuine proletarian *Wohnkultur* was "the culture of objectivity, cleanliness, and clarity":

What [the proletarian] understands by individuality or personal taste is nothing other than the collective expression of other social classes. No matter how impersonal, how little individuality exists in a bourgeois dwelling with all of its deceitfulness, it appears to the worker as something to strive for. He takes over, without a thought, all these obsolete, dusty forms and believes that he has achieved his own domestic culture [Wohnkultur]. He fears simplicity, clarity, and objectivity in his home, fears that if he furnishes it simply and objectively all poetry, culture, and art will disappear from his dwelling.[39]

But Frank found no fault in offering to the proletariat the cultural ideals of the bourgeoisie; far more important for him was that they retained the freedom to make their own choices, even if those choices did not correspond with others' notions about how they should live.

THE HOUSING DEBATE The Klosterneuburg *Siedlung* never proceeded beyond the planning stages; lack of funding and the continuing economic uncertainty eventually doomed the project, as they had the Traiskirchen, Rodaun, Stockerau, and St. Veit an der Triesting *Siedlungen*. Despite his failure to realize most of his projects, Frank continued to work actively with Neurath and the Siedlerverband through 1924. By the end of 1923, however, it was becoming evident that the *Siedlung* movement was losing momentum. One reason for its decline was the steadily improving economic situation. With the Allied blockade now removed, the food scarcity abated and the importance of the garden allotments diminished.

Of even greater consequence was the changing political situation in Vienna. In the first regular general election, held in 1920, the conservative Christian Socialists gained permanent control of the federal government. Shut out on the national level, the Socialists were forced to concentrate their attention on Vienna, where they held a wide margin of seats in the municipal council. Determined to make the city a laboratory of progress, the Social Democratic leadership embarked on an ambitious reform program, pushing through an array of economic, social, and cultural improvements. The centerpiece of the program was an effort to end the city's long-standing housing problem. In the immediate aftermath of the war, the city council issued a series of rent control laws, and in 1921, the authorities set up a separate department charged with overseeing the *Siedlungen*. Adolf Loos was appointed its director and chief architect.[40]

At first, the city *Siedlung* office offered only advice, building materials, and limited financial support. Over the next two years, however, it became increasingly involved in the construction of housing settlements, gradually supplanting the grassroots housing cooperatives. Although the office was able to erect a number of *Siedlungen* within a short time, many within the Social Democratic party hierarchy remained dissatisfied with the program. Citing the high costs of construction, the lack of available building space, and the difficulty of integrating the *Siedlungen* into the existing public transportation network, they urged that they be replaced with large high-density blocks.

Critics of the *Siedlung* idea pointed out, quite correctly, that Vienna had no tradition of single-family housing: even after the turn of the century most middling and haute-bourgeois families had lived in large *Wohnpaläste* (apartment palaces) in the city.[41] As early as 1920, Leopold Bauer, Wagner's successor at the Academy of Fine Arts, had called on the city authorities to end the *Siedlung* program in favor of large multistory housing blocks. The city authorities, he declared, had a responsibility to fulfill not only the housing needs of the masses, but also the "most important demands of daily life." The *Siedlungen* could never satisfy the needs of the masses for communal facilities—laundries, kindergarten, cultural centers, and health clinics. Bauer calculated that to solve the housing problem some 150,000 apartments would be necessary, and that such an effort would only be possible under a city-managed program. He called for the construction of high-density housing blocks, similar to the city's already existing tenements, each with its own garden. In response to Frank and others who advocated single-family houses, Bauer retorted, "For every family a dwelling (not a house!) with a garden!"[42]

Frank answered that high-density blocks were not necessarily cheaper, nor did the construction of *Siedlungen* preclude the social amenities Bauer championed. Frank also saw other advantages in the *Siedlungen*. Like many other Austrians on the political left who had come from the ranks of the upper middle class, he viewed socialism as a way to liberate individuals so that they could cultivate leisure pursuits once reserved for the well-to-do. The socialists' mission was to elevate the proletariat by providing access to bourgeois culture in theater, music, literature, and the fine arts. The single-family house was the first step in this direction, offering unprecedented comfort and opportunities for leisure.

But if Frank saw in the *Siedlung* house "a piece of democracy come true,"[43] many within the Social Democratic party leadership viewed the suburban settlements as reactionary. As early as 1912, Rudolf Müller had warned that single-family houses would undermine the party's efforts to organize and forge solidarity in the ranks of the working class, and weaken "class interests."[44] In the postwar housing debate, others echoed Müller's fears, contending that if the workers became too comfortable a gradual erosion of working-class consciousness would result, which would undermine the workers' movement and perhaps even threaten the existence of the party.

In 1923, in an effort to elicit greater support for the *Siedlung* movement and to convince city officials to dedicate at least some of the open land on the city's periphery for low-density *Siedlungen,* the Siedlerverband commissioned Frank, along with Peter Behrens, Hoffmann, Loos, and Strnad, to draw up a development plan (*Generalarchitekturplan*). The five architects devised a scheme dividing the city into two principal zones: one for high-density housing blocks, which included most of the older central city, and another for a belt of low-density row house *Siedlungen* on its outer edge.[45] Some of the plan's specific proposals were eventually adopted; but the effort to encourage the municipal authorities to expand the *Siedlung* program proved unsuccessful. Throughout 1923, Frank, Loos, Neurath, and other supporters of the *Siedlung* idea continued to hold out in favor of single-family housing. But it was becoming increasingly evident to all that the day of the *Siedlungen* was over. During the first phase of the city-directed housing program, plans called for one-third of the new units constructed to be single-family residences; the remainder, large apartment buildings. As early as 1922, however, the municipal government had decided to place its main effort into constructing large multistory housing blocks.[46]

The decision to scale back the construction of new *Siedlungen* was seen as a serious blow by its supporters. Loos, disillusioned and angry about the dismemberment of the *Siedlung* program and the lack of support from the municipal authorities, resigned from his post as chief architect of the housing office in July 1924 and moved to Paris. Frank continued to advocate the single-family house as the best remedy for the city's housing ills. But the tide had now turned, and he found himself increasingly in the minority.

THE WINARSKY-HOF AND WIEDENHOFER-HOF HOUSING PROJECTS In September 1923, the Socialist city council voted to launch a five-year housing program to build five thousand housing units.[47] With the *Siedlung* movement now all but moribund, the city authorities awarded the Siedlerverband a commission for one of the first large housing blocks and engaged nine architects, including Frank, to design and oversee the construction of the project. The development was located in Brigittenau, a dreary working-class district across the Danube Canal from the inner city. Two separate projects were planned for the site: a smaller, triangular-shaped

65. Winarsky-Hof, Vienna, 1923–25;
site plan. *Die Wohnhausanlage der
Gemeinde Wien: Winarskyhof im
XX. Bezirk* (Vienna, 1926).

housing block adjacent to the nearby rail line (now known as the Otto-Haas-Hof) designed by Loos, Karl Dirnhuber, Schuster, and Lihotzky; and a larger complex, the Winarsky-Hof, assigned to a team of five architects: Behrens, Hoffmann, Strnad, Wlach, and Frank.[48]

Frank and the other four architects met in late 1923 and agreed to divide the project into separate tracts, with each architect solely responsible for his own section. The complex as it was eventually constructed (fig. 65) consisted of three large blocks fronted by the Kaiserwasserstraße (now Winarskystraße), with a side street, the Leystraße, forming the central axis through the project.

Although all of the architects were bound by the same constraints regarding program, apartment size, and building density, each placed his own distinct stamp on his portion of the project. Behrens's section featured thick, imposing walls and raised horizontal bands along the street façade. Hoffmann's tract was the most traditional, with pediments, rounded arches, and other historical references. Strnad and Wlach both produced spare, regular façades, articulated with string courses. Frank's block (figs. 66, 67), a roughly U-shaped section on the southwestern corner of the site, showed the most modern handling. The façades were treated simply, with the mass broken up only by regularly spaced balconies and vertical shafts of windows at the stairwells (fig. 68). On the southwest edge facing the Pasettistraße and Kaiserwasserstraße he inverted the corner, lining it with narrow loggias supported by columns.

The apartments throughout the complex were small, only about 40 square meters, and were certainly not luxurious by any standard. The floor plans of the five architects' blocks were generally similar, although Frank took special pains to ensure that many of the apartments had windows on both the street and courtyard sides, thus ensuring better cross-ventilation (fig. 69).[49]

The outward appearance of the building conformed with the emerging language of functionalism. But while its smoothly surfaced walls had the appearance of the new "machine-age" aesthetic, it was little more than a pretense: behind the skin of stucco was a traditional wall of masonry block. New labor-saving technologies would have reduced the construction costs, but the Social Democratic leadership was adamantly opposed to their introduction because of the growing numbers of jobless workers: with some one hundred thousand Viennese workers unemployed, the Socialists had little choice but to try to provide work for as many artisans and laborers as possible. As a result, experiments with new building techniques were not encouraged, though in later years some elements of the housing projects were standardized.[50]

66. Winarsky-Hof, Vienna, 1923–25, view from the Pasettistraße showing Frank's portion of the project. *L'Architecte* 3 (November 1926).

67. (bottom, left) Winarsky-Hof, Vienna, 1923–25; view from the corner of Pasettistraße and Kaiserwasserstraße. *Moderne Bauformen* 26 (1927).

68. (bottom, right) Winarsky-Hof, Vienna, 1923–25; stairwell in the courtyard. J. G. Wattjes, *Moderne Architektuur* (Amsterdam, 1927).

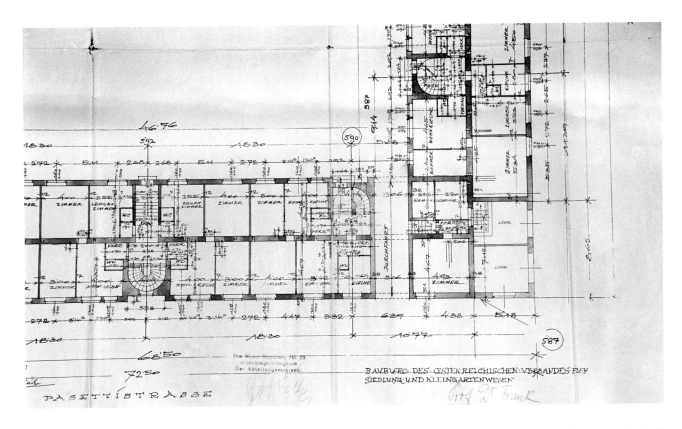

69. Winarsky-Hof, Vienna, 1923–25; ground floor plan (detail). Planarchiv der Stadt Wien (MA 37).

In the late fall of 1923, at the same time that Frank began work on the Winarsky-Hof, the municipal government also commissioned him to design another large housing block in the western end of the city. Frank's first drawing for the project, dated December 1923 (fig. 70), reveals that he originally considered a solution with irregular massing, a flat roof, and a street forming the central axis. In the final version, however, he opted for a more conventional closed-block arrangement, with the building paralleling the streets on all four sides to form a large quadrangle (fig. 71); a smaller block runs through the center forming two enclosed courtyards. In plan, the complex was similar to the standard late-nineteenth-century Viennese apartment blocks. The actual building mass, however, was considerably reduced and much less of the site was covered.

The exterior of the building (fig. 72), known as the Wiedenhofer-Hof, closely resembled the Winarsky-Hof. The façades sported the same highly simplified masses, punctuated by a regular series of windows. Open loggias on the corners and at the center of the building and narrow string courses under the windows served to break up the walls. What set the building off, however, was its warm sienna-red color (plate 5), which immediately earned it the nicknames "Paprika-Kiste," the Paprika Box, or more ominously, "Die rote Festung," the Red Fortress.[51]

PROJEKT
für ein
WOHNHAVS
am
KONGRESSPLATZ

ANSICHT vom KONGRESSPLATZ

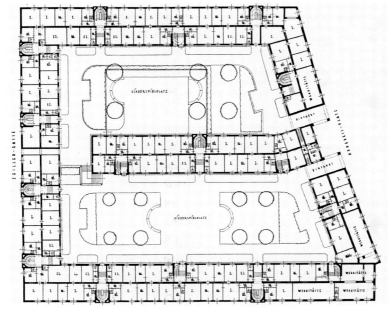

70. Wiedenhofer-Hof, Vienna,
1923–24 (preliminary project); perspective. Pencil, pen and ink on
tracing paper, 32 × 42 cm. Graphische Sammlung Albertina, Vienna.

71. Wiedenhofer-Hof, Vienna,
1923–24; ground-floor plan. *Die
Wohnhausanlage der Gemeinde
Wien: Wiedenhofer-Hof im XVII.
Bezirk* (Vienna, 1926).

Frank's layout of the building's 213 apartments was similar to that of the Winarsky-Hof. At the request of the city authorities, however, he provided a greater diversity of floor plans, ranging from small one-room efficiencies to comparatively large two-bedroom units. As in the Winarsky-Hof, the doors to the stairwells were accessible only from the courtyards, providing both greater privacy and security—and enhancing the building's fortresslike appearance.

When they were completed in 1925 the Winarsky-Hof and Wiedenhofer-Hof drew considerable attention, and over the next several years photographs of the buildings appeared in a wide range of progressive publications, including *Der Neubau, Moderne Bauformen, Wasmuths Monatshefte für Baukunst,* and *L'Architecte.* In spite of their conventional pitched roofs and load-bearing masonry walls, the buildings' austere façades and cubic masses were cited repeatedly as an expression of the new architectural spirit that was beginning to emerge across Europe.

Frank's two housing complexes were among the earliest examples of the new modern building style, or *neues Bauen* as it was called in the German-speaking countries. Numerous architects were beginning to design works in the style, though only a handful of examples had actually been realized by 1924. Otto Haesler's landmark Georgsgarten Siedlung in Celle was finished that year. But the celebrated housing programs in the larger German cities—Berlin, Hamburg, and Frankfurt—were still in the planning stages: Ernst May's Bruchfeldstraße Siedlung in Frankfurt and Taut's Onkel Toms Hütte

73. Project for a terraced restaurant, 1924; model (whereabouts unknown). Alberto Sartoris, *Gli Elementi dell' architettura funzionale* (Milan, 1935).

in Berlin were not completed until the following year; and Walter Gropius's Bauhaus complex in Dessau, which for many would become the quintessential example of the new architecture, was still two years away.

Even more strikingly modern in conception than his two municipal housing blocks was a project for a high-rise building (fig. 73) Frank exhibited at the Jubilee exhibition of the Wiener Kunstgewerbeverein in 1924.[52] Described as a "terraced restaurant" or "casino," the ten-story structure was evidently also intended to house apartments and possibly offices, though neither its proposed site nor complete program was revealed in the show's catalog.[53] Many of the building's features—the checkerboard paving on the terraces, the string courses, and the punctuated fenestration pattern—recalled Frank's earlier designs, but both its scale and arrangement were departures from his previous work. The repeated setbacks suggest that Frank may have drawn on Behrens's 1920 *Ter-rassenhaus* concept or Loos's 1923 project for a terraced apartment block for the Viennese municipality. Frank's interest in designing the ten-story structure, however, was apparently prompted both by the promise of tall buildings for improving the housing situation and by the belief, shared by many architects at the time, that the skyscraper posed an ideal model for a modern, democratic Austria.

Frank's terraced restaurant project was, no doubt, also a response to the countless German proposals for skyscrapers in the early 1920s, which were encouraged by changing building codes that allowed their construction for the first time.[54] Building laws in Vienna at the time, however, precluded the construction of true skyscrapers, which may have dictated Frank's more squat composition. Regardless, the economic and technical realities in Austria would prevent the realization of a skyscraper until the early 1930s, when Siegfried Theiss and Hans Jaksch built the city's first modern high-rise building.

FRANK AND THE "PEOPLE'S PALACES" Although less radical than the terraced restaurant project, Frank's apartment blocks also stood out among the housing projects being erected in Vienna at the time. With their stripped, planar surfaces, they posed a striking contrast to the monumental, Baroque-inspired grandeur of the majority of the city-financed housing blocks. Many of these buildings had been designed by graduates of the Wagnerschule, who in the postwar years had recycled Wagner's simplified classicism, shifting it from bourgeois dwellings and urban monuments to the new worker housing complexes.

Frank viewed this attempt to transfer the imagery of the nineteenth-century bourgeois *Wohnpalast* (apartment palace) to social housing as an indication of a lack of real progress in overcoming the city's low living standard. The "ennoblement" (*Nobilitierung*) of the façades with ornamentation merely concealed the underlying truth: that the apartments within represented at best only a marginal improvement over the prewar tenements. In a satirical article, "The People's Apartment Palace: A Speech Presented on the Occasion of the Groundbreaking That Was Never Delivered" (*Der Volkswohnungspalast. Eine Rede anlässlich der Grundsteinlegung, die nicht gehalten wurde*), published in *Der Aufbau* in the summer of 1926, he lashed out at the notion of erecting *Volkswohnungspaläste* (literally, people's apartment palaces) for the masses. "[W]hen I read these two words together 'Volkswohnung' and 'Palast,' I have the sense that two things have been fused that have never had anything to do with each other and whose union means that one or the other must necessarily come up short, and it would be far preferable if it were the palace."[55]

The specific target of Frank's attack was the Gartenstadt Jedlesee (later renamed the Karl-Seitz-Hof) (fig. 74), designed by Hubert Gessner, the most elaborate and imposing of the municipal housing blocks that had been realized up to that time. With its forceful detailing, axial symmetry, and great semicircular exedra, the massive project was widely lauded both as a monument to the power of the Social Democratic party and its working-class constituency and as a model for future housing projects. For Frank, however, the building demonstrated the failure of the city's housing program to address the real needs of those it was meant to serve. The formal vocabulary of the Jedlesee complex—monumental gates, quoins, and vases—belonged to the symbolic domain of the old aristocracy; it was an expression of feudalism, not of a republic. Not only was the formal language of such *Volkswohnungspaläste* unsuitable for Socialist Vienna, he wrote, but the desire to "maintain the appearance" of grandeur had prompted architects to revisit older design

74. Hubert Gessner, Karl-Seitz-Hof, Vienna, 1926–31. Österreichische Nationalbibliothek, Bildarchiv, Vienna.

conventions that in no way enhanced the quality of living. High-ceilinged rooms, large vestibules, and the axial arrangement of spaces, which mimicked the Baroque palaces of the aristocracy, were vestiges of the long-standing Viennese conviction that comfort and livability had to be sacrificed to image.[56] As a specific example, Frank cited the decision to abandon the *Wohnküche* in the new complex and to provide instead separate kitchen and living areas, which he insisted was a step backward from the *Siedlung* house. The resulting tiny rooms and poorly arranged spaces were not a sign of progress, Frank complained, but a return to the living standards of the old speculative tenement buildings: "Domestic culture is not a matter of the number and size of inhabited rooms, but the manner in which the spaces are used. . . . It is the comprehensive layout of a dwelling, the arrangement of the rooms, that is the fundamental mark of such a culture."[57]

The alternative to such housing blocks, Frank reaffirmed, was the single-family house: "We were perhaps already much closer to [our ideal] than today: that is, the *Siedler* house."[58] "It cannot be emphasized enough that the single-family house is the basis of all of modern architecture and of our cities." To those who extolled new building types, he responded that it was much more important to perfect the house "than to have beautiful factories, offices, and garages." "It is the dream of every Anglo-Saxon person one day to own a house with a garden," Frank avowed, citing the German city planner Werner Hegemann: "To which we should add: every free person. . . . A small house, with a maximum of two stories. . . . that is the palace of the future!"[59]

But Frank's hopes for effecting a fundamental shift in the direction of the municipal housing program were to go unfulfilled. At the time his critique of the *Volkswohnungspalast* appeared, plans were already being made for a series of even larger monumental housing blocks, including the most imposing of all, the mammoth Karl-Marx-Hof.

Frank would continue to design housing blocks for the Vienna municipal housing authority through the early 1930s. But after 1924, he once again focused his attentions on what had been the touchstone of his prewar work: the single-family home and its furnishings.

HAUS & GARTEN

In late 1919, the first large exhibition of handicrafts held in Vienna after the First World War opened at the Museum für Kunst und Industrie. The exhibit featured works by many of Austria's leading designers, among them Josef Hoffmann and the young Dagobert Peche. Although some of the pieces were new, the majority of the hundreds of lavish objects on display had been designed before or during the war, and, in an era of food shortages and economic collapse, they seemed to most observers perversely out of step with the times. The critic Hans Tietze summed up the reactions when he wrote that "in light of the deadly earnest of the present time and of that restriction to barest essentials, . . . the exhibition of a thousand amiable trifles strikes one as untimely, even eerie."[1]

Frank, too, was slow to adapt to the changed realities of the postwar era. Like the majority of the Viennese artists and designers who prior to 1914 had established the city as one of the fertile centers of European decorative arts, he clung to the notion of a modernism rooted in the traditional crafts. His commitment to improving the living standards of the working class notwithstanding, throughout the late 1910s and 1920s Frank remained intent on forging a new bourgeois mode of dwelling based on older ideas of material pleasure. His early postwar designs for the home elaborated and extended the eclectic aesthetic that he, Strnad, and Wlach had pioneered almost a decade before. But by the mid-1920s, Frank would gradually shape his own individual design idiom, one that would not only influence much of later Viennese design but would also come to pose a compelling alternative to the modernist mainstream.

FRANK'S EARLY POSTWAR DESIGNS In 1919, while he was drawing up his first proposals for proletarian *Siedlungen,* Frank was also at work on a commission for the Wiener Werkstätte to design a freestanding silver mirror (fig. 75). The exquisitely crafted piece—only one of which was apparently ever produced—is a testament to the consummate skill of the Werkstätte's craftsmen.[2] Yet it also highlights how reluctant Frank—and, indeed, almost all of the Viennese—were to renounce the aestheticism of the prewar years.

Frank was fully aware of the paradox of pursuing luxury in a time of retrenchment. In an article published in *Der Architekt* in 1921, he conceded that the arts and crafts in Vienna were dying. It was not only the loss of the empire's outlying provinces, from which, as he noted, the city had traditionally drawn much of its artistic stimulus as well as many of its most talented craftsmen that threatened handicraft; rather, Frank wrote, what also had been taken away by the war and its aftermath was "the possibility of quietude and the pleasure one may gain from things that serve no particular purpose [*Freude an Zwecklosem*]."[3] In the harsh new atmosphere of poverty and deprivation, he declared, the arts

75. (left) Design for a silver mirror for the Wiener Werkstätte, 1919. Pencil, pen and ink on paper, 44.5 × 44 cm; (right) the executed design. Österreichisches Museum für angewandte Kunst, Vienna.

and crafts in Vienna had been replaced by a new practicality that allowed little opportunity for quality handwork or contemplation.[4]

While Frank acknowledged that it had become necessary to rethink the arts and crafts and their production—"we will have to begin anew in everything," he wrote—he remained unwilling to abandon completely the old arts and crafts.[5] But unlike Hoffmann and most of the other leading prewar designers who sought to adapt cubism and expressionism to a new decorative language, he continued to find inspiration in older forms, which he sought to interpret in new ways.[6] His 1919 tea table for his wife's sister, Signhild Claëson (plate 6), or the chair he designed for the Lundberg family (fig. 76) illustrate his attempt to readjust his historically based approach to the postwar spirit.

Yet Frank recognized that the profound changes wrought by industrialization necessitated new furniture types and forms: "The furniture of our new 'Machine-Age' will stand apart from any attempt to be merely 'decorative,'" he wrote; instead, it will "represent a minimum of material, space, form, and weight," while at the same time "requiring a minimum of care and upkeep." Such new standard types could not be invented: "they arise on their own."[7] Frank observed, however, that designers could contribute to this process by offering new forms and ideas that would eventually evolve into standard types—like the Windsor chair—that might be used as "ready-mades."

76. Side chair for the Lundberg house, c. 1921. Svenskt Tenn Collection, Josef Frank Archive, Stockholm.

Frank's affirmation of the need for developing new standard types stopped short of a complete endorsement of industrial production of furnishings and other objects of daily use. While conceding that the trend toward machine-made household articles was not to be halted, he insisted that traditional hand-crafted furnishings and other items still had a place in the modern dwelling because they offered qualities that could not be replicated by industrial products: "The mechanized factory can only have one aim, to make its products as useful as possible. It can never go beyond its actual task, to produce objects in the sparest and most precise form possible." Hand-crafted articles, by contrast, because they could be more elaborate and provide evidence of the time and care taken by their maker, fostered a sense of luxury and calm that was lacking in industrially manufactured goods. More important for Frank, handicraft also left room for the "healthy aspiration" of the working man to "find joy" and "heightened intellectual engagement" (*Geistestätigkeit*)[8] and "to express something."[9] Such qualities had allowed the arts and crafts to survive and even prosper in an era that saw increasing competition from the machine. To maintain a living artisanal tradition, however, Frank recognized that it would be necessary to alter the nature of handwork, at once limiting it to objects not intended to be merely functional, and, at the same time, using machines to relieve the craftsman of "worthless labor."[10]

But these changes alone, Frank conceded, would not be enough. A new formal language for handicraft was needed, one that reflected—or at least acknowledged—the realities of machine production. A first step toward this end was to free objects of "mere decoration" (*bloßen Aufputz*), whether traditional or "modern": "a chest painted with cubistic motifs is no more modern than one with Renaissance-style decoration." Needed, too, was a new "eye for the beauties of natural and artificial materials." In spite of such efforts, Frank believed, considerable differences would remain, making a "unified style" as had existed in former times "impossible." The modern home or apartment "required a flexibility" and "variety" that would allow room for these different impulses and forms.[11]

For the next decade, Frank would work to develop a new language for the modern interior—and for its surrounding architectural frame.

THE STIEGL AND CLAËSON HOUSES In the early 1920s, Frank began once more to receive commissions to design single-family residences. In 1923, in addition to the villa for Theo Herzberg-Fränkel in Ortmann, he commenced work on two small summer houses. One of the commissions came from Dr. Felix Bunzl, the brother of Hugo Bunzl, for a site in Wattens, in the Austrian Tyrol. Frank prepared two different versions of the house, one adhering to the traditional vernacular forms of the region, and a second, modernized version. Problems with financing, however, put an end to the project, and the house was never built.

Around the same time, Frank also produced an unrealized design for a summer cottage in Spittal an der Drau, Carinthia, for a client named Otto Stiegl (figs. 77–78). In contrast to the Wattens project, the Stiegl House shows much more modern handling, both inside and out. The main body of the house, a three-story cube, is broken up by balconies, a lower projecting wing, and a pergola. Frank placed the various rooms on different levels: the living room is fifteen centimeters higher than the entry, the dining room, kitchen, and pantry fifty centimeters higher, while the veranda and a terrace on the south side are sunken twenty and forty centimeters, respectively. One would have entered the house on the west side underneath the pergola and climbed up to the main living areas, or alternately, ascended to the upper floors by means of a stairway on the northwest corner.

By removing any barriers between the main living areas on the ground floor, Frank allowed the space to extend freely from side to side. A wall of French doors on the south façade of the house similarly served to break down the distinction between interior and exterior, allowing free access to the terrace and veranda. Although conventional room di-

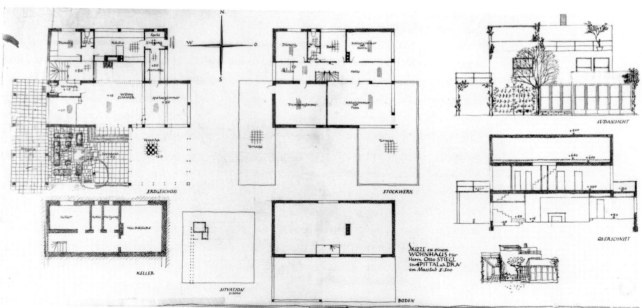

77. Project for a house for Otto Stiegl, Spittal an der Drau, 1924; model (whereabouts unknown). *Moderne Bauformen* 26 (1927).

78. Project for a house for Otto Stiegl, Spittal an der Drau, 1924; site plan 1:1000, plans, elevations, and section 1:100, perspective. Pencil, pen and ink on tracing paper, 30 × 64 cm. Graphische Sammlung Albertina, Vienna.

visions are still preserved in most of the house, Frank's use of large windows and doors gave the entire ensemble an openness absent in his prewar villas.

Frank's interest in free and casual planning was also at the heart of another work, a small beach house for his wife's sister and brother-in-law, Signhild and Axel Claëson. Major Axel Claëson was in the Swedish diplomatic service posted in Paris, but the couple spent the summer months in the seaside resort of Falsterbo on Sweden's southwestern tip. Situated on a narrow, dune- and heather-covered peninsula, the picturesque community of barely two thousand was a favored vacation spot for well-heeled Swedish families from Stockholm and Malmö. Frank and his wife Anna were also regular visitors to the town, and during the 1920s Anna rented a modest house there. The Claëson House was the first of five houses Frank would eventually design for relatives and acquaintances in Falsterbo in the later 1920s and 1930s.[12]

Frank's initial designs for the project date to the summer of 1924, but construction delays—due in large part to the reluctance of the local builder to take on the rather unconventional design fearing that it would "damage his reputation"—prevented its completion until 1927.[13] Over the course of the prolonged design phase, Frank prepared at least four different versions of the house. All of the schemes are based on a two-story brick structure, roughly rectangular in plan, topped with a small wooden lookout, the "cabin," as he referred to it (figs. 79, 80). But Frank varied both the configuration of the main body of the house and balconies and the disposition of the interior spaces, devoting particular attention to the living areas on the ground floor.

With its spare, unadorned façades, blocky massing, and metal railings, the house as it was realized (fig. 81) was Frank's first executed residence to which the stylistic term *modern* may truly apply.[14] The overall design concept and many of the house's features owed much to Frank's efforts to respond to the seaside setting. To shield the house from storms, he specified either small or undivided windows for the south and west sides facing the water, and he opened the house up to the east, which faced a wooded area.[15] Both the third-story "cabin"—intended as a place of work and observation—and the terraces afforded views of the sea and the surrounding countryside. Frank also provided a large, open fireplace on the south end of the upper terrace so that the Claësons and their guests could keep warm during the cool Swedish summer evenings.

The house's interior (fig. 82) was similarly arranged to take advantage of its seaside setting. The second-story bedrooms opened out onto terraces on either side, as did the large L-shaped living and dining area, which occupied much of the space on the ground floor. Frank put special emphasis on fostering an impression of spatial flow, both within the house and between the interior and the outside terraces. Although the house was relatively small, this openness and interconnection imparted an impression of spaciousness.

THE FOUNDING OF HAUS & GARTEN After 1924, Frank began to focus his attentions once more on designing furnishings and other household objects. One reason for his renewed interest in the arts and crafts was the decline of the *Siedlung* program. Even more important, however, was the gradual improvement of the economy. After more than five years of tumult and instability, the financial health of the

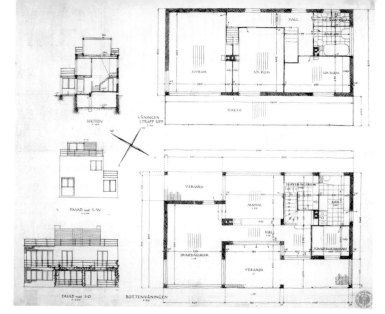

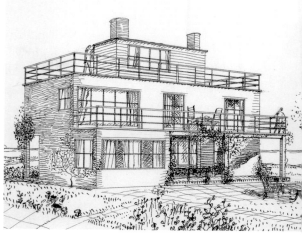

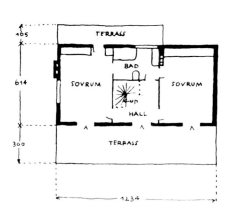

79. (top, left) House for Axel
and Signhild Claëson, Falsterbo,
Sweden, 1924–27; preliminary
version; plans 1:50, elevations, and
section 1:100. Pencil, pen and ink
on tracing paper, 45 × 51.5 cm.
Sammlung, Universität für angewandte Kunst, Vienna.

80. (top, right) House for Axel
and Signhild Claëson, Falsterbo,
Sweden, 1924–27; perspective.
Collection Professor Johannes
Spalt, Vienna.

81. (center) House for Axel and
Signhild Claëson, Falsterbo, Swe-
den, 1924–27; view from the south-
west. Svenskt Tenn Collection,
Josef Frank Archive, Stockholm.
Photograph courtesy of Kristina
Wängberg-Eriksson.

82. (bottom) House for Axel and
Signhild Claëson, Falsterbo, Swe-
den, 1924–27; plans. *Moderne
Bauformen* 28 (1929).

83. Oskar Wlach, c. 1938.
Author's collection.

Austrian Republic started to show sure signs of recovery, and for the next several years—until the worldwide depression set in at the end of the decade—the country experienced a period of brief, if shaky, prosperity.

Encouraged by the upturn, Frank decided to launch his own home furnishings business in the early summer of 1925.[16] He was joined in the enterprise by his former partner, Oskar Wlach (fig. 83).

During the war years, Wlach had been stationed in Albania. He had contracted malaria, and, after a long convalescence, was transferred to Galicia. His illness reoccurred in 1917, and he was removed from the front and reassigned, along with a number of other Austrian architects and technical experts, to Constantinople, to assist the Ottoman government.[17] When the conflict ended, Wlach was interned by the Allies, and he was only able to return to Vienna in the spring of 1919. Like Frank, he participated in the *Siedlung* movement after the war, designing settlement prototypes and, later, several large housing blocks.[18] He also collaborated with Frank on at least one project, a competition design for a housing development in Istanbul in 1920.[19] By 1922, Wlach began once more to concentrate on furniture design and interiors. He and Frank worked together in 1923–24 on the interiors for the villa of the textile magnate David Löbel (fig. 84), which Wlach was remodeling at the time.[20]

Frank and Wlach were joined in the enterprise by a silent partner, Walter Sobotka, a close friend of Frank and Wlach's from their time at the Technische Hochschule.[21] The three architects originally registered the company as "Haus und Garten & Co.," an apparent homage to Scott's *Houses and Gardens*. After Sobotka withdrew from the partnership the following year, Frank and Wlach renamed the company simply "Haus & Garten" (fig. 85).[22]

In the fall of 1925, Frank and Wlach opened a sales outlet (fig. 86) on the Bösendorferstraße, a block from the Opera. They chose the site not only because of its proximity to the fashionable shops along the nearby Ringstrasse, but also because it was adjacent to the main downtown stop of the tram that ran out to the spa resort of Baden, a line many of Vienna's well-to-do regularly rode to take the waters or see the horseraces. To attract potential customers, they changed the shop's windows often, featuring brightly colored fabrics and upholstered furnishings.

On display in the small showroom were samples of the company's product line, which included sofas, chairs, tables, beds, and desks, as well as lamps, pillows, and printed textiles (figs. 87, 88). Most of the pieces, however, were available on a custom-order basis only. Clients could select from among the models on display, or choose pieces or patterns from a series of sample books, specifying particular finishes, sizes, colors, and coverings.

In the first year of the firm's existence, Frank and Wlach produced their own individual designs. But by 1926, Frank took over the role of principal designer, and Wlach as-

HAUS ʊ GARTEN

MÖBEL, LAMPEN,
STOFFE, KERAMIK
VOLLSTÄNDIGE
EINRICHTUNGEN,
ETC.

BUREAU UND ATELIER:
VII., NEUSTIFTGASSE 3
TELEPHON B-35-2-13

AUSSTELLUNG UND VERKAUF:
I., BÖSENDORFERSTRASSE 5
TELEPHON U-47-2-16

84. House for David Löbel,
1923–24; conservatory. *Innen-
Dekoration* 37 (1926).

85. Haus & Garten business card.
Author's collection.

86. Haus & Garten showroom,
Bösendorferstraße 5, c. 1930.
Österreichische Nationalbibliothek,
Bildarchiv, Vienna.

sumed the position of office manager, overseeing the day-to-day operation of the shop and supervising the remodeling jobs and the execution of larger commissions.[23] The arrangement left Frank free to pursue other projects while ensuring that Wlach would attend to the details of the business.

THE 1925 PARIS EXHIBITION

The first public demonstration of Frank's design ideas for Haus & Garten came at the 1925 Paris Exposition Internationale des Arts Décoratifs et Industriels Modernes. In addition to a display of his recent architectural projects, including the terraced restaurant and the Stiegl and Claëson Houses,[24] Frank showed a selection of "practical furniture" (*Nutzmöbel*; fig. 89) in a niche in the central hall of the Austrian pavilion. Though quite small, the exhibit attracted the attention of a number of visitors, among them the young Swedish designer Uno Åhrén, who praised Frank's works for their "freshness," "vigor," and "practical habitability."[25]

These same qualities were also evident in the outdoor "Café viennois" (fig. 90) Frank designed for the pavilion. Wedged in a courtyard framed by Peter Behren's iron and glass pavilion and an organ tower by Strnad, the café proved to be one of the most popular exhibits at the exposition, eliciting praise from a number of critics for its lightness and unaffected atmosphere.[26]

The special character of Frank's design was tied not only to its particular expression but also its underlying message. While Le Corbusier had selected each element of the Pavilion de L'Espirit Nouveau to demonstrate his faith in new materials, standardization, and industrial production,[27] Frank's café seemingly made a plea for a new freedom, one that articulated modernity but left room for comfort and sentimentality. At the same time, Frank pointedly rejected the position of the more conservative French designers, such as Jacques-Emile Ruhlmann or Georges Djo-Bourgeois, who remained wedded to traditional notions of luxury and style. What he offered instead was an attempt to rephrase material enjoyment without resorting either to outmoded forms or new industrial products. It was in this spirit that Frank developed his furnishings and interiors for Haus & Garten over the next decade.

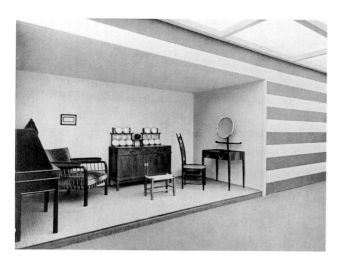

89. Haus & Garten furniture in the
Austrian pavilion at the Exposition
Internationale des Arts Décoratifs
et Industriels Modernes, Paris,
1925. *Moderne Bauformen* 24
(1925).

90. Outdoor coffee house (Café
viennois) for the Austrian pavilion,
Exposition Internationale des Arts
Décoratifs et Industriels Modernes,
Paris, 1925. *Innen-Dekoration* 37
(1926).

DESIGN PRINCIPLES Haus & Garten proved from the start to be a moderate commercial success, and in the summer of 1926 Frank resigned from his teaching position at the Kunstgewerbeschule to devote more of his energy to the undertaking.[28] He and Wlach opened a separate architectural and design office at the corner of Neustiftgasse and Museumstraße in the city's seventh district,[29] but Frank often spent time in the later 1920s at the shop.[30] By 1927—perhaps as early as 1926—Frank and Wlach had also begun to distribute their designs for Haus & Garten in Germany through the Cologne firm Gustav Carl Lehmann.[31] The arrangement with Lehmann allowed Frank and Wlach to gain a foothold in the large German market, and it provided them with greater exposure in the German design press.

The basic design principles Frank developed for Haus & Garten had their anchorage in the eclectic idiom that he and Strnad, working in concert with Wlach, Gorge, and Lurje, had developed before the war.[32] These precepts also came to define the interiors of a whole range of younger Austrian designers—among them Felix Augenfeld, Arthur Berger, Fritz Groß, Karl Hofmann, Julius Jirasek, Otto Niedermoser, Armand Weiser, and Liane Zimbler—whose works were sometimes grouped together under the name "Wiener Wohnkultur" (literally, Viennese dwelling culture).[33] Neither a movement nor a coherent ideology, the Wiener Wohnkultur represented instead a mitigated, cozy modernism, an attempt to wrest some degree of comfort from the mounting drive toward wholesale "purification" and "invention" that characterized the design scene of the later 1920s.

In terms of its product line and client base, Frank and Wlach patterned Haus & Garten after the Wiener Werkstätte. Most of the pieces were expensively produced, incorporating exotic woods or other costly components. Frank and Wlach also insisted on high standards of craftsmanship. As a consequence, the shop's clientele was drawn almost exclusively from the upper middle class, which put it in more or less direct competition with the Wiener Werkstätte. In contrast to the Wiener Werkstätte, however, Haus & Garten had no production facilities of its own; Frank and Wlach sent the various designs out to local artisans, who produced them according to the clients' specifications. But rather than offering groupings or suites of furnishings, as was the standard practice at the Wiener Werkstätte's sale outlets, Frank and Wlach encouraged their clients to choose and match objects at will and to arrange them piecemeal in their rooms. This emphasis on casual arrangement was a marked departure from the Werkstätte's philosophy, which continued to promote carefully coordinated room designs and discouraged the purchase of individual pieces.[34]

In spurning such en suite arrangements, Frank and Wlach rejected not only the idea of unity that had been at the center of Viennese design since the turn of the century, but also the whole notion of the home as a work of art. "A modern living space," Frank wrote in the early 1930s, "is not an art work, it is neither conspicuous, nor effective, nor exciting." Rather, "it is comfortable, without one being able to say why, and the less reason that one can provide the better it is."[35] To engender a sense of rest and pleasure, the home must be free of any pretension, any striving for theatrical or artistic impact.

In the modern dwelling, disorder reigns, which is to say that there are no furnishings that are intended for particular places and that would destroy the harmony of the room if they were moved. One should place each piece of furniture . . . where one needs it at a particular moment.[36]

"The word *Möbel* [furniture]," Frank pointed out,

derives from "mobile," which means movable. That should be taken literally. An armoire is not movable, it forms a "room within a room." . . . It destroys the clarity of a space.[37]

Instead, Frank argued, such "representational" pieces should be replaced by light, easily portable tables and chairs "that assert no [architectonic] influence of any sort." Furniture should be placed in the room "as if by chance," "with no assigned place." Each piece should be "independent of the others," should not "conceal anything," and "constitute a 'grouping' only insofar as they are placed in relation to each other." Our concern is no longer with "installations" (*Einrichtungen*), Frank declared, but "only individual furnishings" (*Einzel-Möbel*).[38]

In extolling diversity and common sense in design, Frank echoed Loos's earlier attacks on the Secessionists and the Werkbund; his notion of a fundamental distinction between the work of art and the object of daily use also undoubtedly derived from Loos.[39] However, Frank parted from Loos on the issue of ornament: while Loos equated the reduction of ornament with cultural progress, Frank maintained that ornament provided a sense of joy and relaxation that was necessary in a time of increasing stress and mental demands:

*Every form of ornament is an expression of play [*Spielerei*], to which is devoted both time for its making and its enjoyment, and which one may reflect on without disruption. For that reason, all ornament of the past has such a remarkably soothing effect (one thinks, for example, of Oriental rugs), whereas all plain industrial products, can immediately be perceived [and] carry over to us a sense of the haste with which they were produced.*[40]

Frank acknowledged that it had become increasingly difficult to generate new forms of ornament in the modern age. His alternative was to borrow from the past: "Because our time is no longer in the position to make decoration and ornament, modern man is compelled to use old fabrics and patterns." The appropriation of older objects and models, he argued, was not mere nostalgia, but a recognition that the modern age did not preclude the past, and that "numerous household objects" represented "perfected types" that had been developed over many years.[41]

Frank believed the way to apply these lessons was not through mimesis or the use of reproductions—as Loos often did in his interiors—but to discern their essence and rephrase it in a new spirit. Most of Frank's designs for Haus & Garten thus drew more or less directly on historical models. The German critic Leopold Greiner, who wrote the first review of Haus & Garten, immediately recognized this debt to the past: The basis of Haus & Garten, he observed, is that "applied forms do not necessarily have to be thoroughly 'new.'"[42]

Yet it was not only Frank's continuing allegiance to history that set his designs apart. Even in his simplest, most radically pared-down pieces (in which the historical models are barely, if at all, discernible) he treated both the surfaces and materials quite differently from most of the other modernists. In place of squared corners and sharply canted edges, Frank specified smoothed, often undulating lines; and he often articulated flat surfaces or ornamented them in some manner. He was especially attentive to any area one might touch or grasp: "The closer one comes into contact with a piece of furniture, the more ungeometric and organic it should be constituted, so that it will fit readily into the hand," he wrote.[43]

This concern with the haptic qualities of surfaces also underlies Frank's preference for wood over metal for furnishings other than lamps. Indeed, Frank's Haus & Garten designs constitute an extended essay on the possibilities of forming and finishing woods, both ordinary and exotic. Frank's preference for wood stemmed in part from his commitment to preserving the nineteenth-century bourgeois ideal of the home as a site of refinement and refuge. Yet, as Greiner recognized, it was also a conscious attempt to maintain a connection with the preindustrial world, and, with it, to a simple and less harried life.[44] In this, Frank anticipated the antitechnological message of later critics of the modern. His aim, however, was not to deny the realities of the machine age or to urge a return to an idealized past but to leave room for other possibilities.

FRANK'S TEXTILE DESIGNS To allow for the greatest flexibility, Frank treated his rooms as more or less neutral containers. Unless a client insisted otherwise, he left the walls white, introducing color principally through the use of Oriental rugs and printed fabrics.

In the earliest Haus & Garten interiors, Frank sometimes employed textiles from other firms, especially Baker's and Heal and Sons in London. But by the end of 1925 he had begun to develop a full line of his own patterns.[45] Frank was no stranger to textile design. Through visits to his father's textile shop[46] and by observing his mother, who was a highly skilled embroiderer[47] Frank had developed an intimate knowledge of the techniques and practices of textile manufacturing. Nor was his interest in textiles unique among his Viennese contemporaries: Hoffmann, Peche, Moser, and many other leading artists and designers produced patterns for the Wiener Werkstätte, Backhausen, and other firms.

However, Frank's textile patterns broke with the prevailing Viennese trends. In place of the heavy stylization that characterized the works of the leading Wiener Werkstätte artists, he substituted a much more freely conceived language of loosely drawn floral or other figurative motifs. Many of the patterns were modeled after the Persian and Indian calicoes that had been imported to Europe in the seventeenth and eighteenth centuries or the later floriferous designs of William Morris and the other British arts and crafts designers.[48] But Frank reconceived these originals, reducing the number of elements while simplifying or otherwise modifying the color schemes. The resulting patterns, such as "Frühling" (Spring; plate 7), retained the decorative qualities of the older designs but in a recognizably modernized form. In some of Frank's textile designs, such as "Fioretti" (plate 8) or "Seegras" (plate 9), he also explored the possibilities of complex geometric patterning based on vegetal models; in others, especially in his carpet designs, he opted for fully abstracted motifs vaguely reminiscent of the form language of contemporary artists Paul Klee and Jóan Miró.

Frank first began experimenting with designing his own printed fabrics during his student years, but he had produced only a handful of patterns prior to the founding of Haus & Garten. Between 1925 and 1930, however, he devised no fewer than thirty new designs, most of them available in several alternative colors combinations.[49] The patterns were block printed on linen or cotton chintz by local craftsmen,[50] a laborious process that involved cutting the design in relief into thick blocks of linden- or pearwood, one for each color, and then applying the dye to the cloth with the separate blocks.

Frank generally confined his use of textiles to curtains or upholstery, but occasionally, especially in his early years, he also applied the fabrics to some of the case pieces as surface decoration, such as his cabinet for the Kalmár Apartment from around 1930 (plate 10). In contrast to the Wiener Werkstätte designers, however, he refrained from using the textiles as wall coverings, regarding them instead as a means to accent rather than to clad large surfaces. As with other Haus & Garten designs, he and Wlach mixed and matched the patterns freely, not infrequently employing several quite dissimilar designs in a single space.

THE EVOLUTION OF HAUS & GARTEN Frank's earliest Haus & Garten interiors retained some of the rigid formality and decorative richness that characterized Viennese houses and apartments of the early postwar years. But after 1926, he began to investigate a more elemental and less ordered approach. The music room of the Bunzl Apartment (fig. 91), which probably dates from late 1925 or early 1926, marks a transition in his designs. Several of the pieces—especially the ample, overstuffed sofas—still have the weightiness of late-nineteenth-century rooms; however, the free arrangement of the furnishings and lamps implies a new ordering concept, one in which the objects exist more or less independently of the space. The architectonic features, in keeping with Frank's precepts, were treated very simply. A dark, narrow molding framed the walls near their junction with the ceiling; otherwise, they were undifferentiated and—aside from the built-in bookcases—the furnishings did not engage them. Instead, the pieces retained their autonomy—from the walls and from each other.

91. Music room, Bunzl Apartment, Vienna, c. 1926. *Innen-Dekoration* 37 (1926).

This move away from conventional ordering is even more pronounced in Frank's rooms of the later 1920s. In the model living room he and Wlach showed at the 1928 *Österreichische Kunstgewerbe-Ausstellung* in Cologne (fig. 92), the chairs, sofas, and tables were arrayed in small informal groupings, an arrangement reminiscent of the Biedermeier idea of a *Wohninsel,* or "living island," which constitute discrete family activity spaces. The pieces were not fixed formally so that the sofa-table-chair combinations could be realigned as desired. Frank and Wlach further enhanced the impression of flexibility and informality through the use of a broad assortment of chairs, tables, rugs, and other elements.

Also notable in the Cologne display is an increasing sense of lightness. Not only have the members of the chairs and other furnishings been pared down, but—which is evident even in the surviving black and white photographs—the color palette is noticeably brighter. This trend toward a lighter, more open, and more colorful décor stands out in Frank's Haus & Garten designs of the early 1930s.

Among the most striking examples of this new simplicity is the living room he designed for the L. R. S. House (fig. 93). Executed around 1933, it demonstrated a new

spareness, one that had already become a distinguishing feature of the interiors of the more radical modernists. In spite of the impulse toward formal reduction, Frank also continued to show an unusual interest in material richness. Works such as the upholstered mahogany chair he designed in the later 1920s (plate 11) attest not only to his allegiance to past models but also to his love for the physical properties of woods and textiles—and how they are formed and finished. Every aspect of its design—from the bamboo staves to the tapering, gently curving stiles—celebrates these qualities of material and fabrication.

The full effect of Frank's interiors derived from the juxtaposition of different objects and accessories, each playing off the others. In the interiors of the Steiner House, one of Haus & Garten's most important and fully realized commissions of the early 1930s (figs. 94, 95), he and Wlach combined a remarkable array of forms, materials, and patterns. Historic designs, such as the Egyptian-inspired three-legged stool[51] in the bedroom, were counterposed with a colorful abstract-patterned rug (plate 12), and these in turn were combined with a rectilinear plant stand, a fabric-covered cabinet, and a Shaker-inspired bed.

But this profusion of elements is not the only feature that distinguished Frank and Wlach's interiors: underlying their evident appeal to the senses is also a vital humanism, an attempt to foster an image that was up-to-date and also adapted to the circumstances of real life. The chairs, sofas, and tables are carefully scaled to accommodate their users, and the gently curving lines,

92. Model living room at the *Öster-reichische Kunstgewerbe-Ausstel-lung*, Cologne, 1928. *Moderne Bauformen* 28 (1929).

93. Living room, L. R. S. House, Vienna, c. 1933. *Innen-Dekoration* 44 (1933).

bright color palette, and medley of forms and patterns represent a concerted effort to please the eye and soothe the psyche (fig. 96).

After 1930, Frank's attempt to forge a personal and responsive modernism assumed an ever greater role in his designs. While not abandoning his commitment to formal variety, he began to explore a softer, more subdued look. In the sitting corner of the W. House (fig. 97), for example, which he designed around 1933, the individual elements have been softened and blended. The result was a more organic conception, one that points firmly in the direction of the modernism of the 1950s.

94. (top, left) Son's room, Steiner House, Vienna, c. 1933.
Innen-Dekoration 44 (1933).

95. (right) Bedroom, Steiner House, Vienna, c. 1933.
Innen-Dekoration 44 (1933).

96. (middle, left) Library, W. House, Vienna, c. 1933.
Innen-Dekoration 44 (1933).

97. (bottom, left) Sitting corner, W. House, Vienna, c. 1933.
Innen-Dekoration 44 (1933).

The same trend toward an integrated design language also appears in Frank's garden furniture of the same period. As the name of the firm suggests, both garden design and garden furniture occupied a central place in the Haus & Garten program. Frank regarded the garden as an extension of the interior living space. Over the years he produced a variety of designs for small landscapes, garden houses, and outdoor furnishings. Frank's design concept, however, was almost invariably the same: a *Wohninsel* framed to provide an intimate, private setting. In his unrealized project for a garden pavilion of around 1926 (fig. 98), the furniture echoed his indoor designs and was only slightly modified for outdoor use. The effect of the ensemble (including the trees trained to espalier along the back wall, which repeat the vegetal designs of his textiles) was intended to produce an impression of fresh-air domesticity. Frank's later garden furnishings, like those he produced for the Steiner House in the early 1930s (fig. 99), were more unified in conception, but his focus on the informal sitting group remained.

If Frank transferred the notion of dwelling to the garden, he sought similarly to break down the distinction between inside and outside. The central place of the garden in Frank's design ideal is reflected, as Greiner had observed early on, in his attempt to use wood and other living materials "to bring a piece of 'nature' into our rooms."[52] It was developed as well in his repeated use of floral patterns and, perhaps most importantly, in his emphasis on establishing direct connections—by means of doors, windows, terraces, and balconies—with the outdoors.

Whether for the inside or the outside, Frank's designs for Haus & Garten explored the rich possibilities of living in the modern age. They were founded not on a new asceticism but on a redefinition of material pleasure. Frank's objects were objects of enjoyment, not statements of a purism or of a machine-age aesthetic. The rich sensuality of the Haus & Garten line provided an alternative form of modern dwelling, one that acknowledged the bourgeois interiors of the past, but was purified of the excesses of historicist taste.

98. Project for a garden pavilion, c. 1926. Alexander Koch, *1000 Ideen zur künstlerischen Ausgestaltung der Wohnung* (Darmstadt, 1926).

99. Garden furniture, Steiner House, Vienna, c. 1933. *Innen-Dekoration* 44 (1933).

1. Student drawing ("Forum"), 1900. Pencil, watercolor on paper, 20.5 × 25 cm. Svenskt Tenn Collection, Josef Frank Archive, Stockholm. Photograph courtesy of Kristina Wängberg-Eriksson.

Inside the drawing:
IOHANES ORICELLARIVS PAV FANSAL MCCCCLXX

VON DER KIRCHE S. MARIA NOVELLA IN FLORENZ ◉ VORDERANSICHT DER KIRCHE IM MASSTAB 1:81

2. Reconstruction of the main façade of Santa Maria Novella, Florence, by Leon Battista Alberti, c. 1910; elevation. Pencil, pen and ink, watercolor on paper, 50.5 × 48.5 cm. Universitätsarchiv, Technische Universität, Vienna.

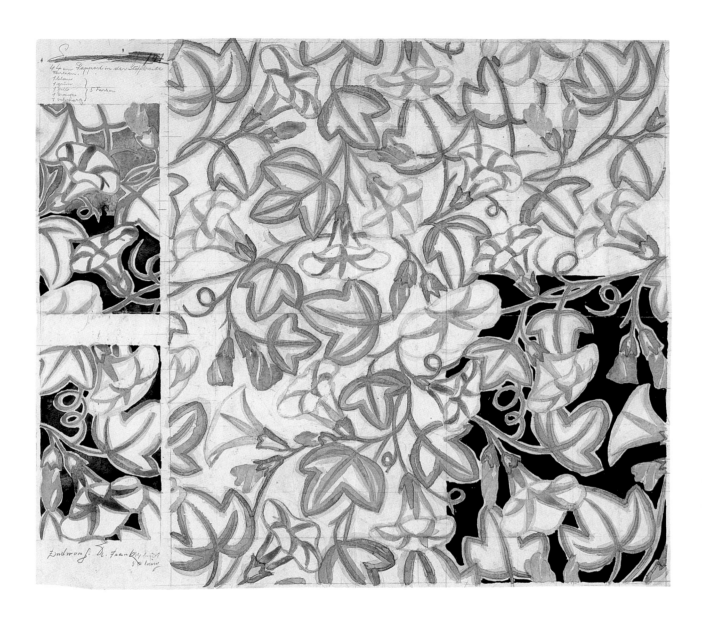

3. Fabric design ("Schöpfung") for the Wiener Werkstätte, 1917. Watercolor and pencil on paper, 50.5 × 69 cm. MAK-Österreichisches Museum für angewandte Kunst, Vienna.

4. Kinderheim, Workers' *Siedlung*, Ortmann, Lower Austria, 1921; hall. Alexander Koch, *Farbige Wohnräume der Neuzeit* (Darmstadt, 1926).

The text on the building plaque reads:

ERBAUT
VON DER
GEMEINDE
WIEN
IM JAHRE
MCMXXIV

5. Wiedenhofer-Hof Housing Project, 1923–24; southwest corner. Photograph by Christopher Long.

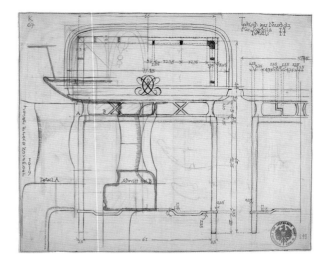

6. Design for a tea table for Signhild Claëson, 1919; elevations, plan, section 1:5; details 1:1. Pen and ink, pencil on paper, 22.5 × 27 cm. Sammlung, Universität für angewandte Kunst, Vienna.

7. "Frühling" fabric sample; printed on linen for Haus & Garten; designed c. 1925–30. Repeat: 38 × 46 cm. Svenskt Tenn Collection, Josef Frank Archive, Stockholm.

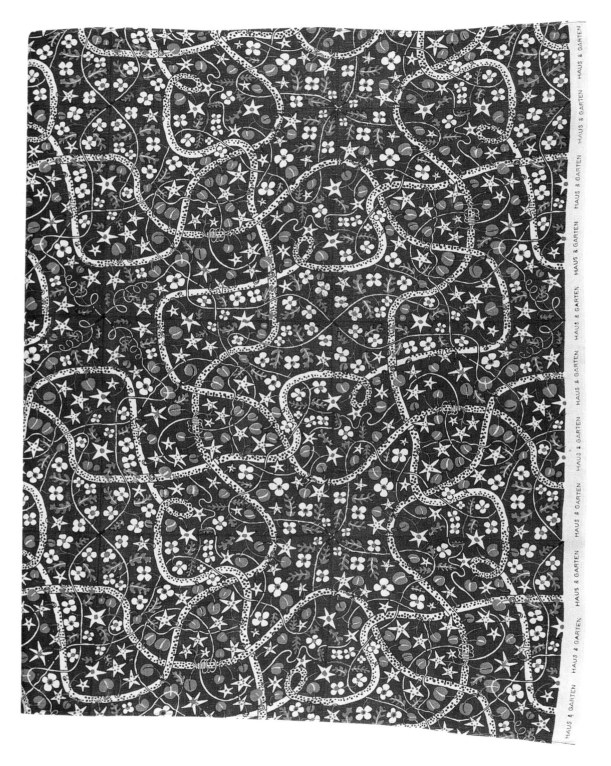

8. "Fioretti" fabric sample; printed on linen for Haus & Garten; designed c. 1925–30. Repeat: 30 × 30 cm. Svenskt Tenn Collection, Josef Frank Archive, Stockholm.

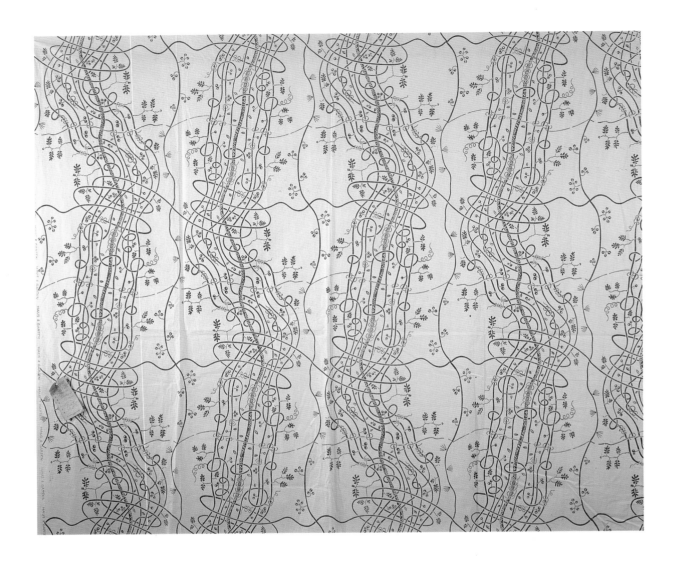

9. "Seegras" fabric sample; printed on chintzed cotton for Haus & Garten; designed c. 1925–30. Repeat 36.5 × 27.5 cm. Courtesy Galerie 16, Vienna.

10. Cabinet covered with "Mirakel" fabric, c. 1930. Collection Ruth Wilson-Kalmár, Vienna.

11. Armchair for Haus & Garten, c. 1930; mahogany and linen. Collection Ruth Wilson-Kalmár, Vienna.

12. Carpet design for Haus & Garten,
c. 1933. Sammlung, Universität für
angewandte Kunst, Vienna.

13. Project for a house in Baden bei Wien,
c. 1927; perspective. *Innen-Dekoration* 39
(1928).

A DISSENTING VOICE The late 1920s and early 1930s marked the pinnacle of Frank's prestige and influence. Though he had realized only a handful of buildings prior to 1927, his designs for the Vienna Municipal Housing Authority and his other published projects had earned him wide recognition in European architectural circles. Photographs of his works, often accompanied by his statements, appeared in most of the leading German-language architectural journals, including *Wasmuths Monatshefte für Baukunst, Deutsche Kunst und Dekoration, Der Neubau,* and *Der Baumeister.* The May 1927 issue of *Moderne Bauformen,* which featured recent works from Viennese architects, devoted a large section to Frank. A brief introduction that preceded the extensive selection of his postwar designs called Frank "a born representative of the '*neue Sachlichkeit.*'" The editors also commended his commitment to the social aspects of the *neues Bauen,* praising his housing projects as "without a doubt the purest and strongest realization of the Viennese communal housing program."[1] The piece concluded with a pronouncement that in only a few years was to have an ironic ring: "Modern architecture cannot be more purely or more significantly advanced than through this one of its leaders."[2]

100. Weissenhofsiedlung, Stuttgart, 1925–27; view toward the south with Frank's double house on the lower left. Zentralinstitut für Kunstgeschichte, Munich.

101. (bottom, left) Double house at the Weissenhofsiedlung, Stuttgart, 1927. Author's collection.

102. (bottom, right) Double house at the Weissenhofsiedlung, Stuttgart, 1927; view from the rear. Bauhaus-Archiv, Berlin.

THE WEISSENHOFSIEDLUNG Confirmation of Frank's rising stature had come the previous fall when he was invited to take part in the second major German Werkbund exhibition, to be held in the Stuttgart suburb of Weissenhof in the summer of 1927. The roster of participants included almost every European modern architect of note: in addition to Le Corbusier and his cousin, Pierre Jeanneret, the list featured a large German contingent consisting of Gropius, Peter Behrens, Richard Döcker, Ludwig Hilbersheimer, Hans Poelzig, Adolf Schneck, Hans Scharoun, Adolf Rading, and Bruno and Max Taut. Also invited were J. J. P. Oud and Mart Stam from the Netherlands and the Belgian Victor Bourgeois.

Frank's selection, however, was not without controversy. Although he was included on the first list of potential participants drawn up by Gustaf Stotz, one of the exhibit's organizers, his name was omitted from the proposal offered by Hugo Häring and Ludwig Mies van der Rohe, who wanted to limit the participants only to "architects of the [artistic] left" and evidently considered Frank too conservative.[3] Frank was eventually reinstated to the list of invitees as a compromise substitute for Loos, who was opposed not only by Mies but also many of the other members of the Werkbund because of his longstanding hostility toward the organization.[4] It is clear, nonetheless, that Mies had a low opinion of the Viennese, whom he believed lagged behind the avantgardists in Germany, France, and the Netherlands. In the end, Frank was the only Austrian invited to build in Stuttgart.[5]

Frank was assigned to devise two single-family units, each suitable for a family with children and a maid. He responded with a rectangular, two-story structure, with the upper story set back to form a continuous terrace on the street side (figs. 100–2). Intended as party wall units, the houses could be built singly, in pairs, or serve as a basic prototype for row houses,

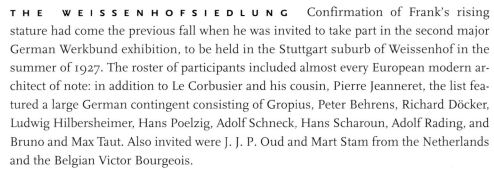

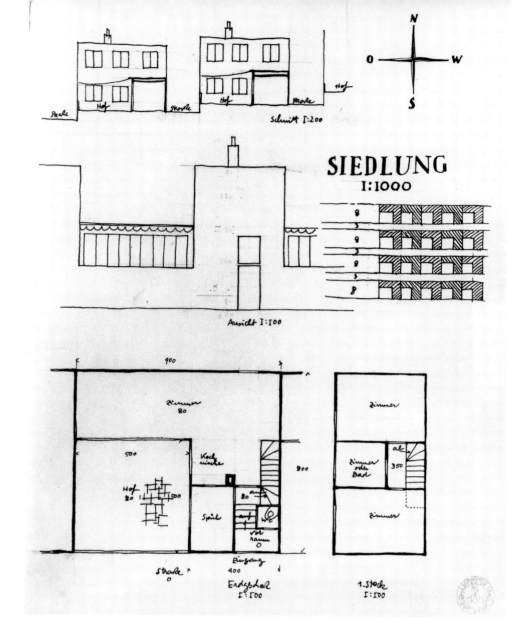

SIEDLUNG
1:1000

Schnitt 1:200

Ansicht 1:100

Erdgeschoß 1:100

1.Stock 1:100

103. Project for a housing settlement, c. 1927; site plan 1:1000, section 1:200, elevation, plans 1:100. Pencil, pen and ink on tracing paper, 29.5 × 22 cm. Graphische Sammlung Albertina, Vienna.

which could be combined to form a larger grouping, not unlike an unrealized project for a housing settlement Frank designed the same year (fig. 103).

The two houses mirrored one another in plan (fig. 104): on the ground floor was a service area with the entrance, kitchen, pantry, and maid's room; adjacent to the service area was a large, L-shaped living and dining area that opened onto a small courtyard. The second floor housed three bedrooms, which faced out onto the terrace. The remainder of the floor was taken up with a bathroom, hall, and closets. Each of the units also had a partial basement with space for a laundry room and storage.

The combined cost of the two units was 39,222 Reichsmarks, although the total expenditure, with the streets, sewers, landscaping, and other features included, brought the

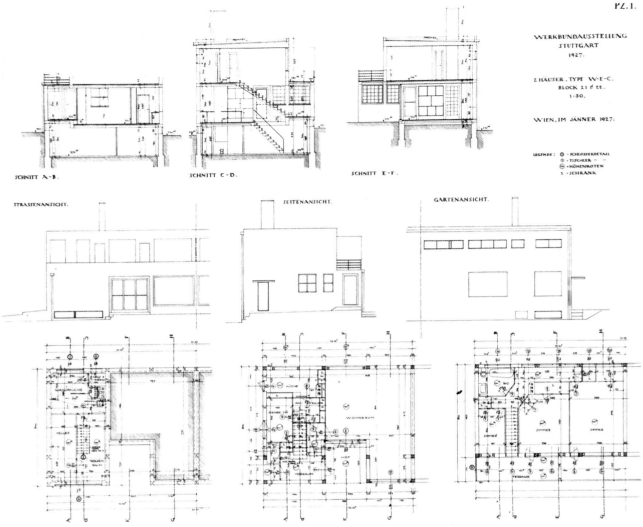

104. Double house at the Weissenhofsiedlung, Stuttgart, 1927; sections, elevations, and plans. Collection Professor Johannes Spalt, Vienna.

price tag to 61,502 marks[6]—a figure that put them well out of reach of proletarian and even many middle-class families (The first tenants were an attorney and an army officer[7]). Despite such extravagance, however, the houses were small and cramped: a sizable portion of the ground floor was taken up by the large entry court, and one of the bedrooms was hardly larger than a closet. Frank's use of hallways of different widths, angles, and axes served only to consume much of the already limited space.

The exterior of the house was finished with smooth, off-white stucco, with the windows set in rather than flush with the walls. In his initial drawings, Frank specified a steel frame structure with block infill, a technique similar to that which Mies employed for his own apartment building. During the late winter, he decided to make use instead of a new construction system developed by German engineer Albert Feifel, which con-

sisted of load-bearing masonry walls made of special L-shaped blocks (fig. 105). These so-called *Feifel-Bausteine* could be arranged in different combinations to create walls of various thicknesses, from 12 to 30 centimeters. Feifel's system offered not only a significant saving of labor—since it required less time to assemble than conventional block construction—but also reduced heat loss because neither the blocks nor the joints extended completely through the wall.[8]

For the interior walls of the house, Frank employed another technical innovation, horizontal gypsum boards with tongue and groove edges that were stacked and held in place by steel stud frames (fig. 106); the light and easily moveable studs doubled as interior door frames. The system, related to American balloon frame construction, was new at the time, but came into general use after the Second World War.[9]

Also widely discussed at the time was the innovative energy concept of Frank's double house. In one unit, all of the appliances were designed to run on gas; in the other, on electricity. The all-electric house, in particular, drew much attention and praise (Stuttgart had only recently been completely electrified, and a fully electric house was a novel idea[10]), although heating costs for both houses in the end proved to be considerably more expensive than coal.[11]

Despite such technical innovations, Frank's double house presented few of the problems for contractors that plagued many of the other designs.[12] He submitted his plans complete and on time, and only a few changes proved necessary, most notably in the size and configuration of the rear windows, which in Frank's original plans were considerably larger.[13] Both houses were finished by opening day. The Electric House was furnished

105. (left) Double house at the Weissenhofsiedlung, Stuttgart, 1927; photograph of the house under construction showing the use of the Feifel blocks. Heinz and Bodo Rasch, *Wie Bauen?* (Stuttgart, 1927).

106. (right) Double house at the Weissenhofsiedlung, Stuttgart, 1927; interior wall system. Bauhaus-Archiv, Berlin.

with pieces from Haus & Garten; the Gas House was only partially furnished until mid-August, when the Württemberg State Crafts Office agreed to underwrite several local designers to complete it.[14]

For all of its advances, the public and many of the critics viewed Frank's double house as reasonable and acceptable, at least in comparison with the other houses.[15] Several reviewers praised its "softened" modernism, its comfortable interiors, and its lack of steel furniture. Julius Zeitler, writing in *Dekorative Kunst,* singled out Frank's house for its "excellent distribution of spaces," adding that its attractive furnishings and ample storage areas "would satisfy even the most demanding."[16] Oskar Wolfer, who reviewed the exhibition for *Die Kunst,* commended Frank for combining the specific needs of the inhabitants with new "technical advances" without allowing the "functional concept" (*Zweckgedanke*) to become "exaggerated."[17] And Willi Fuchs-Röll in *Der Neubau* wrote that Frank's houses represented "a new height in pampered living."[18]

But the houses also drew sharp criticism from a number of architects of the "artistic left," who perceived, quite correctly, that they presented an implicit challenge to the emerging *neue Sachlichkeit* aesthetic.[19] Although Frank had departed from the other architects in several respects in his design of the house's exterior (most notably in his use of sash windows on the upper floor), it was the interiors of the houses—especially the Electric House—that drew most of the fire. While the Gas House combined handcrafted and industrially made pieces (including a bentwood rocking chair Frank had designed for Thonet), the Electric House presented a full range of Haus & Garten furnishings. Some of the spaces, such as the dining room, were rather understated, but the living room (fig. 107) and the bedrooms featured Frank's usual exuberant blend of colors, patterns, and materials.

Compared with many of Frank's Haus & Garten interiors, the Electric House showed a notable degree of restraint. Edgar Wedepohl, who reviewed the exhibit for *Wasmuths Monatshefte,* observed that the house's "predominant color" was "white, enlivened with delicately colored cushions and patterned curtains."[20] The impact of the assorted overstuffed sofas, pillows, and draperies, however, was more than enough to arouse the ire of the radicals. Théo van Doesburg, in his review of the exhibition, charged that while Mies, Stam, and the other functionalists had aimed for "maximal neutralization and austerity in the dwelling," Frank, along with Bruno Taut, Behrens, and Oud, had created "femininely appointed interiors" that were "obtrusive" and "middle-class."[21] Swiss critic Hans Bernoulli wrote that walking around Frank's house had engendered for him a sensation "of being caressed . . . by pillows and a thousand articles of Viennese frippery" (*Gschnas*).[22] Werner Gräff, the press relations chief for the exhibition, went even further, remarking that to him the interiors seemed "almost provocatively conservative."[23] But the most devastating verdict came from Paul Meller, Oud's assistant, who in a letter to Oud dismissed the interiors as "Frank's bordello."[24]

107. Double house at the Weissenhofsiedlung, Stuttgart, 1927; living room of the "Electric House."
Bauhaus-Archiv, Berlin.

Coming to Frank's defense was conservative urban planner Werner Hegemann. In an essay published in *Wasmuths Monatshefte,* Hegemann condemned the "Red Press Agency [*Rote Korrespondenz*], the mouthpiece of the architectural clique which had its say in Stuttgart to the exclusion of all others." While the radicals had admonished Frank for placing "an almost exclusive emphasis on . . . so designing his rooms that they might be thought of as a suitable environment for a lady of breeding," Hegemann charged, they had achieved little beyond functionalized kitchen design. "Indeed," he wrote, "most of what we see in modernist architectural creations does not seem to be made for women of sensibility and education, but for the figures in a Dr. Caligari fantasy film or for the female inmates of a literary coffeehouse."[25]

Frank responded to the criticisms in an article that appeared in *Bau und Wohnung,* one of the exhibition's official publications. Evidently taking his cue from Bernoulli's reference to "Viennese frippery," he entitled the piece "Der Gschnas fürs G'mut und der Gschnas als Problem" (Frippery for the soul and frippery as a problem). To the charge that his interiors were bourgeois, feminine, and old-fashioned, Frank replied that the stripped-down, "functionalist" style of the radical left simply did not respond to most people's psychological needs: "Every person has a certain measure of sentimentality, which he must satisfy."[26] "Frippery," far from being unnecessary and outmoded as the radicals contended, provided a required sense of comfort and well-being.

In the past, Frank explained, traditional artisans had made their pieces one by one, thereby producing multiple versions of a particular object, and this served to meet people's varied requirements. The introduction of industrial production had led to the replacement of this diversity with increasing standardization. In an effort to combat this trend, architects and designers had begun to develop the "arts and crafts." The arts and crafts had become a problem, he asserted, because of an increasing tendency on the part of many to confuse modern realities with fashion. The desire for "Sachlichkeit" not only undermined many traditional objects of daily use—by making them conform to new "rational" standards—but it had also created many articles that were neither practical nor comfortable (in either a physical or a psychological sense). To those who claimed that the machine demanded a radically new design approach, Frank countered that it was "nothing more than a tool, which can produce anything"; it did not dictate a particular formal program.[27] Yet more and more, he claimed, "forms were being sacrificed to the machine," which had become the new "God."[28] Frank observed that while industrialization had brought myriad changes, many old forms retained their usefulness; modern life was rich enough to assimilate many of the things from former times: "One can use everything that is still usable." There was no need for designers to determine what was still serviceable: "Anything that becomes unusable eliminates itself. You cannot ride in Achilles' chariot today any more than you can ride in Napoleon's carriage; but you can sit in their decorated armchairs. And," he added, "who is more modern in his thinking: he who accepts these things as they are, or he who perpetuates what is transient in them by modernizing it?"[29]

FRANK AND THE CIAM Despite the critical reaction to his Stuttgart house, Frank received an invitation in the fall of 1927 to join the newly formed Congrés Internationaux d'Architecture Moderne (CIAM). The first meeting took place in late June 1928 in La Sarraz, Switzerland, at the château of Mme de Mandrot de la Sarraz, who was one of the prime movers behind the idea and had helped finance the venture. Frank once again was the only Austrian representative; among the others in attendance were Le Corbusier, Sigfried Giedion, Hendrik Berlage, Gabriel Guevrékian, Hugo Häring, Ernst May, Hannes Meyer, Gerrit Rietveld, Alberto Sartoris, Hans Schmidt, and Stam (fig. 108).[30]

The program, drawn up by Le Corbusier and Giedion, focused on six major topics: modern technology and its consequences, standardization, economic issues, urban planning, education, and the current state of architecture.[31] Inspired by the Berlin *Ring*, which unified some twenty of the most prominent German modernists, Giedion, Le Corbusier, and the other organizers hoped that the CIAM would bring together the leading progressive architects to discuss the present state and future prospects of modern building. They had expected that the meetings would lead to a consensus about the future of modern building. Yet to the surprise of nearly everyone involved, the discussions immediately became heated. During the first afternoon session, which examined the question

108. Delegates at the first CIAM conference, La Sarraz, Switzerland, June 1928. Standing (from left to right): Richard Dupierre, Mart Stam, Pierre Chareau, Victor Bourgeois, Max Haefeli, Pierre Jeanneret, Gerrit Rietveld, Rudolf Steiger, Ernst May (partially concealed), Alberto Sartoris, Gabriel Guevrékian, Hans Schmidt, Hugo Häring, Zavala, Lucienne Florentin, Le Corbusier, Paul Artaria, Hélène de Mandrot de la Sarraz, Friedrich Gubler, P. Rochat, André Lurçat, Henri Robert von der Mühll, Gino Maggioni, Huib Hoste, Sigfried Giedion, Werner Moser, Josef Frank. Seated (from left to right): Fernando Garcia Mercadal, Molly Weber, Tadevossian. CIAM-Archiv, Eidgenössische Technische Hochschule, Zurich. Courtesy of the Institut für Geschichte und Theorie der Architektur.

of architecture and technology, the exchanges were so vehement Giedion later admitted that he feared that the congress would collapse.[32]

The majority of the architects split into two opposing camps. On one side were Le Corbusier and many of the other non-Germans, including André Lurçat, Sartoris, Pierre Chareau, and A. J. Mercadal, who to varying degrees were concerned with formal aspects of the new building. In the other camp were the more radical German, Dutch, and Swiss architects, including Stam, Schmidt, and Meyer, who urged the elimination of aesthetic conventions in architecture and urban planning and called for greater emphasis on the social aspects of building.[33] The main debate centered on the proposal for a joint manifesto that Le Corbusier and Giedion had drawn up before the conference, which they had hoped the participants would adopt point for point. However, Stam, Schmidt, Häring, and many of the other delegates found that the proposals were too specific and focused too little attention on basic social issues. Even though, as Schmidt later wrote, the architects had agreed on the importance of reform, there remained great differences of opinion about how that goal was to be achieved.[34] In the end, Le Corbusier and Giedion were forced to revise the charter. The final declaration, signed by all present, was considerably shortened, consisting only of general statements and making no mention of architectonic issues.[35]

Frank remained silent throughout most of the conference. During the second session on new construction methods, he spoke out extolling the possibilities of standardized housing, citing, in particular, the widespread use of standardized wood frame houses in the United States: "No one denies the necessity of standardization," he said. "Architects through the ages have always used standardized components." It is simple "common sense." The question, he argued, is how and to what extent architects should utilize this technology.[36]

But if Frank agreed with the more radical functionalists about the importance of exploring new building technologies, he remained wary of the efforts to link ideas of standardization with aesthetic considerations. During the discussions about city planning on the second day, he attacked Lurçat, who had argued for the importance of aesthetic issues in urban design: "If it was really necessary to discuss [aesthetic questions], they should have been placed at the beginning of the program."[37]

As the conference entered its third day, Frank found himself increasingly isolated. On the one hand, he was alarmed by the growing insistence of the radical, mostly German-speaking architects on equating architecture with technology; but he was equally concerned about what he perceived as the development of a new formalism, the tendency to view modernism as a "style." He entertained thoughts of not signing the final joint declaration, and it was only after some persuasion from Giedion that he added his signature. He also pledged to carry on the work of the CIAM in Austria and to participate in future events.

Despite the outward signs of cooperation, Frank, like a number of other delegates, left La Sarraz with a profound feeling of dissatisfaction. In the immediate wake of the conference, Giedion attempted to put the best face on the situation. Ignoring the sometimes bitter infighting that had marred the meeting, he wrote in an article in the *Neue Züricher Zeitung* that the La Sarraz meeting was "a sign that a common and universal advance" was setting in.[38] Yet as Le Corbusier was to reflect a few years later, the conference had in fact revealed deep divisions within the modern movement itself: "The German architects were on the offensive, strong supporters of innumerable so-called modern houses," Le Corbusier wrote. He had attempted to "lead the conference to useful tasks," but found the way "blocked." The Germans called "us 'poets, utopians.'" "I spoke of 'reason' and 'objectivity,' but I wouldn't accept definitions that left architecture under a shadow." The breakdown of the conference, he contended, was the result of the German insistence on *Sachlichkeit,* "which bore fruit and flowered too soon and too suddenly [and] prompted them to begin to sense technical uncertainty opening under their feet."[39]

After the congress, Frank wrote to Giedion promising to organize a local chapter of the CIAM in Austria and to establish contacts with modernist architects in Czechoslovakia, Poland, and Palestine.[40] In Austria, he brought together a small group of dedicated modernists, including Hoffmann's assistant Oswald Haerdtl, Ernst Plischke, and

Sobotka. He also accepted an appointment to the Comité International pour la Réalisation du Problème Architectural Contemporain (CIRPAC), the organizational subcommittee of the CIAM, and attended its first meeting in Basel in February 1929, during which plans were made for a second meeting of the CIAM to be held in the fall.

Frank, however, soon began to have second thoughts about his participation in the CIAM. In a letter to Giedion written after he returned from the Basel conference, he revealed that he thought the meeting had been a failure: "I am of the opinion, one shared by a number of the other [members], that our attention was too divided and that we are still too far removed from our actual task, namely, [to examine] architectonic issues." Frank also alluded to other problems, including growing divisions within the CIAM, which he attributed to both generational and national differences: "What we have in fact is two generations, who will never be able to think the same way." He continued: "And, there is, in addition, which one unfortunately cannot express differently, the German and the non-German view, the one apparently founded on a rational basis, the other resting on an artistic foundation, which, it seems to me, is becoming ever more apparent."[41]

During preparations for a second meeting of the CIAM, Frank wrote again to Giedion, this time questioning whether the CIAM could serve any useful purpose: "The differences of views in modern architecture today are a consequence of tremendous uncertainties, since many peculiarities are exaggerated by their representatives, which is a characteristic of a new movement."[42]

Despite mounting reservations, Frank attended the meeting in Frankfurt in October, which was devoted to examining the question of the "minimum dwelling" (*die Wohnung für das Existenzminimum*).[43] But he returned to Vienna even more dissatisfied than before. Immediately afterward, he wrote again to Giedion, this time announcing his resignation from the CIAM: "The reasons are twofold. . . . the climate of intrigues at the congress, but also . . . its deplorable final results." Citing the "superficiality" of the plenary speeches by Gropius and Schmidt, he also condemned the lack of serious discussion: "I find the entire attitude of the congress completely dishonest. If we are supposed to be discussing modern architecture . . . it is understandable that differences of opinion will occur."[44]

TOWARD A SCIENTIFIC WORLDVIEW Frank's dissatisfaction with the CIAM and its leadership went beyond the backroom politicking and shallow discussion. Even more troubling for him was the notion that modern architecture was being driven by a new irrationalism—what Paul Westheim, the editor of *Das Kunstblatt*, called a "new romanticism of the engineer and the machine."[45] The statements of Gropius, Schmidt, and the other leading radicals smacked to him of a new "pathos," a return to old-fashioned "metaphysical" thinking.

Frank's antipathy toward such a "romanticized" modernism issued from deep within his spiritual and intellectual center. During his student years, Frank had been exposed to the empiricist ideas of Ernst Mach by his older brother Philipp. In 1907, while a physics student at the University of Vienna, Philipp had met Mach, who was then living in retirement after a stroke left him partially paralyzed. Intrigued by Mach's positivism, Philipp began to explore the implications of a critical empiricist philosophy of science with a group of his like-minded friends, including Neurath and Hans Hahn.[46] The philosophy they advanced, logical positivism, was an attempt to purge the interpretation of science of what Philipp called "school philosophy"—unabashed metaphysics.[47]

Frank sometimes joined them; and he often explored the implications of such a position with his friend Neurath. After Philipp moved to Prague in 1912, succeeding Albert Einstein as professor of theoretical physics at the German University in Prague, Frank continued from time to time to sit in on discussions with Neurath, Hahn, and other members of their circle.[48]

When the war ended, Philipp, Neurath, Hahn, and others began meeting regularly again in another discussion group, now centered around Moritz Schlick, professor of the philosophy of physics at the University of Vienna. In 1928, they formed the Verein Ernst Mach, which at Neurath's suggestion became known as the Vienna Circle (Wiener Kreis). The aims of the group were expressed in a pamphlet that appeared in the spring of 1929 soliciting membership: "To all friends of the scientific worldview [*wissenschaftliche Weltauffassung*]," it began. "We live in a critical intellectual [*geistigen*] situation! Metaphysical and theological thought is taking hold in certain groups; astrology, anthroposophy and similar movements are spreading. On the other side: ever more conscious efforts for a scientific worldview, logical-mathematical and empirical thought."[49]

Frank's connection to the Vienna Circle extended beyond his close relationship with Neurath and his brother Philipp.[50] On the roster of charter members of the group, which included Schlick, Rudolf Carnap, and Kurt Gödel, he was listed as one of several "closely connected authors" (*nahestehende Autoren*) who "work on the basis of the scientific world view and are in personal and scientific contact."[51] In addition to discussions and symposia, the activities of the Vienna Circle included a series of public lectures covering such diverse topics as the philosophy of science and mathematics as well as discourses against metaphysics. The first lecture in the series, on 19 April 1929, was given by Frank, who spoke on "The Modern Worldview and Modern Architecture" (fig. 109).[52]

The text of the lecture has not survived, but Frank's plea for a new scientific rationalism resounded in many of his other writings of the time. It is perhaps most clearly articulated in an

A DISSENTING VOICE

article he coauthored with Neurath protesting Meyer's forced resignation from the Bauhaus in 1930. Meyer, who had replaced Gropius as the school's director in 1927, introduced a new curriculum that stressed architecture and the exact sciences, often at the expense of the designers and painters. To promote his view of scientific progressivism, he invited Carnap, Neurath, and Herbert Feigl, another member of the Vienna Circle, to lecture at the school. An avowed Marxist, Meyer also inaugurated courses in Marxism and Leninism in place of the school's traditional anthroposophy. But Meyer's radical ideological and political positions antagonized many of the masters and caused a storm of controversy in local Dessau politics. Eventually, in 1930, he was forced to resign under pressure both from outside the Bauhaus and from within. Frank and Neurath lauded Meyer's emphasis on technical rather than aesthetic subjects and his outspoken criticism of what they described as certain mystical and sectarian tendencies in the school. While Gropius and the other masters continued to emphasize "spiritual" issues, they wrote, Meyer represented the vanguard in the struggle for a world stripped of superstition.[53]

Frank's notion of a *wissenschaftliche Weltauffassung* proved, however, to be a double-edged sword. Although he assailed what he saw as the naively progressivist functionalism of figures like Gropius and Schmidt, he also rejected the penchant many of his fellow Austrians (especially Hoffmann and his circle) showed for a new ornamentalism and nationalism, which Frank claimed were borne of the same sort of "unscientific" thinking.

Frank's attacks, however, amounted to more than a repudiation of the views of the left and right. His satirical and often oblique style of writing has led some to charge that he lacked a coherent ideology.[54] But Frank, in fact, had a very carefully developed position with regard to both modern architecture and politics. While critical of the excesses of the radicals, he remained committed to a modernist program in architecture, and he upheld an ideal of social democracy that celebrated individual freedom and ethical responsibility. The lack of "system" in Frank's writings and work is not unintentional: it is the outcome of his own aversion to totalizing systems, which he regarded as fundamentally antimodern.

Frank shared this abhorrence of "self-referential" systems with his close friend Neurath. During the discussions in the Vienna Circle, Neurath was known to listen vigilantly for metaphysical statements, often interrupting to point out when one of the members lapsed into "unscientific" conjecture.[55] Frank's denunciation of Gropius and Schmidt emanated from a similar distrust of dogmatic views and oversimplification. His sometimes contradictory writings were aimed at opening a broader discourse while avoiding dogma and programmatic statements. Confronted with the mounting passions of the left and the right, Frank sought an appeal to reason and to free discussion. Such views, however, increasingly isolated Frank in the late 1920s and early 1930s.

FRANK'S CRITIQUE OF THE BAUHAUS Frank's antipathy toward "metaphysical systems" also shaped his increasingly critical view of the Bauhaus.

Both he and Neurath had professional as well as personal connections with the Bauhaus and its faculty. But from the start, Frank was skeptical about the school and its intentions. His initial reservations stemmed in part from his aversion to the messianic tone of Gropius's 1919 manifesto and to the esoteric ideas of many of the masters, especially Johannes Itten and Wassily Kandinsky.[56] Frank also had a rather low opinion of Gropius himself. After Gropius lectured in Vienna in 1924, Neurath wrote in a letter: "He brought us nothing new. He himself is certainly not a significant architectural figure"—a view Frank shared.[57]

Even more disquieting for Frank, however, was the stated desire of Gropius and the other masters to create a new "total environment." Far from a progressive step, Frank regarded such a striving toward unity merely as an updated version of the turn-of-century *Gesamtkunstwerk* ideal. As such, it constituted for him a misdirected effort to impose a new style, a goal that Frank, like Loos before him, thought wholly inappropriate for the new age. Frank was troubled as well by the new formalism of the Bauhaus masters and their disciples. The notion that geometric purity should be achieved at the expense of real functionality, which Frank believed was all too often the case in Bauhaus designs, stood opposed to his conviction that true usefulness should take precedence over superficial appearances. The surprising awkwardness of many of the Bauhaus prototypes he ascribed to a new romanticism oblivious of reality. Frank pointed, for example, to the handles developed by the Bauhaus designers (fig. 110), which, he wrote, were indeed "'simple,' but poorly adapted to be grasped by the hand." By contrast, those "produced by industry" fulfill their function but were not conventionally regarded as "functionalistic." The evident shortcomings of the "Bauhaus approach" were a result of "confusing the geometrically simplest form with the most functional form." This search for the most "primitive" expression, Frank argued, was a matter of "fashion"—a desire for decorative effect in no way different from that found in historical period rooms (*Stilzimmer*).[58] Frank was especially critical of the bent tubular steel chairs first developed by Marcel Breuer: "Who would, without a preconceived notion of form [*Formwille*] arrive at the idea of forcing a prismatic shape on a chair and making its surfaces square? The form of a chair must be adapted to the shape of the human body . . . and that has nothing to do with any [regular] geometry." Moreover, Frank insisted, the desire to mimic the flat, clean surfaces of the modern house had resulted in a chair much larger and heavier than was necessary (fig. 111), which "destroys the scale of the room." The basic form of the chair had been established long before, he contended, and it made little sense to alter it.[59]

With Meyer's appointment as director of the Bauhaus in 1928, Frank's views toward the Bauhaus softened for a time. He was encouraged by Meyer's announcement that he would stress the technical and scientific aspects of architecture and put building before aesthetics, which Frank thought would usher in a new direction for the school.[60] Frank's hopes for a fundamental change, however, were soon disappointed, as he learned from

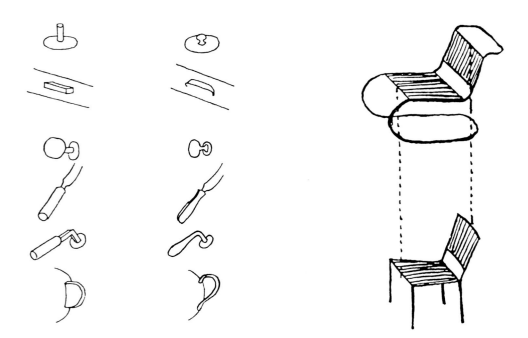

110. (left) "Bauhaus" handles vs. "organic" handles. *Form* 30 (1934).

111. (right) "Bauhaus" chair vs. an "organic" chair. *Form* 30 (1934).

his former student and friend Trude Waehner, who entered the school the same year Meyer became director.

Trude Waehner was to play a crucial role in Frank's life for nearly four decades. She was not only to become his intimate and ally but also his close confidante, with whom he carried on an intense and productive intellectual relationship. During times when they were together, she and Frank had prolonged and deep discussions on architecture and art; when they were apart, as was often the case in later years, they kept up an extensive correspondence. Their surviving letters provide a remarkable chronicle of Frank's evolving ideas—and of his increasingly critical views of modern architecture and design.[61]

Waehner was born in 1900 into a well-to-do middle-class Viennese family. Her father, Dr. Theodor Wähner, was the publisher of the center right—and anti-Semitic—newspaper, the *Deutsche Zeitung,* and he served for a time as a Christian Socialist representative on the city council.[62] Theodor Wähner was also among the earliest supporters of the Viennese Secession and the Hagenbund group of artists and designers. The year his daughter was born, he commissioned Joseph Urban to design the newspaper's offices as well as the family apartment, which were both housed in the same building in the city's eighth district.[63] In the late 1910s and early 1920s, Waehner studied art and design at the Graphische Lehr- und Versuchsanstalt (Graphic Arts School and Institute) and at the Kunstgewerbeschule, where she met Frank. Her interests, however, ranged more widely, and she eventually came into contact with Frank's brother Philipp, Neurath, and the philosopher Karl Popper, among others.[64] She married in 1920, divorced after a short time, and, in 1925, married an attorney, Dr. Friedrich Schmidl. Despite having a child from her first marriage, Waehner decided in 1928 to study at the Bauhaus.[65]

It was apparently Frank who provided a letter of recommendation to Gropius urging that Waehner be admitted directly to the master class in painting taught by Paul Klee without taking the preliminary *Vorkurs*.[66] Prior to her arrival in Dessau, Waehner envisaged the Bauhaus as a bastion of progressivism. She was soon disenchanted, however. She admired Klee and his work, but, as she wrote to Frank, she found the general atmosphere of the school oppressive. She was especially put off by Kandinsky's insistence on abstraction in painting and his "reactionary" search for the "absolute," an experience she compared to a spiritualist séance. She also resented what she saw as a pressure to conform, which she took as a threat to her freedom and individuality.[67]

Waehner's experience only confirmed Frank's worst suspicions. After Meyer's ouster in 1930, he felt that any real chance for reform had passed. In a letter to Meyer in early October, he wrote that he expected the Bauhaus—now under the directorship of Mies—to revert to the status of an ordinary design school:

As far as the Bauhaus is concerned, I think . . . that it will cease to be an important center. . . . It is thus an end to what I had suspected at the time of its founding, that a BAUhaus [a BUILDING institution] cannot in my view support all of these other studies.[68]

Frank continued to take occasional swipes at the Bauhaus and its teachings in the early 1930s. But in the later part of the decade, he became even more outspoken. Convinced that the fanaticism of the Nazis and the radical modernists stemmed from the same German tendency toward authoritarianism, he began to equate the school's modernist "regimentation" with Fascism, a position that was hardly destined to endear him to the architects of the "left."

FRANK AND THE AUSTRIAN WERKBUND After his resignation from the CIAM, Frank turned his attention to reanimating the Austrian Werkbund. In early January 1929, he wrote to Giedion that he hoped the Austrian Werkbund, which he had recently "brought back to life," would soon show new signs of activity.[69] Since its founding before the war as a sister organization of the German Werkbund, the Austrian Werkbund had fallen on hard times. The Austrians had hosted the organization's annual conference in 1912 and had been represented with a pavilion at the 1914 Werkbund exhibition in Cologne. In the years after the war, however, the Austrian Werkbund had been beset by continuous infighting. In 1920, Hoffmann, disgruntled by the direction of the organization and competition for his Wiener Werkstätte, resigned to form his own "Vienna Werkbund."[70] An initial attempt in 1921 to reconcile the warring factions failed, and it was not until 1926 that Frank, Hoffmann, and others made renewed efforts to reunite the organization. Finally, in 1928, after drawn-out negotiations, the two groups were brought together. At a plenary session held in November of that year, a new leadership was chosen. In a conciliatory move aimed at appeasing both conservatives and progressives, Dr. Hermann Neubacher, the well-respected director of the Vienna Cooperative Housing Office, was elected president; Frank and Josef Hoffmann were elected vice-presidents.[71]

While the return of Hoffmann brought renewed prestige to the Werkbund, Frank proved to be the driving force behind the rejuvenation effort. Frank had had a close association with the Werkbund from its early years: while still a student, he attended the inaugural conference of the German Werkbund in Munich in 1908,[72] and he joined the Austrian branch of the organization after its formation in 1912.[73] In the intervening years, he had turned to other concerns, but in the wake of the Weissenhofsiedlung and the first CIAM meetings, he began to consider the Austrian Werkbund as an alternative means for advancing the cause of new design and architecture—and as an avenue for disseminating his own countervailing views.[74]

Frank's "Gespräch über den Werkbund" (Conversation about the Werkbund), which occupied fully a third of the organization's 1929 yearbook, constitutes a restatement of his ideas of the previous decade concerning craft, style, and the role of the machine. Among its recurring themes are his belief in continuity, variety, and his avowal of a craftsmanship ideal. In contrast to the leading *Werkbundler* in Germany, who advocated a closer relationship with industry, Frank remained steadfast in his belief that at least for the immediate future the only rational course for the Austrian Werkbund was to maintain its commitment to handicraft: "Austria today lives in large measure from its production of items of good taste [*Geschmacksindustrie*], better known as arts and crafts; to give that up would naturally be senseless because there is still enough demand for it." Beyond this economic rationale, he also cited sociological and artistic reasons for preserving the traditional crafts: "We also have a large number of mostly older craftsmen, who have a consummate knowledge of their work, and it would be absurd not to use them because in the future there may not be any more like them."[75]

Yet Frank also recognized the necessity of collaborating with the country's struggling industries. In a series of speeches and radio addresses in the later 1920s and early 1930s, he advocated the need for finding new markets for Austrian products and for adapting traditional articles to contemporary tastes. He also made his own contributions to these efforts. In the later 1920s, he designed a modern piano for the Bösendorfer Company, as well as several chairs for Thonet, the famed Viennese maker of bentwood furniture.[76]

Frank's elegantly simplified chairs (fig. 112) posed an attempt to update Thonet's standard models while preserving the hint of Viennese charm and grace that had been their hallmark. As in his designs for Haus & Garten, he emphasized the role of color: the

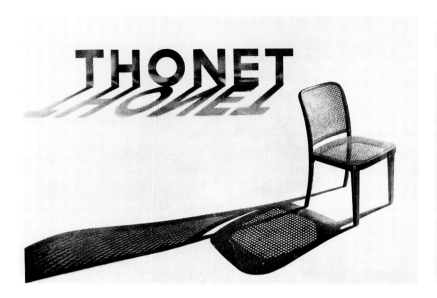

model A 63F chair (fig. 113), for example, was offered in fourteen different colors. His intent was to make the chairs as widely acceptable as possible; but they also expressed an implicit critique of the more severe tubular steel furniture of the German radicals.

THE 1930 WERKBUND CONGRESS Under Frank's leadership, the Werkbund, which had been virtually moribund for a decade, exploded with new activity. Working in close collaboration with Haerdtl, Sobotka, and Neurath, Frank organized a regular series of lectures and radio broadcasts featuring speakers such as Ernst May, Hugo Häring, and German film director Hans Richter. The Werkbund also sponsored a series of exhibitions in Vienna, including the 1929 *Neues Bauen* exhibit and a 1930 show entitled *Film und Foto*, which presented the works of many of Europe's leading avant-garde photographers and filmmakers.[77] *Die Form*, the official organ of the German Werkbund, noting all of the new activity in Vienna, began carrying a regular column on the Austrian Werkbund, and at the 1929 meeting of the German Werkbund in Breslau, the membership voted to accept the Austrian organization's offer to hold the 1930 annual congress in Vienna.[78]

The meeting was held from 22 to 26 June. Delegates arrived from Germany, Austria, Switzerland, and Czechoslovakia, as well as from a number of other countries. The original plans had called for an exhibition of new housing, similar to the Weissenhofsiedlung, on a large open site on the southern edge of the city. Problems with financing and the site, however, forced postponement of the show until 1932. In its stead a large exhibition of recent Austrian design, timed to coincide with the congress, was mounted at the Österreichisches Museum für Kunst und Industrie.

The theme of the exhibit was travel and tourism. In addition to displays of products of Austrian industry, crafts, and fashion, a number of model rooms were created by some of Austria's best-known designers, including Hoffmann (a café), Clemens Holzmeister (a country inn), Ernst Lichtblau (a café with terrace), Strnad (a bar), and Frank (a tearoom). The most noteworthy displays were two elegantly simple steel and glass pavilions in the rear garden of the museum, designed by Haerdtl and Lichtblau.[79]

Frank and Wlach were represented by a selection of Haus & Garten furnishings shown in one of the industry pavilions (fig. 114); but it was Frank's tearoom (fig. 115) that elicited the most comment. The simple arrangement of light-green lacquered chairs and tables (executed by Thonet), red piano, and walls of different pastel colors left a deep impression on many visitors. The Viennese writer Max Ermers was struck by its sense of calm.[80] Another Viennese critic, Soma Morgenstern, a friend of Frank's who reviewed the exhibition for *Die Form,* praised the room's "lightness" and "delicacy." Frank, Morgenstern declared, had created "an atmosphere of peaceful serenity in which all of the new *sachlich* doings are extinguished, and at the same time a new, humane style is fostered."[81]

The same softened, cozy look was also reflected in most of the other exhibits. "Everywhere one turned," another reviewer, Amelia Levetus, wrote, "the personal note 'Viennese' was perceptible, however involuntarily expressed; the Austrian apparently cannot reject it; it comes silently, unurged; he cannot get away from it."[82] For many of the German delegates at the conference, however, the decorative flourishes of the Viennese seemed once more to be a "provocation," prompting a flurry of criticism and disparaging remarks.

114. Display of Haus & Garten furnishings, Austrian Werkbund exhibition, Vienna, 1930. *Innen-Dekoration* 41 (1930).

115. Tearoom, Austrian Werkbund exhibition, Vienna, 1930. Österreichische Nationalbibliothek, Bildarchiv, Vienna.

Frank, who had anticipated the response, provided a reply in the keynote address he delivered at a plenary meeting on the fourth day of the conference. Those present, as Plischke later recalled, expected a genial, light-hearted speech.[83] Instead, Frank launched into an attack on what he called the "Radikal-Modernen." The ninety-minute talk, which he entitled *"Was ist modern?"* (What is modern?), was a rambling, at times disjointed, discourse on modernism and its meanings. It was neither technical skill nor the advent of the machine that separated the present from the past, Frank told the assembled delegates; every age possessed technical knowledge. Rather, it was knowledge about the past, the explosion of historical learning, that set the modern age off from earlier times. "As a result, every struggle against historical knowledge" was "unnecessary and hopeless." It was easier for those living in the past to be "modern" because they were not burdened with the same historical legacy.[84]

In the same way, Frank proclaimed, the growth of the new pluralism that characterized modern society had made futile—at least for the time being—the search for a unified style or expression. The desire of the *Radikal-Modernen* to define and thereby limit modern architecture and design was not the expression of an objective (*sachlich*), scientific view of the world but was driven by a new pathos. Every attempt to forge a single style, whether "in a historical style," the style of "one of the numerous workshops" (*Werkstätten*), "or of tubular steel furniture," was doomed to failure. "They may be charming, practical, or hygienic . . . [but] modern they are not. For in every modern creation there must be a place for all that our time has, and our time includes so much that we cannot begin to compress it into a unified form."[85]

Frank also called into question the assertion that architecture and design were no longer representational. "We use formal symbols just as before, only now they are different ones." Among the best examples of this, he pointed out, was the flat roof. "Without question, the flat roof is modern," not because it is "more practical, cheaper, healthier, faster to put up, or easier to repair," but because it had become "a symbol of our time." It was not, Frank noted, "originally conceived as such," but through its clarity and simplicity the flat roof had become a symbol of modern architecture for champions and detractors alike.[86]

In response to the radicals' assertion that the machine had fundamentally altered the nature of art and design, Frank observed that it was merely a tool, which "dictated no new form"; rather, it simply "made new forms possible."[87] The notion that the "modern architect should work like the engineer," however, was one of the "basic misconceptions" of modern times. While architects worked in the formal realm, engineers were interested solely in fulfilling the "most basic practical need" (*niedrigst-praktischem Zweck*), which, in turn, excluded much of what was important in life and thus was not modern.[88]

What the future would bring, Frank concluded, he could not say; although further "mechanization and rationalization" were unquestionably coming trends. Yet to give a precise answer or to lay down specific rules, he asserted, would be a grievous error; it would be "unmodern." To do so "would lead to the same system, which would again hem us in."[89]

For many of those present, who found the extreme modernism of the radical left cold and unappealing, Frank's speech came as a revelation.[90] Peter Meyer, a moderate member of the Swiss Werkbund, wrote afterward that it was "invigorating" to hear someone put "people rather than machines at the center" of the Werkbund's program.[91] In so doing, Meyer noted, Frank had not only called into question the ideology of the left ("which is already on its way to becoming a new academic, dogmatic aesthetic"); he had also provided a "tacit defense" of the Austrians' position, which was "much closer to reality than all of the theories" of the radicals.[92]

Meyer's was not the sole voice of acclaim. A sizable segment of the Werkbund rank and file, many of whom had already expressed negative reactions to the Weissenhof exhibition three years earlier, found a sympathetic note in Frank's address. Others, however, found his pronouncements rather less comforting. The program provided no time for discussion after the talk, a situation, as Meyer described, that only prompted "more ardent discussion among the members of the audience." A large number of those present voiced their objections, he recorded, contending that Frank's critique offered "no real standpoint" and amounted to a "relativizing" of a "theoretical foundation that had been worked out with so much effort." Moreover, many were indignant that Frank had taken such an occasion to voice his opinions: "The German Werkbund had not come to Vienna to be told that their doctrines were not modern." At the very least, Meyer recounted, many felt Frank should have had the foresight "not to have made such remarks before the public."[93]

Others voiced their criticisms in print. German critic Robert Breuer, who reported on the congress for *Deutsche Kunst und Dekoration*, wrote that Frank had caused the only ripple in the otherwise halcyon atmosphere of the conference: "He set off fireworks . . . polished and scintillating words, precious blasphemies and strange superstitions on the topic: what is modern? He has not answered the question; but the dissonance remained. . . ."[94]

If in Breuer's eyes Frank had failed to supply a satisfactory answer, the speech nevertheless touched off a furious debate within the ranks of the Werkbund about whether the *neue Sachlichkeit* reflected modernism's true spirit. In an effort to head off mounting criticism, the executive committee of the German Werkbund, which was composed mostly of representatives of the radical left, scheduled a special meeting in Stuttgart for 25 October. Frank, who was asked to speak, took part, but neither Mies van der Rohe nor Gropius, aware their ideas would come under attack, opted to attend.

In all, thirty-four delegates spoke, most of them critical of the rational functionalism of the left. Frank repeated his plea that the Werkbund had the "responsibility to deal with all aspects" of contemporary design, not just "the puritanical" ideas "of the Werkbund leadership in Berlin. One should not make imaginary worlds and arbitrarily limit the world," he urged.[95] In response, Marcel Breuer, whom Gropius had asked to represent him, retorted that Frank's charges did not apply to the core group of leading modernists but only to its hangers-on, and that such remarks simply "stood in the way of progress." And Schmidt and Paul Renner reiterated the radicals' view that the architecture of the future should not be based on "an artistic program" but on new technology and "impersonal precision."[96]

The majority of the delegates, however, assailed both the ideas and the arrogance of the left. Even many who had long approved of the general aims of the *neues Bauen* condemned the new *sachlich* architecture as a mechanistic exercise that involved nothing more than engineering and planning.[97]

What the conference revealed, however, was not only the depth of dissatisfaction with the left and with the Werkbund's program, but also a lack of consensus about the direction and meaning of modern architecture and design. Summing up the meeting, Meyer wrote that the delegates had spent "four hours talking past one another."[98]

The debate continued in the pages of *Die Form* and other German-language publications. In an article emphatically entitled "Das ist modern!" (That is modern!), Wilhelm Lotz, one of the editors of *Die Form,* wrote that Frank's attempt to define the modern movement more broadly threatened to undermine all that the Werkbund had sought to achieve: "Certainly it is salutary for someone, in the face of the many radical modern theories, to call attention to the lively multiplicity of modern life." But Frank's skepticism about creating new forms, he added, if taken to its logical end, would spell death for the Werkbund and its program.[99] Lotz's objections were echoed by another Werkbund member, Roger Ginsburger. In a speech given at the opening of an exhibit of French industrial design in Basel at the end of September and subsequently published in *Die Form,* Ginsburger defended the notion of systematically redesigning objects of daily use, arguing that it was an integral part of modern reform efforts.[100]

The idea that modern, *sachlich* design represented a decided improvement was echoed by another German writer, Oskar Schürer. In his essay "On Saving the Honor of the Concept 'Modern,'" which appeared in the December issue of *Deutsche Kunst und Dekoration,* Schürer responded to Frank's call for maintaining living elements from the past. The aim of the modernists in replacing the new for the old, he contended, was "to foster a new correctness" (*Richtigkeit*) and thereby to redeem "the original sense [*Ursinn*] of the forms"—ironically, a formulation nearly identical with Frank's but with a profoundly different intent.[101]

The depth of dissatisfaction that Frank's speech had revealed prompted Walter Riezler, another editor of *Die Form,* to ask in a lead article whether the Werkbund was facing a crisis.[102] Alluding to the speeches at Stuttgart, many of which had focused on the issue of ornament and handicrafts, Riezler attributed much of the dissent to a conservative reaction from the older members, which the Werkbund could "overcome with its own power."[103]

What Riezler overlooked was a rising undercurrent of discontent even among many of those who had comprised the architectural vanguard for the past decade. Writing the same year, Le Corbusier asserted that aesthetics were a "fundamental human function" and thus an integral part of an architect's work. The functionalists' position, he said, was based on the false assumption that "that which is useful is beautiful." In confusing the question of purpose with that of aesthetic quality, the radicals had adopted a "new romanticism, a romanticism of the machine." This "machine aesthetic," Le Corbusier charged, was threatening the traditional concerns of architecture: "Today, in the avant-garde of the *neue Sachlichkeit,* two words have been killed, *Baukunst* (architecture) and *Kunst* (art)."[104] In a letter to Le Corbusier written early in 1929, Mies voiced his own concerns about the radicals: "Especially in Germany, the land of the organizers, it seems to me necessary to emphasize with special clarity that architecture is something other than raw functionalism. In Germany the fight against the rationalists will be more difficult than against the academicians."[105]

ARCHITEKTUR ALS SYMBOL Frank returned from Stuttgart determined to wage his own battle against the left. Throughout the summer and fall of 1930, he worked on a book-length critique of the radical position, which he published at the end of the year under the title *Architektur als Symbol: Elemente deutschen neuen Bauens* (Architecture as symbol: Elements of German modern architecture; fig. 116).

The book repeats and extends many of the ideas he explored in his speech, "Was ist modern?" Though divided into a series of discrete chapters with individual headings, it constitutes an extended essay on what Frank viewed as the problems of contemporary design. At its core, it is a withering attack on the German functionalists; much of the text, however, is an extended discourse on European cultural history and philosophy.[106]

JOSEF FRANK

ARCHITEKTUR
ALS SYMBOL

ELEMENTE
DEUTSCHEN NEUEN BAUENS

1 9 3 1

VERLAG VON ANTON SCHROLL & CO.
WIEN

116. Title page, *Architektur als Symbol* (1930; Vienna, 1931). Harry Ransom Humanities Research Center, The University of Texas at Austin.

The ostensible theme of the book, as its title suggests, is the role of symbolic language in architecture. At its most fundamental level, Frank wrote, architecture is "a symbol of our lives and our times." Every age has had its own architectural expression, its own symbolic language. The "collective appearance" of these symbols "constitutes the style of a [particular] epoch."[107] Countering the radicals, who held that such symbols were no longer meaningful and that architecture could be reduced to its barest use,

Frank argued that modern man also needed a symbolic language. Even functionalism, despite its repudiation of conventional architectural symbols, represented the values and ideals of its makers.

Yet for Frank, the language of functionalism bespoke an alarming trend toward standardization, uniformity, and extremism—and ultimately, even more threateningly, toward German nationalism and militarism.[108] Citing the tubular steel chairs, which he believed summed up the recent tendencies in architecture and design, he wrote sarcastically: "Steel is not a material, but an ideology. These chairs were actually invented to serve as seats for the Commission for War Damage Compensation as a means to show the earnestness of German efforts."[109] Although the chairs had also gained acceptance in other countries, Frank continued, their popularity was merely a fashion. "But the new German feels he is under a moral obligation to sit uncomfortably, and he does not want to know that any other type of chair exists. The God who made iron grow did not want wooden furniture."[110]

The tragedy of the German functionalists' striving "to make something good," Frank wrote, was that it had repeatedly resulted in "artificial and unilateral principles." They had "lacked the courage to rely on any human feeling," which might have been regarded as a "compromise." To preserve the moral authority of such a position, the radicals had been forced to adopt extreme positions. Such posturing, however, "stood in direct contradiction with real life and resulted in the soul-destroying architecture [*Menschenfresserarchitektur;* literally, man-eating architecture] of the present day."[111]

One of the great ironies of "the modern style" Frank noted, was that the proletariat, "for whom it was devised, had not greeted its appearance with enthusiasm." Indeed, their architectural ideal remained identical with that of the nineteenth-century bourgeoisie: wealth and comfort. The aspirations of the working class were not focused on a new architecture of simplicity, but on one that provided the amenities they had long been denied and that, at the same time, expressed their new-found power. And because "power and representation are closely linked," the proletariat distrusted "the symbols that had been given them," which had remained largely the province of "artists living on the margins of society."[112]

The poverty and unfavorable political climate of the postwar years, Frank charged, had kept modern architecture from developing properly. The need to build housing quickly and cheaply had led to the association of architecture with mere "usefulness" (*Nützlichkeit*) and "function" (*Funktion*). Oft-repeated slogans such as Gropius's saying that "[a] work of art must function exactly like a machine" had only confused matters further.[113] Modern man, Frank reiterated, required more than the "basely practical": The true modern building "is one that can accommodate everything vital in our time and yet at the same time remain an organic, living creation. Modern German architecture may be objective, practical, principally correct, often even attractive, but it remains lifeless."[114]

By contrast, Frank insisted, a genuine "new architecture will be born of all the bad taste [*Ungeschmack*] of our time, its intricacy, its diversity, and sentimentality, from everything that is alive and that we experience: at last, an art of the people rather than an art for the people."[115]

Frank also used the opportunity to take a swipe at his more conservative fellow Viennese. While the German modernists' "hunt for the new" had led them astray, he wrote, the Viennese had carried on "without any clue." The striving to forge a regional style (*Heimatstil*) in the form of pseudo-Alpine villas in the city's outlying districts, Frank contended, was nothing more than a naive and misguided attempt to revive traditional symbols that were no longer alive.[116]

But history, Frank asserted, did provide a stock of still living forms: the language of Western classicism. "We have recognized that the forms of antiquity (forms in the widest sense) are the only ones that are self-evident and whose symbols we comprehend, and that to think in the sense of those who created them is our tradition."[117] The forms of the classical past, he proclaimed, are so "clear and yet so manifold" that they can "express every outlook and every emotion; a search for new ones would be hopeless."[118] Frank, however, was not suggesting a direct application of classical motifs: "I understand," he wrote, "by classical tradition not the use of columns and moldings and all other transient forms—which, incidentally, will never wholly disappear—but the striving for organic arrangement of inanimate material; this tradition will dominate our culture as long as man is the measure of all things."[119]

Predictably, the reaction to Frank's book in modernist circles was generally negative. Wilhelm Röhnick, who reviewed it for *Die Form*, found it "disappointing." Although "even richer in clever and surprising" remarks than Frank's 1930 Werkbund address, Röhnick wrote, it was also more full of "paradoxes."[120] Franz Roh, writing in *Das Neue Frankfurt*, was even more critical. Condemning Frank's "unscientific" approach, he accused him of "undervaluing every advance of modern architecture" and of being "a classicist in disguise."[121] Wolfgang Hermann, in *Kunst und Künstler*, questioned how it was possible for someone of Frank's modernist background to produce a book so fraught with "the dangers of eclecticism," which overlooked "all the positive aspects of contemporary and past architecture."[122]

A number of reviewers criticized Frank for the less than systematic presentation of his argument,[123] perhaps forgetting that it was precisely such carefully constructed ideological systems that Frank in fact was rejecting. Hans Eckstein, in *Die Kunst*, gave the book a mixed review, applauding Frank's "healthy" attempt "to link theory with real life" but remarking that his "exaggerated rhetoric and playful delight in paradoxes" had made the book "an embarrassment."[124]

Peter Meyer, who reviewed the book for *Das Werk*, praised the work ("this small book is among the most interesting and important that has been written about modern architecture," he wrote),[125] but he remained very much in the minority. An anonymous review that appeared in the Swiss *Journal de la Construction* offered perhaps the most positive assessment: "Frank, although a member of the avant-garde of the so-called modern architecture, has not allowed himself to be seduced by the superficial formalism of postwar architecture." There were two camps in the vanguard of architecture, the piece continued: "The first, which is pernicious, is composed of those who seek to create a new architecture and abstract everything that came before them, and a second, which unites a somewhat smaller number of persons who are cultivated, who know exactly the value of works of classical antiquity, but possess sufficient powers to create works that are both unique and lasting." Frank, it went on, was representative of the second, one of the few who had the "courage to speak about tradition."[126]

Yet Frank's hope that his book might foster a new critical dialogue on the nature and direction of modern architecture was not to be fulfilled. Aside from the handful of reviews that appeared shortly after the book was published, the response was muted. In the end, Frank's message fell victim to the same dark forces that cut short all of the architectural debate of those years: the deepening economic depression and the rise of Nazism, Fascism, and Stalinism.

THE HOUSE AS PATH AND PLACE

Despite the disappointments of the Weissenhofsiedlung and the CIAM, the late 1920s and early 1930s also brought Frank some notable successes. His increasing international stature translated into numerous invitations to exhibit his work. In addition to regular public showings in Vienna, Frank took part in major exhibitions in Munich, Berlin, Breslau, Cologne, Leipzig, and New York. In 1928, he was also commissioned by the Burgtheater in Vienna to design stage sets for its production of the George Bernard Shaw play *Captain Brassbound's Conversion*. Frank and Wlach continued to enjoy commercial success with Haus & Garten. Sales of individual pieces through the Bösendorferstraße store remained steady, and they received a growing number of commissions to design complete interiors for houses and apartments.

By the late 1920s, however, Frank's work began to undergo noticeable changes. His rejection of the radical modernist line notwithstanding, his buildings and projects displayed a decided shift toward a new simplicity and purity. More important, they also revealed Frank's mounting interest in probing the possibilities of a new and complex vision of space—investigations that would culminate in one of the most re-markable modern houses of the era, his Villa Beer, and in his notion of the "house as path and place."

THE HOUSE PROJECTS OF THE MID-1920S Between 1925 and 1928, Frank produced more than a dozen designs for houses. None of the projects was realized, and little is known about the circumstances surrounding them. It is even uncertain whether Frank had prospective clients for many of the houses or whether the drawings were merely conceptual experiments. For nearly half of the projects there are no surviving plans, so the interior arrangement of spaces cannot be fully recon-structed. Moreover, only a few of the drawings are dated, making it impossible to estab-lish any reliable sequence for the designs.

Among these projects was a house and dance school for a Mr. Ornstein in Tel Aviv, which was first published in *Moderne Bauformen* in 1927.[1] Like Frank's *Siedlung* house prototypes, it was intended as a row house, but the façade design (figs. 117, 118), with its elegant play on mass and void, and its elaborate fenestration pattern, establish it as a middle-class dwelling. Indeed, the massing of the house is reminiscent of Frank's prewar Scholl House.[2] In plan, however, the house was much more ambitious than any of Frank's previous residential designs. He arranged the spaces on a series of different lev-els, connecting them by means of a variety of shorter and longer stairways (fig. 119). The lower portion of the house is functionally divided into two zones: the eastern and rear portions are devoted to the school; the western portion and the upper floors house the private living quarters. From the street-side entry, the main route of penetration leads through the center of the house to the large dance studio and outdoor courtyard at the rear. A second route extends from the veranda up a short flight of stairs to the kitchen and dining room and from there to the bedrooms. Positioned between the ground floor and the upper-level bedrooms is an entresol, or *Zwischenstock,* as Frank describes it on the plan, which is connected to the ground-floor office by a separate spiral staircase. This in-termediate level, which includes a second office, not only serves as a place of observation (from the rear, the room overlooks the dance studio), but it also breaks up the interior volume of the house, forming rooms of various heights.

Frank pushed this idea even further in a residence for Vienna's thirteenth district, which was published in the same issue of *Moderne Bauformen.* The first impression of the House for Vienna XIII gained from a perspective view (fig. 120) is of a three-story structure, with the front portion raised on thin columns. But the accompanying plans and section of the house (fig. 121) reveal that the rooms are actually arranged—if one does not count the basement—on five different levels. Some of the variations are due to Frank's attempt to accommodate the house to its gently sloping hillside site by dividing

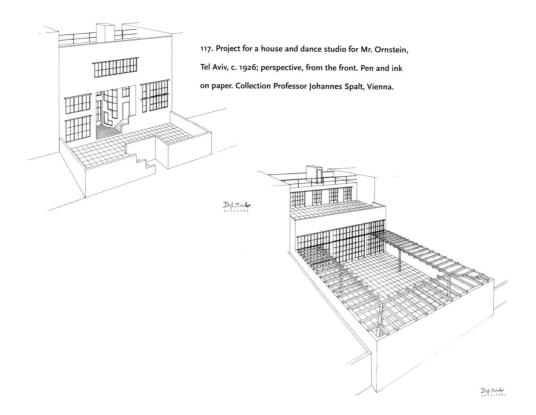

117. Project for a house and dance studio for Mr. Ornstein, Tel Aviv, c. 1926; perspective, from the front. Pen and ink on paper. Collection Professor Johannes Spalt, Vienna.

118. Project for a house and dance studio for Mr. Ornstein, Tel Aviv, c. 1926; perspective, from the rear. Pen and ink on paper. Collection Professor Johannes Spalt, Vienna.

119. Project for a house and dance studio for Mr. Ornstein, Tel Aviv, c. 1926; plans, elevations, section 1:100, plans 1:200. *Moderne Bauformen* 26 (1927).

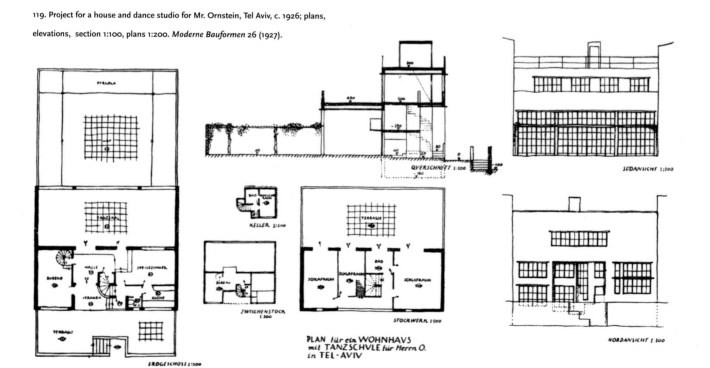

120. (top) Project for a house for Vienna XIII, c. 1926; perspective. *Moderne Bauformen* 26 (1927).

121. (bottom) Project for a house for Vienna XIII, c. 1926; plans, section, elevation 1:200. *Moderne Bauformen* 26 (1927).

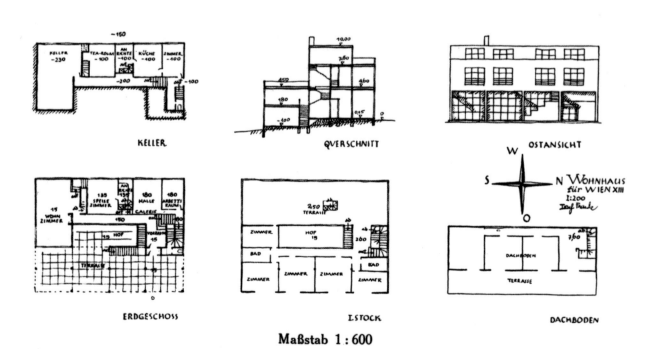

Maßstab 1 : 600

the house into two separate sections, with a courtyard at the center. However, the spaces within the two zones are also differentiated in height so that the open hall at the center of the house extends up to the second floor.

As in the Ornstein House and School, the various levels are connected by a series of stairs, which provide several distinct routes of penetration into and through the house. The sundry levels correspond to the functional divisions within the house: the lower rear portion contains the kitchen, pantry, and other service rooms; the rear section above it houses the main living rooms. But in contrast to the Ornstein House and School in which the divisions and changes in level are employed to separate the public and private areas, the winding paths through the house and the repeated alterations in the floor level appear somewhat forced here.

FRANK, LOOS, AND THE RAUMPLAN The schemes of the Ornstein House and School and the House for Vienna XIII, with their multiple floors and interlocking spaces, are reminiscent of Loos's *Raumplan* houses of the same period. Indeed, many of the standard features of Loos's domestic architectural projects of the 1920s and early 1930s are present: differentiated room levels and heights, open stairwells and large landings, and flowing circulation spaces.[3] Despite these evident parallels, it is unclear to what extent Frank drew on Loos's designs or developed these ideas independently. Frank was, no doubt, aware of Loos's *Raumplan* houses. The two had frequent contact during the early postwar years when Loos headed the city *Siedlung* office, and Frank continued to maintain a cordial if somewhat distant relationship with Loos after the latter returned from Paris in 1928.[4] Loos had been experimenting with the possibilities of "setting the ground plan free in space" (*Das lösen eines grundrisses im raum*), as he once expressed it,[5] from the time prior to the war, but he only fully developed the idea relatively late in life.

Frank's initial spatial planning experiments also dated from the prewar period; but it is important to recall that the impetus for his spatial planning conception initially came not from Loos but from Strnad, and that all three had been strongly influenced by late nineteenth-century English spatial planning precedents.[6] Not only do specific English forms—multistoried halls, outlooks, and continuous, winding stairs—appear in their residential works (albeit usually in a somewhat altered guise), but they also drew from the casual, asymmetrical planning characteristic of the later English "freestyle." Frank, in particular, seems to have heeded Scott's advice to vary the height of the rooms. "The artistic effect of changes in level," Scott wrote in *Houses and Gardens*, "is due to the corresponding changes it affords in point of view"[7]—a formulation that seems to directly presage Frank's own spatial concept.

Frank may well have drawn inspiration from Loos's early *Raumplan* houses, especially the 1922 Rufer and 1923 Moissi Houses. Certain features of the Rufer House—for example, its basic cubic profile and introduction of multiple levels—are also apparent in Frank's designs. But many of the elements of Frank's residential projects of the mid-1920s, such as the use of courtyards or pilotis, find no direct parallels in Loos's work. In several instances, Frank's projects even seem to have anticipated Loos's later villas. The Ornstein House and School and the House for Vienna XIII, for example, in which *Raumplan* ideas are already much more fully evolved than in the Rufer and Moissi Houses, were probably designed in late 1926 or early 1927, and they were published in May 1927 at a time when Loos's Moller House—his first fully realized *Raumplan* work—was still on the drawing board.[8]

Whether Frank drew on Loos's work—or the reverse, which is also possible—there are strong points of convergence in the two architects' residential projects at mid-decade. Perhaps most notable is the way in which they conceive of the room. Unlike later "free plan" designers, Frank and Loos continued to preserve the spatial or room divisions, which allowed them to provide discrete and diverse settings. Because the individual rooms retain their identities, they do not merely merge formlessly into each other but, rather, constitute a succession of defined spaces. The design of the *Raumplan* for both thus entails not only framing and positioning the rooms relative to one another but also establishing the connections between the rooms.

It is the manner in which these spaces are framed and the ways they are connected, however, that define the key points of dissemblance between the two architects' approaches. The rooms in Frank's houses are less sharply delimited: while Loos framed both his rooms and the openings between them with columns, pilasters, or wainscoting, Frank employed only blank white walls, which neither demarcate nor obscure the spatial progression.

Frank and Loos also differed on the ultimate aim of the space-plan idea. For Frank, the discontinuities and displacements of his plans were intended only to generate pleasing and affective spaces—to provide a suitable backdrop for living. Loos, too, shared this desire to "provide warm and livable space,"[9] but he offered another rationale: the *Raumplan,* he contended, also provided a means to save space; the position and height of rooms were based on an economic imperative. The imposition of a *Raumplan,* Loos maintained, allowed him to squeeze more into the container, to redeem space that might otherwise have been wasted. In describing his Michaelerplatz Building in 1910, Loos noted: "The plans [of the competing projects] were all arranged in a plane, while in my opinion the architect must think in terms of spaces, of the cube. . . . A restroom does not need to be as high as a main hall. If one gives each space only the height it naturally requires, then one can build much more economically."[10] Frank, however, had little patience for such arguments, once remarking to his assistant Plischke that the economic bases of Loos's *Raumplan* idea were "simply nonsense" because they often conveyed no real spatial dividend.[11]

Perhaps the most significant point of divergence involved how Frank and Loos established the connections between rooms. In Loos's villas, the rooms are tightly interconnected. There are few conventional axes, however, because the rooms are shifted—either up or down or from side to side, or both. The passage from one room to another occurs directly at these fault lines, either across a displaced threshold or by means of stairs (which are often placed at the edge of the room). Frank, on the other hand, typically separates the individual rooms, using extended halls or stair sequences to join them. In place of the constant progression from room to room of Loos's villas, the spatial sequence in Frank's designs is often punctuated, with prolonged intervening passages; in this way, the plan is divided into a network of rooms and connecting corridors. This notion was already developed in Frank's plans of the mid-1920s, but it became even more pronounced in his later residential designs.

THE PROJECTS FOR HOUSES IN SALZBURG AND SKÄRGÅRDEN The differences between Frank's and Loos's spatial planning strategies are apparent in several other houses Frank designed between 1926 and 1928. In his project for a house in Salzburg (fig. 122), probably executed in late 1926 or early 1927,[12] Frank arranged the house in three adjoining blocks of different heights around a raised central courtyard. He conceived the building from within, devoting considerable attention to the organization and positioning of the living areas and access to the garden. The central focus is a pair of continuous, spiraling paths through and around the house. From the entrance on the northeast, the main route leads into a one-story wing containing the kitchen and other service rooms. From there, it continues along a hallway and up a small stairway through the one-and-a-half-story hall to the main living areas. A second pathway leads up an exterior stairway and across the adjoining terraces to the roof of the three-story block on the south.

At first glance, the composition of the ensemble seems somewhat random, an impression that is enhanced by Frank's freehand rendering. In fact, the plan was based on a carefully conceived quadratic scheme,[13] and Frank took great care to work out not only the dimensions and positioning of the various volumes but also the fenestration pattern. The spatial play both inside and outside the house relied in large measure on the sensation of walking and climbing. But movement within this active field was not necessarily intended to be continuous: along each processional pathway are various stopping points. Frank intended these as places of dwelling, as backdrops for the pursuit of leisured activities (there are, it is worth noting, few sites in Frank's houses specifically devoted to work aside from the servants' domain, which is always carefully isolated). The houses thus function as spheres—or perhaps better, exclusive sanctuaries—for a cultured bourgeoisie, who may take advantage of a variety of picturesque settings to wile away the hours in conversation or contemplation.

WOHNHAUS in SALZBURG

122. Project for a house in Salzburg,
c. 1926; elevations, sections, plans
1:200, perspective. *Moderne
Bauformen* 26 (1927).

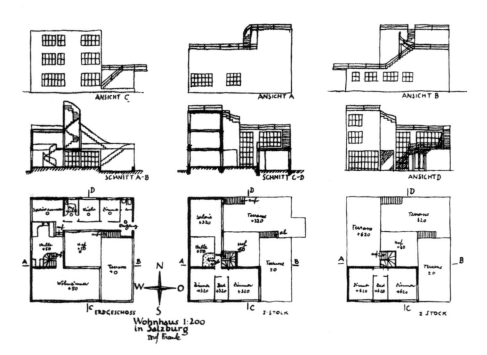

Wohnhaus 1:200
in Salzburg

As in Frank's earlier projects, there is a strong emphasis on the exterior spaces. The large expanses of glass, in fact, establish a certain ambiguity between inside and outside, an impression that is reinforced by Frank's depiction of a *Wohninsel* on the lower roof terrace.

Frank also investigated the potential of a similar courtyard arrangement in another of his house projects of the mid-1920s, a capacious summer villa (fig. 123) in the Skärgården, the archipelago of rocky islets east of Stockholm. The ostensible clients, as the legend on the drawing indicates, was his wife's cousin Dagmar Grill. Both the exaggerated size of the house and its whimsical appearance suggest, however, that it was intended as a fantasy house.

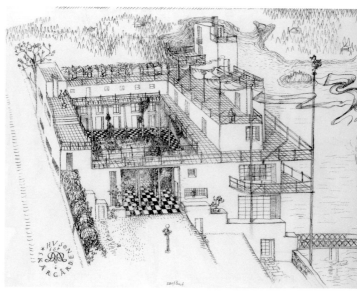

123. Project for a house for Dagmar Grill in Skärgården, Sweden, c. 1926; perspective. Pencil, pen and ink on paper, 34 × 32 cm. Svenskt Tenn Collection, Josef Frank Archive, Stockholm.

Many of the themes of Frank's other houses of this period are apparent here, including the idiosyncratic massing and composition, and multiple levels, balconies, and terraces. Unfortunately, neither a plan nor section of the house has survived so it is not possible to reestablish fully the disposition of its interior. The arrangement of the balconies and terraces and the pattern of fenestration indicate that Frank had in mind a *Raumplan* solution analogous to the Salzburg project. The main entrance appears to be on the right under the bridge joining the open end of the U-shaped structure. The large window on the lower right likely belongs to the living room; the room above was intended perhaps to be a salon or library. The wing on the left is evidently a service block, while the upper stories are no doubt bedrooms and other private dwelling areas. Once more, the controlling idea is a gradual ascent through a series of interlinked spaces to the uppermost levels of the house. In contrast to the Salzburg House, however, the stairs and the main pathways connecting the different volumes are concealed in the interior so that there is a sharper distinction between inside and outside. Also, unlike the Salzburg project, the design exhibits a greater emphasis on the exterior spaces—the balconies, terraces, and courtyard—which dominate the mass of the house.

In the March 1928 issue of *Der Baumeister,* Frank published two related designs, both for country houses.[14] One is a project for a pyramidal hipped-roof house with two terraces (fig. 124); the other, a flat-roofed house with three terraces (fig. 125). Both houses, like Frank's other designs of the period, were certainly influenced by Mediterranean vacation houses. Unlike the Salzburg and Skärgården projects, however, much of the interplay between the inside and outside is lost; and it is from the exterior decks that space develops and expands.

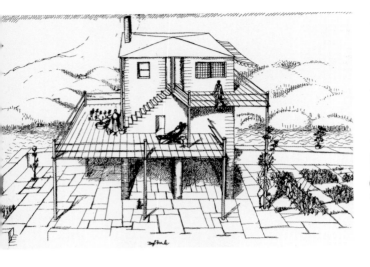
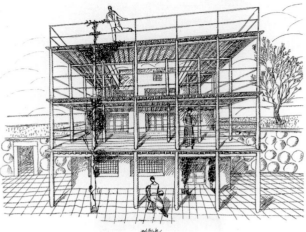

Frank explored many of these same ideas in a project for a house in Baden bei Wien (plate 13), albeit with more conventional results. Although the body of the structure itself appears to consist of three uniform levels, Frank took advantage of the sloping site to provide a gradual descent to the stream, connecting together the different planes by means of a single stairway, which yielded a range of possible stopping and vantage points.

THE HOUSE PROJECTS FOR COLUMBUS, LOS ANGELES, AND PASADENA Three other unrealized house projects, all evidently designed in 1927, chart the trajectory of Frank's rapidly evolving spatial planning ideas and their growing divergence from Loos's *Raumplan* conception. The houses, for sites in Los Angeles and Pasadena, California, and Columbus, Ohio, were apparently intended for American clients, although, as with Frank's other unrealized house projects of this period, little else is known about their circumstances. The houses were likely connected with a trip to the United States that Frank undertook in the spring of 1927 to oversee the installation of the Austrian section at the *Machine-Age Exposition* in New York, held between 16 and 28 May.[15] But it remains unclear whether they represent works Frank included in the exhibition—described only as "country houses" in the catalog[16]—or whether they were actual commissions by American clients Frank encountered before or during his stay. The Los Angeles house is the only one of the three projects that is dated (1927), but the Pasadena House was published in the May 1927 issue of *Moderne Bauformen,* indicating that it predated the exhibition.[17]

The project for a stucco house in Columbus, Ohio (fig. 126), is the most modest of the three. From the west elevation, it resembles Frank's earlier *Siedlung* houses, though it is considerably larger and has a slightly rounded roof in place of Frank's usual flat roof. Also notable is Frank's use of uniform American-style sash windows. As in most of

THE HOUSE AS PATH AND PLACE

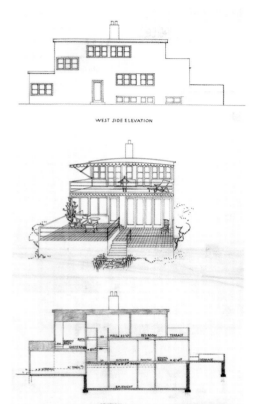

WEST SIDE ELEVATION

SECTION

126. (left) Project for a stucco house for Columbus, Ohio, c. 1928; elevation, perspective, section. Pencil, pen and ink on paper, 60 × 80 cm. Sammlung, Universität für angewandte Kunst, Vienna.

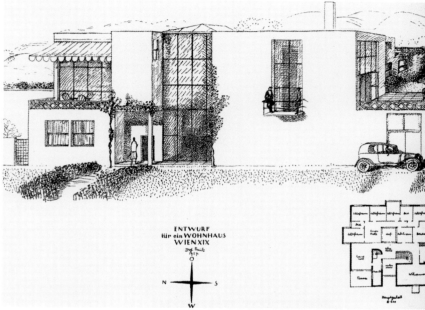

ENTWURF
für ein WOHNHAUS
WIEN XIX

Frank's other houses of this period, the ground-floor rooms are arranged on different levels, with the front alcove, living room, and sun parlor positioned approximately one-third of a meter below the other rooms. The large rear terrace was similarly divided into two levels corresponding to the different heights of the ground floor. Compared with Frank's Salzburg House or the Vienna XIII House, however, the spatial sequence remains relatively straightforward, and there is little attempt—aside from the front guest bedroom and bath—to create interlocking volumes on varying levels.

More complex in spatial terms is Frank's design for the residence for Mr. and Mrs. A. R. G. in Los Angeles (fig. 127). It is not known whether Frank traveled to the West Coast during his 1927 trip to the United States. If so, his goal may have been to visit his fellow Austrians, Richard Neutra and Rudolph M. Schindler, in Los Angeles. Frank knew Schindler from the Technische Hochschule, where their studies had overlapped.[18] He was also surely aware of Neutra's works, which had appeared in many of the leading German-language architecture publications.[19] The A. R. G. House and several subsequent designs for southern California Frank prepared in the late 1920s and in 1930 suggest that

127. (right) Project for a house for Mr. and Mrs. A. R. G., Los Angeles, 1927, plan 1:200, perspective. *Der Baumeister* 26 (1928).

he had familiarity with courtyard houses of the region. His knowledge, however, may have only been secondhand, drawn from American or European publications.[20]

Indeed, despite its relative openness, in formal and compositional terms, the A. R. G. House is closely related to Frank's other residential projects of the time. The living areas are situated on a second-story piano nobile. The primary route of entry extends from the vine-covered porch into a two-story-high glazed hall at the center. From there, a stairway leads up to the second floor. Concealed behind the public areas in the front of the houses is a private domain—a studio, boudoir, and several bedrooms—as well as a separate service wing on the northeast containing the kitchen, pantry, and servants' quarters. The regular horizontal layering of floors is maintained, but the sense of spatial flow and variety is achieved by means of various disjunctures and discontinuities that divide the plan into a series of linked but nonaxial sequences. Much like a maze, the plan forces repeated changes of direction, even requiring one to double back in the same direction. Openings in the walls at various points—for example, the window in the nook overlooking the hall below—would have provided glimpses of other rooms or the vistas outside.

In the A. R. G. House, the pattern of walls and openings, of solids and voids, necessitates constant movement and shifting, entailing not only physical exertion but also a bodily experience of space. But space in Frank's architecture is not only felt. He is also concerned with its mental construction, in the way in which we perceive and then conceptualize it. Indeed, Frank seems to reject the Cartesian schism between the body and mind, seeking instead to affect both. Often, as in the Los Angeles house, the progression of spaces is arranged in such a way as to offer multiple and changing impressions, forcing the observer into active participation. In places, the routing of the promenade may be immediately grasped; but Frank sometimes also positions the walls and openings to first veil and then reveal what lies beyond.[21] However, the pattern of wandering and observing in the A. R. G. House, as in Frank's other residential projects, is never aimless. All of the routes eventually lead to places of dwelling, where one may sit and rest or engage in other activities. In places, the promenade involves merely a directed route across a room; but Frank often attenuates these passages—routing them through hallways or up or down stairs—thereby increasing the distance between one stopping point and the next.

In the residence for Mr. S. H. B. in Pasadena, California (fig. 128), Frank combined this notion of purposeful rambling with elements of the *Raumplan*—in particular, the use of carefully fitted rooms of differing heights—to produce one of his most dynamic and varied spatial arrangements. Unlike his Salzburg and Los Angeles projects, which were still relatively compact, he fragmented the main body of the house into blocks of various sizes and heights and arrayed them along the sloping hillside. These distinct parts, in turn, are shaped and disposed by a series of circulation patterns, which connect together the main living, service, and sleeping areas. The house is mainly conceived from

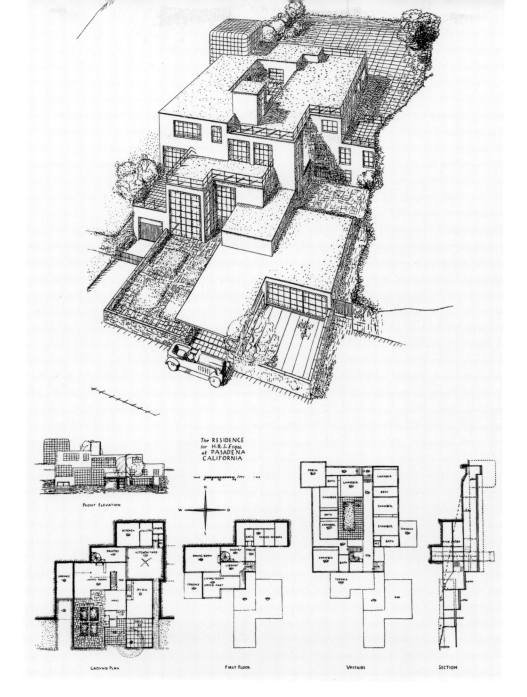

128. Project for a house for Mr. S. H. B., Pasadena, c. 1927; elevation, plans, section 1:200, perspective. *Moderne Bauformen* 26 (1927).

within, with the utmost care focused on its interior spaces—rather, one is tempted to say, to the disadvantage of its overall composition. The somewhat awkward arrangement is especially evident in the bird's-eye perspective, but the effect from street level no doubt would have been more harmonious.

Had they been built, Frank's California house projects would have been among the most modern buildings in the United States at the time. On the West Coast, the only comparable works were those of two of Frank's fellow Austrians, Schindler's Lovell

Beach House, completed in 1926, and Neutra's Jardinette Apartments, finished the following year.

THE CARLSTEN HOUSE Despite this flurry of design activity, however, few commissions materialized.[22] Aside from a small addition to his prewar Strauß House and the Claëson House, designed in 1924, the only other private residence Frank was able to build was another small summer house in Falsterbo in 1927. Commissioned by acquaintances of the Franks, Allan and Signe Carlsten, the house (fig. 129) was situated on a small, roughly triangular-shaped lot a short distance from the Claëson House. Though more modest than the Claëson House both in terms of its architecture and its size, it echoed many of the features of its larger neighbor. In spite of its small scale, the main public areas were open and informal. Terraces on the south and west sides provided ample opportunities to enjoy the out-of-doors. The interior plan was reminiscent of the Claëson House, with a combined living and dining area taking up much of the ground floor. Because of a smaller budget (the Claëson House cost the princely sum of 19,000 Swedish kronor, the Carlsten House, less than half of that), Frank opted for light

129. House for Allan and Signe Carlsten, Falsterbo, Sweden, 1927; plans, elevations, section 1:50. Pencil, pen and ink on tracing paper, 58 × 70 cm. Sammlung, Universität für angewandte Kunst, Vienna.

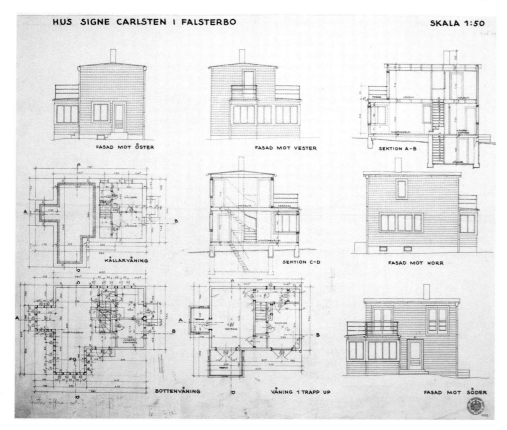

wood frame construction and greatly reduced the size of the terraces. Even so, he managed to preserve the feeling of lightness and spaciousness, producing one of his most effective works.

THE VILLA BEER In 1928—possibly as early as the autumn of 1927—Frank finally received the commission he had long awaited—for a large private villa in the Viennese suburb of Hietzing.[23] He and Wlach labored on the house for the next two years, and it was completed in late August 1930, just at the time Frank began to write *Architektur als Symbol*. Designed during the period when Frank was preoccupied with developing *Raumplan* ideas in his residential projects, it represented the culmination of his early spatial planning experiments. Frank intended the house as a full demonstration of his design principles and, by extension, of his own alternative vision of modernism: many of its features expressed an implicit critique of the radicals, and the work as a whole constituted a provisional answer in built form to the probing questions he posed in "Was ist modern?"

The clients, Dr. Julius Beer and his wife Margarete, were acquaintances of Frank's.[24] Julius Beer was the owner of the Persil Shoe Factory, and both he and his wife were avid devotees of the city's musical culture; they asked Frank and Wlach to design a house suitable for entertaining guests and business associates and for holding musical soirées. Armed with a generous budget, the two architects lavished attention on the project, employing an array of costly materials, including marquetry floors of exotic woods and imported marbles. Frank was largely responsible for designing the 650-square-meter house and most of its furniture; Wlach provided some of the detailing and oversaw the construction of the house and the manufacture of most of the furnishings and their installation.[25]

The house not only was the largest of Frank and Wlach's private commissions, but it also featured their most extensive Haus & Garten interior. The Beers, however, were to occupy the villa only briefly. With the onset of the worldwide depression in 1931, Beer's firm began to experience financial difficulties, and to make ends meet, he and his family moved to the upper floor and rented the lower portion of the house to tenants, among them the famed opera singers Jan Kiepura and Richard Tauber, who stayed there during their engagements in Vienna. Eventually, Beer's firm went into receivership, and the insurance company Österreichische Volksfürsorge, his primary creditor, seized the house. After several unsuccessful attempts to auction the property, it was sold in 1937 to the father of the present owner.[26]

The site was a wooded, roughly trapezoidal lot, sloping gently toward the rear. Frank placed the house close to the street, producing an ample rear garden. The rectangular mass of the house, which extended nearly to the edges of the property on either side, served to screen the garden, providing both privacy and an impression of enclosure.

130. Villa Beer, Vienna, 1928–30.
Innen-Dekoration 42 (1931).

131. Adolf Loos, Moller House,
Vienna, 1928. Österreichische
Nationalbibliothek, Bildarchiv,
Vienna.

Like Frank's unrealized projects of the later 1920s, the Villa Beer is conceived from inside out, its unusual exterior largely a consequence of its interior plan. With its large central oriel, the villa (fig. 130) at first glance bears an unmistakable resemblance to Loos's 1928 Moller House (fig. 131), and indeed, the two houses share a formal kinship. But there are also telling differences, in terms of both their construction and their composition. For one, the projecting bay in Loos's house is cantilevered; Frank, on the other hand, found it necessary to support his much larger extension (which contains two full stories rather than one, as is the case of the Moller House) on thin pilotis. More significant, however, are the dissimilarities in the massing and façade ordonnances of the two houses. While Loos's house was effectively a large cube, the Villa Beer constituted a thin, tall slab with sundry bulges or voids on the front and rear, an impression that is particularly evident in the view from the northeast (fig. 132). The placement of elements in the two houses' façades is also markedly different: whereas Loos's design for the street elevation of the Moller House relies on traditional bilateral symmetry, Frank adopted a much freer ordering principle. Not only are the elements seemingly arranged independently of one another, but Frank employed a wide variety of window types and sizes and door frames. Most conspicuous, however, are the disparities in the treatment of the houses' rear façades. Although the tight cubic form of the Moller House is maintained even on the garden side (fig. 133), Frank allowed the spaces within to cascade outward to form articulated volumes (fig. 134).

It is in the interior, though, that the unique character of Frank's house is fully unmasked. Like most of his unrealized residential projects of the later 1920s, the Villa Beer was arranged around a series of pathways connecting the individual spaces (fig. 135).[27] From the entry—a bright-red lacquered door located underneath the projecting front bay—the principal route of passage led past a small anteroom directly into the two-story

hall (fig. 136). To the rear was a large glassed-in alcove, while off to one side the room opened into the airy dining room (fig. 137). The compositional focus of the space, however, was the dramatic open stair (fig. 138) that linked together the house's different levels.

The impact upon entering this space, as the critic Wolfgang Born wrote, was striking and immediate: "One enters the hall [from the anteroom] through an unobtrusive door and is at once standing, surprised and moved, in the heart of the structure. The first glance instantly offers a clear understanding of the entire arrangement."[28] This impression is enhanced by the spiraling main stair, Born continued, "which simultaneously reveals all of the levels of the house."[29] The open, floating platforms and landings attached to the stair not only disclosed the house's interior order but also constituted a distinctive architectural presence. In contrast to Frank's other unrealized residential projects of this period, in which the stairs serve largely as a means of conveyance linking one space to

132. (left) Villa Beer, Vienna, 1928–30; view from the northeast. Arkitekturmuseet, Stockholm.

133. (top, right) Adolf Loos, Moller House, Vienna, 1928; view from the rear. Österreichische Nationalbibliothek, Bildarchiv, Vienna.

134. (bottom, right) Villa Beer, Vienna, 1928–30; view of the rear. *Innen-Dekoration* 42 (1931).

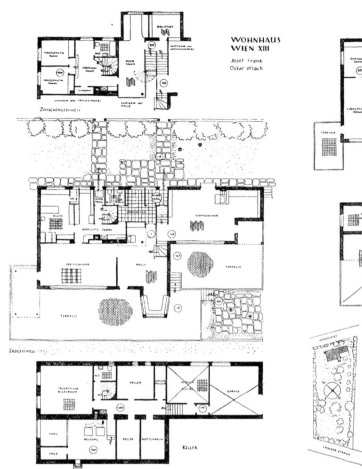

135. (top) Villa Beer, Vienna, 1928–30; plans and section. *Moderne Bauformen* 31 (1932).

136. (bottom, left) Villa Beer, Vienna, 1928–30; main hall. *Innen-Dekoration* 42 (1931).

137. (bottom, right) Villa Beer, Vienna, 1928–30; dining room. *Innen-Dekoration* 42 (1931).

the next, the staircase in the Villa Beer (fig. 139) established a particular spatial identity: it performed as both an avenue leading up through the house and as a series of discrete stopping points.

The living room (fig. 140), which was positioned approximately one and a quarter meters higher than the hall, occupied the first of these stopping points. Above it, on the next level, was an entresol (fig. 141) containing a music room (fig. 142) with an adjoining tearoom (fig. 143) and a small library, the latter two extending into the lower level of the projecting front oriel. Frank's decision to locate the music room on the platform was an adroit response to the wishes of the music-loving Margarete Beer, who wanted music to be at the center of the house.[30] Situating the Bösendorfer grand piano on the open landing accomplished this literally; but it also conferred an acoustic dividend: during music evenings guests could hear the piano or other instruments in any of the principal downstairs rooms.

138. Villa Beer, Vienna, 1928–30; stair from the hall. *Innen-Dekoration* 42 (1931).

139. Villa Beer, Vienna, 1928–30; view of lower portion of the stair leading to the living room. *Innen-Dekoration* 42 (1931).

140. (top, left) Villa Beer, Vienna, 1928–30; view from living room toward the hall. *Innen-Dekoration* 42 (1931).

141. (top, right) Villa Beer, Vienna, 1928–30; view of the entresol and hall from the living room. *Innen-Dekoration* 42 (1931).

142. (bottom) Villa Beer, Vienna, 1928–30; music room. *Innen-Dekoration* 42 (1931).

143. Villa Beer, Vienna, 1928–30; tearoom. *Innen-Dekoration* 42 (1931).

From this intermediate level, the stair continued to the two upper floors—the villa's private sphere comprising the bedrooms, a breakfast nook, several baths, and an exercise room that marked the terminus of the promenade. This elaborate progression, as Born pointed out, resulted from Frank's desire not only to create a visually affective experience but also to integrate it into the house's program: "The essence of this design," he wrote, "is the complete dissolution of all the usual spatial conventions of boxlike rooms, not only in a horizontal sense, in plan, but also in a vertical sense."[31] Yet at the same time, Born noted, the complex "interior spatial configuration . . . arises organically out of the circumstances of 'living'"—as a direct response to the needs of its occupants.[32] The effect, as Born observed, was subtle but noticeable: movement through the house produced "a wonderful sense of relaxation . . . just as the inglenooks invite one to rest, the stairs induce one to climb. But how easy this upward movement is! New views, new surprises constantly present themselves, until one reaches one of the roof terraces (perfectly adapted for sunbathing), which provide the definitive fusion of interior and open-air spaces. Striding through [the house] provides one with an inexhaustible, resounding experience of space."[33]

In his essay "Das Haus als Weg und Platz" (The house as path and place) published a year after the villa was completed, Frank described the ideas that guided its design. He had, he explained, conceived of the Beer House as a city in miniature, with traffic patterns and designated areas for specific activities. "A well-organized house," he wrote, "should be laid out like a city, with streets and alleys that lead inevitably to places that are cut off from traffic, so that one can rest there."[34] Frank emphasized that these pathways should follow natural traffic routes as in the cities of the past, not a simple grid: "A well-laid-out house is comparable to one of those beautiful old cities in which even a stranger immediately knows his way around and can find the city hall and the market square without having to ask."[35]

Frank argued that every aspect of the plan should contribute to this impression. Citing the example of the stairway (fig. 144), he wrote:

[A stairway] must be arranged so that when one approaches and begins to walk up it, he never has the feeling that he has to go back down the same way; one should always go further. . . . Every twist of the stairway serves to heighten this feeling, not to save space. . . . The shortest path is not the most comfortable one and the straight stairway is not always the best, indeed almost never.[36]

144. Villa Beer, Vienna, 1928–30; upper floor landing. *Der Baumeister* 29 (1931).

Frank's language here recalls Viennese urbanist Camillo Sitte's influential text on city planning *Der Städtebau nach seinen künstlerischen Grundsätzen* (City building according to its artistic principles), published in 1889.[37] Despairing over the disquieting results of city expansion and regulations in his own day, Sitte had sought to counter the rational and technical aspects of modern city building by proposing a planning ethic based on the primacy of what was "emotionally effective" and "picturesque." For Sitte, the function of the city was to serve as a forum for its citizenry and as a work of art. "A city," he asserted, quoting Aristotle, "must be so constructed that it makes its citizens at once secure and happy."[38] Accordingly, he focused his attention on the civic functions of streets and plazas, emphasizing their aesthetic and social aspects. Repudiating the uniform urban grid, he strove to recreate, as Carl Schorske wrote, "the free forms of ancient and medieval city-space organization: irregular streets and squares, which arose not on the drawing board but *in natura*."[39] Frank, similarly dissatisfied with the effects of modernization, sought to apply these ideas to the home. Rejecting the call of the functionalists to rationalize the house, he attempted, like Sitte, to create natural, comfortable, and aesthetically pleasing spaces. As Sitte had renounced the straight, wide street and regular monumental plaza, Frank eschewed regular axial planning.

14. Stool (Svenskt Tenn model no. 1063).
Walnut, leather, and brass, 1941. Courtesy
Bukowski Auktioner AB, Stockholm.

15. Table with checkerboard edge inlay
(Svenkst Tenn model no. 2108). Amboyna
with boxwood and ebony inlay, designed
c. 1940. Courtesy Bukowski Auktioner AB,
Stockholm

16. "Anakreon" fabric sample, designed c.
1938. Svenskt Tenn Collection, Josef Frank
Archive, Stockholm.

17. Drawing for a hand-knotted carpet, 1938. Watercolor on paper, 46.7 × 41.3 cm. Svenskt Tenn Collection, Josef Frank Archive, Stockholm.

18. Drawing for "U. S. Tree," 1943–44. Pencil, watercolor and gouache on paper, 90 × 130 cm. Photograph by PeO Eriksson. Svenskt Tenn Collection, Josef Frank Archive, Stockholm.

19. "Vegetable Tree" fabric sample, designed c. 1944. Photograph by PeO Eriksson. Svenskt Tenn Collection, Josef Frank Archive, Stockholm.

20. Drawing for "Rox and Fix," 1943–44. Pencil, watercolor and gouache on paper, 91.4 × 74.6 cm. Svenskt Tenn Collection, Josef Frank Archive, Stockholm.

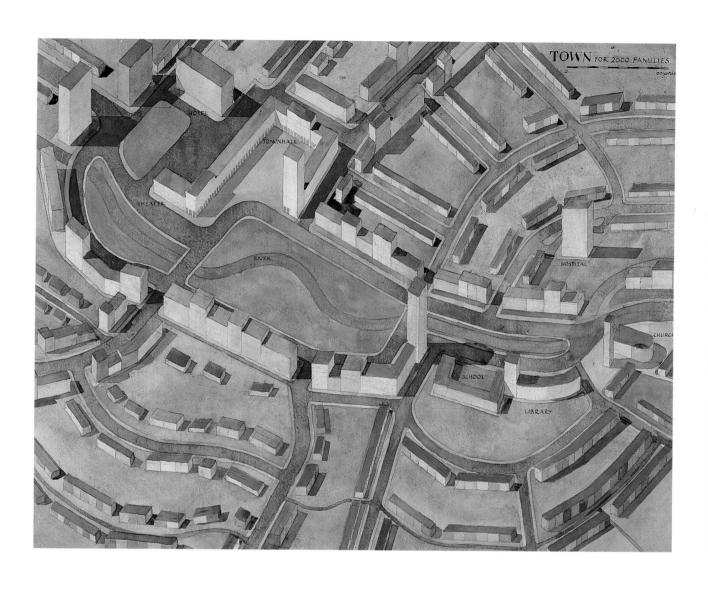

TOWN FOR 2000 FAMILIES

HOTEL

TOWNHALL

THEATER

RIVER

HOSPITAL

CHURCH

SCHOOL

LIBRARY

21. Project for a town for 2,000 families, c. 1950; aerial perspective. Pencil, watercolor on paper, 46.5 × 58 cm. Arkitekturmuseet, Stockholm.

22. Thirteen house designs for Dagmar
Grill; house 9, c. 1953; perspective. Pencil,
watercolor on paper, 29.5 × 42 cm. Graphische Sammlung Albertina, Vienna.

23. D-House with checkerboard parapet, c.
1953; perspective. Pencil, watercolor on
paper, 32 × 51 cm. Graphische Sammlung
Albertina, Vienna.

24. Double D-House 3, c. 1954; perspective.

Pencil, watercolor on paper, 41 × 59.5 cm.

Arkitekturmuseet, Stockholm.

25. Project for a round stone house in Provence, mid-1950s; perspective. Pencil, watercolor on paper, 46.5 × 68 cm. Graphische Sammlung Albertina, Vienna.

26. Project for a house for Trude Waehner,
Provence, late 1950s; perspective. Pencil,
watercolor on paper, 45.5 × 61 cm. Arkitekturmuseet, Stockholm.

But it was in the bohemian artists' garret—from which he argued "the modern house is descended"—that Frank found his direct model for the house. These irregular spaces, "the product of chance," provided for him "all that we seek in vain in the planned and rationally furnished apartments below it: life, large rooms, large windows, multiple corners, angled walls, steps and height differences, pillars and beams—in short, all the variety that we seek in the new house in order to counteract the desolate wasteland of the regular four-cornered room."[40] The real task for the architect, Frank charged, was to reproduce this sense of freedom and spontaneity in the modern dwelling.

Yet the plan of the Beer House was more than an assemblage of haphazard elements: the entire space within was meticulously organized and segmented, with little left to chance. Among the principal divisions was a clear demarcation of the functional and living precincts. The kitchen, pantry, and housekeepers' quarters were confined to a two-story section on the western corner, which had its own entrance and separate stair.[41] These areas were joined in turn with the dining room, music room, and upper floor bedrooms by a series of discreetly placed doors, thus ensuring only limited interaction between the Beers and their servants.

Within the main portion of the house itself were two further divisions, one between zones of movement and rest, and the other between the public and private spheres. Frank usually employed wall or stairs to achieve the separation between spaces of transit and those of stasis; but in places this division was merely intimated so that the two merged formlessly. In the main entry sequence, for example, the cloakroom (fig. 145) was positioned to one side and framed by walls, providing an eddy in the circulation flow. As one entered the main hall, a variety of possibilities opened up: one path led directly back to the sitting area in the rear alcove; another, also plainly indicated, continued up the stairs to the living room and beyond. An additional path went to the right, to the small inglenook underneath the extended gallery of the music room; yet another route took one into the dining room or out into the open area of the hall. Although each alternative path was immediately evident, it was only casually "signed." "It is of the utmost importance," Frank cautioned, that the "path is not marked by some obvious means or decorative scheme, so that the visitor will never have the idea that he is being led around."[42]

The paths invariably terminated in a casual sitting area—the "piazza" of the house, as Frank referred to it.[43] Arranged informally, these spaces—in German *Plätze*, places or squares—assumed a dual character: they have a relaxed quality, but they are also the products of precise manipulation. Paradoxically, the sense of comfort that pervades the house is the product of two seemingly opposite courses of action: a laissez-faire attitude and supreme control.

The understated division between the public and private domains of the house provides a case in point. The break occurred on the landing of the main stairway between the entresol and the first of the upper floors (fig. 146). The spaces beyond were the

145. Villa Beer, Vienna, 1928–30; cloak room. *Innen-Dekoration* 42 (October 1931).

146. Villa Beer, Vienna, 1928–30; main stair from the entresol. *Moderne Bauformen* 31 (1932).

province of the family, while those below or adjacent belonged to the field where guests were received or entertained. Conventionally, a stair would mark this separation. But in the Villa Beer, the staircase acted as a mechanism of conveyance between the places of social gathering on the lower floors. The partition thus had to take place on the stairway itself. Frank achieved a resolution, as he explained, through a subtle treatment of its routing:

One enters the hall facing the stair. The stairway, which turns outward into the room, presents its first step to the person entering. When he begins to climb upward, he can see the first landing and through a large opening into the most important room in the house, the living room. From this level, the stair leads straight up to two rooms, the study and salon, which are concealed from the living room but closely connected to it. At this point, the level housing the main living areas comes to an end. To emphasize this fact, the stairs, which wind in the other direction, lead up to the next floor with the bedrooms, and a clear division of the house is achieved.[44]

The partition of the stair resulted from an alteration of the traffic pattern, rather than by means of a physical barrier or an obvious sign. It arose, as Schmarsow had suggested at the turn of the century, from experience, one that both informed and directly involved the occupant.

In his houses of the 1920s and early 1930s, Loos, too, controlled and manipulated the paths connecting the rooms, but with different results. Like Frank, Loos was concerned with the linkages between the various spaces in his residences. In an oft-cited passage from an interview with Karel Lhota, Loos remarked that the rooms within the space-plan "must be integrated in such a way that the transition is not only imperceptible and natural, but also functional,"[45] a formulation similar to Frank's cautionary statement that the path in the house should "not [be] marked by some obvious means." Loos's practice of fitting his spatial sequences into a tight cubic container, however, ensured that the linkages between the rooms would be generally direct and abrupt, with little separation between areas of movement and rest.

This close integration of path and place is perhaps most pronounced in Loos's Villa Müller in Prague, which was completed in February 1930, a few months before the Villa Beer. In the Müller House, as in the Villa Beer, the stair ascended in stages, connecting

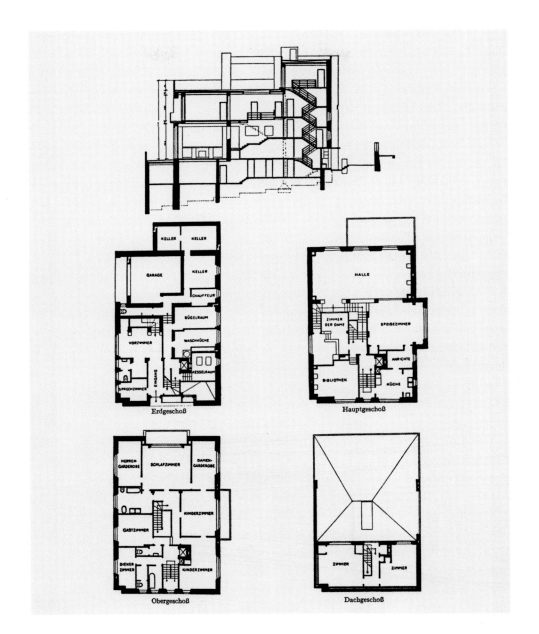

Erdgeschoß

Hauptgeschoß

Obergeschoß

Dachgeschoß

147. Adolf Loos, Müller House, Prague, 1928–30; plans and section. Gustav Adolf Platz, *Wohnräume der Gegenwart* (Berlin, 1933).

rooms on sundry levels; and in like fashion, it also provided dramatic views to and from the hall. But as the plans and section of the house (fig. 147) make evident, the paths between the rooms were highly compressed. The transition from one space to the next was often only a matter of a few steps. This effect was enhanced by Loos's use of marble and wooden cladding along the stairs and hallways, which further served to "reduce" these spaces. Frank, by employing unadorned white walls and similar treatments of the railings, stairs, and other surfaces, ensured a much stronger impression of openness and flow. The result of this expansion was a marked "relaxation" of Loos's notion of the space-plan. In place of Loos's purposeful routing, Frank substituted a freer, less constrained spatial progression. Movements within the Villa Beer constituted a leisurely stroll, and the paths and places were organized in such a manner that many of the routes were never precisely demarcated, thus offering a variety of courses.

But it is not only in the arrangement of the interior that these differences are disclosed. Unlike Loos's Moller and Müller Villas, which, as various commentators have noted, are intently focused inward on themselves,[46] nearly all of Frank's living areas and bedrooms offer direct access to a balcony or terrace, and he provided, in addition, pronounced visual connections with the outside, typically in the form of French doors or large windows. "The natural world surrounding the house," Frank wrote some years later, "should make the transition, in a discreet fashion, into the house itself."[47] A contemporary photograph of the Villa Beer's northeast corner (fig. 148) reveals how Frank carried the notion of the house as path and place outward onto the roof terraces and balconies. These variations in level are repeated in the landscaping, mirroring spatial divisions and alterations of height in the interior. The space-plan not only extends to the exterior, but the freedom and openness of the exterior spaces also pervade the interior spatial field.

148. Villa Beer, Vienna, 1928–30; view of the rear. *Der Baumeister* 29 (1931).

PATTERNS OF DWELLING The development of Frank's notion of *Raumplanung* was driven not only by an attempt to engender a greater sense of freedom but also by his conviction that the spaces in his dwellings should arise from and reflect the changing patterns of everyday living. In "The House as Path and Place," he writes:

The entire struggle for the modern apartment and the modern house has at its heart the goal of freeing people from their bourgeois prejudices and providing them with the possibilities of a bohemian lifestyle. The prim and orderly home in both its old or new guise will become a nightmare in the future.[48]

Rather than jettisoning the past, Frank instead called for a return to earlier forms and patterns. His specific idea of "the house as path and place" issued both from the premodern city and from English domestic planning:

In earlier times, especially in England, to which we owe the modern house form, such arrangements were traditional for cities and houses, but this tradition today has largely died out. The well-laid-out path through the house requires a sensitive understanding, and architects cannot begin anew, which is why it would be important to revive this tradition.[49]

The "well-laid-out path" had its origins in the patterns of normal habits and practices as they developed over time. It was not economic issues or even simple functionality that should determine the ground plan, Frank contended, but a more complex calculus that took into consideration how one actually lived:

All of our objects of daily use, to which we must also accord the house, involve compromises of purpose, material, form, quality, price, and everything else. But the rules for a good house do not in principle change and must be constantly considered anew. How does one enter the garden? What should a path to the main door look like? What form should an anteroom have? How does one proceed from the anteroom past the cloak rack and into the living room? How should a sitting area be positioned in relation to a door or window? How many such questions there are that have to be answered, and from these elements a house arises. That is modern architecture.[50]

For Frank, the role of the designer was to apprehend "the rules of the good house" that had developed through custom and practice and to translate these into built form. The house, he reiterated, was not a work of art, but simply the place in which one lived, unfettered by aesthetic considerations. By examining both our subjective responses and formal and practical considerations, the architect could discern how best to frame the complex patterns of dwelling.

RAUMPLAN AND PLAN LIBRE While Frank and Loos were exploring the spatial possibilities inherent in the concept of the *Raumplan,* other modernists of the time were investigating related ideas. Adolf Rading and Hans Lauterbach, for example, experimented with the use of multiple levels and differentiated room heights; Hans Scharoun and Häring examined the potential of nonorthogonal spaces; and Mies van der Rohe and others pursued strategies of free and open planning. With his use of pathways to connect varied volumes, however, Frank's idea of "the house as path and place" was perhaps closest to Le Corbusier's notion of the *plan libre,* and it is worth dwelling on the comparison for a moment because it reveals important features of Frank's approach.[51] Like Frank, Le Corbusier arranged his houses of the later 1920s along perceptual axes linking the different rooms together to foster a diverse range of spatial and sensory experiences. As Le Corbusier described:

One enters: the architectural spectacle at once offers itself to the eye. One follows an itinerary, and the perspectives develop with great variety, developing a play of light on the walls and making pools of shadow. Large windows open up views of the exterior where the architectural unity is reasserted.[52]

The decisive formative influence for Le Corbusier, as for Frank, was the English country house. But although Le Corbusier adopted the idea of a freely developed interior space, he did so within an architectural order still determined by a classical monumentalism; his residential designs issued from a belief that architecture still belonged to the realm of art. For Frank, by contrast, the house is neither monumental nor—as the radical functionalists held—purely utilitarian; instead, it unfolded as a complex response to the patterns of everyday living.

Frank's idealized inhabitant also lived differently from Le Corbusier's. Le Corbusier's occupant was the modern urban dweller, whose house was an extension of his or her world. For Le Corbusier, as Vincent Scully has written, the house was a place of action; Le Corbusier's tautly stretched boxes were containers for drama, a stage for the play of modern life.[53] For Frank, on the other hand, the house was a refuge, if an illusory one. His heavy masonry walls were screens behind which the human drama occurred offstage, in privacy. The interior of the house for Frank constituted a personal domain, the intimate preserve of the individual and the family. He regarded it not as an extension of the modern world but as a haven from it, a place where one could escape the rigors of contemporary life. Frank employed furniture, rugs, curtains, and other objects to mitigate the impact of the architecture, to soften and "domesticate" the space within. The aggregate effect of these elements served not only to shape the promenade and spatial ordering, but also to provide a note of everyday realism, to cloak the abstract and unyielding nature of the underlying architectural structure.

These differences are also expressed in the spatial sequencing of the two architects' houses. In Le Corbusier's most fully realized *plan libre* designs of the later 1920s, such as the Villa Savoye or the Villa Stein de Monzie, the main passages within the houses are long and straight, with sharp turns and abrupt shifts in direction. The main processional routes rarely provide the inhabitants with places to stop; rather, the arrangement demands full engagement and activity. The ramps in the Villa Savoye ascend without interruption through the house. Although they provide varied prospects of the house and the landscape beyond, they invite continuous movement, not contemplation. By contrast, the paths of the Villa Beer suggested an unhurried stroll; they wound slowly through the spaces allowing ample opportunities to linger. Moreover, while Le Corbusier's ramps, stairs, and hallways were often purposefully detached from the adjacent living areas, in the Villa Beer they merged into the other spaces, leaving little separation between zones of movement and repose.

THE GARDEN AS PATH AND PLACE Frank also applied these same lessons to landscape design. They are most fully displayed in his design for the garden of the Kahane House, which was on the boards at the same time as the Villa Beer. The house, situated on the Hohe Warte in the city's nineteenth district, was designed around 1929 by Viennese architect Arnold Karplus.[54] Frank and Wlach were commissioned to provide all of the furnishings, as well as the landscaping for the new house.[55]

Within the rear garden, Frank established two principal "living areas"—a raised, semicircular terrace attached to the house and a round tea pavilion at the far rear corner (figs. 149, 150). Between these two fixed points for relaxation was a series of paved pathways that allowed one to wander through the garden, passing by its various features. The theme of the design was the juxtaposition of circular or curved elements with squares and straight lines. Most remarkable was the circular, poured concrete tea house, or "tea tent" (*Teezelt*) as Frank refers to it on the plan (fig. 151), the roof of which was supported by a continuous rounded wall on one side and two thin metal columns on the other.

149. Garden for the Kahane House, Vienna, 1929–30; view from the house of the terrace and garden. *Innen-Dekoration* 41 (1930).

(Curtains hanging from a track on the underside of the roof allowed it to be closed entirely, producing a tentlike effect). Though not delimited by walls, the Kahane garden incorporated most of the constituent elements of his interior spatial plans: the use of an architectural promenade (or promenades) to connect the main living areas, the creation of changes in level to enhance the sense of diversity, and the insertion of courtyards or other bordered spaces to provide interruptions within the larger spatial frame. Frank's practice of specifying simple white walls punctuated by bright splashes of color also seems to find its counterpart in his selection of plant material, which relied on isolated masses of flowers or greenery set against

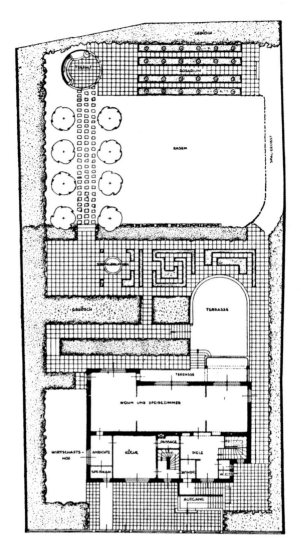

an otherwise understated background. In plan, the arrangement appears highly formalized and rigorously geometric, but the view from any particular position, as the contemporary photographs document, was remarkably complex and varied.

NEW SPATIAL IDEAS Frank, however, was not wholly satisfied with the spatial solution of the Villa Beer. By the middle of 1930, if not before, he began to rethink some of his basic design assumptions, in particular his allegiance to standard orthogonal planning. This shift is already apparent in his essay "The House as Path and Place," which was probably written in the spring or early summer of 1931. Although Frank intended the essay as a statement of his design aims for the villa, also contained within it are unmistakable references to new ideas that would define his architectural philosophy for the next three decades. "The regular four-cornered room," he wrote,

is the least suited to living; it is very practical for a storage space, but not for anything else. I believe that a polygon drawn by chance, whether with right or acute angles, when it is viewed as the plan of a room, is much more appropriate than a regular four-cornered one. Chance also helped in the case of the garret studio, which was always comfortable and impersonal.[56]

In the Beer Villa, as in many of his other residential projects of the later 1920s, Frank had sought to overcome this problem of the "regular four-cornered room" through

150. (left) Garden for the Kahane House, Vienna, 1929–30, plan. *Innen-Dekoration* 41 (1930).

151. (right) Garden for the Kahane House, Vienna, 1929–30; tea pavilion. *Moderne Bauformen* 29 (1930).

THE HOUSE AS PATH AND PLACE

the introduction of various disjunctures and discontinuities. The walls were placed at un-equal intervals; various "interruptions" established complex outlines. Nonetheless, many of the rooms retained a conventional character, which Frank had been forced to amelio-rate with a free placement of the furnishings.

In his unrealized project for the House for M. S., an unknown client in Los Angeles, which likely dates from the second half of 1930, Frank attempted to devise an alternative solution. Three different versions of the house plan have survived, all of them published in the separate section of plates in the same issue of *Der Baumeister* in which "The House as Path and Place" appeared.[57] The overall outlines of the three schemes are similar, showing a rambling, mostly one-story house arranged around one or more interior pa-tios. In two of the schemes (figs. 152, 153), which according to a note by the editors rep-resented the second and third designs, Frank employed standard orthogonal planning. He staggered and shifted the rooms, entries, and hallways, however, shaping a complex network of public and private spaces, paths, sitting areas, and dead ends. To enhance the rambling effect of the plan, Frank also raised or lowered certain rooms or portions of the house. This is particularly pronounced in the third scheme, which has spaces on six dif-ferent levels.

The first of the three schemes (fig. 154), however, departed dramatically from Frank's previous residential projects. Although the outer footprint of the house is similar to the other two designs, Frank abandoned conventional right-angled planning, introducing in-stead curvilinear and oblique lines that produced a series of irregular spaces. Framing the dining room is a long arcing screen. The screen, which is echoed by the outer glass wall of the tearoom, in turn is divided into separate, movable panels, permitting the room to be configured in a number of different ways. Frank had first experimented with the use of such a freestanding rounded screen in a design for the tearoom at the 1930 Werkbund exhibition in Vienna, and the same form appears in the dining room of Mies van der Rohe's Tugendhat House in nearby Brno, which was under construction in the winter of 1929–30 and of which Frank was undoubtedly aware. But in making the panels of the walls adjustable, he created an active plan, quite unlike Mies's more static arrangement. Frank repeated this same idea at the intersection of the dining and living areas, position-ing there a straight sliding door of similar construction, which increased the variety of spatial possibilities.

On the opposite side of the house, Frank splayed the outer edge of the hall, in the process converting several of the bedrooms into irregular polygons. The most severe of these "disruptions" is the long serpentine atrium, which effectively divides the house into two wings, one containing the living room and other public spaces, the other the bed-rooms. Glazed along much of its length on either side, this open patio serves to deform the adjoining spaces, but it also would have yielded complex and constantly changing views as one moved along it. The plan is largely confined to two levels: the bedroom wing

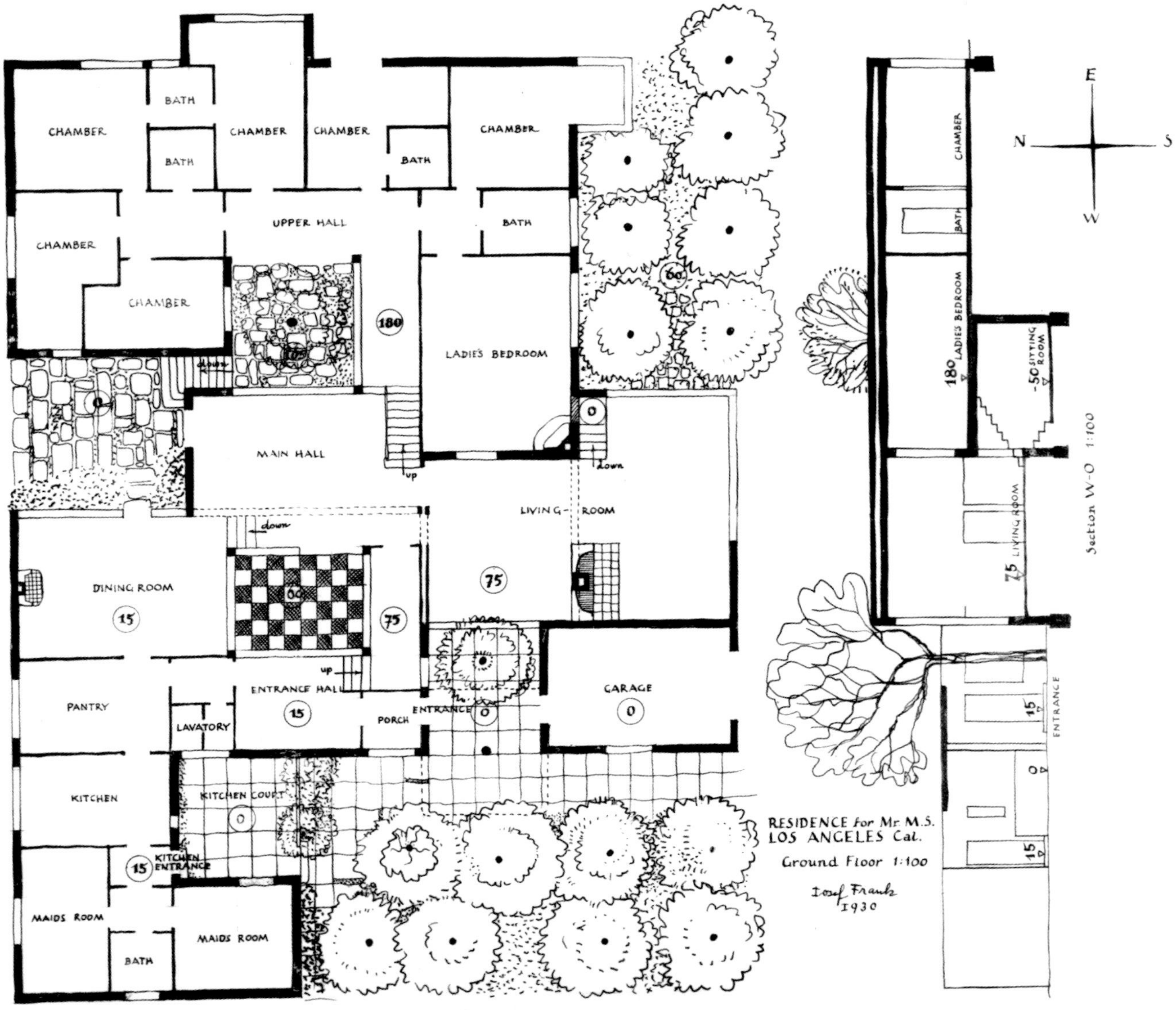
CHAMBER
BATH
CHAMBER
CHAMBER
CHAMBER
BATH
BATH
CHAMBER
UPPER HALL
BATH
CHAMBER
180
LADIES BEDROOM
MAIN HALL
LIVING-ROOM
DINING ROOM
15
75
75
PANTRY
ENTRANCE HALL
15
LAVATORY
PORCH
ENTRANCE
GARAGE
KITCHEN
KITCHEN COURT
KITCHEN ENTRANCE
15
MAIDS ROOM
MAIDS ROOM
BATH
RESIDENCE for Mr. M.S.
LOS ANGELES Cal.
Ground Floor 1:100
Josef Frank
1930
E
N
S
W
Section W-O 1:100
SITTING ROOM
LIVING ROOM
ENTRANCE

152. House for M. S., Los Angeles, 1930; second version; plan, section 1:100. Pencil, pen and ink on tracing paper, 29.5 × 36 cm. Graphische Sammlung Albertina, Vienna.

GROUND FLOOR 1:100

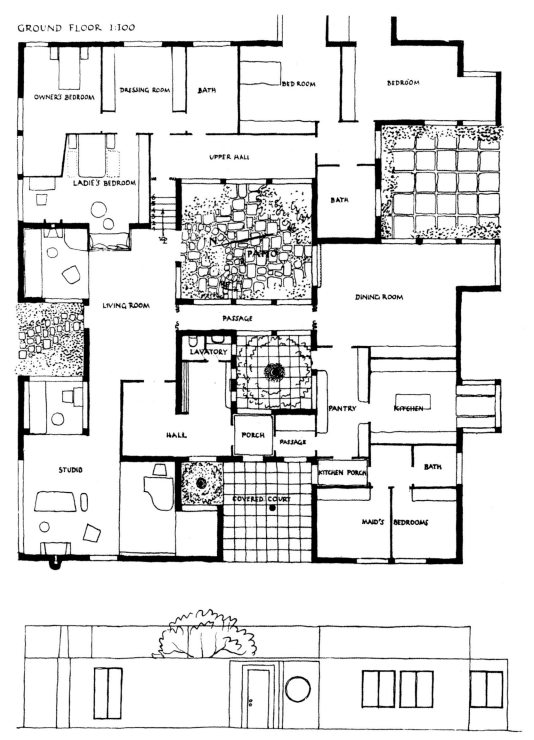

OWNER'S BEDROOM · DRESSING ROOM · BATH · BED ROOM · BEDROOM · LADIE'S BEDROOM · UPPER HALL · BATH · LIVING ROOM · PATIO · DINING ROOM · PASSAGE · LAVATORY · STUDIO · HALL · PORCH · PASSAGE · PANTRY · KITCHEN · COVERED COURT · KITCHEN PORCH · BATH · MAID'S BEDROOMS

153. House for M. S., Los Angeles, 1930; third version; plan, elevation 1:100. *Der Baumeister* 29 (1931).

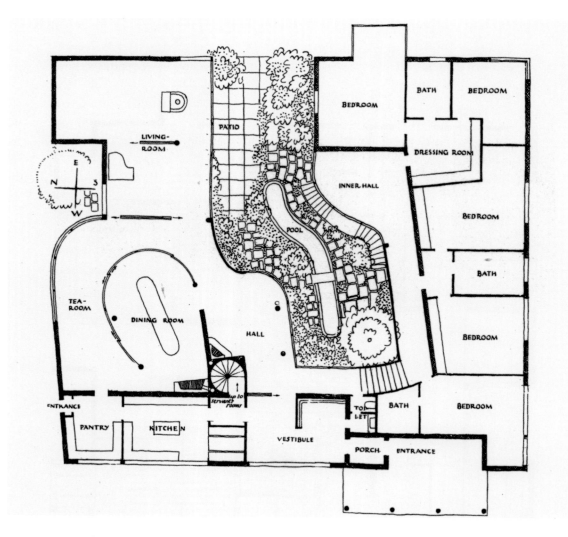

154. House for M. S., Los Angeles,
1930; first version; plan 1:100. *Der
Baumeister* 29 (1931).

is raised approximately a meter and a half above the remainder of the house, while the
servants' quarters are placed on a separate upper story above the kitchen area. Nonetheless, the scheme is replete with the opportunities for spatial play that had been so central
to Frank's architectural work of the later 1920s. Frank would not actually realize this sort
of nonorthogonal planning in one of his residential works for another six years, but the
House for M. S. clearly announced the concerns that were to occupy him for the remainder of his life.[58]

SPACE, TIME, AND PSYCHE The plan of the Villa Beer thus rep-
resents a watershed in Frank's oeuvre. It was not only his most fully realized *Raumplan*
design, but it also marked an end to the design path he had embarked on before the First
World War. Increasingly, after 1930, he would concentrate on the notion of chance or ad-
ditive ordering, using oblique and warped walls to promote an impression of complex, ir-

regular space. In the Villa Beer, however, Frank had managed to add—or perhaps better, extend—at least two important aspects to the development of spatial planning ideas in the interwar years. By merging the notion of the architectural promenade with a spatial partitioning à la Loos, he succeeded in making the idea of the *Raumplan* fully dynamic. It is not only Frank's articulation of space that stands out in the Villa Beer, it is also the way one experiences that space through movement—through changes in spatial and temporal orientation. By carefully determining the "paths" and "places" within the larger spatial continuum, he was able to exploit the inhabitant's perceptual apparatus, to foster a complete experience of space. More important, perhaps, Frank sought to frame this spatial experience in accordance with his understanding of human behavior. His aim was not only to arouse the senses, but also to create an interesting and pleasing environment in which to dwell. The space within the house was not merely a formal exercise; it was also a means of enhancing the rituals of daily life.

WAR ON TWO FRONTS

By 1932, when Josef Frank (fig. 155) turned forty-seven, he could look back upon more than a decade of accomplishment. It was true that the period between the end of the war and the early 1930s had brought hardships and disappointments, but equally it witnessed his steady rise in the ranks of Europe's modernists. Both his buildings and his designs for Haus & Garten continued to win accolades, and he was widely regarded both at home and abroad as the leading voice for modern architecture in Austria. The dawn of the 1930s, however, brought signs that everything was about to change. The years of relative stability and calm were ending. What lay ahead would not only test Frank's resolve, but would force him to rethink his views about architecture and design.

REACTION FROM THE RIGHT

In the late 1920s Frank had directed much of his energy toward combating what he viewed as a "romanticized" modernism. He had not only assailed the position of the radicals but had also challenged some of the very core beliefs of the new architecture. Yet, for all of its stridency, his criticism had always been intended as a contribution to a debate within the modernist camp, and he remained convinced of the fundamental correctness of the modernist vision.

155. Josef Frank, 1932. Österreichische Nationalbibliothek, Bildarchiv, Vienna.

By the early 1930s, however, Frank increasingly found himself forced to fight on two fronts, on the one hand against the pathos of the architectural left, while on the other, against a growing movement that sought to reject modernism and all that it stood for.[1] In 1931, Leo Adler, the influential editor of *Wasmuths Monatshefte*, wrote that in his view the pendulum of architecture, which had been steadily moving in the direction of *Sachlichkeit* for the past decade, had reached its apogee and was beginning to swing back toward "tradition."[2] What Adler had in mind was not a revival of historicism, but the growth of the so-called *Heimatstil,* the quasi folk-idiom, promoted by the *völkisch,* right-wing groups who demanded the "reawakening of a genuine Germanness—*deutsches Volkstum*—in German lands."[3] Led by the outspoken Paul Schultze-Naumburg, who would become the leading architectural authority in Germany after the Nazis seized power, the advocates of *Blut und Boden* (blood and soil) architecture attacked modernism as a foreign style that endangered the German sense of national and racial identity.[4]

The rise of the *Heimatstil* was only the tip of a growing force that threatened to undermine modern architecture. By 1927, politics, though they had never been far from the surface, began to play an ever greater role in the architectural debate. As in neighboring Germany, the political divisions in Austria had deepened in the later 1920s, and political discourse more and more degenerated into street battles.

FRANK'S ENGAGEMENT WITH THE LEFT IN THE LATE 1920S AND EARLY 1930S

Frank spoke out repeatedly in the late 1920s and early 1930s defending the cause of modernism and urging greater tolerance and openness. He also continued to support the attempts of the Socialists to educate and improve the living standards of the Austrian working class.

In 1927, Frank assisted Neurath with the design of the permanent exhibition space for the Gesellschafts- und Wirtschaftsmuseum (Social and Economic Museum).[5] The museum, which opened in December in the *Volkshalle* (hall of the people) on the ground floor of the city hall, was conceived as a "popular" museum, promoting the development of public understanding of the Socialists' programs. As the successor of the earlier Museum für Siedlung und Städtebau (Museum for Settlement and City Planning), the museum displayed the achievements of the municipal building program, and it provided information on the country's social and economic progress. Among the innovative ideas Frank and Neurath incorporated in the museum's installations were a series of moveable panels, sized to fit moldings affixed to the walls, that could be readily rearranged.[6] Frank also took great pains to conceal the neo-Gothic detailing of the museum's two rooms. He covered the floors with a bright red carpet and suspended strong overhead lights above the panels, which set off the charts and left the Gothic vaults above in the dark.[7]

In the late 1920s and early 1930s, Frank took part as well in several exhibitions intended to demonstrate how to furnish the new proletarian dwelling. The most important of these exhibitions was the city-sponsored *Wien und die Wiener* (Vienna and the Viennese), held at the Messepalast in the late spring of 1927. Organized by Neurath's Gesellschafts- und Wirtschaftsmuseum, it included model rooms designed by Frank and a number of other well-known architects, among them Haerdtl, Hoffmann, and Franz Schacherl.[8] The architects collaborated with the Wiener Hausratgesellschaft (Vienna Household Furnishings Company), which had been established to provide furniture for the new apartments in the municipal housing projects, making use of both mass-produced furniture and pieces that they had designed themselves. The purpose of the demonstration was in part practical: the rooms of the new proletarian apartments were lower than those in the prewar tenements, and they typically had a larger number of windows, necessitating smaller-scaled furnishings. The show's organizers and the participating architects, however, were also intent on creating a new, genuinely working-class *Wohnkultur* distinct from the conventional petit-bourgeois style of the time.[9]

Most of the architects did not merely seek to substitute stark "functionalist" objects for the bulky, upholstered, and dark pieces still popular after the war; rather, what they offered was a simplified version of their bourgeois interiors. Frank's design for a living room (fig. 156) stands out in this regard. In place of the integrally designed *Gesamtkunstwerk* ideal of the radical modernists, Frank mixed together sundry inexpensive furnishings, which he assembled piecemeal from different sources. As in his Haus & Garten interiors, he sought to free the furnishings from the walls, and he accented the generally

156. Model room in the exhibition *Wien und die Wiener*, Messepalast, Vienna, 1927. *Moderne Bauformen* 26 (1927).

neutral color scheme with brightly-printed textiles. The individual objects, however, were mostly machine-made or, at least, low-cost examples of handicraft production, not the custom-made items he offered his middle-class customers.

Frank highlighted this same notion of affordability and accessibility in the rooms and objects he designed in several subsequent exhibitions, including *Das neue Wien* (New Vienna), mounted by the Gesellschafts- und Wirtschaftsmuseum in Berlin in 1929, and *Der gute billige Gegenstand* (The Good Inexpensive Object), held at the Österreichisches Museum für Kunst und Industrie in the winter of 1931–32.[10] He also served as a consultant for the Beratungsstelle für Inneneinrichtung und Wohnungshygiene (Advice Center for Interior Design and Domestic Hygiene) housed in the Karl-Marx-Hof. Founded in 1929 as part of the Österreichischer Verband für Wohnungsreform (Austrian Association for Housing Reform), the Beratungsstelle, known by its acronym BEST, served as both an advice office and showroom, advising tenants of the municipal housing projects on how best to furnish their apartments.[11]

But Frank's commitment to the Socialist cause of improving the proletarian *Wohnkultur* was most forcefully expressed in the series of mass housing projects he conceived for the Vienna municipality in the late 1920s and early 1930s. At a time when most of Europe's leading modernists were preoccupied with the practical and technical problems of constructing proletarian housing, Frank continued to raise his voice for an architecture that balanced the functional and pragmatic elements of building with formal variety and social and psychological issues. The financial and political barriers to realizing his ideals, however, were formidable, and in the end, Frank's housing blocks departed only in subtle ways from the modernist mainstream. But contained within those fine differences was an immanent critique of both standard housing practices and contemporary design principles.

THE APARTMENT BLOCK IN SEBASTIAN-KELCH-GASSE Despite his advocacy of the *Siedlung* idea and his vociferous attack on the "peoples' palaces" in 1926, in the later 1920s Frank continued to seek commissions from the municipal building authorities for multistoried housing blocks. The financial incentive—although the fees generated from public works were modest—was undoubtedly one reason. Frank's former assistant Hans Blumenfeld, who worked in his office at the end of the decade, recalled that even with the income generated by Haus & Garten Frank and Wlach were barely able to keep their architecture firm afloat.[12] But Frank's continued engagement with the Socialist building program—his philosophical differences notwithstanding—also issued from a fervent belief in the importance of its mission: the need to "raise the living standard" and to provide "light, air, space, sun, etc.," as he described it.[13]

157. Municipal housing project,
Sebastian-Kelch-Gasse, Vienna,
1928–29. *Moderne Bauformen* 29
(1930).

158. Municipal housing project,
Sebastian-Kelch-Gasse, Vienna,
1928–29. *Moderne Bauformen* 29
(1930).

In 1927, two years after the completion of the Winarsky-Hof and Wiedenhofer-Hof housing projects, the municipal building office awarded Frank a contract to design a small apartment block in the Sebastian-Kelch-Gasse in the city's fourteenth district. The building (figs. 157, 158), completed the following year, reproduced many of the features of his earlier housing blocks: unadorned masonry walls, simple windows cut into the façade and framed with white bands, vertical bands of glazing for the staircases, small cantilevered balconies, and corner loggias. Frank's design, however, diverged from his first apartment houses in a number of ways, particularly in terms of its plan and in the composition of its façades.

The most arresting aspect of the design, the building's unusual asymmetrical footprint (fig. 159), was a response to the site, an awkward trapezoidal-shaped lot bounded on three sides by streets and on the fourth by an existing structure. Rather than building along the outer periphery and leaving a small courtyard in the center, as was the conventional practice in Vienna, Frank opted for an open, H-shaped plan, with the two sides flaring out parallel to the Drechslergasse and Cervantesgasse to form a small front courtyard as well as a smaller rear lightwell. This arrangement served effectively to break up the mass of the building while at the same time providing most of the fifty-three apartments with good cross-ventilation. The resulting complex interaction of forms imparted a certain animated quality, which Frank enhanced through the deliberate juxtaposition of vertical and horizontal elements on the façade. By engendering a careful balance through an irregular distribution of openings and walls, Frank, as he related to Blumenfeld, believed that he could also achieve a sense of uniformity.[14] As he had for the Wiedenhofer-Hof, Frank also used color to further enliven the building's appearance; but rather than a

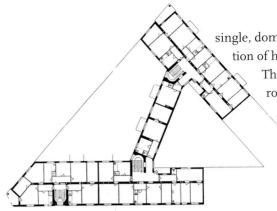

single, dominant color, he divided the structure into sections, applying a selection of hues—white, gray, and a vibrant gold—to the various parts.[15]

The layout of the individual apartments, which ranged from small, one-room flats for single persons to larger, three-room units intended for families, was similar to the other Viennese communal housing blocks, though Frank took particular care to ensure that the majority of the apartments would receive direct sunlight on at least one side.[16] In other respects, however, the building was a departure from the norm. In spite of the formal central entry court, it lacked the monumentality that was a conspicuous feature of the great majority of the municipal blocks. Indeed, Frank's lively handling of the plan and façade lent the building a lightness that contrasted sharply with the fortress-like appearance of many of the larger Socialist housing projects. This feeling of lightness was in part an outcome of his striving to fashion a more amiable living environment; but it was also a direct reply to the changes in the city housing program. Frank, as he told Blumenfeld, was convinced that the decision on the part of the Socialist leadership to scale back the *Siedlungen* in favor of large five-story blocks was the result of "political and military" considerations. In the event of an attack on the city by conservative forces from the provinces, these "workers' fortresses"—many positioned along the main rail lines—would provide stout defensive positions.[17] The openness of the Sebastian-Kelch-Gasse project revealed itself thus also as an ideological statement, a calculated rebuttal to the "militant" housing policy of the city authorities.

THE APARTMENT PROJECT ON THE SITE OF THE OLD BÜRGERVERSORGUNGSHAUS

Frank also investigated other forms for the urban apartment house in this period. His design for a city-sponsored competition for a new residential block on the site of the former Social Security Building (Bürgerversorgungshaus) in the city's ninth district in 1928 (fig. 160) exhibited a radically different and, it must be said, more expressly modern character. Although hints of Frank's personal inflections—such as the small oculus window at the center or complex pattern of fenestration—were still evident, the design as a whole came closer to approximating the standard image of the functionalist idiom than any other of Frank's designs of the 1920s. In contrast to his earlier communal dwellings, in which the windows and doors were set into the wall, the façade of the proposed nine-story building appears almost flat, its taut skin interrupted

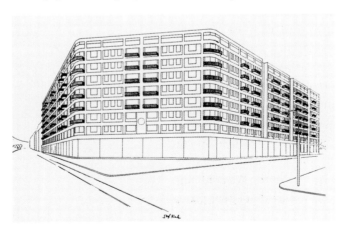

only by small cantilevered balconies. The *sachlich* appearance of the building is further reinforced by its flat roof and by its wide expanses of glass at the street level (the program called for spaces for a bank, post office, branch library, municipal clinic, and an exhibition space for the city gas and electrical utility). What reflected the building's modernist character most vividly, however, was its construction. Unlike Frank's earlier housing projects for the city, which relied on traditional load-bearing masonry walls, the Bürgerversorgungshaus project was intended to have a reinforced concrete frame. The piers and cross-members form a regular grid into which the various window units would be placed.

In siting the building, Frank conformed to local convention. Employing a traditional closed-block system of planning, he set the building at the edge of the two main streets, the Währingerstraße and Spitalgasse, that framed the site (fig. 161).[18] The remainder of the structure followed the perimeter of the available land, leaving an ample courtyard in the center into which he introduced a roughly L-shaped extension.[19] Frank also prepared a second variant of the plan (fig. 162), with the façade facing the Währingerstraße extending in a diagonal line to the Spitalgasse, leaving only a small triangular-shaped plaza on the west side. The effect in either case diverged markedly from the proposals of the other architects who took part in the competition (among them, Rudolf Frass, Rudolf Perco, and Otto Prutscher, as well as the firms of Theiss and Jaksch, and Schmid and Aichinger), all of whom produced monumental blocks reminiscent of the municipal

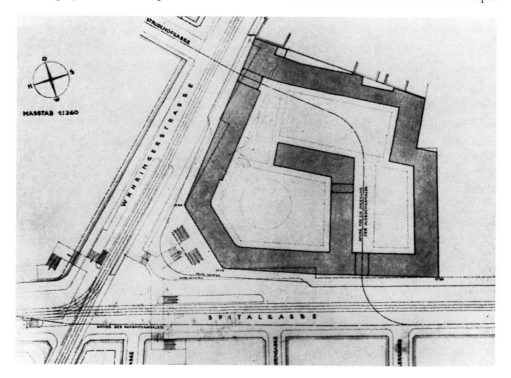

161. Project for an apartment building on the site of the old Bürgerversorgungshauses; site plan 1:3000. *Wasmuths Monatshefte für Baukunst* 13 (1929).

162. Project for an apartment
building on the site of the old
Bürgerversorgungshauses; variant
design. *Wasmuths Monatshefte für
Baukunst* 13 (1929).

housing projects. Frank's design elicited much praise, especially in the German press, but the proposal failed to win over the jury, and the first prize was awarded to Frass.[20]

COMPETITION DESIGN FOR THE REICHSFORSCHUNGSSIED-LUNG IN BERLIN Even more in keeping with the image of functionalism at the end of the decade—at least superficially—was a design Frank submitted to a competition for a housing project in the Berlin suburb of Haselhorst in 1929. The competition was sponsored by the Heimag Building Cooperative, which had acquired 360,000 square meters of open land from the state on the condition that it would construct a "research housing estate" with 3,000 residential units. The main focus of the research was to investigate new building methods, but because of the precise specifications for the competition (including a provision that the apartment blocks be arranged in long, straight rows of blocks—or *Zeilenbau*—with a north-south axis) most of the entries were quite similar. Frank, however, placed his rows on an east-west axis (fig. 163), deviating not only from the rules, but also defying the almost universally held belief at the time that apartment buildings should receive direct natural light on at least two sides. As Frank explained to Blumenfeld (who assisted on the project), he was convinced that it was more important that the main living spaces be oriented to the south allowing them to receive the direct winter sun. In the summer, when direct sun was less desirable, the rooms could be shaded with overhangs or awnings.[21]

Yet Frank also recognized that there were limits to what the architect could determine. Although by the late 1920s those on the left unanimously advocated continued rationalization and standardization, he remained wary of the search for absolute principles. At the International Housing Conference, held in Berlin in June 1931, he spoke out against imposing universal solutions in residential architecture, arguing that the specific location and practices be taken into account:

The positioning of the windows of living rooms, bedrooms, kitchens, etc., in relation to the compass is always undertaken on the assumption that the rooms will be used for the purposes for which the architect intended them, but experience has shown that in practice this assumption is usually wrong. Nor is it possible for the various countries, due to differences in climate and custom, to set up one common standard for all. It is therefore of primary importance that we should find out to what uses the dwellings are put in various countries. We shall then discover that the question of direction is not by any means so important.[22]

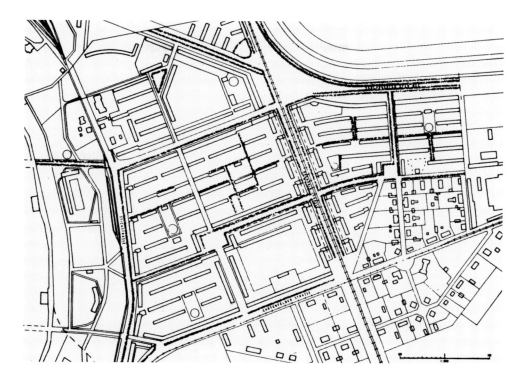

163. Competition design for the
Reichsforschungssiedlung, Berlin-
Haselhorst, 1928–29; site plan.
Author's collection.

Frank's design for the Haselhorst competition departed from the other entries in at least two other respects. While the majority of participants specified large, multistory blocks, Frank's scheme called for two-story row houses, similar in plan and conception to the *Siedlungen* he had designed in the early part of the decade. He also placed some of the rows of houses within the existing grid of the streets, which, in addition to the smaller scale of Frank's design, would have preserved to some extent the suburban character of the area. Several members of the jury, which included Otto Bartning, Ernst May, Fritz Schumacher, and Martin Wagner, preferred Frank's design, but many of the jurors considered it too unorthodox, and the first prize was eventually awarded to Gropius and Stephan Fischer, whose scheme conformed closely to the published program.

THE LAST HOUSING BLOCKS Around 1930, the Vienna city housing office awarded Frank two further commissions for housing blocks. Compared with the Bürgerversorgungshaus project, however, the two buildings represented something of a step backward: although their clean, simple lines set them apart from the mainstream of Viennese communal housing design, both sported traditional saddle roofs and both were of masonry block and stucco construction. There is no evidence that Frank considered a different, more expressly modern and technologically sophisticated design, but it would have made little difference. The realities of the weak Austrian economy and the state of the country's building industry necessitated a more conservative approach, and it is doubtful, even by the early 1930s, that the city authorities would have undertaken a more technically advanced design.

The larger of the two projects, later named the Leopoldine-Glöckel-Hof (fig. 164), was located along the Gürtel, the city's outer beltway, diagonally across from Hubert Gessner's Reumann-Hof, among the most conspicuous examples of the monumental "Baroque" housing projects that Frank had criticized in his 1926 article on the *Volkswohnungspalast*. Unlike the Reumann-Hof, with its central *corps de logis*, flanking wings, and arcuated loggias, the Glöckel-Hof presented a highly simplified, even Spartan, composition. The almost square complex was arranged on a perimeter plan surrounding an immense, park-like interior courtyard. The treatment of the smooth stucco façades on the courtyard side repeated the basic grouping of the Sebastian-Kelch-Gasse, but the street-side elevations were considerably reduced, accented only by a series of vertically aligned balconies with rectilinear grilles. The rhythmical pattern of the windows, balconies, and dormers served to break up the long façades, providing a more varied appearance. Indeed, in spite of the white painted window frames and the conventional pitched roof, the building in the contemporary photographs clearly evokes the image of the *neue Sachlichkeit*.

But here the black and white images do not tell the entire story. As on the Wiedenhofer-Hof and the Sebastian-Kelch-Gasse buildings, Frank employed color to relieve and undermine the long expanses of wall. The façades were partitioned into sections corresponding to the individual stairwells and the stucco painted with different pastel shades—green, blue, yellow, and rose—which promptly earned the building the nickname "Aquarell-Hof," or "watercolor complex."

It was not only the eye-catching color scheme that distinguished the Glöckel-Hof, however. Frank also took special care with the arrangement of the individual units, ensuring that they would receive sufficient natural light and air. A majority of the apartments had at least one room facing the interior courtyard, providing solace from the noise and activity of the busy surrounding streets. This sense of shelter was enhanced through the placement of the stairwells, which on three of the four sides opened only into the interior court (those on the north side opened both to the street and to the court). To meet the varied needs of the building's inhabitants, Frank designed eight basic floor plans, ranging from tiny single rooms of only eighteen square meters to comparatively spacious three-room flats with a total of fifty-three square meters—well beyond the accepted *Existenzminimum*.

With 318 apartments, the Glöckel-Hof was not only the largest of his housing projects, but it was perhaps the most representative of his ideas concerning what could be accomplished within the limitations of the city program. While not achieving the openness and relative privacy of his ear-

164. Leopoldine-Glöckel-Hof, Vienna, 1931–32; view from the southeast. Historisches Museum der Stadt Wien.

lier *Siedlung* designs, it presented a surprisingly livable environment, one greatly enriched by his attention to small details.

By those standards, Frank's last project for the city, a 254-unit apartment house on another major thoroughfare, the Simmeringer Hauptstraße (fig. 165), fell short. Frank had initially proposed at least two different versions for the complex, including a mixed solution (fig. 166) with a closed-block section arrayed along the Simmeringer Hauptstraße and several, angled *Zeilenbau* blocks at the rear of the site. In the second scheme (fig. 167), which was realized, he arranged the building around the perimeter of the site forming a large open

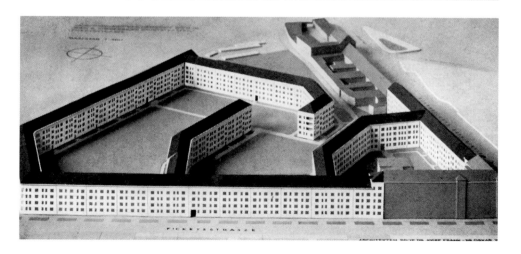

165. (top) Municipal housing project, Simmeringer Hauptstraße, Vienna, 1931–32; view from the east facing the Simmeringer Hauptstraße. Author's collection.

166. (middle) Municipal housing project, Simmeringer Hauptstraße, Vienna, 1931–32; model (whereabouts unknown), first proposed design. *Moderne Bauformen* 29 (1930).

167. (bottom) Municipal housing project, Simmeringer Hauptstraße, Vienna, 1931–32; model (whereabouts unknown), second (realized) design. *Moderne Bauformen* 29 (1930).

space at the center. This courtyard in turn was broken up by several shorter projecting wings angled so as to conceal their full length.[23]

The irregular plan was analogous to Frank's residential layouts, with complex geometries used to foster a sense of visual complexity. This tactic proved partially successful in the interior court, where Frank also employed balconies and open loggias to break up the mass of the building. He was unable, however, to bring the same interest to the façades along the outside perimeter. The banality of the façades is especially evident on the main street-side elevation, which, despite Frank's application of a series of cantilevered three-story bay windows with arched roofs, nonetheless evinces a certain monotony absent in his other housing projects.

THE MODEL ROW HOUSE IN LINZ AND THE PROJECT FOR THE BAHNHOFSVORPLATZ Though Frank's later designs for the Vienna city housing office continued to make use of traditional masonry construction, he had by no means given up his interest in exploring newer building technologies. This was amply demonstrated by the model row house he showed at the *Wohnung und Siedlung* (Dwelling and Settlement) exhibition in Linz in 1929, which took advantage of the most recent prefabrication techniques. The house was based on a system developed by another architect, Alfred Schmid, for the steel house construction firm Gebrüder Böhler & Co. AG in Vienna. Schmid's concept was based on a simple steel frame with modular steel sheets for the walls (fig. 168). To prevent the structure from rusting, the steel plates were screwed to the inside of the structure and thick "Heraklith" rock wool panels were placed over the outside, to which a coat of concrete stucco was applied as a finished surface.[24]

Frank's design was intended as a row house unit, which, like his double house at the Weissenhofsiedlung, could serve as a basic prototype for a large housing settlement. As a result, all of the building's openings and architectural features were confined to the front and rear, although the model house in Linz had a pergola on one side. The interior layout of the two-story structure (fig. 169) resembled his earlier *Siedlung* houses, with a *Wohnküche* on the ground floor, and three small bedrooms and a bath on the upper story. With only forty-one square meters of living area, however, the unit was more compressed than any of the three-room apartments he designed for the Vienna housing authority. To save on construction costs, Frank employed a number of money-saving measures, including the use of stacked plumbing fixtures and standardized windows and doors. While the house's heavy steel members and other materials were comparatively expensive, the labor-saving design made it cheaper than any of the houses exhibited in Linz using traditional block and stucco construction.[25]

Frank's simple and economical solution attracted the attention of the Linz housing authorities, who in 1929 appointed him as a special advisor for housing matters. The fol-

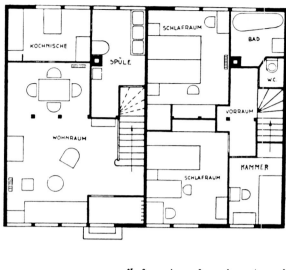

lowing year he was commissioned to design a large housing complex on a site adjacent to the city's main train station. Frank responded with a plan for a five-story U-shaped block with a ten-story tower on one corner (fig. 170). The building, which was never realized, shared many features in common with his Viennese housing blocks of the early 1930s, including the broad white window surrounds and small cantilevered balconies. The project's most noteworthy feature was the construction of the tower block, a concrete frame with brick infill. In most other respects, however, the design was unremarkable. Like Frank's other housing blocks of the period, it showed a development toward a greater structural clarity and simplicity of form. But compared with the visionary skyscrapers of Mies van der Rohe or Le Corbusier, the building is ponderous and ungainly, and, perhaps more damningly, devoid of the softening human touch of Frank's best apartment buildings.

Despite their evident shortcomings, Frank's mass housing projects disclosed his profound desire to forge a more comfortable and life-affirming existence. Yet he recognized, as before, the buildings he was able to realize were at best only a "compromise." Frank had sought to create mass housing that incorporated the best features of his single-family residences; that hope, however, effectively ended with the Semmeringer Hauptstraße and Linz projects. By 1932, the worldwide economic depression and the growing political instability in Austria combined to bring a halt to the city housing program.

Frank would have one last chance to realize his dream of a new mass housing form, a model *Siedlung* in Vienna, developed under the auspices of the Austrian Werkbund, that was planned for the summer of 1932.

168. Model row house at the *Wohnung und Siedlung* exhibition, Linz, 1929; view of the house under construction. *Der Baumeister* 27 (1929).

169. Model row house at the *Wohnung und Siedlung* exhibition, Linz, 1929; plans. *Der Baumeister* 27 (1929).

170. Project for an apartment
house in Linz; model (whereabouts
unknown). Arkitekturmuseet,
Stockholm.

THE VIENNA WERKBUNDSIEDLUNG Despite the mounting threat from the right, Frank focused his attentions on the Austrian Werkbund's plan to mount a large housing exhibition. The exhibit, patterned after the 1927 Weissenhofsiedlung, had originally been timed to coincide with the Werkbund congress in Vienna in the summer of 1930. Many of the architects' plans had been finished as early as 1929, but problems with financing and with the original site had forced its postponement for two years.[26]

Frank was charged with the overall planning and construction of the project. He intended the exhibit, as he wrote, to "show as many architectural solutions as possible to the small one-family house. It is therefore a collection of samples. Every house has been planned to serve as a 'serial house' (row house), or as the ground element for a whole suburban development."[27] As such, it represented one final attempt on Frank's part to respond to the Vienna municipal building program, to demonstrate in concrete terms alternatives to the high-density housing blocks and reawaken interest in the *Siedlung* movement.[28] At the same time, Frank saw in the Vienna Werkbundsiedlung a chance to counter the ideas of the more radical modernists. In drawing up the list of participants, he avoided the leading German and Dutch architects, inviting instead only those architects whom he felt had views more or less in line with his own. None of those who had taken part in the Weissenhofsiedlung, aside from Frank himself, was included. Indeed, the exhibit amounted to a "salon des refusés."[29] Conspicuously absent were most of the best-known members of the avant-garde—Gropius, Le Corbusier, Lissitzky, Mendelsohn, Mies van der Rohe, Oud, Scharoun, and Stam. The only German architect Frank asked to participate was Häring, whose ideas of organic form made him an outsider. The other foreigners invited, Gerrit Rietveld from the Netherlands, and Lurçat and Gabriel Guevrékian from France, had reputations as moderates. All of the remaining participants were Austrians, either older, established figures, like Hoffmann, Strnad, Wlach, and Clemens Holzmeister, or members of the younger, postwar generation of Viennese modernists, such as Karl A. Bieber, Anton Brenner, Haerdtl, Walter Loos, Otto Niedermoser, Schütte-Lihotzky, Plischke, and Hans Vetter.[30] Only two names stood out from the list: Richard Neutra, who had already established a reputation for his authoritative writings and his sleek and technically advanced designs; and Adolf Loos, whom Frank had convinced to take part in spite of his longstanding antipathy toward the Werkbund.[31]

Frank's guiding idea in planning the Werkbundsiedlung was that the most important task was to create a livable environment, not to demonstrate technological progress. If the express purpose of the Stuttgart exhibit had been to explore a new way of building, he intended the Vienna exhibit to show a new way of living. Though most of the architects from abroad, including Rietveld, Häring, and Neutra, would have preferred to use the opportunity to experiment with new building technologies, the city authorities, who were financing the construction, dictated the use of conventional masonry walls for all of the houses, allowing experimentation only with a few cost-saving ideas such as standardized doors and windows.

The differences between the Stuttgart and Vienna *Siedlungen* were also immediately apparent in the houses' interiors. Most of the individual units in Vienna were furnished by local architects or designers. The controlling principle throughout, Frank wrote, "has been that of a complete lack of principle. Everywhere things have been so arranged that not one room should be uniformly furnished. Nowhere the same kind of wood or chintz has been used throughout. Thus it is possible to introduce new things anywhere, to put in new chintzes anywhere, or to hang pictures anywhere."[32] While the interiors of some of the Weissenhofsiedlung houses had featured Breuer's tubular-steel furnishings and Mies's glass tables, most of the houses in Vienna sported the same comfortable modernist idiom that Frank had developed for Haus & Garten in the 1920s. In an effort to further this domestic image, Frank pointedly discouraged the participants from including metal furniture, urging them instead to make use of light, inexpensive wooden pieces.[33]

Frank's plan for the Vienna *Siedlung* was also a departure from the Weissenhofsiedlung. Initially intended as a municipal housing settlement with a mixture of single-family houses and small apartment buildings, it was planned for a large open area on the Triesterstraße on the southern rim of the city. Frank's first site plan (fig. 171) followed the typical *Zeilenbau* arrangement, with the units laid out in rows parallel to the streets. In

171. Preliminary site plan for the
Vienna Werkbundsiedlung, 1930.
Josef Frank, *Die internationale
Werkbundsiedlung Wien 1932*
(Vienna, 1932).

1930, however, the city housing authority decided to finance the project exclusively through the Heimbauhilfe, a municipal fund intended only for single-family houses. Plans to build larger multistory blocks were dropped, and the Werkbund was forced to use another site in the suburb of Lainz, on the western edge of the city.

The new Lainz site proved to be poorly suited for the exhibition. The ground was marshy and sloped steeply in places, necessitating extensive leveling. Even after the land was graded, up to three meters in some areas, most of the houses required cellars, making them significantly more expensive than originally intended. For the new site, Frank completely reworked the plan, this time opting for a more informal arrangement (figs. 172, 173). In contrast to the more rigid ordering of his earlier scheme, the buildings in his final plan were more or less randomly distributed, without any evident underlying order. His intention, as he wrote in the official catalog, was to create the impression of a complex that had "grown up over time" rather than having been planned.[34]

To avoid the monumental effect of the Weissenhofsiedlung, Frank engaged the artist László Gábor, acting secretary of the Austrian Werkbund, to devise a color scheme for the exhibit. After some experimentation, Gábor developed a plan to paint the houses in a range of vibrant pastel shades. The bright colors—yellow, blue, green, pink, and off-white

172. (top) Vienna Werkbundsiedlung, 1932; aerial view. Österreichische Nationalbibliothek, Bildarchiv, Vienna.

173. (bottom) Vienna Werkbundsiedlung, 1932; site plan. Houses 1–5, Hugo Häring; 6–7 Richard Bauer; 8–11, Josef Hoffmann; 12, Josef Frank; 13–14, Oskar Strnad; 15–16, Anton Brenner; 17–18, Karl A. Bieber; 19–20, Walter Loos; 21–22, Eugen Wachberger; 23–24, Clemens Holzmeister; 25–28, André Lurçat; 29–30, Walter Sobotka; 31–32, Oskar Wlach; 33–34, Julius Jirasek; 35–36, Ernst Plischke; 37–38 Josef Wenzel; 39–40, Oswald Haerdtl; 41–42, Ernst Lichtblau; 43–44, Hugo Gorge; 45–46, Jacques Groag; 47, Richard Neutra; 48, Hans Vetter; 49–52, Adolf Loos; 53–56, Gerrit Rietveld; 57–58, Max Fellerer; 60–61, Margarete Schütte–Lihotzky; 63–64, Alfred Grünberger; 65–66, Josef F. Dex; 67–68, Gabriel Guevrékian; 69–70, Helmut Wagner–Freynsheim. Josef Frank, *Die internationale Werkbundsiedlung Wien 1932* (Vienna, 1932).

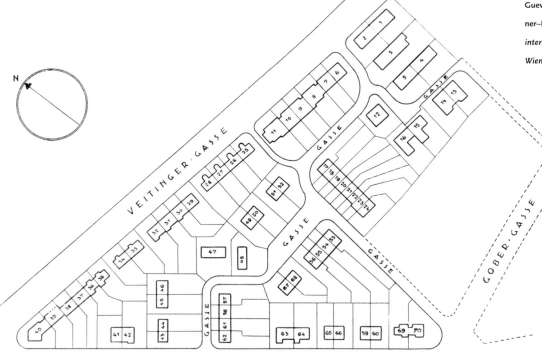

—not only achieved the amiable appearance and sense of delight and novelty that Frank intended, but it also emphasized the modest, villagelike scale of the plan.

The exhibit, which opened on 4 June and ran through 7 August, included seventy houses designed by thirty-one architects, as well as a temporary pavilion designed by Fritz Judtmann and Egon Riss that served as a coffeehouse. Despite the extensive preparations, however, the timing of the show could not have been worse. Unemployment in the country in 1932 reached an unprecedented peak of 470,000, nearly a quarter of the nation's labor force; in some working-class areas in Vienna, nearly one in three was out of work. Nevertheless, nearly 100,000 people toured the exhibit. But for the vast majority, the prospects of ownership remained only a distant dream: while the houses proved to be inexpensive in comparison to privately constructed single-family homes, they remained well out of the reach of most working-class families. The purchasers, as in Stuttgart, came instead almost exclusively from the middle class: white-collar workers, bureaucrats, and teachers. In the end, only fifteen of the units, about a fifth of the total, were sold during and immediately after the exhibit; the city was forced to take over the remainder of the unsold units and rent them out as part of the municipal housing program.

The houses themselves were divided into two groups: attached, or row houses, including those designed by Rietveld, Lurçat, and Hoffmann; and somewhat larger detached or double houses, such as the twin units designed by Strnad. Among the most innovative projects was Loos's double house, which featured a soaring one-and-a-half-story living area. Frank contributed the largest house, a freestanding two-story structure with the upper floor set back to form a large terrace. Viewed from the garden side (fig. 174), it bore a decided resemblance to his double house at the Weissenhofsiedlung, but the plan (fig. 175) diverged in several respects. For one, the two small bedrooms were situated on the ground floor adjacent to the living room. The layout also made no provision for servant's quarters or a separate pantry. Most notable, however, were the changes to the upper floor, which was now given over almost completely to a large family room (*Wohnraum*) that opened out onto the south-facing terrace.

It was not only the distribution of the interior spaces that had changed. If Frank's Weissenhofsiedlung house was attuned to middle-class tastes and requirements, he conceived of the Vienna house as a working-class domicile, but an elevated working class, both culturally and economically. The house was no longer "a compromise" or an interim solution; it was a statement of his vision for the future. Despite its reduced size, it incorporated all of the central elements of his domestic ideal: light, ample living areas, a strong connection between interior and garden, and a physical separation from its neighbors.

The idea of a new proletarian dwelling was also set forth in its interiors (fig. 176), which featured a full array of pieces from Haus & Garten. In his early postwar *Siedlung* houses, Frank had provided an abased version of his bourgeois *Wohnkultur*. The Vienna Werkbundsiedlung house, by contrast, reproduced almost fully the constitutive compo-

174. House 12, Vienna Werkbund-siedlung, 1932; view from the rear garden. Österreichische National-bibliothek, Bildarchiv, Vienna.

KELLER

KOHLE

KELLER

KELLER

W.C.

WASCHKÜCHE

ERDGESCHOSS

KÜCHE

SCHLAFRAUM

VORRAUM

WOHNZIMMER

BAD

KAMMER

SCHLAFRAUM

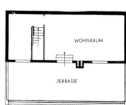

DACHGESCHOSS

WOHNRAUM

TERRASSE

Verbaute Fläche 83 m²
1 Zimmer 7·35 × 3·60 m
2 Zimmer 4·00 × 2·80 ,,
1 Zimmer 6·80 × 3·90 ,,
1 Kammer 2·15 × 2·00 ,,
1 Kammer 3·90 × 2·14 ,,
1 Küche   3·55 × 2·00 ,,
Vorraum, Bad, Waschküche,
Keller, Terrasse

NORDANSICHT

WESTANSICHT

SÜDANSICHT

OSTANSICHT

175. (bottom, left) House 12, Vienna Werkbundsiedlung, 1932; plans and elevations. Josef Frank, *Die interna-tionale Werkbundsiedlung Wien 1932* (Vienna, 1932).

176. (bottom, right) House 12, Vienna Werkbundsiedlung, 1932; living room. Österreichische Na-tionalbibliothek, Bildarchiv, Vienna

nents of his much more costly private villas. While the scale was reduced to accommodate a more modest budget, the promise of the same comfortable lifestyle—only slightly diminished—remained.

Frank elaborated on his concept of a fully developed "serial house" in one of three published projects from the same year that appeared in *Kleine Einfamilienhäuser* (Small single-family houses), a book of model residences edited by Hans Vetter.[35] Two of the three houses were simple attached "cubes," similar to Frank's model row house for the Linz *Wohnung und Siedlung* exhibition. But the third project (fig. 177), a freestanding, split-level dwelling, came perhaps closest to his ideal of the small house with a garden. Not only did its main façade present a distinctive and characteristic image akin to his larger villas, but its plan (fig. 178) echoed their complex spatial ordering. Consistent with the precepts he had outlined in the "The House as Path and Place," the house was organized along a meandering promenade. Although the entire structure, including the second-story atelier (not shown in the plan), had a total area of only seventy-one square meters, it was replete with abrupt turns, changes in level, and shifting vantage points. But, in spite of its small size, its cost remained well beyond the means of Austria's workers. Frank's goal of creating a new proletarian dwelling based on his middle-class villas remained less a model for the present than a representation of future ambition.

177. Project for a house for four persons, c. 1932; perspective. Hans A. Vetter, ed., *Kleine Einfamilienhäuser mit 50 bis 100 Quadratmeter Wohnfläche* (Vienna, 1932).

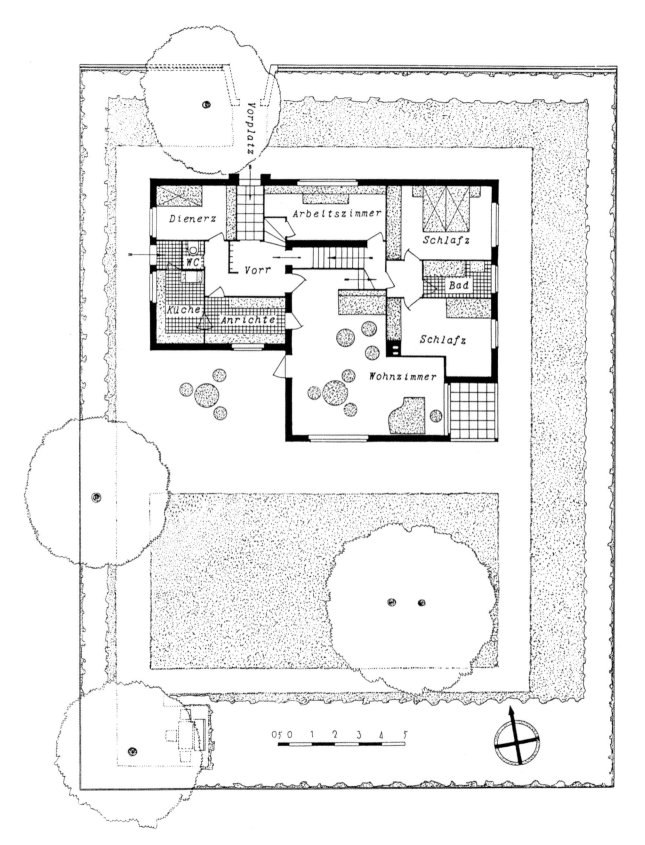

Labels within the plan:

Vorplatz

Dienerz · Arbeitszimmer · Schlafz

WC · Vorr · Bad

Küche · Anrichte · Schlafz

Wohnzimmer

0.50 1 2 3 4 5

178. Project for a house for four persons, c. 1932; ground floor plan. Hans A. Vetter, ed., *Kleine Einfamilienhäuser mit 50 bis 100 Quadratmeter Wohnfläche* (Vienna, 1932).

The same was true of the *Siedlung* as a whole. For many observers, the Vienna Werkbund exhibition symbolized an uneasy compromise between necessity and desire. Most of the critics praised the Austrian Werkbund's attempt to focus on the problem of the small single-family house. The response to the *Siedlung* among the avant-garde, on the other hand, could be at best characterized as unenthusiastic. Frank and the Werkbund both came under attack for not having experimented more with new building technologies[36] and for the houses' comparatively high building cost.[37] A number of observers also found fault with Frank's site plan, which appeared to fly in the face of more rigid "sachlich" and scientific conceptions of ordering. In addition, the exhibition drew fire for its comparatively conservative interpretation of modernist ideas. Wilhelm Lotz, the editor of *Die Form*, was among those critical of its moderate stance. While allowing that the houses "had not been built for building experts or theoreticians," Lotz charged that the settlement was "unproblematic," and "traditional," though, he added grudgingly, it was so "in the best sense."[38]

Several commentators, including Guido Harbers, the editor of *Der Baumeister*, offered a more positive assessment, praising the comfortable interiors of the houses and the "human scale" of the complex.[39] The most thoughtful and incisive commentary, however, came from Häring, who delivered the keynote address at the twentieth annual meeting of the Austrian Werkbund, held while the exhibition was in progress.[40] "Strictly speaking," Häring wrote in a review that appeared a few months later in *Die Form*,

the Viennese are not modern, because they still produce ornament. They emphasize livability [Wohnlichkeit] and keep their distance from Sachlichkeit. *They do not speak about functionalism, they are not searching for the expression of the time, they do not disdainfully turn away when they encounter a historical form. Insofar as the absence of ornament [Ornamentlosigkeit] is a sign of the modern movement, the Viennese are not modern (but then are the painted marble walls of Corbusier not ornament, and is Corbusier not modern?), at least not in terms of the interiors of their houses.*[41]

Despite their tendency to make continued use of ornament, Häring argued that Frank, Wlach, Strnad, and some of the other Austrians had achieved something that had eluded even the most advanced architects in Germany: the creation of an interior that was unencumbered by traditional notions of formal, architectonic style.[42] By rejecting the very idea of style itself, Frank and the other Viennese had come to a new understanding of design. Whether or not the Austrians continued occasionally to employ individual pieces that bore the marks of the past was unimportant, as long as the sense of the "new" remained dominant. In fact, Häring contended, the occasional use of historical objects offered an advantage, for they engendered a feeling for fine quality that was conspicuously lacking in much of modern production.[43]

In spite of the generally critical reaction, the Vienna Werkbundsiedlung marked the high point in Frank's efforts to reinvigorate the Austrian Werkbund. In the face of the ever-worsening economic situation, he had succeeded in mounting a major exhibition that had presented in clear and concrete form his own concept of the modern. In terms of his ambition to influence trends either locally or internationally, however, the Vienna Werkbundsiedlung must be counted as a failure. Frank's more limited objective, that the exhibit would be a model for future *Siedlung* developments, never materialized. The comparatively high cost of the houses and the growing severity of the depression combined to hinder any new experiments with city-funded projects. By the time of the Werkbund exhibit, the *Siedlung* movement had nearly expired, and the Social Democratic administration, which had organized and financed the housing program, would survive only another year and a half. The Vienna Werkbundsiedlung also failed to exert any real influence on the wider modern movement. At the end of July 1932, while the exhibit was still in progress, the Nazi party won a stunning victory in national elections in Germany, outpolling the second-place Social Democrats by a nearly two-to-one margin. The leading German modernists, whose attention Frank had most wanted to engage, were now more concerned with their immediate survival than with specific architectural issues.

THE SPLIT WITHIN THE AUSTRIAN WERKBUND By the early autumn of 1932, Frank, too, found himself under attack at home. In the wake of the exhibition, as he wrote in a letter to Häring, the country's traditional artisans had "organized protests [against the Werkbundsiedlung]—the most recent attended by 2,000 people—in which it is sought—with the aid of *völkischer* arguments—to save handicraft [*Handwerk*]." The voices of dissent could be heard not only in the ranks of the conservative craftsmen; "also in the Werkbund itself," he added, "the opposition is becoming more spirited."[44]

Even before the exhibition had opened there had been signs of mounting tension between Frank and Hoffmann, and between the members of their respective circles. There were numerous reasons for the discord, ideological, as well as personal, political, and economic.[45] Frank and Hoffmann had worked together closely since the resurgence of the Werkbund in the late 1920s, and for years they had been willing to overlook obvious differences in their views. By 1932, however, the deteriorating conditions both in Austria and in the Werkbund itself had made it impossible to ignore the widening gap between them.

Frank, writing many years later, pointed to economic problems as the main cause for the split: "Around this time the only goal Hoffmann and his group had was to keep the Wiener Werkstätte alive, but this was impossible since this luxury was so entirely inappropriate for these impoverished conditions."[46] While Frank's Haus & Garten had been more or less in direct competition with the Wiener Werkstätte, the more immediate source of friction between the two men sprang from deep-seated ideological differences. Although Frank, like Hoffmann, had been unwilling to abandon craft production for machine-manufacturing entirely, he was much more firmly committed to the goal of mass production.[47] Hoffmann, moreover, proved reluctant to accept the changing realities. At a time when architecture and art were striving for ever greater simplicity and abstraction, Hoffmann's continued interest in folk art and traditional ornament fell more and more out of step with "internationalists" like Frank.[48]

Also fuelling the conflict were disagreements about the running of the Werkbund. Shortly after the housing exhibit opened, Hoffmann wrote to Frank accusing him of not carrying out his wishes concerning the organization of the *Siedlung* and of making critical remarks behind his back. Frank responded in a letter to Hoffmann, maintaining that he had never intended to cause a quarrel and vowing that he would take steps to ensure that such misunderstandings would be avoided in the future.[49]

Frank's reassurances, however, did little to stem the increasing tensions between the two men. The matter finally came to a head in early 1933 at a board meeting of the Austrian Werkbund, during which Frank, in an extended monologue, characterized Hoffmann's work as "outdated" and "provincial."[50] The acutely sensitive Hoffmann, who had recently experienced the trauma of the liquidation of his beloved Wiener Werkstätte, regarded the criticism as a personal insult. Adding further fuel to the controversy, Hoffmann accused Frank of maneuvering to ensure that Strnad, and not Hoffmann, would be entrusted with the design of the Austrian exhibit at the 1933 Milan *Triennale*.[51]

Hoffmann responded to Frank's remarks in a letter that he sent to his friend Max Welz, who in turn duplicated it and sent it to the Werkbund membership, along with a cover letter from Hoffmann.[52] In the letter, Hoffmann defended himself, maintaining that what mattered to him above all "were not names or profit or other advantages but only [creating] opportunities for the undisturbed unfolding of those remarkable talents who originated or settled in our homeland." Though not referring to Frank directly, he alluded to "sophistries and malicious remarks . . . about untimeliness or unsalability or lack of usefulness which, no matter how brilliant, [were] always the achievement of a transient, feeble age."[53]

On the surface, Hoffmann seemed to confine his remarks to the state of contemporary design. Yet there are clues in the text that reveal the presence of the political divisions that were slowly tearing the Viennese art world apart. In several passages, Hoffmann wrote of a "feeling for the homeland" (*Heimatgefühl*) and of what "is tied to the soil [*Bodenständig*]," phrases that all too plainly betrayed his growing allegiance to German nationalism:

Everyone who possesses an outspoken feeling for his homeland will be able, if talent exists, to create something worthy of note, something original. The German-Austrian not only possesses a

charming, finely harmonious character, but he also has an understanding for creative volition.
He has to fashion work in which one can sense his homeland and the experience of the period.[54]

Also unmistakable in the rift was the rising tide of anti-Semitism. Protesting the
"Semitization" (*Verjudung*) of the Werkbund, a number of right-wing members resigned
in 1933. The first prominent defector was the president, Hermann Neubacher, at the time
a secret member of the illegal Nazi party and later first mayor of Vienna after the Anschluss, who stepped down, claiming to be "occupationally overburdened."[55] In the following weeks, Hoffmann and his assistant Haerdtl also officially left the Werkbund.

The bitter tenor of the split is vividly demonstrated by remarks Clemens Holzmeister (who, like Behrens, had sided with the "Gruppe Hoffmann") made at a meeting of the
governing board in February 1933. With Frank, Strnad, and Neurath all absent,
Holzmeister took the opportunity to launch a vicious assault on Frank: "If one has not
had the opportunity to achieve anything great, as in the case of Frank, one should not attack men such as Behrens and Hoffmann who have. . . . It seems to me," Holzmeister
went on, "that Frank's position as a creative artist was dealt a decisive blow by the Werkbundsiedlung. . . . The whole concept is such a failure, it is a failure, first and foremost,
in economic terms, it is a failure in terms of what it showed about the technical aspects
of housing construction, it is a failure with regard to the dwelling types it showed, [and]
it is a failure in terms of its site plan."[56]

In a desperate attempt to resolve the differences between the two groups, Strnad,
who had assumed the leadership of the Werkbund in the wake of Neubacher's resignation, called an extraordinary plenary meeting for late June. During the weeks prior to the
meeting, the right-wing members of the "Gruppe Hoffmann" circulated a broadside calling for the election of a new leadership by secret ballot.[57] Strnad countered with a circular pleading for members to keep an open mind.[58] At the meeting, held on 20 June,
some of the moderates interceded, offering a motion to maintain the organization's old
leadership. The measure passed by a margin of 173 to 101.[59] But it was not enough to prevent other right-wing members from walking out.

In the wake of the meeting, Frank, in a last-ditch effort to keep the organization
afloat, extended invitations to several well-known cultural figures, including Oskar
Kokoschka and the composer Ernst Krenek, to join.[60] The move, however, only post-
poned the inevitable. By the end of 1933, the Werkbund had broken into two factions,
one, the "Old Werkbund," almost exclusively Socialist and Jewish and centered around
Frank and Strnad, and a conservative and Roman Catholic "New Werkbund," led by Hoffmann and Holzmeister.[61]

Frank harbored few illusions about what the political convulsions meant. Unlike
many liberal, educated Viennese Jews of the professional classes who simply could not
imagine that the Nazis could seize power in Austria, he had long warned of the impend-

ing disaster. In 1930, even before Hitler's takeover in Germany, he had predicted that the rising tide of Fascism would not be checked: in Austria "we are surrounded by reactionary states," he wrote to Meyer, and "those that are not will follow shortly."[62]

In late 1932, Frank accepted an offer from Estrid Ericson, owner of the interiors firm Svenskt Tenn in Stockholm, to redesign its sales outlet, and by early January 1933 he was in Sweden. Initially, as he wrote to Sobotka, he intended to remain there only "temporarily."[63] But the tide of events over the next year and a half would force him to change his mind. In February 1934, right-wing paramilitary forces and regular troops of the Austrian army attacked the Socialists' strongholds in Vienna, toppling the city government. In the aftermath of the brief civil war, mass arrests of leftists took place and several Socialist leaders were summarily executed; the Social Democratic and Communist parties were outlawed and their property confiscated; and the Austro-Fascists seized control of the Vienna city government. The free trade unions and all Socialist professional and educational societies, cooperatives, and social and welfare organizations were dissolved. Within the space of a few weeks Red Vienna ceased to exist.

After the events of mid-February, numerous organizations, following the lead of the right-wing groups in Germany, began to "purify" their memberships, ousting Jews and anyone suspected of leftist views. On 24 February, the "New Werkbund," now officially renamed the Neuer Werkbund Österreichs, elected its first officers. Holzmeister became the first president, Hoffmann and Behrens the vice-presidents. All Jews and politically leftist members were expelled. A brief statement published in the journal *Das Profil,* which now described itself as the official publication of the "New Werkbund," announced that the organization would henceforth be "the cultural conscience of Austria."[64]

Frank almost immediately came under attack from the journal for critical remarks he allegedly made concerning an exhibit of Austrian arts and crafts, organized by Holzmeister, which opened in London in April 1934.[65] In what was to become an all-too-familiar tactic of those years, the anonymous piece called into question Frank's patriotism, implying none too subtly that his remarks were intended to harm native Austrian craftsmen and designers:

An article by Josef Frank in an English architectural journal makes disparaging remarks concerning the New Austrian Werkbund's works representing the Austrian arts and crafts industries. Unfortunately this article appeared at the same time as an Austrian exhibition in London opened, which was put on to assist our native craftsmen. We only want to mention an English saying, which goes, "Right or wrong, my country."[66]

Frank continued his efforts to support the cause of the "Old Werkbund" for the next several years. By the spring of 1934, however, he had taken up a permanent position as chief designer for Svenskt Tenn, an association that would last for the next three decades.

Although in many respects he remained spiritually tied to Austria and made occasional trips back to Vienna in the years before the German annexation of the country in 1938, Frank's break with his homeland was complete.

SWEDISH MODERN

SWEDISH MODERN Frank's move to Sweden in 1933 signaled a shift in both his architecture and other design work. Though there were tantalizing hints of a new architectural direction in his unrealized design for the M. S. House in Los Angeles at the beginning of the decade, by the mid-1930s Frank would come to abandon strict orthogonal planning in favor of a new, more freely conceived architectonic language. At the same time, Frank's interior and furniture designs, most of them carried out for Svenskt Tenn, became increasingly eclectic, registering his growing love of diversity and originality. In both instances, he anticipated important changes in coming years—the rise of Swedish Modern and new directions in furniture design in the 1950s and, perhaps even more important, the mounting search for alternative forms of modernism.

ESTRID ERICSON AND SVENSKT TENN Frank's decision to seek permanent exile in Sweden was prompted by an offer from Estrid Ericson to work as chief designer for Svenskt Tenn. Imaginative, talented, ambitious, and fiercely determined, Ericson (fig. 179) had managed in the course of a few years to build Svenskt Tenn into one of the foremost design centers in Scandinavia.

179. Estrid Ericson, early 1920s.
Svenskt Tenn Collection, Estrid
Ericson Archive, Stockholm.

Born in 1894 in Öregrund, on the eastern coast of Sweden, Ericson had attended the National College of Arts and Design (Tekniska skolan) in Stockholm, where she earned an art teacher's certificate. Upon graduation in 1918, she taught for a single semester in her hometown of Hjo. But she was dissatisfied with teaching and moved back to Stockholm, where in the early 1920s she worked for the crafts organization Svensk Hemslöjd and the interior design firm Wikman och Wiklund. During her tenure at Wikman och Wiklund, Ericson collaborated with the designer Nils Fougstedt, who aroused her interest in pewter craftsmanship, and in 1924, with a small inheritance from her father, she opened her own pewter workshop.[1]

In its early years, Svenskt Tenn specialized exclusively in pewterware and decorative articles—hence the company's name, which means Swedish pewter. The company quickly developed an international reputation, taking part in the 1925 Paris *Exposition Internationale des Arts Décoratifs et Industriels Modernes*, as well as in exhibitions of Swedish decorative arts in England and the United States.[2]

Hoping to broaden the range of articles Svenskt Tenn offered, Ericson wrote to Frank in 1932 and asked him to send her some designs for furniture.[3] He responded with sketches for several pieces, including a teacart (fig. 180). Their contact remained limited until the following year, however, when she asked Frank to redesign the firm's showrooms.

Frank's arrival in Stockholm came at a time of abrupt transition in the visual arts in Sweden. Despite the country's proximity to Germany, the Swedes had been slow to adopt the new ideology of functionalism. Although the *Jugendstil* had exerted a potent influence after the turn of the century, during the 1920s neoclassicism and a popular folk art revival, later dubbed "national romanticism," dominated the design scene.[4] The impact of both currents was clearly recorded in the early products of Svenskt Tenn, which drew inspiration from both the old pewter of the seventeenth and eighteenth centuries and from the early-twentieth-century classical revival. By the early 1930s, however, functionalism began to assert itself throughout Scandinavia. In Finland, Alvar Aalto developed his own highly individual interpretation of modern architecture based on native building traditions; in Denmark, Kaare Klint won acclaim for his innovative designs that combined simplicity and utility with high standards of craftsmanship; and in Norway, Alf Sture and others created softened, anatomically designed furniture, presaging the biomorphic forms of the 1950s.[5]

However, it was in Sweden, which had the strongest cultural and intellectual ties to Germany, that the trend toward the new functionalist aesthetic was most pronounced.[6] In 1930, the Svenska Slöjdföreningen (Swedish Design Society), which was modeled on the German Werkbund, mounted the first large exhibition of modern architecture and decorative arts in Scandinavia. The exhibit, held in Stockholm during the spring and summer, was planned and overseen by Gunnar Asplund, himself a recent convert from

neoclassicism. Asplund's striking glass and metal pavilions and sign tower announced a dramatic move away
from the region's traditional heavy brick and masonry
construction toward a new architecture of lightness and
spatial clarity.[7] Equally important, the Stockholm exhibit
inaugurated a new attitude toward domestic design in
Scandinavia. Although, like contemporary housing exhibits in Germany, it explored the issues of minimal
space requirements and standardization, the emphasis
was on livability. The dwelling spaces were cheerful and
airy, and the furnishings bold, with basic forms, minimal decoration, and bright, clear colors.[8]

Inspired by the success of the exhibition and by the
new message of *funkis,* as functionalism became known
in Sweden, Ericson opened a furniture and carpet department in the basement of Svenskt Tenn in the fall of
1930.[9] In addition to mass-produced sofas, chairs, and tables from established manufacturers, such as Bodafors
and Gemla, the shop's new furnishings department offered a line of modern furniture specially designed by
Uno Åhrén and the young artist Björn Trägårdh.[10]

An exhibition of Svenskt Tenn's new designs at the
Galleri Modern in September 1931 drew praise from
critic Gotthard Johansson, one of the leading advocates
of functionalism in Sweden, who lauded the "pure
lines" and "modern austerity" of the pieces.[11] Another observer, Gustav Munthe, wrote of
the exhibit that it was "an event that . . . may transform the image of contemporary
Swedish furniture design."[12]

By the early 1930s Ericson's own conversion to functionalism was seemingly complete. In an interview in 1932, she summed up her new design philosophy: "Everything
in the room must be sober and elegant. I always insist on neutral colors where home furnishings are concerned. The room must make a calm and sensible impression; there
should be no exaggerations of color."[13] The furnishings Ericson showed at the Swedish
Society of Industrial Design's homes exhibition in Ålsten in the spring of 1933 (fig. 181)
were characteristic of Svenskt Tenn's style at the time. "Puritanically sober and pragmat-
ically modern," as Johansson described them: "The color scheme is Spartan, with subdued shades of white, dove-gray, moss-green, and earth-brown. The rectilinear furniture
surfaces smooth to the point of anonymity, unstained or plain black. The wife's bedroom
is a symphony in white."[14]

180. (top) Teacart (Svenskt Tenn
model no. 470), birch and beige
linoleum, designed c. 1932.
Courtesy Bukowski Auktioner AB,
Stockholm.

181. (bottom) Estrid Ericson and
Björn Trägårdh, Wife's bedroom,
Swedish Society of Industrial
Design exhibition, Ålsten, Sweden,
1933. Svenskt Tenn Collection,
Stockholm.

FRANK AND THE RISE OF SWEDISH MODERN Frank's arrival in 1933 ushered in a new era for Svenskt Tenn, bringing with it a changing of the firm's design guard. Åhrén, whose crisp geometric designs had defined Svenskt Tenn's aesthetic direction immediately following the Stockholm exhibition, had departed after 1931 to pursue his own projects; and Trägårdh, who had been Ericson's closest associate in the wake of Åhrén's departure, left the firm in 1934 to begin a new life in France as a painter.[15] Frank's impact was almost immediately apparent: within a few months he was able to put his own stamp on the firm's products, substituting his special brand of modernism—vibrant, comfortable, and eclectic—in place of Åhrén and Trägårdh's sober, denuded, functional style.

In spite of her recent vociferous affirmations of the functionalist philosophy, Ericson was quickly won over to Frank's side, and the two soon developed a remarkably close working relationship. Ericson, much as Wlach had done at Haus & Garten, saw to the running of the business, leaving Frank free to pursue his design work. But she also contributed her own ideas, especially in the composition of the interior ensembles. While Frank designed the interior objects Ericson arranged them, transforming the pieces into a finished interior decor.[16]

Frank and Ericson's first collaborative effort came in September 1934, when they exhibited a suite of four model rooms at the Stockholm gallery, Liljevalchs Konsthall.[17] The high point of the show was the striking "Living Room I" (fig. 182), which featured a floral cretonne-covered sofa and matching easy chair. The overall appearance of the room evoked Frank's designs for Haus & Garten. Its proportions, however, were more ample, and its lines, simplified. In place of the polished birch and metal that Åhrén and Trägårdh had favored, Frank introduced mahogany and teak, both soon to become mainstays of the Scandinavian furniture industry. He also employed a broad assortment of exotic materials, including travertine, green marble, and leopard and zebra skin, providing a stunning counterpoint to the earlier Svenskt Tenn designs.

The Liljevalchs exhibit coincided with the opening of Svenskt Tenn's enlarged furniture showrooms on the second floor of its new store on the Strandvägen. The display comprised a model living room, a dining room, and a bedroom, all with pieces Frank had designed since his arrival.[18]

The bedroom (fig. 183), virtually all white, was a successor to the "symphony in white" that Ericson had shown at the Ålsten exhibit in 1933.[19] But although the two rooms bore a superficial resemblance, there were also trenchant differences that went to the heart of the new design style Frank had introduced. The Ålsten bedroom was an exercise in restraint, its crisp lines and sparse appearance a statement of reductive elegance. The Frank white bedroom, by contrast, with its gradations of texture, showed his distinctive imprint, his love of complexity and disjuncture. The space was filled with diverse materials, forms, and ideas: a bed of pale mahogany and cane was paired with a

182. Living room I, Svenskt Tenn
exhibition, Liljevalchs Konsthall,
Stockholm, 1934. Svenskt Tenn
Collection, Estrid Ericson Archive,
Stockholm.

183. Bedroom, Svenskt Tenn
showrooms, Stockholm, 1934.
Svenskt Tenn Collection, Josef
Frank Archive, Stockholm.

plush "polar bear" chair and footstool; a zebra skin lay alongside a long-pile, natural-white rya rug.[20]

Together, the Liljevalchs show and the new furniture display at the Strandvägen shop caused an immediate stir in Swedish design circles and sent ripples throughout Scandinavia.[21] Frank and Ericson's melding of seemingly disparate ideas and their relaxed attitude toward modernism as a whole seemed for many to provide a substitute for the harsh modernism of the German designers.

In an article that appeared at the same time in the Swedish design review *Form,* Frank declared that "the home must not be a mere efficient machine. It must offer comfort, rest, and coziness (soothing to the eye, restful to the soul). . . . [There are] no puritan principles in good interior decoration."[22] Scandinavia, and Sweden in particular, proved to be especially receptive to this message. From the beginning, the Scandinavians had embraced a less dogmatic view of modernism than the German avant-garde. While functionalism had a deep and lasting effect in the region, unlike in Germany, it was ultimately more important in providing a set of general attitudes than in shaping a new universal style.[23] Frank's call for a humane approach, which placed "man, rather than the machine, [at] the symbolic center,"[24] proved in the end appealing to the majority of designers there.

While Frank was no doubt influenced by his contact with the Swedish design world—his color palette, for example, became brighter as a response to Swedish domestic traditions—he had already developed most of the basic forms and ideas in Vienna in the 1920s. The printed textile patterns, such as "Aralia," "Mirakel," and "Primavera," which Frank had designed for Haus & Garten, became mainstays of Svenskt Tenn's product line, and many of the furnishings he introduced in Sweden in the 1930s were based more or less directly on his earlier Viennese works. Frank's sitting corner for the A. W. House (fig. 184), one of the last works he produced before leaving Austria, already exhibited the clean lines and softened shapes that became the hallmarks of Scandinavian modern design.

Yet, ironically, while Frank's works were widely influential and accounted in no small measure for the specific flavor and substance of the aesthetic climate in Scandinavia from the mid-1930s, he remained outside the Swedish design mainstream. Frank's isolation was partly a result of his status as a Jewish exile in a country that at the time was not fully open to outsiders. But it was not only Frank's standing as a foreigner that contributed to his exclusion: his beliefs also ran counter to the nationalistic tenor of the Swedish craft ethos, which remained a powerful current well into the 1950s. Though Frank, like many of the native Swedish designers, sought inspiration in folk culture, he did so as a consequence of a generalized program of eclecticism, not as an attempt to return to specific indigenous folks roots—and Frank's recent experience in Austria of a fervent nationalism did little to make him more receptive to such efforts. Instead, he continued to draw from widely divergent sources, reworking them in his own distinctive manner.

Nonetheless, Frank's oeuvre in the 1930s bore unmistakable parallels with the works of figures such as Carl Malmsten and Gustaf Axel Berg. This was, in part, a consequence of their shared borrowing from the same historical models—folk culture and neoclassicism—which had influenced the course of the decorative arts in Central and Northern Europe from the seventeenth century onward.[25] But the resemblance was only superficial. Frank never belonged to either of the two principal directions of Swedish design in the 1930s—the traditionalists, who advocated a more or less direct return to past forms, or the functionalists who were intent on forging new shapes based on practical requirements. He pursued his own path, shunning any direct allusion to Swedish nationalism while never wholly subscribing to the modernist program of standardization and mechanization.

Despite his isolation, Frank's designs in the mid-1930s underwent subtle changes, in large part due to the influence of Ericson. A small writing space that he and Ericson designed for the Svenskt Tenn's showrooms in the mid-1930s (fig. 185) encapsulates the new, refined synthesis they developed. The desk, chairs, and bookshelves, all the work of Frank, displayed the understated look that he had

begun to explore in his last years in Vienna. To this, Ericson supplied the finishing touches: a pewter lion designed by Anna Petrus, an elephant fabric inspired by a pattern from the Belgian Congo, a woven rug, flowering plants, and a large wall map of the world—all accessories available for purchase in the shop.[26] Such additions served not only to domesticate Frank's works but also to personalize them. The entire ensemble also suggested avenues for making a new type of interior—one that was both pleasant and popular; the appeal and success of Svenskt Tenn rested precisely in Frank and Ericson's facility for fostering an acceptable face for modern design. Many of Frank's designs of the

184. (top) Sitting corner, A. W. House, Vienna, c. 1933. *Innen-Dekoration* 45 (1934).

185. (bottom) Writing corner, Svenskt Tenn, c. 1935. Svenskt Tenn Collection, Josef Frank Archive, Stockholm.

186. Armchair for Svenskt Tenn.
Mahogany and black leather,
mid-1930s. Courtesy Bukowski
Auktioner AB, Stockholm.

1930s and early 1940s, whether based explicitly on historical models, like the leather-covered Egyptian "Tutankhamen" stool (plate 14), or essentially new, like his mahogany and leather armchair (fig. 186), evoked a sense of immediate familiarity. The exotic admixture he and Ericson created was characterized by its diversity and richness, but they were able to fashion an image of a harmonious whole that many found instinctively satisfying.

THE SECOND BUNZL HOUSE While much of his time after 1933 was taken up with his work for Svenskt Tenn, Frank continued to produce designs for Haus & Garten, which Wlach, who had remained in Austria, operated in his absence. In the period prior to the Anschluss in 1938, Frank returned to Vienna regularly to carry out commissions and confer with Wlach on the running of the company. Despite the deteriorating political and economic situation in the country, the two men managed to keep the business afloat. However, sales and commissions dropped off significantly after 1934: the social structure that had sustained Haus & Garten—and, indeed, all of Vienna's modernist culture—was slowly disintegrating. The rift between left and right, between Jews and non-Jews, was growing ever wider: the Nazi movement in Austria was gaining momentum, and after the mid-1930s many Austrians openly boycotted Jewish-owned businesses; by 1937, the shop relied almost exclusively on Jewish customers.[27]

In the face of the mounting political reaction and the worsening economy, Frank also struggled to continue his architectural practice in Austria. In 1935, Hugo Bunzl, who had engaged Frank to design the summer house in Ortmann before the war, once again called on him, this time to build a house on a wooded lot on the Chimanistraße in Vienna's eighteenth district. Frank responded with one of his most accomplished works, a block and stucco structure laid out in the form of a large U. While lacking the spatial drama of the much larger Villa Beer, it provided a convincing and successful display of his planning principles, including split levels, large open spaces, and a carefully determined interior promenade.

The complexity of the plan is plainly registered in the composition of the façades (figs. 187, 188), each of which presented a different look. Inside, Frank divided the house into four functional zones (fig. 189): a two-story wing on the west that housed the entrance and service areas on the ground floor; a front block with three bedrooms; a rear wing containing a large open L-shaped living and dining room; and an upstairs space with two additional bedrooms. The three downstairs areas were linked by a broad hallway (fig. 190) that wrapped around the terrace, providing a main route through the house. Frank took great care to subvert any hints of standard axial planning: throughout the house were subtle programmatic displacements—steps, doors set at unexpected loca-

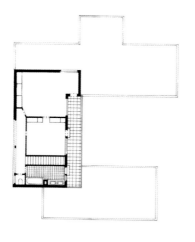

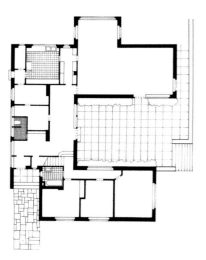

187. (top, left) House for Hugo and Olga Bunzl, Vienna, 1936; view of the southwest corner. Graphische Sammlung Albertina, Vienna.

188. (top, right) House for Hugo and Olga Bunzl, Vienna, 1936; view from the east. MAK-Österreichisches Museum für angewandte Kunst, Vienna.

189. (bottom, left) House for Hugo and Olga Bunzl, Vienna, 1936; upper and ground floor plans. Drawing by Matthew Catterall.

190. (bottom, right) House for Hugo and Olga Bunzl, Vienna, 1936; hallway. Sammlung, Universität für angewandte Kunst, Vienna.

tions, and variations in the width and height of the rooms—all of which reinforced the rambling quality of the spatial progression.

When completed in 1936, the Bunzl House was perhaps the finest modern house built in Vienna during the decade of the 1930s. It proved, however, to be Frank's last building in Austria. The Bunzls were to occupy the house for only another two years, until the Anschluss, when it was seized along with the rest of their property and they were forced to flee Austria.[28]

THE WEHTJE HOUSE As the Bunzl residence was going up, Frank was also at work on several projects in Sweden. Among these were two small summer houses in the resort community of Falsterbo. Located on adjacent lots, the houses (fig. 191) repeated many of the elements of his nearby Carlsten House. Roughly rectangular in plan and the larger of the two, the Låftman House vaguely recalled Frank's experimental house for the 1929 Linz exhibition, while the other residence, the Seth House, with its continuous second-story balcony, bore strong formal similarities to his house at the Weissenhofsiedlung.

191. Låftman House (left) and Seth House, Falsterbo, Sweden. Arkitek- turmuseet, Stockholm.

The houses, both completed in 1935, featured light, airy rooms and clean lines. But neither advanced Frank's ideas of spatial ordering: aside from his effort to establish linkages with the exterior terraces and balconies, the two houses were more or less customary exercises in modernist planning and design. By the summer of 1935, however, Frank was already engaged on a residential project that would push well beyond any of his previous attempts at recasting conventional spatial organization.

The house, for wealthy Stockholm industrialist Walther Wehtje, his wife Gundlar, and their four children, marked a crucial turn in Frank's developing ideas, an attempt to introduce a new irregularity he had first suggested at the end of "The House as Path and Place." Named Solesand, or "Sunny Beach," by the Wehtjes, the house occupied a sandy, pine-studded rise in Falsterbo, a short distance from Frank's other houses there. Like them, it was built as a summer residence, designed, as an article in the *Studio* annual noted, "to make the most" of the short Swedish warm season.[29] The principal rooms were all oriented to the south, with the ample roof deck and second-story living area providing a commanding view of the broad beach and the Baltic Sea beyond.

In plan (figs. 192, 193), the house followed the general outline of the second Bunzl House, with two projecting wings framing a central courtyard to form a broad U. The main entry, however, was from the south, leading through the courtyard (fig. 194), past a towering pine tree and into a large two-story hall.

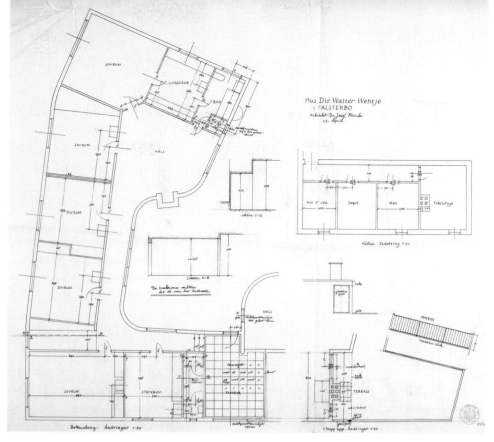

192. (top) House for Walther Wehtje and family, Falsterbo, Sweden, 1936; plans 1:50. Pencil, pen and ink on tracing paper, 60 × 105 cm. Sammlung, Universität für angewandte Kunst, Vienna.

193. (bottom) House for Walther Wehtje and family, Falsterbo, Sweden, 1936; plans 1:50. Pencil, pen and ink on tracing paper, 55 × 60 cm. Sammlung, Universität für angewandte Kunst, Vienna.

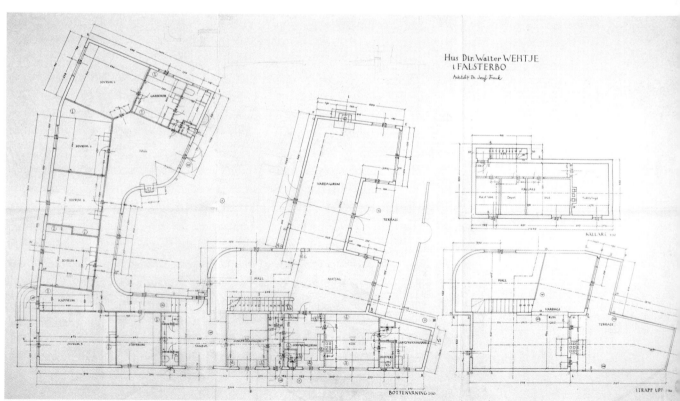

194. House for Walther Wehtje and family, Falsterbo, Sweden, 1936; view of the courtyard from the roof terrace. The siding was added in the 1970s. Photograph by Mikael Bergquist.

But while Frank's plan for the second Bunzl House had remained strictly orthogonal, in the Wehtje House he set several of the walls at oblique angles and gently bent others into soft curvilinear shapes. The arrangement appears to be rather arbitrary; in fact, the footprint of the house was largely determined by the site, which due to the course of the streets formed an irregular polygon. Frank laid the house out with the outer edges parallel to the property lines, in the process carefully wedding the building to its specific location.

As the surviving preliminary drawings show, Frank adopted the overall outlines of the house early on in the design process. The design of the courtyard, however, underwent numerous changes. A sketch dated 24 February reveals that he originally considered having the inner edges of the courtyard parallel the straight lines of outer walls and, by extension, the property lines. He was evidently displeased with the resulting courtyard shape and the disposition of the interiors, which had the dining room along the north wall and the living room at the center of the U. Only three days later, he produced another version of the house, this time introducing curved lines to form a serpentine courtyard, and, in the process, transferring the living and dining spaces to the west wing and replacing them with the large entry hall. The S-shaped court almost certainly derived from the first version for the House for M. S.—the Wehtje plan is almost a mirror image of the house—but Frank greatly enlarged it, removing the pool and instead positioning the entry on the courtyard side. In the final scheme, he widened the opening at the top of the two wings and realigned the inner edges on the east and west so that they ran more or less parallel to each other.

The configuration not only yielded a winding and picturesque entry sequence (which Frank further accentuated with a carefully delineated "natural" paving and planting program), it also generated a series of complex and unusual interior spaces. The most arresting of these were associated with the circulation zone that extended along the inner rim of the U-shaped plan. As in the second Bunzl House, movement along this spatial sequence abounded with repeated shifts, and the general arrangement of elements was both disjointed and asymmetrical. From the French doors on the courtyard side, the main path led around an extended partition into the two-story hall. The curving surface of the outer wall conducted one into the space, which was illuminated by a floor-to-ceiling divided window. Like the great hall in the Villa Beer, the dramatic, two-story volume formed the compositional center of the house, joining together the main public rooms. Despite the views afforded by the stair and the open gallery, however, the assemblage was more understated, presenting the impression of a simple circulation center rather than that of a "main square."

Even with this greater informality, Frank maintained tight control of the distribution and articulation of the paths and places both within and outside the house. The placement of the windows along the main passages and the openings to the exterior provided carefully contrived sensations. Although it was essentially a single-story house with a small rooftop addition, Frank also made use of small alterations in the floor levels (fig. 195)—the bedroom wing is raised approximately a half meter above the main floor of the house—and ceiling heights. This volumetric play is much less pronounced than in the Villa Beer, but the combined effect of the curvilinear and oblique walls actually developed a much wider array of spatial effects.

In functional terms, the main circulation route in the Wehtje House was also more fully integrated into the daily patterns of living than in any of Frank's previous residential works. The hall at the end of the east wing, for example, served simultaneously as the distribution hub for the bedrooms and baths, as a separate entry from the courtyard, and as the children's play area. In the same way, the two-story entry hall constituted a living space, a landing for the stair, and a formal entry to the adjacent living and dining room.

195. House for Walther Wehtje and family, Falsterbo, Sweden, 1936; sections 1:50, site plan 1:200. Pencil, pen and ink on paper, 60 × 100.5 cm. Sammlung, Universität für angewandte Kunst, Vienna.

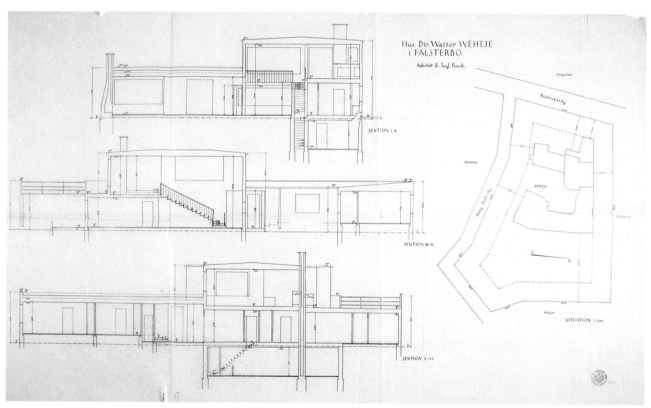

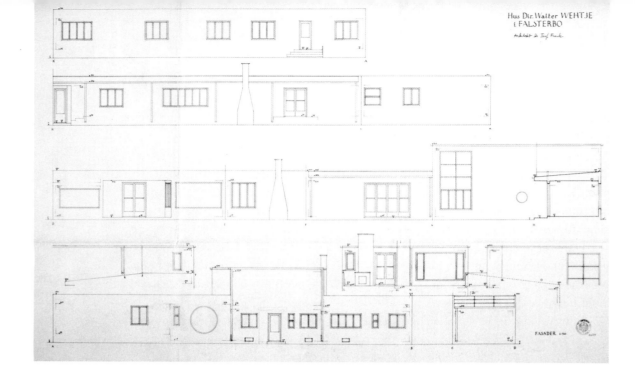

196. House for Walther Wehtje
and family, Falsterbo, Sweden,
1936; elevations 1:50. Pencil, pen
and ink on paper, 60 × 94 cm.
Sammlung, Universität für
angewandte Kunst, Vienna.

While the promenade in the Villa Beer established an almost self-contained architectural feature, in the Wehtje House it merged seamlessly with the other areas of the house leaving virtually no space that was not "living space."

What further set the house apart from any of Frank's earlier designs were its multiple points of access to the outside—there were no fewer than six doors leading directly to the exterior—that afforded a large number of routes to and from the different areas of the villa. While the layout of paths was quite deliberate, Frank's apparently nonchalant arrangement had the effect of making the movement from any one place to the next seem natural and unforced. This impression was bolstered by the unassuming quality of the elevations (fig. 196), which evoked the impression of a traditional Mediterranean village. The house's decided lack of monumentality and the unaffected appearance of the interiors came perhaps closest to fully achieving Frank's ideal of the house as path and place, and in later years it remained one of his personal favorites.[30]

ORGANIC FUNCTIONALISM VERSUS THE FREE PLAN

Frank's departure from right-angle planning in the Wehtje House represented a rejection of the construction-based rationalism of orthodox modernism. If his intention had been to suggest a new architectural approach no longer dependent upon previously held ideas of propriety or conventional ordering, Frank also announced with the house's design an alternative vision of functionalism, one based on the idea of the free plan.

Frank's search for a new architectonic order paralleled that of other Central European modernists of his generation—most notably, Hugo Häring and his disciple, Hans Scharoun. It is unclear, however, to what extent Frank was influenced by either architect. Frank knew Häring from at least the mid-1920s, and the two men met and corresponded regularly from the late 1920s through the mid-1930s.[31] During Frank's first years in Sweden, he returned to Vienna occasionally, sometimes stopping off in Berlin to visit Häring. The bond between them went beyond a collegial relationship: both shared a strong aversion to doctrinaire functionalism, and by the early 1930s they had published works critical of the modernist mainstream. Häring's outspoken denunciations of the "rigid" approach of Gropius, Hilbersheimer, and their followers had endeared him to Frank, and they were behind Frank's invitation to Häring to participate in the 1932 Vienna Werkbundsiedlung.

Frank was also undoubtedly familiar with Häring's notion of organic form in architecture. Häring had first fully spelled out his ideas in his essay "Wege zur Form" (Approaches to form) in 1925.[32] Extending his teacher Theodor Fischer's conviction that buildings should respond directly to place and program and grow "organically from inside outward,"[33] Häring maintained that the aim of functionalism was not mere efficiency but also the creation of an integrated architecture. Like Wright, who had articulated this same idea more than two decades before, Häring stressed the functional elaboration of elements and the nature of materials, but he was less concerned with the idea of artistic expression. At the end of "Wege zur Form" he wrote: "We should not express our own individuality but rather the individuality of things; their expression should be identical with their being."[34] Furthermore, Häring renounced regular geometry as the means of developing organic order, contending that it should arise from the requirements of life and construction. Instead, in the early 1920s, he began to investigate the use of nonorthogonal forms, their arrangement dictated by the specific circumstances of each individual program.

Among the celebrated examples of Häring's new design strategy were the Gut Garkau farmstead (1922–26) and his unrealized villa project of 1923 (fig. 197). The latter, in particular, manifests a number of similarities with Frank's design for the Wehtje House, especially in the organization of its architectural promenade. Häring, too, was interested in movement through spaces and subjective visual experiences: he bent and shaped the contours of his rooms to amplify and define their purpose. He also manipulated the plan to respond to the particular conditions of the site and the building's use.

197. Hugo Häring, Project for a villa, 1923; ground floor plan. Akademie der Künste, Berlin.

Frank's designs of the 1930s stood apart, however, not only in their formal composition but also in terms of their underlying ideological bases. Unlike Häring, Frank never subscribed to a notion of an organic architecture based on "natural forms"; indeed, he explicitly rejected nature as a model: "The architect," he wrote in the early 1940s, "fashions different forms from those of nature; in fact, we could define architecture as being an ordering of nature, with its own individual forms. The further the forms of architecture are from those of nature the better they will be—that is the great lesson of classical art."[35] Frank similarly rejected the charge of formalism, responding that his heterotopic place-making was merely an attempt to adjust to the living needs of the inhabitants. The irregular shapes, he claimed, proceeded from a functional point of view; their purpose was to provide an enhanced feeling of *Wohnlichkeit*. Not only did such rooms heighten the inhabitants' spatial awareness, but they also allowed those within to live freely, unconstrained by fixed hierarchical symmetries.

Whereas Frank renounced biological form, Häring, while acknowledging the necessity of using functional forms determined by life, referred to them as "organhaft" (organlike), fully intending the association with nature. Häring's pronounced emphasis on functionality, moreover, led him to examine the rituals of daily life in greater detail, often elaborating even the smallest features. His works, like Frank's, were shaped by a concern with use; but they are much more determined—even the placement of the furnishings is indicated—and less flexible.[36] The Wehtje House—and indeed Frank's other works of the later 1920s and 1930s—offered a neutral frame for the events of domestic life, engaging them while simultaneously allowing a certain freedom. While Häring's tightly composed plans asserted control, Frank's spaces exuded a sense of ease; they are at once less conspicuously purposeful and constrained.

It is likely nonetheless that Frank found inspiration in Häring's earlier foray into nonorthogonality (by the 1930s, Häring had returned to right-angled design for the bulk of his works).[37] But Maria Welzig's assertion that the Wehtje House "could not have come about without Häring's stimulus" disregards the development of Frank's ideas of space extending all the way back to his prewar interiors.[38] Indeed, in light of Frank's increasing dissatisfaction with "the regular, four-cornered room" in the early 1930s, his embrace of nonorthogonality was an obvious and logical move. Frank found in the free plan not a wholly new design system, but a means of more fully realizing long-held intentions.

Any direct influence by Scharoun on Frank seems less likely. In the 1930s, it was Scharoun, far more than Häring, who was able to translate the ideas of an organic functionalism into built form.[39] Though inspired by Häring, Scharoun's experiments with free planning and spatial fluidity were more radical, especially in their use of modern building methods and materials. But Frank's early investigations into nonorthogonality—the first version of the House for M. S. in Los Angeles was made in 1930—predate Scharoun's Schminke House (1932–33) and his other revolutionary residential designs of the period before the Second World War. Frank's houses may have superficially resembled Scharoun's, but they sprang from different sources and attitudes.

THE BAHRKE HOUSE AND THE PROJECT FOR THE AUSTRIAN PAVILION AT THE 1937 PARIS EXPOSITION

During the mid-1930s, Frank designed at least one additional house for Falsterbo, an unrealized project for a client named Bahrke. The elevations in the surviving rendering (fig. 198) resembled those of the Wehtje House, but the project as a whole

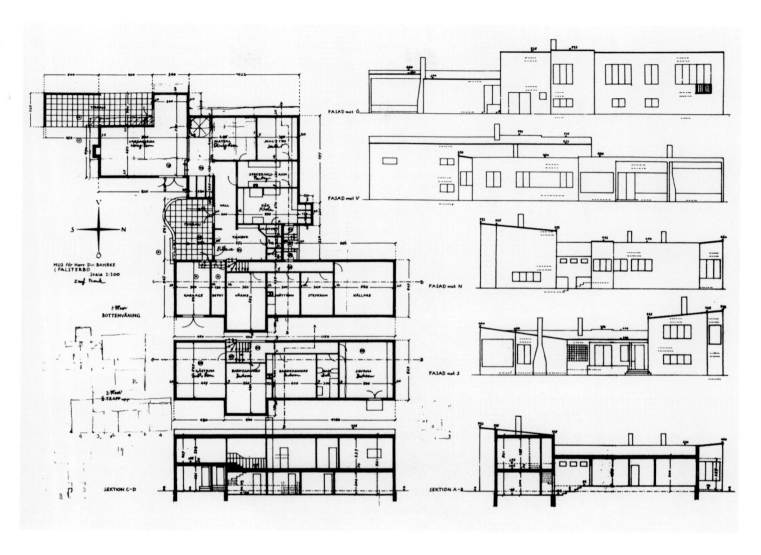

was decidedly more conventional. For one, the house is not arrayed around a courtyard but rather consists of a central core with wings on the east and west projecting in opposite directions. The larger, two-story block on the east would have contained several bedrooms and a guest room; downstairs, the plans called for a garage, sewing room, furnace, and storage spaces. The shorter, one-story wing on the west houses a separate dining room and a large L-shaped living area, and the central portion of the house is given over to an entry hall, kitchen, and other service areas. More important, however, aside from the low curving wall along the front terrace, is the fact that the design is strictly orthogonal. Despite the several shifts in level, the plan displays few of the spatial disjunctures that Frank had introduced in the Wehtje House.

198. Project for the Bahrke House, Falsterbo, Sweden, c. 1936; elevations, plans, section 1:100. Pencil, pen and ink on tracing paper, 40 × 38 cm. Arkitekturmuseet, Stockholm

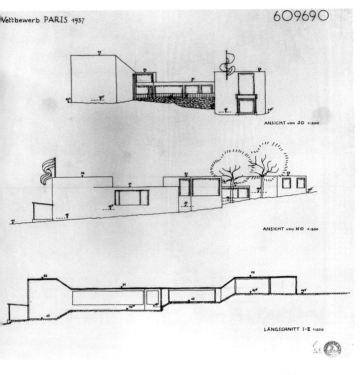

Wettbewerb PARIS 1937

609690

ANSICHT von SO 1:200

ANSICHT von NO 1:200

LÄNGSCHNITT I–II 1:200

199. Project for the Austrian pavilion at the 1937 Paris *Exposition Internationale*; elevations and section 1:200. Pencil, pen and ink on tracing paper, 36 × 36 cm. Graphische Sammlung Albertina, Vienna.

Closely related to the Bahrke House is another project from the same year, a design Frank submitted to a competition for the Austrian Pavilion for the 1937 Paris *Exposition Internationale* (fig. 199). The roughly U-shaped pavilion resembles the Bahrke House in several key respects, including its blocky, asymmetrical massing and irregularly composed façades. Frank refrained from using the curvilinear lines of the Wehtje House, however, instead achieving the building's complex spatial plan through the imposition of obliquely angled walls. In contrast to the Bahrke project, the spaces within would have been much more freely constituted: despite the generally linear progression of the long side, it is clear from the longitudinal section (no ground plan has survived) that Frank's use of volumes of varied shapes and sizes, each lit in a different way, would have provided an extraordinary spatial sequence.

Also conspicuous in the design is Frank's use of contrasting surfaces—smooth stucco and rubble masonry—not unlike Le Corbusier's houses of the early 1930s that would become a pronounced feature of his later architectural designs. The application of a rubble veneer to the lower portion of the central block serves a formal purpose—to underscore the connection between the two projecting wings at either end and to provide a transition with the landscape. It also further strengthens the impression of diversity and complexity while at the same time undermining the building's monumentality.

THE PROJECT FOR THE WEHTJE HOUSE IN DJURSHOLM   Two years after the Wehtje House in Falsterbo was completed, Wehtje asked Frank to design a house for his family in the Stockholm suburb of Djursholm. Although it was never realized, Frank's design (fig. 200) represents the fulfillment of his spatial planning ideas of the 1930s. The roughly L-shaped villa reproduces many of the basic ideas of the first Wehtje House, including, most notably, its emphasis on complex geometries. However, it is even more idiosyncratic in the development of its interior spaces. Aside from the kitchen, the bathrooms, and an upstairs maid's room, none of the spaces is a regular standard rectangle: instead, each of the rooms is arranged more or less freely, its form determined by Frank's sense of what would be most emotionally effective.

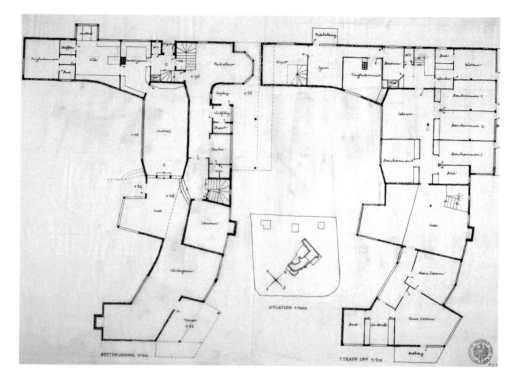

200. Project for the Wehtje House in Djursholm, Sweden, 1938; plans 1:100, site plan 1:1000. Pencil, pen and ink on tracing paper, 36 × 52.5 cm. Sammlung, Universität für angewandte Kunst, Vienna.

The principal axis through the house is laid out in a more or less direct line, but the irregularly formed walls and spaces along its route, combined with subtle alterations in lighting and level, would have achieved much the same results as Frank's more meandering promenades. It is the fracturing and disordering of the individual rooms themselves, however, that sets the project apart from his previous attempts to subvert traditional orthogonal planning. Not only do the "paths" constitute spatial episodes, each "place" also establishes particular vistas and sensations. The disruptions and irregularities abound everywhere, leaving almost no trace of conventional symmetrical arrangement.

The Wehtje project for Djursholm would be Frank's last experiment of its kind for nearly a decade. After 1937, he concentrated almost exclusively on furniture and textile design. The Wehtje House in Falsterbo, completed two years before, was to be among his last built works. Frank's abandonment of architecture was in part due to his relative isolation in Sweden, which made it difficult for him to find commissions. But perhaps even more, it was a result of his own decided lack of enthusiasm for the practice of architecture. Years later he would write that he had given up building because the process was, in his words, "too complicated" and "for the most part it consisted of dealing with customers, bureaucrats, and suppliers."[40] At Svenskt Tenn, Ericson saw to it that Frank was spared such concerns; and he found the situation far too agreeable to ever again undertake the running of his own architectural firm.

THE TRIUMPH OF SWEDISH MODERN The years from 1936 to 1941 were among Frank's most prolific as a furniture designer. Although his basic philosophy remained unchanged after 1935, his work began to undergo a subtle but discernible transformation. As before, he continued to mine the past for ideas: a large secretary he designed in 1936 (fig. 201) drew inspiration from Renaissance case pieces and eighteenth-century English cabinetry, while his rocking chair of 1940 (fig. 202) borrowed directly from American Shaker and folk design. More and more, however, his products bore indications of a growing elegance and refinement. Many of the designs, such as a dining table with an inlaid edge (plate 15) or his numerous brass lamps and ceiling fixtures (fig. 203), repeated themes he had developed in his work for Haus & Garten; but the finishes and execution of the pieces betrayed a growing sophistication, reflecting Ericson's desire to appeal to an upscale clientele.

The stress on finish in Frank's furnishings was accompanied by a trend toward greater clarity and simplicity of form. The result was not merely a slimmed-down version of his earlier aesthetic: rather, Frank began to investigate the possibilities of a historicized modernism that fused together the language of functionalism and historical precedent. Pieces such as the remarkable cabinet-on-stand he designed in 1938 (fig. 204) presented—even more than his works of the 1920s and early 1930s—a complex merging of old and new.

Frank's penchant for reusing older forms also appears in his textile designs. His pattern "Anakreon" (plate 16), designed in 1938, for example, was based on fragments of

201. (left) Drop-front desk (Svenskt Tenn model no. 1036). Pyramid wood with boxwood inlay, 1936. Courtesy Bukowski Auktioner AB, Stockholm.

202. (middle) Rocking chair (Svenskt Tenn model no. 997). Oak with green leather, 1940. Courtesy Bukowski Auktioner AB, Stockholm.

203. (right) Ceiling lamp (Svenskt Tenn model no. 2357/8). Polished brass, designed in the 1930s. Courtesy Bukowski Auktioner AB, Stockholm.

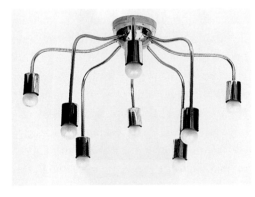

frescos from the New Palace of Knossos (1600–1400 B.C.) on Crete, excavated by Arthur Evans a few years before. Frank made few changes to the original composition, adding only ivy leaves, a few flowers, and a bird's nest, and altering the colors. [41] But his repetition of the forms and his vibrant color scheme yielded a powerful, and decidedly modern, effect.

The same blending of historical forms and intricate patterning is evident as well in Frank's carpet designs of the period. During the late 1930s and early 1940s, Frank created a number of carpets; eventually, he would produce some thirty patterns in all. Unlike his textiles, which were generally based on vegetal and animal forms, most featured simple geometric shapes. But even in his design for a hand-knotted carpet from 1938 (plate 17), which appears at first to be wholly modern in conception, Frank provided a historical allusion: the rounded, five-pointed star derived from a footstool discovered in Tutankhamen's tomb; it was a favorite motif of his, and it appeared in a number of his carpet designs.[42]

In addition to producing new designs for Svenskt Tenn, during the late 1930s Frank was busy with the preparations for several international exhibitions. At the 1937 Paris *Exposition*, his work was presented in both the Austrian and Swedish Pavilions. The Austrian Pavilion, designed by Haerdtl, included interiors by Hoffmann (a boudoir), Max Fellerer (president's office), and Karl Witzmann (reception hall), among others.[43] In a conciliatory gesture, Frank and Wlach were asked to provide a living room with furnishings from Haus & Garten. The room (fig. 205), which looked out onto a small interior courtyard, was typical of Frank and Wlach's designs of the 1930s—open, varied, and relaxed. Its most striking feature, the freestanding fireplace in the center of the space, repeated the bottle-shaped profile of the chimneys on the exterior of the Wehtje House in Falsterbo. Consistent with Frank's ideas of not concealing the room's architectonic sur-

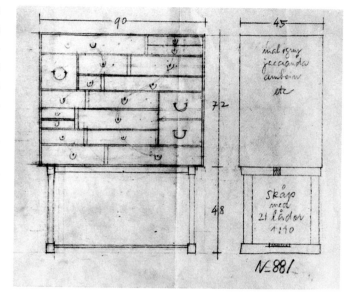

204. (top) Drawing for a cabinet-on-stand, c. 1938. Pencil on tracing paper, 15.9 × 9.4 cm. Svenskt Tenn Collection, Josef Frank Archive, Stockholm.

205. (bottom) Living room with free-standing fireplace, Haus & Garten display, *Exposition internationale des arts décoratifs*, Paris, 1937. Sammlung, Universität für angewandte Kunst, Vienna.

206. Svenskt Tenn display, 1937
Paris *Exposition*; view of the terrace
looking toward the Seine. Svenskt
Tenn Collection, Josef Frank
Archive, Stockholm.

faces, however, it was raised from the floor, establishing a spatial field of its own. Notable also was the room's irregular plan—actually a consequence of Haerdtl's design and not of Frank's making—which nevertheless provided a poignant demonstration of how the spaces in the second Wehtje House might have appeared had it been realized.

Frank's display for the Swedish Pavilion (fig. 206), on the other hand, was more reserved. The small terrace overlooking the Seine presented his usual medley of chairs and tables, all executed in rattan, as a well as a polished, silver-plated copper fountain; but the overall look of the ensemble was almost classical in comparison with the Haus & Garten display.

Yet it was Frank's work at the Swedish Pavilion that attracted the greater notice. Together with interiors by Berg, Malmsten, and other leading Swedish designers, the pavilion captivated visitors. Modern and up-to-date yet unpretentious and comfortable, the new "Swedish Modern" style appealed to those who sought an accessible modernism, and almost overnight it was picked up and copied by designers and companies in a number of other countries, especially the United States.[44]

The growing popularity of the style was also bolstered by a series of smaller exhibitions of Swedish products abroad sponsored by the Svenska Slöjdföreningen, including a traveling show of Svenskt Tenn products in Warsaw and Prague that Frank and Ericson prepared in 1938.[45] The most important affirmation of the Swedish Modern design approach, however, came the following year at the New York World's Fair.

FRANK AND THE 1939 NEW YORK WORLD'S FAIR
The Swedish Pavilion at the New York World's Fair, designed by Sven Markelius, proved to be among the most popular of the foreign pavilions. Situated away from the other national exhibits in the shadow of the Trylon and Perisphere at the center of the grounds, the building's eloquent simplicity provided for many an agreeable contrast to the overblown architecture of many of the exhibition's other structures. So impressed was the reviewer for *Architectural Forum* that he declared that it was "unquestionably the most civilized piece of modern architecture in the entire Fair grounds."[46]

The casual informality of the Swedish Pavilion was also repeated in its displays of modern furniture and applied arts, which incorporated five model rooms arranged by some of the country's leading designers, among them Berg, Malmsten, Axel Larsson, and Elias Svedberg.[47] Frank and Ericson were represented with a studio (fig. 207) featuring an array of recent Svenskt Tenn furnishings in the company's now familiar softened modernist style, including a kidney-shaped teakwood writing desk and a low sofa, both of which would become standard elements of Scandinavian design in the 1950s.

The "humanistic modernism" of Frank and Ericson's studio was also evident in the displays of the other designers, which sported similar light, comfortable, and attractive furnishings. For many observers, the Swedish display constituted a welcome relief from the other furniture exhibits. Walter Rendell Storey, design critic for the *New York Times*, summed up the reactions, praising the Swedish interiors for their "lightness of effect and simplicity," which he found posed a healthy alternative to the austerity of German functionalism and the lush decorative affectations of French art deco.[48] After more than a decade of modernist excess, Swedish Modern appeared to offer, as the pavilion's official catalog announced, "A Movement toward Sanity in Design."

Frank and Ericson were also represented at the Swedish Pavilion at the 1939 *Golden Gate Exhibition* in San Francisco.[49] The Svenskt Tenn exhibit, a combination bedroom and boudoir, presented a number of Frank's by now standard pieces, including a rattan-and-wood bed and a dressing table with three mirrors (fig. 208). But the display exposed the divide between his ideas and those like Bruno Mathsson, who favored simpler, cleaner lines, suggesting the wide diversity of design idioms that had been lumped under

207. Svenskt Tenn exhibit, New York *World's Fair*, 1939. Svenskt Tenn Collection, Josef Frank Archive, Stockholm.

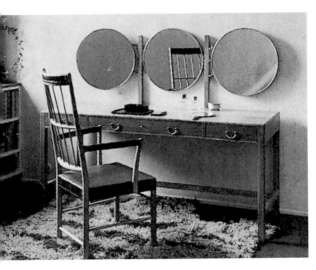

208. Dressing table with three mirrors, *Golden Gate Exhibition*, San Francisco, 1939. Svenskt Tenn Collection, Josef Frank Archive, Stockholm.

the name "Swedish Modern." As Berg wrote in *American Home* magazine, the Swedish Modern style was not a style at all, "but an attitude to life—the modern attitude." The interiors were "[n]ot based on any inherited Swedish tradition but created according to our new conceptions of art and what is pleasant and delightful."[50]

THE END OF HAUS & GARTEN Even while Frank was enjoying unprecedented success with his designs for Svenskt Tenn, he was worried about the tide of events in Austria. After German troops marched into the country in March 1938, Jews were beaten in the streets and Jewish-owned businesses were boycotted and plundered. Frank was immediately concerned with the welfare of his relatives and friends there, especially his elderly mother (his father had died in 1921), who was too frail to start a new life elsewhere.[51] Frank was also confronted with the question of what to do with Haus & Garten after the imposition of new laws prohibiting Jewish ownership of property.[52] Faced with the prospect of having the firm confiscated, he and Wlach sold it to a gentile friend, Julius Kalmár, who owned a similar furnishings store on the Bennogasse in Vienna's eighth district.[53] Kalmár eventually turned the running of Haus & Garten over to his niece, Lea Calice, and architect Anna-Lülja Praun, who continued to operate the business under the same name until 1958, when they were forced to close it in the face of dwindling sales and losses due to embezzlement by the firm's ac-

209. Frank with the composer Ernst Krenek in Stockholm, 1938. Author's collection.

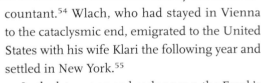

countant.[54] Wlach, who had stayed in Vienna to the cataclysmic end, emigrated to the United States with his wife Klari the following year and settled in New York.[55]

In the late 1930s and early 1940s, the Frank's apartment on Rindögatan became a haven for Austrian and German émigrés fleeing the Nazis. Among them were many Social Democrats, as well as noted cultural figures, including Bertold Brecht and Ernst Krenek (fig. 209).[56] Elsa Björkman-Goldschmidt, a friend of the Franks whose husband, Walter Goldschmidt, had been a physician in Vienna, later recalled that the Frank's small three-room flat offered "a space to breathe" for the many exiles who passed through Sweden on their way elsewhere.[57] All day and long into the evening friends and acquaintances came and went, often sitting for hours discussing current cultural issues and the ominous events in Europe.

In November 1938, after the Swedish government declared its intention to help free Jews imprisoned in the German concentration camps, Frank supplied the authorities with names and information of Viennese detainees, among them psychologist Bruno Bettelheim, who was released from Buchenwald the same year. He also assisted many others with finding papers and financial affidavits that would permit them entry in the United States.[58]

TOLVEKARNA Despite the increasingly threatening signs of war, the early 1940s were a busy time for Frank. He continued to add to the ever-growing range of furnishings and objects for Svenskt Tenn, producing, on average, one new design every week.[59] He also undertook the adaptation of Ericson's summer house in the village of Tyresö southeast of Stockholm.

Ericson had rented the house, which she called Tolvekarna, or Twelve Oaks, since 1931.[60] She purchased it in 1941, and a short time later she asked Frank to make extensive changes to both the interior and exterior.[61] He expanded the simple board and batten structure (fig. 210), adding a bedroom wing fitted out to resemble a ship's cabin for Ericson's future husband, Sigfrid Ericson, who was captain of the Swedish passenger liner SS *Gripsholm*. He also created an ample glass-roofed terrace facing out onto the Stockholm archipelago.

Most of Frank's changes were straightforward, but his configuration of the interior hall where the existing house and addition were joined provided a compelling statement of his spatial ideas. Rather than continuing the lines of the existing house for the addition, Frank set the two wings at an angle (fig. 211), interposing a connecting corridor that served as the entry and circulation hub for the house. The intersection of the two wings produced an intricate, twisting volume in which the various paths through the house converged (fig. 212). The stair, which led down to a partially subterranean bedroom and workshop, served as the visual pivot within the space. In contrast to the stair of the Villa Beer a decade before, however, its role as a distributor of movement within the space was subordinate to the part it assumed in breaking the inflected axes. This fracturing was enhanced further through the imposition of the broken stone floor, which seemingly mimicked, on a smaller scale, the impression of a geometric bricolage.

210. Tolvekarna, Estrid Ericson's country house, Tyresö, Sweden, 1941. Svenskt Tenn Collection, Josef Frank Archive, Stockholm.

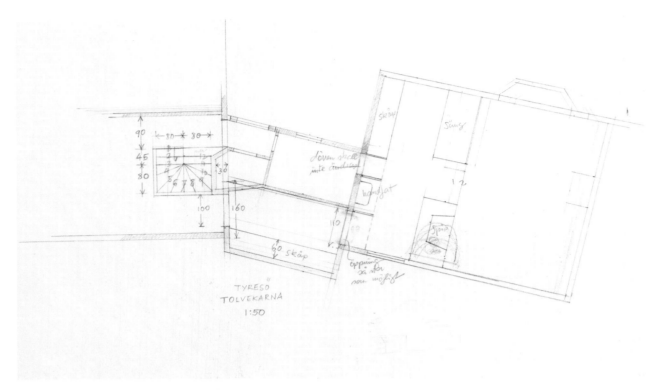

TYRESÖ
TOLVEKARNA
1:50

211. Tolvekarna, Estrid Ericson's country house, Tyresö, Sweden, 1941; plan 1:50. Collection Gun Jacobson, Tyresö, Sweden.

212. Tolvekarna, Estrid Ericson's country house, Tyresö, Sweden, 1941; hall. Svenskt Tenn Collection, Josef Frank Archive, Stockholm.

Like the visionary works of the expressionists of the late 1910s and early 1920s or those of later architects such as Frank Gehry and Coop Himmelblau, Frank's bending of the architectural frame provided a richly variegated promenade as well as perspectival distortions. But he achieved these effects without fundamentally altering the rules of architecture; his spatial disordering did not overlook the need to provide comprehensible reference points. Ericson's additions—the furniture, maps, seashells in the vitrine window, and other objects—served to normalize the spaces, to impart, as Frank intended, an atmosphere of serenity. Together, the amalgam of textures, colors, and lighting effects formed a complex whole that summarized Frank's ideas of the previous decade.

Work on the house stretched into the summer of 1942, but by then Frank had already left for New York, where he would spend the next four years. Despite the war's interruption of his work for Svenskt Tenn, Frank would continue his collaboration with Ericson through the early 1960s. Increasingly, however, his thoughts turned to larger questions about the future of modern architecture and design.

N E W   Y O R K   In 1938, shortly after the German occupation of Austria, Frank began to explore the possibility of immigrating to the United States. The same year, he turned to his brother Philipp (who by chance had been in the United States on a lecture tour at the time of the Anschluss and subsequently managed to find a temporary teaching position at Harvard[1]) to secure the necessary financial affidavits and to help him find suitable work. Philipp arranged for one of the affidavits, and László Gábor, Frank's former colleague from the Austrian Werkbund who was living in Pittsburgh, supplied the other. In the late fall of 1940, with Philipp's assistance, Frank received an invitation from Alvin Johnson, president of the New School for Social Research in New York City, to teach in the art history department.[2]

The news arrived at a critical moment. After the German occupation of Denmark and Norway in April 1940, it was no longer certain that Swedish neutrality could be guaranteed, and rumors circulated of an impending invasion or even a possible Nazi coup d'état. Armed with the requisite papers, Frank and his wife Anna embarked from Southhampton on the SS *Santa Rosa* in early December 1941. While aboard ship, they received news of the Japanese attack on Pearl Harbor and the United States's declaration of war.[3]

He and Anna moved into a comfortable, if modest, two-room apartment on the upper end of Manhattan at 50 Park Terrace East. But the transition to American life was by no means without its difficulties for Frank. Aside from the usual problems with language and having to endure the separation from his close friends in Sweden, he was forced to give up the financial stability that his position with Svenskt Tenn provided. Frank's cultural adjustment to life in New York was eased by his reacquaintance with many of his former Viennese friends and colleagues, most of whom had left Austria in the months immediately after the Anschluss. Besides Wlach and his wife Klari, who had found an apartment on the city's Upper East Side, he met up again with Felix Augenfeld, Ernst Lichtblau, and many others. Frank was also reunited with Trude Waehner, who lived a short distance away at 31 Park Terrace West.[4]

THE NEW SCHOOL Frank was similarly in good company at Alvin Johnson's "university in exile" at the New School. The faculty included many illustrious émigrés, among them the dramatist Erwin Piscator, the psychologists Alfred Adler and Karen Horney, and urban planner Werner Hegemann. Recognizing early the threat that the rise of Hitler and Mussolini presented for European intellectuals, particularly Jews and those on the left, Johnson offered temporary positions to as many refugees as possible, using the jobs as a means to sidestep the country's strict immigration requirements.[5] Still, the New School was more than a haven for those fleeing Fascism; Johnson envisioned it as a center of modern culture, a place where adults could learn about the newest currents in ideas and art. Unconventional thinking and intellectual debate were welcomed, and faculty members were given wide latitude in their selection of courses.

As a latecomer, Frank was assigned to the school's continuing education division, joining an art faculty that counted the painter Amédée Ozenfant and art historians Meyer Schapiro and Paul Zucker. He taught one evening course per semester, beginning in the spring term of 1942.[6] With little else to occupy his time, Frank used the opportunity to collect and refine his thoughts about the contemporary state of architecture and design, carefully writing out his lectures in German and then passing them along to Waehner, who translated them into English.[7] The lectures, a number of which have survived in manuscript form, are, like his earlier writings, intertwined with historical facts, conjectures, and observations. But though often repeating familiar positions, they also offer hints of his changing ideas about modernism that would emerge in his postwar works.

Frank's first course, "The Future of Architecture and Interior Decoration," explored the evolution of nineteenth-century architecture and design, the rise of modernism, and its prospects. He concluded the lecture series, as a brief preview in the course catalog noted, with the contention that the only proper path was away from standardization and collectivism:

The goal of modern architecture is greater freedom. Failure to obtain it in times past was due not only to more primitive construction but primarily to the superstition that our surroundings required formal unity, style.

The more scientific modern approach has made for greater variety and greater individuality among works of architecture, engineering, and decoration. We shall, therefore, never again have a style in the old sense. Attempts to create one today, whether modern or modernized historical, have a reactionary and totalitarian effect.[8]

His arguments, however, as he reported in a letter to Sobotka, who was now teaching in Pittsburgh, went well over the heads of his handful of students:

I have six female students. The first lecture was definitely too high despite all precaution; I will now have to reduce all that; the main interests of the female students is, of course, interior decoration. Thus, I have to revise the whole program, unless new ones appear—not to be expected during this term. . . .[9]

In his second lecture series, "Introduction to Modern Art and Architecture," given in the fall of 1942, Frank took a more basic approach, breaking the course down into individual discussions of fundamental concepts. The lecture titles included, "What is style?" "What is tradition?" "What is functional?" and "What is practical?"—all aimed at uncovering what Frank considered the fallacies of much of contemporary building and design.[10] His course for the spring term of 1943, "Post War Problems of Art" (fig. 213), followed a similar format, but it betrayed an even stronger undercurrent of criticism. One lecture, "Past and future of non-objective art," developed a critique of abstract art, which Frank argued had become irrelevant and even passé. More telling, however, was his lecture on "the totalitarian arts," which posed the question: "How totalitarian ideas were spread by so-called functionalism, that tried to make the world uniform with a new, universal style. Will this style ever come?"[11]

The eleventh lecture in the course, "How to Plan a House," which has survived in manuscript form, is significant for the insight it provides into Frank's changing ideas of spatial ordering and, more generally, of modern architecture.[12] Much of the discussion is a detailed addendum to the arguments he first presented in "The House as Path as Place" concerning the proper alignment of rooms and connecting sequences. More strident than ever before, however, is Frank's assertion that only free and irregular planning could overcome the dead hand of history and the "tyranny" of what he increasingly referred to as "Bauhaus-Funktionalismus":

The form of the house will, it is true, never produce a new society; but it can contribute to inspiring a person to freer thinking; if he understands that conventions, prejudices, and symbols

213. Announcement for

Frank's course, "Post War

Problems of Art," New

School of Social Research,

New York, Winter 1942.

Author's collection.

THE NEW SCHOOL
FOR SOCIAL RESEARCH
66 W TWELFTH ST   NEW YORK

POST WAR PROBLEMS OF ART

15 weeks. Tuesdays, 8:20-10 P.M. $12.50.   Josef Frank

Beginning February 2. The war may be expected to create new forms of our human society. These new forms influence the arts, and not all the trends of our time will survive as we know by experience. The artist must find his place in the new world.

Feb.   2   Art and war
Will the war influence art and evaluation of specific art works? Can art help win the war?

Feb.   9   Art and ideology
Art in our daily life; how many people are interested in art? Is it possible to increase public interest?

Feb.   16   Architecture and society
The relation between different forms of society and their architecture. Can we predict the change in architecture after the war?

Feb.   23   Art and science
Will the growth of scientific thinking destroy art? In what ways is art influenced by superstition?

Mar.   2   Art and nationalism
Will increasing nationalism disturb the internationalism of culture and result in national arts that differ from each other?

Mar.   9   The way the wind blows
What possibilities still exist for the decorative arts? What development is desirable, what probable?

Mar.   16   The industrial designer
The industrial designer and progressive mechanization. Is there still a chance for handicraft in the decorative arts?

Mar.   23   The totalitarian arts
How totalitarian ideas were spread by so called functionalism, that tried to make the world uniform with a new, universal style. Will this new style ever come?

Mar   30   The modern home
The home for people or people for the home?

April   6   The modern house in a historic neighborhood
How would we live today if people had always built their houses in the style of former times?

April 13   How to plan a house
What demands are basic for a modern house other than the fulfillment of practical necessities? How can they be achieved?

April 20   The future of architecture as art
Is the pressure of business, industrialization, standardization and mechanization so strong that architecture as art will disappear? Is this desirable?

April 27   City planning
What do we demand of the future city? Under what conditions would it be possible?

May   4   Past and future of non-objective art
Is non-objective art the latest and the only recent step in the development of art? Is realism dead for ever?

May   11   Art critic
What influence has the art critic on the development of art, the work of artists and the taste of the public? The difference between art criticism and art history.

EXHIBITION OF ARCHITECTURE
by Josef Frank
will be held at the New School
from January 18 to February 9.

that are very old can be done away with, and that their abolition brings with it advantages, then he can be influenced that this is also desirable in other spheres of life.[13]

An architecture founded on "the belief in systematic ordering," he charged, was a product of "being reared in an atmosphere lacking in freedom," and such buildings constituted symbols of bondage and servitude, or of Fascism. Regular, right-angled planning had come about not because "such rooms are especially suited for living, because even squared corners exact a certain coercion," but in order to satisfy the need to array houses in an orderly fashion in the city and to form regular streets. The "desire for straight streets," which was "inevitably representative" of some political or social hierarchy, "was always exaggerated." Yet, for cities, as for houses, Frank claimed, orthogonal planning did not imply real comfort: "The more irregular the streets, the more livable the city." If straight streets were sometimes necessary "for the purpose of traffic circulation and real estate," this was not true for the house: "modern technology allows every free division of the interior." This yearning for complex and varied spaces, he asserted, was universal. "It is no wonder that people have a greater sense of well-being in casually remodeled barns and adapted windmills than in a carefully planned house with scientifically determined divisions into functional areas, and that they seek reprieve from the convenience of the city in the primitive conditions of the countryside."[14]

Frank insisted, however, that it was impossible to wholly ignore such functional considerations: "We cannot, of course, assemble a house only from 'accidents' [*Zufälligkeiten*], we require a conscious plan, one that first and foremost fulfills practical requirements."[15] While not fully embracing randomization as an ordering principle, the text points firmly toward the possibility of allowing such "accidents" to play a greater role in determining the house form, an idea Frank would pursue further in the later 1940s.

THE NEW YORK SLUM CLEARANCE PROJECTS In an effort to increase his visibility in the city and attract commissions, Frank mounted an exhibition of his work during the winter of 1943 at the New School's main building on West Twelfth Street. The show, which ran from 18 January to 9 February, included his most recent houses in Austria and Sweden, as well as several of the Viennese housing blocks and a number of unrealized projects. The display drew some interest from the German-speaking refugee community,[16] but on the whole it elicited little comment. The absence of most of the younger American architects, who were away serving in the armed forces, was doubtless one reason for the scant response. Yet, as Frank himself observed in a letter to Lurçat in 1945, it was also a consequence of the American modernists' acceptance of the German approach:

Within the image:
CITY of NEW YORK
SLUM CLEARENCE
Actual condition of 4 Blocks

*Josef Frank
New York 1942*

214. Project for slum clearance in New York, 1942; aerial perspective. Pencil, pen and ink, watercolor on paper, 55 × 65 cm. Graphische Sammlung Albertina, Vienna.

The German architects, who have been here longer, have had great success. Gropius, Breuer, Mies, Hilbersheimer are professors and have influenced architecture (mainly on paper and not in reality). But the American architects . . . are convinced that the Bauhaus and modern architecture are one and the same.[17]

Among the projects Frank apparently exhibited at the New School was a proposal for a slum clearance for a site on New York's Lower East Side (fig. 214). It is unlikely that Frank actually was commissioned to produce the design; it was probably an attempt to demonstrate his own approach to the housing problem. By 1942, discussions were already underway concerning the rebuilding of much of the area along the East River north of Fourteenth Street. Frank proposed to redevelop a four-block area between First and Second avenues bounded on the south by Twelfth Street and on the north by Sixteenth Street.[18] In place of the existing four- and five-story tenements, he called for the erection of eight, twenty-four-story high rises, containing a total of 1,824 units, as well as a school facing Sixteenth Street. Though reminiscent of other well-known modernist urban designs, such as Hilbersheimer's 1927 "Welfare City" (*Wohlfahrtsstadt*) or Le Corbusier's "Plan Voisin" of 1922–25, Frank's layout of the grounds was less regimented, offering in place of a grid a number of gently curving pathways that wound through the parklike setting. As he had on his earlier communal apartment buildings in Vienna, Frank cloaked the façades in various bright colors—yellow, rose, green, and mauve—and introduced variations in the buildings' geometry as a means to avoid the impression of monotony. The trim, modular towers were perhaps his most successful large-scale designs, well-proportioned and appealingly composed.

The following year Frank prepared a second slum clearance proposal, a schematic plan for an adjacent site just to the east of First Avenue (fig. 215). The project was a response to the published plans designed by architect Irwin Clavan for a housing estate in the so-called "gashouse district" extending from Fourteenth Street up to Twentieth Street (fig. 216).[19] The huge residential community, eventually named Stuyvesant Town, was a

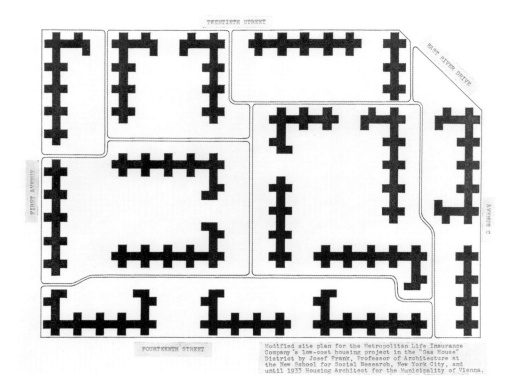

215. Frank's "modified site plan" for Stuyvesant Town, New York, 1943. Ink and typewritten legends on board, 27 × 35.5 cm. Graphische Sammlung Albertina, Vienna.

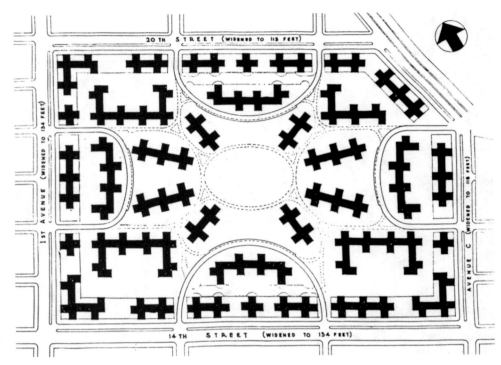

216. Irwin Clavan, preliminary design for Stuyvesant Town, New York, 1943. *Pencil Points* 24 (May 1943).

private development of the Metropolitan Life Insurance Company. First announced in the spring of 1943, construction was slated to begin after the war.[20] Frank intended his design as a counterproposal to Clavan's regular, symmetrical site plan. Relying once more on intentional irregularities and "picturesque" planning, it repeated, on an urban scale, features of his ideas on domestic planning. The individual ten- to twelve-story buildings were organized to form large open commons. These common areas, in turn, were connected through a series of pathways, which, although linear, provided interruptions to the surrounding grid.

Although Frank's modified plan might have lessened somewhat the tedium of the complex, one suspects that, given the density and design of apartment blocks, the differences would have been negligible. Frank may have intended to present his alternate scheme to the City Planning Commission, perhaps in an effort to attract future work.[21] A number of prominent architects and urban authorities publicly criticized Clavan's plan at a May 1943 meeting of the commission shortly after the project was announced, but there is no record that Frank was among the speakers.[22] In any event, nothing came of Frank's urban renewal projects, and he soon abandoned the effort.

FRANK'S LATER YEARS IN NEW YORK Frank gave one additional course—"Appreciation of Architecture"—at the New School in the fall of 1943.[23]

But for reasons unknown he resigned his teaching position there at the beginning of 1944. For the next two years, Frank mostly occupied himself with designing lamps and, especially, textiles.

Frank had been encouraged to take up textile design again after learning in 1942 that Ericson, who was no longer able to import cretonnes from England because of the German blockade, had begun to have some of Frank's earlier designs printed in Sweden.[24] By 1944, Frank had completed some two dozen new patterns, which he sent to Ericson on the occasion of her fiftieth birthday in September 1944.[25] Many of the designs, such as "U.S. Tree" (plate 18) or "Vegetable Tree" (plate 19), were based on the illustrations in several small inexpensive pocket guides to North American flora and fauna that Frank had picked up at New York bookstores.[26] He mixed and matched the motifs, depicting a variety of different plants "growing" on the same branch, at the same time altering their colors and scale. He also drew inspiration from the worlds of art and architecture: "Rox and Fix" (plate 20), for example, was modeled after Chinese scroll paintings from the Ming dynasty that he had seen at the Metropolitan Museum of Art.[27]

Frank's new designs departed from his earlier Haus & Garten textiles. Rather than focusing on intricate patterning, he concentrated on the motifs themselves, which were larger and more freely drawn than in his previous textile designs. Frank's depictions of flora and fauna also became more personalized, yielding a distinctive and recognizable style.[28] By the end of 1945, he had produced nearly sixty new patterns. Due to wartime shortages and technical problems with the printing process, most of the patterns were not printed until the later 1940s. Initially, the bright, richly colored designs failed to attract Swedish consumers, who were accustomed to more a sedate look. Eventually, however, they became the most popular items at Svenskt Tenn, their sales far outstripping any of Frank's other designs.[29]

The textile designs also helped to relieve the Franks' increasingly tightened financial circumstances, which had grown precarious after his teaching stint at the New School ended. During their first years in New York, the Franks lived mainly on Josef's share from the sale of Haus & Garten, but by 1943 the funds had been expended, and they needed additional income. At one point, they had so little money that Anna was forced to take a job sewing gloves.[30]

To help make ends meet, Frank created a line of textiles for the New York firm F. Schumacher & Co.[31] The company eventually produced several patterns: "Victory Garden," "Citrus Garden," "Baranquilla," and "Dehli." "Citrus Garden," in particular, available in three different color combinations, sold well, and the firm continued to produce it until 1962.[32] Frank, however, was never fully satisfied with the quality of Schumacher's printing and he finally ended his relationship with the company in the later 1940s.[33]

With little else to fill his days, Frank turned to writing, a pastime he had taken up in his last years in Vienna. In Stockholm in the early 1940s, he had worked on a novel, *The*

History of the Thirty Years War, Volume II covering the first years of the Second World War; and shortly after arriving in New York, in 1942, he wrote *The Peace Conference*, a satire poking fun at the American belief in progress and its messianic role in world affairs. Sometime later, he penned two plays, one, entitled *Woch*, dealing with Nazism and anti-Semitism, and a comedy, *Träume* (Dreams). The works, however, were far from literary masterpieces, and none was ever published.[34] Frank also failed in his efforts to find an American publisher for *Architektur als Symbol* and for his lecture series "Postwar Problems of Art," which he revised into book form between 1943 and 1946. He engaged a literary agent, and later he asked Waehner to approach publisher Alfred A. Knopf.[35] But U.S. publishing houses showed little interest, correctly surmising that Frank's ideas ran counter to the prevailing mood in architecture.

In spite of the poor reception he found for his ideas in the United States, Frank never shared the condescending attitudes many of his fellow European émigrés had for the American way of life. Like Loos, who had regaled Frank during his student days with tales of his years in the New World, he was fascinated with the practicality and comfort of American dwellings. Even before he had first traveled to the United States in 1927, Frank had collected images of American houses and interiors, and he later often showed examples of American rooms and furnishings in his lectures.[36] He also regularly kept up with the latest developments in American domestic design through popular magazines, such as *House and Garden* and *House Beautiful*.[37] It was not only the pragmatic nature of the American house that appealed to Frank: he also admired American individuality and openness, especially with regard to the issues of form and style.[38]

Though sometimes troubled by American materialism, Frank found life in New York congenial. He reveled in the newness and the diversity of the city, which he looked upon as an invigorating contrast to an "antiquated" Europe. He took especially great pleasure in what he saw as an absence of ideologies in American artistic and intellectual life, which he believed had plagued Europe prior to the war.

Much as he had in Sweden, however, Frank remained isolated from the architectural community in the United States. He made only a few fainthearted efforts to establish professional connections or to seek commissions, preferring, it would seem, the status of the outsider. Frank's alienation from the design establishment stemmed not only from his ambivalence about practicing architecture again; it also grew out of his recognition that American modernists showed little interest in the "Viennese approach," which for them seemed to lack the "purity" and forcefulness of contemporary German and Dutch design.[39] Frank was not the only Viennese exile who proved unable to find a place in the United States: of the more than a dozen well-known Viennese architects and designers who fled to the United States after the Anschluss—among them, Augenfeld, Lichtblau, Sobotka, and Bernard Rudofsky—only Victor Gruen, who was younger than most of the émigrés and was able to adapt more readily to the changed realities, succeeded in building a thriving practice. Most of the others eked out a living with small projects or found positions in education.[40] Frank, who was already in his late fifties when he arrived in New York and was virtually unknown in the United States, indeed found himself at a decided disadvantage compared with figures like Gropius, Mies, Breuer, and Hilbersheimer.

One of the few American architects Frank sought out was Frank Lloyd Wright. Frank particularly admired Wright's later designs, which he thought exemplified a freedom and inventiveness lacking in much of modern architecture.[41] Meeting Wright, however, as he wrote to Lurçat, proved to be a disappointment:

I also saw Frank Lloyd Wright and his work yesterday. He is a man of great imagination, he is seventy-six years and still working. Unfortunately, it is difficult to talk to him, he is too much of a Nazi. The first thing he said to me was, "There is no difference between Roosevelt and Stalin."[42]

Nonetheless, Frank, as he later confided to Sobotka, still preferred Wright's work, which he thought was a better "influence . . . than the Bauhaus-Corbusier's [sic] which had led to basic stiffness and boredom."[43] Frank's fervent wish, however, that a new organicism would dominate postwar American architecture, would remain unfulfilled.

In late January 1946, only a few months before his sixty-first birthday, Frank and Anna sailed back to Stockholm, where they took up residence once more at their apartment on Rindögatan. Frank, however, kept the apartment in New York, returning annually to the United States, usually during the winter and early spring.[44] He resumed his work for Svenskt Tenn, but he also produced designs for lamps and other articles for the New York interior design shop Plus, operated by one of his old acquaintances from Vienna, Anna Epstein-Guttmann. In addition, Frank designed several interiors for friends in the New York area, among them actress Dolly Haas-Hirschfeld and her husband, caricaturist Al Hirschfeld.[45] But Frank was never able to establish himself in the United States. In the early 1950s he gave up the attempt, turning his sights once more to Europe and to new ideas of modern architecture and design.

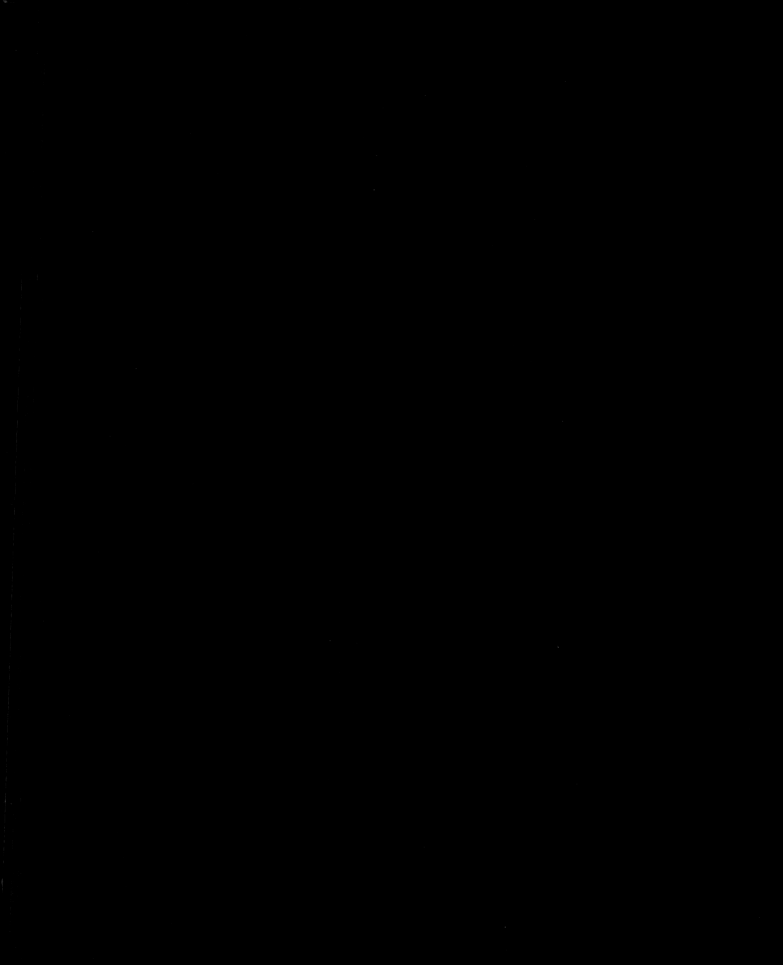

R E V I S I O N S The two decades following the Second World War were a time both of triumph and of change in the fortunes of modern architecture. The era witnessed the construction of some of modernism's most impressive monuments: Mies van der Rohe's Farnsworth House (1946–50) and Seagram Building (1958), Le Corbusier's Unité d'Habitation (1947–52) and Chandigarh complex (1957–65), Neutra's Kaufmann House (1946), and Oscar Niemeyer's Brasilia (1956–63). But even as modernism dominated the world building scene, it was subjected to increasingly intense questioning. Scientific planning, standardized housing, and the introduction of new materials and construction methods, while providing tremendous technical advantages, did not guarantee the continuation of humane values in architecture. The postwar years also saw the proliferation of a huge volume of buildings that imitated the forms of the early "international style," while falling well short of its crisp, minimalist serenity.

Symptomatic of the time was an ongoing reexamination of many of modernism's principles. In contrast to the prewar era, the cultural critique of the new architecture now came largely from within the ranks of the avant-garde. Challenging the doctrines of the old functionalism, various writers called for the reintroduction of symbolic representation, historical forms, and aesthetic expressiveness. As he had before the war, Frank joined those demanding reform. In the last two decades of his life, he became increasingly preoccupied with the search for alternatives to mainstream architecture and design. Decrying the "dullness" of postwar architecture, he sought novel approaches, not only to contemporary building but also to design and urban planning. Although his late works often reflected his earlier concerns and ideas—especially the new design directions he had explored in the later 1930s—they also broke fresh ground, presaging the coming revolt of the 1960s and 1970s.

NEW DESIGNS FOR SVENSKT TENN   After returning to Stockholm in 1946, Frank once more took up his design work for Svenskt Tenn. Besides adding to the company's already considerable array of furniture, textiles, and other objects, he assisted Ericson in the arrangement of its showroom displays and in the planning of several exhibitions, among them a large retrospective in 1949 marking the twenty-fifth anniversary of the company.[1] He also consulted on the creation of interiors for the firm's ever-expanding list of clients. The phenomenal postwar success of Swedish Modern—now more commonly lumped together with the works of designers in Finland, Norway, and Denmark and referred to simply as "Scandinavian Design"—translated into numerous commissions for the company. The impressive list of Frank's projects of the late 1940s and early 1950s included interiors for the home of the noted Swedish sculptor Carl Milles (fig. 217) and for two large Stockholm banks, the Handelsbanken and Stockholm Enskilda Bank, as well as the furnishings for many of Sweden's embassies and consulates around the world.

217. Anne's House, Millesgården, Stockholm, c. 1950. Seated at the desk are Carl and Olga Milles. Svenskt Tenn Collection, Josef Frank Archive, Stockholm.

In 1951, Frank also mounted an exhibition of his designs for Svenskt Tenn in the United States. The venue was Kaufmann's Department Store in Pittsburgh. Owned by Edgar Kaufmann, Sr., and his family, the clients for both Wright's Fallingwater house and the desert house in Palm Springs designed by Neutra, the store, following the tastes of the Kaufmanns themselves, mounted frequent displays of the newest design trends.[2]

Frank's connection to Kaufmann's was through his old friend László Gábor, who was the store's artistic director. The designs were displayed in five large show windows facing Smith Street in downtown Pittsburgh. Each window featured a complete room, including a living room, a dining room, a garden room, a study, and a bedroom (fig. 218).[3] In keeping with Frank's ideas, the pieces were arranged informally, each installation featuring a diversity of colors and patterns. The show received exten-

218. Bedroom exhibited at
Kaufmann's Department Store,
Pittsburgh, 1951. Svenskt Tenn
Collection, Josef Frank Archive,
Stockholm.

sive coverage in the local Pittsburgh press and was generally well received by the public. But sales proved to be disappointing, and after the show closed, Kaufmann's declined to continue the association with Svenskt Tenn. The exhibition proved to be the last of Frank's work in the United States during his lifetime, and it effectively ended his efforts to establish himself in the country.[4]

Frank's designs of the postwar years continued the trend of his works of the late 1930s toward a softened, comfortable, and eclectic modernism. But many of his works of the later 1940s and early 1950s also evinced a growing mannerism. At a time when the other leading Scandinavian designers were moving toward a pared-down look based on natural woods and colors, Frank's designs often displayed a decided bent for quirky form and unconventional contrasts (fig. 219). Ever in search of variety, he continued to pursue new means to recast modernist simplicity with richness and complexity. His vitrine-on-stand, designed in 1946 (fig. 220), for example, combined plain lines with thin spindles on the feet. In the same way, the model no. 1179 chair he designed in 1947 (fig. 221) brought together such diverse materials as mahogany, bamboo, and leather, as well as ball joints and a sweeping curvilinear crest.

With their luxurious materials and delicate joinery, Frank's furnishings for Svenskt Tenn also ran counter to the postwar trend in Scandinavia toward a more popular, affordable design style. While furniture makers such as Kaare Klint stressed the importance of adapting their ideas to mass-production methods, Frank and Ericson insisted on

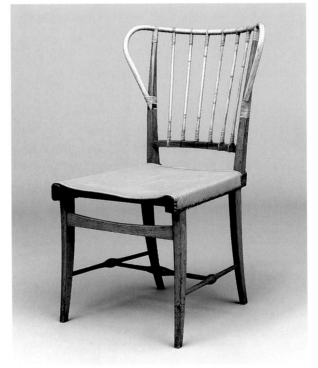

219. (left) Living room, Tolvekarna, Estrid Ericson's country house, Tyresö, Sweden, late 1940s. Svenskt Tenn Collection, Josef Frank Archive, Stockholm.

220. (top, right) Vitrine-on-stand (Svenskt Tenn model no. 2077). Cherrywood and glass, 1946. Courtesy Bukowski Auktioner AB, Stockholm.

221. (bottom, right) Chair (Svenskt Tenn model no. 1020), Mahogany, bamboo and leather, 1947. Courtesy Bukowski Auktioner AB, Stockholm.

the highest standards of materials and craftsmanship. As a result, most of the pieces were expensive, and Svenskt Tenn's clientele was confined to a small elite drawn largely from the Swedish bourgeoisie and from well-to-do customers from other European countries and the United States. The shop prospered due to the patronage of a small coterie of devoted clients, who returned regularly over the years to add to their collections of Frank pieces and fabrics (figs. 222, 223). Frank's oft-stated wish in the 1920s and 1930s, to bring good design to the broader public through large scale manufacturing, was only realized in later years by designers who drew on his ideas but simplified them so that they could be reproduced inexpensively.[5]

222. (left) Textile department at Svenskt Tenn, c. 1950. Svenskt Tenn Collection, Josef Frank Archive, Stockholm.

223. (right) Pewter objects for Svenskt Tenn, designed late 1940s. Svenskt Tenn Collection, Josef Frank Archive, Stockholm.

Frank churned out new works for Svenskt Tenn through the late 1950s, but his interest in furniture design, as he confessed in a series of letters in 1946 to Waehner, had begun to wane. While admitting that he still enjoyed "doodling" new textile patterns, he confided that he increasingly resented having to produce works for an "empty-headed decadent bourgeoisie" who live "as if nothing has changed."[6]

Nevertheless, Frank's work and ideas continued to have an impact on the development of Swedish Modern. Not only did his notion of a flexible, undogmatic interior design aesthetic exert a profound influence in design circles, but his use of natural materials and bright, bold patterns became common features in homes throughout Scandinavia. Yet Frank's most important and enduring contribution was doubtless the introduction of a more humane modernism, a message that reached beyond Scandinavia to the rest of Europe and the United States.

RETURN TO VIENNA   In 1947, Frank received an invitation to attend a conference in the small village of Alpbach in the Tyrolean Alps. After long hesitation he decided to accept, although he felt deeply uncomfortable about returning to Austria. His talk, which examined the role of architecture in the postwar era, offered little new, but his presence in the country raised questions about whether he might return permanently.[7] The following year, in January, Frank accepted an invitation from Vienna mayor Theodor Körner to present an address on "Architecture and City Planning in the United States and Sweden" at the auditorium of the Österreichischer Ingenieur- und Architektenverein (Association of the Austrian Engineers and Architects). The response to the lecture was so great that Frank was asked to repeat it the following week at a larger hall in the working-class district of Ottakring.[8]

Frank also presented a lecture on 28 January on "Art and Society" (*Kunst und Gesellschaft*) under the auspices of the Austrian CIAM group. Any possibility that he would go back to Austria to live and work, however, he quickly dispelled at the beginning of the talk. As Herbert Thurner later recalled, he startled those present with the—typically Frankian—acid remark: "I see sitting in the front row the same gentlemen, who in the old days, with flags flying and their tails between their legs, went running from the old Werkbund to the new one."[9] It was to be Frank's only postwar trip to Vienna: although he traveled extensively during the next two decades, never again did he return to the city of his youth.[10]

CITY PLANNING IDEAS   At the end of 1948, however, Frank accepted a call from Haerdtl, who was president of the Austrian CIAM chapter, to submit a proposal for the rebuilding of the war-damaged area around St. Stephen's Cathedral in Vienna's center.[11] Rather than preparing a specific proposal, Frank, in two published articles, laid out his ideas of basic principles for reconfiguring the space. He pointed out that there were two fundamental types of squares: those that had arisen over time; and those that were designed by a single architect as a total concept: "St. Peter's Square in Rome or the Place Vendôme, both of which were planned from the beginning, he wrote, are beautiful but uninspiring. The Piazza San Marco [in Venice] arose more through chance, for who knew at the time the church was built what the colonnade would look like?"[12] The Stephansplatz, Frank noted, was an example of a square that was a product of gradual accretion, and it made little sense to attempt to create a more unified square, as some had suggested; instead, an irregular building line consisting of individually designed structures would result in a more interesting and pleasing space and not undermine the monumentality of the cathedral itself.

Rather than endorsing a single plan, Frank discussed three general schemes (fig. 224), each of which explored how to best arrange the space around the cathedral while maintaining existing traffic patterns. His two preferred options called for a large open area to serve as a central square in front of the cathedral. He was particularly concerned that the space not become a mere utilitarian passageway connecting the main downtown streets, but a genuine agora, an island for the human community within the city. In this, as in his house planning schemes, Frank's proposals were very much in the spirit of Sitte, who viewed the square as a theater of everyday life. Frank hoped that the square around St. Stephan's—like the "squares" or places in his houses—would beckon passersby to stop and spend time, to relax and contemplate their surroundings. At the same time, he hoped the square would establish a feeling of variety and provide a sense of scale and embellishment to the adjoining structures. In the second of the two published articles, Frank warned against creating a unified, monumental effect: "Unfortunately, the architects of our time (or better put: of the recent past), think too much about standardization." Drawing once more a comparison between the ideologies of "simplicity" and "unity" with the currents of totalitarianism and militarism, he maintained that it was time for architects "to learn to think again, to find an individual solution for each problem, and to stop considering the stencil [Schablone] as an ideal."[13]

In the later 1940s, Frank sought to work out ways to bring new life to the modern cityscape. Not long after returning to Stockholm, he wrote to Waehner: "I am now preoccupied here with the problem of boredom in art and architecture. Why, one must ask oneself, are the streets and dwellings here so uninteresting?"[14] Comparing the rich vitality of New York with the well-ordered monotony he found in European cities, Frank pondered whether the American pattern was not the better model for modern times: "I gen-

224. Project for rebuilding St. Stephan's Square, Vienna; variant plans. *Wiener Tageszeitung*, 1 May 1949.

uinely prefer the rawness [*Roheit*] there [in America]," he wrote.[15] "I very much miss the whole Dyckman Street. What good is the art here and *carefullness* [English in the original] in building if everything is so dull? I am now completely of the opinion that much that is good comes about merely through chance and not through careful planning."[16]

Frank's rejection of uniformity and standardization was at the heart of several unrealized town planning projects he drew up in the late 1940s and early 1950s. One of the projects, for a community of 1,200 families (fig. 225), featured a curving thoroughfare leading to a central square with shops, a hotel, a theater, and a town hall; arrayed around this core is a network of residential streets, with lots presumably intended for single-family housing. The roughly circular pattern of streets suggests the influence of Ebenezer Howard's widely published scheme for an ideal garden city, but the plan is punctuated with deliberate breaks, along the lines of U.S. suburban developments, which Frank no doubt saw during his stays in the United States. The perspective view Frank made of the main square (fig. 226), on the other hand, is clearly modeled after the Piazza San Marco, with a six-story hotel tower substituted for the campanile. Yet Frank was unable to avoid the unified and monotonous effect he had condemned in planned spaces: indeed, the square, in spite of its calculated irregularities, is among the least appealing of his later works, a design that has more in common with Hilbersheimer's starkly rational *Zeilenbau* projects of the 1920s and early 1930s than the casual informality that characterized Frank's postwar interiors.

Another town planning project Frank prepared during the same period, the City for 2,000 Families (plate 21), exhibits a much less ordered arrangement.[17] The streets are laid out irregularly, with the structures clustered to form civic plazas and shopping areas. Large green spaces separate the buildings, again evoking Howard's garden city plans. But the buildings, which are depicted only schematically, are at a much greater scale, suggesting a hybrid between standard suburban and urban patterns. The city center in the plan repeats the basic layout of the Piazza San Marco, with a tower on one corner of a square. The tight ordering is partially offset by the haphazard arrangement of the streets, but the effect, despite Frank's intentions, is still that of a planned settlement rather than a population center that had evolved over an extended period without a formal program.

Frank repeated many of these same ideas in his entry for a 1952 competition to redesign the Kungsträdgården in Stockholm, an old park in the center of the city, which had once been the royal family's vegetable garden. Rather than converting the site to a paved square as many of the submissions recommended, Frank's proposal (which he submitted under the name "Rome," presumably because of its "organic" design) called for maintaining it as a park. As in his other city planning schemes, he sought to soften the effect of the surrounding urban grid with a series of meandering footpaths. The placement of the paths, as he explained in a written statement that accompanied his proposal, was dictated in part by his desire to save as many of the old trees as possible and

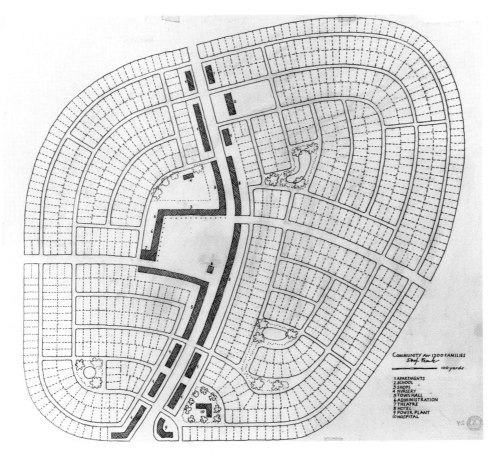

COMMUNITY for 1200 FAMILIES
Prof Frank
100 yards

1 APARTMENTS
2 SCHOOL
3 SHOPS
4 NURSERY
5 TOWN HALL
6 ADMINISTRATION
7 THEATRE
8 HOTEL
9 POWER PLANT
10 HOSPITAL

225. (top) Project for a town for 1,200 families, c. 1950; site plan. Pencil, pen and ink on tracing paper, 47 × 53 cm. Graphische Sammlung Albertina, Vienna.

226. (bottom) Project for a town for 1,200 families, c. 1950; perspective. Pencil, watercolor on paper, 22. 5 × 49 cm. Graphische Sammlung Albertina, Vienna.

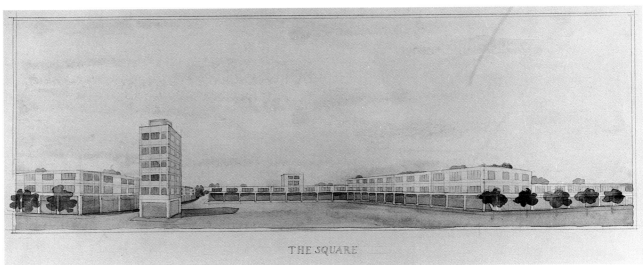

THE SQUARE

thus provide more green space in an area with few parks.[18] Frank's proposal, however, not only considered the park itself; he extended the design to encompass the nearby square before the Royal Palace and the Parliament building on the opposite side of the estuary, thereby greatly exceeding the parameters of the competition. In addition to re-aligning the shoreline to form a more ample open space, he suggested adding a twenty-story tower (fig. 227) to the Parliament and converting the adjacent area to a formal park framed by parallel rows of trees—all in an effort to establish a formal entrance to the palace and provide a visual separation between the Palace and the turn-of-the-century Parliament. The effect, which repeated Frank's notion of a square and campanile, was awkward at best, and the proposal was strongly rejected by the jury.

The proposed Parliament Tower itself harked back to another of Frank's unrealized designs of the late 1940s, a proposal for the new United Nations Building in New York (fig. 228). Frank probably prepared the project around 1947; it is unclear, however, whether he actually intended to submit it to the competition or whether he merely re-garded it as a statement of his ideas. The structure and form of the three towers, with their thinly stretched glass skins and crisp massing, were expressly modern; the shortest of the three is even raised on slender pilotis. But Frank's introduction of complex geo-metric patterning on the surfaces of the buildings—reminiscent of Hoffmann and Moser's decorative style at the turn of the century—served to diminish the hard-edged ef-fect, giving the buildings the appearance of large decorated jewel boxes, a profoundly dif-ferent look from the purist skyscrapers of the period. Years later, Frank wrote to Sobotka that the worst aspect of postwar architecture was "the loss of everything personal and everything following only a set pattern . . . Therefore, I believe that such buildings like the Seagram Building, the Unesco in Paris (Breuer), etc., are so unpleasant, because they all have even divisions without any three-dimensional or any other idea."[19]

In his designs of the late 1940s and early 1950s, Frank occasionally resorted to sculp-ture or other historical forms in an effort to engender greater architectonic diversity. His unrealized design for a Theater for 1,200 (fig. 229), for example, sported four large human figures symbolizing the four performing arts of music, opera, dance, and drama.

Frank, however, remained dissatisfied with the results. Writing to Haerdtl in 1949, he questioned whether the modern movement had not reached a dead end: "The ideals of [the prewar period] are in fact no longer (nor should they be) those of the present and therefore they are also not good models. I think that all the veterans of modern architecture of that time think basically the same thing, but just keep muddling along, because they do not re-ally know what one should do now, which I, by the way, also no longer know."[20]

THE THIRTEEN HOUSES FOR DAGMAR GRILL Frank's own response to this mounting crisis of confidence was most dramatically expressed in a series of house designs he produced in the last two decades of his life. Most were fantasy

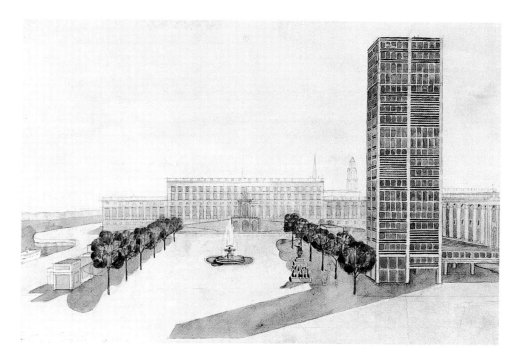

227. Project for the reconfiguration of the Kungsträdgården, Stockholm, 1952; perspective showing the extension of Helgeandsholmen and an addition to the Parliament. Arkitekturmuseet, Stockholm.

THE U.N. headquarters

228. (bottom, left) Project for the United Nations Building, New York, c. 1947; perspective. Pencil, pen and ink, watercolor on paper, 67.5 × 55.5 cm. Graphische Sammlung Albertina, Vienna.

229. (bottom, right) Project for a theater for 1,200, c. 1950; perspective. Pencil, watercolor on paper, 46.5 × 61 cm. Graphische Sammlung Albertina, Vienna.

houses, which, like his projects of the 1920s, were produced not in response to specific commissions but as part of his ongoing meditations about the nature of the home and his dissatisfaction with modernism.

The earliest of these designs appeared in a group of letters he wrote to his wife's cousin, Dagmar Grill. Frank had known Grill since the early 1910s. Trained as a physiotherapist, she had moved to Vienna to work at the Strömberg-Palm Gymnastics School; later, in the 1920s, she worked in the Haus & Garten showroom, and after his wife's death in 1957, she and Frank lived together in Stockholm. In the late 1940s, Grill lived outside Stockholm in the suburb of Djursholm, and the two carried on a correspondence when they were unable to meet.[21] For some time, he and Grill discussed alternatives to conventional modernist planning. In Grill's absence, Frank took the opportunity to explore the problem in depth. The letters, seven in all, written between 22 July and 15 August and mailed to Sätra Brun, where Grill worked, included sketches of thirteen houses as well as Frank's commentary on them.[22] Sometime later, Frank collected the designs and reproduced them in india ink on three sheets of tracing paper (figs. 230, 231, 232). He numbered the houses 1 through 13, producing large watercolor renderings of his favorite designs. (In the process, Frank changed the numbering of the houses from their original chronological order, which is 1, 2, 5, 6, 7, 4, 3, 9, 8, 10, 11, 12, 13.)[23]

The first four designs are variations on the houses he had designed in Sweden and Austria in the late 1930s, with complex interior plans juxtaposing right-angled and freely formed spaces. House 7, the fifth of the series, however, marks a departure. Not only does it include a series of low hipped roofs, but the columns that support the roofs and upper stories are no longer aligned but rather arranged more or less randomly. In the letter that included the drawing, Frank wrote of the house: "with a roof, but complex [krångligt]."

The next two houses, numbers 4 and 3, are based on a rigid rectangular grid within which the plans are developed freely.[24] For House 9 (plate 22, fig. 233) which followed, Frank wholly abandoned regular orthogonal arrangement, creating two different and irregular floor plans, with one superimposed upon the other. Writing to Grill, he noted that this house was "the most complex so far."[25] In the letter, he also came back to a point he had first made in his essay "The House as Path and Place" about the superiority of irregular spaces over rectangular ones: "When one draws a crooked line, without thinking about it, as a plan, it is still better than the carefully crafted rectangles of a *funkis* (functionalist) architect, is that not so?"[26] With its completely free and unpredictable spaces, House 9 summed up Frank's yearning for architecture that broke completely away from the rationalist spirit of modernism.

For the next house in the series, House 8 (figs. 234, 235), Frank again returned to the rectangular grid. This time he experimented with breaking up the building mass through a number of terraces and further elaborating the façade by using windows of different shapes and sizes, as well as with different building materials—field stones, stucco, and

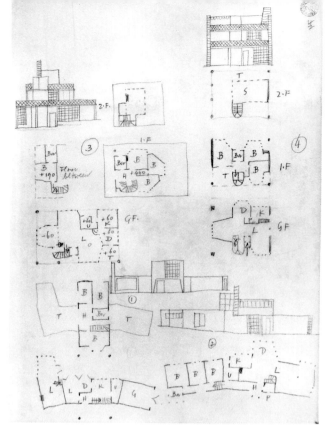

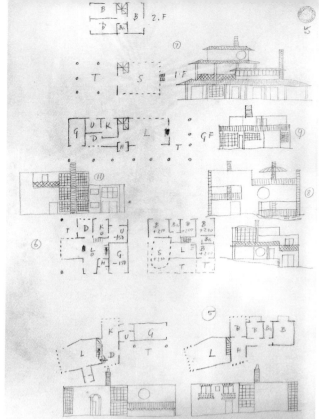

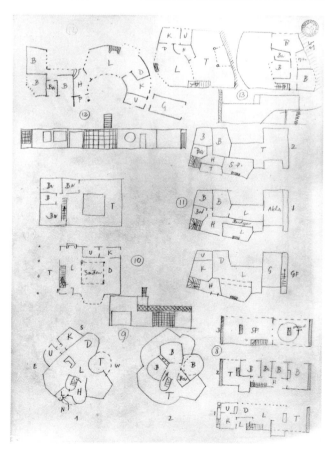

230. (top, left) Thirteen house designs for Dagmar Grill, 1947; houses 1, 2, 3, and 4, elevations and plans. Pencil on tracing paper, 42 × 29 cm. Graphische Sammlung Albertina, Vienna.

231. (right) Thirteen house designs for Dagmar Grill, 1947; houses 5, 6, 7, 8, 9, and 11, elevations and plans. Pencil on tracing paper, 42 × 29 cm. Graphische Sammlung Albertina, Vienna.

232. (bottom, left) Thirteen house designs for Dagmar Grill, 1947; houses 8, 9, 10, 11, 12, and 13, elevations and plans. Pencil on tracing paper, 42 × 29 cm. Graphische Sammlung Albertina, Vienna.

233. Thirteen house designs for
Dagmar Grill; house 9, c. 1953;
plans 1:100. Pencil, pen and ink on
tracing paper, 23 × 36 cm. Graphische Sammlung Albertina, Vienna.

234. Thirteen house designs for
Dagmar Grill; house 8, c. 1953;
perspective. Pencil, watercolor on
paper, 45 × 50.5 cm. Graphische
Sammlung Albertina, Vienna.

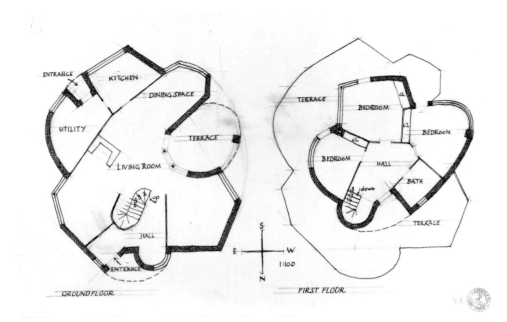

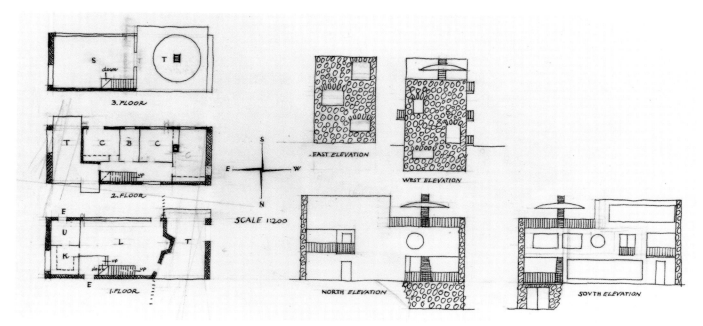

235. Thirteen house designs for Dagmar Grill; house 8, c. 1953; plans and elevations 1:200. Pencil, pen and ink on tracing paper, 29.5 × 42 cm. Graphische Sammlung Albertina, Vienna.

poured concrete. He was apparently not completely happy with the effect, for he wrote to Grill that "the house is not very complex, only a little. We can vary it later on."[27] House 10, which followed, is similar to House 8 in most respects, although it employed an atrium at the center to bring light into the volume.

For the last three houses, numbers 11, 12, and 13, Frank once more renounced the rectangular grid. House 12, which is arranged around a small semicircular courtyard, is reminiscent of the prewar Wehtje House, with a curving path that formed a continuous progression through the rooms. The other two houses, however, like House 9, are composed of wholly irregular spaces that seem to follow no discernible order and lack any overt sense of planned spatial sequence or hierarchy.

THE D-HOUSES Frank returned to these same ideas in another series of four unrealized houses he designed for Grill in December 1953. In contrast to the Thirteen Houses of 1947, all four of these houses share a similar program—a large living room and kitchen on the ground floor, and on the second floor, two bedrooms and a bath—suggesting that Grill may actually have had an intention to build a small residence. Like Frank's earlier designs for her, the houses also represent an attempt to reconstitute the modern dwelling, to generate a sense of interest and vitality through complex and composite arrangement. The first, third, and fourth of the houses, dated 2 December, combine regular orthogonal and irregular spaces in a manner similar to houses 4 and 13 from the 1947 series. The second house (plate 23), however, dated 3 December, constitutes an even more willful renunciation of modernist beliefs in purity and clarity of expression. The oddly disjunctive appearance of the house points in the direction of Frank's more eccentric furniture designs for Svenskt Tenn; but it goes even further in its rejection of precedent, adding wholly new elements—the checkerboard parapet, for example—while at the same time playing freely with accepted ideas of scale and composition. Even more than the Thirteen Houses, it also suggests a calculated ambiguity in the relationships of its parts and their purpose. What is contained within the upper story? How are the other sides of the house framed? What could the meaning of these various gestures possibly be? The façade is both strangely simple and elaborate—a paradox that provides a disquieting tension and accounts for much of its visual impact.

This free mixing of compositional ideas, however, was only partially an attempt to find an alternative to conventional modernist codes. Frank also sought a form language that could articulate, as completely as possible, his conviction that modern architecture had to relate the full variety of modern life: not only its richness but also its unevenness and its contradictions. In his houses of the 1920s and early 1930s, he had conceived of their exteriors as screens that concealed the diversity within. With the Thirteen Houses, and especially D-House 2, he began to allow the variegated forms that defined his interiors to be expressed externally.

Frank's desire to allow a field for all that life offered, from the serious to the purely frivolous, is also displayed in a third set of houses he designed for Grill. The houses, six in number, are all double houses or duplexes, each with one unit for Grill, and a second to be rented out, as the descriptions on several of the drawings indicate, to a grocer. Although none of the drawings are dated, Frank probably designed them after the other D-Houses, perhaps in 1954 or 1955. The intended location (as was the case in all likelihood for the four original D-Houses) was the villa colony of Djursholm, where Grill lived, but the drawings reveal no information concerning a specific site.[28] In all six designs, the program of the unit for Grill is identical with that of the four earlier D-Houses except for a separate or designated space for a dining room; the "grocer's house" is analogous, but with an additional upstairs bedroom. The layout of the two units in each case, however, is dissimilar: the side for Grill is spatially much more complex, whereas the other unit, as Frank noted on the plan of the sixth house, was "to be rented out and therefore [was] more conventional."

The first two houses in the series, which Frank designated "A D-House" and "Another D-House" (fig. 236), largely maintain a standard orthogonal layout, but the units for Grill feature slight variations in floor height and, in the case of the latter, a gallery on the second level that looks down on the living room below. In House 3 (plate 24), Frank introduced a curving, nearly semicircular court on the entry side, which also carries over into the interior spaces. The layout is similar to House 12 in the series of Thirteen Houses from 1947, but it is two stories rather than one, with a stairway placed along the outer wall connecting the floors. It is not the spatial arrangement of the interior that stands out most; rather, it is the composition of the front façade, with its nine oculi,

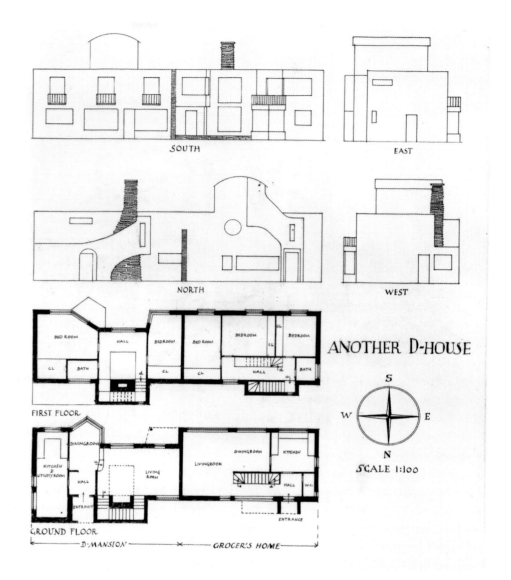

SOUTH

EAST

NORTH

WEST

FIRST FLOOR

GROUND FLOOR

D-MANSION — GROCER'S HOME

ANOTHER D-HOUSE

SCALE 1:100

236. Double D-House 2 ("Another D-House"), c. 1954; elevations, plans 1:100. Pencil, pen and ink on tracing paper, 49 × 38 cm. Graphische Sammlung Albertina, Vienna.

chimneys, and other diverse and discordant elements, which together establish its distinctive and startling identity. The combination of these sundry parts, which seem almost to exist independently of each other, form one of Frank's most arresting solecisms, a complex assemblage that explodes all conventional systems of ordering. The visual impact of the house, however, results not only from its apparent incongruities, but also from its oddly matter-of-fact presentation, suggesting an air of whimsy.

In the fourth of the Double D-Houses (fig. 237), this element of detached irony is even more pronounced: the pink stucco façades and the fieldstone chimneys—which re-

237. Double D-House 4, c. 1954; perspective. Pencil, watercolor on paper, 36. 5 × 59 cm. Graphische Sammlung Albertina, Vienna.

semble, as Kristina Wängberg-Eriksson has observed, abstracted giraffes—seemingly pose a rather precious joke. Frank no doubt intended this sense of playfulness, but the plans and elevations (fig. 238) also show that he had carefully worked out the arrangement of the rooms and the spatial sequencing. Indeed, it is clear from the plans that the articulation of the façades is largely a result of the logic of the two units' interior schemes. In the elevations, which certainly predate the watercolor perspective, the chimneys are of brick construction and thus mostly avoid the whimsical effect. Frank's subsequent changes suggest that he may have considered the design too severe and therefore sought to further "enliven" it. Whatever the case, the house as shown in the perspective rendering exhibits an undeniable element of kitsch, one that seems firmly to underscore Frank's conviction that personality and sentimentality still had an important place in modern life. "Every great work of art," Frank wrote in one of his unpublished writings, "must border on kitsch. If people are so charmed by kitsch, then that at least is a genuine sentiment; they aren't putting on airs. The work of art must speak to this legitimate feeling and shape it into a meaningful form."[29]

Double D-House 5, the next in the series, is similar in plan, but the façades are less mannered. For the sixth Double D-House (fig. 239), Frank returned to more or less orthogonal planning, the complexities introduced largely through various spatial shifts, much like his houses of the late 1920s and 1930s. The corners in most of the rooms in the unit intended for Grill, however, are cut at forty-five-degree angles, with the result that only the two upstairs bedrooms are regular, right-angled spaces. The intricate and composite quality of the interior spaces reveals no immediately discernible compositional

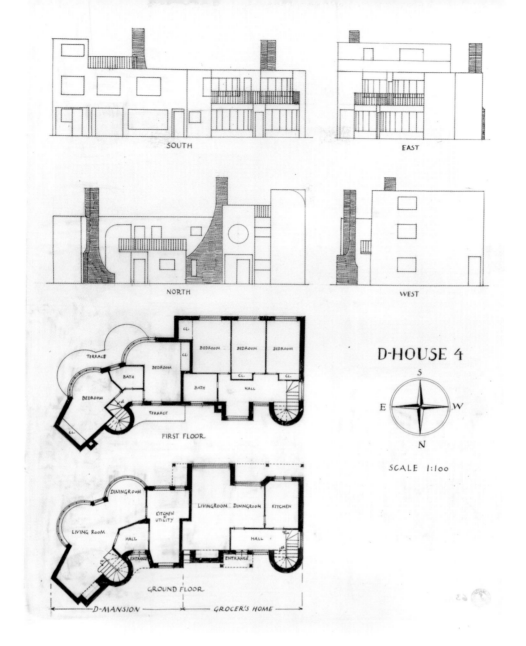

SOUTH

EAST

NORTH

WEST

D-HOUSE 4

SCALE 1:100

TERRACE
BEDROOM
BATH
BEDROOM
BEDROOM
BEDROOM
BEDROOM
CL.
CL.
CL.
CL.
BATH
HALL
TERRACE

FIRST FLOOR

DININGROOM
KITCHEN & UTILITY
LIVINGROOM DININGROOM
KITCHEN
LIVING ROOM
HALL
ENTRANCE
HALL
ENTRANCE

GROUND FLOOR

— D-MANSION —   — GROCER'S HOME —

238. Double D-House 4, c. 1954; elevations, plans 1:100. Pencil, pen and ink on tracing paper, 54.5 × 40 cm. Graphische Sammlung Albertina, Vienna.

order. Instead, it seems to imply that it was nothing more than a collection of mostly un-related parts, a haphazard assemblage brought about by accident.

This notion of happenstance emerged as the central idea of Frank's work in the 1950s. During the interwar years, he had sought to substitute an architecture that was "emotionally effective" for the strict scientific rationalism of the functionalists. To this, he now offered a new vision of an architecture whose foundation rested not on the scientif-ically planned but on the random and the spontaneous. The houses of the postwar years were based on Frank's observation that those places that seemed most inviting and agree-able had developed over time, without planning. Such an evolutionary process, he be-

239. Double D-House 6, c. 1954, plans. *Form* 54 (1958).

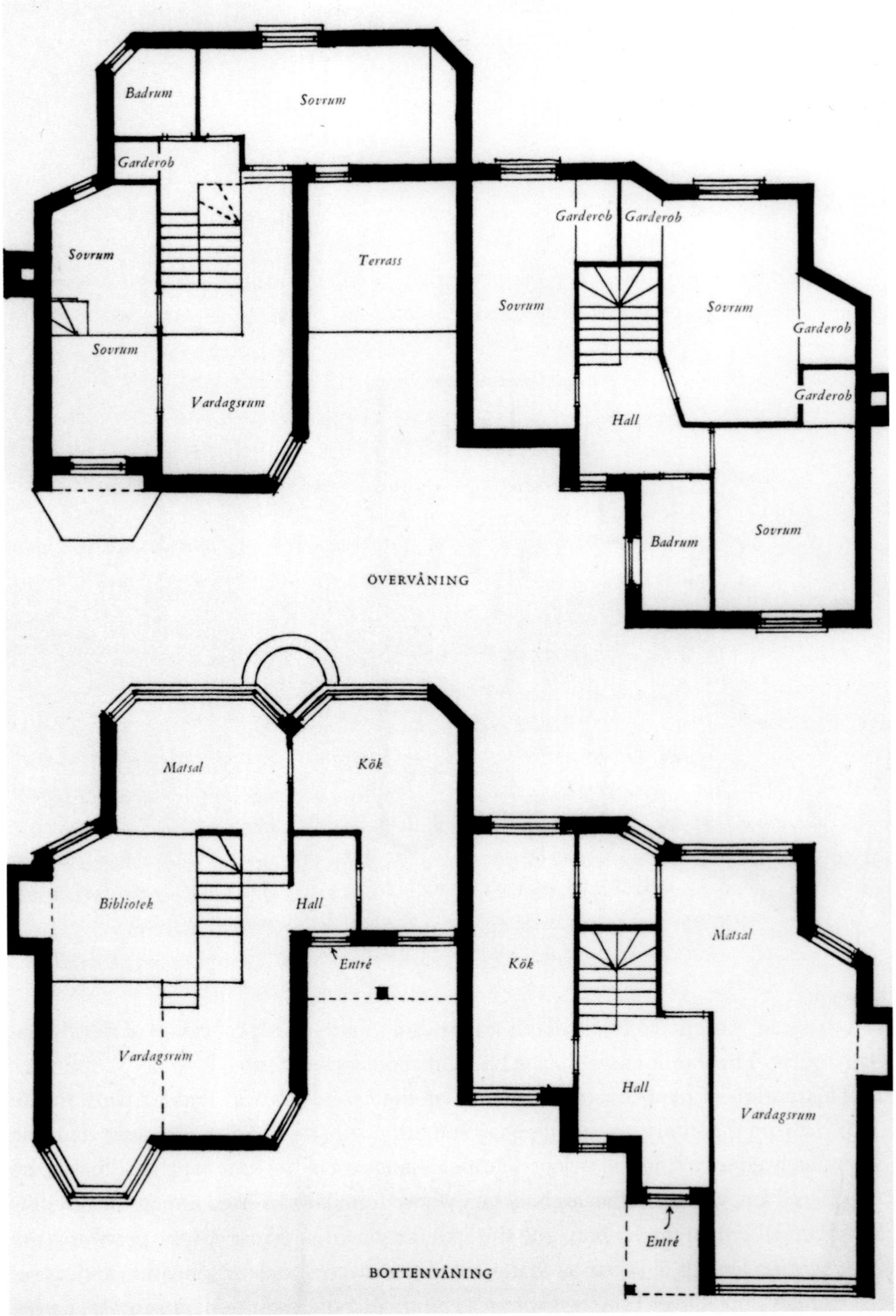
Badrum
Sovrum
Garderob
Sovrum
Terrass
Garderob
Garderob
Sovrum
Sovrum
Sovrum
Garderob
Vardagsrum
Garderob
Hall
Badrum
Sovrum
ÖVERVÅNING
Matsal
Kök
Bibliotek
Hall
Entré
Matsal
Kök
Vardagsrum
Hall
Vardagsrum
Entré
BOTTENVÅNING

lieved, inevitably involved some element of chance, with each generation leaving its own individual imprint. For Frank, this randomness provided a necessary feeling of variety, which rationally planned places and buildings lacked. The challenge for the architect, he reasoned, was to create this sort of "traditional" disorder intentionally.

ACCIDENTISM Frank developed these thoughts in an article entitled "Accidentism," published in the Swedish journal *Form* in 1958. Part antimodernist manifesto, part formal statement of his intentions in his house designs for Grill, it began, as had so many of his essays, with a discussion of the place of history in modern architecture and design. The gradual erosion of tradition, he wrote, had made it necessary for the modernists to invent their own artistic rules. To give their new aesthetic the greatest intellectual and moral force, they had adopted an art of purism, in which "much is forbidden, but little is allowed." In this way, Frank explained, "an art arose that [had] little connection to our actual lifestyle, but in fact quite nearly symbolized its opposite." People began to "yearn again for spaces that allowed some room for fantasy" and for streets "that were something other than solutions to traffic problems."[30]

The alternative, Frank argued, was not another "style" but a fundamentally new way of thinking about art and design. "What we need," he wrote,

is a much greater elasticity, not strict formal rules. A demonumentalization, without recourse to historical styles. Those styles are and will remain dead. What I call modern architecture in the long run is fundamentally different from any historical architecture. . . . Every human needs a certain degree of sentimentality to feel free. . . . What we need is variety and not stereotyped monumentality. No one feels comfortable in an order that has been forced upon him, even if it has been doused in a sauce of beauty. Therefore, what I suggest are not new rules and forms but a radically different attitude toward art. Away with universal styles, away with the equalization of art and industry, away with the whole system that has become popular under the name functionalism. This new architectural system . . . I would like to give a name in the manner that is currently fashionable. . . . I will call it Accidentism *for the time being, and by that I mean that we should design our surroundings as if they originated by chance.*[31]

For Frank, this new architecture of accidentism offered a means to recreate the pleasing diversity found in old cities and buildings:

Every place where one feels comfortable—rooms, streets, and cities—has originated by chance. Buildings of all epochs stand harmoniously next to one another in cities that have grown organically. Something of this nature of course cannot be attained today, but I am convinced that uniformity is not the result of necessity but of an ideology that is not even our own. . . . A theater does not have to look like a factory, and the hall of a bank like a pastry shop.[32]

Accompanying Frank's text were illustrations of three of his postwar works—House 9 from the 1947 series (perspective), Double D-House 6 (plans and perspective), and a perspective of an unrealized project for a hotel from around 1958 (fig. 240)—each intended to demonstrate his principles. Though quite different in terms of planning and composition, all three present a vision of an architecture based on "difficulty" and "multiplicity" resulting from a seemingly undetermined design process: the various elements were intended to suggest the actions of happenstance rather than intent. But if Frank drew on the notion of chance, his architecture and urban plans were never purely aleatoric. While some of the young cultural *revoltés* of the postwar years—such as Jackson Pollock or John Cage—sought an art of no order, no structure, and no control, Frank merely attempted to impart the impression of disorder. The designs remain as rigorously controlled as any of Frank's earlier works. The apparent diversity of ideas is, quite ironically, the outcome of careful regulation and manipulation.

Frank was not alone in his desire to introduce a less structured architecture. Strains of "antirationalism" sounded in many theoretical writings of the late 1950s and early 1960s, from those of William Katavolos to the painter Friedrich Hundertwasser. Frank, however, remained almost completely detached from the contemporary architectural discourse. "Accidentism" was reprinted in German in *Baukunst und Werkform* in 1961, but it attracted scant attention. Many of the same themes, however, resounded in Robert Venturi's powerful critique of modernism, *Complexity and Contradiction in Architecture,* published eight years later, in 1966. Frank almost certainly never saw it; he died only a few months after the book's appearance. But Venturi's call for "messy vitality over obvious unity"[33] summed up ideas Frank had been developing over the previous three decades; and many of the principles Venturi laid out seem to be foreshadowed in Frank's late architectural projects.

THE LATE HOUSES In his designs for the Thirteen Houses and the two series of D-Houses, Frank had investigated how the standard modernist vocabulary might be adapted to present an architecture of complexity and apparent disorder. In the mid- to late 1950s, he also began to examine ways to integrate historical and modern forms to forge a new composite language. The inspiration for this melding of old and new derived in part from Frank's frequent visits to Provence, where Waehner had purchased a small summer house. Over the years, Frank made several additions to the traditional stone building, perched on a hillside high above the village of Dieulefit, including a long pergola and an outdoor fireplace.[34] Taken with the simple rustic architecture of the region—"the southern architecture is probably the best of what exists in Europe," he wrote to Sobotka[35]—Frank in the early 1950s began to incorporate elements of the Mediterranean vernacular in his designs. In some of his projects, such as his design for a house with a stone entry (fig. 241), this interest is revealed largely through the massing, which suggests the volumes of the hillside villages of the region. Increasingly, however, he began to make direct quotations, siting the houses in his renderings in the Provençal countryside and employing both rustic stone masonry and stucco walls. In his design for a round stone house of the mid-1950s (plate 25, fig. 242), Frank, perhaps inspired by the prehistoric dwellings of the Mediterranean, also explored the possibilities of older free-form designs.

None of the works was constructed: aside from a commission for a villa for a client named Albrée in Grasse on the Riviera, which never came to fruition,[36] all of Frank's late designs were evidently fantasy houses, created without any real prospects for realization. Like his earlier fantasy houses, Frank's projects of the mid- to late 1950s expressed his accidentist principles. But more and more he sought to use a historical frame for his complex spatial and compositional ideas.

This is most strikingly apparent in a project for a house for Waehner in Provence, which he designed in the late 1950s (plate 26, fig. 243). Like the works of Venturi and Charles Moore of the 1960s and 1970s, it quoted boldly from history. The façade, which included two existing buildings, sported elements of the Provençal vernacular—whitewashed stucco, rubble masonry, and red tile roofs.[37] Into this "quasi-historicist" assem-

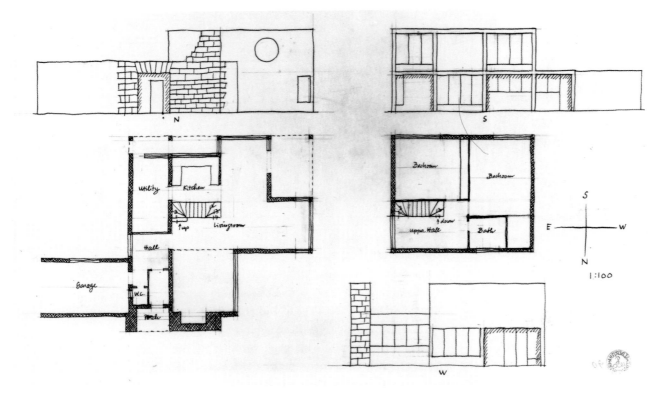

241. (top) Project for a house with
stone entry, mid-1950s; elevations,
plans 1:100. Pencil, pen and ink on
tracing paper, 29.5 × 42 cm.
Graphische Sammlung Albertina,
Vienna.

242. (bottom) Project for a round
stone house in Provence, mid-
1950s; plans and elevations 1:100.
Pencil, pen and ink on tracing
paper, 27.5 × 42.5 cm. Graphische
Sammlung Albertina, Vienna.

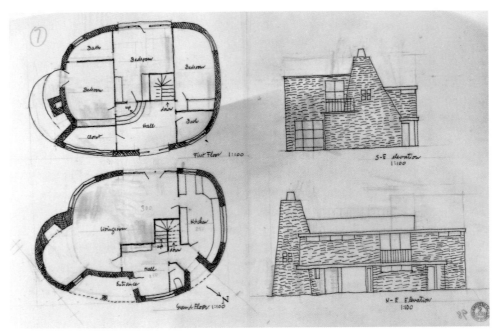

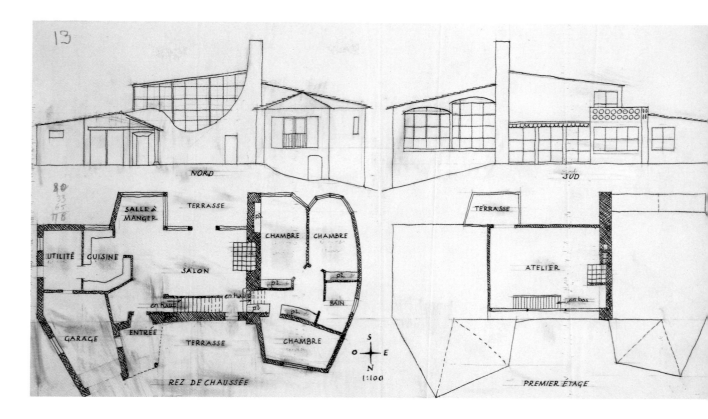

blage, Frank introduced a "modern" glass atelier, the framing members painted a vibrant red. But all of these various constituent parts have been warped and deformed, at once redefining their relationships and revealing the idiosyncratic spatial order within. This merging of old and new, of complexities and distortions, served to foster a symbolic image of sophistication and eccentricity, while at the same time making a potent statement about the possibilities for a new kind of architecture.

If, in the last two decades of his life, Frank's designs and writings boldly preached a new eclecticism, he lacked the sense of confidence of mission of Venturi and the other young postmodernists. Indeed, many of his later writings reveal a sense of a deep resignation. As early as 1948, he had written to Waehner, "I don't believe anymore that I can accomplish anything; it will still be necessary for me to do a little something to earn a living, [but] I have closed out my life's work so to speak." He added: "It is not the life's work that I imagined and that had been my goal and what I could have done and wanted to do, but that which I was able to accomplish under these circumstances; and when I look back on it, it looks very sad."[38]

Despite failing health, Frank continued to work sporadically for Svenskt Tenn through the late 1950s. While in Stockholm, he would stop by the shop daily, meeting

243. Project for a house for Trude Waehner, Provence, late 1950s; elevations and plans. Pencil, pen and ink on paper, 26 × 47.5 cm. Graphische Sammlung Albertina, Vienna.

with Ericson to confer on the details of his latest works (fig. 244). He wrote little after "Accidentism," although he presented several public lectures in Stockholm in the mid-1960s, including talks on *Jugendstil* and on the Austrian architecture of the interwar years. In his last years, Frank lived quietly in Stockholm, still musing about the problems of modern architecture. He reflected little on his previous accomplishments, preferring as he once wrote, "not to dig into the past."[39] In 1965, when Viennese critic and historian Viktor Matejka asked him about his hopes for the future of architecture, he answered simply, "more personality and the avoidance of uniformity for its own sake."[40] He added that he was gratified to see that a growing number of younger architects shared his dissatisfaction with modern architecture. The reason for their displeasure, he asserted, was that modernism was now "exhausted." Before it had become so commonplace, "its principles had a persuasive power," but by the 1960s it had become "tedious." Only "in the Mediterranean countries," he wrote, "where the classical tradition still survived, was that not the case."[41]

In 1965, through the efforts of a group of younger Viennese architects and historians, including Friedrich Achleitner, Hermann Czech, Friedrich Kurrent, and Johannes Spalt, Frank was awarded the Austrian State Prize for Architecture, the country's highest honor for a living architect. Frank, however, who was about to turn eighty, was too weak to travel to Vienna to accept the award. He died in Stockholm a little more than a year and a half later on 8 January 1967.

244. Frank with Estrid Ericson at Svenskt Tenn, 1964. Photograph by Lennart Nilsson. Svenskt Tenn Collection, Josef Frank Archive, Stockholm

EPILOGUE: FRANK AND MODERNISM Frank's passing came at a time when the reaction to modernism was just beginning to gather force. The deaths of the last surviving modern masters—Le Corbusier died the year before, and Gropius and Mies both expired in 1969—signaled the start of a new age and, at the same time, a period of reappraisal of the modern movement and its history. But though Frank had long been among the most persistent of the small chorus of voices calling for reform, little notice was taken of his death. Apart from a brief memoir in the Italian journal *Domus* written by Carmela Haerdtl, the wife of Oswald Haerdtl, and obituaries in newspapers in Austria and Sweden, Frank's death went unrecorded, a telling sign of how far he had fallen in the estimation of his contemporaries.

The question of Frank's importance in the story of modernism is a complex one. His output as an architect, in comparison with figures like Wright or Mies, was quite small. During his peak years of building, from 1919 to 1936, he was able to erect only a handful of works; and many of them, because of the economic woes of post–First World War Austria, were modest at best. Yet Frank also built two of the landmark houses of the interwar years, the Villa Beer in Vienna and the Wehtje House in Falsterbo, which although still surprisingly little known, articulated new ideas of space and place-making as powerfully as any of the works of Mies, Loos, or Wright. Indeed, it is in his expansion of the possibilities of space and spatial experience that Frank's significance partially resides. Architecture, for Frank, was fundamentally about providing room for human experience; he understood buildings as the background and framework for the events of daily life. The purpose of that frame was not to determine human actions but to allow the inhabitants to live as they wanted, freely and without fixed rules. His concern for movement and bodily experience grew out of his abiding interest in both use and comfort.

Frank's work as a designer issued from the same belief in the importance of combining the utilitarian with the concept of pleasure. His furnishings and objects for Haus & Garten and Svenskt Tenn (fig. 245) were always conceived as articles to fulfill their assigned tasks *and* provide enjoyment. Formal issues in Frank's designs never took precedence over matters of human delight. At a time in modern design when pure geometry seemingly threatened to sweep away any vestige of elaboration, Frank produced modern, up-to-date pieces that nonetheless preserved older aesthetic conventions. As one of the spiritual founders of Swedish Modern, he also helped to forge the groundwork for one of the most important reappraisals of functionalism.

Frank's most important contribution, however, centers on his role as a critic and reformer of modernism. During the later 1920s and early 1930s, he was among the most prominent of those calling for a reexamination of modern architecture and modern life. And although his pleas went largely unheeded at the time, they raised meaningful issues about both that still hold relevance in our time. In a letter to his cousin Helene Eisenkolb written only a month before his death, Frank closed with what might have been a fitting

245. Living room at the *Josef Frank Memorial Exhibition* at Svenskt Tenn, Stockholm, 1968. Photograph by C. J. Rönn. Svenskt Tenn Collection, Josef Frank Archive, Stockholm.

epitaph. "Otherwise," he concluded, "there is absolutely nothing new, and that is all well and good, because when everything is new it is usually not so beautiful [*denn alles neue ist gewöhnlich nicht so schön*]."[42] It was, in so many ways, a characteristic remark for Frank. Throughout his life he had fought passionately against the notion of novelty for its own sake, against the easy association of the "new" with the "modern." Rather than attempting to forge a wholly new style, he attempted to reconcile past and present.

Frank's careful mining of the past, however, was more than mere nostalgia. Above all, he had sought answers to the problem of how modern man should live. That question, in turn, led him to seek solutions to the basic problems of architecture and design. Often the conclusions he arrived at placed him outside the mainstream of the modern movement. Indeed, even in his most pointedly promodernist work and writings, there are repeated suggestions that he was out of touch with the spirit of that movement, that, much like Loos, he had never really been part of it. He shared neither the radical modernists' affirmations of a new purism nor their firm faith in the virtues of the machine age. In his later years, he grew increasingly opposed to the ideas of rationalization and standardization. During the late 1940s and 1950s, when the world architecture scene was dominated by a combination of austerity and cool formalism, Frank preached a new eclecticism that had at its heart a rejection of the twin pillars of unity and technical prowess upon which the widely accepted view of modernism rested.

Yet in other respects Frank was very much a part of the story of modern architecture. In his early years, he had been deeply influenced by its generative ideas, and he had personally contributed much to its rise in the 1920s. But more significantly, Frank's life experiences, his search for a new way of living, and his successes and failures, had highlighted the ongoing development of modern architecture. By probing its limits and assumptions and by pointing out its faults and its inherent deficiencies, he brought the problems of modernism into high relief.

It is tempting to view Frank as a precursor of the postmodernist revolt of the 1960s and 1970s. Many of his criticisms of modern architecture seem to reverberate in the writings and works of Venturi, Charles Moore, and those who came after them. But in the end, Frank's attack on the ideology of the avant-garde was not an effort to subvert modernism but to find a way to remake it. His aim was to forge a modern architecture freed of the problems of style and of ideological demands, at the same time reestablishing a genuine tie to the past.

Indeed, it seems now that Frank was eager to weave so many elements together, not out of some empty eclecticism, but in the belief that this synthesis might redeem architecture and design. His late call for a new architecture of accidentism was not an attempt to hasten the death of modernism but to find a way to save it, recast it, and give it new life. In so doing, he pointed simultaneously in two directions, back to the past and forward to the future.

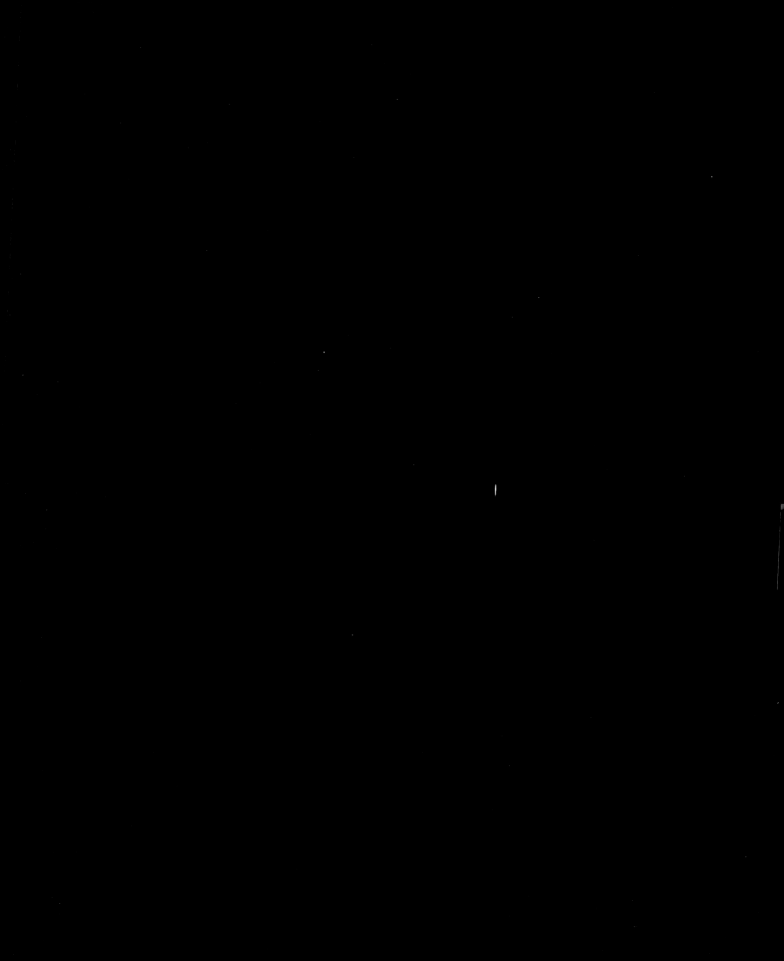

NOTES

PROLOGUE

1   Josef Frank, "Was ist modern?" *Die Form* 5 (1 August 1930): 400.

2   Frank, "Was ist modern?" 399.

CHAPTER ONE

1   *Lehmanns Allgemeiner Wohnungsanzeiger nebst Handels- und Gewerbe-Adreßbuch für die k. u. k. Reichs- Haupt- und Residenzstadt und Umgebung* (Vienna, 1870–1910). On Frank's early life see also Wilfried Posch, "Josef Frank, eine bedeutende Persönlichkeit des österreichischen Kulturliberalismus," *Um Bau* 10 (August 1986), 21–22.

2   Letter to the author from Anni Feilendorf (Frank's cousin), 30 December 1993. Ignaz (1851–1921) and Jenny Frank (1861–1941) first lived at Liechtensteinstraße 61 in the city's ninth district. Around 1900, they moved to an apartment at Augustengasse 4 (now Gölsdorfgasse) in the first district. Jenny Frank continued to reside there until the time of her death. Records, Wiener Stadt- und Landesarchiv.

3   Records, Israelitische Kultusgemeinde, Vienna; and Magistrat der Stadt Wien (MA 61).

4   Birth register, Israelitische Kultusgemeinde, Vienna.

5   Helene Eisenkolb (Frank's cousin),
    interview by author, 12 June 1987.

6   A. Feilendorf, letter.

7   Also among those who attended the
    school during the same years was the fu-
    ture composer Alban Berg, who for a time
    was one of Frank's classmates. Records,
    Wiener k. k. Staatsoberrealschule im 1.
    Bezirke, Vienna.

8   Stephanie Feilendorf (Frank's cousin),
    interview by author, New York, 15 July
    1987.

9   "Hauptkatalogue der V. Classe"
    (1899–1900, 1900–1901), and "Hauptkat-
    alogue der VII. Classe" (1902–1903).
    Wiener k. k. Staatsoberrealschule im 1.
    Bezirke.

10 S. Feilendorf, interview, 15 July 1987.

11 Otto Wagner, *Moderne Architektur* (Vi-
    enna: Anton Schroll, 1896), 4.

12 Marco Pozzetto, "Karl König und die Ar-
    chitektur der Wiener Technischen
    Hochschule," in *Wien um 1900: Kunst und
    Kultur*, edited by Maria Auböck and Maria
    Marchetti, exhibition catalog (Vienna:
    Christian Brandstätter, 1985), 305. On the
    Königschule, see also Christopher Long,
    "An Alternative Path to Modernism: Carl
    König and Architectural Education at the
    Vienna Technische Hochschule,
    1890–1913," *Journal of Architectural
    Education* 55 (September 2001): 21–30.

13 On König's life and work, see Markus
    Kristan, *Carl König, 1841–1915: Ein
    neubarocker Großstadtarchitekt in Wien*, ex-
    hibition catalog (Vienna: Jüdisches Mu-
    seum der Stadt Wien, 1999). See also *Carl
    König, Bauten und Entwürfe von Carl König
    herausgegeben von seinen Schülern* (Vienna:
    Gerlach & Wiedling, 1910), 5–6; Karl
    Mayreder, *Zu Karl Königs siebzigstem
    Geburtstag* (Vienna: Karl König-Komitees,
    1912); "Karl König," in *Allgemeines Lexikon
    der bildenden Künstler von der Antike bis zur
    Gegenwart*, edited by Ulrich Thieme and
    Felix Becker (Leipzig: E. A. Seemann,
    1935), 21: 157–58; and Renate Wagner-
    Rieger, "Karl König," *Österreichisches Bi-
    ographisches Lexikon, 1815–1950* (Vienna:
    Böhlau, 1969), 36–37.

14 Walter Sobotka, "Principles of Design,"
    MS 368, Sobotka Papers, Avery Architec-
    tural and Fine Arts Library, Columbia
    University, 400. Sobotka studied at the
    Technische Hochschule from 1907 to
    1912. He and Frank corresponded in later
    years, reminiscing about their years at the
    school. Frank, in one of his letters (from
    March 1962, translated by Sobotka and
    included in the appendix of his manu-
    script), remembered: "I have learned a lot
    from König and this was a good founda-
    tion."

15 In the years after the turn of the century,
    nearly one-third of all of the architecture
    students at the Technische Hochschule
    were Jewish. By contrast, the Academy of
    Fine Arts, the other important training
    ground for architects at the time, enrolled
    very few Jews. Of the 190 students who
    studied in the Wagnerschule between
    1894 and 1914, for example, only one,
    Ernst Lichtblau, was Jewish. The anti-Se-
    mitic atmosphere of the school was doubt-
    less one reason why Frank never applied
    for admission to the Academy of Fine
    Arts, a route a number of his fellow stu-
    dents from Technische Hochschule took,
    among them Rudolph M. Schindler,
    Oskar Laske, and Emil Pirchan. See Ur-
    sula Prokop, *Wien, Aufbruch zur Metro-
    pole: Geschäfts- und Wohnhäuser der Innen-
    stadt 1910 bis 1914* (Vienna: Böhlau,
    1994), 65.

16 "Die Wissenschaft von der Architektur und ihre praktische Bedeutung," reprinted in *Bauten und Entwürfe von Carl König*, 9.

17 See Max Fabiani, "Karl König," *Wiener Bauindustrie Zeitung* 32 (May 1915): 61.

18 Sobotka, "Principles of Design," 400.

19 See Pozzetto, "Karl König," 305–6, and Long, "An Alternative Path to Modernism," esp. 25–28.

20 Fabiani, "Karl König," 61.

21 Although on a number of occasions Frank later wrote of König's importance for his development, he never mentioned Fabiani's influence. In a letter written in 1967 to Carmela Haerdtl, however, Sobotka confirmed that Frank had been a student of Fabiani's: "When I entered [the school]," Sobotka wrote, "Frank was in his next to last or last year. So I know for certain that Frank was his [Fabiani's] student." Marco Pozzetto, *Max Fabiani: Ein Architekt der Monarchie* (Vienna: Edition Tusch, 1983), 18. On Fabiani's influence on Frank, see also Maria Welzig, *Josef Frank, 1885–1967: Das architektonische Werk* (Vienna, Cologne, and Weimar: Böhlau, 1998), 14–16.

22 On Fabiani's work and ideas, see Pozzetto, *Max Fabiani: Ein Architekt der Monarchie*; and idem, *Max Fabiani* (Trieste: MGS Press, 1998).

23 Fabiani, "Die deutsche, italienische und französiche Komposition," quoted in Pozzetto, *Max Fabiani: Ein Architekt der Monarchie*, 19.

24 Letter from Frank to Walter Sobotka, 23 April 1964, quoted in Sobotka, "Principles of Design," 409.

25 See Max Fabiani, *Regulierung der Stadt Bielitz—Erläuterungsbericht zum General-Regulierungs-Pläne der Stadt Bielitz* (Vienna, 1899).

26 J. P. Hodin, *Oskar Kokoschka: The Artist and His Time. A Biographical Study* (London: Cory, Adams & Mackay, 1966), 76.

27 Felix Augenfeld, "Erinnerungen an Adolf Loos," *Bauwelt* 72 (6 November 1981): 1907. Loos, in an article entitled "Meine bauschule" published in *Der Architekt* in 1913, responded characteristically: "A professor at one of our universities in the middle of the school year forbade his students to attend my lectures. I owe him a debt of gratitude. Those with character remained, and he has freed me of the others." The article was later reprinted in Adolf Loos, *Trotzdem, 1900–1930* (Innsbruck: Brenner, 1931), 66.

28 Loos, in a handwritten note in the Loos Papers at the Graphische Sammlung Albertina, mentions that he and Frank attended the German Werkbund conference held in Munich in June of that year, and refers to Frank as "von mir hochgeschätzen Kollegen Dr. Frank" (my highly esteemed colleague Dr. Frank). See Burkhardt Rukschcio and Roland L. Schachel, *Adolf Loos: Leben und Werk* (Salzburg and Vienna: Residenz, 1982), 114.

29 Originally a market hall, the building had been adapted by Joseph Urban for use by the Hagenbund artists group just after the turn of the century. In 1907, in conjunction with the forthcoming Eighth International Congress of Architects, plans were formulated to erect a new structure on the site. The competition, sponsored by the Österreichischer Ingenieur- und Architektenverein (Austrian Engineer and Architects Association), ran from 5 to 25 April 1907. *Wiener Bauindustrie Zeitung* 24 (3 May 1907): 271. For a discussion of the general context of the competition, see

Matthias Boeckl, "Die Mode-Moderne mit dem fabriciertem Stimmungs-Dusel," in *Die verlorene Moderne: Der Künstlerbund Hagen, 1900–1938*, edited by Günter Natter, exhibition catalog (Vienna: Österreichische Galerie, 1993), 64–65.

30 "Konkurrenz für eine Ausstellungshalle," *Der Architekt* 13 (September 1907): 49–52.

31 Frank, curriculum vitae (1910); and Rigorosenakt, vol. 304 (1909–10), Universitätsarchiv, Technische Universität, Vienna.

32 Prüfungsprotokoll, II. Staatsprüfung, (4–13 July 1908), Universitätsarchiv, Technische Universität, Vienna.

33 Frank, curriculum vitae.

34 See Anthony Alofsin, *Frank Lloyd Wright, the Lost Years, 1910–1922: A Study of Influence* (Chicago and London: University of Chicago Press, 1993), 12–13.

35 Lewerentz worked in Möhring's office from the summer of 1908 through February 1909, when he left to take up an apprenticeship in the office of Theodor Fischer in Munich. See Janne Ahlin, *Sigurd Lewerentz, Architect, 1885–1975* (Cambridge, Mass.: MIT Press, 1987), 14.

36 For a complete list of Möhring's work, see Ines Wagemann, *Der Architekt Bruno Möhring, 1863–1929* (Witterschlick: M. Wehle, 1992), 216–20.

37 See Welzig, *Josef Frank*, 20–21. Only one of the perspectives published in *Stein und Eisen* is likely by Frank. Welzig attributes a second drawing to Frank, which is reproduced in her book; it exhibits a very different rendering technique and almost certainly is not his work.

38 See Rudolf Eberstadt, Bruno Möhring, and Richard Petersen, *Groß-Berlin. Ein Programm für die Planung der neuzeitlichen Groß-Stadt* (Berlin: Ernst Wasmuth, 1910). Möhring's plan was not adopted, but it later influenced Albert Speer's design for the city.

39 Frank, curriculum vitae.

40 Frank, "Vom neuen Stil," *Baukunst* 3 (August 1927): 234.

41 Rigorosenakt.

CHAPTER TWO

1 Esther Strömberg, who taught therapeutic gymnastics, had moved to Vienna in 1902 and later founded the school with Harald Palm. During the same period he worked on the school, Frank also designed the interiors for the apartment of Strömberg and her husband, the writer Stefan Großmann. See Welzig, *Josef Frank*, 23–27.

2 Carl Larsson's paintings of domestic interiors were widely published in the German-speaking world after the turn of the century. Larsson's book, *Ett hem* (Stockholm: A. Bonnier, 1899), published in a revised version in German (*Das Haus in der Sonne* [Düsseldorf and Leipzig: K. R. Langewiesche, 1909]), included not only images of the novel program of interior decoration that he and his wife Karin had developed for their house in Sundborn, Sweden, but also a text expounding the Larssons' ideas. Frank, who two years later included several of Larsson's watercolors in his room at the spring exhibition, undoubtedly was aware of his work. What attracted Frank was not only Larsson's use of Swedish folk elements but also his skillful synthesis of traditional motifs with ideas drawn from the English arts and crafts movement, Japonisme, and art nouveau. On the ideas and influence of the Larssons, see Michael Snodin and Elisabet Stavenow-Hidemark, eds., *Carl and Karin Larsson: Creators of the Swedish Style*, exhibition catalog (Boston:

Little, Brown, 1997). On the exhibition of Swedish folk arts and cottage industries, see *Ausstellung schwedischer Volkskunst und Hausindustrie,* exhibition catalog (Vienna: Österreichisches Museum für Kunst und Industrie, 1910).

3   On the design of the vitrine, see Nina Stritzler-Levine, ed., *Josef Frank, Architect and Designer: An Alternative Vision of the Modern Home,* exhibition catalog (New Haven and London: Yale University Press, 1996), 159. Maria Welzig has argued that the vitrine is the work of Strnad (Welzig, *Josef Frank,* 23, 28), but Oskar Wlach in his article on Frank clearly identifies it as Frank's work. See Oskar Wlach, "Zu den Arbeiten von Josef Frank," *Das Interieur* 13 (1912), plate 44.

4   Wlach, "Zu den Arbeiten von Josef Frank," 42.

5   Hermann Bahr, *Secession* (Vienna: L. Rosner, 1900), 33–34.

6   Wlach, "Zu den Arbeiten von Josef Frank," 45.

7   Wlach, "Zu den Arbeiten von Josef Frank," 42–43.

8   Strnad (1879–1935) had studied at the Technische Hochschule from 1898 to 1904; Lurje (1883-?) from 1901 to 1907; and Wlach (1881–1963) from 1898 to 1903. Gorge (1883–1934), however, had studied at the Academy of Fine Arts with Friedrich Ohmann and probably knew Strnad from Friedrich Ohmann's office, where he worked from 1903 to 1910.

9   On Strnad's life and work, see "Oskar Strnad zum 50. Geburtstag," *Deutsche Kunst und Dekoration* 33 (January 1930): 253–68; Max Eisler, *Oskar Strnad* (Vienna: Gerlach & Wiedling, 1936); Joseph Gregor, *Rede auf Oskar Strnad* (Vienna: Herbert Reicher, 1936); Otto Niedermoser, *Oskar Strnad,*

1879–1935 (Vienna: Bergland, 1935); and Johannes Spalt, ed., *Der Architekt Oskar Strnad. Zum hundertsten Geburtstag am 26. Oktober 1979* (Vienna: Hochschule für angewandte Kunst, 1979).

10   Strnad's first project with Wlach was for a competition for the new chamber of commerce in Brünn (Brno). The two also collaborated on an entry for the War Ministry competition in 1908 and for a theater in Brüx (Most) in 1909. In 1909, Strnad and Lurje collaborated on a competition for a colonnade in Karlsbad (Karlovy Vary). On the formation and early work of the Strnad circle, see Welzig, *Josef Frank,* 31–37.

11   Cf. Frank's article "Die Einrichtung des Wohnzimmers," *Innen-Dekoration* 30 (December 1919): 416–17, with Strnad's 1913 lecture "Einiges Theoretische zur Raumgestaltung," *Deutsche Kunst und Dekoration* 41 (October 1917): 39–69.

12   Hartwig Fischel, "Die Ausstellung österreichischer Kunstgewerbe im k.k. österreichischen Museum für Kunst und Industrie," *Kunst und Kunsthandwerk* 14 (1911): 626.

13   Fischel, "Die Ausstellung österreichischer Kunstgewerbe," 626.

14   Österreichisches Museum für Kunst und Industrie, *Frühjahrsausstellung österreichischer Kunstgewerbe, verbunden mit einer Ausstellung der k. k. Kunstgewerbeschule Wien. Mai–Juli 1912,* exhibition catalog (Vienna, 1912). On the exhibition, see also Sabine Forsthuber, *Moderne Raumkunst: Wiener Ausstellungsbauten von 1898 bis 1914* (Vienna: Picus, 1991), 152–58; and Christopher Long, "'A Symptom of the Werkbund': The Spring 1912 Exhibition at the Austrian Museum of Art and Industry, Vienna," *Studies in the Decorative Arts* 7 (spring–summer 2000): 91–121.

15 Christian Witt-Dörring, "'Steel Is Not a Raw Material; Steel Is a *Weltanschauung*': The Early Furniture Designs of Josef Frank, 1910–1933," in Nina Stritzler-Levine, ed., *Josef Frank, Architect and Designer: An Alternative Vision of the Modern* (New Haven and London: Yale University Press, 1996), 107.

16 "[T]he much freer and lighter furnishings of the English home," Frank wrote many years later, presented "the best solution of the interior problem." English houses "had not merged their domestic identity in rigid theories. They seemed to have the advantage of retaining something 'human' in their appearance." "An Austrian Architect Looks at England," *Architectural Review* 73 (June 1933): 268.

17 Hoffmann and Loos were fervent Anglophiles and shared a penchant for English tailoring and furnishings with many of Vienna's avant-garde. The *Studio*, the leading English arts publication at the turn of the century, was widely circulated in Vienna, and after 1900 most of the leading German and Austrian architectural and interior design journals, including *Deutsche Kunst und Dekoration, Innen-Dekoration, Dekorative Kunst,* and *Kunst und Kunsthandwerk,* regularly kept their readers abreast of the most recent English developments. See, for example, Amelia S. Levetus, "The European Influence of the Studio," *Studio* 105 (1933): 257–58.

18 Witt-Dörring, "'Steel Is Not a Raw Material,'" in Stritzler-Levine, *Josef Frank, Architect and Designer,* 107–8.

19 Fritz Planer, "Die Ausstellung im Österreichischen Museum für Kunst und Industrie 1912," *Deutsche Kunst und Dekoration* 31 (October 1912): 180.

20 *Kunst und Kunsthandwerk* 15 (1912), 345.

21 Frank, "Die Einrichtung des Wohnzimmers," 417.

22 Frank, "Die Einrichtung des Wohnzimmers," 417.

23 Adolf Fischer (1856–1914) initially prepared to join his father in running the family concerns. His first love remained the theater, however, and during the late 1870s and early 1880s he studied with the well-known Viennese actor Josef Lewinsky. From 1883 to 1886, he served as director of the *Stadttheater* in Königsberg, but eventually gave up the theater to devote himself to the study of art. During the 1890s, he made the first of several trips to China and Japan, and over the course of the next decade he assembled an impressive collection of East Asian art. He mounted several exhibitions of his collection around the turn of the century, including the sixth exhibition of the Vienna Secession, held from 20 January through 15 February 1900, which was devoted to Japanese art and design. On Fischer's life and the history of the museum, see Adolf Fischer, *Führer durch das Museum für Ostasiatische Kunst der Stadt Cöln* (Cologne: M. Dumont Schauberg, 1913); and Ulrich Wiesner, *Museum für Ostasiatische Kunst Köln. Zum 75jährigen Jubiläum des Museums* (Cologne: Museum für Ostasiatische Kunst der Stadt Köln, 1984).

24 Hoffmann evidently became acquainted with Frank through Strnad, who knew Hoffmann quite well. During his time in Cologne, Frank regularly wrote to Hoffmann updating him on his progress. Two of the surviving letters have been preserved in the collection of the Wiener Stadt- und Landesbibliothek, I.N. 158.556 and I.N. 158.557.

25   The interior configuration for the annex had already been worked out by the municipal architect in the city of Kiel, which had initially committed to build the museum. Brantzky was forced to adapt the plans for the Cologne site, wedging it into a corner of the already complete Museum of Arts and Crafts. Fischer was also involved in the design process, but the design work was finished before Frank arrived in Cologne. Wiesner, *Museum für Ostasiatische Kunst Köln*, 18–19.

26   Letter, Frank to Hoffmann, 20 November 1912, Wiener Stadt- und Landesbibliothek, I.N. 158.556.

27   Frank, "Über die Aufstellung des 'Museums für Ostasiatische Kunst' in Köln," *Der Architekt* 22 (1919): 170.

28   Wiesner, *Museum für Ostasiatische Kunst Köln*, 26.

29   Curt Glaser, "Ein Museum ostasiatischer Kunst," *Kunst und Künstler* 12 (1913–14): 287.

30   See, for example, M. Osborn, "Ostasien in Köln," *Berliner Zeitung*, 24 October 1913; R. Petrucci, "Das Museum für ostasiatische Kunst," *Frankfurter Zeitung*, 27 October 1913; and F. Stahl, "Das Kölner Museum für ostasiatiche Kunst," *Berliner Tagblatt*, 27 October 1913. Clipping files, Museum für Ostasiatische Kunst, Cologne. The building and all of the installations were destroyed during the Second World War.

31   Stephanie Feilendorf, interview by author, New York, 14 July 1987.

32   Personal papers of Anna Sebenius Frank and Josef Frank, Svenskt Tenn Collection, Josef Frank Archive, Stockholm. See also Kristina Wängberg-Eriksson, *Josef Frank— Livsträd i krigens skugga* (Lund: Bokförlaget Signum, 1994), 45–46.

33   S. Feilendorf, interview, 14 July 1987.

34   Welzig, *Josef Frank*, 38–39.

35   Oskar Wlach, "Professional Career of Dr. Oskar Wlach," n.d. Photocopy in possession of the author.

36   Karl Tedesco, who was married to Frank's sister Hedwig, was Hugo Bunzl's cousin. Frank's mother Jenny was also related to both the Tedescos and the Bunzls. Letter, Elisabeth Pelc-Bunzl to the author, 3 January 1988.

37   Hermann Muthesius, *Das englische Haus: Entwicklung, Bedingungen, Anlage, Aufbau, Einrichtung und Innenraum*, 3 vols. (Berlin: Ernst Wasmuth, 1904–5).

38   M. H. Baillie Scott, *Houses and Garden* (London: George Newnes, Ltd., 1906).

39   M. H. Baillie Scott, *Häuser und Gärten*, translated by Wilhelm Schölermann (Berlin: E. Wasmuth, 1912).

40   M. H. Baillie Scott, *Houses and Gardens*, 7.

41   Scott, *Houses and Gardens*, 10.

42   Scott, *Houses and Gardens*, 10–11.

43   Scott, *Houses and Gardens*, 3.

44   "Das neuzeitliche Landhaus," *Innen-Dekoration* 30 (December 1919): 410–12.

45   On the influence of Webb, Shaw, and other English architects on the Viennese, see Julius Posener, "Der Raumplan. Vorläufer und Zeitgenossen von Adolf Loos," in *Adolf Loos, 1870–1933 Raumplan-Wohnungsbau*, edited by Dietrich Worbs, exhibition catalog (Berlin: Akademie der Künste, 1984), 53–63.

46   Frank, "Das neuzeitliche Landhaus," 412.

47   Frank, "Das neuzeitliche Landhaus," 412. On Frank's views on the flat roof, see also his article "Das steile Dach ist ein Rest aus dem romantischen Zeitalter," *Das neue Frankfurt* 1 (October–December 1927): 194–96.

48 See Adolf Loos, "Regeln für den, der in den bergen baut," first published in *Jahrbuch der Schwarzwald'schen Schulanstalten* (1913), reprinted in *Trotzdem* (Innsbruck: Brenner, 1931): 133–34. Loos writes: "Changes in the old building methods are only allowed when they mean an improvement, otherwise stay with the old" (134).

49 Eduard F. Sekler, *Josef Hoffmann: The Architectural Work* (Princeton: Princeton University Press, 1985), 23.

50 Strnad presented the lecture on 17 January 1913 to the Österreichischer Ingenieur- und Architektenverein in Vienna. The text of talk was published in 1917 under the title "Einiges Theoretische zur Raumgestaltung," *Deutsche Kunst und Dekoration* 41 (October 1917): 39–40, 49–50, 62, 65–69. It was reprinted under the title "Raumgestaltung und Raumgelenke" in *Innen-Dekoration* 30 (July–August 1919): 254–58, 292–93.

51 Strnad, "Einiges Theoretische zur Raumgestaltung," 68.

52 Architektur ist keineswegs eine reine sichtbare Welt, sondern ist aus unendlich vielen Imponderabilien zusammengesetzt. Ein architektonisches Konzept entsteht durch die Konzentrationskraft der Vorstellung sowohl der Bewegungsmöglichkeit (als absolutes Raumgefühl) wie auch der Wirkung des Lichts (Farbe der Materie), des Geruchs, des Gehörs und des Tatsinns (Materie) . . . Die Behandlung der Oberfläche der Materie darf keinesfalls nur aus ästhetischen Gründen erfunden werden, sondern aus viel tieferen, nicht zu erklärenden seelischen. Strnad, "Gedanken beim Entwurf eines Grundrisses (1913)," reprinted in Niedermoser, *Oskar Strnad*, 17–18. The original manuscript of the lecture is preserved at the archive of Universität für angewandte Kunst, manuscript 4648/Q/5. It was published posthumously in Eisler, *Oskar Strnad*, 56–57. For a discussion of Strnad's spatial planning ideas, see Ulla Weich, "Die theoretischen Ansichten des Architekten und Lehrers Oskar Strnad" (M.A. thesis, Universität Wien, 1995), 49–53, 105–6.

53 See Ernest K. Mundt, "Three Aspects of German Aesthetic Theory," *Journal of Aesthetics and Art Criticism* 17 (March 1959): 287–310; and the introduction to *Empathy, Form, and Space: Problems in German Aesthetics, 1873–1893*, edited by Harry Francis Mallgrave and Eleftherios Ikonomou (Santa Monica, Calif.: Getty Center for the History of Art and the Humanities, 1994), esp. 57–66.

54 Adolf Hildebrand, *Das Problem der Form in der bildenden Künste* (Strasbourg: Heitz & Mündel, 1893).

55 See August Schmarsow, *Unser Verhältnis zu den Bildenden Künsten: Sechs Vorträge über Kunst und Erziehung* (Leipzig: B. G. Teubner, 1903); and *Grundbegriffe der Kunstwissenschaft* (Leipzig: B. G. Teubner, 1905). See also Mitchell W. Schwarzer, "The Emergence of Architectural Space: August Schmarsow's Theory of *Raumgestaltung*," *Assemblage* 15 (August 1991): 48–61; and Ernst Ullmann, "Der Beitrag August Schmarsows zur Architekturtheorie" (unpublished Habilitationsschrift, Institute für Kunstgeschichte und Kunsterziehung, Universität Leipzig, 1967).

56 See Schwarzer, "The Emergence of Architectural Space," 55.

57 Although neither Strnad nor Frank refers explicitly to Schmarsow (they may indeed have encountered his ideas second- or

even thirdhand), it is clear from their writings that they were acquainted with the main outlines of the debate and with the application of the new spatial concepts in the works of historians such as Alois Riegl and Paul Frankl.

58 The ideas of Hildebrand, Schmarsow, Riegl, and others involved in the discussions of space at the time were certainly familiar to Loos, who must have similarly drawn important lessons from them.

59 Loos, "Das Prinzip der Bekleidung," first published in *Neue Freie Presse,* 4 September 1898, reprinted in Adolf Loos, *Ins Leere gesprochen,* 108–9.

60 On the development of the idea of empathy in Germany and Austria, see Mallgrave and Ikonomou's introduction to *Empathy, Form, and Space,* 17–29.

61 Max Eisler, "Oskar Strnad," *Dekorative Kunst* 21 (February 1918): 153.

62 See Sekler, *Josef Hoffmann,* 83–84.

63 Ferdinand von Feldegg, "Maria am Gestade im Gefahr," *Wiener Bauindustrie-Zeitung* 33 (June 1916): 65–68.

64 Eisler, "Oskar Strnad," 153.

65 Leopold Kleiner, "Wien," *Wasmuths Monatshefte für Baukunst* 6 (1921): 178.

66 See Max Eisler, *Österreichische Werkkultur* (Vienna: Anton Schroll, 1916), 81–95.

67 Margarete Schütte-Lihotzky later recalled that while she was a student in the late 1910s the two Wilbrandtgasse houses were widely discussed in Viennese architectural circles, provoking "bitter debates." "Erinnerungen an Josef Frank," *Bauwelt* 26 (12 July 1985): 1052.

68 In Frank's absence, Strnad took over the task of making the final corrections to the houses, and he signed the revised drawings. Archives, Baupolizei, Vienna XIX (MA37).

69 Military service records, Österreichisches Staatsarchiv-Kriegsarchiv, Vienna.

70 Although Frank's years in the Imperial army proved largely uneventful, his military service records reveal that during the war he was brought up on charges of striking a fellow officer. The incident took place in November 1915, while Frank was still in training. After another cadet made an anti-Semitic remark and refused to take the statement back, Frank "struck him in the face with his hand." The case dragged through the military courts for several years, until finally, in March 1918, Frank was convicted and sentenced to three days house arrest. Military service records, Österreichisches Staatsarchiv-Kriegsarchiv, Vienna, Dok. Präs. 14/672/1 (14 March 1918), and 25 6/197–2 (30 March 1918).

71 See Angela Völker, *Textiles of the Wiener Werkstätte, 1910–1932* (London: Thames and Hudson, 1994), 214, 252; and Werner J. Schweiger, *Wiener Werkstätte: Design in Vienna, 1903–1932* (New York: Abbeville Press, 1984), 259.

CHAPTER THREE

1 Stefan Zweig, *Die Welt von Gestern. Erinnerungen eines Europäers* (London: H. Hamilton, 1941), translated as *The World of Yesterday: An Autobiography* (New York: Viking Press, 1943), 281.

2 Schweiger, *Wiener Werkstätte,* 109–10, 259; Kristina Wängberg-Eriksson, *Josef Frank: Textile Designs* (Lund: Bokförlaget Signum, 1999), 150.

3 Karl A. Bieber, interview by author, Graz, 1 July 1986.

4 Herbert Thurner, "Über Josef Frank," in Johannes Spalt and Hermann Czech, eds.,

Josef Frank, 1885–1967 (Vienna: Hochschule für angewandte Kunst), 7.

5   Thurner, "Über Josef Frank."

6   Thurner, "Über Josef Frank."

7   Johannes Itten, *Design and Form: The Basic Course at the Bauhaus* (London: Thames and Hudson, 1964), 9.

8   Karl A. Bieber, interview by author, 1 July 1986.

9   See Frank, "Wiens moderne Architektur bis 1914," *Der Aufbau* 1 (September 1926), 168.

10 Adolf Loos, "Wohnen lernen!" *Neues Wiener Tagblatt*, 15 May 1921, reprinted in Loos, *Trotzdem*, 165.

11 On the *Siedlerbewegung*, see Robert Hoffmann, "Entproletarisierung durch Siedlung? Die Siedlungbewegung in Österreich 1918 bis 1938," in *Bewegung und Klasse. Studien zur österreichischen Arbeitergeschichte*, edited by Gerhard Botz et al. (Vienna, Munich, and Zurich: Europa, 1978): 713–42; Wolfgang Förster, "Die Wiener Arbeitersiedlungsbewegung vor dem Zweiten Weltkrieg—Eine Alternative zum kommunalen Wohnbauprogram," *Der Aufbau* 35, no. 12 (1980): 405–10; Klaus Novy, "Selbsthilfe als Reformbewegung: Der Kampf der Wiener Siedler nach dem 1. Weltkrieg," *Arch+* 55 (February 1981): 26–40; Klaus Novy and Günther Uhlig, *Die Wiener Siedlungsbewegung, 1918–1934*, exhibition catalog (Cologne: Arch+, 1982); Helmut Weihsmann, *Das rote Wien: Sozialdemokratische Architektur und Kommunalpolitik, 1919–1934* (Vienna: Promedia, 1985), 114–18; Robert Hoffmann, *Nimm Hack' und Spaten—: Siedlung und Siedlerbewegung in Österreich 1918–1938* (Vienna: Verlag für Gesellschaftskritik, 1987); and Eve Blau, *The Architecture of Red Vienna, 1919–1934*

(Cambridge, Mass.: MIT Press, 1999), chap. 3.

12 Ernst A. Plischke, interview by author, Vienna, 17 November 1986.

13 Josef Frank, Hugo Fuchs, and Franz Zettinig, "Wohnhäuser aus Gußbeton. Ein Vorschlag zur Lösung der Wohnungsfrage," *Der Architekt* 22 (1919): 36.

14 Frank does not cite specific examples of U.S. concrete housing construction. Among the contemporary works on the subject were *Concrete Houses and Cottages*, 2 vols. (New York: Atlas P. Cement Co., 1909); Oswald C. Hering, *Concrete and Stucco Houses* (New York: McBridge, Nast & Co., 1912); and *The Manufacture of Standardized Houses* (New York: Standardized Housing Corporation, 1917). Frank, who regularly read U.S. architectural publications, was also, no doubt, aware of Thomas A. Edison's experiments with concrete construction during the early years of the new century.

15 Frank et al., "Wohnhäuser aus Gußbeton," 34–37.

16 Frank et al., "Wohnhäuser aus Gußbeton," 36.

17 Letter, Elisabeth Pelc-Bunzl to author, 22 November 1987; and biographical entry on Hugo Bunzl in *International Biographical Dictionary of Central European Émigrés, 1933–1945*, edited by Herbert A. Strauss et al., 3 vols. (Munich: K. G. Saur, 1980–83), 1: 104.

18 Frank, "Die Arbeiter-Kolonie in Ortmann," *Deutsche Kunst und Dekoration* 48 (September 1921): 307.

19 See Paul Mebes, *Um 1800, Architektur und Handwerk im letzten Jahrhundert ihrer traditionellen Entwicklung*, 2 vols. (Munich: F. Bruckmann, 1908); Heinrich Tessenow, *Die Wohnhausbau* (Munich: G. D. W. Call-

wey, 1909); and Paul Schultze-Naumburg, *Kulturarbeiten*, 9 vols. (Munich: G. D. W. Callwey, 1902–7). Related designs appear in the works of a number of other architects and planners who proposed similar garden cities during and after the war, including Peter Behrens and Heinrich de Fries, who coauthored the work *Vom sparsamen Bauen: Ein Beitrag zur Siedlungsfrage* (Berlin: Bauwelt, 1918), and Hermann Muthesius, who the same year published *Kleinhaus und Kleinsiedlung* (Munich: F. Bruckmann, 1918).

20 On Tessenow's tenure in Vienna, see Herbert Sommer, ed., *Heinrich Tessenow* (Vienna: Hochschule für angewandte Kunst, 1976).

21 Frank, "Die Arbeiter-Kolonie in Ortmann," 307.

22 Josef Frank, "Die Wiener Siedlung," *Der Neubau* 6 (10 February 1924): 25.

23 Frank, "Die Wiener Siedlung," 25.

24 Frank, "Die Wiener Siedlung," 25.

25 See Philipp Frank, *Modern Science and Its Philosophy* (Cambridge, Mass.: Harvard University Press, 1949), 1–52; and Rudolf Haller, "Der erste Wiener Kreis," in *Fragen zu Wittgenstein und Aufsätze zur österreichischen Philosophie*, edited by Rudolf Haller (Amsterdam: Rodopi, 1986): 89–107.

26 Frank was also close friends with Neurath's second wife, Olga Hahn-Neurath, who was the sister of Hans Hahn. Olga had lost her sight at the age of twenty-two, and Frank regularly accompanied her on long evening walks. Paul Neurath (Otto Neurath's son), interview by author, Vienna, 30 August 1990.

27 Margarete Schütte-Lihotzky, "Mein Freund Otto Neurath," in Friedrich Stadler, ed., *Arbeiterbildung in der Zwischenkriegszeit,*

Otto Neurath-Gerd Arntz (Vienna: Löcker, 1982), 40.

28 On Neurath's life and work, see Elisabeth Nemeth and Friedrich Stadler, eds., *Encyclopedia and Utopia: The Life and Work of Otto Neurath, 1882–1945* (Dordrecht and Boston: Kluwer, 1996); and William M. Johnston, *The Austrian Mind: An Intellectual and Social History, 1848–1938* (Berkeley, Los Angeles, and London: University of California Press, 1972), 192–95. See also Paul Neurath, "Wieder in Wien: Generalsekretär des österreichischen Verbandes für Siedlungs- und Kleingartenwesen (1920–1925)," in Paul Neurath and Elisabeth Nemeth, eds., *Otto Neurath: Oder die Einheit von Wissenschaft und Gesellschaft,* Monographien zur österreichischen Kultur und Geistesgeschichte, vol. 6 (Vienna: Böhlau, 1994): 53–58; and Robert Hoffmann, "Proletarisches Siedeln: Otto Neuraths Engagement für die Wiener Siedlungsbewegung und den Gildensozialismus 1920 bis 1925," in Stadler, *Arbeiterbildung in der Zwischenkriegszeit*, 140–48.

29 On the courses taught in the *Siedlerschule,* see Renate Allmeyer-Beck, Susanne Baumgartner-Haindl, Marion Lindner-Gross, and Christine Zwingl, eds., *Margarete Schütte-Lihotzky: Soziale Architektur, Zeitzeugin eines Jahrhunderts* (Vienna: Böhlau, 1996), 22.

30 Allmeyer-Beck et al., *Margarete Schütte-Lihotzky: Soziale Architektur,* 25.

31 Blau, *The Architecture of Red Vienna,* 116.

32 Otto Kapfinger, "Josef Frank—Siedlungen und Siedlungsprojekte 1919–1932," *Um Bau* 10 (August 1986): 48.

33 Klaus Novy and Wolfgang Förster, *Einfach bauen, Genossenschaftliche Selbsthilfe nach der Jahrhundertwende: Zur Rekonstruktion*

der Wiener Siedlerbewegung (Vienna: Verein für moderne Kommunalpolitik), 159.

34 Otto Neurath, *Österreichs Kleingärtner- und Siedlerorganisation* (Vienna: Wiener Volksbuchhandlung, 1923), 34.

35 Werner Hegemann, "Kritisches zu den Wohnbauten der Stadt Wien," *Wasmuths Monatshefte für Baukunst und Städtebau* 10 (1926): 365–66. In a letter to the critic Franz Roh, Neurath noted that Frank "was the one socialist [architect] who attempts to make his style accessible to young people, the settlers, the municipal authorities"—although it is clear that his assessment in the end was not fully shared by the settlers themselves. Letter, Neurath to Franz Roh, 19 June 1924, Franz Roh Papers, file 850120, Getty Research Institute for the History of Art and the Humanities, Los Angeles.

36 On the competition, see Carol Herselle Krinsky, *Synagogues of Europe: Architecture, History, Meaning* (New York: Architectural History Foundation and Cambridge, Mass.: MIT Press, 1985), 258–60.

37 Although included with the drawings of the Klosterneuburg *Siedlung*, the plans do not correspond to the configuration of the rooms, which Frank evidently intended to be illustrations of a different, "future" settlement. Frank, "Einzelmöbel und Kunsthandwerk," *Innen-Dekoration* 34 (November 1923): 336–38.

38 Frank, "Einzelmöbel und Kunsthandwerk," 337–38.

39 Franz Schuster and Franz Schacherl, "Proletarische Architektur," *Der Kampf* 19 (1926): 37–38, quoted in Blau, *The Architecture of Red Vienna*, 194.

40 Rukschcio and Schachel, *Adolf Loos*, 243ff.

41 During the latter half of the nineteenth century, several experimental suburban communities had been built in Vienna, among them an area known as "Cottage," begun in 1873 in the district of Währing. Heinrich von Ferstel, one of the leading Ringstrasse architects, served as architectural advisor. Some 350 houses were eventually constructed. But the idea of single-family housing failed to gain popularity among the Viennese middle class, and in later years many of the villas were divided up into apartments. See Donald Olsen, *The City as a Work of Art: London, Paris, Vienna* (New Haven and London: Yale University Press, 1986), 172ff.

42 Quoted in Jan Tabor, "Der unsichere Boden der Tradition," *Wien aktuell* 89 (October 1984): 24–25.

43 Wilfried Posch, "Die Wiener Gartenstadtbewegung-Der Streit um Wohn- und Hausform," in *Reflexionen und Aphorismen zur österreichischen Architektur*, edited by Viktor Hufnagl (Vienna: Georg Prachner, 1984), 341.

44 Rudolf Müller, "Die Kehrseite des Eigenhauses," *Der Kampf. Sozialdemokratische Monatsschrift* 5 (1912): 172.

45 On the details of the plan, see Max Ermers, "Groß-Wiens Stadterweiterung und der neue General-Architekturplan," *Der Tag*, 25 November 1923, 6; Otto Neurath, "Generalarchitekturplan," *Das Kunstblatt* 7 (April 1924): 105–8; and Blau, *The Architecture of Red Vienna*, 160–66.

46 Although the actual number of *Siedlung* houses continued to grow during the 1920s, their percentage of the city's entire building program decreased steadily: in 1921, *Siedlung* houses accounted for slightly more than half of the housing units built; in 1923, they made up less than one-third; and by 1925, they consti-

tuted only 4 percent of the total. Wilfried Posch, "Die Gartenstadtbewegung in Wien," *Bauforum* [Vienna] 13, nos. 77–78 (1980): 17. After 1926, the settlements were constructed almost exclusively under the direction of Gemeinwirtschaftliche Siedlungs- und Baustoffanstalt (GESIBA), with financial support coming directly from the government. On the dissolution of the *Siedlung* movement, see Blau, *The Architecture of Red Vienna,* 128–33.

47 On the Viennese communal housing program, see Deutsch-Österreichischer Städtebund, *Die Wohnungspolitik der Gemeinde Wien. Ein Überblick über die Tätigkeit der Stadt Wien seit der Bekämpfung der Wohnungsnot und zur Hebung der Wohnkultur* (Vienna, 1926); Josef Bittner, *Neubauten der Stadt Wien,* 2 vols., Die Quelle, 14 (Vienna and New York: Gerlach & Wiedling, 1926–30); Robert Dannenberg, *Zehn Jahre Neues Wien* (Vienna: Wiener Volksbuchhandlung, 1929); Charles O. Hardy, assisted by Robert R. Kuczynski, *The Housing Program of the City of Vienna* (Washington, D.C.: Brookings Institution, 1934); Helfried Kodré, "Die Entwicklung des Wiener sozialen Wohnungsbaues in den Jahren 1919–1938," *Der Aufbau* 19 (September 1964): 343–50; Peter Haiko and Mara Reissberger, "Die Wohnhausbauten der Gemeinde Wien 1919–1934," *Architese* 12 (1974): 49–54; Karl Mang and Eva Mang-Frimmel, eds., *Kommunaler Wohnbau in Wien: Aufbruch 1923–1934 Ausstrahlung* (Vienna: Presse- und Informationsdienst der Stadt Wien, 1977); Hans Hautmann and Rudolf Hautmann, *Die Gemeindebauten des Roten Wien 1919–1934* (Vienna: Schönbrunn, 1980); Manfredo Tafuri, ed., *Vienna Rossa: La politica residenziale nella*

Vienna socialista, 1919–1923 (Milan: Electa Editrice, 1980); Weihsmann, *Das rote Wien;* Helmut Gruber, *Red Vienna: Experiment in Working-Class Culture, 1919–1934* (New York: Oxford University Press, 1991); and Blau, *The Architecture of Red Vienna.*

48 See Blau, *The Architecture of Red Vienna,* 303.

49 Dietrich Worbs, "Josef Franks Wiener Massenwohnungsbau—Ein pragmatischer Versuch," *Bauwelt* 76 (12 July 1985): 1049.

50 Friedrich Achleitner, "Viennese Architecture between the Wars: First Split between the Form and Content of Modernity," *Lotus International* 29 (1981): 123.

51 Max Ermers, "Die 'Paprikakiste' am Kongreßplatz," *Der Tag,* 1 August 1926, 9.

52 Wiener Kunstgewerbeverein, *Katalog der Jubiläumsausstellung,* exhibition catalog (Vienna, 1924).

53 Photographs of the model were also published in *Österreichische Kunst* 1 (1927): 120, and in Alberto Sartoris's compilation of modernist architecture, *Gli elementi dell' architettura funzionale* (Milan: Hoepli, 1935), 72.

54 See Dietrich Neumann, *Die Wolkenkratzer kommen: Deutsche Hochhäuser der Zwanziger Jahre* (Wiesbaden: Vieweg, 1995).

55 Frank, "Der Volkswohnungspalast. Eine Rede anlässlich der Grundsteinlegung, die nicht gehalten wurde," *Der Aufbau* 1 (August 1926): 107.

56 Frank, "Der Volkswohnungspalast," 107–9.

57 Frank, "Der Volkswohnungspalast," 109.

58 Frank, "Der Volkswohnungspalast," 110.

59 Frank, "Der Volkswohnungspalast," 110–11.

CHAPTER FOUR

1 Hans Tietze in *Der Neue Tag* (Vienna), 1 February 1920, quoted in Schweiger, *Wiener Werkstätte: Design in Vienna,* 106.

2 Frank's silver mirror was among the objects illustrated in the catalog of the New York branch of the Wiener Werkstätte operated by Joseph Urban. A surviving copy of the catalog (which incorrectly identifies the mirror as a work of Strnad's) with handwritten prices lists the mirror at $1,200, a large sum at the time. Urban opened the shop in June 1922, in part to help his fellow architects and designers in Vienna. But it seems unlikely, given the considerable gap between the time Frank designed the piece in 1919 and Urban opened the New York showroom, that it was originally intended for the U.S. market. See Jane Kallir, *Viennese Design and the Wiener Werkstätte,* exhibition catalog (New York: George Braziller, 1986), 31.

3 Frank, "Über die Zukunft des Wiener Kunstgewerbes," *Der Architekt* 24 (1921–22): 42.

4 Frank, "Über die Zukunft des Wiener Kunstgewerbes," 37.

5 Frank, "Über die Zukunft des Wiener Kunstgewerbes," 42.

6 Frank was particularly critical of what he viewed as a growing tendency on the part of many Viennese designers to divorce their work from the new reality. In a 1923 essay, he singled out Dagobert Peche, who emerged in the postwar period as the most innovative form-giver among the Wiener Werkstätte's artists and designers. Although Frank recognized Peche's consummate skill as a draftsman and his "magnificent imagination," he complained that Peche "had almost lost sight of the organic relationship that exists between material and its treatment." As a result, he continued, the works of Peche and his followers "are exercises of the imagination comparable to the boldest experiments in painting, the cubist and expressionist tendencies, but no longer have any relation to the more ordered art of architecture." Frank, "Le Métier d'Art," *L'Amour de l'Art* 4 (August 1923): 652.

7 Frank, "Einzelmöbel und Kunsthandwerk," *Innen-Dekoration* 34 (November 1923): 337.

8 Frank, "Handwerks- und Maschinen-Erzeugnis. Die Abgrenzung Beider Gebiete," *Innen-Dekoration* 34 (August 1922): 243.

9 Frank, "Handwerks- und Maschinen-Erzeugnis," 241.

10 Frank, "Kunst, Kunsthandwerk und Machine," *Die Ware* 1 (1923): 70.

11 Frank, "Kunst, Kunsthandwerk und Machine," 70.

12 On Frank's Falsterbo houses, see Mikael Bergquist and Olof Michélsen, *Josef Frank, Falsterbovillorna* (Stockholm: Arkitektur, 1998).

13 "Haus Claëson in Falsterbo, Schweden," *Moderne Bauformen* 28 (1929): 44.

14 The Claëson House was also, it is worth noting, among the earliest "functionalist" buildings constructed in Sweden. On the rise of modernism in Sweden, see Marion C. Donnelly, *Architecture in the Scandinavian Countries* (Cambridge, Mass.: MIT Press, 1992).

15 See the interview with Frank, "Franksk funktionalism i Falsterbo," *Veckojournalen* 40 (1929): 33–35.

16 As Gmeiner and Pirhofer note, the decision on the part of Frank and his partners to launch the business was "a calculated

response" to the changing marketplace. Although most middle-class families still lacked the savings to build new housing, many were able to afford to replace or augment their old prewar furnishings, providing a demand that Frank and his partners hoped to fill. Astrid Gmeiner and Gottfried Pirhofer, *Der Österreichische Werkbund: Alternative zur klassischen Moderne in Architektur, Raum- und Produktgestaltung* (Salzburg: Residenz, 1985), 111.

17 While in Turkey, Wlach undertook a number of projects, including a plan to rebuild the Stambul and Galata quarters of Constantinople that had been destroyed by fire. He also designed a central slaughterhouse for the city and a city plan for Smyrna. "Oskar Wlach, Bewerbung für die Aufnahme in die Liste der Sachverständigen für Architektur und Hochbaufach," 18 June 1924; and "Professional Career of Dr. Oskar Wlach, April 1958." Copies in possession of the author.

18 On Wlach's postwar housing designs, see, for example, "Einküchenhaus," *Der Architekt* 22 (1919): 121–22.

19 "Oskar Wlach, Bewerbung für die Aufnahme in die Liste der Sachverständigen für Architektur und Hochbaufach," 18 June 1924, 2. Copy in possession of the author. Cf. n. 17.

20 Welzig, *Josef Frank*, 81. The interiors of the Löbel House are shown in the early publications on Haus & Garten. See Leopold Greiner, "Möbel und Einrichtung der Neuzeit. Arbeiten der Werkstätten 'Haus & Garten'-Wien," *Innen-Dekoration* 37 (October 1926): 348, 362–63, 368, 370–72, 384; and "Josef Frank," *Moderne Bauformen* 26 (May 1927): 177.

21 Sobotka (1888–1972) entered the Technische Hochschule in 1907, the year before

Frank left for Berlin. After the war, he worked as an architect and designer for Karl Korn and others, and he subsequently launched his own architecture and interior design firm. In 1938, he fled to New York, where he found work as a designer with the U.S. branch of the Thonet Company. Later, he taught interior design at the Carnegie Institute of Technology (now Carnegie Mellon University) in Pittsburgh. He and Frank carried on a correspondence into the early 1960s. See Maria Welzig, "Entwurzelt: Sobotka, Wlach und Frank in Pittsburgh und New York," in Matthias Boeckl, ed., *Visionäre und Vertriebene: Österreichische Spuren in der modernen amerikanischen Architektur* (Berlin: Ernst & Sohn, 1995), 204–11, which also includes a biography of Sobotka (344–45).

22 The company was officially registered on 6 June 1925. It was renamed "Haus & Garten, Frank und Wlach" on 22 January 1926 after Sobotka's departure. Central registration archives of the City of Vienna (MA 63).

23 Plischke, interview, 17 November 1986.

24 See *L'Autriche à l'exposition internationale des arts décoratifs et industriels modernes Paris 1925*, exhibition catalog (Vienna: Commission Exécutive Instituée pour la Participation de L'Autriche à L'Exposition, 1925).

25 Quoted in Kristina Wängberg-Eriksson, "The Interior Designer," in Monica Boman, ed., *Estrid Ericson: Founder of Svenskt Tenn*, translated by Roger G. Tanner (Stockholm: Carlsson, 1989), 102.

26 English critic H. C. Bradshaw, for example, wrote that the "design of the teahouse and garden was one of the best in the Exhibition and cleverly combined a

sheltered garden and terraces overlooking the river with the Pavilion itself." Bradshaw, "The Architecture of the Paris Exhibition, 1925," in H. Llewellyn Smith, *Report on the Present Position and Tendencies of the Industrial Arts As Indicated at the International Exhibition of Modern Decorative and Industrial Arts, Paris, 1925* (London: Department of Oversees Trade, 1927), 45.

27 See Nancy J. Troy, *Modernism and the Decorative Arts in France: Art Nouveau to Le Corbusier* (New Haven and London: Yale University Press, 1991), 220–26.

28 Josef Frank file, Personnel records, Universität für angewandte Kunst, Vienna.

29 From about 1926 to 1929, the address of their atelier was listed as Museumstraße 5a. After 1929, it was given as Neustiftgasse 3. *Lehmanns Wohnungsanzeiger für Wien* (1925–30). This change is also reflected on Frank's drawings, providing an indication of the design dates for his furnishings and buildings of the period.

30 Plischke, interview, Vienna, 28 November 1986.

31 Gustav Carl Lehmann originally specialized in wallpaper and linoleum, but during the 1920s the company expanded their product range to include furniture, textiles, and other household objects. It is unknown precisely when the company started selling Haus & Garten designs, but the association between the two firms had been formed by 1927 when Lehmann produced the upholstered furnishings for Frank's double house at the Stuttgart Weissenhofsiedlung. See Welzig, *Josef Frank*, 164. In the late 1920s and early 1930s, Frank and Wlach mounted regular exhibitions of their newest products at Lehmann's. Frank also redesigned the Cologne shop's exterior and furnished the reception area in the early 1930s. Frank's connection to the firm was through one of the co-owners of the enterprise, Artur Wachsberger, a Viennese whom Frank had met while working for Fischer at the East Asian Art Museum prior to the war. At the time, Wachsberger was one of Josef Strzygowski's assistants at the Kunsthistorisches Institut in Vienna. Strzygowski recommended him to Fischer, who employed him for eight months at the museum beginning in early 1913. During that time, he and Frank formed a friendship that lasted for many years. Welzig, *Josef Frank*, 50–51.

32 It was Strnad, in fact, in an article published in *Innen-Dekoration* in 1922, who articulated most fully the principles of the new design direction. Home furnishings, Strnad wrote, should be light, moveable, and carefully scaled to human dimensions. They should be placed independently of the room and arrayed so that the walls, ceiling, corners, and floor be left visible: "One should never attempt to make 'architecture' with furniture," nor should furnishings be used to divide or organize the room. The walls should be treated simply—in most instances merely painted white, which, he argued, would enhance the feeling of spaciousness by heightening a sense of the walls' immateriality. Brightly colored Oriental rugs and fabrics could be added to "dress" [*ver-kleiden*] and accent the room, Strnad asserted, but industrially produced articles should be avoided because they engendered a sense of "unease." Strnad, "Neue Wege in der Wohnraum-Einrichtung," *Innen-Dekoration* 33 (October 1922): 323–24.

33 On the origins and development of the Wiener Wohnkultur, see Christian Witt-Dörring, Eva Mang, and Karl Mang, eds., *Neues Wohnen. Wiener Innenraumgestaltung, 1918–1938,* exhibition catalog (Vienna: Österreichisches Museum für angewandte Kunst, 1980); and Christopher Long, "*Wiener Wohnkultur*: Interior Design in Vienna, 1910–1938," *Studies in the Decorative Arts* 5 (fall–winter 1997–98): 29–51.

34 See Witt-Dörring, "Steel Is Not a Material," in Stritzler-Levine, *Josef Frank, Architect and Designer,* 110–14.

35 Frank, "Rum och inredning," *Form* 30 (1934); translated into German under the title "Raum und Einrichtung," in Spalt and Czech, *Josef Frank 1885–1967,* 97.

36 Frank, "Raum and Einrichtung," 97.

37 Frank, "Einzelmöbel und Kunsthandwerk," 337.

38 Frank, "Einzelmöbel und Kunsthandwerk," 338. Wlach also advocated this new emphasis on individual furnishings in his work and writings in this period. See, for example, Wlach's essay, "Einheit und Lebendigkeit," *Innen-Dekoration* 33 (January–February 1922): 59–65.

39 See Eva B. Ottillinger, *Adolf Loos: Wohnkonzepte und Möbelentwürfe* (Salzburg and Vienna: Residenz, 1994), esp. 24–28, 90, 120–21, 124, and 132.

40 Frank, *Architektur als Symbol,* 150.

41 Frank, "Die moderne Einrichtung des Wohnhauses," in Werner Gräff, ed., *Innenräume. Räume und Inneneinrichtungsgegenstände aus der Werkbundausstellung "Die Wohnung"* (Stuttgart: Dr. Fr. Wedekind & Co., 1928), 126.

42 Greiner, "Möbel und Einrichtung der Neuzeit," 355.

43 Frank, "Raum und Einrichtung," 97.

44 Greiner, "Möbel und Einrichtung der Neuzeit," 355.

45 On Frank's early development as a textile designer, see Kristina Wängberg-Eriksson, "Geometry in Disguise: A Modernist's Vision of Textile Design," in Nina Stritzler-Levine, ed., *Josef Frank, Architect and Designer: An Alternative Vision of the Modern Home* (New Haven and London: Yale University Press, 1996), 140–44; and idem, *Josef Frank: Textile Designs,* translated by Christopher Long, Jan Christer Eriksson, and Kristina Wängberg-Eriksson (Lund: Bokförlaget Signum, 1999); originally published as *Pepis flora: Josef Frank som mönsterkonstnär* (Lund: Bokförlaget Signum, 1998), 10–15, 35–58.

46 S. Feilendorf, interview, 15 July 1987.

47 Jenny Frank produced many of the pieces for family and friends. Frank occasionally made use of her works in exhibitions and interiors for clients, and he evidently arranged to have some of her pieces exhibited in the Austrian Pavilion at the 1925 Paris *Exposition Internationale.* See *L'Autriche à l'exposition internationale des arts décoratifs et industriels modernes Paris 1925,* 41.

48 Wängberg-Eriksson, *Josef Frank: Textile Designs,* chaps. 2 and 3.

49 See the complete list of Frank's textiles in Wängberg-Eriksson, *Josef Frank: Textile Designs,* 147–51.

50 Around 1930, Frank began having the textiles printed by the English firm of G. P. and J. Baker. Wängberg-Eriksson, *Josef Frank: Textile Designs,* 59–62.

51 Frank produced several different versions of this Egyptian stool, which is based on a surviving example from circa 1300 B.C. Reproductions of the stool were sold by Liberty's in London from 1884 on, and it

was introduced into Vienna by Adolf Loos around the turn of the century. A few years later, Loos designed his own variant of the stool, which can be see in photographs of many of his domestic interiors in the 1920s and early 1930s. Frank's version, which he also used in a number of his interiors during this period, has a somewhat thinner saddle seat, with a carrying hole in the center. The edges are also more rounded, and the legs, rather than angling away from the seat, continue straight-down, similar to the legs of a table. On the history of the stool and Loos and Frank's models, see Ottillinger, *Adolf Loos: Wohnkonzepte und Möbelentwürfe,* 124–26.

52 Greiner, "Möbel und Einrichtung der Neuzeit," 355.

CHAPTER FIVE

1 "Josef Frank," *Moderne Bauformen* 26 (May 1927): 172.

2 "Josef Frank," 173.

3 Letter, Mies van der Rohe to Gustaf Stotz, 26 September 1925. Mies van der Rohe Archive, Museum of Modern Art, New York. On the selection process see Karin Kirsch, *Die Weissenhofsiedlung: Werkbund-Ausstellung "Die Wohnung" Stuttgart 1927* (Stuttgart: Deutsche Verlags-Anstalt, 1987), 53–58; Richard Pommer and Christian F. Otto, *Weissenhof 1927 and the Modern Movement in Architecture* (Chicago and London: University of Chicago Press, 1991), 45–55, 173–77; and Wolf Tegethoff, "Weißenhof 1927: Der Sieg des neuen Bauens?" in *Jahrbuch des Zentralinstituts für Kunstgeschichte* (Munich: C. H. Beck, 1987), 3: 211–22. Much of the original correspondence is reprinted in Karin Kirsch, ed., *Briefe zur Weißenhofsiedlung* (Stuttgart: Deutsche Verlags-Anstalt, 1997). See also idem, "Weissenhofsiedlung Stuttgart 1927," *Arquitectura* 70 (May–August 1989): 51–73.

4 Pommer and Otto, *Weissenhof 1927,* 47.

5 Mies also proposed to include Anton Brenner, another young Viennese architect, but he was excluded from the final roster. Frank, concerned that the Austrians were not better represented, wrote to Mies requesting that a cross-section of "the best and most important works of Austrian architects" be included. Letter, Frank to Mies, 9 April 1927. Mies van der Rohe Archive, Museum of Modern Art, New York. Eventually, several other well-known Viennese figures were invited to show their work at the exhibition, including Sobotka and Wlach, who designed interiors for Behrens's apartment block, and Schütte-Lihotzky, whose space-saving "Frankfurt kitchen" and *Plattenhaus* were displayed.

6 This smaller figure is from a list compiled by Richard Döcker late in 1927. The higher cost is the estimate from Stuttgart Hochbauamt, who oversaw the construction of the project. See Pommer and Otto, *Weissenhof 1927,* 146, 178–79; and Franz Hoffmann, "Kritisches über die Stuttgarter Werkbundsiedlung," *Bauwelt* 41 (1927): 1020.

7 Jürgen Joedicke, *Architektur der Zukunft der Architektur,* exhibition catalog (Stuttgart: Universität Stuttgart, 1980), 56.

8 "Feifel-Bausteine," in Günther Wasmuth and Leo Adler, *Wasmuths Lexikon der Baukunst* (Berlin: E. Wasmuth, 1930), 2: 429–30.

9 Thomas Fisher, "Low Cost, High Design," *Progressive Architecture* 10 (October 1988): 98, 104.

10 Kirsch, *Die Weissenhofsiedlung*, 174.

11 "Wie sind die Häuser der Werkbundsiedlung zu heizen?" *Württembergische Zeitung*, 10 January 1928.

12 Kirsch, *Die Weissenhofsiedlung*, 172.

13 Pommer and Otto, *Weissenhof 1927*, 99.

14 Kirsch, *Die Weissenhofsiedlung*, 172.

15 Kirsch, *Die Weissenhofsiedlung*, 172.

16 Julius Zeitler, "Die Werkbundausstellung 'Die Wohnung' in Stuttgart," *Dekorative Kunst* 31 (1927–28): 34–35.

17 Oskar Wolfer, "Die Werkbundausstellung 'Die Wohnung' in Stuttgart," *Die Kunst: Angewandte Kunst* 58 (October 1927): 57.

18 Willi P. Fuchs-Röll, "'Neues Wohnen.' Werkbundausstellung in Stuttgart 1927," *Der Neubau* 9 (10 September 1927): 201.

19 See Wilfried Wang, "Orthodoxy and Immanent Criticism: On Josef Frank's Contribution to the Stuttgart Weissenhofsiedlung, 1926–1927," in Alexander von Hoffmann, ed., *Form, Modernism, and History: Essays in Honor of Eduard F. Sekler* (Cambridge, Mass., and London: Harvard University Press, 1996): 63–70.

20 Edgar Wedepohl, "Die Weissenhofsiedlung der Werkbundausstellung 'Die Wohnung' Stuttgart 1927," *Wasmuths Monatshefte für Baukunst* 11 (1927): 397–98.

21 "Die Wohnung," *Het Bouwbedrijf* 4 (November 1927): 556–59; reprinted in Théo van Doesburg, *On European Architecture. Complete Essays from Het Bouwbedrijf, 1924–1931*, trans. Charlotte I. Loeb and Arthur L. Loeb (Basel and Boston: Birkhäuser, 1990), 172.

22 Bei Frank-Wien fühlt man sich in ebenso atavistischer wie angenehmer Weise von Kissen und tausenderlei Wiener Gschnas umschmeichelt. Hans Bernoulli, "Die Wohnungsausstellung Stuttgart 1927," *Das Werk* 14, no. 9 (1927): 265.

23 Werner Gräff, "Hinter den Kulissen der Weissenhofsiedlung," Werner-Gräff-Archiv, Mülheim, quoted in Kirsch, *Die Weissenhofsiedlung*, 174.

24 Letter, Paul Meller to J. J. P. Oud, 31 August 1927, Oud Archive, Rotterdam, reprinted in Kirsch, *Briefe zur Weißenhofsiedlung*, 201–2.

25 Werner Hegemann, "Stuttgarter Schildbürgerstreiche und die Berliner Bauausstellung 1930," *Wasmuths Monatshefte für Baukunst* 12, no. 1 (1928): 11.

26 Frank, "Der Gschnas fürs G'müt und der Gschnas als Problem," in Deutscher Werkbund, *Bau und Wohnung*, exhibition catalog (Stuttgart: Dr. Fr. Wedekind & Co., 1927), 49.

27 Frank, "Der Gschnas fürs G'müt," 55.

28 Frank, "Der Gschnas fürs G'müt," 58.

29 Frank, "Der Gschnas fürs G'müt." See also Frank's article "Drei Behauptungen und ihre Folgen," *Die Form* 2, no. 9 (1927): 289–91.

30 Conspicuously absent were Gropius, who was busy resettling in Berlin after his resignation from the Bauhaus, and Mies van der Rohe. Lissitzky had been invited to attend, but received his visa too late and did not arrive until the last day of the conference. Also missing were most of the older representatives of the new architecture, including Tony Garnier, Loos, Karl Moser, and Auguste Perret. Hendrik Berlage arrived on the second day of the congress but did not take part in the discussions. See *CIAM Dokumente, 1928–1939*, edited by Martin Steinmann (Basel and Stuttgart: Birkhäuser, 1979), 22.

31 "Congrès Préparatoire International d'Architecture Moderne," reproduced in *CIAM Dokumente, 1928–1939*, 15–21.

32 Letter, Giedion to Gropius, 5 July 1928, quoted in *CIAM Dokumente, 1928–1939,* 26.

33 See Giorgio Ciucci, "The Invention of the Modern Movement," *Oppositions* 24 (spring 1981): 75; and Eric Mumford, *The CIAM Discourse on Urbanism, 1928–1960* (Cambridge, Mass.: MIT Press, 2000), 19–26. See also *CIAM Dokumente, 1928–1939,* 16–30.

34 *CIAM Dokumente, 1928–1939,* 16–17.

35 The charter was issued in both German and French, though with some important differences. *CIAM Dokumente, 1928–1939,* 28–31. See also Jacques Gubler, *Nationalisme et internationalisme dans l'architecture moderne de la Suisse* (Lausanne: L'Age d'Homme, 1975), 145–61; and Mumford, *The CIAM Discourse on Urbanism,* 24–26.

36 Transcripts of the CIAM conference, Fonds Arnold Hoechel, Ecole d'Architecture, CRR, Geneva. See also Armand Brulhart, "Josef Frank und die CIAM bis zum Bruch 1928–1929," *Bauwelt* 26 (12 July 1985): 1058–60.

37 Brulhart, "Josef Frank und die CIAM bis zum Bruch 1928–1929."

38 Sigfried Giedion, "Der Zusammenschluss des Neuen Bauens," *Neue Züricher Zeitung,* 15 July 1928, quoted in *CIAM Dokumente, 1928–1939,* 28.

39 Le Corbusier, "Défense de l'architecture," *L'architecture d'aujourd'hui* 6, no. 10 (1933): 33–61. See *Oppositions* 4 (1974): 107, n2.

40 Letter, Frank to Giedion, 19 August 1928, CIAM-Archiv, Institut für Geschichte und Theorie der Architektur, Eidgenössische Technische Hochschule, Zurich.

41 Letter, Frank to Giedion, 25 May 1929, CIAM-Archiv.

42 Letter, Frank to Giedion, 6 July 1929, CIAM-Archiv.

43 See *CIAM Dokumente, 1928–1939,* 36–71.

44 Letter, Frank to Giedion, 5 November 1929, CIAM-Archiv. Frank also mentioned the same reasons for his resignation in a letter to Hannes Meyer the following year. He writes that he resigned from the CIAM: "[W]eil ich nach dem niederschmetternden Resultat dieses Kongresses nicht mehr die Möglichkeit gesehen habe, dass dieser wieder zu brauchbaren Resultaten gelangen kann. Was dort verhandelt worden ist, war ja schlisslich [sic] nichts anderes wie das, was auf jedem Wohnungskongress in viel gründlicher Weise und mit viel mehr Kenntnis der Sachlage besprochen wird, wobei sich aber sehr viele verschleierte Sonderinteressen gezeigt haben. Ausserdem war alles voll von Intriguen aller art [sic], die ich nicht habe durchschauen können, so dass die ganze Atmosphäre nicht angenehm war. So ungern ich sonst internationale Zusammenschlüsse aufgebe oder gar störe, schien es mir doch so am besten, da ja schliesslich und endlich Architektur keine Politik ist und nicht diese Art geheimnissevoller Kompromisse verlangt." Letter, Frank to Hannes Meyer, 7 October 1930, Bauhaus Correspondence, file 870570, Special Collections, Library, Getty Research Institute, Los Angeles.

45 Paul Westheim, "Architektur-Entwicklung," *Die Glocke* 10 (1924): 181–85. Westheim's remarks were echoed by Walter Müller-Wulckow, author of the Blauen Bücher series on modern architecture, who argued that the new architectural style "is characterized by a passionate desire for pure forms, a desire that penetrates deeper into the idea and essence of reality than a mere love of ornament ever could. Strange as it may sound, these logi-

cally planned and constructed buildings embody a metaphysical yearning. These creations of the machine age reflect a new fantasy of the spirit and a new mysticism of the soul." *Bauten der Arbeit,* 10 (Königstein im Taunus and Leipzig: K. R. Langewiesche, 1929), quoted in Barbara Miller Lane, *Architecture and Politics in Germany, 1918–1945* (Cambridge, Mass.: Harvard University Press, 1985), 132.

46 See Philipp Frank, *Modern Science and Its Philosophy,* 1–52; and Rudolf Haller, "Der erste Wiener Kreis," in Haller, *Fragen zu Wittgenstein und Aufsätze zur österreichischen Philosophie* (Amsterdam: Rodopi, 1986): 89–107; and Gerald Holton, "Ernst Mach and the Fortunes of Positivism in America," *Isis* 83 (1992): 42. On the Vienna Circle and Frank's association with the members of the group, see also Rudolf Haller, "Otto Neurath—For and Against," in Nemeth and Stadler, *Encyclopedia and Utopia,* 33. On Philipp's life and ideas, see Gerald Holton and Robert S. Cohen, "Philipp Frank," in *Dictionary of Scientific Biography,* edited by Charles C. Gillispie (New York: Charles Scribner's Sons, 1972), 5: 122–23.

47 Jeremy Bernstein, *The Life It Brings: One Physicist's Beginnings* (New York: Ticknor & Fields, 1987), 49.

48 Neurath, interview.

49 Verein Ernst Mach, "An alle Freunde wissenschaftlicher Weltauffassung!" (1929), quoted in Peter Galison, "Aufbau/Bauhaus: Logical Positivism and Architectural Modernism," *Critical Inquiry* 16 (summer 1990): 720.

50 See Margerethe Engelhardt-Krajanek, "Der Werkbundgedanke und seine Verbindung zum Wiener Kreis am Beispiel Josef Frank," in Volker Thurm-

Nemeth, ed., *Konstruktion zwischen Werkbund und Bauhaus: Wissenschaft—Architektur—Wiener Kreis,* Wissenschaftliche Weltauffassung und Kunst, vol. 4 (Vienna: Hölder-Pichler-Tempsky, 1998): 79–122; and Friedrich Stadler, *Studien zum Wiener Kreis: Ursprung, Entwicklung und Wirkung des Logischen Empirismus im Kontext* (Frankfurt am Main: Suhrkamp, 1997), esp. 68–73, 375, 590, 614, 832–35.

51 Hans Hahn, Otto Neurath, and Rudolf Carnap, *Wissenschaftliche Weltauffassung. Der Wiener Kreis* (Vienna: Verein Ernst Mach/Artur Wolf, 1929), 48.

52 Verein Ernst Mach flyer, "Freunde wissenschaftlicher Weltauffassung! . . . Vorträge" (n.d.), document 029–30–01, Carnap Papers in the Archives of Scientific Philosophy, University of Pittsburgh Libraries, University of Pittsburgh. On the close connections between Frank and other architects and the Vienna Circle, see Galison, "Aufbau/Bauhaus," 709–52; and Lucian Krukowski, "Aufbau and Bauhaus: A Cross-realm Comparison," *Journal of Aesthetics and Art Criticism* 50 (summer 1992): 197–209.

53 Josef Frank and Otto Neurath, "Hannes Meyer," *Der Klassenkampf: Sozialistische Politik und Wissenschaft* 3 (1930): 574. See also Galison, "Aufbau/Bauhaus," 718–20.

54 Pommer and Otto, for example, in *Weissenhof 1927,* 234, n120 write: "It must be recognized that no coherent architectural theory or point of view emerges from these often elusive discussions. . . . Frank employs statement and denial, indefinite or epigrammatic phrases and satire, all of which work against establishing a set of principles for architectural design generally or specifically for the house." See also Martin Steinmann, "Frank?—Kenn' ich

nicht!" *Um Bau* 10 (August 1986): 95–104.

55 "If ever [Neurath] heard another member make a scientifically empty claim, he called out, 'Metaphysics!' During the discussions of Wittgenstein's *Tractatus* Neurath interrupted continuously. Finally it was suggested that he should hum 'M-m-m-m' instead. Neurath answered that it would be more efficient if he were simply to say 'not-M' whenever they were not misled into talking metaphysics." Quoted in Nancy Cartwright and Thomas E. Uebel, "Philosophy in the Earthly Plane," in Elisabeth Nemeth and Friedrich Stadler, eds., *Encyclopedia and Utopia: The Life and Work of Otto Neurath* (Dordrecht and Boston: Kluwer, 1996), 40.

56 Plischke, interview, 17 November 1986. In the Bauhaus program, for example, Gropius wrote: "Together let us desire, conceive, and create the new structure of the future, which will embrace architecture and sculpture and painting in one unity and which will one day rise toward heaven from the hands of a million workers like the crystal symbol of a new faith." Walter Gropius, "Programme of the Staatliches Bauhaus in Weimar," in Ulrich Conrads, ed., *Programs and Manifestoes on 20th-Century Architecture* (Cambridge, Mass.: MIT Press, 1971), 49.

57 Letter, Neurath to Franz Roh, n.d., Franz Roh Papers, Library, Getty Research Institute. On Neurath's views of the Bauhaus, see also his article "Das Neue Bauhaus in Dessau," *Der Aufbau* 1, nos. 11–12 (1926): 210–11.

58 Frank, "Rum och inredning," 99–101.

59 Frank, "Rum och inredning," 100.

60 See Hannes Meyer, "Bauen" in Hannes Meyer et al., *Bauhaus. Zeitschrift für Gestaltung* 4, no. 2 (Dessau: Bauhaus, 1928). Frank's view that Meyer had affected a fundamental change in the school is articulated in his and Neurath's 1930 article in *Der Klassenkampf* protesting Meyer's ouster. Frank, however, in contrast to Neurath, never developed the same enthusiasm for a purely "scientific" building approach, and in later years he sometimes made fun of Meyer's zealousness.

61 Some 350 of Frank's letters to Waehner have survived, which are in private collections in Vienna. Waehner also wrote an unpublished autobiography in Italian, *Una sola cosa*, around 1976, which has survived in manuscript form. See Sabine Plakolm-Forsthuber, "Josef Frank an Trude Waehner (1938–1965): Das Nachleben des Werkbundes in der Kritik am Bauhaus," in *Konstruktion zwischen Werkbund und Bauhaus: Wissenschaft—Architektur—Wiener Kreis*, edited by Volker Thurm-Nemeth (Vienna: Hölder-Pichler-Tempsky, 1998), 123–24.

62 While living abroad, Waehner changed the spelling of the family name, dropping the umlaut. Plakolm-Forsthuber, "Josef Frank an Trude Waehner," 125. On Trude Waehner's life, see also her autobiographical sketches in *Trude Waehner*, exhibition catalog (Ravenna: Galleria Bottega, 1971); *Ausstellung Trude Waehner: Zeichnungen und Aquarelle*, exhibition catalog (Vienna: Österreichische Kulturvereinigung, 1966); and Gustav Szekely, *Aus dem Leben der Malerin Trude Waehner berichtet von ihren Sohn* (Vienna: Löcker, 2000).

63 The building was located at Buchfeldgasse 6. On Urban's extensive interiors, see Markus Kristan, *Joseph Urban: Die Wiener Jahre des Jugendstilarchitekten und Illustrators, 1872–1911* (Vienna: Böhlau, 2000),

224–35. Wähner was also involved in awarding the important commission for the "Rathauskeller" in the Vienna city hall to Urban in 1898.

64 Waehner's atelier, housed in the attic of same building in the eighth district where her parents lived, became a meeting place for artists, scholars, and intellectuals. Her broad circle of acquaintances also included Hans Buschbeck, Ernst Garger, Felix Kaufmann, Ernst Kris, and Franz Münz. Plakolm-Forsthuber, "Josef Frank an Trude Waehner," 125–26.

65 Plakolm-Forsthuber, "Josef Frank an Trude Waehner," 125–26. As Plakolm-Forsthuber notes, Waehner's decision to attend the Bauhaus was somewhat unexpected. Though one of the best known of the Bauhaus masters, Johannes Itten, had taught in Vienna prior to going to Weimar in 1919, Bauhaus ideas had little currency in the city, and only a small number of Viennese studied at the school, among them Friedl Dicker and Franz Singer, who followed Itten there. Dicker and Singer returned to Vienna, but they remained outsiders because of their very different design approach. See Friedrich Achleitner, " . . . sondern der Zukunft," in Georg Schrom and Stefanie Trautmannsdorff, eds., *Bauhaus in Wien: Franz Singer/Friedl Decker,* exhibition catalog (Vienna: Hochschule für angewandte Kunst, 1988), 6–7.

66 Plakolm-Forsthuber, "Josef Frank an Trude Waehner," 129.

67 Plakolm-Forsthuber, "Josef Frank an Trude Waehner," 130.

68 The entire section reads: "Was das Bauhaus betrifft, so glaube ich, dass es nun zu einer normalen, mehr oder weniger modern eingerichteten Kunst-gewerbeschule werden wird, die aber kaum mehr einen Anziehungspunkt bedeuten wird, da es ja derartiges auch in anderen geeignetren Städten gibt. Es ist dies aber ein Ende, das ich schon bei seiner Begründung geahnt habe, denn ein BAUhaus [emphasis in the original] verträgt meiner Ansicht nach diese übrigen Lehrfächer nicht und muss sich notwendigerweise um Lehrer und Schüler zu beschäftigen auf anderes konzentrieren, da ja bekanntlich Maler sich immer zurückgesetzt fühlen, wenn sie mit Architekten zusammenkommen; denn sie fühlen sehr gut, dass das grosse Publikum für sie heute kein besonderes Interesse hat." Letter, Frank to Hannes Meyer, 7 October 1930, Bauhaus Correspondence, file 870570, Library, Getty Research Institute.

69 Letter, Frank to Giedion, 1 January 1929, CIAM-Archiv.

70 Although aesthetic and philosophical issues were at the heart of the controversy, another of the principal reasons for the break was Hoffmann's insistence that the Werkbund close its sales shop, which he saw as unwelcome competition for his Wiener Werkstätte. Hoffmann's request, which would have eliminated the most important sales outlet for many of the Werkbund members, was rejected by most of the rank and file, prompting his resignation. See Gmeiner and Pirhofer, *Der Österreichische Werkbund,* 51ff; Arthur Roessler, "Kunstschau, Kunstgewerbeschule, Wiener Werkstätte und Österreichischer Werkbund," *Die Wage* 2 (2 October 1920): 15; Hans Tietze, "Die Wiener Kunstschau, die Wiener Werkstätte und der Österreichische Werkbund," *Kunstchronik und Kunstmarkt* 54,

no. 46 (1920): 892; and Schweiger, *Wiener Werkstätte*, 106–11.

71 Gmeiner and Pirhofer, 123–28. See also Wilfried Posch, "Die Österreichische Werkbundbewegung 1907–1912," in *Geistiges Leben im Österreich der Ersten Republik*, edited by Isabella Ackerl and Rudolf Neck (Vienna: Verlag für Geschichte und Politik, 1986), 279–312.

72 Rukschcio and Schachel, *Adolf Loos*, 114.

73 See the membership list in the 1912 German Werkbund yearbook, *Die Durchgeistigung der deutschen Arbeit: Wege und Ziele im Zusammenhang von Industrie, Handwerk und Kunst* (Jena: Eugen Dietrichs, 1912).

74 See Plakolm-Forsthuber, "Josef Frank an Trude Waehner," 132–38.

75 Josef Frank, "Gespräch über den Werkbund," in *Österreichischer Werkbund* (1929), 11.

76 On Frank's piano design for Bösendorfer, see, e.g., *Profil* 2 (June 1934): 171.

77 Gmeiner and Pirhofer, *Der Österreichische Werkbund*, 125–28.

78 Frank took part in the Breslau meeting along with several other prominent Werkbund figures, including László Gábor, Oswald Haerdtl, Julius Kalmár, Walter Sobotka, and Hermann Neubacher.

79 *Werkbundausstellung 1930. Juni bis Oktober,* exhibition catalog (Vienna: Österreichischer Werkbund, 1930). See also Wolfgang Born, "Ausstellung des Österreichischen Werkbundes in Wien," *Deutsche Kunst und Dekoration* 66 (August 1930): 305–23; and Max Eisler, "Österreichischer Werkbund 1930," *Moderne Bauformen* 29 (August 1930): 333–48.

80 Max Ermers, "Bildberichte—Ausstellung des Österreichischen Werkbundes in Wien," *Bauwelt* 21 (3 July 1930): 839.

81 "In einer selbstverständlichen Vollkommenheit, in solenner Formeinheit spricht der Teesalon von Frank an. Farbe an Farbe, zart und leicht erzeugt hier eine reinliche Atmosphäre der geselligen Serenität, die alles neusachliche Getue auslöscht und gleichsam einen neu-humanen Stil in sich begründet." Soma Morgenstern, "Die Ausstellung des Österreichischen Werkbundes," *Die Form* 5 (1 July 1930): 330.

82 Amelia S. Levetus, "The Austrian Werkbund Exhibition in Vienna," *American Magazine of Art* 21 (October 1930): 585.

83 Plischke, interview, 17 November 1986.

84 "Was ist modern?" reprinted in *Die Form* 5 (1 August 1930): 399.

85 "Was ist modern?" 400.

86 "Was ist modern?" 400–1.

87 "Was ist modern?" 401.

88 "Was ist modern?" 402.

89 "Was ist modern?" 404, 406.

90 An editorial in *Bauwelt* noted: "Im gleichen Sinne wie die Äußerungen eines Teiles der Werkbund-Mitglieder über eine einseitige Festlegung, ist wohl eine Stelle in seinem Vortrag zu verstehen, wenn er sich gegen ein Festnageln auf bestimmte Regeln und gegen enge dogmatische Definition dessen, was man als gut und modern bezeichnen soll, wendet." "Der Werkbund tagt in Wien," *Bauwelt* 21 (3 July 1930): 838.

91 Peter Meyer, "Der Deutsche Werkbund in Wien," *Neue Züricher Zeitung,* 8 July 1930, 4–5.

92 Peter Meyer, "Der Deutsche Werkbund in Wien," *Das Werk* 17 (August 1930), 252.

93 Meyer, "Der Deutsche Werkbund in Wien."

94 Breuer added sarcastically that "one was hardly cross with the witty speaker (*witzi-*

gen Plauderer); he was merely a part of that which one was supposed to enjoy: Viennese atmosphere." Robert Breuer, "Werkbund-Tagung in Wien," *Deutsche Kunst und Dekoration* 66 (August 1930): 322.

95   The remarks of Frank and a number of other delegates are summarized in "Diskussionsreferat zur Stuttgarter Werkbundtagung v. 25.10.30," *Der Baumeister* 28, supplement (December 1930): B 223. See also "Die Ziele des Deutschen Werkbundes," *Die Form* 5 (1930): 612–14.

96   "Diskussionsreferat zur Stuttgarter Werkbundtagung v. 25.10.30," B 223.

97   Joan Campbell, *The German Werkbund: The Politics of Reform in the Applied Arts* (Princeton: Princeton University Press, 1978), 214–15. See also Guido Harbers, "Die Zukunft des Deutschen Werkbundes," *Der Baumeister* 28, supplement (December 1930): B 223–24.

98   Peter Meyer, "Die Stuttgarter Aussprache über die Ziele des Deutschen Werkbundes," *Frankfurter Zeitung*, 30 October 1930, 1. See also Meyer, "Die Ziele des Deutschen Werkbundes," *Neue Züricher Zeitung*, 29 October 1930, 1; and P. [?], "Der Deutsche Werkbund in Stuttgart," *Bauwelt* 21, no. 44 (1930), 1450.

99   Wilhelm Lotz, "Das ist modern!" *Die Form* 5 (15 September 1930): 494.

100 Roger Ginsburger, "Was ist modern?" *Die Form* 6, no. 1 (1931): 6–11. On the generational split in the Werkbund, see also Fritz Hellmut Ehmcke, "Die Stuttgarter Werkbundtagung," in Ehmcke, *Geordnetes und Gültiges: Gesammelte Aufsätzen und Arbeiten aud den letzten 25 Jahren* (Munich: C. H. Beck, 1955), 39.

101 Oskar Schürer, "Zur Ehrenrettung des Begriffs 'modern,'" *Deutsche Kunst und Dekoration* 67 (December 1930): 165.

102 Walter Riezler, "Werkbundkrisis?" *Die Form* 6, no. 1 (1931): 1–3.

103 Riezler, "Werkbundkrisis?" 3.

104 Le Corbusier's comments were written in 1929 in response to Karel Teige's critique of his Mundaneum project, which Teige, who sided with the radical functionalists, had attacked as "archaic" and "metaphysical" architecture. The piece, however, was not published until 1933. Le Corbusier, "Défense de l'architecture," *L'architecture d'aujourd'hui* 6, no. 10 (1933): 33–61.

105 Letter, Mies to Le Corbusier, 1 February 1929, Fondacion Le Corbusier, Paris.

106 See Karin Lindegren, *Architektur als Symbol:* Theory and Polemic," in Nina Stritzler-Levine, ed., *Josef Frank, Architect and Designer: An Alternative Vision of the Modern Home* (New Haven and London: Yale University Press, 1996), 98.

107 Frank, *Architektur als Symbol*, 16.

108 Years later, in a letter to Viktor Matejka, Frank explained that he had never meant to imply that the radical modernists were Fascists, only that their ideas shared a similar underlying philosophy. "Es war mir damals mehr darum zu tun, den Zusammenhang zwischen der standardisierten unorganischen Architektur und dem Aufflammen des Nazitums zu zeigen, was deshalb nicht verstanden worden ist, da die modernen Architekten alles eher Nazis waren, aber deren Werke haben den gleichen Geist der Uniformierung gezeigt und damit geistige Propaganda gemacht." Letter, Frank to Victor Matejka, 11 August 1965, reprinted in Viktor Matejka, "12 Fragen an Josef Frank," *Bauwelt* 76 (12 July 1985), 1064.

109 Frank, *Architektur als Symbol*, 132–33.

110 Frank, *Architektur als Symbol*, 133. "Der Gott, der Eisen wachsen ließ, der wollte

keine Holzmöbel." The phrase is Frank's satirical takeoff of the first verse of composer Ernst Moritz Arndt's national hymn ("Vaterlandlied" [1812]), which had been popular during the Napoleonic Wars and had regained popularity again during the First World War. The original line is "Der Gott, der Eisen wachsen ließ, der wollte keine Knechte" (The God who made iron grow, he wanted no farmhands), a reference to German preparedness for war. See Welzig, *Josef Frank*, 141.

111 Frank, *Architektur als Symbol*, 134–35.

112 Frank, *Architektur als Symbol*, 116.

113 Frank, *Architektur als Symbol*, 139. In the text, Frank does not identify Gropius by name. However, the quotation, with attribution, also appears in the book's frontispiece.

114 Frank, *Architektur als Symbol*, 135.

115 Frank, *Architektur als Symbol*, 188.

116 Frank, *Architektur als Symbol*, 140–44.

117 Frank, *Architektur als Symbol*, 180.

118 Frank, *Architektur als Symbol*, 124–25.

119 Frank, *Architektur als Symbol*, 22.

120 Wilhelm Röhnick, review of *Architektur als Symbol*, *Die Form* 6 (15 March 1931), 120. See also Paul Klopfer, "*Architektur als Symbol*: Nachdenkliches über Josef Frank's gleichnamiges Buch," *Stein, Holz, Eisen* 45 (5 March 1931): 81–84.

121 [Franz] Roh, review of *Architektur als Symbol*, *Das Neue Frankfurt* 5 (March 1931), 59.

122 Wolfgang Hermann, review of *Architektur als Symbol*, *Kunst und Künstler* 29 (September 1931): 464.

123 For example, Dutch architectural critic J. G. Wattjes wrote: "With all the valuable and striking things that the author has to say, it is unfortunate that the material is not more strictly ordered and put in a more logical form. In its present state it is a wild stream of thoughts, which only occasionally hits the mark." J. G. Wattjes, review of *Architektur als Symbol*, *Het Bouwbedrijf* 8 (23 October 1931), 489. See also Fritz Tamms, review of *Architektur als Symbol*, *Die Baugilde* 13 (10 March 1931): 416.

124 Hans Eckstein, "Bürgerlicher Wohnbau (*Architektur als Symbol*)," *Die Kunst* 68 (January 1933): 89.

125 Peter Meyer, review of *Architektur als Symbol*, *Das Werk* 17 (November 1930): xlvii.

126 Review of *Architektur als Symbol*, *Journal de la Construction de la suisse romande* 7 (15 August 1932): 469.

CHAPTER SIX

1 "Josef Frank," *Moderne Bauformen* 26 (1927): 185.

2 The large glazed surfaces, especially on the south-facing rear courtyard, would have been impractical in the hot climate of Tel Aviv. Had it been realized, Frank's Ornstein House and Dance School would have been among the first modern buildings in Tel Aviv. Later modern architects, many of them immigrants from Central and Eastern Europe, soon learned not to employ such large expanses of glass. See Winfried Nerdinger, ed., *Tel Aviv Modern Architecture, 1930–1939* (Tübingen: Wasmuth, 1994).

3 On Loos's *Raumplan* idea, see Dietrich Worbs, ed., *Adolf Loos, 1870–1933: Raumplan—Wohungsbau* (Berlin: Akademie der Künste, 1983); idem, "Der Raumplan in der Architektur von Adolf Loos" (Ph.D. diss., Technische Universität Stuttgart, 1981); Werner Oechslin, "*Raumplan* versus *Plan libre*," *Daidalos* (December 1991): 76–83; and Julius Posener, "Adolf

Loos–Der Raumplan," *Arch+* 53 (1980): 36–40.

4 Plischke, who worked for Frank as draftsman in the late 1920s, reported that though Frank and Loos only met infrequently after Loos returned from France, they remained on good terms. Plischke recalled that it was Frank, in fact, who mounted the drive to collect money to pay for Loos's funeral expenses after his death in 1933. Ernst A. Plischke, interview by author, Vienna, 25 August 1986.

5 Adolf Loos, "Josef Veillich," *Frankfurter Zeitung,* 21 March 1929, reprinted in Loos, *Trotzdem,* 248–49.

6 See Julius Posener, "Der Raumplan. Vorläufer und Zeitgenossen von Adolf Loos," in Worbs, *Adolf Loos,* 52–64; and Johannes Spalt, "The Form of Dwelling: Drawings of Josef Frank before 1934," *Lotus International* 29 (1981): 111–13.

7 Scott, *Houses and Gardens,* 36.

8 According to Rukschcio and Schachel, Loos did not begin work on the Moller House until early 1927, and construction work only commenced in October of the same year. Given the likely delay between the design and publication of Frank's two houses, they were probably drawn in late 1926 or early 1927, suggesting that Frank had not seen Loos's design. Rukschcio and Schachel, *Adolf Loos: Leben und Werk,* 600.

9 Loos, "Das Prinzip der Bekleidung," in Loos, *Ins Leere gesprochen,* 108

10 Loos, "Mein Haus am Michaelerplatz," in *Aufbruch zur Jahrhundertwende: Der Künstlerkreis um Adolf Loos,* edited by Charlotte Kreuzmayr, *Parnass,* special issue, no. 2 (Linz: C. & E. Grosser, 1985), iii.

11 Ernst A. Plischke, interview by author, Vienna, 25 August 1986.

12 The project was among those Frank published in the May issue of *Moderne Bauformen.* On the original drawing, now in the Graphische Sammlung Albertina, Frank has written in the names of the various rooms in English over the German originals, suggesting that he may have had a prospective American client or that he may have included the design in the *Machine-Age Exposition* in New York in May 1927.

13 See Welzig, *Josef Frank,* 121–22.

14 "Einiges von Land- und Sommerhäuser." *Der Baumeister* 26 (March 1928), 94–102.

15 The exhibition was sponsored by the *Little Review,* the New York avant-garde literary journal edited by Jane Heap. The artistic steering committee included a number of leading modernists, among them Alexander Archipenko, Charles Demuth, Marcel Duchamp, Hugh Ferriss, and Man Ray. Frank's invitation to take part in the exhibition came from André Lurçat, who had been asked by Heap to assist in planning the architecture section. Letter from Frank to Lurçat, 10 January 1927, Fonds Lurçat, Archives nationales, Paris. Frank's trip to the United States was confirmed by Philip Ginther, who was working in Frank's office at the time, in an interview in 1991. Welzig, *Josef Frank,* 198.

16 The catalog lists five works by Frank, three listed as "Perspectives of Country Houses," one as "Ground Plan and 2 Perspectives of Country Houses," and one as "Ground Plan and 1 Perspective of Country House." These may have included the three American houses, or some of the other "country houses" Frank published in *Moderne Bauformen* in May 1927. The Pasadena House was published in the issue, so it was certainly designed before

the exhibition. In addition to his own drawings, Frank included works by Wlach, Hoffmann, Haerdtl, and seven of Hoffmann's students, among them Philip Ginther. *Machine-Age Exposition*, edited by Jane Heap, exhibition catalog (New York: Little Review, 1927), 10–12.

17 The original drawing in the Graphische Sammlung Albertina in Vienna is labeled "Residence for Mr. S. H. B. at Pasadena, California," but the identical drawing published in *Moderne Bauformen* bears the legend "The Residence for H. R. S. Esqu at Pasadena California." The Los Angeles house also appears with two different legends. The original in the Albertina is labeled "Residence for Mr. and Mrs. A. R. G. Los Angeles," but when Frank published it in *Der Baumeister* in 1928, he changed the description to "House for Vienna XIX," suggesting that the commission had fallen through and that he may have had other prospective clients for the project. See *Der Baumeister* 26 (March 1928): 98.

18 Schindler studied with König and others at the Technische Hochschule from 1906 to 1911. Karl Bieber, Frank's former student who was a cousin of Schindler's, confirmed that Frank and Schindler were acquainted with each other. Bieber, interview.

19 It is possible that Frank also knew Neutra during the prewar years, although Neutra did not enter the Technische Hochschule until the fall of 1911, almost a year after Frank had graduated. Frank later was responsible for Neutra's invitation to take part in the 1932 Vienna Werkbundsiedlung. Frank may have also been acquainted with Artur Grünberger (1882–1935), another former student of

König's at the Technische Hochschule, who moved to the United States and, in 1926, settled in Los Angeles, where he designed sets for the film industry. Like Neutra, Grünberger participated in the 1932 Vienna Werkbundsiedlung. See Boeckl, *Visionäre und Vertriebene*, 333.

20 References to American houses and the American way of life abound in Frank's writings of the late 1920s and early 1930s. Frank was a regular reader of American architecture magazines, and he was also undoubtedly familiar with publications such as Neutra's *Wie baut Amerika* (Stuttgart: Julius Hoffmann, 1927). See Welzig, *Josef Frank*, 198–201.

21 Frank argued that this notion of gradual disclosure should dictate even the way doors are hung. He often remarked that doors should open toward a wall or the shorter side of the room so that one's prospect of the space would slowly unfold. Plischke, interview, 25 August 1986.

22 With few commissions coming in, Frank's architectural office staff remained small, rarely consisting of more than a single assistant. Plischke remembered that Frank appeared at the office infrequently, "once every week or two." His room, Plischke described, was almost empty: a table, but no drawing board or parallel bar (by the late 1920s, Frank drew virtually everything freehand and, when necessary, turned over the sketches to an assistant to produce working drawings), and a bookcase with only a single book: Adolf Behne's *Der moderne Zweckbau* (The modern functional building). Plischke, interview, 17 November 1986. See also Ernst A. Plischke, *Ein Leben mit Architektur*, 90–91.

23 Philip Ginther, who worked in Frank's office at the time, revealed in a 1991 inter-

view with Maria Welzig that the house was originally planned for another location and later transferred to the Wenzgasse site. Welzig, *Josef Frank*, 135.

24 Plischke, interview, 17 November 1986.

25 This division of labor was confirmed by Plischke, who worked as an assistant for Frank around this time. Plischke, interview, 25 August 1986.

26 Adolph Stiller, "Coloured Dots on a Grey Background: Six Key Buildings of Modern Architecture in Central Europe," in *On Continuity*, edited by Rosamund Diamond and Wilfried Wang, 9H, no. 9 (Cambridge, Mass.: 9H Publications, 1995; distributed by Princeton Architectural Press), 27. Unfortunately, the house has recently undergone extensive alterations that have compromised the interior spatial concept.

27 For a discussion of the Villa Beer's spatial plan, see Guido Beltramini, "La casa sensibile," in *La casa isolata dalla tautologia alla banalità: Letture, trascrizioni, variazioni su testi di Wittgenstein, Loos, Frank*, edited by Giovanni Fraziano (Venice: Cluva Editrice, 1989): 83–85; Julius Posener, "Der Raumplan: Vorläufer und Zeitgenossen von Adolf Loos," in *Adolf Loos 1870–1933: Raumplan–Wohnungsbau*, edited by Dietrich Worbs. (Berlin: Akademie der Künste, 1984), 52; Arthur Rüegg and Adolph Stiller, *Sechs Häuser: Nach Aufnahmen korrigierte Grundrisse der Wohngeschosse sechs bedeutender Häuser der Moderne im Dreieck Prag-Leipzig-Wien* (Zurich: Eidgenössische Technische Hochschule, 1992); and Welzig, *Josef Frank*, 129–35. For contemporary articles on the house and its interior spaces, see Wolfgang Born, "Ein Haus in Wien-Hietzing," *Innen-Dekoration* 42 (September 1931): 363–98; Carmela Haerdtl, "Una

nuova casa di Josef Frank," *Domus* 4 (August 1931): 48–51; and "Una casa privata a Vienna degli architetti Josef Frank e Oscar [*sic*] Wlach," *Domus* 4 (July 1931): 28–30, 77; Max Eisler, "Ein Wohnhaus von Josef Frank und Oskar Wlach, Wien," *Moderne Bauformen* 31 (1932): 88–95; and "Una casa en las proximidades de Viena," *Viviendas* 4 (June 1935): 6–15.

28 Born, "Ein Haus in Wien-Hietzing," 364.

29 Born, "Ein Haus in Wien-Hietzing," 366.

30 Born, "Ein Haus in Wien-Hietzing," 363.

31 Born, "Ein Haus in Wien-Hietzing," 364–65.

32 Born, "Ein Haus in Wien-Hietzing," 363.

33 Born, "Ein Haus in Wien-Hietzing," 373.

34 Josef Frank, "Das Haus als Weg und Platz," *Der Baumeister* 29 (August 1931): 316–17.

35 Frank, "Das Haus als Weg und Platz," 317, 319.

36 Frank, "Das Haus als Weg und Platz," 319.

37 Camillo Sitte, *Der Städtebau nach seinen künstlerischen Grundsätzen: Ein Beitrag zur Lösung moderner Fragen der Architektur und monumentalen Plastik unter besonderer Beziehung auf Wien*, 5th ed. (1889; Vienna: Karl Graeser, 1922), translated by George Rosenborough Collins and Christiane Crasemann Collins as *The Birth of Modern City Planning* (New York: Rizzoli, 1986). See also the discussion of Sitte's ideas in Carl E. Schorske, *Fin-de-siècle Vienna: Politics and Culture* (New York: Knopf, 1980), 62–72. Stiller has also noted the relationship between Sitte's urban planning ideas and Frank's notion of "the house as path and place": "In the course of redrawing the ground floor [of the Villa Beer] this idea of organizing the rooms in the tradition of tangentially (grown) accessed

urban spaces, could be impressively com-
prehended; these figures also recall certain schematic drawings by Camillo Sitte
from *Der Städtebau.*" Stiller, "Coloured
Dots on a Grey Background," 35. Sitte's
ideas also apparently influenced Frank's
later urbanistic designs.

38 Sitte, *Der Städtebau,* 2.

39 Schorske, *Fin-de-siècle Vienna,* 63.

40 Frank, "Das Haus als Weg und Platz," 316.

41 A surviving set of plans in the archives of
the *Baupolizei* in the city's thirteenth district (MA 37) shows an unrealized rectangular wing on the house's southwest corner that would have contained several
additional servants' rooms. The plans are
dated October 1929, when the house was
already under construction, but there is
no evidence that any work on the wing
was undertaken.

42 Frank, "Das Haus als Weg und Platz," 317.

43 Frank, "Das Haus als Weg und Platz," 321.

44 Frank, "Das Haus als Weg und Platz,"
319.

45 Karel Lhota, "Architekt Adolf Loos," *Architekt SIA* 32, no. 9 (1933), 143.

46 See Beatriz Colomina, "Intimacy and
Spectacle: The Interiors of Adolf Loos,"
AA Files 20 (fall 1990): 5–15; idem, "The
Split Wall: Domestic Voyeurism," in *Sexu-
ality and Space,* edited by Beatriz Colom-
ina (New York: Princeton Architectural
Press, 1992): 73–80; Leslie van Duzer and
Kent Kleinman, *Villa Müller: A Work of
Adolf Loos* (New York: Princeton Architec-
tural Press, 1994), 38–57. See also Christ-
ian Kühn, *Das Schöne, das Wahre und das
Richtige: Adolf Loos und das Haus Müller in
Prag* (Braunschweig and Wiesbaden:
Friedr. Vieweg & Sohn, 1989), 13–62.

47 To make this transition, Frank continues,
"often only a few changes will suffice: the

pavings and plantings become more regular, the door is placed in a niche that pre-
pares one to go inside while one is standing outside." Josef Frank, "How to Plan a
House," lecture presented at the New
School for Social Research, New York, 13
April 1943, reprinted in Johannes Spalt,
ed., *Josef Frank, 1885–1967: Möbel & Geräte
& Theoretisches* (Vienna: Hochschule für
angewandte Kunst, 1981), 165.

48 Frank, "Das Haus als Weg und Platz," 316.

49 Frank, "Das Haus als Weg und Platz," 317.

50 Frank, "Das Haus als Weg und Platz," 323.

51 For a comparison of Loos's *Raumplan* and
the *Plan libre,* see Oechslin, "*Raumplan
versus Plan libre,* 76–83; and Max Risselada, ed., *Raumplan Versus Plan Libre:
Adolf Loos and Le Corbusier, 1919–1930*
(New York: Rizzoli, 1988).

52 Le Corbusier and Pierre Jeanneret, *Oeuvre
complète,* vol. 1 (Zurich: Editions d'Architecture Erlenbach, 1935), 60.

53 Vincent Scully, Jr., *Modern Architecture:
The Architecture of Democracy,* revised ed.
(New York: George Braziller, 1982), 42.

54 Arnold Karplus (1877–1968) was born in
Wigstadtl, Austrian Silesia, and studied
architecture with Friedrich Ohmann at
the Technische Hochschule in Prague,
graduating in 1905. He later moved to Vienna, where he designed a number of
apartment houses and other buildings. He
emigrated from Austria at the time of the
Anschluss and died in Caracas,
Venezuela. I would like to extend my gratitude to Helmut Weihsmann, who generously shared with me information on
Karplus and the house.

55 Photographs of the interiors of the house
as well as of the gardens were reproduced
in the November 1930 issue of *Innen-
Dekoration* and in Max Eisler, "Neue

Bauten und Innenräume von Josef Frank, Oskar Wlach ("Haus und Garten")—Arnold Karplus, Wohnhaus auf der Hohen Warte in Wien," *Moderne Bauformen* 29 (1930): 432–44. See also *Arnold Karplus—Gerhard Karplus,* Wiener Architekten, Band 14 (Vienna and Leipzig: Elbemühle, 1935), 21–23; and *House and Garden* 60 (September 1931): 56.

56 Frank, "Das Haus als Weg und Platz," 319–20.

57 *Der Baumeister* 29 (August 1931): plates 82–83. The original drawings for the second and third schemes are preserved in the Graphische Sammlung Albertina in Vienna (Frank-Archiv numbers 29 and 30); the whereabouts of the first are unknown.

58 On Frank's later designs, see Hermann Czech, "Josef Frank—The Accidental House: The Thirteen Designs in Letters to Dagmar Grill, " *Lotus International* 29 (1980): 108–110; Christopher Long, "Space for Living: The Architecture of Josef Frank," in Nina Stritzler-Levine, *Josef Frank, Architect and Designer: An Alternative Vision of the Modern Home,* 90–94; and Welzig, *Josef Frank,* chaps. 3 and 4.

CHAPTER SEVEN

1 See Friedrich Achleitner, "Wiener Architektur der Zwischenkriegszeit: Kontinuität, Irritation, Resignation," in *Das geistige Leben Wiens in der Zwischenkriegszeit,* edited by Peter Heintel, Norbert Leser, Gerald Stourzh, and Adam Wandruszka (Vienna: Österreichischer Bundesverlag, 1981), 290–91.

2 Leo Adler, *Neuzeitliche Miethäuser und Siedlungen* (Berlin and Charlottenburg: Ernst Pollak, 1931), ix.

3 Ernst Buske, "Jugend und Volk," in *Grundschriften der deutschen Jugendbewegung,* edited by Werner Kindt (1963), quoted in Peter Gay, *Weimar Culture: The Insider as Outsider* (New York: Harper & Row, 1970), 79.

4 See, for example, Paul Schultze-Naumburg, *Kunst und Rasse* (Munich, 1928); *Das Gesicht des deutschen Hauses* (Munich, 1929); and "Müssen wir in Zukunft in asiatischen Häusern wohnen?" *Das neue Deutschland* 1 (1931): 88–91.

5 On Frank's role in the planning and design of the Gesellschafts- und Wirtschaftsmuseum, see Stadler, *Arbeiterbildung in der Zwischenkriegszeit.*

6 Frank's architectural ideas had a marked impact on Neurath's thinking and on his museum program. As Blau writes: "Frank's ideas on architectural semantics resonate throughout Neurath's descriptions of the museum, its purposes, and the techniques of presentation developed." Blau, *The Architecture of Red Vienna,* 393. For the museum, Neurath, working with the graphic designers Erwin Bernath and Gerd Arntz, also pioneered new methods of visual representation. See Stadler, *Arbeiterbildung in der Zwischenkriegszeit;* Robin Kinross, "Otto Neurath et la communication visuelle," in Jean Sebestik and Antonia Soulez, eds., *Le Cercle de Vienne, doctrines et controverses* (Paris: Klincksieck, 1986): 271–78; Rudolf Haller and Robin Kinross, eds., *Gesammelte bildpädagogische Schriften, Otto Neurath,* Band 3 (Vienna: Hölder-Pichler-Tempsky, 1991); and Nemeth and Stadler, *Encyclopedia and Utopia,* 135–200.

7 Marie Neurath, "Memories of Otto Neurath," in *Empiricism and Sociology,* edited by Marie Neurath and Robert S. Cohen

(Dordrecht and Boston: Reidel, 1973), 58–59. In a letter to German art critic Franz Roh, Neurath wrote of the new installations: "The museum overflows with the old *Sachlichkeit*. Wholly geometrical. Everywhere, tables of commensurable quantities, and the whole assembled with open space surrounding the tables." Letter, Neurath to Franz Roh, n.d., Franz Roh Papers, file 850120, Library, Getty Research Institute. Neurath also described the installations in an article on the museum: "Even the furniture of the exhibition is to serve the Museum's purpose only and not detract by sentimental or monumental effects. Size and position of a chart is such that it can be viewed comfortably. A four foot square became the basic unit. By sub-divisions and additions, a number of basic sizes of charts were found which can always be fitted together and also allow different proportions for single charts as required for different representations. The frames are narrow and of a light colour so that they do not detract from the charts themselves. Charts are held together by specially designed wooden rails out of which they can be lifted for exchange. The exhibition stands themselves are composed of units which can form larger or smaller compartments. They are plain and of a light colour, the atmosphere that of a club; the museum's architect Josef Frank planned an arrangement and lighting in which the charts attract the main attention." Otto Neurath, "From Vienna Method to Isotype," in Neurath and S. Cohen, *Empiricism and Sociology*, 216. See also Neurath, *Die bunte Welt* (Vienna: Arthur Wolf, 1929), and idem, "Das Gesellschafts- und Wirtschaftsmuseum

in Wien," in *Minerva-Zeitschrift* 7, nos. 9–10 (1931): 153–56.

8   Österreichisches Gesellschafts- und Wirtschaftsmuseum, *Wien und die Wiener*, exhibition catalog (Vienna: Messepalast, 1927).

9   Blau, *The Architecture of Red Vienna*, 191.

10 Österreichischer Werkbund (Vienna, 1929), 14; and Österreichischer Werkbund, *Der gute billige Gegenstand. Ausstellung im Österreichischen Museum für Kunst und Industrie November 1931—Jänner 1932*, exhibition catalog (Vienna, 1931).

11 On the Beratungsstelle and its activities, see its official publication, *Die Wohnungsreform. Offizielles Organ des österreichischen Verbands für Wohnungsreform* (Vienna, 1929–31); August Sarnitz, *Ernst Lichtblau, Architekt, 1883–1963* (Vienna, Cologne, and Weimar: Böhlau, 1994), 86–88; and Blau, *The Architecture of Red Vienna*, 191–92.

12 Hans Blumenfeld, "Meine Arbeit mit Josef Frank, 1928/29," *Bauwelt* 76 (12 July 1985): 1057.

13 Frank, "Der Volkswohungspalast," 142.

14 Blumenfeld, "Meine Arbeit mit Josef Frank, 1928/29," 1057.

15 Frank, like Bruno Taut and a number of other modernists in this period, had begun to advocate for more color in architecture. New mineral-based colors (*Keim*), which had recently begun to appear on the market, enabled architects to produce a much greater range of color effects on their façades.

16 See Dietrich Worbs, "Josef Franks Wiener Massenwohnungsbau—Ein pragmatischer Versuch," *Bauwelt* 76 (12 July 1985): 1049–50.

17 Blumenfeld, "Meine Arbeit mit Josef Frank, 1928/29," 1057.

18 See Stefanie Frischauer, "Das erste Hochhaus in Wien," *Wasmuths Monatshefte für Baukunst* 13 (1929): 495.

19 Frischauer, "Das erste Hochhaus in Wien," 496–97.

20 Frischauer, "Das erste Hochhaus in Wien," 495–97.

21 Blumenfeld, "Meine Arbeit mit Josef Frank, 1928/29," 1057.

22 Quoted in "Diskussion zu Thema II, 'Der Bau von Kleinwohnungen mit tragbaren Mieten,' International Housing Conference, Berlin, 1931," *Wohnen und Bauen* 3, nos. 5–6 (1931): 257.

23 Eisler, "Neue Bauten und Innenräume von Josef Frank," 430.

24 Kurt Junghanns, *Das Haus für Alle: Zur Geschichte der Vorfertigung in Deutschland* (Berlin: Ernst & Sohn, 1994), 225–26.

25 "Ausstellung 'Wohnung und Siedlung,' Linz 1929," *Der Baumeister* 27 (December 1929): 410–11.

26 On the genesis and construction of the Vienna Werkbundsiedlung, see Josef Frank, ed., *Die internationale Werkbundsiedlung. Wien, 1932,* exhibition catalog (Vienna: Anton Schroll & Co., 1932); Wolfdieter Dreibholz, "Die Internationale Werkbundsiedlung, Wien, 1932," *Bauforum* 10, no. 61 (1977): 19–22; Gmeiner and Pirhofer, *Der Österreichische Werkbund,* esp. 155–79; Adolf Krischanitz and Otto Kapfinger, *Die Wiener Werkbundsiedlung. Dokumentation einer Erneuerung* (Vienna: Compress, 1985); Jan Tabor, "Die erneuerte Vision. Die Wiener Werkbundsiedlung, 1932–1984," in *Reflexionen und Aphorismen zur österreichischen Architektur,* edited by Viktor Hufnagl (Vienna: Georg Prachner, 1984): 346–52; Liselotte Ungers, *Die Suche nach einer neuen Wohnform: Siedlungen der zwanziger Jahre damals und heute* (Stuttgart: Deutsche Verlags-Anstalt, 1983); and "Werkbund Siedlung 1932," *Arquitectura* 70 (May-August 1989): 74–87.

27 Josef Frank, "International Housing Exposition, Vienna, Austria," *Architectural Forum* [New York] 57 (October 1932): 325.

28 Otto Kapfinger, "Position einer liberalen Moderne. Die Wiener Werkbundsiedlung—1932," in Astrid Gmeiner and Gottfried Pirhofer, eds., *Der Österreichische Werkbund: Alternative zur klassischen Moderne in Architektur, Raum- und Produktgestaltung* (Salzburg: Residenz, 1985), 174.

29 Dreibholz, "Die Internationale Werkbundsiedlung, Wien, 1932," 22.

30 Also missing from the list were the leading conservative architects of the Wagnerschule: Karl Ehn, Hubert Gessner, Emil Hoppe, Rudolf Perco, and Otto Schönthal. The only well-known Wagner student was Ernst Lichtblau, who was a professor at the Kunstgewerbeschule.

31 Loos had been invited to design a bar for the 1930 Vienna Werkbund exhibit, but he had refused to take part in the exhibition, citing his usual objections to the organization and its aims. Frank, however, who remained on friendly terms with Loos, persuaded him to submit a design for the housing exhibition, arguing that it would constitute an alternative to previous exhibitions. A number of those close to Loos also participated, among them, Helmut Wagner-Freynsheim, Otto Breuer, Jacques Groag, Gabriel Guevrékian, Lurçat, Neutra, and Schütte-Lihotzky. See Rukschcio and Schachel, *Adolf Loos: Leben und Werk,* 355–56.

32 Frank, "International Housing Exposition, Vienna, Austria," 328.

33 Plischke, interview, 17 November 1986. Nonetheless, a number of the houses included tubular-steel furniture, including those by Rietveld, Josef Dex, and Lurçat, which featured pieces from the local Thonet-Mundus Company. See, for example, *Bau- und Werkkunst* 8 (1932), 190ff.

34 Frank, *Die internationale Werkbundsiedlung Wien 1932*, 8.

35 Hans Vetter, ed., *Kleine Einfamilienhäuser mit 50 bis 100 Quadratmeter Wohnfläche* (Vienna: Anton Schroll, 1932), 6–7, 10, 76–77.

36 See, for example, Oskar Hellwig, "Die Werkbundsiedlung," *Neue Freie Presse*, 4 June 1932, 8. For an extensive list of contemporary reviews, see Krischanitz and Kapfinger, *Die Wiener Werkbundsiedlung*, 126–27.

37 Franz Kaym, "Die Werkbundsiedlung," *Neue Freie Presse*, 6 July 1932, 2.

38 Wilhelm Lotz, "Die Wiener Werkbundsiedlung," *Die Form* 7 (15 July 1932): 201, 204.

39 Guido Harbers, "'Moderne Linie,' Wohnkultur und Stagnation: Abschliessende Randbemerkungen zur Wiener Werkbundsiedlung," *Der Baumeister* 30 (October 1932): 367, 70. See also "Die Werkbundsiedlung Wien-Lainz" *Bauwelt* 23 (16 June 1932): 598.

40 Hugo Häring, "Versuch einer Orientierung," *Die Form* 7 (15 July 1932): 218–23.

41 Hugo Häring, "Bemerkungen zur Werkbundsiedlung Wien-Lainz 1932," *Die Form* 7 (15 July 1932), 204.

42 Häring, "Bemerkungen zur Werkbundsiedlung Wien-Lainz 1932," 205.

43 Häring, "Bemerkungen zur Werkbundsiedlung Wien-Lainz 1932."

44 Letter, Frank to Häring, 19 July 1932, Nachlaß Hugo Häring, Akademie der Künste, Berlin, quoted in *Hugo Häring: Schriften, Entwürfe, Bauten*, edited by Heinrich Lauterbach und Jürgen Joedicke (Stuttgart: Karl Krämer, 1965), 11–12.

45 See Eduard F. Sekler, "The Architectural Reaction in Austria," *Journal of the Society of Architectural Historians* 24 (March 1965): 67–70.

46 Letter, Frank to Eduard F. Sekler, 7 April 1964, quoted in Sekler, *Josef Hoffmann*, 208.

47 In his monograph on Hoffmann, Sekler writes: "The consistent pursuit of his own ideas from the year 1921 on forced Frank to become more and more critical of the arts and crafts, and finally to condemn completely what he called the arts and crafts mentality, the striving 'to unify formally everything that exists.' He described work by Dagobert Peche as 'vacuous banality,' said of ornament that it 'had always destroyed form,' and commented during a Werkbund discussion in 1932 that 'mere decoration' is 'uncreative.' He also did not hesitate to publicly criticize a door handle from Peter Behrens's early period; but while Behrens received such criticism calmly, Hoffmann, on a similar occasion requested the appointment of a court of honor by the president of the Werkbund." Sekler, *Josef Hoffmann*, 209. On the growing conflict between Hoffmann and Frank, see also Giovanni Fanelli and Ezio Godoli, *La Vienna di Hoffmann, architetto della qualità* (Rome and Bari: Laterza, 1981), 401ff; and Gmeiner and Pirhofer, *Der Österreichische Werkbund*, 184.

48 As late at the early 1930s, Hoffmann remarked to a former student: "If I were to build a house now, I would decorate it from top to bottom." Quoted in Sekler, *Josef Hoffmann*, 213.

49 Letter from Frank to Hoffmann, 12 July 1932, Wiener Stadt- und Landesbibliothek, Handschriftensammlung, I.N. 158.558. The text reads:

SEHR VEREHRTER HERR OBERBAURAT,
ich danke Ihnen bestens für Ihr freundliches Schreiben und ich kann Ihnen nur versichern, daß ich diesen Zwischenfall auf das tiefste bedaure und Sie dürfen überzeugt sein, daß ich alles tun werde, ihn aus der Welt zu schaffen. Es wäre sicherlich nie dazu gekommen, wenn ich nicht vollkommen überrascht worden wäre, da bis dahin von irgendwelchen Differenzen innerhalb des Werkbundes weder mir noch den anderen Vorstandsmitgliedern irgend etwas bekannt war, da ich bis dahin immer nur gesehen habe, daß sämtliche Absichten von Ihnen in so weitgehender Weise unterstützt worden sind. Ebenso kann ich mich nicht daran erinnern, daß irgendwelche Ihrer Anträge oder Absichten nicht ausgeführt worden sind. Es wird dies selbstverständlich an den Protokollen leicht nachweisbar sein, ebenso, daß ich die mir vorgeworfenen Aussprüche niemals getan habe. Ich muß in diesem letzteren Fall leider annehmen, daß Ihnen verschiedens falsch berichtet worden ist und zwar von Leuten, die ein Interesse daran zu haben glauben, dies zu tun. Deshalb bin ich Ihnen auch sehr dankbar, daß Sie bereit [sic], diesen Zwischenfall auf diese Weise zu erledigen und ich hoffe daß dies dazu beitragen wird, alle scheinbaren Differenzen endgültig zu erledigen.
— *HOCHACHTUNGSVOLL, IHR ERGEBENER, JOSEF FRANK*

———————

MOST ESTEEMED HERR OBERBAURAT,
I want to thank you very much for your friendly letter and to assure you that I deeply regret this incident and will do everything possible to settle this matter. It would never have come to this point had I not been completely surprised, because up to that time neither I nor any of the other members of the board were aware of any differences within the Werkbund, since until then I had always thought that all of your ideas had been thoroughly supported. Moreover, I cannot recall that any of your requests or wishes were not carried out. This, of course, would be easy to demonstrate from the minutes, just as it could be shown that I never made the statements attributed to me. As for the latter, I must assume that something different was reported to you by persons who believed they had a reason to do so. Therefore, I am very thankful that you are prepared to settle this matter, and I hope that this will help to finally dispose of all apparent differences.
— *RESPECTFULLY, YOURS TRULY,*
JOSEF FRANK

50 See Sekler, *Josef Hoffmann,* 209.

51 Bieber, interview.

52 Sekler, "The Architectural Reaction in Austria," 67.

53 Letter, Hoffmann to Max Welz, 26 March 1933. The letter is reprinted in its entirety in Sekler, *Josef Hoffmann,* 497–99. Hoffmann also chose to direct some of his ire at Adolf Loos, whom he accused of being a "model for some of today's actions," but adding—clearly with Frank in mind—that "[Loos] was at least original in his method."

54 Sekler, *Josef Hoffmann,* 497.

55 Friedrich Achleitner, "Der Österreichische Werkbund und seine Beziehung zum Deutschen Werkbund," in *Der Werkbund in Deutschland, Österreich und der Schweiz,* edited by Lucius Burkhardt (Stuttgart: Deutsche Verlags-Anstalt, 1978), 111. Despite Neubacher's association with the

Nazis, Frank later noted that during Neubacher's tenure as president of the Werkbund he had behaved quite well, choosing to remain above the political squabbling.

56 Österreichischer Werkbund, "Protokoll der Sitzung des Gesamtvorstandes des Architektur- und Kunstgewerbeausschusses vom Freitag, den 24. Februar 1933, 18 Uhr." Collection of Eduard F. Sekler, Cambridge, Mass., quoted in Posch, "Josef Frank," 652. An even more vicious attack on Frank appeared in the right-wing newspaper *12-Uhr-Blatt* at the end of December 1933:
The main exponent of the foreign element [fremdrassig] in the Austrian Werkbund was Professor Dr. Josef Frank. Frank is an exponent of the mathematical tendency in modern art. He is for an international art and rejects the national element, which alone has the capacity to be creative. In particular, Frank is for the ideas of the French architect Le Corbusier. Frank (who is clearly of Jewish descent) formed a group around him that, because of their racial differences, kept to themselves and that had as their goal, wherever possible, to stifle creative Aryan artists.
Quoted in Posch, "Josef Frank," 653.

57 Clemens Holzmeister, Paul Seifert, Max Welz, and Max Fellerer, "Wortlaut der Anträge der 'Gruppe Hoffmann' zur Ausserordentlichen Vollversammlung des Österreichischen Werkbundes am 20. Juni 1933," facsimile reprinted in Gmeiner and Pirhofer, *Der Österreichische Werkbund*, 185.

58 Der Vorstand des Österreichischen Werkbundes, "Zur ausserordentlichen Vollversammlung am 20. Juni 1933." Photocopy in possession of the author.

59 Achleitner, "Der Österreichische Werkbund," 111.

60 Achleitner, "Der Österreichische Werkbund," 111. Kokoschka, who had managed to maintain cordial relations with both Hoffmann and Frank, attempted to mediate between the feuding parties, but was unsuccessful. Letter, Hoffmann to Oskar Kokoschka, 1 March 1934, Wiener Stadt- und Landesbibliothek, Handschriftensammlung, I.N. 172.570.

61 On the formation of the "New" Werkbund, see "Verein: Neuer Werkbund Österreichs in Wien, Bildung," Österreichisches Staatsarchiv, Allgemeines Verwaltungsarchiv, file Zl. 254.167-GD2/1933. See also *Das befreite Handwerk*, exhibition catalog (Vienna: Österreichisches Museum für Kunst und Industrie, 1934).

62 Letter, Frank to Hannes Meyer, 7 October 1930, Bauhaus Correspondence, Getty Research Institute.

63 Letter, Frank to Walter Sobotka, 1 January 1933, Sobotka Papers, Avery Library, Columbia University. The Franks moved to Stockholm permanently in December 1933.

64 "Neuer Werkbund Österreichs," *Profil* 3 (March 1934): vii.

65 Despite a diligent search, I have been unable to locate any such source.

66 "Professor Frank und die Ausstellung in London," *Das Profil* 2 (May 1934): vii. The text reads:
Ein Artikel Josef Franks in einer englischen Architekturzeitschrift nimmt gegen die vom Neuen Werkbund Österreichs vertretenen Erzeugnisse österreichischen Kunstgewerbes in abfälliger Weise Stellung. Leider erschien dieser Artikel anläßlich der Eröffnung der österreichischen Ausstellung in London, die zur Förderung unserer heimischen Handwerker veranstaltet wurde. Wir wollen nur an ein englisches Sprichwort erinnern,

welches heißt: "Right or wrong, my country."

An even more virulent attack on
Frank that appeared in an unpublished
essay on Rudolf Perco, written by Franz
Kaym prior to 1940, provides a taste of the
contemporary discourse:

*Im Bilde der Zeit darf das jüdische Kleeblatt
Strnad, Frank, Wlach nicht fehlen. Sie kommen nur vom Intellekt her und sind äs-
thetisierende Eklektiker, von jedem Baum der
Erkenntnis pflückend, geistige Nomaden,
denen kein Volksgut der Welt heilig ist.
Charakteristisch ist ihr Durchrasen aller
durch Bücher erreichbaren Kulturen mit
einem Einfühlungsvermögen, das einem
Deutschen unfassbar ist. Ihr Dogma ist heute
Mykenä, morgen Alt-Wien, ein andermal po-
linesiche Primitive, ja, hie und da sogar
ehrliches, gutes Handwerk. Welcher
Weihrauch ist um sie und wehe dem, der
heute noch ala [sic] Negerkultur macht,
wenn seit gestern schon dalmatinische Volkskunst Mode ist.*

———————

*[In our discussion of that period, one cannot
forget the Jewish triad of Strnad, Frank,
Wlach. They are products of pure intellect,
eclectic aesthetes, who pick from every tree of
knowledge—spiritual nomads, for whom no
people's culture is holy. Characteristic is the
way in which they flip through the books of
every culture in the world with an empathy
that is incomprehensible for a German. Their
dogma is: today Mycenaean, tomorrow old
Viennese, and the next time Polynesian
primitive, and here and there, even good,
honest craftsmanship. Who knows what in-
cense they are bathed in, and woe to him who
designs in the spirit of African art when,
since yesterday, Dalmatian folk art is the current fashion.]*

Franz Kaym, unpublished manuscript on
Rudolf Perco, n.d. 12, Perco Papers,
Wiener Stadt- und Landesbibliothek. My
thanks to Monika Platzer for sharing this
document with me.

CHAPTER EIGHT

1 On Ericson's life and work, see Boman,
   Estrid Ericson; Elisabeth Aschehoug, "Dis-
   tinguished Leader in Swedish Modern,"
   American Swedish Monthly 33 (February
   1939): 8–10; 35; and Kristina Wängberg-
   Eriksson, *Svenskt Tenn. Josef Frank och
   Estrid Ericson. En konsthistorisk studie*
   (Stockholm: Stockholms universitet, 1985).

2 Pieces from Svenskt Tenn were included
   in an exhibition of Swedish decorative art
   that opened at the Metropolitan Museum
   of Art in New York on 17 January 1927,
   and later traveled to Detroit and Chicago.
   See Metropolitan Museum of Art, *Decora-
   tive Arts from Sweden*, exhibition catalog
   (New York: The Museum, 1927). Svenskt
   Tenn was also represented in a display of
   Swedish arts and crafts at the Wanamaker
   Department Store in New York in December of the same year and at Altman &
   Company in New York in September 1928.
   Monika Eriksson, "A Time for Pewter," in
   Estrid Ericson: Founder of Svenskt Tenn, ed-
   ited by Monica Boman, translated by
   Roger G. Tanner (Stockholm: Carlsson,
   1989), 68–72. See also I. Bergström,
   "Pewter: A Swedish Revival. New Applica-
   tions by the Firma Svenskt Tenn," *Studio*
   111 (February 1936): 97–99.

3 Kristina Wängberg-Eriksson has suggested that Ericson may have first encountered Frank's work as early as 1917 while
   she was still a student. Among her papers
   is a copy of the 1916 Austrian Werkbund

annual—which included a number of Frank's designs—inscribed with her signature and the date 1917. Ericson's first documented contact with Frank's work came in 1921 at the home of relatives of her friend Ragnhild Lundberg, for whom Frank had designed a dining room suite the same year. See Kristina Wängberg-Eriksson, "The Interior Designer," in *Estrid Ericson: Founder of Svenskt Tenn*, edited by Monica Boman, translated by Roger G. Tanner (Stockholm: Carlsson, 1989), 101–04.

4   See David McFadden, ed., *Scandinavian Modern Design, 1880–1980*, exhibition catalog (New York: Harry N. Abrams, 1982), especially the essays by Elisabet Stavenow-Hidemark, Erik Lassen, and Jarno Peltonen; and Kerstin Wickman, "Homes," in *20th-Century Architecture, Sweden*, edited by Claes Caldenby, Jöran Lindvall, and Wilfried Wang, exhibition catalog (Munich and New York: Prestel, 1998), 199–207.

5   Jarno Peltonen, "The 1930s: A New Function for Design," in *Scandinavian Modern Design 1880–1980*, edited by David McFadden (New York: Harry N. Abrams, 1982), 113–28.

6   On the impact of functionalism on Swedish design, see, for example, Åke H. Huldt, ed., *Konsthantverk och hemslöjd i Sverige, 1930–1940* (Göteborg: Bokförmedlingen, 1941); and *Mellan funkis och framtid: Svensk Form, 1930–80*, exhibition catalog (Stockholm: Svensk Form, 1980).

7   *Stockholmsutställningen 1930 av konstindustri, konsthantverk och hemslöjd*, exhibition catalog (Uppsala: Almqvist & Wiksells, 1930). See also Kenneth Frampton, "Stockholm 1930: Asplund and the Legacy of the Funkis," in *Asplund*, edited by Claes

Caldenby and Olof Hulten (New York: Rizzoli, 1986), 35–39; Eva Rudberg, *The 1930 Stockholm Exhibition: Modernism's Breakthrough in Swedish Architecture* (Stockholm: Stockholmia, 1999); idem, "Early Functionalism," in Calenby et al., *20th-Century Architecture, Sweden*, 81–109; and Bernt Nyberg, Olof Hultin, and Sylvia Johnson, eds., *Aufbruch und Krise des Funktionalismus: Bauen und Wohnen in Schweden, 1930–80*, exhibition catalog (Stockholm: Sveriges arkitekturmuseum, 1976).

8   Peltonen, "The 1930s: A New Function for Design," in McFadden, *Scandinavian Modern Design 1880–1980*, 108.

9   During the previous year, Ericson had taken part in an exhibit of modern decorative art at the Swedish Nationalmuseum in Stockholm, the centerpiece of which was a striking "functionalist" dining suite made of mahogany and lined with pewter and brass designed by Uno Åhrén. See Eriksson, "A Time for Pewter," 76–79.

10 Kristina Wängberg-Eriksson, "The Interior Designer," in *Estrid Ericson: Founder of Svenskt Tenn*, edited by Monica Boman, translated by Roger G. Tanner (Stockholm: Carlsson, 1989), 91–92. See also Wängberg-Eriksson's pamphlet, *Svenskt Tenn—A Short Account of Its History* (Stockholm: Svenskt Tenn, n.d.), and idem, *Svenskt Tenn*, esp. 12–55. On Åhrén and his work for Svenskt Tenn, see Eva Rudberg, *Uno Åhrén: En föregångsman inom 1900-talets arkitektur och samhällsplanering* (Stockholm: Byggforskningsrådet, 1981).

11 Quoted in Eriksson, "A Time for Pewter," 85.

12 Quoted in Monika Lindahl Åkerman, "A Working Life," in *Estrid Ericson: Founder of*

Svenskt Tenn, edited by Monica Boman, translated by Roger B. Tanner (Stockholm: Carlsson, 1989), 12.

13 Åkerman, "A Working Life," 13.

14 Åkerman, "A Working Life," 12–13.

15 Wängberg-Eriksson, "The Interior Designer," 107.

16 Wängberg-Eriksson, "The Interior Designer," 107.

17 The exhibit also included rooms by David Blomberg, Elsa Gullberg, and Carl Malmsten, as well as Märta Måås-Fjätterström's textile group and Gefle Porslinsfabrik. Sven A. Gustafsson, *Liljevalchsutställningen 15 september—14 oktober 1934*, exhibition catalog (Stockholm, 1934); Gunnar Mascoll Silfverstolpe, "Hemutställningen i Liljevalchs," *Stockholms Tidningen*, 15 September 1934; "Svensk konstslöjd hos Liljevalchs: Sex separatutställningar av svensk heminredningskonst," *Nya Dagligt Allehanda*, 14 September 1934; "Vackra varor i Liljevalchs," *Dagens Nyheter*, 14 September 1934; and Wängberg-Eriksson, *Svenskt Tenn*, 89–93.

18 On the exhibit, see Heinrich Ritter, "Wohnräume aus Schweden," *Innen-Dekoration* 46 (March 1935): 92–98; and Wängberg-Eriksson, *Svenskt Tenn*, 94–98.

19 Wängberg-Eriksson, "The Interior Designer," 99–100.

20 Wängberg-Eriksson, "The Interior Designer," 106–7.

21 Many years later, Frank recalled the impact of the exhibition: "In the spring [sic] of 1934, I had a large exhibition of interiors with more or less the same things that I had made in Vienna, but which were unknown to the general public [in Stockholm]. Its success was very surprising, and the pieces were not only recognized, but also widely imitated. Within a short

time the entire Swedish furniture industry was focused in that direction, and later also the Danish, and this style is known throughout the world as Scandinavian, its origin unknown. These furnishings are now exported in large quantities around the world, which Austria could have also done, had anyone done something about it." Letter, Frank to Viktor Matejka, 11 August 1965, quoted in Spalt, *Josef Frank, 1885–1967*, 4.

22 Frank, "Rum och inredning," 217–25.

23 Peltonen, "The 1930s: A New Function for Design," 128. See also Penny Sparke, "Fashion of the Fifties: The Emergence of 'Swedish Modern,'" *Industrial Design* 29 (May–June 1982): 35–37.

24 Penny Sparke, *Furniture: Twentieth Century Design* (New York: E. P. Dutton, 1986), 34.

25 Penny Sparke, "'Convenience and Pleasantness': Josef Frank and the Swedish Modern Movement in Design," in Nina Stritzler-Levine, ed., *Josef Frank, Architect and Designer: An Alternative Vision of the Modern Home* (New Haven and London: Yale University Press, 1996), 120–21.

26 Wängberg-Eriksson, "The Interior Designer," 103.

27 Plischke, interview, 25 August 1986.

28 Feilendorf, interview, 14 July 1987.

29 "Solesand," *Decorative Art: The Studio Yearbook* (London: The Studio, 1938), 20.

30 Letter from Frank to Trude Waehner, 11 July 1946. Collection Professor Johannes Spalt, Vienna.

31 Welzig, *Josef Frank*, 187.

32 Hugo Häring, "Wege zur Form," *Die Form* 1 (October 1925): 3–5. On Häring's work and his ideas of organic architecture, see Peter Blundell Jones, *Hugo Häring: The Organic versus the Geometric* (Stuttgart and

London: Edition Axel Menges, 1999), esp. chaps. 6–8; Jürgen Joedicke, ed., *Das andere Bauen: Gedanken und Zeichnungen von Hugo Häring* (Stuttgart: Karl Krämer, 1982); Jürgen Joedicke and Heinrich Lauterbach, eds., *Hugo Häring: Schriften, Entwürfe, Bauten* (Stuttgart: Karl Krämer, 1965); Sabine Kremer, *Hugo Häring (1882–1958)—Wohnungsbau: Theorie und Praxis* (Stuttgart: Karl Krämer, 1984).

33   Theodor Fischer, from a speech delivered at the opening of his workers' hostel in Munich, published in *Die Bauzeitung*, 1927, quoted in Jones, *Hugo Häring: The Organic versus the Geometric*, 19.

34   Häring, "Wege zur Form," 5.

35   Frank, "How to Plan a House," manuscript of a lecture presented at the New School for Social Research, c. 1942, reprinted in Spalt, *Josef Frank 1885–1967*, 165.

36   Especially noteworthy is Häring's continued allegiance to the regular layering of floors. The spatial distortions within his plans take place almost exclusively along the horizontal plane.

37   Blundell-Jones, *Hugo Häring: The Organic versus the Geometric*, 153.

38   Welzig, *Josef Frank*, 189.

39   On Scharoun and Häring's influence on his work, see J. Christoph Bürkle, *Hans Scharoun und die Moderne: Ideen, Projekte, Theaterbau* (Frankfurt am Main: Campus, 1986), idem, *Hans Scharoun* (Artemis: Zurich, 1993); Eckehard Janofske, *Architektur-Räume: Idee und Gestalt bei Hans Scharoun* (Braunschweig and Wiesbaden: Vieweg & Sohn, 1984); Peter Blundell-Jones, *Hans Scharoun* (London: Phaidon, 1995); idem, "Scharoun, Häring and Organic Functionalism," *Architecture Association Quarterly* 5 (January 1973): 48–57;

idem, "Organic versus Classic," *Architecture Association Quarterly* 10 (January 1978): 10–20; Jörg C. Kirschenmann and Eberhard Syring, *Hans Scharoun: Die Forderung des Unvollendeten* (Stuttgart: Deutsche Verlags-Anstalt, 1993); Peter Pfankuch, ed., *Hans Scharoun: Bauten, Entwürfe, Texte* (Berlin: Akademie der Künste, 1974); Achim Wendschuh, ed., *Hans Scharoun: Zeichnungen, Aquarelle, Texte*, exhibition catalog (Berlin: Akademie der Künste, 1993).

40   Letter, Frank to Viktor Matejka, 11 August 1965, quoted in Matejka, "12 Fragen an Josef Frank," 1065.

41   As Wängberg-Eriksson has documented, the idea of using the blue bird fresco as the basis for a pattern came from Ericson. See her catalog entry on "Anakreon" in Stritzler-Levine, *Josef Frank: Architect and Designer*, 228–29.

42   See Wängberg-Eriksson's description of the rug designs in Stritzler-Levine, *Josef Frank: Architect and Designer*, 240–43. The rugs, which were intended to be hand-knotted, using either a rya or pile technique, proved to be unpopular, and only a small number were produced at the time.

43   See *L'Autriche a l'exposition internationale de Paris 1937*, exhibition catalog (Vienna: Wiener Ausstellungsausschuß/Brüder Rosenbaum, 1937).

44   By 1938, a number of U.S. furniture manufacturers, including Conant-Ball, Dunbar, Heywood-Wakefield, and the Michigan Seating Company, were offering their own "Swedish Modern" pieces. Articles also appeared in many of the country's popular home furnishings magazines offering advice on how to reproduce the look. On the influence of Swedish Modern in the United States, see, for example,

Creative Design in Home Furnishings 3 (February 1938): 27, and (April–May 1938): 1; "We Give You a Liveable Modern—and It's Called 'Swedish Modern,'" *American Home* 20 (October 1938): 12–13, 74; "Swedish Modern," *House and Garden* 73 (February 1938): 50–51; and "Swedish Modern in the U.S.A.," *American Home* 22 (July 1939): 24, 64.

45 See Åke Hult, "I Warszawa och Praha," *Svenska hem i ord och bilder* 26 (May 1938): vi-vii; and Wängberg-Eriksson, *Svenskt Tenn*, 149–50, 153.

46 *Architectural Forum* 70 (June 1939): special issue, World's Fairs, n.p.

47 Larsson and Malmsten both showed living rooms; Svedberg exhibited a combination living and informal dining room; and Berg, Åke Huldt, and Horlen Mattis collaborated on a farm kitchen. On the exhibit and its reception, see Åke Stavenow et al., eds., *Swedish Arts and Crafts. Swedish Modern—A Movement toward Sanity in Design*, exhibition catalog (New York: Royal Swedish Commission, New York World's Fair, 1939); Elisabeth Aschehoug, "Beauty and Comfort for All," *American Swedish Monthly* (May 1939): esp. 12–13; Martin Strömberg, "Swedish Modern: Svensk lösen i New York," *Svenska hem i ord och bilder* 27 (April 1939): 89–93; "Svenskt Tenn i interiör i New York," in *Nyt Tidskrift for Konstindustrie* 13 (March 1940); "Sweden Offers a New Modern," *House and Garden* 76 (July 1939): 16–17; and Wängberg-Eriksson, *Svenskt Tenn*, 142–48.

48 Walter Rendell Storey, "Home Decoration: A World of Furniture at the Fair," *New York Times*, 4 June 1939, B8.

49 On the Swedish exhibit, see Gunvor Björkman, "Svenskt på Golden Gate,"

Svenska hem i ord och bilder 27 (February 1939): 34–40.

50 G. A. Berg, "What Swedish Modern Is in Sweden," *American Home* 22 (July 1939): 22. For other contemporary accounts of Swedish Modern, see also G. A. Berg, "Swedish Modern," *Form* 34, no. 7 (1938): 162–68; and Philip Gustafson, "Swedish Modern—A Way of Living," *Country Life* 76 (June 1939): 52–53.

51 Protected by a friend of the family's who worked for the Bulgarian Embassy, Jenny Frank remained in Vienna until her death in 1941.

52 After the Anschluss, the Nazi authorities also declared the Austrian Werkbund "a Jewish institution," seized its assets, and forced its disbandment. Österreichisches Staatsarchiv, Akten der Stillhaltekommission 37A/1, 13 December 1938.

53 Lea Calice, in an interview with Monika Platzer in 1986, recalled that due to the chaotic circumstances of the company's transfer, many of its records, including the customer files, were lost, and she and Praun were forced to reconstruct the client list from order books. After the firm was disbanded, most of the remaining records were destroyed. Some of Frank's drawings and the original textile printing blocks, however, have survived, and they are now in private hands. Several sets of blocks are in the collections of the Österreichisches Museum für angewandte Kunst and Svenskt Tenn. Platzer, "Einrichtungshaus 'Haus & Garten,'" 5.

54 Kristina Wängberg-Eriksson, "Life in Exile: Josef Frank in Sweden and the United States, 1933–1967," in *Josef Frank, Architect and Designer: An Alternative Vision of the Modern Home*, edited by Nina Stritzler-Levine (New Haven and London:

Yale University Press, 1996), 69. The remaining inventory, primarily textiles, was sold off to several competing Viennese firms, among them Backhausen & Söhne.

55 Frank, who was especially concerned about Wlach, purchased an interior design shop for him in Haifa. Wlach, however, did not accept the offer and eventually opted to go to the United States. Plakholm-Forsthuber, "Josef Frank an Trude Waehner," 146. Over the next two decades, Wlach collaborated with several architects and construction companies in New York, specializing in interior design and focusing particularly on ship interiors. He also designed number of homes in the early 1940s, but as a result of the outbreak of the Second World War none of the projects was realized. After the war, Wlach worked with the interior design firm Hopeman Bros., Inc. In the early 1950s, he tried unsuccessfully to open an interior design shop based on Haus & Garten. He retired in 1958 and lived in the Bronx until his death on 16 August 1963. Wlach's wife Klari (née Krausz, born in Budapest in 1896) died in New York in 1990. Information courtesy of Rebecca Lehrman and Wlach's nephew Tobias Walch. "Professional Career of Dr. Oskar Wlach," typescript, dated April 1958. Copy in possession of the author. See also Wlach's obituary in the *New York Times*, 20 August 1963, 33; and Boeckl, *Visionäre und Vertriebene*, esp. 211–15, 348–49.

56 Wängberg-Eriksson, *Josef Frank—Livsträd i krigens skugga*, 193, 196.

57 Elsa Björkman-Goldschmidt, *Vad sedan hände* (Stockholm: Norstedts, 1964), 237.

58 Plakolm-Forsthuber, "Josef Frank an Trude Waehner," 146–47.

59 Wängberg-Eriksson, *Josef Frank: Textile Designs*, 99.

60 See Kristina Wängberg-Eriksson, "Tolvekarna Tyresö," Form 80, no. 627 (1984): 49–53; and *Josef Frank—Livsträd i krigens skugga*, 169–76.

61 The purchase agreement and other relevant papers, including a number drawings by Frank for the addition and alterations, are in the possession of Gun Jacobson, the house's current owner.

CHAPTER NINE

1 Holton, "Ernst Mach and the Fortunes of Positivism in America," 57–59.

2 Welzig, "Entwurzelt," 215. A number of others also tried to help Frank, among them Hugo Breitner, the former city councilman and principal author of Red Vienna's tax system, which had enabled the city housing projects and many other programs. Breitner attempted to find an academic post for Frank but ran into difficulties because Frank, unlike the leading German modernists, was virtually unknown in the United States. Plakolm-Forsthuber, "Josef Frank an Trude Waehner," 147.

3 Wängberg-Eriksson, Josef Frank—*Livsträd i krigens skugga*, 197.

4 In late 1938, Waehner emigrated to the United States by way of Paris. During the war years, she taught at Sarah Lawrence College, and she gave lectures on the psychology of art at the New School and at the Metropolitan Museum of Art. Later, she taught studio art at Moravian College for Women in Bethlehem, Pennsylvania. She remained in the United States until 1953. Welzig, *Josef Frank, 1885–1967*, 205.

5   In all, 178 European intellectuals received appointments to the various divisions of the New School, most of them arriving between 1933 and the U.S. entry into the war in December 1941. On the history of the school and the experience of the émigrés who taught there, see Peter M. Rutkoff and William B. Scott, *New School: A History of the New School for Social Research* (New York: Free Press, 1986), esp. chaps. 5 and 7.

6   Course catalogs for the spring 1942, fall 1942, spring 1943, and fall 1943 terms. Archive of the New School for Social Research, New York.

7   Welzig, "Entwurzelt," 215.

8   Course catalog, New School for Social Research, spring 1942. Archive of the New School for Social Research, New York.

9   Frank, letter to Walter Sobotka, 8 February 1942, quoted in Sobotka, "Principles of Design," 368.

10 Course catalog, New School for Social Research, fall 1942. Archive of the New School for Social Research, New York.

11 Course catalog, New School for Social Research, spring 1943. Archive of the New School for Social Research, New York.

12 The original manuscripts are in the collection of Hermann Czech in Vienna. Only the titles are in English; all of the surviving texts are in German.

13 Frank, "How to Plan a House," in Spalt, *Josef Frank, 1885–1967*, 162.

14 Spalt, *Josef Frank, 1885–1967*, 163.

15 Spalt, *Josef Frank, 1885–1967*, 163.

16 See the write-up of the show by Else J. Hofmann, "J. Frank, Wiener Architekt, ist Schöpfer des hier 'Swedish Modern' gennanten Möbelstils," *New York Staatszeitung und Herold*, 6 February 1943, 7.

17 Frank, letter to André Lurçat, 15 September 1945, Fonds Lurçat, Archives nationales, Paris, quoted in Welzig, *Josef Frank*, 206.

18 On Frank's modified site plan on the upper right of the perspective view, he incorrectly labeled the western edge of the development as Third Avenue.

19 See "Metropolitan Project to House 30,000," *Pencil Points* 24 (May 1943): 19, 23.

20 The Stuyvesant Town project immediately ran into trouble due to questions concerning tax exemptions and condemnation procedures. Metropolitan Life also encountered public resistance because of the company's announced intentions to exclude African Americans. Eventually, Mayor Fiorello La Guardia and Robert Moses, the powerful head of the City Planning Commission, pushed the project through. Construction began in 1946 and was completed in 1948. The community, which encompassed thirty-five apartment buildings and housing more than 24,000 residents, was among the largest and best known of the postwar urban renewal developments. See "Parkchester 2 for 194X," *Architectural Forum* 78 (May 1943): 66, 160; "Stuyvesant Saga," *Architectural Forum* 79 (July 1943): 40–41; "Stuyvesant Town," *NAHO* News 6 (16 July 1943): 61; "Met Housing in Trouble," *Architectural Forum* 79 (September 1943): 112; "Stuyvesant Town: Metropolitan's newest housing giant is nearing completion despite material and labor shortages," *Architectural Forum* 86 (April 1947): 74–75; "Stuyvesant Town: A Commercial Housing Development, New York," *Builder* 173 (21 November 1947): 572–73; "Stuyvesant Town: Rebuilding a Blighted City Area," *Engineering News Record* 140 (5 February 1948): 73–96; "Stuyvesant Town:

Borough of Manhattan, New York City," *Architect and Engineer* 174 (August 1948): 27–29; "They Live in Stuyvesant Town," *House and Garden* 94 (September 1948): 118–21; and Robert Caro, *The Power Broker: Robert Moses and the Fall of New York* (New York: Knopf, 1974), esp. 7, 805, 961, 968.

21 The typewritten legends on the board allude to Frank's previous work for the Vienna Municipal Housing Authority.

22 Among those who spoke out in opposition to the design were Harold Buttenheim, Arthur C. Holden, and Simon Breines. See "No Holds Barred," *Architectural Forum* 78 (June 1943): 50.

23 Course catalog, New School for Social Research, fall 1943. Archive of the New School for Social Research, New York.

24 Wängberg-Eriksson, *Josef Frank: Textile Designs*, 80–81.

25 Captain Sigfrid Ericson, who married Estrid Ericson on her fiftieth birthday and regularly sailed to New York during the war years, evidently transported the master drawings to Sweden. Wängberg-Eriksson, *Josef Frank: Textile Designs*, 146, n. 2.

26 Wängberg-Eriksson, *Josef Frank: Textile Designs*, 101.

27 Wängberg-Eriksson, *Josef Frank: Textile Designs*, 107, 109, 112.

28 Wängberg-Eriksson, *Josef Frank: Textile Designs*, 99.

29 Wängberg-Eriksson, *Josef Frank: Textile Designs*, 101.

30 Wängberg-Eriksson, "Josef Frank in Sweden and the United States," 76, n. 25.

31 Wängberg-Eriksson, *Josef Frank: Textile Designs*, 99.

32 "New Fabrics for Fall Decorating," *House and Garden* 94 (October 1948): 127–28; and *Interiors* 108 (April 1948): 142. See also Wängberg-Eriksson, *Josef Frank: Textile Designs*, 114

33 After the war, Frank also designed five wallpaper patterns for Schumacher. Welzig, *Josef Frank*, 209.

34 For a discussion of Frank's literary writings, see Georg Schöllhammer, "Zum literarischen Werk Josef Franks," *Um Bau* 10 (August 1986): 133–45.

35 Welzig, *Josef Frank*, 207.

36 Among Frank's drawings and photographs preserved in the archive at the Arkitekturmuseet in Stockholm are 152 large format diapositives, which include a number of American examples, Frank-Arkiv no. 1968-102-(1–152). I am grateful to Cecilia Währner at the Arkitekturmuseet for sharing photocopies of all of the slides with me.

37 Estrid Ericson had subscriptions to a number of popular U.S. design magazines. Many of her issues from the 1940s, 1950s, and 1960s, which Ericson kept at Tolvekarna, are now in the collection of Gun Jacobson.

38 In a letter to Sobotka in 1942, Frank observed: "For America, these questions play no part at all, because these problems do not exist, in fact, neither form nor style are problems; most new things are style-less in a way unknown in Europe, which, however, does not make them more beautiful." Letter, Frank to Sobotka, 8 February 1942, reprinted in Sobotka, "Principles of Design," 367.

39 At the landmark "Modern Architecture" exhibition at the Museum of Modern Art in New York in 1932, for example, only two Austrian architects, Neutra (who by then had been living in Los Angeles for a nearly a decade) and Lois Welzenbacher (whose work was more in tune with Ger-

man trends) were included. Hitchcock and Johnson also completely excluded Austria from their chapter in the show's catalog discussing "The Extent of Modern Architecture," a reflection of the low esteem with which they held Frank and the other Viennese. Henry-Russell Hitchcock, Jr., and Philip Johnson, *Modern Architecture,* exhibition catalog (New York: Museum of Modern Art, 1932), 21–24.

40 Also among the noted Viennese architects and designers who found exile in the United States after 1938 were Rudolf Baumfeld, Wilhelm Baumgarten, Josef Franz Dex, Gerhard Karplus, Leopold Kleiner, Emanuel Neubrunn, Simon Schmiderer, Ernst Schwadron, Wlach, and Liane Zimbler. See Matthias Boeckl and Otto Kapfinger, "Visionäre und Vertriebene: Österreichische Spuren in der modernen amerikanischen Architektur," in Boeckl, *Visionäre und Vertriebene,* 36–41.

41 Welzig, *Josef Frank,* 206.

42 Frank, letter to Lurçat, 15 September 1945, Fonds Lurçat, Archives nationales, Paris, quoted in Welzig, *Josef Frank,* 206.

43 Letter, Frank to Sobotka, 9 September 1961, quoted in Sobotka, "Principles of Design," 396.

44 Welzig, *Josef Frank,* 210.

45 Welzig, *Josef Frank,* 209.

CHAPTER TEN

1 On the exhibition, see Sven Erik Skawonius, "Svenskt Tenn 25 år," *Form* 45 (1949): 164–65.

2 See Richard Cleary, *Merchant Prince and Master Builder: Edgar J. Kaufmann and Frank Lloyd Wright,* exhibition catalog (Pittsburgh: Heinz Architectural Center, Carnegie Museum of Art/Seattle and London: University of Washington Press, 1999), 17–35.

3 Wängberg-Eriksson, "Josef Frank im Exil auf Manhattan 1942–46," 198.

4 See, for example, "Swedish Articles on Display Here," *Pittsburgh Post-Gazette,* 6 February 1951; and "Swedish Expert Here Gives Philosophy on Art," *Pittsburgh Sun-Telegraph,* 7 February 1951.

5 Ultimately, the most successful of the firms was the IKEA chain, founded by Ingvar Kamprad in 1965. IKEA's product line was influenced by the works of Frank and other leading postwar designers as well as by the exhibitions by the Svenska Slöjdföreningen and the Stockholm department store NK, and *Allt i hemmet,* then the best-selling home furnishings periodical in Sweden. On the emergence of IKEA in Sweden, see Wickman, "Homes," 220–25.

6 Letter, Frank to Trude Waehner, 14 March 1946, quoted in Plakholm-Forsthuber, "Josef Frank an Trude Waehner," 152.

7 Frank's talk at the Alpbach Forum was published the following year as "Die Rolle der Architektur," *Europäische Rundschau* 17 (1948): 777–81.

8 Welzig, *Josef Frank,* 211. On the talk and the public response to it, see Margarete Schütte-Lihotzky, "Professor Frank im Ottakringer Volksheim," *Österreichische Zeitung,* 4 February 1948.

9 Herbert Thurner, quoted in Friedrich Kurrent, "Frank und frei," *Um Bau* 10 (August 1986): 88. Lotte Schwarz, who met Frank many years later, recalled asking him why he had not returned to Vienna after the war. According to Schwarz, he replied that "never could he forgive, never could he breathe freely in a city in which an obdurate Fascism perpetuated by village

idiots [*Dorftrottelfaschismus*] had brought such disaster." Lotte Schwarz, "Eine Begegnung mit Josef Frank in Dieulefit," *Bauwelt* 76 (12 July 1986): 1069.

10 Frank confided in a letter to Waehner that he no longer had an interest in Vienna or the works of local architects and designers, only for a few "individuals." Plakholm-Forsthuber, "Josef Frank an Trude Waehner," 151.

11 Frank "Großstädisch gedacht," *Film* 36 (March 1949): 11–12. See also Frank's article "Zur Neugestaltung des Stephansplatzes," *Wiener Tageszeitung*, 1 May 1948, 3.

12 Letter, Frank to Waehner, 30 May 1946, quoted in Welzig, *Josef Frank*, 235.

13. Frank, "Großstädisch gedacht," 11–12.

14 Letter, Frank to Waehner, 2 March 1946, quoted in Welzig, *Josef Frank*, 235.

15 Letter, Frank to Waehner, 4 May 1946, quoted in Welzig, *Josef Frank*, 235.

16 Letter, Frank to Waehner, 30 May 1946, quoted in Welzig, *Josef Frank*, 235.

17 It is unclear precisely when or why Frank prepared the schemes. The Town for 2,000 Families, like the Community for 1,200 Families, has inscriptions in English, and on the back of a photograph of the former is a notation that it was "for Wisconsin." The Town for 15,000, on the other hand, has legends in French, and the Residential District for 20,000 Residents, in Swedish. Welzig has suggested that the Town for 2,000 Families and the Residential District for 20,000 Residents were designed after the other two, but it is also possible that they were all executed around the same time in the late 1940s or early 1950s. Welzig, *Josef Frank, 228–29.*

18 "Tävlingsförslag till Kungsträdgården i Stockholm, Beskrivning," typescript (in German), Arkitekturmuseet, Stockholm.

19 Letter, Frank to Walter Sobotka, 2 May 1958, quoted in Sobotka, "Principles of Design," 380.

20 Letter, Frank to Oswald Haerdtl, 12 January 1949, reprinted in Spalt and Czech, *Josef Frank, 1885–1967,* 162.

21 On the genesis and development of the late houses, see Spalt and Czech, *Josef Frank, 1885–1967,* 218–237; Hermann Czech, "The Accidental House: The Thirteen Designs in Letters to Dagmar Grill," *Lotus International* 29, no. 4 (1981): 108–10, 114–15; and Welzig, *Josef Frank,* 214–19.

22 Only photocopies of some of the letters (now in the collection of Johannes Spalt) have survived; the originals have been lost, making it difficult to trace fully the development of the house designs.

23 Czech, "The Accidental House," 115.

24 Czech has argued that the "underlying assumption" for House 3 was Le Corbusier's "'Dom-Ino' and 'plan libre' used here with a trace of irony." "The Accidental House," 115. The scheme, however, may also be viewed as an extension of the "columnar" house projects Frank had designed in Vienna in the mid-1920s, in which he had experimented with various *Raumplan* ideas.

25 Letter, Frank to Dagmar Grill, 12 August 1947, quoted in Czech, "The Accidental House," 115.

26 Letter, Frank to Grill, 4 August 1947, quoted in Hermann Czech, "Ein Begriffsraster zur aktuellen Interpretation Josef Franks," *Um Bau* 10 (August 1986), 113.

27 Letter, Frank to Grill, 12 August 1947, quoted in Czech, "The Accidental House," 115.

28 A number of the D-Houses are depicted in a "Provence-like" landscape, an attempt, as he wrote to Waehner, "to warm myself inside." Plakolm-Forsthuber, "Josef Frank an Trude Waehner," 149.

29 Frank, unpublished writings, quoted in Hermann Czech, "A Mode for the Current Interpretation of Josef Frank," *Architecture and Urbanism* 254 (November 1991): 24.

30 Josef Frank, "Accidentism," *Form* 54 (1958): 161–62.

31 Frank, "Accidentism," 163–65. The idea for the term "accidentism" evidently came from Waehner, who in a 1946 letter suggested it to describe Frank's notion of chance ordering. Frank initially did not think that the term was quite right, but eventually adopted it. See Plakolm-Forsthuber, "Josef Frank an Trude Waehner," 149; and Johannes Spalt, "Moderne Weltauffassung und moderne Architektur," *Bauwelt* 76 (12 July 1985): 1067.

32 Frank, "Accidentism," 165.

33 Robert Venturi, *Complexity and Contradiction in Architecture,* 2d. ed. (New York: Museum of Modern Art, 1977), 16.

34 See Schwarz, "Eine Begegnung mit Josef Frank in Dieulefit," 1069.

35 Letter, Frank to Sobotka, 13 April 1960, quoted in Sobotka, "Principles of Design," 390.

36 The project, as Frank wrote to Sobotka in 1960, was fraught with financial problems from the start, due in large measure to the instability of the French franc. Initially, Albrée asked Frank to design a new house, but concerned with financing, he later asked Frank to adapt a small seventeenth-century farmhouse. Neither project was realized. Letter, Frank to Sobotka, 13 April 1960, quoted in Sobotka, "Principles of Design," 390.

37 Plakholm-Forsthuber, "Josef Frank an Trude Waehner," 149.

38 Letter, Frank to Waehner, 23 May 1948, quoted in Johannes Spalt, "Zu Josef Frank," in *Josef Frank 1885–1967. Stoffe, Tapeten, Teppiche,* edited by Johannes Spalt, exhibition catalog (Vienna: Hochschule für angewandte Kunst, 1986), 7.

39 Letter, Frank to Viktor Matejka, 11 August 1965, reprinted in Matejka, "12 Fragen an Josef Frank," 1064.

40 Matejka, "12 Fragen an Josef Frank," 1065.

41 Matejka, "12 Fragen an Josef Frank," 1065.

42 Letter, Frank to Helene Eisenkolb, 19 November 1966, in possession of the author.

ABBREVIATIONS

Architekt *Der Architekt* [Vienna]
Arkitekturmuseet Arkitektur-
museet, Stockholm
Albertina Graphische Sammlung
Albertina, Vienna
Aufbau *Der Aufbau* [Vienna]
Bauhaus-Archiv Bauhaus-Archiv,
Museum für Gestaltung,
Berlin
Baumeister *Der Baumeister* [Mu-
nich]
Bergquist and Michélsen 1994
Mikael Bergquist and Olof
Michélsen, *Josef Frank—
arkitektur* (Stockholm, 1994)
Bergquist and Michélsen 1998
Mikael Bergquist and Olof
Michélsen, *Josef Frank Falster-
bovillorna* (Stockholm, 1998)
Blau 1999 Eve Blau, *The Architec-
ture of Red Vienna, 1919–1934*
(Cambridge, Mass., 1999)
BuWK *Bau- und Werkkunst* [Vi-
enna]
DB *Deutsche Baukunst* [Lübeck]
DK *Dekorative Kunst* [Munich]
DKuD *Deutsche Kunst und Dekora-
tion* [Darmstadt]
Form *Die Form* [Berlin]
Frank 1968 Nationalmuseum,
*Josef Frank 1885–1967. Min-
nesutställning* (Stockholm,
1968)

Frank 1981 Johannes Spalt and
Hermann Czech, eds., *Josef
Frank 1885–1967* (Vienna,
1981)
Frank 1985 Johannes Spalt, ed.,
*Josef Frank zum 100. Geburt-
stag am 15. Juli 1985* (Vienna,
1985)
Getty Getty Research Institute,
Los Angeles
HMSW Historisches Museum
der Stadt Wien
ID *Zeitschrift für Innendekoration,*
later *Innen-Dekoration* [Darm-
stadt]
Josef Frank 100 år Rikard Jacob-
son, ed., *Josef Frank 100 år Ju-
bileumsutställning hösten 1985*
(Stockholm, 1985)
KuKhw *Kunst und Kunsthandwerk*
[Vienna]
MBF *Moderne Bauformen*
[Stuttgart]
Möbel-Geräte-Theoretisches Jo-
hannes Spalt, ed., *Josef Frank,
1885–1967: Möbel & Geräte &
Theoretisches* (Vienna, 1981)
Neubau *Der Neubau* [Berlin]
ÖK *Österreichische Kunst* [Vienna]
ÖNB-BA Österreichische Nation-
albibliothek, Bildarchiv,
Vienna
ÖW Max Eisler, *Österreichische
Werkkultur* (Vienna, 1916)

Stein Holz Eisen *Stein Holz Eisen*
[Frankfurt am Main]
Stritzler-Levine 1996 Nina
Stritzler-Levine, ed. *Josef
Frank, Architect and Designer:
An Alternative Vision of the
Modern Home* (New Haven,
1996)
Studio Yearbook *The Studio Year-
book of Decorative Art* [London]
Svenskt Tenn Svenskt Tenn
Archive, Stockholm.
UfaK Sammlung, Universität für
angewandte Kunst, Vienna
Wängberg-Eriksson 1994
Kristina Wängberg-Eriksson,
*Josef Frank—Livsträd i krigens
skugga* (Lund, 1994)
Weihsmann 1985 Helmut Weihs-
mann, *Das Rote Wien.
Sozialdemokratisches Architek-
tur und Kommunalpolitik
1919–1934* (Vienna, 1985)
Welzig 1998 Maria Welzig, *Josef
Frank, 1885–1967: Das architek-
tonische Werk* (Vienna, 1998)
WM *Wasmuths Monatshefte für
Baukunst* [Berlin]

CATALOG OF WORKS
Buildings, Projects, and Interiors

1907
Competition project for the renovation of the Zedlitzhalle, Vienna
VIENNA I, ZELITZGASSE/
LIEBENBERGGASSE

———

Wiener Bauindustriezeitung, 5 April 1907; *Architekt* 13 (Sept. 1907): 48–52; Matthias Boeckl, "Die Mode-Moderne mit dem fabriciertem Stimmungs-Dusel," in *Die verlorene Moderne* (exhib. cat.; Vienna, 1993), 64–65; Stritzler-Levine 1996: 78–79; Welzig 1998: 16–19, 240.

1909
Competition drawing for a Zeppelin hangar
ZEPPELIN WERKE, FRIEDRICHSHAFEN, GERMANY
(Design: Bruno Möhring)

———

Stein und Eisen (Berlin, 1908); Welzig 1998: 20–21.

1909–10
Reconstructions of the churches of Leon Battista Alberti
Drawings: Universitätsarchiv, Technische Universität, Vienna

———

Josef Frank, "Über die ursprüngliche Gestalt der krichlichen Bauten des

Leone Battista Alberti" (Ph.D. diss., Technische Hochschule, 1910); Wängberg-Eriksson 1994: 26–27, 49; Stritzler-Levine 1996: 156–57; Welzig 1998: 21–22, 240, plate 1.

1910

Furnishings for the apartment of Karl and Hedwig Tedesco

VIENNA III, UNTERE VIADUKTGASSE 16
Photographs: UfaK; Collection Prof. Johannes Spalt, Vienna

————

Das Interieur 13 (June 1912): 41–48, plates 41–47; *Studio Yearbook* (1913): 190; *ÖW*: 87, 89, 91; *Frank 1981*: 57; *Möbel-Geräte-Theoretisches* 90; *Um Bau* 10 (Aug. 1986): 75; Wängberg-Eriksson 1994: 31–32; Stritzler-Levine 1996: 47, 104–5, 160; Welzig 1998: 23–25, 32–33, 240.

Interiors for the Strömberg-Palm Swedish Gymnastics School

VIENNA I, FLEISCHMARKT I
Photographs: Collection Prof. Johannes Spalt, Vienna

————

Das Interieur 13 (June 1912): 41–48, plates 41–47; *Frank 1981*: 248; Stritzler-Levine 1996: 47; Welzig 1998: 23, 25–27, 29, 240.

1911

Furnishings for the apartment of Stefan and Esther Grossmann

VIENNA (ADDRESS UNKNOWN)

————

Welzig 1998: 27, 240.

1911–12

Design for an exhibition room, Jahresausstellung Österreichischer Kunstgewerbe

ÖSTERREICHISCHES MUSEUM FÜR KUNST UND IN-
DUSTRIE, VIENNA
(with Hugo Gorge, Viktor Lurje, and Oskar Strnad)
Photographs: MAK-Österreichisches Museum für angewante Kunst, Vienna

————

Das Interieur 12 (Dec. 1911): 89–92; *Kunst und Kunsthandwerk* 14 (1911): 621, 626–30; Sabine Forsthuber, *Moderne Raumkunst: Wiener Ausstellungsbauten von 1898–1914* (Vienna, 1991), 151–52; Stritzler-Levine 1996: 106; Welzig 1998: 32, 240.

1912

Design for a living room in a country house, Spring Exhibition of Austrian Arts and Crafts

ÖSTERREICHISCHES MUSEUM FÜR KUNST UND
INDUSTRIE, VIENNA
Photographs: UfaK; Collection Prof. Johannes Spalt, Vienna; MAK-Österreichisches Museum für angewante Kunst

————

Österreichisches Museum für Kunst und Industrie, *Frühjahrsausstellung österreichischer Kunstgewerbe, verbunden mit einer Ausstellung der k.k. Kunstgewerbeschule Wien. Mai-Juli 1912* (exhib. cat.; Vienna, 1912); Benotto, "Frühjahrsausstellung im Österreichischen Museum," *Das Interieur* 13 (1912); *Kunst und Kunsthandwerk* 15 (1912): 345; *DKuD* 31 (Oct. 1912): 89–107, 190–91; Fritz Planer, "Die Frühjahrsausstellung 1912 im Österreichischen Museum für Kunst und Industrie"; Kunstrevue, *Österreichische Illustrierte Zeitung* 41 (June 1912): 1009; F. Stern, "Die Frühjahrsausstellung des Österreichischen Museum," in *Neues Wiener Tagblatt*, 4 June 1912; Alexander Koch, *Handbuch neuzeitlicher Wohnungskultur. Das vornehm-bürgerliches Heim* (Darmstadt, 1922), 16; *Das Zelt* 1, no. 10 (1924): 353; Alexander Koch, *1000 Ideen zur künst-*

lerischen Ausgestaltung der Wohnung (Darmstadt, 1926), 16; Christian Witt-Dörring, *Wiener Innenraumgestaltung* (Vienna, 1981), 26, 31; *Frank 1981:* 57; *Möbel-Geräte-Theoretisches*, 89; *Josef Frank 100 år*, 14; Sabine Forsthuber, *Moderne Raumkunst: Wiener Ausstellungsbauten von 1898–1914* (Vienna, 1991), 152–58; Wängberg-Eriksson 1994: 38; Stritzler-Levine 1996: 107, 161; Welzig 1998: 28–30; Christopher Long, "A Symptom of the Werkbund," *Studies in the Decorative Arts* 7 (spring–summer 2000): 96–97, 101.

Furnishings for the apartment of Emma and Malte Jacobsson

ASCHEBERGSGATAN, GÖTEBORG

————

ID 33 (Sept. 1922): 329; Wängberg-Eriksson 1994: 91; Welzig 1998: 240.

1912–13

Interiors for the Museum für Ostasiatische Kunst

HANSARING 32A/BREMER STRASSE (NOW ADOLF-FISCHER-STRASSE)/GEREONSWALL, COLOGNE (DESTROYED 1944)

Photographs: Museum für Ostasiatische Kunst, Cologne; Rheinisches Bildarchiv, Cologne

————

Adolf Fischer, *Führer durch das Museum für ostasiatische Kunst der Stadt Cöln* (Cologne, 1913); *Kunst und Künstler* 12 (1913–14): 286–88; *Kölnische Zeitung*, 25 Oct. 1913 (Morgen–Ausgabe), 25 Oct. 1913 (Abend-Ausgabe), 7 Nov. 1913 (Mittags-Ausgabe); M. Osborn, "Ostasien in Köln," *B.Z. am Mittag*, 4 Oct. 1913; R. Petrucci, "Das Museum für Osasiatische Kunst," *Frankfurter Zeitung*, 27 Oct. 1913; F. Stahl, "Das Kölner Museum für ostasiatische Kunst," *Berliner Tageblatt*, 27 Oct. 1913; Adolf Fischer, "Das Museum für ostasiatische Kunst der Stadt Cöln," *Museumskunde* 10 (1914): 71–107; *ÖW*: 95; *Architekt* 22 (1919): 169–74; Joseph Thiele and Adam Wrede, eds., *Köln als Stätte der Bildung*

(Cologne, 1922): 161–66, plates 12, 13; Frieda Fischer-Wieruszowki, "Das Museum für ostasiatische Kunst der Stadt Köln," *DKuD* 51 (Oct. 1922): 33–42; *Frank 1981*: 170; Ulrich Wiesner, *Museum für Ostasiatische Kunst Köln. Zum 75jährigen Jubiläum des Museums* (Cologne, 1984); Wängberg-Eriksson 1994: 42–45; Stritzler-Levine 1996: 48; Welzig 1998: 48–51.

1913

Furnishings of Frank's own apartment

VIENNA IV, WIEDNER HAUPTSTRASSE 64/4/10

Photographs: MAK-Österreichisches Museum für angewante Kunst, Vienna

————

Architekt 21 (1916–18); supplement, *Die Bildenden Künste*: 17; *ID* 30 (Dec. 1919): 416; *Baukunst* 3 (Aug. 1927): 244; *Frank 1981*: 58–59; *Ottagano* 16 (Sept. 1981): 28; Sylvia Mattl-Wurm, ed., *Interieurs: Wiener Künstlerwohnungen 1830–1930* (exhib. cat.; Vienna, 1991), 122; Bergquist and Michélsen 1994: 12; Wängberg-Eriksson 1994: 45–47; Stritzler-Levine 1996: 109; Welzig 1998: 30–31.

Designs for the exhibition of the Austrian wallpaper and linoleum industry

ÖSTERREICHISCHES MUSEUM FÜR KUNST UND INDUSTRIE, VIENNA

————

DKuD 33 (1913–14): 155–56; *Kunst und Kunsthandwerk* 16 (1913): 400; Berta Zuckerkandl, "Die Tapetenausstellung," *Wiener Allgemeine Zeitung*, 28 May 1913; Sabine Forsthuber, *Moderne Raumkunst: Wiener Ausstellungsbauten von 1898–1914* (Vienna, 1991), 159–62.

1913–14

Villa for Dr. Emil and Agnes Scholl

VIENNA XVIII (NOW VIENNA XIX),
WILBRANDTGASSE 3

Drawings: Planarchiv der Stadt Wien (MA 37)
Photographs: Arkitekturmuseet; Getty; UfaK; Collection Prof. Johannes Spalt, Vienna

———

WM 2 (1915–16): 522–24; *ÖW*: 83, 84; *ID* 30 (Dec. 1919): 241–43; *Aufbau* 1 (Sept. 1926): 168; *Frank 1981*: 16–18; Helmut Weihsmann, *Wiener Moderne* (n.p., n.d); *Bauwelt* 76 (12 July 1985): 1046; Astrid Gmeiner and Pirhofer Gottfried, *Der Österreichische Werkbund* (Salzburg and Vienna, 1985), 112; Ákos Moravánszky, *Die Architektur der Donaumonarchie* (Berlin, 1988), 171, 174; Bergquist and Michélsen 1994: 95–96; Wängberg-Eriksson 1994: 47–48, 50; Stritzler-Levine 1996: 80–81, 164–65; Welzig 1998: 53–57, plate 2.

1914

Villa for Oskar and Hanny Strauß

VIENNA XVIII (NOW VIENNA XIX),
WILBRANDTGASSE II

Drawings: Planarchiv der Stadt Wien (MA 37)
Photographs: Arkitekturmuseet; Bauhaus-Archiv; Getty; Collection Prof. Johannes Spalt, Vienna

———

WM 6 (1921): 176; *Das Zelt* 1, no. 10 (1924): 350; *Frank 1981*: 19; *Bauwelt* 76 (12 July 1985): 1046; Bergquist and Michélsen 1994: 144; Stritzler-Levine 1996: 49; Welzig 1998: 57–60.

Country house for Hugo Bunzl

ORTMANN 16 (NOW KITZBERGHÖHE 2,
NEUSIEDL), ORTMANN BEI PERNITZ, LOWER
AUSTRIA

Drawings: UfaK 1216, 1221, 1222
Photographs: Albertina; UfaK; Collection Prof. Johannes Spalt, Vienna

———

WM 2 (1915–16): 515–17; *ÖW*: 82, 86, 91; *Architekt* 21 (1916–18), supplement, *Die Bildenden Künste*, 19; *ID* 30 (Dec. 1919): 410–15, 419; Alexander Koch, *Handbuch neuzeitlicher Wohnungskultur. Das vornehmbürgerliche Heim* (Darmstadt, 1922), 35, 53; *DKuD* 54 (1924): 100; *Das Zelt* 1, no. 10 (1924): 349; *Frank 1981*: 12–14; *Möbel-Geräte-Theoretisches*: 90; Ákos Moravánszky, *Die Architektur der Donaumonarchie* (Berlin, 1988), 171, 174; Bergquist and Michélsen 1994: 25, 93; Wängberg-Eriksson 1994: 35–37, 47–48, 71; Stritzler-Levine 1996: 78, 80–81, 110, 114, 163; Welzig 1998: 60–65, plate 3.

Project: Office building near the Church of Maria am Gestade

VIENNA I, CORNER OF AM GESTADE AND
TIEFER-GRABEN

(with Oskar Strnad and Oskar Wlach)
Photographs: Albertina; Arkitekturmuseet; MAK-Österreichisches Museum für angewante Kunst, Vienna; Collection Prof. Johannes Spalt, Vienna

———

DK 21 (Feb. 1918): 153; *WM* 6 (1921): 178; *Aufbau* 1 (Sept. 1926): 168; Max Eisler, *Oskar Strnad* (Vienna, 1936), 20–21; Otto Niedermoser, *Oskar Strnad* (Vienna, 1965), 19; Bergquist and Michélsen 1994: 145; Welzig 1998: 70–72.

Project: Four houses in the Wilbrandtgasse

VIENNA XVIII

Photographs: Arkitekturmuseet; Collection Prof. Johannes Spalt, Vienna

———

Frank 1981: 15; *Bauwelt* 76 (12 July 1985): 1052; Bergquist and Michélsen 1994: 11; Wängberg-Eriksson 1994: 46; Welzig 1998: 60.

1918–19

Project: Housing development with poured concrete buildings

(with Hugo Fuchs and Franz Zettinig)

———

Architekt 22 (1919): 33–37; *Frank 1981*: 112–15; Bergquist and Michélsen 1994: 18; Kurt Junghanns, *Das Haus für Alle: Zur Geschichte der Vorfertigung in Deutschland* (Berlin, 1994), 107; Welzig 1998: 241; Blau 1999: 433.

1919

Workers' housing project for the Bunzl and Biach paper factory (phase 1)

ORTMANN BEI PERNITZ, LOWER AUSTRIA

Drawings: Gemeindeamt Waidmannsfeld

Photograph: Arkitekturmuseet

———

KuKhw (1920): 269; *DKuD* 48 (Sept. 1921): 307–10; *Um Bau* 10 (Aug. 1986): 40–42; Bergquist and Michélsen 1994: 18, 56–57; Wängberg-Eriksson 1994: 54–55; Stritzler-Levine 1996: 49–50; Welzig 1998: 86–87, 242.

1920

Project: Competition for a housing development in Istanbul

(with Oskar Wlach)

———

Oskar Wlach, "Bewerbung für Aufnahme in die Liste der Sachverständingen für Architektur und das Hochfachbau" (1924), and "Professional Career of Dr. Oskar Wlach" (1958). Copies in possession of the author.

Kitchen/living room and bedroom for a worker's home at the exhibition Einfacher Hausrat

ÖSTERREICHISCHES MUSEUM FÜR KUNST UND INDUSTRIE

———

Einfacher Hausrat (exhib. cat.; Vienna, 1920); *ID* 23 (Nov.–Dec. 1920): 81; *Architekt* 23 (1920–21): 83–84; *KuKhw* (1920): 260–61; *ID* 32 (June 1921): 190, 192; *Studio Yearbook* (1922): 141; *Frank 1981*: 117; *Möbel-Geräte-Theoretisches*: 73; Christian Witt-Dörring, *Wiener Innenraumgestaltung* (Vienna, 1981), 35, 43–44; Astrid Gmeiner and Gottfried Pirhofer, *Der Österreichische Werkbund* (Salzburg and Vienna, 1985), 102–3; Welzig 1998: 45.

1920–22

Workers' housing project for the Bunzl and Biach paper factory (phase 2)

ORTMANN BEI PERNITZ, LOWER AUSTRIA

(Landscape design by Albert Esch)

Drawings: Gemeindeamt Waidmannsfeld

Photographs: UfaK; Collection Prof. Johannes Spalt, Vienna

———

DKuD 54 (1924): 102–3; *Neubau* 6 (10 Feb. 1924): 24–29; *MBF* 26 (May 1927): 176; *Frank 1981*: 116–18; *Um Bau* 10 (Aug. 1986): 43–45; *Möbel-Geräte-Theoretisches*: 73; Bergquist and Michélsen 1994: 57; Welzig 1998: 87–89, plate 4.

1921

Nursery school (Kinderheim) for the Bunzl and Biach paper factory

ORTMANN BEI PERNITZ, LOWER AUSTRIA

Drawings: Gemeindeamt Waidmannsfeld; Collection Prof. Johannes Spalt, Vienna

Photographs: Arkitekturmuseet; Collection Prof. Johannes Spalt, Vienna

———

DKuD 54 (1924): 101; *Neubau* 6 (10 Feb. 1924): 25, 27; *Das Zelt* 1, no. 10 (1924): 351; *ID* 36 (Feb. 1925): 70; Alexander Koch, *Farbige Wohnräume der Neuzeit* (Darmstadt, 1926), 60; *MBF* 26 (May 1927): 174; *Stein Holz Eisen* 41 (1927), Sondernr. 1: 2; Bruno Taut, *Die neue Baukunst in Europa und Amerika*

(Stuttgart, 1929), 202, translated as *Modern Architecture* (London, 1929), 178; *Frank 1981*: 120–23; Bergquist and Michélsen 1994: 58; Stritzler-Levine 1996: 97; Welzig 1998: 90–92, 242, plates 4, 5.

Project: Housing settlement in Traiskirchen, Lower Austria (two versions)

Drawings: Albertina, Frank-Archiv 48, 49

———

Neubau 6 (10 Feb. 1924): 28; *Stein Holz Eisen* 43 (1929): 319; Karl Mang and Eva Mang, *Viennese Architecture, 1860–1930, in Drawings* (New York, 1979), 114; *Frank 1981*: 126; *Um Bau* 10 (Aug. 1986): 46–47; Bergquist and Michélsen 1994: 146; Stritzler-Levine 1996: 172; Welzig 1998: 94, 242.

1921–25

Hoffingergasse housing project

286 row houses

VIENNA XII, HOFFINGERGASSE, FRÜHWIRTHGASSE, STEGMAYERGASSE, ELSNIGGASSE, SONNERGASSE, SCHNEIDERHAHNGASSE, OSWALDGASSE

(with Erich Faber)

Drawings: Planarchiv der Stadt Wien (MA 37)
Photographs: HMSW; Collection Prof. Johannes Spalt, Vienna

———

Arbeiter-Zeitung [Vienna], 16 March 1921; 31 July 1921; 7 Oct. 1921; 30 Dec. 1921; 22 Jan. 1922; 31 May 1922; 12 June 1922; 1 July 1922; 28 Oct. 1922; 4 Nov. 1922; *DKuD* 54 (1924): 100, 102; *Neubau* 6 (10 June 1924): 118, 120; Hans Kampffmeyer, *Siedlung und Kleingarten* (Vienna, 1926), 67, 142–43; *WM* 10 (1926): 365; *MBF* 26 (May 1927): 176; Grete Dexel and W. Dexel, *Das Wohnhaus von heute* (Leipzig, 1928), 67; Österreichisches Gesellschafts- und Wirtschaftsmuseum, *Die Wohnungspolitik der Gemeinde Wien* (Vienna, 1929), 38; *Stein Holz Eisen* 43 (1929): 316, 318; Charles O. Hardy, *The Housing Program of the City of Vienna* (Washington, D.C., 1934), facing 68; Manfredo Tafuri, *Vienna Rossa. La*

politica residenziale nella Vienna socialista, 1919–1933 (Milan, 1980), 17; *Frank 1981*: 124–25; Weihsmann 1985: 214; *Um Bau* 10 (Aug. 1986): 47–49; Friedrich Achleitner, *Österreichische Architektur im 20. Jahrhundert*, vol. 3, no. 1. (Vienna 1990), 324; Bergquist and Michélsen 1994: 17–19; Stritzler-Levine 1996: 81–82; Welzig 1998: 92–93, 242; Blau 1999: 114–17, 131.

1922

Project: Model settlement row house, "type 1"

Drawing: UfaK 1224

———

Frank 1981: 127; Stritzler-Levine 1996: 173; Welzig 1998: 243.

Project: Model settlement row house, "type 127"

Drawing: Collection Professor Johannes Spalt, Vienna

Project: Settlement house with the smallest possible plan

———

Neubau 6 (10 Feb. 1924): 26; *Frank 1981*: 130; Welzig 1998: 243.

Project: Expandable settlement house

———

Neubau 6 (10 Feb. 1924): 26; Welzig 1998: 243.

Project: Housing settlement for Rodaun

VIENNA XXII, BREITENFURTER STRASSE

Drawing: UfaK 1223

———

Neubau 6 (10 Feb. 1924): 26–27; *Frank 1981*: 127; Welzig 1998: 243.

Project: Row house for the Stockerau housing settlement
Drawing: Collection Prof. Johannes Spalt, Vienna

———

Frank 1981: 127; Welzig 1998: 243.

Project: Housing settlement in St. Veit an der Treisting, Lower Austria
Drawing: UfaK 1238

———

Frank 1981: 127; Welzig 1998: 243.

Project: Manager housing in Ortmann bei Pernitz, Lower Austria
Drawing: UfaK 1235

———

Frank 1981: 123; Welzig 1998: 243.

Project: Elementary school in Tiberias, Palestine
Drawing: Albertina, Frank-Archiv 23

———

Frank 1981: 177; Stritzler-Levine 1996: 174; Welzig 1998: 243.

1922–23
Project: Housing settlement in Klosterneuburg, Lower Austria
Drawing: Albertina, Frank-Archiv 20
Photograph: Arkitekturmuseet

———

ID 34 (August 1923): 336–38; *Das Kunstblatt* 7 (1924): 109; *Neubau* 6 (10 Feb. 1924): 26; *Frank 1981*: 128–29; *Um Bau* 10 (Aug. 1986): 49–51; Bergquist and Michélsen 1994: 19, 60–62; Stritzler-Levine 1996: 175; Welzig 1998: 94–95, 154, 244.

Project: Wohnküche for a Siedlung house

———

ID 34 (August 1923): 337; *Frank 1981*: 128; Bergquist and Michélsen 1994: 63; Welzig 1998: 244.

Project: Two living room designs for settlement houses

———

ID 34 (August 1923): 336–37; Bergquist and Michélsen 1994: 61, 63; Welzig 1998: 244.

1923
Furnishings for a salon in the exhibition Modernes österreichisches Kunsthandwerk
OSTERREICHISCHES MUSEUM FÜR KUNST UND INDUSTRIE, VIENNA

———

DKuD 54 (1924): 40.

Project: General architecture plan for Vienna
(with Peter Behrens, Josef Hoffmann, Adolf Loos, and Oskar Strnad)

———

Max Ermers, "Groß-Wiens Stadterweiterung und der neue General-Architekturplan," *Der Tag*, 25 Nov. 1923: 6; *Die Neue Wirtschaft*, 29 Nov. 1923: 11, 31 Jan. 1924: 11; Otto Neurath, "Generalarchitekturplan," *Das Kunstblatt* 7 (April 1924): 105–8; Wilfried Posch, "Die Gartenstadtbewegung in Wien," *Bauforum* 13, nos. 77–78 (1980): 19; Burkhardt Rukschcio and Roland Schachel, *Adolf Loos. Leben und Werk* (Salzburg and Vienna, 1982), 533–34; Blau 1999: 161–65.

Project: Main square for the Ortmann housing settlement
ORTMANN BEI PERNITZ, LOWER AUSTRIA
Drawing: UfaK 1243

———

Frank 1981: 119; Bergquist and Michélsen 1994: 59; Stritzler-Levine 1996: 176; Welzig 1998: 86, 90, 244.

**Project: Housing block for foremen of the
Škoda-Wetzler Company**

―――――

Frank 1981: 130; *Welzig 1998*: 244.

Project: Synagogue in Antwerp, Belgium
Photograph: Collection Prof. Johannes Spalt, Vienna

―――――

L'Amour de l'art 4 (Aug. 1923): 634; *Menorah* 7
(1929): 557; *Frank 1981*: 174; Carol Herselle Krinsky,
Synagogues of Europe (New York and Cambridge,
Mass., 1985), 258–60.

1923–24
Villa for Dr. Theo Herzberg-Fränkel
ORTMANN 50 (NOW VICTOR BUNZLSTRASSE 2) ORT-
MANN BEI PERNITZ, LOWER AUSTRIA
Drawing: Gemeindeamt Waidmannsfeld; Collection
Prof. Johannes Spalt, Vienna
Photograph: Arkitekturmuseet

―――――

Das Zelt 1, no. 10 (1924): 352; *MBF* 26 (May 1927):
172–73; *Frank 1981*: 20–21; Bergquist and
Michélsen 1994: 64–65; *Welzig 1998*: 118–20, 244.

**Project: Summer house for Dr. Felix Bunzl in
Wattens, Tyrol (two versions)**
Drawings: UfaK 1228; Collection Prof. Johannes
Spalt, Vienna

―――――

Frank 1981: 191; Bergquist and Michélsen 1994:
147; *Welzig 1998*: 117–19, 244.

Project: Housing project on the Sandleitengasse

―――――

Die neue Wirtschaft, 29 Nov. 1923: 11; *Die neue
Wirtschaft*, 31 Jan. 1924: 11; *Siedler und Kleingärtner*
3, no. 12 (1923): 1; *Siedler und Kleingärtner* 4, no. 1
(1924): 1; *Welzig 1998*: 244–45; Blau 1999: 447.

Interiors and garden for the house of David Löbel
VIENNA XIII, GEYLINGGASSE 13
(with Oskar Wlach and Robert Obsieger)
Drawings: UfaK 368, 369, 385, 387, 403; Collection
Prof. Johannes Spalt, Vienna

―――――

ID 37 (Oct. 1926): 348, 362–63, 368, 370–72, 384;
MBF 26 (May 1927): 177; André Lurçat, ed., *Ter-
rasses et jardines* (Paris, 1929): 1; *Frank 1981*: 86;
Möbel-Geräte-Theoretisches: 103, 111, 114; Welzig
1998: 82, 244, plate 7.

Wiedenhofer-Hof housing project
213 units
VIENNA XVII, ZEILERGASSE 7–11, BERINGGASSE 15,
LIEBKNECHTGASSE 10–12, PRETSCHGOGASSE 5
(with Oskar Wlach)
Drawings: Albertina, Frank-Archiv 39, 40;
Planarchiv der Stadt Wien (MA 37)
Photographs: Arkitekturmuseet; HMSW; Collection
Prof. Johannes Spalt, Vienna; Wiener Stadt- und
Landesarchiv

―――――

Gemeinde Wien, *Die Wohnhausanlage der Gemeinde
Wien. Wiedenhoferhof im XVII. Bezirk* (Vienna,
1926); *Neubau* 6 (10 June 1924): 119; *L'Architecture
vivante* (winter 1926): plate 42; *Der Tag*, 1 Aug.
1926: 9; *Menorah* 6 (Sept. 1926): facing 519;
Neubau 8 (10 Oct. 1926): 224–26; *WM* 10 (1926):
366ff.; Ludwig Hilbersheimer, *Internationale
Baukunst* (Stuttgart, 1927): 45; *MBF* 26 (May 1927):
171; *WM* 11 (1927): 381ff.; Grete Dexel and W. Dexel,
Das Wohnhaus von heute (Leipzig, 1928), 188; *Architekten* [Copenhagen] 30 (1928): 206; Bruno Taut,
Modern Architecture (London 1929), 116; Karl Mang
and Eva Mang, *Viennese Architecture, 1860–1930, in
Drawings* (New York, 1979), 116–17; Manfredo
Tafuri, *Vienna Rossa. La politica residenziale nella Vi-
enna socialista, 1919–1933* (Milan, 1980), 38, 172;
Frank 1981: 134–37; *Bauwelt* 76 (12 July 1985):
1049–50; Astrid Gmeiner and Gottfried Pirhofer,
Der Österreichische Werkbund (Salzburg and Vienna,

1985), 108–9; Weihsmann 1985: 306; Bergquist and Michélsen 1994: 20–21; Wängberg-Eriksson 1994: 58–59, 63; Stritzler-Levine 1996: 50–51, 83, 177; Welzig 1998: 95–97, 245; Blau 1999: 317–18, 320, 378–79, plate 20.

1923–25

Winarsky-Hof housing project

123 units

VIENNA XX, STROMSTRASSE 36–38, VORGARTENSTRASSE, LEYSTRASSE, PASETTISTRASSE, KAISERWASSERSTRASSE (NOW WINARSKYSTRASSE)

(with Peter Behrens, Josef Hoffmann, Oskar Strnad, Oskar Wlach)

Drawings: Planarchiv der Stadt Wien (MA 37)
Photographs: Arkitekturmuseet; Collection Prof. Johannes Spalt, Vienna; Wiener Stadt- und Landesarchiv

———

Gemeinde Wien, *Die Wohnhausanlage der Gemeinde Wien. Winarskyhof im XX. Bezirk* (Vienna 1926); *L'Architecte* 3 (Nov. 1926): 87, plates 64, 65; Josef Bittner, *Die Neubauten der Stadt Wien* (Vienna, 1926), 24–25, plates 21–23; J. G. Wattjes, *Moderne Architektur* (Amsterdam, 1927), 148–49; *MBF* 26 (May 1927): 170; Walter Curt Behrendt, *Der Sieg des neuen Baustils* (Stuttgart, 1927), 7; *Bauwelt* 19 (11 Oct. 1928): 3; *Baumeister* 27 (July 1929): 245–46; Bruno Taut, *Modern Architecture* (London 1929), 105; Walter Müller-Wulckow, *Wohnbauten und Siedlungen aus deutscher Gegenwart* (Königstein im Taunus, 1929), 95; *Das Wohnungswesen der Stadt Wien* (Stuttgart, 1933), 36; *Form* 63 (1967): 177; *Frank 1968*: 17; Karl Mang et al., *Kommunaler Wohnbau in Wien* (Vienna, [1978]); Manfredo Tafuri, *Vienna Rossa. La politica residenziale nella Vienna socialista, 1919–1933* (Milan, 1980), 50, 158ff., 178–79; *Frank 1981*: 138–39; *Bauwelt* 76 (12 July 1985): 1048–49; Astrid Gmeiner and Gottfried Pirhofer, *Der Österreichische Werkbund* (Salzburg and Vienna, 1985), 109;

Weihsmann 1985: 284–85; Bergquist and Michélsen 1994: 148; Welzig 1998: 97–98, 245, plate 9; Blau 1999: 303–10, 378–79.

1924

Project: House for Otto Stiegl in Spittal an der Drau, Carinthia

Drawing: Albertina; Frank-Archiv 71
Photographs: Collection Prof. Johannes Spalt, Vienna

———

MBF 26 (May 1927): 175; Karl Mang and Eva Mang, *Viennese Architecture, 1860–1930, in Drawings* (New York, 1979), 115; *Frank 1981*: 195; Bergquist and Michélsen 1994: 149; Stritzler-Levine 1996: 195; Welzig 1998: 126, 246.

Project: Terraced restaurant

Photographs: Arkitekturmuseet

———

Katalog der Jubiläumsausstellung (Vienna, 1924); *ÖK* 1 (1927): 120; *Baukunst* (1927): 253; Alberto Sartoris, *Gli elementi dell' architecttura funzionale* (Milan, 1935), 72; *Frank 1981*: 181; Bergquist and Michélsen 1994: 23; Welzig 1998: 246.

Project: House in Falsterbo

Drawing: Collection Prof. Johannes Spalt, Vienna
Welzig 1998: 246.

Project: Gravestone for the Schwitzer family

ZENTRALFRIEDHOF, I. TOR, VIENNA
Drawing: UfaK 1247

———

Frank 1981: 175; Welzig 1998: 245.

Project: Gravestone for the Askonas family

DÖBLINGER FRIEDHOF, VIENNA

———

Frank 1981: 175; Welzig 1998: 245.

Project: Funerary urn for Malwine Lang

URNENHAIN, RING 2, GRUPPE 9, GRABPLATZ 178

Drawing: UfaK 1218

————

Frank 1981: 175; Welzig 1998: 245.

c. 1924

Project: Garden pavilion

————

ID 35 (April 1924): 119; Alexander Koch, *1000 Ideen zur künstlerischen Ausgestaltung der Wohnung* (Darmstadt, 1926), 64; *Frank 1981*: 173; Welzig 1998: 156–57, 245.

1924–27

House for Axel and Signhild Claëson

ROSTOCKERVÄGEN I, FALSTERBO, SWEDEN

Drawings: UfaK 1231; Collection Prof. Johannes Spalt, Vienna

Photographs: Arkitekturmuseet; UfaK

————

MBF 26 (May 1927): 182; *Baumeister* 26 (March 1928): 100; Richard Döcker, *Terrassentyp* (Stuttgart, [1929]), 100; Herbert Hoffmann, *Neue Villen* (Stuttgart, 1929), 44; *MBF* 28 (1929): 44; *Ord och bild* I (14 Jan. 1929): 59; *Österreichischer Werkbund* (Vienna, 1929), 30; *Studio Yearbook* (1929): 14, 50; *Veckojournalen* 40 (1929): 33–36; Hans Eckstein, *Neue Wohnbauten* (Munich, 1932), 50; *Frank 1968*: 18; *Frank 1981*: 22–29; *Möbel-Geräte-Theoretisches*: 10; Bergquist and Michélsen 1994: 14, 98–101; Wängberg-Eriksson 1994: 100, 130–34; Stritzler-Levine 1996: 83–84, 86, 197–98; Bergquist and Michélsen 1998: 21–29, 54; Welzig 1998: 111–17, 137, 246, plate 8.

1925

Strauß House, addition and alterations

VIENNA XVIII, WILBRANDTGASSE II

————

Frank 1981: 19.

Showroom for Haus und Garten

VIENNA I, BÖSENDORFERSTR. 5

(with Oskar Wlach)

Photographs: UfaK; ÖNB-BA

————

ID 37 (Oct. 1926): 374, 376; Wängberg-Eriksson 1994: 78, 89.

Outdoor café and furniture (Haus & Garten) in the Austrian Pavilion at the Exposition des Art Décoratifs et Industriels Modernes, *Paris*

(Opening: 28 April 1925)

QUAI DE LA CONFÉRANCE, EAST OF THE PONT ALEXANDRE III

————

Catalogue general officiel. Exposition des arts décoratifs et industriels modernes (Paris, 1925); *L'Autriche à Paris, Guide* (Vienna, 1925); *Art et décoration* 29 (Sept. 1925): 120–32; *ÖBuWK* 1 (1925): 296ff.; *L'Architecte* 2 (1925): plate 68; L. W. Rochowanski, "Österreich auf der Pariser Ausstellung," *DKuD* 57 (Oct. 1925): 69–76; *ID* 37 (Oct. 1926): 383; *Exposition internationale des arts décoratifs, Rapport genéral* (Paris, 1928), vol. 2; *BuWK* 6 (1929–30): 235; Christian Witt-Dörring, *Wiener Innenraumgestaltung* (Vienna, 1981), 50; *Frank 1981*: 210; Astrid Gmeiner and Gottfried Pirhofer, *Der Österreichische Werkbund* (Salzburg and Vienna, 1985), 99–100; Kristina Wängberg-Eriksson, *Svenskt Tenn. Josef Frank och Estrid Ericson* (Stockholm, 1985), 8–10; Monica Boman, ed., *Estrid Ericson* (Stockholm, 1989), 102; Wängberg-Eriksson 1994: 73–75; Stritzler-Levine 1996: 131; Welzig 1998: 246.

Furnishings for the apartment of Viktor Aufricht
VIENNA III, AUENBRUGGERGASSE 2
Drawing: Collection Prof. Johannes Spalt, Vienna
————
Frank 1981: 92–93; Welzig 1998: 246.

c. 1925
Project: Garden pavilion
Drawing: Collection Prof. Johannes Spalt, Vienna
————
Frank 1981: 173; Welzig 1998: 156–57, 257.

1926
Living room at the Weihnachtsschau exhibition
KÜNSTLERHAUS, VIENNA
(Haus & Garten; with Oskar Wlach)
————
BuWK 3 (1926–27): 76; Welzig 1998: 247.

c. 1926
Project: House in Salzburg
Drawings: Albertina, Frank-Archiv 38; Collection
Prof. Johannes Spalt, Vienna; Collection Friedrich
Kurrent, Munich
————
MBF 26 (May 1927): 184; *Frank 1981*: 186; *Lotus International* 29 (1981): 112–13; *Bauwelt* 76 (12 July 1985): 1068; *Frank 1985*: 38–39; *Um Bau* 10 (Aug. 1986): 68–69; Bergquist and Michélsen 1994: 35–36; Stritzler-Levine 1996: 200–1; Welzig 1998: 121–23, 247.

Project: House for Vienna XIII
Drawings: Albertina, Frank-Archiv 33; Collection
Prof. Johannes Spalt, Vienna
————
MBF 26 (May 1927): 183; *Frank 1981*: 184; *Lotus International* 29 (1981): 112–13; *Ottagano* 16 (Sept. 1981): 27; *Um Bau* 10 (Aug. 1981): 66–67;

Bergquist and Michélsen 1994: 34; Stritzler-Levine 1996: 51–52; Welzig 1998: 123–25, 247.

**Project: House with a dance school for
Mr. Ornstein, Tel Aviv**
Drawings: Albertina, Frank-Archiv 17; Collection
Prof. Johannes Spalt, Vienna
————
MBF: 26 (May 1927): 185; *Frank 1981*: 201; *Frank 1985*: 40–41; Bergquist and Michélsen 1994: 150; Stritzler-Levine 1996: 196; Welzig 1998: 128, 247.

**Project: House for Dagmar Grill in Skärgården,
Sweden**
Drawing: Svenskt Tenn
————
Frank 1981: 187; Bergquist and Michélsen 1994: 38; Stritzler-Levine 1996: 202; Welzig 1998: 121, 159–60, 218, 247.

Interiors for the B. [Bunzl?] apartment
VIENNA (ADDRESS UNKNOWN)
(Haus & Garten; with Oskar Wlach)
————
ID 37 (Oct. 1926): 350–61; Welzig 1998: 246.

Interiors for the S. apartment
VIENNA (ADDRESS UNKNOWN)
(Haus & Garten; with Oskar Wlach)
————
ID 37 (Oct. 1926): 366–67, 369; Welzig 1998: 246.

Interiors for the A. [Aufricht?] apartment
VIENNA (ADDRESS UNKNOWN)
(Haus & Garten; with Oskar Wlach)
————
ID 37 (Oct. 1926): 378; *MBF* 26 (1927): 178; Welzig 1998: 246.

Project: Villa in Ankara

Jahresausstellung der Genossenschaft Bildender Künstler Wiens (exhib. cat.; Vienna: Künstlerhaus 1926), Nr. 554; Welzig 1998: 246.

Project: Bank building in Ankara

Jahresausstellung der Genossenschaft Bildender Künstler Wiens (exhib. cat.; Vienna: Künstlerhaus 1926): Nr. 558; Welzig 1998: 247.

1926–27
Double house at the Weissenhofsiedlung International Exhibition

STUTTGART-WEISSENHOF, RATHENAUSTRASSE 13–15

Drawings: Bauaktei, Stuttgart; Bauhaus-Archiv; Museum of Modern Art, New York; Mies van der Rohe Archive: 4.26; Collection Prof. Johannes Spalt, Vienna

Photographs: Arkitekturmuseet; Bauhaus-Archiv; Getty; UfaK; Collection Prof. Johannes Spalt, Vienna; Württembergische Landesbildstelle, Stuttgart

Amtlicher Katalog. Werkbund-Ausstellung "Die Wohnung" (Stuttgart, 1927); Deutscher Werkbund, *Bau und Wohnung* (Stuttgart, 1927); Werner Gräff, ed., *Innenräume* (Stuttgart, 1928); Heinz Rasch and Bodo Rasch, *Wie Bauen?* (Stuttgart, 1927), 29–31; *Art et décoration* 52 (1927): 189; *Bauwelt* 18 (28 July 1927): 737; *DKuD* 61 (Oct. 1927): 95, 98; *Form* 2 (1927): 290–91; *Das Kunstblatt* 11 (1927): 334, 340; *Neubau* 9 (10 Sept. 1927): 200ff.; *ID* 38 (Dec. 1927): 456ff.; *WM* 11 (1927): 397–98; *DK* 31 (1927–28): 34ff.; Grete Dexel and W. Dexel, *Das Wohnhaus von heute* (Leipzig, 1928), 146; *L'Architecte* 5 (March 1928): 20, plate 16; *ID* 39 (Dec. 1928): 4–51; *Menorah* 6 (Feb. 1928): 121; Richard Döcker, *Terrassentyp* (Stuttgart, 1929), 100–1; *Studio Yearbook* (1929): 50; Sheldon Cheney, *The New*

World Architecture (London and New York, 1930), 260; Hans Eckstein, *Die schöne Wohnung* (Munich, 1931), 28; Ludwig Hilbersheimer, *Contemporary Architecture* (Chicago, 1964), 156; *Form* 63 (1967): 177; *Frank 1968*: 18; Jürgen Joedicke and Christian Plath, *Die Weissenhofsiedlung Stuttgart* (Stuttgart, 1977), 28; *Frank 1981*: 33–35; *Domus* 649 (April 1984): 11; *Bauwelt* 76 (12 July 1985): 1054–56; Astrid Gmeiner and Gottfried Pirhofer, *Der Österreichische Werkbund* (Salzburg and Vienna, 1985), 156; Karin Kirsch, *Die Weissenhofsiedlung* (Stuttgart, 1987), 172–75; *Progressive Architecture* 10 (Oct. 1988): 104; Richard Pommer and Christian F. Otto, *Weissenhof 1927 and the Modern Movement in Architecture* (Chicago, 1991), 99–100; Bergquist and Michélsen 1994: 18, 103, 106, 109–10; Wängberg-Eriksson 1994: 92–96, 98; Stritzler-Levine 1996: 23–24, 53–54, 114; Welzig 1998: 101–4, 247; Blau 1999: 114, 433.

Allan and Signe Carlsten house

FYRVÄGEN 26, FALSTERBO, SWEDEN

Drawing: UfaK 1229

Photographs: Arkitekturmuseet

Hans Eckstein, *Neue Wohnbauten* (Munich, 1932), 49–50; *Frank 1981*: 30–31; Bergquist and Michélsen 1994: 66–69; Wängberg-Eriksson 1994: 101, 104–5, 108–9, 134–36; Stritzler-Levine 1996: 199; Bergquist and Michélsen 1998: 30–37, 55; Welzig 1998: 117–18, 247.

Project: Palace for the League of Nations, Geneva
(with Oskar Wlach)

Ohmann-Gedächtnis-Ausstellung (exhib. cat.; Vienna, 1928); Welzig 1998: 247.

1927

Furnishing of a model living room for Vienna municipal housing projects for the exhibition Wien und die Wiener

MESSEPALAST, VIENNA (MAY–JUNE 1927)

———————

Österreichisches Gesellschafts- und Wirtschaftsmuseum, *Wien und die Wiener* (exhib. cat.; Vienna 1927); *MBF* 26 (1927): 398; Christian Witt-Dörring, *Wiener Innenraumgestaltung* (Vienna, 1981), 45–46; Welzig 1998: 248; Blau 1999: 189–91.

Exhibition designs for Kunstschau 1927

ÖSTERREICHISCHES MUSEUM FÜR KUNST UND INDUSTRIE, VIENNA

Photographs: UfaK

———————

Österreichisches Museum für Kunst und Industrie, *Kunstschau Wien 1927* (exhib. cat.; Berlin, 1927); *DKuD* 61 (Oct. 1928): 80; *MBF* 26 (1927): 394; *ÖK* 1 (15 July–15 Aug. 1927): 120–29; *Frank 1968*: 18; Christian Witt-Dörring, *Wiener Innenraumgestaltung* (Vienna, 1981), 50–51; *Möbel-Geräte-Theoretisches*: 94; Astrid Gmeiner and Gottfried Pirhofer, *Der Österreichische Werkbund* (Salzburg and Vienna, 1985), 124; Welzig 1998: 248.

Permanent exhibition design for the Österreichisches Gesellschafts- und Wirtschaftsmuseum

VIENNA I, RATHAUS

Photographs: Wiener Stadt- und Landesarchiv

———————

[Otto Neurath], "Aufgaben des Gesellschafts- und Wirtschafts Museum in Wien," *Der Aufbau* 1 (Sept. 1926): 169–70, [Otto Neurath], "Der Weg des Gesellschafts- und Wirtschaftsmuseum in Wien," *Österreichische Gemeinde-Zeitung* 4, nos. 3–5 (1927); Otto Neurath, *Die bunte Welt* (Vienna, 1929), "Das Gesellschafts- und Wirtschaftsmuseum in Wien," *Minerva-Zeitschrift* 7, nos. 9–10 (1931): 153–56; Marie Neurath and Robert S. Cohen, *Otto Neurath-Empiricism and Sociology* (Dordrecht and Boston,

1973), 58–59, 216–17; Friedrich Stadler, ed., *Arbeiterbildung in der Zwischenkriegszeit: Otto Neurath-Gerd Arntz* (exhib. cat.; Vienna, 1982); Welzig 1998: 248; Blau 1999: 390–93.

c. 1927

Project: **Country house with two terraces**

Drawing: Albertina, Frank-Archiv 37

———————

Baumeister 26 (March 1928): 99; *Frank 1981*: 182; *Bauwelt* 76 (12 July 1985): 1069; Bergquist and Michélsen 1994: 149; Welzig 1998: 147, 248.

Project: **Summer house with three terraces**

Drawing: Albertina, Frank-Archiv 31

———————

Baumeister 26 (March 1928): 97; *Form* 63 (1967): 176; *Frank 1981*: 183; *Lotus International* 29 (1981): 116; Bergquist and Michélsen 1994: 22; Wängberg-Eriksson 1994: 80; Welzig 1998: 158, 248.

Furnishing for the Cassirer apartment

BRESLAU (ADDRESS UNKNOWN)

(Haus & Garten; with Oskar Wlach)

Drawing: UfaK 334

———————

MBF 26 (1927): 179; Welzig 1998: 247.

Furnishings for the apartment of F.

ADDRESS UNKNOWN

(Haus & Garten; with Oskar Wlach)

———————

MBF 26 (1927): 179.

Furnishings for the home of Mr. W.

ADDRESS UNKNOWN

(Haus & Garten; with Oskar Wlach and Robert Obsieger)

———————

MBF 26 (1927): 177.

Furnishings for a villa in Vienna XIII
ADDRESS UNKNOWN
(Haus & Garten; with Oskar Wlach)
———

MBF 26 (1927): 178.

Furnishings for a lady's bedroom
ADDRESS UNKNOWN
(Haus & Garten; with Oskar Wlach)
———

MBF 26 (1927): 178.

Project: Country house with a terrace
BADEN, LOWER AUSTRIA
———

ID 39 (Dec. 1928): 450; *Frank 1981*: 176; Welzig
1998: 248–49.

**Project: Residence for Mr. and Mrs. A. R. G.,
Los Angeles/House in Vienna XIX**
Drawing: Albertina, Frank-Archiv 28
———

Baumeister 26 (March 1928): 98; Karl M. Grimme,
Das Eigenheim (Berlin, 1929), 25; *Frank 1981*: 185;
Lotus International 29 (1981): 111; *Um Bau* 10 (Aug.
1986): 69; Bergquist and Michélsen 1994: 37; Stritzler-Levine 1996: 204; Welzig 1998: 191, 193–95,
248.

**Project: House for Mr. S. H. B. in Pasadena,
California (also H. R. S. Esq., Pasadena)**
Drawing: Albertina, Frank-Archiv 27
———

MBF 26 (May 1927): 181; *Frank 1981*: 198; *Lotus International* 29 (1981): 113; Bergquist and Michélsen
1994: 151; Stritzler-Levine 1996: 85–88, 205; Welzig
1998: 191–92, 247.

Project: Stucco house in Columbus, Ohio
(with Ernst A. Plischke)
Drawing: UfaK 1234
———

Frank 1981: 8, 200; Ernst A. Plischke, *Ein Leben mit
Architektur* (Vienna, 1989), 92; Bergquist and
Michélsen 1994: 152; Welzig 1998: 135, 148–50,
191, 197–98, 248.

Project: Row house settlement
(with Ernst A. Plischke)
Drawing: Albertina, Frank-Archiv 50
———

Baukunst 3 (Aug. 1927): 252; *Ord och bild* 38 (14 Jan.
1929): 56; *Frank 1981*: 9, 133; Bergquist and
Michélsen 1994: 151; Wängberg-Eriksson 1994: 58;
Stritzler-Levine 1996: 206; Welzig 1998: 100, 248.

1927–28
**Additions and alterations for the house of
Robert and Anna Lang**
VIENNA XIX, COBENZLGASSE 54
(Haus & Garten; with Oskar Wlach and Ernst A.
Plischke)
Drawings: Albertina, Frank-Archiv 21; Planarchiv
der Stadt Wien (MA 37)
———

Ernst A. Plischke, *Ein Leben mit Architektur* (Vienna, 1989), 89; Welzig 1998: 148–49, 248.

1928
Apartment house for the City of Vienna
VIENNA XIV, SEBASTIAN-KELCH-GASSE 1–3, CER-
VANTESGASSE, DRECHSLERGASSE
53 units
(with Oskar Wlach and Ernst A. Plischke)
Drawings: Planarchiv der Stadt Wien (MA 37)
Photographs: Arkitekturmuseet; Wiener Stadt- und
Landesarchiv
———

Form 5 (1 March 1932): 129–30; Charles O. Hardy, *The Housing Program of the City of Vienna* (Washington, D.C., 1934), facing 63; *Frank 1968*: 17; *Frank 1981*: 140; *Bauwelt* 76 (12 July 1985): 1050; Weihsmann 1985: 340–41; Ernst A. Plischke, *Ein Leben mit Architektur* (Vienna, 1989), 90, 99; Bergquist and Michélsen 1994: 26; Welzig 1998: 98–99, 249, plates 10, 11; Blau 1999: 319–20, 379–80, plates 21, 22.

Stage sets for the play Captain Brassbound's Conversion by George Bernard Shaw performed at the Burgtheater in Vienna
(Director: Hans Brahm; première, 3 November 1928)
Photographs: ÖNB-BA; Österreichisches Theatermuseum, Vienna

———

Frank 1981: 249; Welzig 1998: 248.

Four-room apartment for a four- to five-member family at the exhibition Heim und Technik, Munich

———

Baumeister 26 (July 1928): 202, 212–13; *Heim und Technik* (exhib. cat.; Munich, 1928), 39; *Frank 1981*: 32; Welzig 1998: 249.

Living room and bedroom at the exhibition Österreichische Kunstgewerbe, Cologne
(Haus & Garten; with Oskar Wlach)

———

MBF 38 (Feb. 1929): 79; *Möbel-Geräte-Theoretisches*: 92; Welzig 1998: 249.

Furnishings for the villa of H. and M. Blitz
VIENNA (ADDRESS UNKNOWN)
(Haus & Garten; with Oskar Wlach and Ernst Epstein)
Photographs: UfaK

———

ID 39 (Dec. 1928): 451–88; *Frank 1981*: 8, 86, 89; *Möbel-Geräte-Theoretisches*: 109; Stritzler-Levine 1996: 111; Welzig 1998: 248.

Project: Competition design for the Reichsforschungssiedlung
BERLIN-HASELHORST GARTENFELDERSTRASSE 104–140, BURSCHEIDER WEG 1–61, DAUMSTRASSE 2–10, HASELHORSTER DAMM 1–25, 2–48, RIENSBERGSTRASSE 61–77
(with Hans Blumenfeld)

———

Bauwelt 76 (12 July 1985): 1057; Welzig 1998: 249.

1928–29
Competition project for an apartment house on the site of the old Bürgerversorgungshaus
VIENNA IX, CORNER OF WÄHRINGERSTRASSE AND SPITALGASSE

———

BuWK 5 (1928–29): 187; *WM* 13 (1929): 495–97; *Frank 1981*: 144–45.

1929
Model row house at the exhibition Wohnung und Siedlung in Linz
(with Alfred Schmid)

———

Wohnung und Siedlung in Stadt und Land (exhib. cat.; Linz, 1929); *Wiener Allgemeine Zeitung*, 12 April 1929, 4; *Baumeister* 27 (Dec. 1929): 410–11; *Frank 1981*: 152; Kurt Junghanns, *Das Haus für Alle: Zur Geschichte der Vorfertigung in Deutschland* (Berlin, 1994), 223, 225–26; Annette Becker, Dietmar Steiner, and Wilfried Wang, eds., *Architektur im 20. Jahrhundert: Österreich* (Munich and New York, 1995), 80; Welzig 1998: 100–1, 250.

Living room at the exhibition Wiener Raumkünstler
KÜNSTLERHAUS, VIENNA
(Haus & Garten; with Oskar Wlach)

———

Österreichisches Museum für Kunst und Industrie, *Wiener Raumkünstler* (exhib. cat.; Vienna, 1929);

Neue Freie Presse, 5 Dec. 1929; *DKuD* 65 (March 1930): 417, 422–23; *ID* 44 (June 1933): 190, 208; Welzig 1998: 249.

Living room at the exhibition Das neue Wien
BERLIN-KREUZBERG, MOUNTED BY THE
ÖSTERREICHISCHES GESELLSCHAFTS- UND
WIRTSCHAFTSMUSEUM

————

Österreichischer Werkbund, Vienna, 1929), 14; Astrid Gmeiner and Gottfried Pirhofer, *Der Österreichische Werkbund* (Salzburg and Vienna, 1985), 125; Welzig 1998: 249.

Project: Courtyard house
Drawing: Collection Prof. Johannes Spalt, Vienna
Welzig 1998: 196–97; 250.

1929–30
Villa for Julius and Margarete Beer
VIENNA XIII, WENZGASSE 12
(Haus & Garten; with Oskar Wlach)
Drawings: Planarchiv der Stadt Wien (MA 37); Collection Prof. Johannes Spalt, Vienna
Photographs: MAK-Österreichisches Museum für angewandte Kunst, Vienna; Collection Prof. Johannes Spalt, Vienna

————

Baumeister 29 (Aug. 1931): 316–23; *MBF* 31 (1932): 88–95; *Form* 7 (15 March 1932): 76; Gustav A. Platz, *Wohnräume der Gegenwart* (Berlin, 1933), 415; Roberto Aloi, *L'arredamento moderno* (Milan, 1934), plates 386, 555; *Viviendas* 4 (June 1935): 6–15; *Architectural Review* 83 (April 1938): 170; Gerd H. Sonnek, "Wien: Haus Wenzgasse," in Christine Wessely, *Paläste und Bürgerhäuser in Österreich* (Vienna, 1970), 225–28; *Casabella* 345 (Feb. 1970): 45; Christian Witt-Dörring, *Wiener Innenraumgestaltung* (Vienna, 1981), 33–35; *Frank 1981*: 37–43, 88–91; *Lotus International* 29 (1981): 108–13; *Möbel-Geräte-Theoretisches*: 57, 95, 118; Johann Kräftner, *Bauen in*

Österreich (Vienna, 1983), 30ff.; *Bauwelt* 76 (12 July 1985): 1042, 1044–47; *Frank 1985*: 22–31; Astrid Gmeiner and Gottfried Pirhofer, *Der Österreichische Werkbund* (Salzburg and Vienna, 1985), 118–22; *Arkitektur* 86 (April 1986): 29; *Um Bau* 10 (Aug. 1986): 70–71; Arthur Rüegg and Adolph Stiller, eds., *Sechs Häuser* (Zurich, 1992); Roberto Schezen and Peter Haiko, *Vienna, 1850–1930: Architecture* (New York, 1992), 24, 248–51; Bergquist and Michélsen 1994, 38, 120–31; Wängberg-Eriksson 1994: 97, 114–15, 118–21; Annette Becker, Dietmar Steiner, and Wilfried Wang, eds., *Architektur im 20. Jahrhundert*: Österreich(Munich, 1995), 152–53; Stritzler-Levine 1996: 87–89, 112, 134–35, 208–9; Welzig 1998: 129–35, 250, plates XIV–XVI.

Project: Housing settlement for the City of Vienna near the Spinnerin am Kreuz Monument
VIENNA X, TRIESTER STRASSE

————

Form 5 (15 April 1930): 224; Josef Frank, *Die internationale Werkbundsiedlung Wien 1932* (exhib. cat.; Vienna, 1932), 7–8; Welzig 1998: 104–6; 250–51.

1930

Façade renovation of an existing building
(for Firma Gustav Carl Lehmann)
HOHENZOLLERN RING 48, COLOGNE I
Photographs: Rheinisches Bildarchiv, Cologne; Collection Prof. Johannes Spalt, Vienna

————

Frank 1981: 251; Welzig 1998: 144–45, 252.

Tea salon, furnishings at the 1930 Austrian Werkbund exhibition
(Opening: 30 June 1930)
ÖSTERREICHISCHES MUSEUM FÜR KUNST UND
INDUSTRIE, VIENNA
Photographs: Arkitekturmuseet; ÖNB-BA

————

Österreichischer Werkbund, *Werkbundausstellung 1930* (exhib. cat.; Vienna 1930), 40–41; *Form* 5 (1

July 1930): 329–30; *MBF* 29 (August 1930): 334–35; *BuWK* 6 (1929–30): 225ff.; *ID* 41 (Nov. 1930): 432; Klaus-Jürgen Sembach, *Stil 1930* (Tübingen, 1971), plate 54; *Frank 1981*: 211; *Möbel-Geräte-Theoretisches*: 52; Astrid Gmeiner and Gottfried Pirhofer, *Der Österreichische Werkbund* (Salzburg and Vienna, 1985), 132, 136; Bergquist and Michélsen 1994: 15, 114; Wängberg-Eriksson 1994: 99, 102–3, 106; Welzig 1998: 155, 250.

Furnishings, garden, and tea pavilion for the Kahane House

VIENNA XIX, FÜRFANGGASSE 2
(Architect: Arnold Karplus; Haus & Garten; with Oskar Wlach)
Photographs: UfaK

————

MBF 39 (Oct. 1930): 429–48, Mitteilungen: 212; *ID* 41 (Nov. 1930): 402–9, 411, 424–26, 427; House & Garden 60 (Sept. 1931): 56; *Menorah* 9 (Jan.–Feb. 1931): 38–39, 41–42; *Arnold Karplus-Gerhard Karplus* (Vienna and Leipzig, 1935), 21ff.; *Frank 1981*: 173; Astrid Gmeiner and Gottfried Pirhofer, *Der Österreichische Werkbund* (Salzburg and Vienna, 1985), 118; Welzig 1998: 250.

Project: House for M. S. in Los Angeles, California

Drawings: Albertina, Frank-Archiv 29, 30

————

Baumeister 29 (Aug. 1931): Tafel 82–83; *Frank 1981*: 199; *Lotus International* 29 (1981): 113; *Um Bau* 10 (Aug. 1986): 72; Bergquist and Michélsen 1994: 39–40; Stritzler-Levine 1996: 89–90, 210–11; Welzig 1998: 127, 174–77, 185–86, 191, 194–95, 197, 201, 232, 250.

Project: House for California

Drawings: Collection Prof. Johannes Spalt, Vienna
Welzig 1998: 250.

Project: Apartment complex on the Bahnhofsvorplatz, Linz

Photographs: Arkitekturmuseet; Collection Prof. Johannes Spalt, Vienna

————

Alberto Sartoris, *Gli elementi dell' architettura funzionale* (Milan, 1932), 66; *Frank 1981*: 151; Welzig 1998: 251.

c. 1930
Furnishings for the Epstein House

VIENNA XIII, GLORIETTEGASSE
(Haus & Garten; with Oskar Wlach)

————

ID 41 (Nov. 1930): 410, 417; Welzig 1998: 250.

Dining room for Emil Bunzl

VIENNA III, AM HEUMARKT 27
Drawing: Collection Prof. Johannes Spalt, Vienna

Furnishings for the house of Dr. W. B.

VIENNA (ADDRESS UNKNOWN)
(Haus & Garten; with Oskar Wlach)

————

MBF 29 (Oct. 1930): 445; *ID* 41 (Nov. 1930): 413–16, 418–19, Welzig 1998: 250.

Furnishings for the house of L. E. R.

VIENNA (ADDRESS UNKNOWN)
(Haus & Garten; with Oskar Wlach)

————

MBF 29 (Oct. 1930): 446; *ID* 41 (Nov. 1930): 420–21, 423; Welzig 1998: 250.

Furnishings for the house of A. T.

COLOGNE (ADDRESS UNKNOWN)
(Haus & Garten; with Oskar Wlach)

————

ID 41 (Nov. 1930): 433.

Project: House in Vienna XVIII

Drawing: Albertina, Frank-Archiv 34

———

Frank 1981: 194; Welzig 1998: 257.

Project: House in Vienna XIX

Drawing: Albertina, Frank-Archiv 35

———

Frank 1981: 192; Bergquist and Michélsen 1994:
155; Stritzler-Levine 1996: 203; Welzig 1998: 127,
257.

Project: House with two doors in Vienna XIX

Drawing: Albertina, Frank-Archiv 36

———

Frank 1981: 193; Bergquist and Michélsen 1994:
154; Welzig 1998: 257.

Project: Courtyard house for Sweden

Drawing: UfaK 1241

———

Welzig 1998: 197, 250.

1931–32

**Apartment building for the City of Vienna
(now Leopoldine-Glöckel-Hof)**

VIENNA XII, STEINBAUERGASSE I–7,
GAUDENZDORFER GÜRTEL

318 units

(with Oskar Wlach)

Drawing: Planarchiv der Stadt Wien (MA 37)

Photographs: Collection Prof. Johannes Spalt, Vienna; HMSW; Wiener Stadt- und Landesarchiv

Frank 1981: 148–49; *Lotus International* 29 (1981):
108–9; *Bauwelt* 76 (12 July 1985): 1050–51; Weihsmann 1985: 201; Friedrich Achleitner, *Österreichische Architektur im 20. Jahrhundert*, vol. 3, no. 1 (Vienna 1990), 322; Bergquist and Michélsen 1994:
152; Welzig 1998: 251; Blau 1999: 320, 379, 467.

Apartment building for the City of Vienna

VIENNA XI, SIMMERINGER HAUPTSTRASSE I42–50,
FICKEYSTRASSE 8, PLEISCHLGASSE, STRACHEGASSE

254 units

(with Oskar Wlach)

Drawing: Planarchiv der Stadt Wien (MA 37)

Photographs: Wiener Stadt- und Landesarchiv

Manfredo Tafuri, *Vienna Rossa. La politica residenziale nella Vienna socialista, 1919–1933* (Milan,
1980), 138; *Frank 1981*: 150; Johann Kräftner, *Bauen
in Österreich* (Vienna, 1983), 31; *Bauwelt* 76 (12 July
1985): 1051; Weihsmann 1985: 242; Friedrich
Achleitner, *Österreichische Architektur im 20.
Jahrhundert*, vol. 3, no. 1 (Vienna 1990), 300;
Welzig 1998: 251; Blau 1999: 320.

Project: Kindergarten in Vienna XII

VIENNA XII, HASENLEITENSTRASSE 9

(with Oskar Wlach)

Drawing: Planarchiv der Stadt Wien (MA 37)

———

Friedrich Achleitner, *Österreichische Architektur im
20. Jahrhundert*, vol. 3, no. 1 (Vienna 1990), 296;
Welzig 1998: 251.

**Plan for the Vienna International Werkbund
Exhibition *(final version)***

VIENNA XIII, JAGDSCHLOSSGASSE, VEITINGER-
GASSE, WOINOVICHGASSE, JAGICGASSE, ENGEL-
BRECHTWEG

Drawings: Planarchiv der Stadt Wien (MA 37)

Photographs: Arkitekturmuseet, Albertina, UfaK,
ÖNB-BA; Wiener Stadt- und Landesarchiv

———

Josef Frank, *Die internationale Werkbundsiedlung:
Wien 1932* (exhib. cat.; Vienna), 1932; *Architectural
Forum* 58 (Oct. 1932): 325–38; *Baumeister* 30 (Oct.
1932): 367–73; *Bauwelt* 23 (16 June 1932): 1–8;
BuWK 8 (1932): 169–79; *DKuD* 70 (1932): 227–28;
Form 7 (15 March 1932): 84–85; *Form* 7 (15 July
1932): 201–23; *ID* 43 (Aug. 1932): 273–75; *DK* 66
(Sept. 1932): 269–75; *MBF* 31 (1932): 39; *Zentral-*

blatt der Bauverwaltung [Berlin] 52 (1932): 365–70; *Bauforum* 61 (1977): 19–28; *Frank 1981*: 153–55; *Bauwelt* 76 (12 July 1985): 1052; Adolf Krischanitz and Otto Kapfinger, *Die Wiener Werkbundsiedlung* (Vienna, 1985); Astrid Gmeiner and Gottfried Pirhofer, *Der Österreichische Werkbund* (Salzburg and Vienna, 1985), 155–78; *Weihsmann 1985*: 347ff.; *Um Bau* 10 (Aug. 1986): 51–53; Bergquist and Michélsen 1994: 70–71; Wängberg-Eriksson 1994: 121–22, 124–25; Annette Becker, Dietmar Steiner, and Wilfried Wang, eds., *Architektur im 20. Jahrhundert: Österreich* (Munich and New York, 1995), 158–59; *Stritzler-Levine 1996*, 56–58; *Welzig 1998*: 104–7, 250–51; *Blau 1999*: 132–33.

House in the Vienna International Werkbund Exhibition

VIENNA XIII, WOINOVICHGASSE 32
Drawings: Planarchiv der Stadt Wien (MA 37)
Photographs: Arkitekturmuseet; UfaK; ÖNB-BA; Collection Prof. Johannes Spalt, Vienna

———

Josef Frank, *Die internationale Werkbundsiedlung Wien 1932* (exhib. cat.; Vienna, 1932), figs. 39–47; *BuWK* 8 (1932): 189; *Baumeister* 30 (1932): 371; *Bauwelt* 23 (16 June 1932): 4; *Form* 7 (15 July 1932): 210ff.; *DK* 33 (Sept. 1932): 273, 275; *MBF* 31 (1932): 437, 453; *Zentralblatt der Bauverwaltung* [Berlin]: 365ff.; *Das Wohnungswesen der Stadt Wien* (Stuttgart, 1933), 47; *ID* 44 (June 1933): 204, 210; Alberto Sartoris, *Gli elementi dell'architettura funzionale* (Milan, 1935), 71; F. R. S. Yorke, *The Modern House* (Surrey, 1944), 26; *Bauforum* 61 (1977): 23ff.; Christian Witt-Dörring, *Wiener Innenraumgestaltung* (Vienna, 1981), 52–53; *Frank 1981*: 157; *Möbel-Geräte-Theoretisches* 91, 129; *Bauwelt* 76 (12 July 1985): 1047, 1053; Astrid Gmeiner and Gottfried Pirhofer, *Der Österreichische Werkbund* (Salzburg and Vienna, 1985), 148, 170–72; *Weihsmann 1985*: 350–51; Johannes Spalt, ed., *Josef Frank: Stoffe-Tapeten-Teppiche* (Vienna, 1986), 6; Bergquist and Michélsen 1994: 72–73; Wängberg-Eriksson 1994:

121–25; *Stritzler-Levine 1996*: 57, 144; *Welzig 1998*: 107–9, 251, plates 12, 13.

1932
Project: Single-family house for five persons

———

Hans A. Vetter, *Kleine Familienhäuser* (Vienna, 1932), 6–7; *Frank 1981*: 152; *Welzig 1998*: 252.

Project: Single-family house for six persons

———

Hans A. Vetter, *Kleine Familienhäuser* (Vienna, 1932), 10; *Frank 1981*: 152; *Welzig 1998*: 252.

Project: Two-story house for four persons

———

Hans A. Vetter, *Kleine Familienhäuser* (Vienna, 1932), 76–77; *Frank 1981*: 152; *Welzig 1998*: 252.

c. 1933
Furnishings for a villa for A. F. Steiner

VIENNA XIII (ADDRESS UNKNOWN)
(Haus & Garten; with Oskar Wlach)

———

ID 44 (June 1933): 184, 186–87, 189, 197, 200, 202–3, 208, 210; *MBF* 32 (1933): 356–57, 364; *Frank 1981*: 85, 89; *Möbel-Geräte-Theoretisches*: 109; Johannes Spalt, ed., *Josef Frank: Stoffe-Tapeten-Teppiche* (Vienna, 1986), 73–75; Bergquist and Michélsen 1994: 29; Wängberg-Eriksson 1994: 81; *Stritzler-Levine 1996*: 39, 51, 179; *Welzig 1998*: 252.

Furnishings for a house for L. R. S.

VIENNA XIII (ADDRESS UNKNOWN)
(Haus & Garten; with Oskar Wlach)

———

ID 44 (June 1933): 186–87, 189, 206–7; *MBF* 32 (1933): 357, 362–63; *Welzig 1998*: 252.

Furnishings for a house for R. B.
ADDRESS UNKNOWN
(Haus & Garten; with Oskar Wlach)

———

ID 44 (June 1933): 188–89, 192–93; Johannes Spalt,
ed., *Josef Frank: Stoffe-Tapeten-Teppiche* (Vienna,
1986), 10; Welzig 1998: 252.

Furnishings for the house of Dr. D.
VIENNA (ADDRESS UNKNOWN)
(Haus & Garten; with Oskar Wlach)

———

ID 44 (June 1933): 189–91, 198–99; *MBF* 32 (1933):
361; *Frank 1981*: 85; 87; Johannes Spalt, ed., *Josef
Frank: Stoffe-Tapeten-Teppiche* (Vienna, 1986), 10,
73; Welzig 1998: 252.

Furnishings for the house of A. L. H.
VIENNA XIX (ADDRESS UNKNOWN)
(Haus & Garten; with Oskar Wlach)

———

ID 44 (June 1933): 190, 205, 207; *MBF* 32 (1933):
360; Welzig 1998: 252.

Furnishings for the house of W.
ADDRESS UNKNOWN
(Haus & Garten; with Oskar Wlach)

———

ID 44 (June 1933): 189–90, 194–96, 209; *MBF* 32
(1933): 364; Christian Witt-Dörring, *Wiener Innenraumgestaltung* (Vienna, 1981), 30; *Frank 1981*: 85,
87; *Möbel-Geräte-Theoretisches*: 91, 112; Welzig 1998:
252.

Furnishings for the house of Dr. H. F.
VIENNA (ADDRESS UNKNOWN)
(Haus & Garten; with Oskar Wlach)

———

MBF 32 (1933): 358–59; Welzig 1998: 252.

Furnishings for the house of W. W.
VIENNA XIII (ADDRESS UNKNOWN)
(Haus & Garten; with Oskar Wlach)

———

MBF 32 (1933): 365; Welzig 1998: 252.

Exhibition at Gustav Carl Lehmann
COLOGNE I, HOHENZOLLERN RING 48
(Haus & Garten; with Oskar Wlach)

———

ID 44 (June 1933): 185, 190; Welzig 1998: 252.

1933–34
Showrooms for Svenskt Tenn
STRANDVÄGEN 5A, STOCKHOLM
(with Estrid Ericson)
Photographs: UfaK; Svenskt Tenn

———

Heinrich Ritter, "Wohnräume aus Schweden,"
Innen-Dekoration 46 (March 1935): 92–98; Kristina
Wängberg-Eriksson, *Svenskt Tenn. Josef Frank och
Estrid Ericson* (Stockholm, 1985), 94–98; Monica
Boman, ed., *Estrid Ericson* (Stockholm, 1989),
14–15, 106–7; Wängberg-Eriksson 1994: 87, 154;
Welzig 1998: 252.

1934
Studio addition to the house of Anders Österling
FIDDELEDET 7, FALSTERBO, SWEDEN

———

Bergquist and Michélsen 1998: 38, 56; Welzig
1998: 165, 179, 182, 184–85, 253.

Exhibition at Liljevalchs konsthall
DJURGÅRDSVÄGEN 60, STOCKHOLM
(Svenskt Tenn; with Estrid Ericson)

———

Josef Frank 100 år, 18; *Um Bau* 10 (Aug. 1986):
77–78; Kristina Wängberg-Eriksson, *Svenskt Tenn.
Josef Frank och Estrid Ericson* (Stockholm, 1985),

89–93; Monica Boman, ed., *Estrid Ericson* (Stockholm, 1989), 104–5, 107; Wängberg-Eriksson 1994: 150–51; Stritzler-Levine 1996: 64–65, 217; Welzig 1998: 253.

c. 1934

Furnishings of a house for J. B. (Julius Bunzl?)
VIENNA (ADDRESS UNKNOWN)
(Haus & Garten; with Oskar Wlach)

————

ID 45 (Oct. 1934): 314–19; *Frank 1981*: 85; *Möbel-Geräte-Theoretisches*: 117; Welzig 1998: 252.

Furnishings of a house for Ernst Krenek
VIENNA (ADDRESS UNKNOWN)
(Haus & Garten; with Oskar Wlach)

————

ID 45 (Oct. 1934): 316, 320–23; *Frank 1981*: 87; Johannes Spalt, ed., *Josef Frank: Stoffe-Tapeten-Teppiche* (Vienna, 1986), 12; Welzig 1998: 252.

Furnishings of a house for A. W.
VIENNA (ADDRESS UNKNOWN)
(Haus & Garten; with Oskar Wlach)

————

ID 45 (Oct. 1934): 317, 324–34; *Frank 1981*: 85, 88–89; *Möbel-Geräte-Theoretisches*: 108, 119; Stritzler-Levine 1996: 112; Welzig 1998: 252.

Furnishings for the apartment of Max Eisler
VIENNA III, UNTERE WEISSGERBERSTRASSE 37
(Haus & Garten; with Oskar Wlach)

————

Roberto Aloi, *L'arredamento moderno* (Milan, 1934).

1934–35

Låftman House
FYRVÄGEN 15, FALSTERBO, SWEDEN
Drawings: Vellinge Municipal Archive
Photographs: Arkitekturmuseet; Collection
Prof. Johannes Spalt, Vienna

————

Frank 1981: 44–45; Bergquist and Michélsen 1994: 74–75; Bergquist and Michélsen 1998: 39, 41–43; Welzig 1998: 117, 132, 165, 178, 182, 184, 253.

Seth House
FYRVÄGEN 13, FALSTERBO, SWEDEN
Drawings: Vellinge Municipal Archive
Photographs: Arkitekturmuseet; Collection
Prof. Johannes Spalt, Vienna

————

Frank 1981: 44–45; Bergquist and Michélsen 1994: 74–75; Bergquist and Michélsen 1998: 40–42, 57; Welzig 1998: 117–18, 132, 165, 178, 182–84, 253.

1935

Bedroom for the guest cottage of Hjalmar Olson
SWEDEN (ADDRESS UNKNOWN)
(Svenskt Tenn, with Estrid Ericson)
Photographs: UfaK; Svenskt Tenn

————

Kristina Wängberg-Eriksson, *Svenskt Tenn. Josef Frank och Estrid Ericson* (Stockholm, 1985), 109, 111; Wängberg-Eriksson 1994: 185; Stritzler-Levine 1996: 121.

1935–36

House for Hugo and Olga Bunzl
VIENNA XVIII, CHIMANISTRASSE 18
(Haus & Garten; with Oskar Wlach)
Drawings: UfaK 1220; Planarchiv der Stadt Wien (MA 37)
Photographs: Albertina; UfaK; HMSW; Collection
Prof. Johannes Spalt, Vienna

Architectural Review 83 (April 1938): 169; *Svenska hem i ord och bilder* 36 (1948): 97; *Form* 63 (1967): 176; *Frank* 1968: 20; *Frank* 1981: 46–48; Johann Kräftner, *Bauen in Österreich* (Vienna, 1983), 31ff.; *Bauwelt* 76 (12 July 1985): 1047; Astrid Gmeiner and Gottfried Pirhofer, *Der Österreichische Werkbund* (Salzburg and Vienna, 1985), 121; Bergquist and Michélsen 1994: 76–79; Stritzler-Levine 1996: 219; Welzig 1998: 118, 165, 176–79, 253, plate 17.

House for Walther and Gundlar Wehtje (Solesand)

ROSTOCKERVÄGEN 4, FALSTERBO, SWEDEN
Drawings: Arkitekturmuseet 1968–12–17; UfaK 1225, 1226, 1227, 1230; Collection Prof. Johannes Spalt, Vienna; Vellinge Municipal Archive
Photographs: Arkitekturmuseet; Collection Prof. Johannes Spalt, Vienna

Studio Yearbook (1938): 20; *Frank* 1981: 49–51; Bergquist and Michélsen 1994: 80–83; Wängberg-Eriksson 1994: 136–41; Stritzler-Levine 1996: 220–21; Bergquist and Michélsen 1998: 44–51, 58–60; Welzig 1998: 127, 152–53, 165–74, 176–77, 179, 186, 188–89, 197, 201, 232, 253, plate 17.

1936

Furnishings for the apartment of Emma and Malte Jacobsson

ASCHEBERGSGATAN, GÖTEBORG
Photographs: Svenskt Tenn

Gotthard Johansson, *Josef Frank: Tjugo år i Svenskt Tenn* (exhib. cat.; Stockholm, 1952), n.p.; Wängberg-Eriksson 1994: 219–21.

Project: Austrian Pavilion, 1937 Paris Exposition Internationale

Drawings: Albertina, Frank-Archiv 32; Collection Prof. Johannes Spalt, Vienna

Frank 1981: 210; Bergquist and Michélsen 1994: 153; Stritzler-Levine 1996: 222; Welzig 1998: 253.

Project: The Bahrke House in Falsterbo, Sweden

Drawings: Arkitekturmuseet; UfaK 1232

Frank 1981: 53; Welzig 1998: 179–80, 253.

c. 1936

Project: Small one-story patio house

Drawing: Collection Prof. Johannes Spalt, Vienna

Welzig 1998: 178–79, 257.

1937–1938

Project: House for Walther Wehtje in Djursholm, Sweden

Drawings: UfaK 1233; Collection Prof. Johannes Spalt, Vienna

Frank 1981: 52; Bergquist and Michélsen 1994: 41; Stritzler-Levine 1996: 223; Welzig 1998: 180–81, 189–90, 214, 222, 232, 254.

Garden terrace for the Swedish Pavilion at the 1937 Paris Exposition Internationale

(Svenskt Tenn; with Estrid Ericson)
Photographs: Svenskt Tenn

Byggmästaren 32 (1937): 364; *Styl* 21, no. 1 (1938): 3–6; *Möbel-Geräte-Theoretisches*: 92; *Josef Frank 100 år*: 22; Kristina Wängberg-Eriksson, *Svenskt Tenn. Josef Frank och Estrid Ericson* (Stockholm, 1985), 137–42; Monica Boman, ed., *Estrid Ericson* (Stockholm, 1989), 112, 115; Wängberg-Eriksson 1994: 181, 184, 236; Stritzler-Levine 1996: 125; Welzig 1998: 254.

Living room for Haus & Garten in the Austrian
Pavilion at the 1937 Paris Exposition Internationale
(Haus & Garten; with Oskar Wlach)
Photographs: UfaK; Svenskt Tenn

———

Frank 1981: 92; *Um Bau 10* (Aug. 1986): 79; Welzig
1998: 254.

1938

Furnishings for exhibitions of Swedish design in
Warsaw and Prague
(Svenskt Tenn; with Estrid Ericson)
Photographs: Svenskt Tenn

———

Instytut Propagandy Sztuki, *Wystawa Szwedzkiego*
Przemystu Artystyczneco (exhib. cat.; Warsaw, 1938);
Svenska hem 26 (1938): vi–vii; *Josef Frank 100 år*: 23;
Kristina Wängberg-Eriksson, *Svenskt Tenn. Josef*
Frank och Estrid Ericson (Stockholm, 1985), 149–50;
Wängberg-Eriksson 1994: 223; Welzig 1998: 254.

Furnishing for the Swedish Ambassador's House in
Tokyo, Japan
(Svenskt Tenn; with Estrid Ericson)

Design for an exhibition of the work of
William Morris at Svenskt Tenn
(Svenskt Tenn; with Estrid Ericson)

———

Wängberg-Eriksson 1994: 205; Stritzler-Levine
1996: 145; Welzig 1998: 254.

1938–39

Furnishings for the Swedish Pavilion at the Golden
Gate Exposition, San Francisco
(Svenskt Tenn; with Estrid Ericson)
Drawings: Svenskt Tenn
Photographs: Svenskt Tenn

———

Svenska hem 27 (1939): 34–40; *Architectural Forum*

70 (June 1939); *Form 63* (1967): 178; *Josef Frank 100*
år: 26–27; Kristina Wängberg-Eriksson, *Svenskt*
Tenn. Josef Frank och Estrid Ericson (Stockholm,
1985), 147–48; *Möbel-Geräte-Theoretisches*: 115; *Frank*
1981: 87; Johannes Spalt, ed., *Josef Frank: Stoffe-*
Tapeten-Teppiche (Vienna, 1986), 35; Monica
Boman, ed., *Estrid Ericson* (Stockholm, 1989),
114–15; Wängberg-Eriksson 1994: 186–87, 188–89;
Stritzler-Levine 1996: 236; Welzig 1998: 254.

Interiors for the Swedish Pavilion at the
New York World's Fair
(Svenskt Tenn; with Estrid Ericson)
Drawing: Svenskt Tenn
Photographs: UfaK; Svenskt Tenn

———

Åke Stavenow et al., eds., *Swedish Arts and*
Crafts/Swedish Modern—A Movement toward Sanity
in Design (exhib. cat.; New York, 1939); *American*
Swedish Monthly 33 (May 1939): 11–15, 96–97; *Ar-*
chitectural Forum 70 (June 1939); *New York Times*, 4
June 1939, B8; *House and Garden 76* (July 1939):
16; *Bauwelt 76* (12 July 1985): 1061; *Josef Frank 100*
år: 24; Kristina Wängberg-Eriksson, *Svenskt Tenn.*
Josef Frank och Estrid Ericson (Stockholm, 1985),
142–44, 148; *Um Bau 10* (Aug. 1986): 78–79; Monica Boman, ed., *Estrid Ericson* (Stockholm, 1989),
114–15; Wängberg-Eriksson 1994: 184–85; Stritzler-
Levine 1996: 68–69, 234–35; Welzig 1998: 254.

1940

Project: Garden pavilion
Drawing: Collection Prof. Johannes Spalt, Vienna

———

Frank 1981: 214; Bergquist and Michélsen 1994:
154; Welzig 1998: 254.

1941–42

Additions and furnishings for Estrid Ericson´s summer house "Tolvekarna"

TYRESÖ, SWEDEN

(Svenskt Tenn; with Estrid Ericson)

Drawings: Collection Gun Jacobson, Tyresö, Sweden

Photographs: Svenskt Tenn

———

Form 80, no. 627 (1984): 49–53; *Josef Frank 100 år*: 36; Kristina Wängberg-Eriksson, *Svenskt Tenn. Josef Frank och Estrid Ericson* (Stockholm, 1985), 103–7, 167; *Um Bau* 10 (Aug. 1986): 77–78; Monica Boman, ed., *Estrid Ericson* (Stockholm, 1989), 36–40, 110–12; Wängberg-Eriksson 1994: 172–73, 176; Stritzler-Levine 1996: 121–22.

1942

Project: "City of New York Slum Clearance"

FIRST AVENUE, TWELFTH STREET, THIRD AVENUE, SIXTEENTH STREET, NEW YORK CITY

Drawing: Albertina, Frank-Archiv 41

———

Frank 1981: 160; Wängberg-Eriksson 1994: 203; Maria Welzig, "Entwurzelt," in Matthias Boeckl, ed., *Visionäre und Vertriebene* (Berlin, 1995), 216–18; Welzig 1998: 208, 232, 254, plate 20.

1943

Project: Alternative site plan for the low-cost housing project of the Metropolitan Life Insurance Company ("Stuyvesant Town")

FIRST AVENUE, TWENTIETH STREET, EAST RIVER DRIVE, AVENUE C, FOURTEENTH STREET, NEW YORK CITY

Drawing: Albertina, Frank-Archiv 19

———

Frank 1981: 160; Maria Welzig, "Entwurzelt," in Matthias Boeckl, ed., *Visionäre und Vertriebene* (Berlin, 1995), 218; Welzig 1998: 208, 254.

1945–55

Furnishing for Swedish Consulates and Embassies

(In Addis Ababa, Algiers, Ankara, Antwerp, Bagdad, Beijing, Beirut, Berlin, Belgrade, Bonn, Budapest, Buenos Aires, Canberra, Caracas, Dar es Salaam, Djakarta, Geneva, Guatemala City, Den Haag, Hamburg, Hong Kong, Istanbul, Jiddah, Cairo, Karachi, Khartoum, Lagos, Madrid, Monrovia, Montreal, Moscow, Nairobi, New Delhi, New York, Oslo, Ottawa, Paris, Pretoria, Prague, Quito, Reykjavik, Rio de Janeiro, Rome, San Francisco, Santiago, Sofia, Teheran, Tel Aviv, Tunis, Vienna, Warsaw, Washington, and Wellington)

(Svenskt Tenn; with Estrid Ericson)

Drawings: Svenskt Tenn

Photographs: Svenskt Tenn

———

Gotthard Johannson, *Josef Frank: Tjugo år i Svenskt Tenn* (exhib. cat.; Stockholm, 1952); *Möbel-Geräte-Theoretisches*: 141; *Frank 1981*: 91; Stritzler-Levine 1996: 277–78.

1947

Project: United Nations Headquarters, New York

Drawing: Albertina, Frank-Archiv 18

———

Frank 1981: 240; Bergquist and Michélsen 1994: 48; Wängberg-Eriksson 1994: 203, 232; Maria Welzig, "Entwurzelt," in Matthias Boeckl, ed., *Visionäre und Vertriebene* (Berlin, 1995), 219; Stritzler-Levine 1996: 264; Welzig 1998: 231–32, 254, plate 29.

1947–early 1950s

Thirteen house designs for Dagmar Grill

Drawings: Albertina, Frank-Archiv 72–74

———

Frank 1981: 218–19; *Lotus International* 29 (1981): 109–16; Bergquist and Michélsen 1994: 84–87; Wängberg-Eriksson 1994: 228–31; Stritzler-Levine 1996: 91–92; Welzig 1998: 213–19.

House 1 (22 July 1947)
Drawings: Albertina, Frank-Archiv 81
Welzig 1998: 255.

House 2 (23 July 1947)
Drawings: Albertina, Frank-Archiv 80
Welzig 1998: 214, 255.

House 3 (1 August 1947)
Drawings: Albertina, Frank-Archiv 79
Frank 1981: 222; *Bauwelt* 76 (12 July 1985): 1066;
Bergquist and Michélsen 1994: 47, 89; Welzig
1998: 216, 255.

House 4 (31 July 1947)
Drawings: Albertina, Frank-Archiv 78
Frank 1981: 221; Bergquist and Michélsen 1994: 88;
Welzig 1998: 255.

House 5 (25 July 1947)
Drawings: Albertina, Frank-Archiv 77
Welzig 1998: 255.

House 6 (29 July 1947)
Drawings: Albertina, Frank-Archiv 76
Welzig 1998: 215, 255.

House 7 (30 July 1947)
Drawings: Albertina, Frank-Archiv 75
Frank 1981: 220; Bergquist and Michélsen 1994:
88; Welzig 1998: 215, 255.

House 8 (5 August 1947)
Drawings: Albertina, Frank-Archiv 82, 104
Form 54 (1958): 162; *Frank 1981*: 226–27; Stritzler-
Levine 1996: 267–68; Welzig 1998: 217, 255.

House 9 (4 August 1947)
Drawings: Albertina, Frank-Archiv 83, 88
Frank 1981: 223–25; *Bauwelt* 76 (12 July 1985): 1067;
Bergquist and Michélsen 1994: 47, 89; Wängberg-
Eriksson 1994: 199; Stritzler-Levine 1996: 268–69;
Welzig 1998: 216, 255.

House 10 (6 August 1947)
Drawings: Albertina, Frank-Archiv 84
Welzig 1998: 217, 255.

House 11 (12 August 1947)
Drawings: Albertina, Frank-Archiv 5
Welzig 1998: 255.

House 12 (14 August 1947)
Drawings: Albertina, Frank-Archiv 6
Welzig 1998: 221, 255.

House 13 (15 August 1947)
Drawings: Albertina, Frank-Archiv 6, 87, 89
Welzig 1998: 218, 255, plate 22.

1948–49
Project: Plan for rebuilding St. Stephan's Square, Vienna
————

Josef Frank, "Zur Neugestaltung des Stephan-
platzes," *Wiener Tageszeitung*, 1 May 1949, 3; *Film*
36 (March 1949): 11ff.; *Frank 1981*: 162–65; *Transparent* 3–5 (1987): 17–21; Welzig 1998: 229, 255.

1949
Furnishings for the Israeli Embassy, Moscow
(Svenskt Tenn; with Estrid Ericson)
Photographs: Svenskt Tenn

————

Gotthard Johansson, *Josef Frank: Tjugo år i Svenskt
Tenn* (exhib. cat.; Stockholm, 1952), n.p.; Welzig
1998: 256.

1949–51

Furnishings for various branches of the Enskilda Bank, Stockholm

(Svenskt Tenn; with Estrid Ericson)

(In 1949, Sturegatan; in 1950, Odengatan; in 1950, Sundbyberg; in 1950, Södertälje; in 1951, Konserthuset; in 1951, Solna)

Photographs: Svenskt Tenn

———

Gotthard Johansson, *Josef Frank*: *Tjugo år i Svenskt Tenn* (exhib. cat.; Stockholm, 1952), n.p.

c. 1950

Furnishings for the house of Anne Hedmark, Millesgården

CARL MILLES VÄG 2, LIDINGÖ, STOCKHOLM

(Svenskt Tenn; with Estrid Ericson)

Photographs: Svenskt Tenn

———

Gotthard Johansson, *Josef Frank*: *Tjugo år i Svenskt Tenn* (exhib. cat.; Stockholm, 1952), n.p.; *Josef Frank 100 år*: 35; *Um Bau* 10 (Aug. 1986): 81; Kristina Wängberg-Eriksson, *Svenskt Tenn. Josef Frank och Estrid Ericson* (Stockholm, 1985), 158; Wängberg-Eriksson 1994: 221–22; Stritzler-Levine 1996: 148–49; Welzig 1998: 255.

Interiors for the Solliden Restaurant

SKANSEN, STOCKHOLM

(Svenskt Tenn; with Estrid Ericson)

Drawing: Svenskt Tenn

———

Welzig 1998: 258.

Prior to 1951

Project: Town for 2,000 families

WISCONSIN

Drawing: Arkitekturmuseet 1968–12–07

———

Frank 1981: 167; Bergquist and Michélsen 1994: 45; Maria Welzig, "Entwurzelt," in Matthias Boeckl, ed., *Visionäre und Vertriebene* (Berlin, 1995), 217, 219; Stritzler-Levine 1996: 266; Welzig 1998: 228, 255.

Project: Residential district for 20,000 residents

Drawing: Albertina, Frank-Archiv 9

———

Frank 1981: 167; Welzig 1998: 228–29, 255–56.

1951

Exhibition of five model rooms at Kaufmann's Department Store

PITTSBURGH

(Svenskt Tenn; with Estrid Ericson)

Photographs: Svenskt Tenn

———

Wängberg-Eriksson 1994: 214–15; Kristina Wängberg-Eriksson, "Josef Frank im Exil auf Manhattan, 1942–46," in Matthias Boeckl, ed., *Visionäre und Vertriebene* (Berlin, 1995), 198–99; Maria Welzig, "Entwurzelt," in Matthias Boeckl, ed., *Visionäre und Vertriebene* (Berlin, 1995), 202–3; Stritzler-Levine 1996: 71; Welzig 1998: 256.

Prior to 1952

Furnishings for a restaurant

(Svenskt Tenn; with Estrid Ericson)

Photographs: Svenskt Tenn

———

Gotthard Johansson, *Josef Frank*: *Tjugo år i Svenskt Tenn* (exhib. cat.; Stockholm, 1952), n.p.; Welzig 1998: 256.

Furnishings for the Allmänna
Pensionsförsäkringsbolaget, Stockholm
(Svenskt Tenn; with Estrid Ericson)
Photographs: Svenskt Tenn

————

Gotthard Johansson, Josef Frank: Tjugo år i Svenskt Tenn (exhib. cat.; Stockholm, 1952), n.p.; Welzig 1998: 256.

1952
Project: Competition design for the reconfiguration of the Kungsträdgården, Stockholm
Drawing: Arkitekturmuseet 1968–12–20

————

Frank 1981: 161; Bergquist and Michélsen 1994: 155; Wängberg-Eriksson 1994: 202, 231–32; Stritzler-Levine 1996: 265; Welzig 1998: 230–32, 256.

1953
Project: Four D-houses for Dagmar Grill

————

Frank 1985: 44–45; Welzig 1998: 219–20.

D-House
Drawings: Albertina, Frank-Archiv 25, 26, 53
Welzig 1998: 219, 256.

D-House with checkerboard parapet
Drawings: Albertina, Frank-Archiv 15, 54
Frank 1981: 236–37; Welzig 1998: 220, 256.

D-House
Drawings: Albertina, Frank-Archiv 53
Welzig 1998: 256.

D-House
Drawings: Albertina, Frank-Archiv 52
Stritzler-Levine 1996: 271; Welzig 1998: 256.

1954
Furnishings for the Israeli Embassy in Ottawa, Canada
(Svenskt Tenn; with Estrid Ericson)
Photographs: Svenskt Tenn

c. 1954
Project: Six Double D-houses for Dagmar Grill

————

A D-House
Drawings: Albertina, Frank-Archiv 69; Arkitekturmuseet
Welzig 1998: 256.

Another D-House
Drawings: Albertina, Frank-Archiv 67
Bergquist and Michélsen 1994: 30; Stritzler-Levine 1996: 92; Welzig 1998: 256.

D-House 3
Drawings: Albertina, Frank-Archiv 64; Arkitekturmuseet 1968–12–04
Stritzler-Levine 1996: 282; Welzig 1998: plate 23, 221, 256.

D-House Four ("Giraffe house")
Drawings: Albertina, Frank-Archiv 14, 63
Frank 1981: 234–35; Bergquist and Michélsen 1994: 132–33; Wängberg-Eriksson 1994: 198; Stritzler-Levine 1996: 270; Welzig 1998: 222, 256.

D- House 5
Drawings: Albertina, Frank-Archiv 60
Welzig 1998: 257.

D-House 6
Drawings: Albertina, Frank-Archiv 56, 57; Arkitekturmuseet
Form 54 (1958): 160–61; *Frank 1981*: 243; Bergquist and Michélsen 1994: 30; Welzig 1998: 257.

1955

Project: House with an atelier

Drawings: Albertina, Frank-Archiv 19, 103

————

Frank 1981: 228–29; Welzig 1998: 221, 224, 256.

Undated works after 1946

Furnishings for the Svenska Handelsbanken in Stockholm

(Svenskt Tenn; with Estrid Ericson)

Drawing: Svenskt Tenn

————

Frank 1981: 101; Welzig 1998: 258.

Project: Community of 1,200 families

Drawings: Albertina, Frank-Archiv 22, 24

————

Frank 1981: 158–59; *Um Bau* 10 (1986): 53; Maria Welzig, "Entwurzelt," in Matthias Boeckl, ed., *Visionäre und Vertriebene* (Berlin, 1995), 217, 219; Welzig 1998: 228–29, 259, plate 20.

Project: Residential district for 15,000 residents

Drawing: Albertina, Frank-Archiv 10

————

Welzig 1998: 259, plate 21.

Project: Horns Department Store

Drawing: Albertina, Frank-Archiv 46

————

Welzig 1998: 231–32, 259, plate 31.

Project: Hotel on a boulevard

Drawing: Albertina, Frank-Archiv 3

————

Form 54 (1958): 163; Welzig 1998: 257, plate 30.

Project: High-rise apartment house

Drawing: Alberina, Frank-Archiv 45

————

Welzig 1998: 232, 259, plate 32.

Project: Theater for 1,200

Drawing: Albertina, Frank-Archiv 4; Arkitektur-museet

————

Frank 1981: 239; Welzig 1998: 17, 19, 259.

Project: Three row house designs ("Motto: DBL")

Drawings: UfaK 1236; Albertina, Frank-Archiv 42, 43, 44; Collection Prof. Johannes Spalt, Vienna

————

Frank 1981: 159; Welzig 1998: 257.

Pergola and other additions to Trude Waehner´s house, Dieulefit, France

Bauwelt 26 (12 July 1985): 1069.

Project: House for Trude Waehner in Dieulefit, France

Drawings: Albertina, Frank-Archiv 101; Arkitektur-museet 1968–12–01, 1968–12–02; UfaK 1242

————

Bauforum 10 (1977): 29; *Frank 1981*: 230–31; *Arkitektur* 86 (April 1986): 29; Bergquist and Michélsen 1994: 140; Wängberg-Eriksson 1994: 199, 233; Stritzler-Levine 1996: 93–94, 285–86; Welzig 1998: 223–24, 256.

Project: House with a large round window and atelier

Drawings: Albertina, Frank-Archiv 16, 97

————

Stritzler-Levine 1996: 279; Welzig 1998: 258.

Project: Round stone house

Drawings: Albertina, Frank-Archiv 1, 98

————

Frank 1981: 232–33; Bergquist and Michélsen 1994: 136–37; Stritzler-Levine 1996: 283; Welzig 1998: 258–59.

Project: Blue house for Stockholm

Drawings: Albertina, Frank-Archiv 7, 100

———

Stritzler-Levine 1996: 281; Welzig 1998: 224–25, 258, plate 28.

Project: House at Hovslagaregatan 3

Drawings: UfaK 1240

———

Welzig 1998: 257.

Project: House based on three cylinders

Drawings: Albertina, Frank Archiv 11, 102

———

Frank 1985: 42–43; Welzig 1998: 225–26, 259, plate XXVII.

Project: House with stone entry

Drawings: Albertina, Frank-Archiv 90

———

Stritzler-Levine 1996: 280; Welzig 1998: 259.

Project: House with flat roofs

Drawings: Albertina, Frank-Archiv 91

———

Welzig 1998: 259.

Project: H-shaped house in Sweden

Drawing: Albertina, Frank-Archiv 92

———

Welzig 1998: 257.

Project: Double house

Drawings: Albertina, Frank-Archiv 93

———

Welzig 1998: 259.

Project: Triple house

Drawings: Albertina, Frank-Archiv 96; Arkitekturmuseet

———

Um Bau 10 (Aug. 1986): 115; Welzig 1998: 227, 259, plate XXVI.

Project: Villa on the Mediterranean

Drawings: Albertina, Frank-Archiv 12, 13, 99

———

Welzig 1998: 224–25, 258, plate XXIV.

Project: House on a hill in southern France

Drawings: Albertina, Frank-Archiv 2, 95

———

Welzig 1998: 258, plate XXV.

Project: Villa for M. Albrée in southern France

Drawings: Collection Prof. Johannes Spalt, Vienna

———

Welzig 1998: 227, 259.

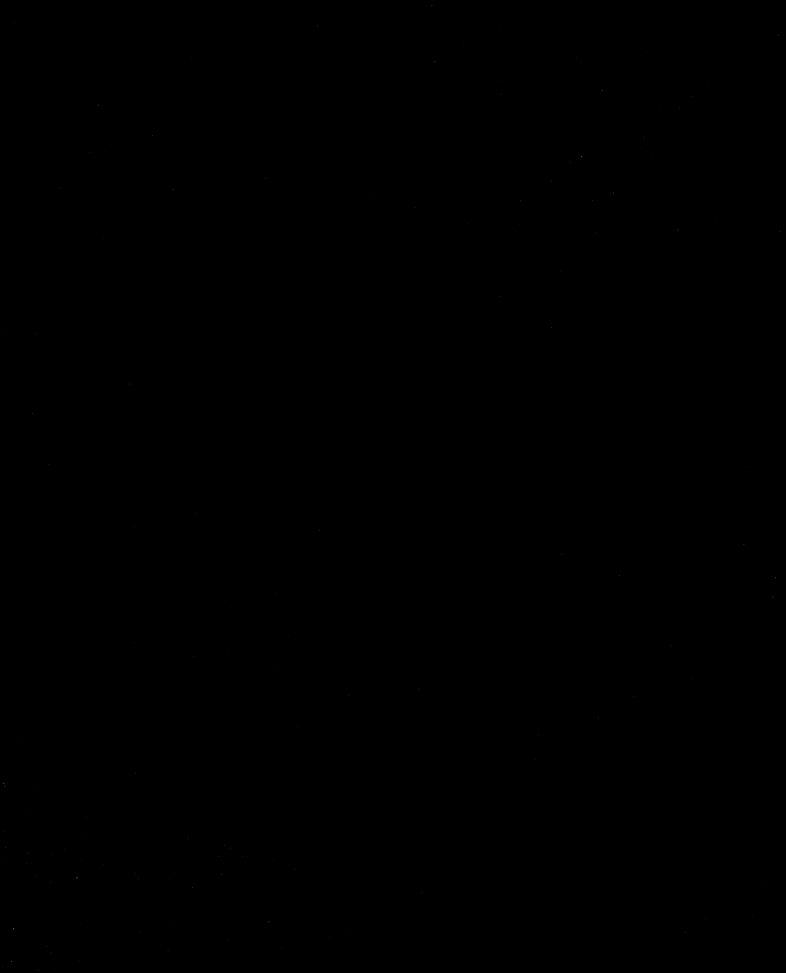

LIST OF EXHIBITIONS

1911–12
Jahresausstellung (Annual exhibition),
Österreichisches Museum für Kunst
und Industrie, Vienna

1912
Frühjahrsausstellung (Spring exhibition),
Österreichisches Museum für Kunst
und Industrie, Vienna

1913
*Ausstellung österreichischer Tapeten,
Linkrusta- und Linoleum-Industrie*
(Exhibition of the Austrian wallpa-
per and linoleum industry), Österre-
ichisches Museum für Kunst und
Industrie, Vienna

1920
Kunstschau (Art exhibition) 1920,
Österreichisches Museum für Kunst
und Industrie, Vienna

1920–21
Einfacher Hausrat (Simple home furnishings), Österreichisches Museum für Kunst und Industrie, Vienna

1923
Dagobert Peche Gedächtnis-Ausstellung
(Dagobert Peche memorial exhibi-
tion), Österreichisches Museum für
Kunst und Industrie, Vienna
Wohnraum-Ausstellung (Living space
exhibition), Österreichisches
Museum für Kunst und Industrie,
Vienna

1924

Jubiläumsausstellung des Wiener Kunstgewerbe-Vereins (Jubilee exhibition of the Vienna Arts and Crafts Association), Österreichisches Museum für Kunst und Industrie, Vienna

1925

Exposition des Arts Décoratifs et Industrieles Modernes, Paris

1926

Internationale Städtebau-Ausstellung (International city planning exhibition), Künstlerhaus, Vienna

Deuxième Exposition Annuelle du Comité Nancy-Paris, Nancy

Jahresausstellung der Genossenschaft Bildender Künstler Wiens (Annual exhibition of the Association of Fine Artists), Künstlerhaus, Vienna

Kunstgewerbe- und Architektur-Ausstellung (Arts and crafts and architecture exhibition), Breslau

Weihnachtsschau der Genossenschaft Bildender Künstler Wiens, Künstlerhaus (Christmas exhibition of the Vienna Association of Fine Artists), Vienna

1927

Kunstschau (Art exhibition), 1927, Österreichisches Museum für Kunst und Industrie, Vienna

Machine-Age Exposition, New York

Ausstellung Europäischer Kunstgewerbe (Exhibition of European arts and crafts), Grassi-Museum, Leipzig

Die Wohnung (The dwelling), German Werkbund exhibition, Stuttgart-Weissenhof

Ausstellung Österreichischer Kunstgewerbe (Exhibition of Austrian arts and crafts), Hotel Königshof, Essen

Wien und die Wiener (Vienna and the Viennese, Messepalast, Vienna

1928

Heim und Technik (Home and technology), Munich

Die neuzeitliche Wohnung (The contemporary dwelling), Österreichisches Museum für Kunst und Industrie, Vienna

Österreichische Kunstgewerbe-Ausstellung (Austrian exhibition of arts and crafts), Cologne

Haus und Garten, Firma Gustav Carl Lehmann, Cologne

1929

Das neue Wien (New Vienna), Berlin-Kreuzberg

Neues Bauen (Modern architecture), Österreichisches Museum für Kunst und Industrie, Vienna

Wohnung und Siedlung (Dwelling and settlement), Linz

Wohnung und Werkraum (Dwelling and work space), Breslau

Wiener Raumkünstler (Vienna interior designers), Österreichisches Museum für Kunst und Industrie, Vienna

1930

Werkbundausstellung (Werkbund exhibition) 1930, Österreichisches Museum für Kunst und Industrie, Vienna

Triennale, Milan

Die Kunst in unserer Zeit (Art in our time), *Künstlerhaus*, Vienna

1931–32

Der gute billige Gegenstand (The good inexpensive object), Österreichisches Museum für Kunst und Industrie, Vienna

1932

Vienna Werkbundsiedlung

1933

Triennale, Milan

Firma Gustav Carl Lehmann, Cologne

1934

Standard 1934, Liljevalchs konsthall, Stockholm

En serie utställningar, Liljevalchs konsthall, Stockholm

1935

Exposition Internationale, Brussels

1936

Triennale, Milan

1937

Austrian Pavilion, *Exposition Internationale*, Paris

Swedish Pavilion, *Exposition Internationale*, Paris

1938

Exhibitions for Svenskt Tenn, Warsaw and Prague

1939

Swedish Pavilion, New York World's Fair

Swedish Pavilion, *Golden Gate Fair*, San Francisco

1942

Svensk Form (Swedish form), Konstindustrimuséet, Copenhagen

1943

New School for Social Research, New York

1949

25 Years Svenskt Tenn, Stockholm

1951

Kaufmann's Department Store, Pittsburgh

1952

Josef Frank: Tjugo år i Svenskt Tenn (Josef Frank: Twenty years at Svenskt Tenn), Nationalmuseum, Stockholm

1958

Josef Frank, Svenskt Tenn, Stockholm

1965

Josef Frank, Österreichische Gesellschaft für Architektur, Vienna

1968

Josef Frank-Minnesutställning (Josef Frank memorial exhibition), Nationalmuseum, Stockholm

1975

Möbel nach Maß (Furniture by measure), Österreichisches Museum für angewandte Kunst, Vienna

1981

Josef Frank—Architektur, Möbel, Textil (Josef Frank—Architecture, furniture, textiles), Österreichisches Museum für angewandte Kunst, Vienna

Josef Frank—Graphik, Textil, Entwürfe (Josef Frank—Graphic designs, textiles, projects), Galerie Brandstetter, Vienna

1985

Josef Frank—100 år Jubileumsutsällning hösten 1985 (Josef Frank—100 year jubilee exhibition), Svenskt Tenn, Stockholm

Josef Frank-Siedlungsbau (Josef Frank—Siedlung designs), Werkbundsiedlung, Vienna

Josef Frank—Wohnbauten, Architektur (Josef Frank—Residential designs, architecture), Technische Universität, Munich

1986

Josef Frank—Stoffe, Tapeten und Teppiche (Josef Frank—Fabric designs, wallpaper, carpets), Galerie in der Staatsoper, Vienna

1987

Josef Frank—Tapeten und Stoffe (Josef Frank—Wallpaper and fabric designs), Einrichtungshaus
Kalmár, Vienna

1994

Josef Frank—arkitektur (Josef Frank—Architecture),
Arkitekturmuseet, Stockholm

Josef Frank—inredning (Josef Frank—Interior design), Millesgården, Stockholm

1996

*Josef Frank, Architect and Designer: An Alternative
Vision of the Modern Home*, Bard Graduate Center for Studies in the Decorative Arts, New York

1998

Josef Frank, Varning för god smak (Josef Frank, Be-
ware of good taste), Kulturhuset, Stockholm.

BIBLIOGRAPHY

ARCHIVAL SOURCES

A note on the archival sources:
After Josef Frank's death in 1967, the majority of his surviving drawings and original photographs of his works were donated to archives in Austria and Sweden. The most important collections of his architectural drawings are now housed in the Josef Frank Archive at Graphische Sammlung Albertina in Vienna, at the Arkitekturmuseet in Stockholm, and the Universität für angewandte Kunst in Vienna. Professor Johannes Spalt in Vienna also has an important collection of Frank's architectural drawings and related materials. The vast majority of Frank's numerous drawings for furnishings and other objects are preserved in the Josef Frank Collection in the Svenskt Tenn Archive in Stockholm.

Archives nationales, Paris; Fonds André Lurçat (correspondence between Frank and André Lurçat)

Akademie der Künste, Berlin; Hugo Häring Papers (correspondence between Frank and Hugo Häring)

Avery Architectural and Fine Arts Library, Columbia University, New York; Walter Sobotka Papers (correspondence between Frank and Walter Sobotka)

Bauaktei, Stuttgart (records and drawings relating to the Weissenhofsiedlung)

Baupolizei, Vienna; MA 37 (plans for Frank's buildings in Vienna)

Bauhaus-Archiv, Berlin (photographs of Frank's houses in Vienna and Stuttgart)

Berlinische Galerie, Landesmuseum für Moderne Kunst, Photographie und Architektur, Berlin (photographs of Bruno Möhring's works)

Ecole d'Architecture, CRR, Geneva; Fonds Arnold Hoechel (transcripts of the first CIAM conference)

Getty Research Insitute, Library, Los Angeles; Franz Roh Papers; Bauhaus Correspondence (correspondence between Otto Neurath and Franz Roh, correspondence between Frank and Hannes Meyer)

Graphische Sammlung Albertina, Vienna; Josef Frank Archiv (Frank's architectural drawings, photographs of his works, and other related materials)

Historisches Museum der Stadt Wien, Vienna (photographs of Frank's works for the Vienna municipality)

Institut für Geschichte und Theorie der Architektur, Eidgenössische Technische Hochschule, Zurich; CIAM-Archiv (correspondence between Frank and Sigfried Giedion, photographs and other materials associated with the CIAM congresses)

Israelitische Kultusgemeinde, Vienna (birth and death records for the Frank family)

Gun Jacobson, Tyresö, Sweden (Frank's drawings for the alterations to Estrid Ericson's country house)

MAK-Österreichisches Museum für angewandte Kunst, Vienna (photographs of Frank's exhibition designs at the Österreichisches Museum für Kunst und Industrie; drawings and photographs of his Wiener Werkstätte designs)

Museum of Modern Art, New York; Ludwig Mies van der Rohe Archive (correspondence and drawings relating to Frank's participation in the Weissenhofsiedlung)

Museum für Ostasiatische Kunst, Cologne (clipping files relating to Frank's design for the museum's interiors)

National Gallery of Art, Stockholm; Estrid Ericson Archive (correspondence to and from Frank and Estrid Ericson, photographs, and other materials documenting to his work for Svenskt Tenn)

Österreichische Nationalbibliothek-Bildarchiv, Vienna (photographs relating to Frank's life and his built works; photographs of Adolf Loos's houses)

Österreichisches Staatsarchiv, Allgemeines Verwaltungsarchiv, Vienna (Haus & Garten business records)

Österreichisches Staatsarchiv, Kriegsarchiv, Vienna (Frank's military service records)

Rheinisches Bildarchiv, Cologne (photographs of Frank's installations for the Museum für Ostasiatische Kunst, Cologne)

Universität für angewandte Kunst—Sammlung, Vienna (Frank's architectural and furniture drawings, photographs of his works, and his personnel records)

University of Pittsburgh Libraries, Archives of Scientific Philosophy, Pittsburgh; Carnap Papers (photographs and papers relating to the Vienna Circle)

Professor Johannes Spalt, Vienna (Frank's architectural drawings, photographs, correspondence with Trude Waehner, and other related materials)

Svenskt Tenn Archive, Stockholm; Josef Frank Collection (drawings, photographs, correspondence, and other materials documenting Frank's work for Svenskt Tenn)

Gustav Szekely, Vienna (correspondence between Frank and Trude Waehner)

Technische Universität, Vienna, Universitätsarchiv (Frank's university records, dissertation, and dissertation drawings)

Vitra Design Museum, Weil am Rhein, Germany (catalogs featuring Frank's designs for
Thonet)

Wiener Stadt- und Landesbibliothek-Hand-
schriftensammlung, Vienna (correspondence from Frank to Josef Hoffmann)

Wiener Stadt- und Landesarchiv, Vienna (photographs of Frank's buildings for the Vienna
municipality)

Zentralinstitut für Kunstgeschichte, Munich
(photographs of the Weissenhofsiedlung)

F R A N K ' S   W R I T I N G S

1910

Über die ursprüngliche Gestalt der kirchlichen
Bauten des Leone Battista Alberti. Ph.D.
diss., Technische Hochschule, Vienna, 1910.

1919

———, Hugo Fuchs, and Franz Zettinig.
"Wohnhäuser aus Gußbeton. Ein Vorschlag
zur Lösung der Wohnungsfrage." *Der Architekt* 22 (1919): 33–37.

"Über die Aufstellung des 'Museums für Ostasiatische Kunst' in Köln." *Der Architekt* 22
(1919): 169–74.

"Das neuzeitliche Landhaus." *Innen-Dekoration*
30 (December 1919): 410–15.

"Die Einrichtung des Wohnzimmers." *Innen-
Dekoration* 30 (December 1919): 416–17.

1921

"Die Arbeiter-Kolonie in Ortmann." *Deutsche
Kunst und Dekoration* 48 (September 1921):
307–10.

"Über die Zukunft des Wiener Kunstgewerbes." *Der Architekt* 24 (1921–22):
37–44.

1923

"Kunst, Kunsthandwerk und Maschine." *Die
Ware* 1 (1923): 70.

"Handwerks- und Maschinen-Erzeugnis. Die
Abgrenzung beider Gebiete." *Innen-Dekoration* 34 (August 1923): 241, 243.

"Le Métier d'Art." *L'Amour de l'Art* 4 (August
1923): 646–52.

"Einzelmöbel und Kunsthandwerk." *Innen-
Dekoration* 34 (November 1923): 336–38.

1924

"Die Wiener Siedlung." *Der Neubau* 6 (10 February 1924): 24–29.

"Siedlung und Normen." *Die neue Wirtschaft* 1
(14 February 1924): 9.

"Siedlungshäuser." *Deutsche Kunst und Dekoration* 54 (May 1924): 100–3.

"Volkswohnhaus und Individualismus." *Der
Neubau* 6 (10 June 1924): 118–21.

1926

"Erziehung zum Architekten." *Soziale
Bauwirtschaft* 3 (1926): 166–68.

"Formprobleme. Die Erziehung zum Architekten und die Titelfrage." *Der Aufbau* 1 (May
1926): 59–62.

"Der Volkswohnungspalast. Eine Rede, anläßlich der Grundsteinlegung, die nicht
gehalten wurde." *Der Aufbau* 1 (August
1926): 107–11.

"Wiens moderne Architektur bis 1914." *Der
Aufbau* 1 (September 1926): 162–68.

1927

"Drei Behauptungen und ihre Folgen." *Die
Form* 2 (1927): 289–91.

"Die Großstadtwohnung unserer Zeit." *Moderne Bauformen* 26 (1927), Beilage, 11: "Mitteilungen aus der Fachwelt."

"Der Gschnas fürs G'müt und der Gschnas als
Problem." In Deutscher Werkbund. *Bau und*

Wohnung, 48–57. Exhibition catalog. Stuttgart: Dr. Fr. Wedekind & Co., 1927.

"Vom neuen Stil." *Baukunst* 3 (August 1927): 234–49.

"Das steile Dach ist ein Rest aus dem romantischen Zeitalter." *Das neue Frankfurt* 1 (October–December 1927): 194–96.

1928

"Die moderne Einrichtung des Wohnhauses." In *Innenräume. Räume und Inneneinrichtungsgegenstände aus der Werkbundausstellung "Die Wohnung."* Edited by Werner Gräff, 126–27. Stuttgart: Dr. Fr. Wedekind & Co., 1928.

"Das Wohnhaus unserer Zeit. Die möglichst gute Wohnung ist Ziel." *Innen-Dekoration* 39 (January 1928): 33.

"Vom neuen Stil. Einige Fragen und Antworten." *Innen-Dekoration* 39 (February 1928): 103.

"Fassade und Interieur." *Deutsche Kunst und Dekoration* 62 (June 1928): 187–89.

1929

"Probleme des Neuen Bauens. Vortrag des Professor Josef Frank." *Architektur und Bautechnik* 16, no. 7 (1929): 111. Reprinted in *Wiener Allgemeine Zeitung*, 12 April 1929, 4.

"Gespräch über den Werkbund." In *Österreichischer Werkbund, 1929*, 3–13. Vienna: 1929.

"Muster-Reihenhaus in Böhler-Stahlbauweise," In *Wohnung und Siedlung in Stadt und Land*, 127–29. Exhibition catalog. Linz, 1929.

1930

Adolf Loos zum 60. Geburtstag am 10. Dezember 1930, 20. Vienna: Buchhandlung Richard Lanyi, 1930.

Josef Hoffmann zum sechszigsten Geburtstag 15. Dezember 1930, 13. Vienna: Sonderveröffentlichung der Zeitschrift Almanach der Dame, 1930.

"Wiener Bauten und Wohnungen." In *Wohnungsfragen in Österreich*. Part 3 of *Beiträge zur städtische Wohn- und Siedelwirtschaft*, 37–44. Edited by Julius Bunzel. Munich: Dunckert & Humboldt, 1930.

Untitled article in special issue, "Oskar Strnad zum 50. Geburtstag." *Deutsche Kunst und Dekoration*, 65 (January 1930): 255.

"Was ist modern?" *Die Form* 5 (1 August 1930): 399–406. Reprinted in *Der Baumeister* 28 (October 1930): 388–411.

"Ein Briefwechsel über Mode." *Die Form* 5 (15 August 1930): 413.

"Geltungswille." *Innen-Dekoration* 41 (November 1930): 406.

Architektur als Symbol. Elemente deutschen Neuen Bauens [1930]. Vienna: Anton Schroll & Co., 1931. Reprint, Vienna: Löcker, 1981.

———, and Otto Neurath. "Hannes Meyer." *Der Klassenkampf: Sozialistische Politik und Wissenschaft* 3 (1930): 573–75.

1931

"Das Profil der Herrengasse." *Wiener Allgemeine Zeitung*, 20 February 1931.

"Das Haus als Weg und Platz." *Der Baumeister* 29 (August 1931): 316–23.

"Zum Formproblem." In Österreichischer Werkbund. *Der gute billige Gegenstand. Ausstellung im Österreichischen Museum für Kunst und Industrie November 1931—Jänner 1932*, 12–16. Exhibition catalog. Vienna, 1931. Reprinted in *Bau und Werkkunst* 8 (1932): 16–24.

1932

———, ed. *Die internationale Werkbundsiedlung. Wien, 1932*. Neues Bauen in der Welt,

4. Exhibition catalog. Vienna: Anton Schroll & Co., 1932.

"Zur Entstehung der Werkbundsiedlung." *Bau und Werkkunst* 8 (1932): 169–70.

————, and Oskar Strnad. "Arch. Prof. Dr. Oskar Strnad und Arch. Prof. Dr. Josef Frank äußern sich zur Museumsfrage." *Österreichische Kunst* 3 (January 1932): 13–15.

"Quale sarà la nostra casa, domani." *Domus* (February 1932): 68–69.

"Brauchbare Typen." *Innen-Dekoration* 43 (June 1932): 224.

"Die Siedlungsbau in der modernen Architektur." *Radio Wien* 8 (10 June 1932): 16–17.

"Der Verteidiger der Zwergsiedlung hat das Wort!" *Der Morgen*, 18 July 1932, 5–6.

"Werkbund-Siedlung, Internationale Ausstellung Wien 1932." *Innen-Dekoration* 43 (August 1932): 273–75.

"Die Werkbundsiedlung Internationale Ausstellung Wien 1932." *Deutsche Kunst und Dekoration* 70 (August 1932): 227–28.

"International Housing Exposition, Vienna, Austria." *Architectural Forum* [New York] 57 (October 1932): 325–38.

1933
"Modefragen." *Die neue Wohnung, Österreichische Möbelzeitschrift* 5 (1933): 6–7.

1934
"Rum och inredning." *Form* 30 (1934): 217–25. Translated into German under the title "Raum und Einrichtung," in *Josef Frank, 1885–1967*. Edited by Johannes Spalt and Hermann Czech, 95–101. Vienna: Hochschule für angewandte Kunst, 1981.

1948
"Zur Neugestaltung des Stephansplatzes." *Wiener Tageszeitung*, 1 May 1948, 3. Reprinted in *Transparent* 3–5 (1987): 17–18.

"Die Rolle der Architektur." *Europäische Rundschau* [Vienna] 17 (1948): 777–81.

"Hur skall tapeten användas?" *Vi Bo. Tidskrift för god heminredning* 12 (1948): 12.

1949
"Die vorliegenden Tapeten." *Architektur und Wohnform* 4 (1949): 84–86. Reprinted in *Tapetenzeitung* 5 (1949): 98–99.

"Großstädtisch gedacht." *Film* 36 (March 1949): 11–13.

1950
"Modern Architecture and the Symbols of Statics." *Synthese: An International Journal for the Logical Study of the Foundations of Science* 7 (1950–51): 342–49.

1955
"Trenger vi en moderne stil?" *Bonytt* (February 1955): 36–38.

1958
"Accidentism." *Form* 54 (1958): 160–65.

1960
"Is There a Modern Style?" *Industrial Design* 7 (March 1960): 39–42.

1961
"Akzidentismus." *Baukunst und Werkform* 14 (1961): 216–18. Reprinted in *Die Furche* [Vienna] 3 (1966): 9.

1977
"Selbstdarstellung." *Bauforum* 10, no. 61 (1977): 29.

1980

"Accidentism" [excerpts]. *Archetype* 1, no. 4 (1980): 38–39.

1981

"How to Plan a House." In *Josef Frank, 1885–1967: Möbel & Geräte & Theoretisches.* Exhibition catalog. Edited by Johannes Spalt, 156–67. Vienna: Hochschule für angewandte Kunst, 1981.

1982

"The House as Street and Square." *9H* 3 (1982): 9–12.

1986

Architettura come simbolo. Elementi del nuovo edificio tedesco. Translated by Ferruccio Della Giacoma and Stefano Zagoni. Introuction by Hermann Czech. Biographical note by Giuliano Gresleri. Bologna: Zanichelli Editore, 1986.

1995

Arkitektur som symbol: Element i tyskt Neues Bauens. Translated by Karin Lindegren. Introduction by Karin Lindegren. Lund: ellerströms, 1995.

Lectures and other unpublished writings

"Grundlagen der modernen Architektur." Lecture presented in Graz, 18 October 1930.

"Das moderne Haus und seine Einrichtung." Lecture presented in Salzburg, 23 October 1930.

Lecture series presented at the New School for Social Research, New York (texts are in German and English; not all of the lectures have survived): "The Future of Architecture and Interior Decoration" (1942), "Introduction to Modern Art and Architecture" (1942), "Ap-

preciation of Architecture" (1943), "Post War Problems of Art" (1943).

"The Peace Conference" (1942).

"Schweden kämpft gegen die Wohnungsnot" (Vienna, 1958).

"Antwort auf 12 Fragen von Viktor Matejka" (1965).

"Über den Jugendstil" (Stockholm, 25 February 1965).

"Zwischenkriegsarchitektur in Österreich" (Stockholm, 5 March 1965).

Undated Manuscripts

"Von der Schönheit und vom Ornament."

"Brauchen wir einen modernen Stil?"

"The Four Freedoms."

The History of the Thirty Years War (novel).

Das Leben des Malers Lucien Sander (novel).

Träume. Komödie in fünf Akten (play).

Woch (play).

WORKS ABOUT FRANK

Note: Only the most significant articles and books about Frank are listed here. Works illustrating individual pieces of furniture and objects are also included. For specific references to Frank's architectonic works, see the Catalog of Buildings, Projects, and Interiors.

1912

Wlach, Oskar. "Zu den Arbeiten von Josef Frank." *Das Interieur* 13 (1912): 41–45.

1913

Levetus, Amelia S. "Austrian Architecture and Decoration." *Studio Yearbook of Decorative Art* (1913): 187–88, 190.

1915

Eisler, Max. "Wiener Stadtvillen und Land-
    häuser." *Wasmuths Monatshefte für Baukunst*
    2 (1915–16): 491–524.

1916

Eisler, Max. *Österreichische Werkkultur*. Vienna:
    Anton Schroll & Co., 1916, 82–87, 89, 91,
    94–95, 139.

1922

Holme, Geoffrey, ed. *Studio Yearbook of Decora-
    tive Art*, 141. London: The Studio, 1922.
Innen-Dekoration 33 (May 1922): 191.
Innen-Dekoration 33 (September 1922): 315–20.
Innen-Dekoration 33 (October 1922): 329.

1924

Eisler, Max. "Die schöne Wohnung." *Das Zelt* 1,
    no. 3 (1924): 106–10.
Hahn, Josef. "Josef Frank." *Das Zelt* 1, no. 10
    (1924): 349–53.

1925

Innen-Dekoration 34 (February 1925): 70.

1926

Eisler, Max. "Neue Wiener Nutzbauten." *Mod-
    erne Bauformen* 25 (September 1926):
    233–37.
Ermers, Max. "Die 'Paprikakiste' am Kongreß-
    platz." *Der Tag*, 1 August 1926, 9.
Fuchs-Röll, Willy P. "Wiener Volkswohnungs-
    bauten." *Der Neubau* 8 (10 October 1926):
    221–26.
Greiner, Leopold. "Möbel und Einrichtung der
    Neuzeit. Arbeiten der Werkstätten 'Haus &
    Garten'-Wien." *Innen-Dekoration* 37 (October
    1926): 348–84.
Holme, Geoffrey, ed. *Studio Yearbook of Decora-
    tive Art*, 169. London: The Studio, 1926.

1927

Bernoulli, Hans. "Die Wohnungsausstellung
    Stuttgart 1927." *Das Werk* 14, no. 9 (1927):
    265.
Eisler, Max. "Neu-Wiener Innenräume." *Mod-
    erne Bauformen* 26 (1927): 388–409.
Holme, Geoffrey, ed. *Studio Yearbook of Deco-
    rative Art*, 70. London: The Studio, 1927.
"Josef Frank." *Moderne Bauformen* 26 (1927):
    170–85.

1928

"Einiges von Land- und Sommerhäuser." *Der
    Baumeister* 26 (March 1928): 94–102.
Hegemann, Werner. "Stuttgarter Schildbürger-
    streiche und die Berliner Bauausstellung
    1930." *Wasmuths Monatshefte für Baukunst*
    12, no. 1 (1928): 8–12.
Hoffmann, Else. "Das Haus H. und M. Blitz in
    Wien." *Innen-Dekoration* 39 (December
    1928): 451–88.
Holme, Geoffrey, ed. *Decorative Art: The Studio
    Yearbook*, 113. London: The Studio, 1928.

1929

Eisler, Max. "Haus und Garten." *Moderne Bau-
    formen* 28 (1929): 79–85.
"Franksk funktionalism i Falsterbo." *Veckojour-
    nalen* 40 (1929): 33–35.
"Haus Claëson in Falsterbo, Schweden." *Mod-
    erne Bauformen* 28 (1929): 44.
Holme, Geoffrey, ed. *Decorative Art 1929: The
    Studio Yearbook*, 14, 50, 137. London: The
    Studio, 1929.
Noreen, Ärland. "Den nyaste byggnadskon-
    sten." *Ord och bild* 1 (14 January 1929):
    49–60.
"Professor Josef Frank über Probleme des
    neuen Bauens." *Wiener Allgemeine Zeitung*,
    12 April 1929, 4.

1930

Eisler, Max. "Neue Bauten und Innenräume von Josef Frank, Oskar Wlach ('Haus und Garten')—Arnold Karplus Wohnhaus auf der Hohen Warte in Wien." *Moderne Bauformen*, 39 (1930): 429–48.

Holme, Geoffrey, ed. *Decorative Art: The Studio Yearbook*, 129–30. London: The Studio, 1930

"Josef Frank." In *Dresslers Kunsthandbuch*. Vol. 2. Edited by Willy O. Dressler, 267. Berlin: Karl Curtius, 1930.

Meyer, Peter. Review of *Architektur als Symbol*. *Das Werk* 17 (November 1930): xlvii.

"Werkstätten 'Haus & Garten' in Wien." *Innen-Dekoration* 41 (November 1930): 402–34.

1931

Born, Wolfgang. "Ein Haus in Wien-Hietzing." *Innen-Dekoration* 42 (September 1931): 362–98.

Eisler, Max. "Von der neuen Baukunst." *Menorah* 9 (January–February 1931): 35–42.

Haerdtl, Carmela. "Una casa nuova di Josef Frank." *Domus* (July 1931): 48–51.

———. "Una casa privata a Vienna degli architetti Josef Frank e Oscar [*sic*] Wlach." *Domus* (August 1931), 28–30, 77.

Hermann, Wolfgang. Review of *Architektur als Symbol*. *Kunst und Künstler* 29 (September 1931): 464.

Holme, Geoffrey, ed. *Decorative Art 1931: The Studio Yearbook*, 92, 94. London: The Studio, 1931.

Klopfer, Paul. "*Architektur als Symbol*: Nachdenkliches über Josef Frank's gleichnamiges Buch." *Stein Holz Eisen* 45 (5 March 1931): 81–84.

Review of *Architektur als Symbol*. *Cahiers d'Art* 6, no. 2 (1931): 116.

Roh, [Franz]. Review of *Architektur als Symbol*. *Das Neue Frankfurt* 5 (March 1931): 59.

R[iezler], W[alter]. Review of *Architektur als Symbol*. *Die Form* 6 (15 March 1931): 120.

Röhnick, Wilhelm. Review of *Architektur als Symbol*. *Die Form* 6 (15 March 1931): 120.

Tamms, [Fritz]. Review of *Architektur als Symbol*. *Die Baugilde* 13 (10 March 1931): 416.

Wattjes, J. G. Review of *Architektur als Symbol*. *Het Bouwbedrijf* 8 (23 October 1931): 488–89.

1932

Review of *Architektur als Symbol*. *Journal de la construction de la suisse romande* 7 (15 August 1932): 469.

Eisler, Max. "Ein Wohnhaus von Josef Frank und Oskar Wlach, Wien." *Moderne Bauformen* 31 (1932): 88–95.

Holme, Geoffrey, ed. *Decorative Art 1932: The Studio Yearbook*, 72. London: The Studio, 1932.

M[ayreder, Friedrich]. Review of *Die internationale Werkbundsiedlung Wien 1932*. *Die Baugilde* 14 (25 September 1932): 900.

1933

"An Austrian Architect Looks at England." *Architectural Review* 73 (June 1933): 268.

Boltenstern, Erich, ed. *Wiener Möbel in Lichtbildern und maßstäblichen Rissen*, 11–18, 40–41, 43, 50–51, 72–73, 87, 90, 96. Stuttgart: Julius Hoffmann, 1933.

Born, Wolfgang. "Neue Innenräume von Haus & Garten." *Innen-Dekoration* 44 (June 1933): 184–210.

Eckstein, Hans. "Bürgerlicher Wohnbau (*Architektur als Symbol*)." *Die Kunst* 68 (January 1933): 89–96. Reprinted in *Schöne Heim* 36 (January 1933): 113–16, 120.

"Räume und Möbel von Josef Frank und Oskar Wlach, Wien." *Moderne Bauformen* 32 (1933): 355–66.

1934

Ritter, Heinrich. "Neue Wohnungen von 'Haus und Garten.'" *Innen-Dekoration* 45 (October 1934): 314–34.

"Professor Frank und die österreichische Ausstellung in London." *Profil* 2 (May 1934): vii.

1935

Eisler, Max. "Das Wiener Möbel von heute." *Moderne Bauformen* 34 (June 1935): 314–24.

Holme, Geoffrey, ed. *Decorative Art 1935: The Studio Yearbook*, 69. London: The Studio, 1935.

Ritter, Heinrich. "Wohnräume aus Schweden." *Innen-Dekoration* 46 (March 1935): 92–98.

"Una casa en las proximidades de Viena." *Viviendas* 4 (June 1935): 6–15.

1936

Ponti, Gio. "Espressione e carattere nell'opera di Frank e Wlach." *Domus* (March 1936): 10–15.

1937

Holme, Geoffrey, ed. *Decorative Art 1937: The Studio Yearbook*, 49, 80, 133. London: The Studio, 1937.

1938

Holme, Geoffrey, ed. *Decorative Art 1938: The Studio Yearbook*, 20. London: The Studio, 1938.

1939

Ericson, Estrid. *Inrednings-Katekes*. Stockholm, 1939.

Hoffmann, Herbert. "Schwedische Wohnkultur von heute, II." *Moderne Bauformen* 38 (May 1939): 277–92.

Holme, Geoffrey, ed. *Decorative Art 1939: The Studio Yearbook*, 135. London: The Studio, 1939.

1940

Belysningar från Svenskt Tenn. Exhibition catalog. Stockholm, 1940.

Hodin, Josef Paul. "En mänsklig bostadkultur." *Form* 7 (1940): 147–54.

Holme, Geoffrey, ed. *Decorative Art 1940: The Studio Yearbook*, 98. London: The Studio, 1940.

1943

Hofmann, Else J. "J. Frank, Wiener Architekt, ist Schöpfer des hier 'Swedish Modern' gennanten Möbelstils." *New York Staatszeitung und Herold*, 6 February 1943, 7.

"Portrait of Dr. Josef Frank by Trude Schmidl-Waehner. At Bonestell to Feb. 13." *Art Digest* 17 (1 February 1943): 19.

"Ein Wiener Handwerker." *Austro-American Tribune* (December 1943): 3.

1946

"Spring." *Studio* 131 (May 1946): 151.

1948

Björkman, Gunvor. "Josef Frank—wienerstilens mästare." *Svenska hem i ord och bilder* 36 (1948): 94–97.

"Geplantes und privates Bauen." *Österreichische Volksstimme*, 10 February 1948, 4.

"Gespräch mit Josef Frank." *Die Presse*, 17 January 1948, 6.

Huldt, Åke H., and Eva Benedicks. *Design in Sweden Today*, 44–45. Stockholm and New York: Albert Bonnier, 1948.

Schütte, Wilhelm. "Josef Frank über das Bauen." *Österreichisches Tagebuch* 3 (30 January 1948): 11–12.

Sch[ütte]-L[ihotzky, Margarete]. "Professor Frank im Ottakringer Volksheim." *Österreichische Zeitung*, 4 February 1948.

"Schweden kämpft gegen die Wohnungsnot." *Wiener Kurier*, 2 February 1948, 6.

1949

Skawonius, Sven-Erik. "Svenskt Tenn 25 år." *Form* 45 (1949): 164–65.

1950

Svenskt Tenn, Strandvägen 5A, Stockholm. Stockholm: Svenskt Tenn, 1950.

Decorative Art, 1950–51: The Studio Yearbook, 50–51, 102. London: The Studio, 1950.

1951

Hald, Arthur, and Sven Erik Skawonius. *Contemporary Swedish Design*, 29, 33, 36, 38, 45, 53, 60–61, 68–69, 79, 82, 90, 132, 150. Stockholm: Nordisk Rotogravyr, 1951.

"Swedish Articles on Display Here." *Pittsburgh Post-Gazette*, 6 February 1951.

"Swedish Expert Here Gives Philosophy on Art." *Pittsburgh Sun-Telegraph*, 7 February 1951.

1952

Björkman, Gunvor. "Två möbelprofeter Josef Frank och Carl Malmsten." *Ord och bild* 61 (1952): 543–52.

Decorative Art, 1952–53: The Studio Yearbook, 80. London: The Studio, 1952.

Johansson, Gotthard. *Josef Frank: Tjugo år i Svenskt Tenn.* Exhibition catalog. Stockholm: Nationalmuseum, 1952.

———. "Josef Frank—Tjugo år i Svenskt Tenn." *Form* 48 (1952): 100–1.

Ullrich, Erik. "Josef Frank på Nationalmuseum." *Svenska hem i ord och bilder* 40 (1952): 78–80.

1953

Decorative Art, 1953–54: The Studio Yearbook, 34, 40, 62. London: The Studio, 1953.

1954

Belysningar från Svenskt Tenn. Exhibition catalog. Stockholm, 1954.

Decorative Art, 1954–55: The Studio Yearbook, 34, 38. London: The Studio, 1954.

1955

Decorative Art, 1955–56: The Studio Yearbook, 58. London: The Studio, 1955.

"Josef Frank 70 Jahre Alt." *Arbeiter Zeitung*, 17 July 1955, 14.

"Josef Frank 70 Jahre Alt." *Die Presse*, 26 July 1955, 4.

1956

Decorative Art, 1956–57: The Studio Yearbook, 33, 44, 54. London: The Studio, 1956.

1958

Lagercrantz, Bo. "Har funktionalismen moraliserat sönder hemmiljön?" *Expressen*, 11 January 1958, 4.

Tidholm, Kajs. "Ett hem att trivas i." *Husmodern* 48 (25 November–2 December 1958): 24–27, 69–70.

1960

Nordström, Thyra. "Bättre mönster på tapeten." *Form* 56 (1960): 464–76.

1963

Hård af Segerstad, Ulf. *Modern Scandinavian Furniture.* London: The Studio, 1963.

Zahle, Erik, ed. *Scandinavian Domestic Design.* London: Methuen, 1963.

1965

Achleitner, Friedrich. "Ohne Dogma und Pathos." *Die Presse,* 24 December 1965, 9.

———. "Repräsentant Wiener Architektur. Staatspreisträger Josef Frank begeht in Schweden seiner 80. Geburtstag." *Die Presse,* 17–18 July 1965, 9.

Kurrent, Friedrich, and Johannes Spalt. "Ein Architekt aus Wien." *Die Furche,* 29 (1965): 10.

———, eds. *Josef Frank.* Exhibition catalog. Vienna: Hochschule für angewandte Kunst, 1965.

Thurner, Herbert. "Josef Frank—Österreichischer Staatspreisträger." *Bau: Schrift für Architektur und Städtebau* 3 (1965): 66.

1967

"Josef Frank—Intellekt, Liebenswürdigkeit, Ironie." *Die Furche* 3 (21 January 1967): 4.

Haerdtl, Carmela. "Un ricordo di Josef Frank." *Domus* 449 (4 April 1967): 6.

Kurrent, Friedrich. "Um Fortsetzung bemüht." *Die Presse,* 11 January 1967, 6.

Hård af Segerstad, Ulf. "Josef Frank in memoriam." *Svenska Dagbladet,* 10 January 1967, 4.

———. "Josef Frank." *Form* 63 (1967): 176–80.

1968

Ericson, Estrid, ed. *Josef Frank, 1885–1967. Minnesutställning 4 April–19 Maj 1968.* Exhibition catalog. Stockholm: Nationalmuseum, 1968.

1970

"Una casa d'abitazione di Josef Frank e Oskar Wlach." *Casabella* 345 (February 1970): 45.

1975

Windisch-Graetz, Franz. *Möbel nach Maß: Frank, Malmsten, Raab, Asmussen.* Exhibition catalog. Vienna: Hochschule für angewandte Kunst, 1975.

1979

Hård af Segerstad, Ulf. "Josef Frank." *Mobilia* 282 (1979): 34–39.

Mang, Karl, and Eva Mang. *Viennese Architecture, 1860–1930, in Drawings,* 114–17. New York: Rizzoli, 1979.

1980

Czech, Hermann. "Josef Frank." *Archetype* 1 (winter 1980): 37–39.

1981

Baroni, Danile, and Antonio D'Auria. "Protagonisti del movimento moderno: Josef Frank." *Ottagano* 16 (September 1981): 26–33.

Baumer, Dorothea. "Wohnungen, in denen man frei denken kann. Das Werk des österreichischen Architekten Josef Frank wird in einer Ausstellung wiederentdeckt." *Süddeutsche Zeitung,* 9 June 1981, 28.

Czech, Hermann. "Josef Frank, The Accidental House: The Thirteen Designs in Letters to Dagmar Grill." *Lotus International* 29 (1981): 108–10, 114–15.

Kapfinger, Otto. "Der schöpferische Skeptiker. Zur Ausstellung 'Josef Frank 1885 bis 1967.'" *Die Presse,* 2–3 May 1981, 6.

Spalt, Johannes. "The Form of Dwelling: Drawings of Josef Frank before 1934." *Lotus International* 29 (1981): 111–13.

———, ed. *Josef Frank, 1885–1967: Möbel & Geräte & Theoretisches.* Exhibition catalog. Vienna: Hochschule für angewandte Kunst, 1981.

———, and Hermann Czech, eds. *Josef Frank, 1885–1967.* Exhibition catalog. Vienna: Hochschule für angewandte Kunst, 1981.

1982

Kapfinger, Otto. "Wie ist das mit Josef Frank?" *Architese* 12 (May–June 1982): 11–13, 54.

Sack, Manfred. "Modern geblieben." *Die Zeit,* 17 September 1982, 44.

1984

Wängberg-Eriksson, Kristina. "Tolvekarna Tyresö" *Form* 80, no. 627 (1984): 49–53.

1985

Blumenfeld, Hans. "Meine Arbeit mit Josef Frank, 1928/29." *Bauwelt* 26 (12 July 1985): 1057.

Brulhart, Armand. "Josef Frank und die CIAM bis zum Bruch 1928–1929." *Bauwelt* 26 (12 July 1985): 1058–60.

Jacobson, Rikard. *Josef Frank 100 år, Jubileumsutställning hösten 1985.* Exhibition catalog. Stockholm: Svenskt Tenn, 1985.

Jung, Karin Carmen. "Das moderne Wohnhaus als 'zweckloser' Gebrauchsgegenstand." *Bauwelt* 26 (12 July 1985): 1044–47.

———, and Dietrich Worbs. "Josef Frank: Funktionalismuskritik und moderne Architekturkonzeption. Zur Aktualität von Josef Frank." *Bauwelt* 26 (12 July 1985): 1042–43.

Kapfinger, Otto. "Ein Haus ist ein Haus. Zum hundertsten Geburtstag des Architekten Josef Frank." *Die Presse,* 13–14 July 1985, 7.

Kirsch, Karin. "Franks Doppelhaus in der Weißenhofsiedlung." *Bauwelt* 26 (12 July 1985): 1054–56.

Kurrent, Friedrich. "Die 'Rückkehr' Josef Franks aus der Emigration." *Bauwelt* 26 (12 July 1985): 1068–69.

Lutteman, Helena Dahlbäck. "Josef Frank 100 år." *Form* 81, no. 8 (1985): 47.

Matejka, Viktor. "12 Fragen an Josef Frank." *Bauwelt* 26 (12 July 1985): 1064–65.

Munck af Rosenschöld, Malin. "Aus meiner Zusammenarbeit mit Josef Frank." *Bauwelt* 26 (12 July 1985): 1060.

Schütte-Lihotzky, Margarete. "Erinnerungen an Josef Frank." *Bauwelt* 26 (12 July 1985): 1052–53.

Spalt, Johannes. "Josef Frank zum 100. Geburtstag." *Bauforum* 18 (1985): 25–27.

———. "Moderne Weltauffassung und moderne Architektur." *Bauwelt* 26 (12 July 1985): 1066–67.

———, ed. *Josef Frank zum 100. Geburtstag am 15. Juli 1985.* Exhibition catalog. Vienna: Hochschule für angewandte Kunst, 1985.

Schwarz, Lotte. "Eine Begegnung mit Josef Frank in Dieulefit." *Bauwelt* 26 (12 July 1985): 1069.

Wängberg-Eriksson, Kristina. "Josef Frank und Svenskt Tenn." *Bauwelt* 26 (12 July 1985): 1061–63.

———. *Svenskt Tenn: Josef Frank och Estrid Ericson. En konsthistorisk studie.* Stockholm: Stockholms universitet, 1985.

Worbs, Dietrich. "Josef Franks Wiener Massenwohnungsbau—Ein pragmatischer Versuch." *Bauwelt* 26 (12 July 1985): 1048–51.

1986

Achleitner, Friedrich. "Franks Weiterwirken in der neueren Wiener Architektur." *Um Bau* 10 (August 1986): 121–31.

———. "Josef Frank et l'architecture viennoise de l'entre-deux-guerres." In *Vienne, 1880–1930: L'apocalypse joyeuse,* 619–25. Exhibition catalog. Paris: Centre Pompidou, 1986.

Czech, Hermann. "Ett sätt att förstå Josef Frank idag." *Arkitektur* 86 (April 1986): 28–29.

———. "Ein Begriffsraster zur aktuellen Interpretation Josef Franks." *Um Bau* 10 (August 1986): 105–20.

Grimmer, Vera. "Simpozij o Jozefu Franku." *Covjek i Prostor* 33 (February 1986): 26–27.

Kapfinger, Otto. "Josef Frank—Siedlungen und Siedlungsprojekte, 1919–1932." *Um Bau* 10 (August 1986): 39–58.

Kurrent, Friedrich. "Frank und frei." *Um Bau* 10 (August 1986): 85–93.

Mizrahil, Monique. "Josef Frank: le opere e i giorni." *Interni* 359 (April 1986): 14–17.

Platzer, Monika. "Einrichtungshaus 'Haus & Garten,' Josef Frank." Unpublished manuscript. University of Vienna, 1986.

Posch, Wilfried. "Josef Frank, eine bedeutende Persönlichkeit des österreichischen Kulturliberalismus." *Um Bau* 10 (August 1986): 21–22.

Schöllhammer, Georg. "Zum literarischen Werk Josef Franks." *Um Bau* 10 (August 1986): 133–45.

Spalt, Johannes. "Josef Frank und die räumliche Konzeption seiner Hausentwürfe." *Um Bau* 10 (August 1986): 59–74.

———. "The Form of Dwelling: Drawings of Josef Frank before 1934." *Lotus International* 29 (1981): 111–13.

———, ed. *Josef Frank, 1885–1967. Stoffe, Tapeten, Teppiche.* Exhibition catalog. Vienna: Hochschule für angewandte Kunst, 1986.

Steinmann, Martin. "Frank?—Kenn' ich nicht!" *Um Bau* 10 (August 1986): 95–104.

Wängberg-Eriksson, Kristina. "Josef Frank bei Svenskt Tenn in Schweden." *Um Bau* 10 (August 1986): 75–84.

1987

Kapfinger, Otto. "Eine neue Josef-Frank-Ausstellung." *Bauforum* 20 (1987): 54–55.

Koller, Gabriele. "Der Taktile Widerstand." In *Die Radikalisierung der Phantasie: Design aus Österreich*, 260–75. Salzburg and Vienna: Residenz, 1987.

Zucchi, Cino. Review of the Italian translation of *Architektur als Symbol. Domus* 682 (April 1987): vi.

1988

Posch, Wilfried. "Josef Frank." In *Vertriebe Vernuft II. Emigration und Exil österreichischer Wissenschaft. Internationales Symposion 19. bis 23. Oktober in Wien.* Edited by Friedrich Stadler, 645–58. Vienna and Munich: Jugend & Volk, 1988.

1989

Beltramini, Guido. "La casa sensibile." In *La casa isolata: dalla tautologia alla banalità: Letture, trascrizioni, variazioni su testi di Wittgenstein, Loos, Frank.* Edited by Giovanni Fraziano, 81–91. Venice: Cluva Editrice, 1989.

Wängberg-Erkisson, Kristina. "The Interior Designer." In *Estrid Ericson: Founder of Svenskt Tenn.* Edited by Monica Boman. Translated by Roger G. Tanner, 90–123. Stockholm: Carlsson, 1989.

1990

Mayer, Margit J. "Gefühl und Qualität." *Der Standard*, 18–19 August 1990, 12.

Wängberg-Eriksson, Kristina. "Josef Frank." In *Svenska möbler, 1890–1990.* Edited by Monica Boman, 194–95. Lund: Signum, 1991.

1991

Czech, Hermann. "A Mode for the Current Interpretation of Josef Frank." *Architecture and Urbanism* 254 (November 1991): 20–37.

1992

Rüegg, Arthur, and Adolph Stiller. *Sechs Häuser.* Zurich: ETH, 1992.

1993

Long, Christopher. "Josef Frank and the Crisis of Modern Architecture." Ph.D. diss., University of Texas at Austin, 1993.

Meder, Iris. "Josef Franks Wiener Einfamilienhäuser." M.A. thesis, Universität Stuttgart, 1993.

1994

Bergquist, Mikael, and Olof Michélsen. "Arkitekten Josef Frank." *Arkitektur* 5 (July-August 1994): 48–55.

———, eds. *Josef Frank—arkitektur.* Exhibition catalog. Stockholm: Arkitekturmuseet, 1994. Translated into German as *Josef Frank—Architektur.* Basel: Birkhäuser, 1995.

Boman, Monica, ed. *Josef Frank—inredning.* Exhibition catalog. Stockholm: Millesgården, 1994.

Mæchel, Ingela. "Aktuell Frank." *Form* 696, no. 6 (1994): 94–95.

Wängberg-Eriksson, Kristina. *Josef Frank—Livsträd i krigens skugga.* Lund: Signum, 1994.

Welzig, Maria. "Die Wiener Internationalität Josef Franks. Das Werk des Architekten bis 1938." Ph.D. diss., Universität Wien, 1994.

1995

Collotti, Francesco. "Josef Frank, Architektur." *Architese* 25 (September–October 1995): 68–69.

Morganti, R. "L'architettura di Joseph Frank in monstra a Stoccolma." *Industria delle Construzioni* 29 (March 1995): 50–52.

Stiller, Adolph. "Colored Dots on a Grey Background: Six Key Buildings of Modern Architecture in Central Europe." In *On Continuity.* Edited by Rosamund Diamond and Wilfried Wang, 24–41. 9H, no. 9. Cambridge, Mass.: 9H Publications, 1995; distributed by Princeton Architectural Press.

Wängberg-Eriksson, Kristina. "Josef Frank im Exil auf Manhattan, 1942–46." In *Visionäre und Vertriebene: Österreichische Spuren in der modernen amerikanischen Architektur.* Edited by Matthias Boeckl, 189–99. Exhibtion catalog. Berlin: Ernst & Sohn, 1995.

Welzig, Maria. "Entwurzelt: Sobotka, Wlach und Frank in Pittsburgh und New York." In *Visionäre und Vertriebene: Österreichische Spuren in der modernen amerikanischen Architektur.* Edited by Matthias Boeckl, 201–23. Exhibition catalog. Berlin: Ernst & Sohn, 1995.

1996

Achleitner, Friedrich. "Josef Frank und die Wiener Architektur der Zwischenkriegszeit." In *Wiener Architektur: Zwischen typologischem Fatalismus und semantischen Schlamassel,* 81–87. Vienna: Böhlau, 1996.

Busch, Akiko. "Josef Frank: The Roots of Swedish Modern." *Metropolis* 15 (May 1996): 90–91, 127–29.

Casciani, Stefano. "Josef Frank: La diaspora del genio." *Abitare* 335 (October 1996): 180–86.

Czech, Hermann. "Selbstkritiker der Moderne: Josef Frank." *Der Architekt* 1 (January 1996): 27–30.

Petkanas, Christopher. "Freely Modern." *House Beautiful* 138 (June 1996): 68–69.

Stritzler-Levine, Nina, ed. *Josef Frank, Architect and Designer: An Alternative Vision of the Modern Home.* Exhibition catalog. New Haven and London: Yale University Press, 1996.

Wang, Wilfried. "Orthodoxy and Immanent Criticism: On Josef Frank's Contribution to the Stuttgart Weissenhofsiedlung, 1926–1927." In *Form, Modernism, and History: Essays in Honor of Eduard F. Sekler.* Edited by Alexander von Hoffman, 62–70.

BIBLIOGRAPHY

Cambridge, Mass.: Harvard University Press, 1996.

1997

Achleitner, Friedrich. "Josef Frank and the Viennese Architecture of the Inter-War Period." *Zlatý řez* 14 (spring 1997): 8–10.

Long, Christopher. "Josef Frank's Critique of Functionalism." *Zlatý řez* 14 (spring 1997): 4–7.

Templ, Stephan. "A House Which Can Accommodate Our Whole Lives." *Zlatý řez* 14 (spring 1997): 10–11.

1998

Bergquist, Mikael, and Olof Michélsen. *Josef Frank: Falsterbovillorna.* Stockholm: Arkitektur, 1998.

Overy, Paul. "Josef Frank, Architect and Designer: An Alternative Vision of the Modern Home." *Journal of Design History* 11, no. 3 (1998): 253–58.

Thurm-Nemeth, Volker, ed. *Konstruktion zwischen Werkbund und Bauhaus: Wissenschaft—Architektur—Wiener Kries.* Wissenschaftliche Weltauffassung und Kunst, vol. 4. Vienna: Hölder-Pichler-Tempsky, 1998.

Welzig, Maria. *Josef Frank, 1885–1967: Das architektonische Werk.* Vienna, Cologne, and Weimar: Böhlau, 1998.

Wängberg-Eriksson, Kristina. *Josef Frank: Textile Designs.* Translated by Christopher Long, Jan Christer Eriksson, and Kristina Wängberg-Eriksson. Lund: Bokförlaget Signum, 1999. Originally published as *Pepis flora: Josef Frank som mönsterkonstnär* (Lund: Bokförlaget Signum, 1998).

1999

Long, Christopher. Review of *Josef Frank, 1885–1967: Das architektonische Werk* by Maria Welzig. *Journal of the Society of Architectural Historians* 58 (June 1999): 214–16.

———. "The Other Modern Dwelling: Josef Frank and Haus & Garten." Working Papers in Austrian Studies, 98-2. Minneapolis: Center for Austrian Studies, University of Minnesota, 1999.

2000

Long, Christopher. "The House as Path and Place: Spatial Planning in Josef Frank's Villa Beer, 1928–1930." *Journal of the Society of Architectural Historians* 59 (December 2000): 478–501.

OTHER SOURCES CITED IN TEXT

Primary sources

Adler, Leo. *Neuzeitliche Miethäuser und Siedlungen.* Berlin and Charlottenburg: Ernst Pollak, 1931.

Ankwicz-Kleehoven, Hans. "Kunstgewerbe." In Carl Brockhausen, *Österreich in Wort und Bild*, 44–47. Berlin, Vienna, and Leipzig: Franz Schneider, 1924.

———. "Die internationale Werkbundsiedlung Wien 1932." *Wiener Zeitung*, 5 August 1932: 4–6.

Aschehoug, Elisabeth. "Distinguished Leader in Swedish Modern." *American Swedish Monthly* 33 (February 1939): 8–10, 35.

———. "Beauty and Comfort for All." *American Swedish Monthly* (May 1939): 11–15, 96–97.

Augenfeld, Felix. "Modern Austria: Personalities and Style." *Architectural Review* 83 (April 1938): 165–74.

———. "Erinnerungen an Adolf Loos." *Bauwelt* 72 (6 November 1981): 1907.

Ausstellung schwedischer Volkskunst und Hausindustrie. Exhibition catalog. Vienna: Österreichisches Museum für Kunst und Industrie, 1910.

"Ausstellung 'Wohnung und Siedlung,' Linz 1929." *Der Baumeister* 27 (December 1929): 410–11.

L'Autriche a l'exposition internationale de Paris 1937. Vienna: Wiener Ausstellungsausschuß/Brüder Rosenbaum, 1937.

Bahr, Hermann. *Secession.* Vienna: L. Rosner, 1900.

Bauten und Entwürfe von Carl König herausgegeben von seinen Schülern. Vienna: Gerlach & Wiedling, 1910.

Das befreite Handwerk. Exhibition catalog. Vienna: Österreichisches Museum für Kunst und Industrie, 1934.

Behne, Adolf. *Der moderne Zweckbau.* Munich: Drei Masken, 1926.

Behrendt, Walter Curt. *Der Sieg des neuen Baustils.* Stuttgart: Dr. Fr. Wedekind & Co., 1927.

Behrens, Peter, and Heinrich de Fries. *Vom sparsamen Bauen: Ein Beitrag zur Siedlungsfrage.* Berlin: Bauwelt, 1918.

Berg, G. A. "Swedish Modern." *Form* 34 (1938): 162–68.

———. "What Swedish Modern Is in Sweden." *American Home* 22 (July 1939): 22–23, 65–67.

Bieber, Karl A. Interview by author. Graz, 1 July 1986.

Boltenstern, Erich. *Wiener Möbel.* Stuttgart: Julius Hoffmann, 1935.

Born, Wolfgang. "Ausstellung des Österreichischen Werkbundes in Wien." *Deutsche Kunst und Dekoration* 66 (August 1930): 305–23.

———. "Der Aufbau der Siedlung." *Innen-Dekoration* 43 (August 1932): 276–88, 295–96.

Brenner, Anton. "Was lehrt die Wiener Werkbundausstellung?" *Bauwelt* 47 (1933): 167.

Breuer, Robert. "Werkbund-Tagung in Wien." *Deutsche Kunst und Dekoration* 66 (August 1930): 321–22.

CIAM Dokumente, 1928–1939. Edited by Martin Steinmann. Basel and Stuttgart: Birkhäuser, 1979.

Concrete Houses and Cottages. 2 vols. New York: Atlas P. Cement Co., 1909.

Conrads, Ulrich, ed. *Programs and Manifestoes on 20th-Century Architecture.* Cambridge, Mass.: MIT Press, 1971.

Dannenberg, Robert. *Zehn Jahre Neues Wien.* Vienna: Wiener Volksbuchhandlung, 1929.

Deutsch-Österreichischer Städtebund. *Die Wohnungspolitik der Gemeinde Wien. Ein Überblick über die Tätigkeit der Stadt Wien seit der Bekämpfung der Wohnungsnot und zur Hebung der Wohnkultur.* Vienna, 1926.

Deutscher Werkbund. *Die Durchgeistigung der deutschen Arbeit: Wege und Ziele im Zusammenhang von Industrie, Handwerk und Kunst.* Jena: Eugen Dietrichs, 1912.

———. *Bau und Wohnung.* Stuttgart: Dr. Fr. Wedekind & Co., 1927.

———. *Werkbund-Ausstellung "Die Wohnung" Stuttgart 1927 23 Juli–9 Okt.* Exhibition catalog. Stuttgart, 1927.

"Der Deutscher Werkbund in Stuttgart." *Bauwelt* 21 (1930): 1450.

"Diskussion zu Thema II, 'Der Bau von Kleinwohnungen mit tragbaren Mieten,' International Housing Conference, Berlin, 1931." *Wohnen und Bauen* 3, nos. 5–6 (1931): 257.

Eberstadt, Rudolf, Bruno Möhring, and Richard Petersen. *Groß-Berlin. Ein Programm für die Planung der neuzeitlichen Groß-Stadt.* Berlin: Ernst Wasmuth, 1910.

Ehmke, Fritz Helmut. *Geordnetes und Gültiges. Gesammelte Aufsätze und Arbeiten aus den letzten 25 Jahren.* Munich: C. H. Beck, 1955.

Eisenkolb, Helene. Interview by author. Vienna, 12 June 1987.

Eisler, Max. *Österreichische Werkkultur.* Vienna: Anton Schroll, 1916.

———. "Oskar Strnad." *Dekorative Kunst* 21 (February 1918): 145–54.

———. "L'Architecture, la décoration intérieur et l'ameublement." *L'Amour de l'art* 4 (August 1923): 633–45.

———. "Österreich in Paris 1925." *Moderne Bauformen* 24 (1925): 249–88.

———. "Vom neuen Geist in der jüdischen Baukunst." *Menorah* 6 (September 1926): 519–27.

———. "Kunst und Gemeinde." *Menorah* 6 (February 1928): 118–24.

———. "Neues aus Wien und Brünn." *Moderne Bauformen* 28 (1929): 393–432.

———. "Neue Wiener Innenräume." *Moderne Bauformen* 29 (1930): 78–99.

———. "Österreichischer Werkbund 1930." *Moderne Bauformen* 29 (August 1930): 333–48.

———. "Was gefällt Ihnen nicht an der Werkbundausstellung?" *Der Morgen* 4 (July 1932): 10–11.

———. "Was gefällt Ihnen nicht an der Werkbundausstellung? Reaktionen der Redaktion und von Max Eisler auf den Artikel von P. A. R. und die Antwort Franks." *Der Morgen* (5 July 1932): 8.

———. "Die Werkbundsiedlung in Wien." *Moderne Bauformen* 31 (1932): 435–58.

———. "Viennese Architecture." *Architectural Forum* 58 (1932): 500–18.

———. *Oskar Strnad.* Vienna: Gerlach & Wiedling, 1936.

Ermers, Max. "Groß-Wiens Stadterweiterung und der neue General-Architekturplan." *Der Tag*, 25 November 1923, 6.

———. "Eine baurevolutionäre Ausstellung. Werkbundschau 'Neues Bauen' in der Hofburg." *Der Tag*, 7 April 1929, 4.

———. "Die Werkbundsiedlung Wien-Lainz, Gesamtplanung Prof. Josef Frank, Wien." *Bauwelt* 23 (16 June 1932): 1–8.

———. "Bildberichte—Ausstellung des Österreichischen Werkbundes in Wien." *Bauwelt* 21 (3 July 1930): 839.

Fabiani, Max. *Regulierung der Stadt Bielitz—Erläuterungsbericht zum General-Regulierungs-Pläne der Stadt Bielitz.* Vienna, 1899.

———. "Karl König. Gedenkrede, gehalten in der Zentralvereinigung der Architekten." *Wiener Bauindustrie Zeitung*, 32, no. 38 (May 1915): 59–61.

Feilendorf, Anni. Letter to author. 30 December 1993.

Feilendorf, Stephanie. Interview by author. New York, 14 July 1987.

———. Interview by author. New York, 15 July 1987.

Feldegg, Ferdinand von. "Maria am Gestade im Gefahr." *Wiener Bauindustrie-Zeitung* 33 (June 1916): 65–68.

Fischel, Hartwig. "Die Ausstellung österreichischer Kunstgewerbe im k.k. österreichischen Museum für Kunst und Industrie." *Kunst und Kunsthandwerk* 14 (1911): 626.

———. "Die Frühjahrsaustellung österreichischer Kunstgewerbe und die k. k. Kunstgewerbeschule im Österreichischen Museum." *Kunst und Kunsthandwerk* 15 (1912): 329–45.

Fischer, Adolf. *Führer durch das Museum für Ostasiatische Kunst der Stadt Cöln.* Cologne: M. Dumont Schauberg, 1913.

Fischer-Wieruszowski, Frieda. "Das Museum für ostasiatische Kunst der Stadt Köln." *Deutsche Kunst und Dekoration* 49 (October 1922): 33–42.

Frank, Philipp. *Modern Science and Its Philosophy.* Cambridge, Mass.: Harvard University Press, 1949.

Frischauer, Stefanie. "Das erste Hochhaus in Wien." *Wasmuths Monatshefte für Baukunst* 13 (1929): 495–97.

Fuchs-Röll, Willi P. "'Neues Wohnen.' Werkbundaustellung in Stuttgart 1927." *Der Neubau* 9 (10 September 1927): 201.

Gábor, László. "Wesentliches über die Werkbundsiedlung." *Neues Wiener Tagblatt*, 18 June 1932, 8.

Ginsburger, Roger. "Was ist modern?" *Die Form* 6, no. 1 (1931): 6–11.

Glaser, Curt. "Ein Museum ostasiatischer Kunst." *Kunst und Künstler* 12 (1913–14): 286–88.

Gräff, Werner, ed. *Innenräume. Räume und Inneneinrichtungsgegenstände aus der Werkbundausstellung "Die Wohnung."* Stuttgart: Dr. Fr. Wedekind & Co., 1928.

Gregor, Joseph. *Rede auf Oskar Strnad.* Vienna: Herbert Reicher, 1936.

Grimme, Karl Maria. "Das neue Heim. Kritischer Führer durch die Werkbundsiedlung in Wien." *Der getreue Eckart* 10 (1932): 65–72.

Gustafson, Philip. "Swedish Modern—A Way of Living." *Country Life* 76 (June 1939): 52–53.

Gustafsson, Sven A. *Liljevalchsutställningen 15 september—14 oktober 1934.* Exhibition catalog. Stockholm, 1934.

Hahn, Hans, Otto Neurath, and Rudolf Carnap. *Wissenschaftliche Weltauffassung. Der Wiener Kreis.* Vienna: Verein Ernst Mach/Artur Wolf, 1929.

Harbers, Guido. "Die Zukunft des Deutschen Werkbundes." *Der Baumeister* 28 supplement (December 1930): B223–24.

———. "'Moderne Linie,' Wohnkultur und Stagnation. Abschliessende Randbemerkungen zur Wiener Werkbundsiedlung." *Der Baumeister* 30 (October 1932): 367–73.

———. "Die Werkbundsiedlung Wien-Lainz." *Bauwelt* 23 (16 June 1932): 593–600.

Hardy, Charles O., assisted by Robert R. Kuczynski. *The Housing Program of the City of Vienna.* Washington, D.C.: Brookings Institution, 1934.

Häring, Hugo. "Wege zur Form." *Die Form* 1 (October 1925): 3–5.

———. "Bemerkungen zum ästhetischen Problem des neuen Bauens." *Bauwelt* 52 (1931): 614–15.

———. "Bemerkungen zur Werkbundsiedlung Wien-Lainz 1932." *Die Form* 7 (15 July 1932): 204–8.

———. "Versuch einer Orientierung." *Die Form* 7 (15 July 1932): 218–23.

———. "Werkbundsiedlung in Wien." *Zentralblatt der Bauverwaltung* 52 (1932): 365–70.

Hegemann, Werner. "Kritisches zu den Wohnbauten der Stadt Wien." *Wasmuths Monatshefte für Baukunst und Städtebau* 10 (1926): 365–66.

Hering, Oswald C. *Concrete and Stucco Houses.* New York: McBridge, Nast & Co., 1912.

Hildebrand, Adolf. *Das Problem der Form in der bildenden Künste.* Strasbourg: Heitz & Mündel, 1893.

Hitchcock, Henry-Russell, Jr., and Philip Johnson. *Modern Architecture.* Exhibition catalog. New York: Museum of Modern Art, 1932.

Hoffmann, Franz. "Kritisches über die Stuttgarter Werkbundsiedlung." *Bauwelt* 41 (1927): 1020.

Holey, Karl. "Karl König, sein Schaffen und seine Persönlichkeit." *Zeitschrift des Österreichischen Ingenieur- und Architekten-Vereins* 68 (January 1916): 1–13.

Huldt, Åke H. "I Warszawa och Praha." *Svenska hem i ord och bilder* 26 (May 1938): vi–vii.

———, ed. *Konsthantverk och hemslöjd i Sverige, 1930–40.* Göteborg: Bokformedlingen, 1941.

Kleiner, Leopold. "Wien." *Wasmuths Monatshefte für Baukunst* 6 (1921): 178.

Koch, Alexander. *Das neue Kunsthandwerk in Deutschland und Österreich*. Darmstadt: Alexander Koch, 1923.

"Konkurrenz für eine Ausstellungshalle." *Der Architekt* 13 (September 1907): 49–52.

Krukowski, Lucian. "Aufbau and Bauhaus: A Cross-realm Comparison." *Journal of Aesthetics and Art Criticism* 50 (summer 1992): 197–209.

Kulka, Heinrich. *Adolf Loos. Das Werk des Architekten*. Vienna: Anton Schroll & Co., 1931.

Le Corbusier. "Défense de l'architecture." *L'architecture d'aujourd'hui* 6, no. 10 (1933): 33–61.

Lehmanns Allgemeiner Wohnungsanzeiger nebst Handels- und Gewerbe-Adreßbuch für die k. u. k. Reichs- Haupt- und Residenzstadt und Umgebung. Vienna, 1870–1910.

Lhota, Karel. "Architekt Adolf Loos." *Architekt SIA* 32, no. 9 (1933): 137–43.

Loos, Adolf. *Trotzdem, 1900–1930*. Innsbruck: Brenner, 1931.

———. "Mein Haus am Michaelerplatz." In *Aufbruch zur Jahrhundertwende: Der Künstlerkreis um Adolf Loos*. Edited by Charlotte Kreuzmayr. *Parnass*, special issue, no. 2. Linz, Austria: C. & E. Grosser, 1985.

———. *Ins Leere gesprochen, 1897–1930*. Paris: Éditions George Crès et Cie, 1921.

Lotz, Wilhelm. "Das ist modern!" *Die Form* 5 (15 September 1930): 494–95.

———. "Die Wiener Werkbundsiedlung." *Die Form* (12 July 1932): 201–4.

Machine-Age Exposition. Edited by Jane Heap. Exhibition catalog. New York: Little Review, 1927.

The Manufacture of Standardized Houses. New York: Standardized Housing Corporation, 1917.

Mayreder, Friedrich. *Zu Karl Königs siebzigstem Geburtstag*. Vienna: Karl König-Komitees, 1912.

———. "Werkbundsiedlung in Wien." *Die Baugilde* 14 (10 June 1932): 541–42.

Mebes, Paul. *Um 1800, Architektur und Handwerk im letzten Jahrhundert ihrer traditionellen Entwicklung*. 2 vols. Munich: F. Bruckmann, 1908.

"Met Housing in Trouble." *Architectural Forum* 79 (September 1943): 112.

Metropolitan Museum of Art. *Decorative Arts from Sweden*. Exhibition catalog. New York: The Museum, 1927.

"Metropolitan Project to House 30,000." *Pencil Points* 24 (May 1943): 19, 23.

Meyer, Hannes, et al. *Bauhaus. Zeitschrift für Gestaltung*. No. 2. Dessau: Bauhaus, 1928.

Meyer, Peter. *Moderne Architektur und Tradition*. Zurich: H. Ginsberger, 1928.

———. "Der Deutsche Werkbund in Wien." *Neue Züricher Zeitung*, 8 July 1930, 4–5.

———. "Der Deutsche Werkbund in Wien." *Das Werk* 17 (August 1930): 249–52.

———. "Die Ziele des Deutschen Werkbundes." *Neue Züricher Zeitung*, 29 October 1930, 1.

———. "Die Stuttgarter Aussprache über die Ziele des Deutschen Werkbundes." *Frankfurter Zeitung*, 30 October 1930, 1–2.

Michel, Wilhelm. "Die Weissenhof-Siedlung–Stuttgart. Erwägungen zur Werkbund-Ausstellung 1927." *Innen-Dekoration* 38 (1927): 440–78.

Morgenstern, Soma. "Die Ausstellung des Österreichischen Werkbundes." *Die Form* 5 (1 July 1930): 329–36.

Müller, Rudolf. "Die Kehrseite des Eigenhauses," *Der Kampf. Sozialdemokratische Monatschrift* 5 (1912): 172.

Muthesius, Hermann. *Das englische Haus: Entwicklung, Bedingungen, Anlage, Aufbau, Einrichtung und Innenraum*. 3 vols. Berlin: Ernst Wasmuth, 1904–5.

———. *Kleinhaus und Kleinsiedlung*. Munich: F. Bruckmann, 1918.

"Neuer Werkbund Österreichs." *Profil* 3 (March 1934): vii.

Neurath, Marie. "Memories of Otto Neurath." In *Empiricism and Sociology*. Edited by Marie Neurath and Robert S. Cohen. Dordrecht and Boston: Reidel, 1973.

Neurath, Otto. *Österreichs Kleingärtner- und Siedlerorganisation*. Vienna: Wiener Volksbuchhandlung, 1923.

———. "Generalarchitekturplan." *Das Kunstblatt* 7 (April 1924): 105–8.

———. "Das Neue Bauhaus in Dessau." *Der Aufbau* 1, nos. 11–12 (1926): 210–11.

———. *Die bunte Welt*. Vienna: Arthur Wolf, 1929.

———. "Das Gesellschafts- und Wirtschaftsmuseum in Wien." *Minerva-Zeitschrift* 7, nos. 9–10 (1931): 153–56.

Neurath, Paul. Interview by author. Vienna, 30 August 1990.

Neurath, Paul, and Elisabeth Nemeth, eds. *Otto Neurath: Oder die Einheit von Wissenschaft und Gesellschaft*. Monographien zur österreichischen Kultur und Geistesgeschichte, 6. Vienna: Böhlau, 1994.

Neutra, Richard. *Wie baut Amerika*. Stuttgart: Julius Hoffmann, 1927.

"Oskar Strnad zum 50. Geburtstag." *Deutsche Kunst und Dekoration* 33 (January 1930): 253–68.

"Oskar Wlach" [obituary]. *New York Times*, 20 August 1963, 33.

Österreichischer Werkbund. Vienna, 1929.

Österreichischer Werkbund. *Werkbundausstellung 1930, Juni bis Oktober*. Exhibition catalog. Vienna: Österreichisches Museum für Kunst und Industrie, 1930.

———. *Werkbundausstellung. Internationale Ausstellung Wien 1932*. Exhibition catalog. Vienna, 1932.

Österreichisches Museum für Kunst und Industrie. *Frühjahrsausstellung österreichischer Kunstgewerbe, verbunden mit einer Ausstellung der k. k. Kunstgewerbeschule Wien, Mai-Juli 1912*. Exhibition catalog. Vienna, 1912.

———. *Kunstschau Wien 1927*. Exhibition catalog. Berlin: Eugen Diehl, 1927.

———. *Wien und die Wiener*. Exhibition catalog. Vienna, 1927.

———. *Wiener Raumkünstler*. Exhibition catalog. Vienna, 1929.

"Parkchester 2 for 194X." *Architectural Forum* 78 (May 1943): 66, 160.

"Philipp Frank" [obituary]. *New York Times*, 23 July 1966, 25.

Planer, Fritz. "Die Ausstellung im Österreichischen Museum für Kunst und Industrie 1912." *Deutsche Kunst und Dekoration* 31 (October 1912): 180, 190–91.

Platz, Gustav Adolf. *Die Baukunst der neuesten Zeit*. Berlin: Propyläen, 1927.

———. *Wohnräume der Gegenwart*. Berlin: Propyläen, 1933.

Plischke, Ernst. Interview by author. Vienna, 25 August 1986.

———. Interview by author. Vienna, 17 November 1986.

———. Interview by author. Vienna, 28 November 1986.

———. *Ein Leben mit Architektur*. Vienna: Löcker, 1989.

Rabén, Hans, ed. *Det moderna hemmet. Inredningskonst i sverige och andra länder*. Stockholm: Natur och Kultur, 1937.

Rares, Paul A. "Siedlungsbauten für Zwerge: Unsachmäßige Bemerkungen zur Werkbund-Wochenschau." *Der Morgen*, 11 July 1932, 6.

Rasch, Heinz, and Bodo Rasch. *Wie Bauen? Bau und Einrichtung der Werkbundsiedlung am Weissenhof in Stuttgart 1927*. Stuttgart: Dr. Fr. Wedekind & Co., 1927.

Riezler, Walter. "Werkbundkrisis?" *Die Form* 6, no. 1 (1931): 1–3.

Rochowanski, Leopold Wolfgang. "Für und Wider der Wohnsachlichkeit." *Deutsche Kunst und Dekoration* 65 (March 1930): 423, 426–30.

———. "Österreich auf der Pariser Ausstellung." *Deutsche Kunst und Dekoration* 58 (October 1925): 69–76.

———. "Wiener Notizen." *Die Form* 5 (1 March 1930): 129–32.

———. "Wiener Wohnungskunst und Kunstgewerbe." *Deutsche Kunst und Dekoration* 65 (March 1930): 417–18.

———, ed. *Ein Führer durch das österreichische Kunstgewerbe.* Leipzig, Vienna, and Troppau: Heinz, 1930.

Roessler, Arthur. "Kunstschau, Kunstgewerbeschule, Wiener Werkstätte und Österreichischer Werkbund." *Die Wage* 2 (2 October 1920): 15.

Sartoris, Alberto. *Gli elementi dell' architettura funzionale.* Milan: Hoepli, 1935.

Schmarsow, August. *Unser Verhältnis zu den Bildenden Künsten: Sechs Vorträge über Kunst und Erziehung.* Leipzig: B. G. Teubner, 1903.

———. *Grundbegriffe der Kunstwissenschaft.* Leipzig: B. G. Teubner, 1905.

Schulte, Julius August, Eduard Eberhard Thumb, and Oskar Wlach, eds. *Wiener Türmer. Ein Almanach auf das Jahr 1904.* Vienna: Akademischer Verein Konkurrenz-Klub, 1904.

Schultze-Naumburg, Paul. *Kunst und Rasse.* Munich, 1928.

———. *Das Gesicht des deutschen Hauses.* Munich, 1929.

———. "Müssen wir in Zukunft in asiatischen Häusern wohnen?" *Das neue Deutschland* 1 (1931): 88–91.

Schürer, Oskar. "Zur Ehrenrettung des Begriffs 'modern.'" *Deutsche Kunst und Dekoration* 67 (December 1930): 165.

Scott, M. H. Baillie. *Houses and Gardens.* London: George Newnes, Ltd., 1906. Translated by Wilhelm Schölermann as *Häuser und Gärten* (Berlin: E. Wasmuth, 1912).

Sitte, Camillo. *Der Städtebau nach seinen künstlerischen Grundsätzen: Ein Beitrag zur Lösung moderner Fragen der Architektur und monumentalen Plastik unter besonderer Beziehung auf Wien.* 5th ed. Vienna: Karl Graeser, 1922. Translated by George Rosenborough Collins and Christiane Crasemann Collins as *The Birth of Modern City Planning* (New York: Rizzoli, 1986).

Skawonius, Sven Erik. "Svenskt Tenn 25 år." *Form* 45 (1949): 164–65.

Smith, H. Llewellyn. *Report on the Present Position and Tendencies of the Industrial Arts As Indicated at the International Exhibition of Modern Decorative and Industrial Arts, Paris, 1925.* London: Department of Oversees Trade, 1927.

Sobotka, Walter. "Principles of Design." MS 368. Sobotka Papers, Avery Library, Columbia University, New York.

"Solesand." *Decorative Art: The Studio Yearbook.* London: The Studio, 1938, 20.

Stavenow, Åke, et al., eds. *Swedish Arts and Crafts. Swedish Modern—A Movement toward Sanity in Design.* New York: Royal Swedish Commission, New York World's Fair, 1939.

Stockholms utställningen 1930 av konstindustri, konsthantverk och hemslöjd. Exhibition catalog. Uppsala: Almqvist & Wiksells, 1930.

Storey, Walter Rendell. "Home Decoration: A World of Furniture at the Fair." *New York Times,* 4 June 1939, 2, 8.

Strnad, Oskar. "Einiges Theoretische zur Raumgestaltung." *Deutsche Kunst und Dekoration* 41 (October 1917): 39–40, 49–50, 62,

65–68. Reprinted as "Raumgestaltung und Raumgelenke," *Innen-Dekoration* 30 (July–August 1919): 254–58, 292–93.

———. "Neue Wege in der Wohnraum-Einrichtung." *Innen-Dekoration* 33 (October 1922): 323–24.

Strömberg, Martin. "Swedish Modern: Svensk lösen i New York." *Svenska hem i ord och bilder* 27 (April 1939): 89–93.

"Stuyvesant Saga." *Architectural Forum* 79 (July 1943): 40–41.

"Stuyvesant Town." *NAHO News* 6 (16 July 1943): 61.

"Stuyvesant Town: Borough of Manhattan, New York City." *Architect and Engineer* 174 (August 1948): 27–29.

"Stuyvesant Town: A Commercial Housing Development, New York." *Builder* 173 (21 November 1947): 572–73.

"Stuyvesant Town: Metropolitan's Newest Housing Giant Is Nearing Completion Despite Material and Labor Shortages." *Architectural Forum* 86 (April 1947): 74–75.

"Stuyvesant Town: Rebuilding a Blighted City Area." *Engineering News Record* 140 (5 February 1948): 73–96.

Taut, Bruno. *Modern Architecture.* London: The Studio, 1929.

Tessenow, Heinrich. *Die Wohnhausbau.* Munich: G. D. W. Callwey, 1909.

"They Live in Stuyvesant Town." *House and Garden* 94 (September 1948): 118–21.

Tietze, Hans. "Die Wiener Kunstschau, die Wiener Werkstätte und der Österreichische Werkbund." *Kunstchronik und Kunstmarkt* 54, no. 46 (1920): 892.

Vetter, Hans, ed. *Kleine Einfamilienhäuser mit 50 bis 100 Quadratmeter Wohnfläche.* Vienna: Anton Schroll, 1932.

Verein Ernst Mach. *Wissenschaftliche Weltauffassung. Der Wiener Kreis.* Vienna: Artur Wolf, 1929.

"Der Werkbund tagt in Wien." *Bauwelt* 21 (3 July 1930): 838.

Wiener Kunstgewerbeverein. *Katalog der Jubiläumsausstellung.* Exhibition catalog. Vienna, 1924.

Wasmuth, Günther, and Leo Adler, eds. *Wasmuths Lexikon der Baukunst.* 5 vols. Berlin: E. Wasmuth, 1927–37.

Wedepohl, Edgar. "Die Weissenhofsiedlung der Werkbundausstellung 'Die Wohnung' Stuttgart 1927." *Wasmuths Monatshefte für Baukunst* 11 (1927): 397–98.

"We Give You Liveable Modern—and It's Called 'Swedish Modern.'" *American Home* 20 (October 1938): 12–13, 74.

Werkbundausstellung 1930. Juni bis Oktober. Exhibition catalog. Vienna: Österreichischer Werkbund, 1930.

Westheim, Paul. "Architektur-Entwicklung." *Die Glocke* 10 (1924): 181–85.

Wlach, Oskar. "Einheit und Lebendigkeit." *Innen-Dekoration* 33 (January–February 1922): 59–65.

Die Wohnungsreform. Offizielles Organ des österreichischen Verbands für Wohnungsreform. Vienna, 1929–31.

Wolfer, Oskar. "Die Werkbundausstellung 'Die Wohnung' in Stuttgart." *Die Kunst* 58, *Angewandte Kunst* (October 1927): 33–45.

"Die Ziele des Deutschen Werkbundes." *Die Form* 5 (1930): 612–14.

Zeitler, Julius. "Die Werkbundausstellung 'Die Wohnung' in Stuttgart." *Dekorative Kunst* 31 (1927–28): 34–35.

Zweig, Stefan. *Die Welt von Gestern. Erinnerungen eines Europäers.* London: H. Hamilton, 1941. Translated as *The World of Yesterday: An Autobiography.* New York: Viking Press, 1943.

SECONDARY LITERATURE

Achleitner, Friedrich. "Der Österreichische Werkbund und seine Beziehung zum Deutschen Werkbund." In *Der Werkbund in Deutschland, Österreich und der Schweiz*. Edited by Lucius Burkhardt, 102–13. Stuttgart: Deutsche Verlags-Anstalt, 1978.

———. "Viennese Architecture between the Wars: First Split between the Form and Content of Modernity." *Lotus International* 29 (1981): 117–27.

———. "Wiener Architektur der Zwischenkriegszeit: Kontinuität, Irritation, Resignation." In *Das geistige Leben Wiens in der Zwischenkriegszeit*. Edited by Peter Heintel, Norbert Leser, Gerald Stourzh, and Adam Wandruszka, 277–94. Vienna: Österreichischer Bundesverlag, 1981.

———. ". . . sondern der Zukunft." In *Bauhaus in Wien: Franz Singer/Friedl Decker*. Edited by Georg Schrom and Stefanie Trautmannsdorff, 6. Vienna: Hochschule für angewandte Kunst, 1988.

Ackerl, Isabella, and Rudolf Neck, eds. *Geistiges Leben im Österreich der Ersten Republik*. Vienna: Geschichte und Politik, 1986.

Ahlin, Janne. *Sigurd Lewerentz, Architect, 1885–1975*. Cambridge, Mass.: MIT Press, 1987.

Allmeyer-Beck, Renate, Susanne Baumgartner-Haindl, Marion Lindner-Gross, and Christine Zwingl, eds. *Margarete Schütte-Lihotzky: Soziale Architektur, Zeitzeugin eines Jahrhunderts*. Vienna: Böhlau, 1996.

Alofsin, Anthony. *Frank Lloyd Wright, The Lost Years, 1910–1922: A Study of Influence*. Chicago and London: University of Chicago Press, 1993.

Ausstellung Trude Waehner: Zeichnungen und Aquarelle. Exhibition catalog. Vienna: Österreichische Kulturvereinigung, 1966.

Berg, G. A. "Swedish Modern." *Form* 34, no. 7 (1938): 162–68.

———. "What Swedish Modern Is in Sweden." *American Home* 22 (July 1939): 22.

Bergström, I. "Pewter: A Swedish Revival. New Applications by the Firma Svenskt Tenn." *Studio* 111 (February 1936): 97–99.

Bernstein, Jeremy. *The Life It Brings: One Physicist's Beginnings*. New York: Ticknor & Fields, 1987.

Bittner, Josef. *Neubauten der Stadt Wien*. 2 vols. Die Quelle, 14. Vienna and New York: Gerlach & Wiedling, 1926–30.

Björkman, Gunvor. "Svenskt på Golden Gate." *Svenska hem i ord och bilder* 27 (February 1939): 34–40.

Björkman-Goldschmidt, Elsa. *Vad sedan hände*. Stockholm: Norstedts, 1964.

Blau, Eve. *The Architecture of Red Vienna, 1919–1934*. Cambridge, Mass.: MIT Press, 1999.

Blundell Jones, Peter. "Scharoun, Häring and Organic Functionalism." *Architecture Association Quarterly* 5 (January 1973): 48–57.

———. "Organic versus Classic." *Architecture Association Quarterly* 10 (January 1978): 10–20.

———. *Hans Scharoun*. London: Phaidon, 1995.

——— *Hugo Häring: The Organic versus the Geometric*. Stuttgart and London: Edition Axel Menges, 1999.

Boeckl, Matthias. "Die Mode-Moderne mit dem fabriciertem Stimmungs-Dusel." In *Die verlorene Moderne: Der Künstlerbund Hagen, 1900–1938*. Edited by Günter Natter. Exhibition catalog. Vienna: Österreichische Galerie, 1993.

———, ed. *Visionäre und Vertriebene: Österreichische Spuren in der modernen amerikanischen Architektur*. Berlin: Ernst & Sohn, 1995.

Boman, Monica, ed. *Estrid Ericson: Founder of Svenskt Tenn*. Translated by Roger G. Tanner.

Stockholm: Carlsson, 1989. Originally published as *Estrid Ericson—Orkidé i vinterlandet* (Stockholm: Carlsson Bokförlag, 1989).

Burkhardt, Lucius, ed. *Der Werkbund in Deutschland, Österreich und der Schweiz.* Stuttgart: Deutsche Verlags-Anstalt, 1978.

Bürkle, J. Christoph. *Hans Scharoun und die Moderne: Ideen, Projekte, Theaterbau.* Frankfurt am Main: Campus, 1986.

———. *Hans Scharoun.* Artemis: Zurich, 1993.

Campbell, Joan. *The German Werkbund: The Politics of Reform in the Applied Arts.* Princeton: Princeton University Press, 1978.

Caro, Robert. *The Power Broker: Robert Moses and the Fall of New York.* New York: Knopf, 1974.

Ciucci, Giorgio. "The Invention of the Modern Movement." *Oppositions* 24 (spring 1981): 68–91.

Cleary, Richard. *Merchant Prince and Master Builder: Edgar J. Kaufmann and Frank Lloyd Wright.* Exhibition catalog. Pittsburgh: Heinz Architectural Center, Carnegie Museum of Art, in association with University of Washington (Seattle) Press, 1999.

Colomina, Beatriz. "Intimacy and Spectacle: The Interiors of Adolf Loos." *AA Files* 20 (fall 1990): 5–15.

———. "The Split Wall: Domestic Voyeurism." In *Sexuality and Space.* Edited by Beatriz Colomina, 73–80. New York: Princeton Architectural Press, 1992.

Doesburg, Théo van. *On European Architecture. Complete Essays from Het Bouwbedrijf, 1924–1931.* Translated by Charlotte I. Loeb and Arthur L. Loeb. Basel and Boston: Birkhäuser, 1990.

Donnelly, Marion C. *Architecture in the Scandinavian Countries.* Cambridge, Mass.: MIT Press, 1992.

Dimitriou, Sokratis. "Zwischen Kunst und Politik. Gedanken zum Österreichischen Werkbund." *Bauforum* 10, no. 61 (1977): 12.

Dreibholz, Wolfdieter. "Die Internationale Werkbundsiedlung, Wien 1932." *Bauforum* 10, no. 61 (1977): 19–22.

Eriksson, Monika. "A Time for Pewter." In *Estrid Ericson: Founder of Svenskt Tenn.* Edited by Monica Boman. Translated by Roger G. Tanner. Stockholm: Carlsson, 1989.

Fanelli, Giovanni, and Ezio Godoli. *La Vienna di Hoffmann, architetto della qualità.* Rome and Bari: Laterza, 1981.

Fisher, Thomas. "Low Cost, High Design." *Progressive Architecture* 10 (October 1988): 98–109.

Förster, Wolfgang. "Die Wiener Arbeitersiedlungsbewegung vor dem Zweiten Weltkrieg—Eine Alternative zum kommunalen Wohnbauprogram." *Der Aufbau* 35, no. 12 (1980): 405–10.

Forsthuber, Sabine. *Moderne Raumkunst: Wiener Ausstellungsbauten von 1898 bis 1914.* Vienna: Picus, 1991.

Frampton, Kenneth. "Stockholm 1930: Asplund and the Legacy of the Funkis." In *Asplund.* Edited by Claes Caldenby and Olof Hultin. New York: Rizzoli, 1986.

Frank, Philipp. *Modern Science and Its Philosophy.* Cambridge, Mass.: Harvard University Press, 1949.

Gay, Peter, *Weimar Culture: The Insider as Outsider.* New York: Harper & Row, 1970.

Galison, Peter. "Aufbau/Bauhaus: Logical Positivism and Architectural Modernism." *Critical Inquiry* 16 (summer 1990): 709–52.

Gmeiner, Astrid, and Gottfried Pirhofer, eds. *Der Österreichische Werkbund: Alternative zur klassischen Moderne in Architektur, Raum- und Produktgestaltung.* Salzburg: Residenz, 1985.

Gruber, Helmut. *Red Vienna: Experiment in Working-Class Culture, 1919–1934.* New York: Oxford University Press, 1991.

Gubler, Jacques. *Nationalisme et internationalisme dans l'architecture moderne de la Suisse.* Lausanne: L'Age d'Homme, 1975.

Haiko, Peter, and Mara Reissberger, "Die Wohnhausbauten der Gemeinde Wien 1919–1934." *Architese* 12 (1974): 49–54.

Haller, Rudolf. "Der erste Wiener Kreis." In Haller, *Fragen zu Wittgenstein und Aufsätze zur österreichischen Philosophie*. Amsterdam: Rodopi, 1986, 89–107.

———. *Fragen zu Wittgenstein und Aufsätze zur österreichischen Philosophie*. Amsterdam: Rodopi, 1986.

Haller, Rudolf, and Robin Kinross, eds. *Gesammelte bildpädagogische Schriften, Otto Neurath*. Band 3. Vienna: Hölder-Pichler-Tempsky, 1991.

Hautmann, Hans, and Rudolf Hautmann. *Die Gemeindebauten des Roten Wien, 1919–1934*. Vienna: Schönbrunn, 1980.

Hodin, J. P. *Oskar Kokoschka: The Artist and His Time. A Biographical Study*. London: Cory, Adams & Mackay, 1966.

Holton, Gerald. "Ernst Mach and the Fortunes of Positivism in America." *Isis* 83 (1992): 27–60.

Hoffmann, Robert. "Entproletarisierung durch Siedung? Die Siedlungbewegung in Österreich 1918 bis 1938." In *Bewegung und Klasse. Studien zur österreichischen Arbeitergeschichte*. Edited by Gerhard Botz et al., 713–42. Vienna, Munich, and Zurich: Europa, 1978.

———. *Nimm Hack' und Spaten—: Siedlung und Siedlerbewegung in Österreich, 1918–1938*. Vienna: Gesellschaftskritik, 1987.

Holton, Gerald, and Robert S. Cohen. "Philipp Frank." In *Dictionary of Scientific Biography*. Edited by Charles C. Gillispie 5: 122–23. New York: Charles Scribner's Sons, 1972.

Hufnagl, Viktor, ed. *Reflexionen und Aphorismen zur österreichischen Architektur*. Vienna: Georg Prachner, 1984.

Huldt, Åke H., ed. *Konsthantverk och hemslöjd i Sverige, 1930–1940*. Göteborg: Bokförmedlingen, 1941.

———. *Mellan funkis och framtid: Svensk Form 1930–80*. Stockholm: Svensk Form, 1980.

International Biographical Dictionary of Central European Émigrés, 1933–1945. Edited by Herbert A. Strauss et al. 3 vols. Munich: K. G. Saur, 1980–83.

Itten, Johannes. *Design and Form: The Basic Course at the Bauhaus*. London: Thames and Hudson, 1964.

Joedicke, Jürgen. *Architektur der Zukunft der Architektur*. Stuttgart: Universität Stuttgart, 1980.

———, ed. *Das andere Bauen: Gedanken und Zeichnungen von Hugo Häring*. Stuttgart: Karl Krämer, 1982.

Joedicke, Jürgen, and Heinrich Lauterbach, eds. *Hugo Häring: Schriften, Entwürfe, Bauten*. Stuttgart: Karl Krämer, 1965.

Johnston, William M. *The Austrian Mind: An Intellectual and Social History, 1848–1938*. Berkeley, Los Angeles, and London: University of California Press, 1972.

Junghanns, Kurt. *Das Haus für Alle: Zur Geschichte der Vorfertigung in Deutschland*. Berlin: Ernst & Sohn, 1994.

Kallir, Jane. *Viennese Design and the Wiener Werkstätte*. New York: George Braziller, 1986.

"Karl König." In *Allgemeines Lexikon der bildenden Künstler von der Antike bis zur Gegenwart*. Edited by Ulrich Thieme and Felix Becker. Vol. 21. Leipzig: E. A. Seemann, 1935: 157–58.

Kirsch, Karin. "Weissenhofsiedlung Stuttgart 1927." *Arquitectura* 70 (May–August 1989]): 51–73.

———, ed. *Briefe zur Weißenhofsiedlung*. Stuttgart: Deutsche Verlags-Anstalt, 1997.

———, and Gerhard Kirsch. *Die Weissenhofsiedlung: Werkbund-Ausstellung "Die Woh-*

nung" Stuttgart 1927. Stuttgart: Deutsche Verlags-Anstalt, 1987.

Kirschenmann, Jörg C., and Eberhard Syring. *Hans Scharoun: Die Forderung des Unvollendeten*. Stuttgart: Deutsche Verlags-Anstalt, 1993.

Kodré, Helfried. "Die Entwicklung des Wiener sozialen Wohnungsbaues in den Jahren 1919–1938." *Der Aufbau* 19 (September 1964): 343–50.

Kinross, Robin. "Otto Neurath et la communication visuelle." In *Le Cercle de Vienne, doctrines et controverses*. Edited by Jean Sebestik and Antonia Soulez, 271–78. Paris: Klincksieck, 1986.

Kremer, Sabine. *Hugo Häring (1882–1958)—Wohnungsbau: Theorie und Praxis*. Stuttgart: Karl Krämer, 1984.

Krischanitz, Adolf, and Otto Kapfinger. *Die Wiener Werkbundsiedlung. Dokumentation einer Erneuerung*. Vienna: Compress, 1985.

Krinsky, Carol Herselle. *Synagogues of Europe: Architecture, History, Meaning*. New York: Architectural History Foundation and Cambridge, Mass.: MIT Press, 1985.

Kristan, Markus. *Carl König, 1841–1915: Ein neubarocker Großstadtarchitekt in Wien*. Exhibition catalog. Vienna: Jüdisches Museum der Stadt Wien, 1999.

———. *Joseph Urban: Die Wiener Jahre des Jugendstilarchitekten und Illustrators, 1872–1911*. Vienna: Böhlau, 2000.

Kühn, Christian. *Das Schöne, das Wahre und das Richtige: Adolf Loos und das Haus Müller in Prag*. Braunschweig and Wiesbaden: Friedr. Vieweg & Sohn, 1989.

Kurrent, Friedrich, and Johannes Spalt. "Österreichische Wohnhäuser der dreissiger Jahre." *Der Aufbau* 19 (November–December 1964): 439–44.

Lane, Barbara Miller. *Architecture and Politics in Germany, 1918–1945*. Cambridge, Mass: Harvard University Press, 1968.

Lauterbach, Heinrich, and Jürgen Joedicke, eds. *Hugo Häring: Schriften, Entwürfe, Bauten*. Stuttgart and Bern: Karl Krämer, 1965.

Levetus, Amelia S. "The Austrian Werkbund Exhibition in Vienna." *American Magazine of Art* 21 (October 1930): 581–87.

Long, Christopher. "*Wiener Wohnkultur*: Interior Design in Vienna, 1910–1938." *Studies in the Decorative Arts* 5 (fall–winter 1997–98): 29–51.

———. "'A Symptom of the Werkbund': The Spring 1912 Exhibition at the Austrian Museum of Art and Industry, Vienna." *Studies in the Decorative Arts* 7 (spring–summer 2000): 91–121.

———. "An Alternative Path to Modernism: Carl König and Architectural Education at the Vienna Technische Hochschule, 1890–1913." *Journal of Architectural Education* 55 (Sept. 2001): 21–30.

McFadden, David, ed. *Scandinavian Modern Design, 1880–1980*. New York: Harry N. Abrams, 1982.

Mallgrave, Harry Francis, and Eleftherios Ikonomou, eds. *Empathy, Form, and Space: Problems in German Aesthetics, 1873–1893*. Santa Monica, Calif.: Getty Center for the History of Art and the Humanities, 1994.

Mang, Karl, and Eva Mang-Frimmel, eds. *Kommunaler Wohnbau in Wien: Aufbruch 1923–1934 Ausstrahlung*. Vienna: Presse- und Informationsdienst der Stadt Wien, 1977.

Morvánszky, Ákos. *Die Erneuerung der Baukunst. Wege zur Moderne in Mitteleuropa 1900–1940*. Salzburg and Vienna: Residenz, 1988.

Mumford, Eric. *The CIAM Discourse on Urbanism, 1928–1960.* Cambridge, Mass., and London: MIT Press, 2000.

Mundt, Ernest K. "Three Aspects of German Aesthetic Theory." *Journal of Aesthetics and Art Criticism* 17 (March 1959): 287–310.

Naylor, Gillian. "Swedish Grace . . . or the Acceptable Face of Modernism?" In *Modernism in Design.* Edited by Peter Greenhalgh, 164–83. London: Reaktion, 1990.

Nemeth, Elisabeth, and Friedrich Stadler, eds. *Encyclopedia and Utopia: The Life and Work of Otto Neurath, 1882–1945.* Dordrecht and Boston: Kluwer, 1996.

Nerdinger, Winfried, ed. *Tel Aviv Modern Architecture, 1930–1939.* Tübingen: Wasmuth, 1994.

Neumann, Dietrich. *Die Wolkenkratzer kommen: Deutsche Hochhäuser der Zwanziger Jahre.* Wiesbaden: Vieweg, 1995.

Neurath, Marie, and Robert S. Cohen, eds. *Empiricism and Sociology.* Dordrecht and Boston: Reidel, 1973.

Niedermoser, Otto. *Oskar Strnad, 1879–1935.* Vienna: Bergland, 1935.

Novy, Klaus. "Selbsthilfe als Reformbewegung: Der Kampf der Wiener Siedler nach dem 1. Weltkrieg." *Arch+* 55 (February 1981): 26–40.

Novy, Klaus, and Wolfgang Förster. *Einfach bauen, Genossenschaftliche Selbsthilfe nach der Jahrhundertwende: Zur Rekonstruktion der Wiener Siedlerbewegung.* Vienna: Verein für moderne Kommunalpolitik, 1991.

Novy, Klaus, and Günther Uhlig. *Die Wiener Siedlungsbewegung, 1918–1934.* Cologne: Arch+, 1982.

Nyberg, Bernt, Olof Hultin, and Sylvia Johnsson, eds. *Aufbruch und Krise des Funktionalismus: Bauen und Wohnen in Schweden, 1930–80.* Stockholm: Sveriges arkitekturmuseum, 1976.

Oechslin, Werner. "*Raumplan* versus *Plan libre.*" *Daidalos* (December 1991): 76–83.

Olsen, Donald. *The City as a Work of Art: London, Paris, Vienna.* New Haven and London: Yale University Press, 1986.

Ottillinger, Eva B. *Adolf Loos: Wohnkonzepte und Möbelentwürfe.* Salzburg and Vienna: Residenz, 1994.

Patka, Erika, ed. *Kunst—Anspruch und Gegenstand: Von der Kunstgewerbeschule zur Hochschule für angewandte Kunst in Wien 1918-1991.* Vienna and Salzburg: Residenz, 1991.

Pfankuch, Peter, ed. *Hans Scharoun: Bauten, Entwürfe, Texte.* Berlin: Akademie der Künste, 1974.

Pommer, Richard, and Christian F. Otto. *Weissenhof 1927 and the Modern Movement in Architecture.* Chicago and London: University of Chicago Press, 1991.

Posch, Wilfried. "Die Gartenstadtbewegung in Wien." *Bauforum* [Vienna] 13, nos. 77–78 (1980): 9–24.

———. *Die Wiener Gartenstadtbewegung: Reformversuch zwischen erster und zweiter Gründerzeit.* Vienna: Tusch-Urbanistica, 1981.

———. "Die Österreichische Werkbundbewegung, 1907–1912." In *Geistiges Leben im Österreich der Ersten Republik.* Edited by Isabella Ackerl and Rudolf Neck, 279–312. Vienna: Verlag für Geschichte und Politik, 1986.

Posener, Julius. "Adolf Loos-Der Raumplan." *Arch+* 53 (1980): 36–40.

———, ed. *Adolf Loos, 1870–1933: Ein Vortrag.* Berlin: Akademie der Künste, 1984.

Pozzetto, Marco. *Max Fabiani: Ein Architekt der Monarchie.* Vienna: Edition Tusch, 1983.

———. "Karl König und die Architektur der Wiener Technischen Hochschule." In *Wien um 1900: Kunst und Kultur.* Edited by Maria Auböck and Maria Marchetti, 305–6. Exhibition catalog. Vienna: Christian Brandstätter, 1985.

———. *Max Fabiani*. Trieste: MGS Press, 1998.

Prokop, Ursula. *Wien, Aufbruch zur Metropole: Geschäfts- und Wohnhäuser der Innenstadt 1910 bis 1914*. Vienna: Böhlau, 1994.

Risselada, Max, ed. *Raumplan Versus Plan Libre: Adolf Loos and Le Corbusier, 1919–1930*. New York: Rizzoli, 1988.

Rudberg, Eva. *Uno Åhrén: En föregångsman inom 1900-talets arkitektur och samhällsplanering*. Stockholm: Byggsforskningsrådet, 1981.

———. "Early Functionalism." In *20th-Century Sweden*. Edited by Claes Caldenby, Jöran Lindvall, and Wilfried Wang, 81–109. Munich and New York: Prestel, 1998.

———. *The 1930 Stockholm Exhibition: Modernism's Breakthrough in Swedish Architecture*. Stockholm: Stockholmia, 1999.

Rüegg, Arthur, and Adolph Stiller. *Sechs Häuser: Nach Aufnahmen korrigierte Grundrisse der Wohngeschosse sechs bedeutender Häuser der Moderne im Dreieck Prag-Leipzig-Wien*. Zurich: Eidgenössiche Technische Hochschule, 1992.

Rukschcio, Burkhardt, and Roland L. Schachel. *Adolf Loos: Leben und Werk*. Salzburg and Vienna: Residenz, 1982.

Rutkoff, Peter M., and William B. Scott. *New School: A History of the New School for Social Research*. New York: Free Press, 1986.

Sarnitz, August. *Ernst Lichtblau, Architekt, 1883–1963*. Vienna, Cologne, and Weimar: Böhlau, 1994.

Schorske, Carl E. *Fin-de-siècle Vienna: Politics and Culture*. New York: Knopf, 1980.

Schwarzer, Mitchell W. "The Emergence of Architectural Space: August Schmarsow's Theory of *Raumgestaltung*." *Assemblage* 15 (August 1991): 48–61.

Schweiger, Werner J. *Wiener Werkstätte: Design in Vienna, 1903–1932*. New York: Abbeville Press, 1984.

Scully, Vincent, Jr. *Modern Architecture: The Architecture of Democracy*. Revised edition. New York: George Braziller, 1982.

Sekler, Eduard F. "The Architectural Reaction in Austria." *Journal of the Society of Architectural Historians* 24 (March 1965): 67–70.

———. *Josef Hoffmann: The Architectural Work*. Princeton: Princeton University Press, 1985.

Snodin, Michael, and Elisabet Stavenow-Hidemark, eds. *Carl and Karin Larsson: Creators of the Swedish Style*. Boston: Little, Brown and Company, 1997.

Sommer, Herbert, ed. *Heinrich Tessenow*. Vienna: Hochschule für angewandte Kunst, 1976.

Spalt, Johannes, ed. *Der Architekt Oskar Strnad. Zum hundertsten Geburtstag am 26. Oktober 1979*. Vienna: Hochschule für angewandte Kunst, 1979.

Sparke, Penny. "Fashion of the Fifties: The Emergence of 'Swedish Modern.'" *Industrial Design* 29 (May–June 1982): 35–37.

———. *Furniture: Twentieth-Century Design*. New York: E. P. Dutton, 1986.

Stadler, Friedrich. *Studien zum Wiener Kreis: Ursprung, Entwicklung und Wirkung des Logischen Empirismus im Kontext*. Frankfurt am Main: Suhrkamp, 1997.

———, ed. *Arbeiterbildung in der Zwischenkriegszeit: Otto Neurath-Gerd Arntz*. Vienna: Löcker, 1982.

Steinmann, Martin, ed. *CIAM: Dokumente 1928–1939*. Basel and Stuttgart: Birkhäuser, 1979.

Sterk, Harald. *Industrie Kultur in Österreich. Der Wandel in Architektur, Kunst und Gesellschaft im Fabrikszeitalter, 1873–1950*. 4 vols. Vienna and Munich: Christian Brandstätter, 1984–87.

Szekely, Gustav. *Aus dem Leben der Malerin Trude Waehner berichtet von ihren Sohn.* Vienna: Löcker, 2000.

Tabor, Jan. "Der unsichere Boden der Tradition." *Wien aktuell* 89 (October 1984): 23–25.

———. "Die erneuerte Vision. Die Wiener Werkbundsiedlung, 1932–1984." In *Reflexionen und Aphorismen zur österreichischen Architektur.* Edited by Viktor Hufnagl, 346–52. Vienna: Georg Prachner, 1984.

Tafuri, Manfredo, ed. *Vienna Rossa: La politica residenziale nella Vienna socialista, 1919–1923.* Milan: Electa Editrice, 1980.

Tegethoff, Wolf. "Weißenhof 1927: Der Sieg des neuen Bauens?" In *Jahrbuch des Zentralinstituts für Kunstgeschichte,* 3: 195–228. Munich: C. H. Beck, 1987.

Troy, Nancy J. *Modernism and the Decorative Arts in France: Art Nouveau to Le Corbusier.* New Haven and London: Yale University Press, 1991.

Trude Waehner. Exhibition catalog. Ravenna: Galleria Bottega, 1971.

Ullmann, Ernst. "Der Beitrag August Schmarsows zur Architekturtheorie." Unpublished Habilitationsschrift, Institut für Kunstgeschichte und Kunsterziehung, Universität Leipzig, 1967.

Ungers, Liselotte. *Die Suche nach einer neuen Wohnform: Siedlungen der zwanziger Jahre damals und heute.* Stuttgart: Deutsche Verlags-Anstalt, 1983.

———. "Werkbund Siedlung, 1932." *Arquitectura* 70 (May–August 1989): 74–87.

van Duzer, Leslie, and Kent Kleinman. *Villa Müller: A Work of Adolf Loos.* New York: Princeton Architectural Press, 1994.

Venturi, Robert. *Complexity and Contradiction in Architecture.* 2d. ed. New York: Museum of Modern Art, 1977.

Völker, Angela. *Textiles of the Wiener Werkstätte, 1910–1932.* London: Thames and Hudson, 1994.

Wagemann, Ines. *Der Architekt Bruno Möhring, 1863–1929.* Witterschlick: M. Wehle, 1992.

Wagner-Rieger, Renate. "Karl König." In *Österreichisches Biographisches Lexikon, 1815–1950,* 36–37. Vienna: Böhlau, 1969.

Wängberg-Eriksson, Kristina. *Svenskt Tenn—A Short Account of Its History.* Stockholm: Svenskt Tenn, n.d.

Weich, Ulla. "Die theoretischen Ansichten des Architekten und Lehrers Oskar Strnad." M.A. thesis, Universität Wien, 1995.

Weihsmann, Helmut. *Das rote Wien: Sozialdemokratische Architektur und Kommunalpolitik, 1919–1934.* Vienna: Promedia, 1985.

Wendschuh, Achim, ed. *Hans Scharoun: Zeichnungen, Aquarelle, Texte.* Berlin: Akademie der Künste, 1993.

Wickman, Kerstin. "Homes." In *20th-Century Sweden.* Edited by Claes Caldenby, Jöran Lindvall, and Wilfried Wang, 199–207. Munich and New York: Prestel, 1998.

Wiesner, Ulrich. *Museum für Ostasiatische Kunst Köln. Zum 75jährigen Jubiläum des Museums.* Cologne: Museum für Ostasiatische Kunst der Stadt Köln, 1984.

Wilson, Colin St. John. *The Other Tradition of Modern Arhcitecture: The Uncompleted Project.* London: Academy, 1995.

Witt-Dörring, Christian, Eva Mang, and Karl Mang, eds. *Neues Wohnen. Wiener Innenraumgestaltung, 1918–1938.* Exhibition catalog. Vienna: Österreichisches Museum für angewandte Kunst, 1980.

Worbs, Dietrich. "Der Raumplan in der Architektur von Adolf Loos." Ph.D. diss., Technische Universität Stuttgart, 1981.

————, ed. *Adolf Loos, 1870–1933: Raumplan—Wohnungsbau.* Exhibition catalog. Berlin: Akademie der Künste, 1983.

Zucker, Paul. "The Paradox of Architectural Theories at the Beginning of the Modern Movement." *Journal of the Society of Architectural Historians* 10 (October 1951): 8–14.

INDEX (References to figures are indicated by *f.*)

ence, 40; modernism, 87; Paris *Exposition Internationale*, 1937, 213; Primavesi Country House, 31; Secession movement, 7; support for Frank, 23, 27, 50; textile design, 98; urban development plan, 75; Vienna Werkbundsiedlung exhibition, 179, 182; Wiener Werkstätte, 187–89; *Wien und die Wiener* exhibition, 167; Winarsky-Hof, 76

Hoffmann, Karl, 95

Holzmeister, Clemens, 121, 179, 189–90

Hoppe, Emil, 295n30

Horner House, 12, 39

Horney, Karen, 222

Hotel project, 254, 254f

House and Garden, 230

"The House as Path and Place" (Frank), 158–62, 206, 223. *See also* architectural promenade

House Beautiful, 230

House for four persons, 184, 185f

House for Vienna XIII, 130, 132f, 133, 134

House for Vienna XIX, 290n17

Houses and Gardens (Scott), 33, 133

housing blocks, 74–84, 103, 166–86; Bürgerversorgungshaus, 170–72, 170–72f; Leopoldine-Glöckel-Hof housing project, 174–75, 174f; Linz apartment project, 177, 178f; New York City slum clearance projects, 226–28, 226–28f; Reichsforschungssiedlung competition, 172–73, 173f; Sebastian-Kelch-Gasse housing block, 168–70, 169–70f; Simmeringer Hauptstraße housing project, 175–76, 175f; vs. single-family housing, 74, 82–84

housing cooperatives. *See* Siedlerverband

Howard, Ebenezer, 240, 241f

H. R. S. House. *See* S. H. B. House

Huldt, Åke, 303n47

Hundertwasser, Friedrich, 254

IKEA, 307n5

industrialization, 15; Austrian Werkbund disputes, 187–88; furniture production, 87–88; Le Corbusier, 94; radical left, 122–23; use of concrete, 52–54, 53f; Winarsky-

Hof, 76

Innen-Dekoration, 34, 71, 278n32

interior design, 156; American, 230; Bunzl House, 34; Carl Larsson's work, 266–67n2; color, 16, 98–99, 119–20, 196, 198; configuration of spaces, 27; decoration, 85–88, 95–97, 115, 296n47; eclecticism, 22, 25–27, 31–32, 86, 95–97, 99, 278n32; exotic materials, 196; furniture placement, 26–27, 86–88, 90–102; informality, 33–35; materials, 238, 276n6; model living room, 98, 99f; proletarian *Wohnkultur*, 166–68, 167f; public and private domains of houses, 151–52; Strnad group, 22–27; Svenskt Tenn, 234–38; Tedesco apartment, 21–22; uniformity, 88; vernacular design, 20–21; Vienna Werkbundsiedlung exhibition, 179, 182–84, 183f; wall covering, 44–45; Weissenhofsiedlung double houses, 108–10; *Wohnkultur*, 71–73, 72f. *See also* arts and crafts; spatial effects

International Housing Conference, 1931, 172

irregularity, 158–62, 223, 225; late houses, 244–53; Wehtje Houses, 202–8, 210–12, 211f. *See also* asymmetry

Itten, Johannes, 51, 285n65

Jacobson, Gun, 304n61

Jaksch, Hans, 82

Jardinette Apartments (Neutra), 142

Jeanneret, Charles-Édouard. *See* Le Corbusier

Jeanneret, Pierre, 104

Jews, 4–5, 7–8, 264n15. *See also* anti-Semitism

Jirasek, Julius, 95

Johansson, Gotthard, 196

Johnson, Alvin, 221

Johnson, Philip, 306–7n39

Journal de la Construction, 128

Judtman, Fritz, 182

Jugendstil, 6, 12, 19, 21, 258

Kahane House garden, 157–58, 157–58f

Kalmár, Julius, 216

Kalmár Apartment, 98

Kandinsky, Wassily, 118

Karl-Marx-Hof, 84

Karl-Seitz-Hof, 82–83, 83f

Karplus, Arnold, 157, 292n54

Karplus, Gerhard, 307n40

Katavolos, William, 254

Kaufmann, Edgar, Sr., 217

Kaufmann Department Store exhibition, 217–18, 218f

Kaufmann House (Neutra), 233–34

Kaym, Franz, 298–99n66

Kiepura, Jan, 143

Kinderheim in Ortmann, 61–65, 63–65f, plate 4

kitsch, 250

Klee, Paul, 98, 118

Kleine Einfamilienhäuser, 184

Kleiner, Leopold, 307n40

Klimt, Gustav, 6, 11–12

Klint, Kaare, 194

Klosterneuburg *Siedlung*, 68, 70–71f, 71, 73, 274n37

Kokoschka, Oskar, 11, 189, 198n60

König, Carl, 7–10, 16–17, 264n14, 265n21; opinion of Loos, 11, 265n27; students, 22

Korn, Karl, 277n21

Körner, Theodor, 238

Kornhäusel, Josef, 4

Krenek, Ernst, 189

Krinsky, Carol Herselle, 68

Kungsträdgården design competition, 240–42

Kunstgewerbeschule (School of Arts and Crafts), 7, 55; Frank's position as teacher, 50–52, 95; Strnad's position, 23, 31

Kunsthistorisches Institut, Vienna, 278n31

Künstlergenossenschaft (Artist's Association), 6

Kunst und Künstler, 30, 127

Kurrent, Friedrich, 258

L. R. S. House, 98–99, 99f

labor issues, 60–61

Låftman House, 202, 202f

La Guardia, Fiorello, 305–6n20

landscaping, 154, 157–58, 204. *See also* gardens

L'Architecte, 80

Larsson, Axel, 214, 303n47

Larsson, Carl, 21, 25, 266n2

Laske, Oskar, 264n15

Lauterbach, Hans, 155–56